CONSPIRACY / THEORY

CONSPIRACY
/THEORY

EDITED BY JOSEPH MASCO AND LISA WEDEEN

DUKE UNIVERSITY PRESS DURHAM & LONDON 2024

Project Editor: Bird Williams
Designed by Matthew Tauch
Typeset in Alegreya and Degular by Westchester Publishing Services

Library of Congress Cataloging-in-Publication Data
Names: Masco, Joseph, [date] editor. | Wedeen, Lisa, editor.
Title: Conspiracy/Theory / edited by Joseph Masco and Lisa Wedeen.
Other titles: Conspiracy Theory
Description: Durham : Duke University Press, 2024. | Include bibli-
ographical references and index.
Identifiers: LCCN 2023015289 (print)
LCCN 2023015290 (ebook)
ISBN 9781478025559 (paperback)
ISBN 9781478020813 (hardcover)
ISBN 9781478027676 (ebook)
Subjects: LCSH: Conspiracy theories. | Conspiracy. | Critical theory. |
Truthfulness and falsehood. | BISAC: SOCIAL SCIENCE / Anthropology /
Cultural & Social | SOCIAL SCIENCE / Conspiracy Theories
Classification: LCC HV6275 .C667 2024 (print)
LCC HV6275 (ebook)
DDC 001.9/8—dc23/eng/20231023
LC record available at https://lccn.loc.gov/2023015289
LC ebook record available at https://lccn.loc.gov/2023015290

CONTENTS

JOSEPH MASCO AND LISA WEDEEN

INTRODUCTION
CONSPIRACY/
THEORY

The twenty-first century has dawned as an era of generalized epistemic crisis, an age of propaganda, of wall-to-wall psyops, disorientation campaigns, and attentional hacks. The narrative techniques being drawn on stem from ancient practices as well as from technological revolutions in digital communication of all kinds. Social media and smart phones deploying novel product designs based on the latest algorithms and theories of subjectivity have become pervasive and highly efficient in capturing, controlling, and directing attention. As the weaponization of the infosphere intensifies, individuals being targeted for influence are left to their own evaluative capacities and are challenged to explain to themselves a world that abandons and obfuscates, misinforms, and routinely injures and kills. The origins of this distributed, direct, and indirect violence must be understood in terms of how information technologies are used to organize and narrativize the ways we apprehend problems, turning the sensory regimes and mass-mediated experiences of life into arguments about what hurts and why, about the potentials and dangers of the moment, and about the prospects of creating some kind of collective future. The response of mainstream journalists to this situation of intensified epistemic precarity has mostly been to declare the arrival of a new "golden age" of conspiracy theory.

Obscured by this blanket characterization is the fact that conspiracy theories come in many varieties, and they appeal unevenly and in different ways to whatever audiences they successfully hail. Most generally, a distinction can be made between speculative narratives that are demonstrably preposterous (that the COVID-19 pandemic is a global hoax) and those that are more or less plausible because, for example, they speak to long-standing structural inequalities or can be proven, in retrospect, to have been true (such as racist redlining in housing). Plausible narratives are undergirded by what Hannah Arendt (2006a, 218) calls "factual truths," which are by no means self-evident but are subject to communal, public adjudication. For Arendt, politics takes place within a domain of plural, contingent opinions, presupposing an understanding of freedom rooted in an appreciation of the human capacity for speech and other kinds of action, and where the establishment, maintenance, and constructive disputation of what counts as a fact are all important parts of sustaining political life. Facts, although vulnerable, are also stubborn, according to Arendt, so that airbrushing Trotsky out of Soviet images of the Russian Revolution did not render him a nonparticipant in its history.

Arendt tells us that the exercise of sound political judgment depends on people acting together in the inevitably messy world of human opinion and sharing a common world, which the erosion of a fact-based discourse undermines. However, even in a world of too much information, often the facts are not available or are subject to the distortion of a globalized economy, a planetary scale environmental disruption, or the compounding effects of covert institutions and activities. To think collectively in this current era requires the cultivation of new practices of attunement that simultaneously disrupt status-quo conventionality and induce solidarity across existing fault lines. Addressing others who may be very different from oneself suggests opening up styles of thinking that embrace ambiguity and foster curiosity, regenerating what Kant called a "sensus communis" or "common sense." This *sensus communis* is always contingent, indeterminate, open to revision, and a product of ongoing exploration and disagreement. But admittedly, a Kantian-Arendtian common sense is often not nearly enough; individuals can live in siloed communities, not sharing basic orientations toward politics, factual evidence, or concepts of agency within a broader public. There are also ontological differences in worlds, based on historical experience, religious viewpoints, and radical differences in obligations to land, environment, and futurity (e.g., see Jackson 2008; Turner 1993). So, in the contemporary moment of intensifying wealth consolidation, dirty wars, and new expressions of right-wing populism, individuals feel the need to activate other sensibilities as well, modalities of thought that are intuitive, anticipatory, and skeptical and that employ modes of serious speculation often as techniques for basic survival.

Conspiracy/Theory interrogates—despite real and consequential differences, as noted above—the elective affinities between *aspects* of conspiratorial thinking and our intellectual practice of critical theory, an acknowledgment of the ways in which people—in their individual capacities as experts, theorists, and/or ordinary citizens—are motivated to find patterns, uncover what is hidden, and attend to dimensions of life that might be hiding in plain sight. Both plausible and not-so-plausible, offensive and admirable explorations of events and issues depend on "connecting the dots." It is by rendering complex and confusing appearances coherent, or by revealing logics that have hitherto eluded big-picture scrutiny, that patterns are perceived. Not all these activities and accounts are equally salutary, of course, and some are surely pernicious for politics, but they are nonetheless symptomatic and indicative of current conditions.

Although much has been made of digital forms of "surveillance capitalism" in industrial and postindustrialized spaces (Zuboff 2019), our interest here is more on the ways in which the practice of questioning the terms of a shared reality appears in the form of efficacious and at times highly profitable social media enterprises, which has implications for the exercise of political judgment and the attention evaluation requires. Put differently, the multiplatform social media revolution since the advent of the twenty-first century has worked to democratize psyops—allowing individuals across the world to influence perceptions on a population scale in a way that was formerly possible only for large corporations and nation-states (see Donovan et al. 2021).[1] This means that for every progressive activist working to advance the common cause, other players, both foreign and domestic, are waging sophisticated disorientation campaigns, some of which are overtly designed to attack the very possibility of collectivity itself, with the effect of stalling, confusing, or preventing action on a vast array of unfolding problems that we do share in common (Curtis 2016).

The informational practices democratizing psyops, perhaps counterintuitively, are highly conducive to new forms of authoritarianism and to intensifying strains of authoritarianism in democracies. They operate by fomenting competing and irreconcilable framings of reality, by disputing recorded facts and documented actions, and by committing explicitly to speech as a dedicated form of information warfare. As a consequence, theorizing contemporary conditions requires a combination of judgment and intuition if we are to cut through the informational distortion fields and find both refuge and allies in the search for positive collective futures.

We know from concrete examples that authoritarian regimes are able to enforce obedience not only or even necessarily by cultivating belief but also by using information technologies to sow confusion and paralysis among some citizens, to polarize others, and to generate widespread political despondency by forcing people constantly to address the very thing they want to dismiss. The atmosphere of epistemic murk we find in authoritarian systems today works by generating conditions of uncertainty that make political judgment all the more difficult. To keep up with the barrage of information and misinformation coming at them, people toggle between belief and unbelief, and between regimes, states, cultural producers, and civil society organizations, undergoing micropolitical encounters inside an affective environment that complicates the fundamental binary between belief and unbelief, such that one can know something and not know it at the same time, just as one can feel something and know something else. Apprehension, not only in the sense of anxiety but also as information comprehension and capture, is part and parcel of authoritarian politics today; it helps shape and intensify the attraction of conspiracy theorizing (see Wedeen 2019, and this volume).

These modalities of control, labeled authoritarian, are not confined to autocracies, of course, as our examples of social media and our theoretical positioning make clear. The US national security state functions more-or-less openly by manipulating perception, emotions, and imaginations. It does so in large part by fomenting images of dangerous others that require and enable a vast range of political and military projects which could not be otherwise pursued through formal democratic means (see Masco 2014, and this volume). Indeed, the United States rides on the foundational contradiction of being a country that formally espouses democratic principles and equality while officially pursuing permanent warfare, white supremacy, and radical class consolidation (see Rana 2010). The daily structure of democratic discourse and practice in the United States involves negotiating this split not only at the level of policy but also at the level of imaginations and affects. Historically, this structural contradiction has been managed by undertaking covert military actions abroad and by engaging in democracy-reduction techniques at home (Singh 2017; C. Anderson 2018)—both of which depend on social mechanisms to silence voices, induce amnesia, or render valid critiques a form of unreason.

Given the inequality with which social orders are generally afflicted, anticipation, intuition, skepticism, and suspicion have become necessary modes of attention for dealing with the unpredictable daily "weather," as Christina Sharpe (2016) might say of racism; they are ways of navigating long-standing and explicit forms of structural violence that can erupt at any moment with ferocious intensity. In the twenty-first century we are seeing powerful recursive interactions among militarism, corporate financial interests, environmental destabilization, and revolutionary information technologies that attack perception itself in the pursuit of profits. In the United States, foundational violences in the forms of anti-blackness, indigenous dispossession, immigrant exclusion, and predatory whiteness meet in the twenty-first century with the rebounding effects of industrial capital (Who lost their job or home today because of global finance?), militarization (What drone attack or police intervention took a child's life today?), and corporate forces opposed to addressing climate change (Who, at the moment, is experiencing fire, flood, storm, or drought?). These compounding conditions add new forms of collective stress and injury to long-standing inequalities, the effects of which are felt on enormous collective scales with highly variable temporalities and local intensities. What is the right language for the imbrication of these forces and their consequences for any individual? And who is so confident, or comfortable, in their everyday life that they are not pressed to theorize a current state of being?

THE POWER OF PLOT

As a term, *conspiracy theory* has a surprisingly short history in the English language, originating in the context of Cold War politics in the mid-twentieth-century United States. Despite its short existence, however, the term has played an outsized role in policing what counts as acceptable modes of political discourse (see Melley 2000, and this volume). As an accusation, a mode of dismissal, conspiracy theory has proven key in maintaining and regulating inequality, militarism, white supremacy, and geopolitical hegemony. The CIA, for example, advised all its branches to designate those criticizing the Warren Report or other federal judgments as "conspiracy theorists"—deploying the term from 1967 on as a method of patrolling speech and undermining critics (see deHaven-Smith 2013). Since then, conspiracy theory has also become a literary genre, appearing as a narrative form with entertainment value across print, film, radio, and the internet. And it operates in support of multimodal forms of information warfare, a means of spreading disruptive information for political advantage or, in today's commitments to online lulz, for subversive counterinstitutional individual pleasure (Coleman 2014) or for political or financial profit (e.g., Rush Limbaugh's or Glenn Beck's radio shows or Alex Jones's online *Infowars*).

Here it is important to note how politically vulnerable media platforms have become to misinformation campaigns in the twenty-first century. One of Vladimir Putin's first acts as president of Russia in 2000 was to take control of television networks, allowing the Kremlin, as Peter Pomerantsev writes (2014, 231), to finally master "the art of fusing reality TV and authoritarianism to keep the great, 140-million-strong population, entertained, distracted, and constantly exposed to geopolitical nightmares, which if repeated enough times can become infectious," and thus enabling conspiracy theories to overwhelm any possibility for citizens to maintain a stable view of the world. The goal of authoritarian conspiracy theory is to create a world not where truth does not exist but where finding it is too exhausting for the individual, thus encouraging a relinquishing of judgment to the state or to a particular site's seductive narrative, a project that is familiar to us today from Orban's Hungary, Bolsonaro's Brazil, and Trump's United States. Trump's presidency was supported by Fox News and a network of reinforcing radio and internet programs, but it was enabled by Twitter and Facebook, which allowed him to have direct communication with his supporters. Only on these social media platforms could Trump bypass fact-checking reviews, demonize opponents, test messaging for affective appeal, and construct an alternative political narrative, all while raising money.

That said, for generations, to be accused of being a "conspiracy theorist" was to have one's perspective devalued, relegated to the unserious, the deranged, the untrustworthy, even the pathological. But pause here for a moment to consider how often you as a reader have had access to all the information needed to evaluate collective conditions across economy, politics, and environment. A more complex infosphere has come with more narrowly specialized experts, yet each of us is in some sense responsible for judging the whole, for discerning truths and dangers, who to be with and which encounters to avoid. This is not to deny the distinction to be made between rigorous theoretical discourse that is consciously based on some substantial empirical exercise and the profusion of conspiratorial assertions devoted to demonizing the political opposition (for profit or for control or both) that attempts to displace possibilities for substantive intellectual interrogation.

What we *are* suggesting is that the array of epistemological conundrums to be identified makes it often difficult to find the appropriate interpretative voice to engage the local effects of global political problems. Anthropogenic global warming—a consolidated effect of a century of petrochemical capitalism—was well understood by Big Oil as a cost of their industry as early as the 1980s. Exxon, Shell, and other oil companies made corporate decisions in the early 1990s to gaslight on a planetary scale; to obfuscate the environmental science their own research teams had produced; to find people with PhDs for hire, some of whom hailed from fields with no relation to the environment, and to deploy them to dispute the findings of climate scientists. A well-funded and substantial enterprise has been responsible for setting up think tanks and sophisticated information warfare operations to convince various publics that virtually the entire population of working environmental scientists do not know what they are talking about (Oreskes and Conway 2010). This is an explicit petrochemical program to protect profits—literally at the cost of the planetary biosphere—a corporate conspiracy against collective life and the very idea of environmental governance.

Or, from another angle, how should citizens understand current messages from the US security state in light of previous histories of disinformation? The George W. Bush administration's 2001–3 domestic psyops campaign (in which then-Iraqi president Saddam Hussein was held responsible for the suicide-hijacker attacks on 9/11 and was allegedly in possession of illegal weapons of mass destruction with which he intended to imminently attack the United States) is one dramatic example of an all-too-familiar system of strategic lying in international politics that transformed both domestic and global worlds in the process. These particular falsehoods were orchestrated directly from the White House and disseminated through the United States' most reputable news media (the *New York Times, Washington Post,* CNN), with the effect of converting a real and devastating attack on US citizens into an illegal assault on a completely uninvolved state, resulting in the deaths of hundreds of thousands of Iraqis, with millions more displaced throughout the region. The Bush administration's hoax was a foundational act in what became a global "war on terror," with its attendant practices of US torture and illegal detention. And it involved a vast domestic surveillance system that depended on the complicity of most of the major information technology companies in the world (AT&T, Google, Facebook, Microsoft). What, exactly, is the appropriate analytic stance toward politics in the aftermath of such consequential revelations of governmental mendacity, domestic psyops campaigns, officially sanctioned illegality, and commercial tech giants' complicity?

Isn't the stance of the caricatured conspiracy theorist—the one worried about government surveillance, public deception, and the disruption of ordinary life by state and corporate entities—closer to the truth than that of the normative political subject who doubts that such things are done, but, if they have been done, trusts it must have been "necessary," that is, a subject who chooses to refuse to question, let alone judge?

These conundrums raise the question of how one disagrees with the ideological recruitment techniques of the moment, how one challenges the veracity of governmental actions that are cloaked by national security protocols, or how one challenges corporate programs that stack the scientific debate to get the answer that is most profitable. For example, in the late 1990s, Purdue Pharma marketed its new prescription drug oxycontin as a nonaddictive form of pain relief. It was touted as a major medical breakthrough that offered a safe medication for people enduring terrible suffering. But rather than relieving pain, oxycontin produced an opioid epidemic in the United States that has claimed well over half a million lives since 1998. How is one to act in a world where government-approved drugs, prescribed by credentialed doctors to treat real pain, produce a cumulative domestic death rate greater than the number of US soldiers who died fighting in World War II?

Or, to put this differently: calling a given line of thought a conspiracy theory opens a complex rather than self-evident political field. The term has been weaponized for generations to discount, dismiss, and contain people's expressions of what they are actually experiencing in their lives and what they, based on limited information at hand, are trying to understand. The charge has been used to dismiss those who claim the state is using its powers to surveil citizens, misdirect debate, and kill with impunity, even as the state does so. Many conspiratorial narratives remain at the margins because practices of state secrecy create a de facto alibi for antidemocratic actions, for imperial and police violence, for financial corruption and lousy policy. Because individuals lack substantial documentation, the appropriate credentials, and authorized legal standing, they wind up disempowered, cast as irrational subjects. Thus, for every anti-vaxxer who denies the value of biomedicine and for every 9/11-truther insisting that the United States or the Mossad bombed the World Trade Center to unlock a new world order—views presumably few readers would embrace without convincing evidence and more questioning—there is a vast section of the population experiencing material and psychic distress and working to survive in a violent world while not able to trust officials who are known to lie, or experts who are frequently bought, or mass media that all too readily propagandize for profit.

It is not at all a simple thing in the twenty-first century to assess or locate the origins of harm within a globalized, mass-mediated, late-industrial society that is proliferating violences that are both fast (i.e., warfare, police oppression, gun violence) and slow (poverty, pollution, climate disruption) and that operate with a wide range of intensities and concentrations (see Nixon 2011). How can or should one orient oneself from within complex global networks and systems that are both emergent and experimental as well as frequently occluded (either secret or privatized), while also being recursive to one another and unpredictable in their interactions? What, for example, are the foundational conditions for the figure of the "climate refugee" today? Is the primary force behind this monumental displacement of vulnerable people industrial, financial, military, or the historically complex imbrication of all three? And who, as a displaced person, is in a position to correctly diagnose such a problem, let alone address the foundational structures that created such radical inequalities and occluded forces?

Perhaps the most popularized conspiracy theorists in the West are the UFO believers. In Susan Lepselter's chapter, we encounter the figure who sees lights in the night sky, casts them as from another world, and worries about their intent. The public anxiety about lights in the night sky was amplified by the Cold War arms race, which rehearsed the idea of missiles coming over the horizon without warning as a perverse form of nation-building (see Masco 2014). That alone might be enough to explain the ongoing public fascination with and worry about UFOS. But then, consider the post–Cold War confession of CIA agents admitting to generating media stories about UFOS to provide cover for secret US aeronautical research, fabricating tales of extraterrestrial visitors to explain away the anomalous things people were actually seeing in the sky, seeking to cultivate an inchoate brew of Soviet nuclear aggression and extraterrestrial invasion in the service of strategic misdirection.

Some religious doctrines function very much like conspiracy theories. The teleological modes of thinking characteristic of evangelical Christianity, for example, claim to understand how the world ends, which makes the present an occluded field in need of analytic interpretation, and the construction of one's current status and position in relation to the inevitable end (see Stewart and Harding 1999). While differing in some ways from classic conspiracy theory, this mode of the anticipatory shares with conspiracy theories a subject position in which an ego "in the know" is tasked to read the signs of everyday life as landmarks in the inevitable path that only some can see clearly (Stewart 1999). In this way, conspiracy theory can be an ego-trip, a powerful mode of self-fashioning, one that frequently recruits those at the margins of society to assume the position of expert. To cultivate such a point of view, regardless of the veracity of judgment, can thus be satisfying, empowering, and even a mode of resistance.

KEY TERMS

This volume seeks to align this complex political field with the no less complicated but much less maligned field of critical theory. We realize this may appear as our own effort to connect disparate dots, to indulge in a scholarly apophenia (see Lepselter, this volume), but historically the two terms actually share important parallels. The Ngram citational study from Google Books shows that the appearances of the term *conspiracy theory* emerge together with *critical theory* as textual concerns in the 1960s, mirroring each other as modes of interpretive assessment.[2] This book seeks to understand why that is. We want to account for the elective affinities between the two ideas while moving beyond what Paul Ricoeur (1970) powerfully identified as a "hermeneutics of suspicion," which puts the analytic focus on the relation of surface to depth. Looking back on more than thirty years of critical theory, Eve Sedgwick saw in Ricoeur's hermeneutics of suspicion a "paranoid style of reading," for it assumes that distrusting surface forms in favor of excavating the depths leads to greater truths being revealed—an inherently conspiratorial approach to social life and meaning. Sedgwick sees paranoia in critical thought as a kind of anticipatory politics:

> Whatever account it may give of its own motivation, paranoia is characterized by placing, in practice, an extraordinary stress on the efficacy of knowledge per se—knowledge in the form of exposure. Maybe that's why paranoid knowing is so inescapably narrative. Like the deinstitutionalized person on the street who, betrayed and plotted against by everyone else in the city, still urges on you the finger-worn dossier bristling with his precious correspondence, paranoia for all its vaunted suspicion acts as though

its work would be accomplished if only it could finally, this time, somehow get its story truly known. That a fully initiated listener could still remain indifferent or inimical, or might have no help to offer, is hardly treated as a possibility. It's strange that a hermeneutics of suspicion would appear so trusting. (Sedgwick 2003b, 138)

In university circles these interpretive logics inform what is still called "critical theory"—designating a mode of professional practice seeking to move beyond mere appearances to discern the structure of politics, economy, and communication in an effort to render them less conducive to structures of oppression across the lines of race, class, gender, or geopolitics. In Walter Benjamin's (2007, 257) terms, to carry out interpretation of this type is to "brush history against the grain," revealing how normative structures of inequality inform peoples' understandings of history, politics, and economy. The "critical" aspect of theory in this formulation lies then in the imperative to activate readers, mobilizing an analytic narrative to reveal the structural inequalities within an existing social order in the hope of altering its future condition. The implicit assumption of critical theory is that the most powerful forms of violence are loaded into the everyday, built into infrastructures of production and consumption, language, governance and media, institutions and identarian categories; and it is in this way that they are rendered naturalized and occluded, made into powers that determine people's prospects from behind the scenes. Their effects are intense but also hidden, networked, and powerful, which is to say, properly conspiratorial.

So, to say the least, *Conspiracy/Theory* addresses a moment when what people know or think they know about public life, the utility of theory, and the logistics of conspiracy touch directly on the kinds of collective worlds individuals can recognize in common and want to live in. The book also attempts to forge a shared diagnostic understanding of the worlds people actually find themselves inhabiting. Thus, the project is comparative in both a historical and ethnographic sense, a concerted effort to break out of the narrow framing of conspiratorial reason and to avoid allowing the US framing of the problem to dominate discussion. In this spirit, it is worth exploring in greater detail some key terms.

Conspiracy refers to a subversive act undertaken by people for some kind of gain—literally to plot with others an alternate future. While it is commonly marked as illicit or criminal behavior conducted in secret and, thus, appears predominantly in contemporary discourse as pejorative and antidemocratic, conspiracy also describes any activist project attempting to improve the world. Etymologically, conspiracy simply means to "breathe together," which puts at its core some notion of an activated, engaged solidarity. As a political practice, conspiracy has an ancient history and, as Demetra Kasimis reveals in her chapter, informs foundational debates about democracy itself. Conspiracy has appeared in well-documented forms across the political spectrum, making it something revolutionary insurrectionists have in common with the covert government agents opposing them, and something that is shared by both with criminals. The list of high-order state and corporate conspiracies runs deep and goes on, linking "black" operations conducted by military states, to democracy-reduction techniques pursued by oligarchs, to the user agreements on social media platforms that infotech giants rely on to relieve themselves of liability while misleading consumers as to how their data are actually being used.

Nevertheless, as Kimberley Ban (2019) argues, and as our invocation of "breathing together" suggests, conspiracy also has an inherent, undeniable, element of fugitivity. It entails departing from a social code or norm, regardless of the reasons or motives for undertaking such a departure. From this point of view, a world without conspiracy is one without the possibility of liberation, without the possibility of reimagining new potentials and possibilities, without justice. This is not to ignore the formal criminal connotations of the term, whether in standard legal definitions (such as the Racketeer Influenced and Corrupt Organizations Act [RICO] devised to prosecute the Mafia) or in singular institutions like the Nuremburg Codes, but to underscore that collective action is impossible absent some sort of shared fugitivity. Any collective pursuing change is going to be working to some extent outside the norm, the public eye, or formal governance.

Conspiracy is thus a fundamental point of origin for world-making, a condition of responding to imperialism, white supremacy, indigenous dispossession, dictatorial rule, and systemic forms of global inequality. As Tim Choy (2021, 251–52) defines it: "To conspire is to avow embodied complicities and intimacies, both those activated in breathing together and those circulating as the surround. It is to pose historical and future-oriented questions of the conditions that sustain or deplete you: What conditions the differential distribution of the difficulties or impossibilities of breath for particular forms of life here in the atmosphere?" For Choy, the necessary affirmative project of twenty-first-century conspiracy calls for assembling all breathing life forms, bound as we all are by the distributed deadly effects of industrial pollution, to create a less toxic, more verdant biosphere in support of all life. To recover and acknowledge a robust notion of conspiracy in this sense is one commitment of this volume.

Theory advances propositions about the social or material structure of things. In the form of critical theory, it draws on Marxism and psychoanalysis to unpack the psychosocial order of political economy. Adopted initially by the Frankfurt School in the 1930s, the term has come to connote a wide range of analytic approaches (Marxist, psychoanalytic, poststructuralist, new historicist, deconstructionist, feminist, critical race theoretical, affect theoretical) that work with differences between surfaces and depths to unpack social practices, texts, and mass-mediated forms. Critical theorists, to varying degrees, assume that truths are hidden, often in plain sight. Critical practices attune us to what we already know, or they make visible what has been masked. Across profound and generative disagreements, the core concepts are those of analytic reason and immanent critique, so that close readings, combined with an account of structural oppression and attention to the minute and contradictory aspects of social and textual practice, hold the promise of at least a diagnosis and perhaps even move toward political transformation and social justice. Critical theory has always promised that authoritarian and imperialist formations can be understood, if not necessarily avoided, via critical assessment and public exposure. Critical theory also demonstrates both the subversive power of mass mediation and popular susceptibilities to fascistic recruitment (Horkheimer and Adorno 2002; Marcuse 1955). The terrain that matters for critical theory arguably ends up being reason itself, a commitment to the analytic value of denaturalization, temporal dislocation, alternative genealogies, and alienation for purposes of revealing the constructedness of social life and, consequently, opening up possibilities for life to be otherwise. The speculative nature of critical theory is thus modulated by analytic rigor, intellectual intensity, and the assembling of evidence as well as, foundationally, by the rejection of any association with its necessary twin-other: conspiracy theory.

Conspiracy theory is similarly an analytic, a mode of speculative appraisal seeking to understand current conditions in the absence of access to all the necessary data. Sometimes the data exist but are kept secret. And sometimes data are lacking because the situation is unknowable or redacted. Whatever the conditions of the not known, however, conspiracy theory has at its center elements of intuition, anticipation, projection, and investment. In current usage, it merges hyperbolic modes of fantastical narration with the considerable set of survival skills needed to navigate a permanent warfare, plutocrat-dominated, and climate-disrupted world. Staying ahead of the curve—seeing the violence coming and gathering those you care about to get as far out of the way as possible—requires intuition, anticipation, and a theory of how the world works (see Thomas and Masco 2023). As a mode of thinking, conspiracy theory can be wrong in its interpretive conclusions, but it remains a way of animating analytic capacities in a world that is ambivalent to, or that actually embraces, *longue durée* oppressive practices, distributing them in ways that reinforce (settler-)colonial, racist, sexist, homophobic, and antidemocratic worldviews.

After the 9/11 attacks, for example, citizens in the United States and elsewhere who attempted to raise concern about the emergence of a new digital COINTELPRO, or the negative global implications of the USA PATRIOT Act, found themselves accused by government officials of dealing in "conspiracy theory," in the now iconic usage designed to deauthorize claims by processing them as a degraded form of reason, a half-step above madness, and verging on the pathological. Given the now verifiable truth behind their warnings (as documented by Edward Snowden and Wikileaks, among other whistleblowers), it is important to pause and ask about the terms of veracity and truth-telling that are accepted at any given historical moment as well as about the modalities of deauthorization that prevent those insights from being acknowledged. In other words, the accusation of conspiracy theory is overloaded today precisely because it is so politically useful. It is useful to states as a means of denying secret operations and limiting modes of critique. It is efficacious to corporations because it helps them avoid accountability for their toxicity by hiding behind plaintiffs' lack of perfect documentation of injury. It is instrumental for intelligence agencies because it disrupts the terms of domestic discourse and allows plausible deniability. And it is useful to unscrupulous individuals who make their livelihoods on social media by spreading outrageous claims or who just enjoy seeing their fictions go viral. The connecting element here lies in how conspiracy theory seeks to activate attention, to recruit others into an interpretive frame, to see the world differently, and to overcome the opacity and historical embeddedness of powerful entities. Given these powerful dynamics and institutional commitments that seem devoted to destabilizing the contemporary order, it is important not to lose sight of the fact that conspiracy theory is also a survival tactic, a mode of deliberation and intuition that for those not in power is frequently a necessary form, a way to break free of normative political imaginaries and to foment new futurities.

If the substantial overlap between conspiracy theory and critical theory as genres of contemporary thought is obvious, there is still a powerful policing of the boundary between the two. Conspiracy theory is frequently portrayed as misguided and untrustworthy, while critical theory is authorized and professionally sanctioned. A lot of intellectual energy goes into keeping the respectable form from being contaminated by its other—a project that this book seeks to unpack and expose.

Conspiracy/theory is helpful as a concept in our effort to explore the analytic overlap between critical theory and conspiracy theory. The slash in *conspiracy/theory* is meant to work as an invitation to consider the terms not only separately but also as imbricated in each other. It is designed to focus attention on the overlap as an epistemological dilemma, providing a standpoint from which we interrogate the analytic challenges of life in a mass-mediated and hyperviolent society that has normalized powerful forms of exclusion, dehumanization, and environmental destruction and that denies doing so. The concept *conspiracy/theory* offers an opportunity to review and refine a number of prevailing assumptions found in both academic discourse and political life, and to consider how narrative frames and specific forms and agendas of world-making are reciprocally constitutive. Exploring the conditions for knowing in a world beset by too much and too little information at the same time, this book asks how and when characteristics such as intuition, viewpoint, experience, and anxiety become marked as either conspiratorial or theoretical. When is it impossible to separate what the two terms reference, and when are they synonymous? Understanding the affinities between conspiracy and theory, while appreciating the seductions of each, the chapters in this book engage, from different historical and regional perspectives, the theoretical in conspiracy and the conspiratorial in theory, grappling simultaneously with the ways in which suspicion, opacity, networks, uncertainty, silencing, judgment, affect, and mass-mediation function.

In adopting such an approach, this volume is radically at odds with the conventional split between conspiracy and theory made famous in Richard Hofstadter's 1964 essay "The Paranoid Style in American Politics." Hofstadter takes as his object a "style of thought" based in "heated exaggeration, suspiciousness and conspiratorial fantasy" that is devoted to defending a "way of life" perceived to be under attack. Focusing on far-right movements in the United States, he identifies the paranoid style of thinking as a long-standing aspect of American thought, while also diagnosing it as a pathological formation of the liberal order. Hofstadter's essay has been essential reading about US public intellectual life for over half a century; it has been cited on an almost weekly basis in mass media to explain the Trump phenomenon, the popularity of alt-right media sites, and new authoritarian movements. The popularity of Hofstadter's essay today, however, says more about its political utility for normative power structures than about its analytic reach (see also Marasco 2016). Hofstadter marks conspiracy thinking as excessive and irrational, a pathology to be excised from public life. In his hands, the "paranoid style" is a political theology, a modern form of superstition or the supernatural, a collection of beliefs that should be eliminated in favor of serious political discourse and modernist rationality. And crucially, he knows exactly where to draw the line.

Consider, however, the era in which Hofstadter was writing. The formal objects of his study were McCarthyism and the rise of the John Birch Society, both of which rallied public passions against global communism as a multifaceted conspiracy against American life, a force behind every welfare-state initiative and civil rights mobilization. McCarthy's exaggerated allegation that the US government was filled with communists is now foundational to the public conception of conspiracy theory as a damaging and socially corroding form. It also provided direct rhetorical resources to Donald Trump, who declared—long before he was in office—the presence of a "deep state" set against his future administration, seeking to turn every investigation of his behavior into an illustration of a corrupt and occluded center of power (which became a centerpiece of the QAnon movement). By focusing on such forms, Hofstadter conjures and then dismisses the paranoid style as an abjuration of the democratic form. But Hofstadter was writing at a time of accelerating US covert actions around the world, repeated nuclear confrontation and explicit overt and covert efforts to manipulate public life and opinion in the service of mobilizing support for the project of the Cold War. It was the era in which Frank Wisner, head of the political warfare unit at the CIA, could describe controlling US media like a "mighty Wurlitzer" organ, as it was capable of "playing any propaganda tune he desired" to the listening American public—even while his agency was legally prohibited from conducting operations inside the United States (Wilford 2009, 7). Hofstadter's essay came after Rachel Carson's *Silent Spring*, published in 1962, which alerted the world to the plague of invisible and unregulated industrial pollution—showing how deadly privatized profits, marketed as modernist achievements in chemistry, can be. And it came just after the signing of the Limited Test Ban Treaty in 1963, with an emerging antinuclear movement joining with environmental activists to resist a military-industrial world committed to death on a new kind of scale. The essay appeared before the passage of the 1965 Voting Rights Act, a vital first step in addressing systemic voter suppression and racism in the United States. Yet the essay includes no discussion of the Jim Crow system or the logics of indigenous dispossession or anti-immigration campaigns. Hofstadter first presented the paper at Oxford the very month President John F. Kennedy was shot, one of a series of political assassinations in the 1960s involving civil rights activists (Medgar Evers, Malcolm X, Martin Luther King) and other politicians (Robert Kennedy), alongside church bombings by the KKK (the 16th Street Baptist Church in Birmingham, Alabama) that fundamentally confirmed the deadly reality of conspiracies.

In short, Hofstadter gave no consideration to the possibility that contemporary political, environmental, military, and financial conditions might call for something more than idle suspicion from the citizen-subject. Similarly, the liberal "we" implicitly evoked throughout the essay takes no account of the foundational histories in the United States of settler-colonial and anti-Black violence. At the time Hofstadter wrote, basic rights of citizenship were still being hard won on paper for many who continued to live with no assurance of personal safety or fairness in their everyday interactions with police, courts, housing, and employment (Martinot and Sexton 2003). Given the magnitude of contextual omissions in the essay, it is no mystery why Hofstadter remains the go-to expert on conspiracy theory to this day: he authorizes the dismissal of paranoid reason as pathological and uninformed, even as consequential conspiratorial projects stack up in all directions. The point here, considering structural constraints and global conditions, is that a paranoid style of thought might just be for many a necessary skill set—even a basic survival strategy—for those living in political orders committed to maintaining extreme inequalities.

Conspiracy/Theory moves beyond Hofstadter's comfortable defense of liberal reason; its contributors are willing to sit with the uncomfortable reality that people narrate the world and might not always have the best factual evidence or perspective. The book also moves beyond a US focus by thinking in multisited and implicitly comparative ways about the myriad conspiracy theories in circulation today—some constrained by incomplete data; some requiring speculation on the unknowable; some in the service of stabilizing military, imperial, and/or authoritarian projects; and some as a way of surviving such conditions or encouraging a revolutionary otherwise to contemporary politics. *Conspiracy/Theory* demonstrates across historical periods and state projects the vital place of speculation in both making and evaluating collective conditions.

OVERVIEW

Part I. Organizing Fictions

Walter Benjamin (2007, 257) argued that the "tradition of the oppressed teaches us that the 'state of emergency' in which we live is not the exception but the rule," underscoring the power of historical narrative as a means of consolidating social power and establishing a false promise of "progress." Part I of *Conspiracy/Theory*, "Organizing Fictions," explores the psychosocial necessity and force of narrative, accepting our inherent human reliance on storytelling to shape, craft, and engage social reality. George Shulman frames this dynamic via a forceful critique of Hofstadter's essay, arguing that its quick dismissal of paranoia and its identification of the conspiratorial as primarily a right-wing seduction is a fundamental misreading of human nature and of American politics. Turning to Melville and Pynchon for guidance on grappling with unavoidable paranoia in everyday life, Shulman argues for the power and necessity of organizing fictions in "political culture." The necessary response to an authoritarian moment, for Shulman, is not to be found in the simple recitation of factual evidence. To trust that facts alone can redirect political energies is to ignore the power of affect, fantasy, fear, and cathexis in politics. Factual claims are never enough to create social investment, cohesion, and collectivity. Shulman argues that the establishment of counternarratives elevating different values and different understandings of collective life is not only essential, but the only way to create a political culture that is more equal, less violent, and more democratic.

A central insight of "Organizing Fictions" is that expert knowledge is never enough to mobilize social commitment. But in that case, how do people come to know the origins of calamities such as a monumental outbreak of infectious disease? The COVID-19 pandemic radically and suddenly altered the terms of life and death in December 2019, producing a vast range of reframings and resistances to public health expertise. Looking back at the origins of another global infectious disease outbreak, that of HIV/AIDS, Lochlann Jain questions the existing biomedical expert consensus that the virus jumped from animals to humans in Africa via meat consumption, thereby initiating an unavoidable local zoonotic outbreak that led to a global infection. Tracking an alternative hypothesis, which is extensively investigated in Edward Hooper's *The River* (2000), Jain asks how biomedicine polices its own narrative. Jain explores an evidentiary chain of events before the emergence of HIV/AIDS, connecting medical experimentation on subaltern populations to a global movement of blood plasma and the search for novel vaccines. Interrogating a historic moment of loose ethical controls but globally expansive experimental circuits, Jain seeks to understand how medical logics and experimental practices as well as the availability of certain subjects became globally linked in ways which just might have inadvertently produced a novel and deadly global infection. In his larger research on what he calls the Wet Net, Jain's consideration of why Hooper's book was preemptively dismissed without serious review by the Royal Society—despite its voluminous presentation of evidence—reveals the threatening power of a counternarrative, one that requires medical experts to recognize their historical use of dangerous experimental practices. In Jain's telling, the counternarrative calls on experts to consider their complicity not simply in preventing, treating, or creating disease but in exploiting vulnerable humans and nonhumans to do so.

Responsibility for violent global outcomes is also the subject of Joseph Masco's chapter, which tracks how the duplicity of authority is constitutive of US politics. Working with Michael Rogin's notion of political demonology and the logics of WWE (World Wrestling Entertainment) wrestling, Masco explores how oppositional structures and affect mobilization create a psychosocial space of projection and misrecognition. Unpacking "national security" as a set of projections, orchestrated appearances, and self-deceptions, Masco asks how it is that imperial projects proceed alongside loudly voiced democratic commitments. Misdirection, deception, and fantasy are essential to such a project, constituting a reliance on "false flag" operations. Masco argues that an inherent danger in American life is the call to flatten out experience into a simple for-or-against political framework along the lines of WWE wrestling—as Donald Trump (and before him George W. Bush) demanded. These mechanisms of polarization have historical depth in the United States and are today amplified by both siloed social media publics and the secrecy of the security state. One consequence of these forms, Masco shows, is that people now find themselves constantly subject to recruitment into a style of thought that reduces the complexity and quality of judgment, of conspiratorial reason itself, to friend/enemy distinctions functioning primarily to enable affective and imaginative capture.

This question of how to assess collective conditions in the absence of coherent memory is at the center of Elizabeth Anne Davis's chapter on "conspiracy attunement" in Cyprus. Davis considers the epistemological problems that arise for subjects in a historically contested place, attached to competing Greek-Cypriot and Turkish-Cypriot national narratives, riven by the multigenerational psychosocial consequences of unsettled atrocity, all while navigating the untrustworthiness of mass mediation in an era of global money-laundering on the island—with the latter relying precisely on the uncertainty of jurisdiction in Cyprus. Davis focuses on the narrative forms called forth in the attempt to explain contemporary conditions—narratives that involve the CIA, KGB, global bankers, oligarchs, and drug dealers—attuning us to the expert judgments that go into conspiratorial interpretations. Here, conspiracy attunement is not only a basic political skill, a way of judging the motives behind political narratives, but also an aesthetic form. Davis's narrative allows us to appreciate the terms, logics, and qualities of thought that promote an explanatory form without necessarily believing in any one story. Davis shows us how a sophisticated conspiracy attunement operates in Cyprus, hard-won via war, atrocity, and geopolitical manipulations of local politics. Her portrait is at once a sophisticated assessment of political consciousness in Cyprus and an example of a mode of interpretation that *Conspiracy/Theory* argues is increasingly ascendent in the contemporary world. Davis deftly shows how conspiracy attunement can be a mode for engaging the complexity of the world rather than for flattening it out, offering a highly self-conscious approach to the power of plot, the techniques of propaganda and their implications for political judgment, the workings of finance capital, the constant pull of misrecognition, and desires for a better world.

If doubt is now a strategic achievement, the intended and unintended work of social media networks, intelligence agencies, corporations, political parties, and dedicated individuals, then how is the democratic form, based at least in part and in principle on transparency and trust, to operate—let alone thrive? Timothy Melley addresses this question directly in his chapter on the "post-truth" public sphere in the Trump era. Building on his important study of a "covert sphere" in US politics after World War II (see Melley 2012), Melley traces the ideological development of the term *conspiracy theory* in the United States since 1945. He focuses on how the paranoia of the Cold War system infiltrated interpretive realms in multiple registers, linking the fiction-making of novelists and Hollywood filmmakers to the security state itself. The resulting public understanding that the government is keeping secrets has a dual effect of creating a will to know and a distrust of all available information. He concludes with a discussion of Donald Trump's strategy of running for elected office in 2016 while declaring that all elections are rigged, via fake media, against him. A commitment to a "post-truth politics"—that is, the willful constitution of an instrumental alternative reality—rides on the achievements of security state media projects that go back for generations now, in an ongoing effort to artificially craft politically efficacious realities. Melley shows how this strategy has become literally infectious in the twenty-first century and now poses serious problems for civic judgment.

Part II. Atmospheres of Doubt

The Latin roots of conspiracy—*con* (with or together) and *spirare* (to breath)—show why it is essential to any project of social change as a marker of shared space, conversation, strategic thinking, and collective dreaming. Part II, "Atmospheres of Doubt," explores the multivalent possibilities of breathing together, from the utopian possibility of remaking the world to reactionary mobilizations against any such project. Both are equally conspiratorial. Frantz Fanon (2004) articulated the complexity of this dilemma in his theorization of the psychosocial effects of colonization, showing how imposed hierarchies are embedded not just in social institutions, behaviors, and language but in self-images and ultimately in desire itself. Thus, for Fanon, a project of liberation is at once political and libidinal, and he sought to authorize readers to demand not simply a modification of existing conditions but an entirely new world, fomenting a conspiracy on a global scale. But we should note here how often liberatory moments have been converted into new modes of policing, into a defense of property and hierarchy that undercuts the idea of actual liberation while acting formally in its name—mobilizing revolutionary energies against revolution itself (see James Siegel 1998; Benjamin 1978).

Breathing together, in other words, sounds self-evident, but it is always highly challenged, contested, and fraught. In her chapter, Lisa Wedeen investigates the "conditions of generalized uncertainty" that work to polarize some communities while blocking judgment in others during the 2011–14 revolutionary mobilizations in Syria. Analyzing systemic distortions in news media, Wedeen considers the risks of political judgment and the techniques of mystification in a world of complex social media and multifaceted disinformation campaigns, ones that raise the stakes of radical speech and (other forms of) action to an all but impossible level. The questions around the alleged killing of a Syrian singer are considered against the work of a politically oriented Syrian film collective and a terrifying chemical weapons attack, which was globally contested in terms of authorship but frequently attributed to the ruling regime in Syria. While then President Obama was drawing and then erasing red lines about chemical weapons attacks, threatening what for some Syrians would have been welcome US intervention (and for others a new catastrophe), Syrians and global actors alike were obliged to navigate the uncertainty of attribution for the use of the weapons. Was it the Syrian regime, a rival revolutionary faction, or an outside party? In dealing with these life-and-death circumstances of epistemic insecurity, Wedeen posits—following Arendt—the frightening loss of a "common world," meaning that the basic coordinates for collective life have been undercut by the absence of a shared informational circuit capable of coordinating both understanding and action. All people then have to work with is their intuitive interpretation of events, as they are constrained to convince others amid a surplus of information that is more confusing than it is clarifying—or what is generally disparaged as conspiracy theory.

The resources for such counternarratives are all around us. Here, Susan Lepselter's focus on the power of apophenia—or the making of connection between seemingly unrelated things—shows how connecting the dots is not simply a game of perception but of both world-making and judgment. Her interlocutors navigate not only traumatic forces in the US West but also the fragility of social orders, thinking from the margins about how to make sense of what has already happened and how power operates. Following people who believe they have been abducted by extraterrestrial beings, Lepselter tracks the uncanny resonances that endow autobiographical narrative with the possibility of both recovering lost histories and recalibrating contemporary life. Many of Lepselter's interlocutors feel their economic marginality from the position of settler-colonial whiteness in the 1990s, a moment that Lepselter notes falls between the Cold War and the war on terror but that remains filled with fears of invasion and capture. This constellation of after-ness and not-yet-ness opens up a conceptual space that, for some, requires narration. From Texas to Nevada, individuals look up into the night sky and not only see the marvel of a bigger universe of nonhuman possibility but also generate a narrative understanding that something out there might literally be coming for them.

Public perception is a dedicated target of political manipulation, and the liberal democratic form, as ideal type, is always subject to attempts to shape collective understanding, whether by persuading people to support some political projects as opposed to others, or by trying to dismantle the possibility of collective understanding. Demetra Kasimis suggests in her chapter that democracy itself, in its primary formation, has always been constituted by and in relation to conspiracy. Reading Plato's *Republic* as a conspiratorial text, Kasimis finds evidence of conspiracy in the whisperings of those in power, whose multiple fears of rebellion erode notions of public trust and the capacity for judgment. Drawing out the implications for a post–Cold War retheorization of Athenian democracy, Kasimis shows that the conspiratorial is not a pathology to be excised from the public sphere but a constant presence within it, infusing as well as imperiling the democratic project. Secrecy, rumors, and plots abound in the *Republic*, both cultivating democracy and threatening its demise. Kasimis establishes a foundational conspiratorial dimension within political theory: in other words, speaking in the hypothetical about social order is simultaneously a way of making future worlds and establishing their very boundaries, defining the limits of both thought and political desire.

The forms of political manipulation that the chapters in this part lay bare are, in Nadia Abu El-Haj's chapter, keyed into the conspiratorial terms of US warfare. Exploring the psychosocial mechanisms of displacement and erasure for soldiers suffering the mental aftereffects of combat, Abu El-Haj shows how victimization and sacrifice have been rescripted in the twenty-first century in ways that thwart accountability, allowing US forever wars to continue unimpeded by ethical review. The campaign to forestall public critique of militarism, ascendant since the first Gulf War in 1990, has now been consolidated into a gestural civilian "thank you for your service" to soldiers. Abu El-Haj reads this reflex as a way of supplanting critical judgment, with the effect that American responsibility for its violence around the world is avoided, a theme central to this part's concerns with judgment. This automatic "thank you" for unexamined activities preempts any discussion about the legitimacy of US wars and ignores whatever crimes any given soldier may have perpetrated. After decades of US covert and overt warfare, and despite public knowledge of atrocities committed by soldiers against civilians accumulating in the course of failed military operations in Afghanistan, Iraq, Pakistan, and Somalia (to name a few examples), one might have expected a political debate about US militarism. Abu El-Haj details how it has been short-circuited. But her concerns are not only about judgment. They also highlight the co-implication of militarism with the logics of enmity more broadly, examining how the psychiatric sciences, in tandem with imperial power, create political conditions conducive to the reproduction of global conflict by reconfiguring warfare as an injury—not to citizens of other countries being killed or displaced but to soldiers tasked with violence. She chronicles the emergence of a new diagnostic category of "moral injury," a pathology related to but different from post-traumatic stress disorder. Abu El-Haj, in this way, demonstrates how soldiers who have killed civilians in the war on terror have come to be constituted as victims for having been ordered to do it, rather than as subjects to be held accountable for the violence they visited on civilian others. To limit recognition of suffering to the morally injured soldier is to fundamentally recast the citizen-soldier relationship in the United States by disqualifying concern for non-American victims, amounting to a profound nationwide conspiracy against both self-assessment and the very possibility of peace.

Part III. The Force of Capital

To *speculate* is at once to imagine and to place a bet on a future outcome, linking expertise to theorizing to magical thinking to just plain dumb luck. Or, on this critical world-making point, we might consider the proposition of Peter Thiel (a cofounder of PayPal, a first investor in Facebook, and creator of Palantir—the controversial data analytics company built with CIA start-up money to generate tools for predictive policing, counterterrorism, and immigration control), who tells his readers that a great business is nothing less than "a conspiracy to change the world" (Thiel 2014, 93). For Thiel, the corporation is a world engine, perhaps *the* world engine, a way of shaping the social order as well as consolidating financial and political power. His corporate conspiracy relies on what Adam Smith famously called the "invisible hand," that elusive force that orchestrates wealth, possibility, and ruin in the economy. Since the 1980s, the globalization of financial capital has vastly remade labor conditions around the world, creating ever more unstable local conditions, as corporations chase the cheapest labor by arranging ever more complicated supply chains and take advantage of tax-evasion schemes wherever they can. Part III, "The Force of Capital," brings together assessments of market violence, interrogating the "profit motive" as a conspiratorial modality that provokes its own response in the form of vital intellectual efforts that have coalesced to locally diagnose, account for, and intervene in the disruptive forces of globalized finance.

Rosalind C. Morris explores value and loss in her ethnographic consideration of gold miners in South Africa, where groups of refugees from neighboring states find their way into informal settlements. Speaking no common language but what they concoct in the mines, they are brought together by their hopes of recovering valuable residues in mined-out shafts long abandoned by the companies that created them. Here, the lure of gold, that primary form of value, is theorized against all the missing aspects of state provisioning—water, electricity, security, and health—creating a zone of highly charged attention to the details of everyday life. Mining the residuals of corporate extraction, in Morris's hands, is conceptual as well as material, a problem of value as well as of interpretation. The assembled miners, known as the *zama-zamas* and drawn from difficult conditions across the hemisphere, work to craft a life from within the dangers of underground extraction, experiencing simultaneously the abandonment of the state and the conflicting political and linguistic spaces of nation, tribe, gender, and sexuality. Morris interrogates the historical conditions that generate the necessity for so many of informal gold mining's practices (often illegal and always dangerous) while also acknowledging the conceptual pull of gold. Gold is frequently the object of conspiratorial thought and a dynamic part of a global system of exchange. The logic of buried treasure thus posits a survivalist outside, enabling a fantasy of pure escape, as the gold becomes an agreed-upon form that can seem to make coherent the fantastic diversity of people, cultural practices, and languages that meet in the dark tunnels miles underground to chip away at the rock face. In this way, Morris considers how much the conceptual universe of the *zama-zamas* offers a compelling version of life in the twenty-first century, where the objects of desire, the conditions of social life, and the mercilessness of the market define in ways difficult to fully account for—even in the minute-to-minute search for gold—the terms of living and dying, of hope and misery, and of collectivity and profit.

The commitment to growth, Joseph Dumit shows in his interrogation of the corporate logics of Big Pharma, Big Oil, and Higher Education, is antihuman. For what does it mean that human society is organized around an institutional form—the corporation—that is concerned solely with its own expansion, that is willing to destroy health, education, and the planet in the endless pursuit of profit? Dumit exposes, at the center of the modern world system, a conspiracy against life, one that is unintentional and headless but still all pervasive. The pharmaceutical companies, which treat health risk rather than symptoms as a way to increase the number of drugs prescribed per person, meet in his assessment with the global project of Big Oil, committed to petrochemical extraction in all its forms despite rising sea levels and a destabilizing climate. The corporate imperative to grow seamlessly and endlessly works to convert healthcare into its opposite, even as Exxon's climate scientists measure, while its publicists deny, the catastrophe of anthropogenic climate change that it is producing. Dumit asks a profound question about large-scale institutions like health care, energy, and the university: are they inherently conspiratorial? But even more, he asks where such conspiracies are located and considers how such violent forms are normalized, loaded into individual nervous systems as modes of desire and habitual relations that ensure the destruction of the world. On this point he turns to the philosopher-artist Adrian Piper, who assesses the way the university functions as a corporation, tracking how claims about sexual and racial harassment are naturalized as a form of bullying, requiring heroic self-sacrifice on the part of anyone who would call out the system or demand structural change. In this way, Dumit, via Piper, considers how race and capital are intertwined conspiracies fomenting vast scales of self-destructive social behavior, and he ponders an alternative, life-affirming conspiracy—that is, the one informing demands for an entirely different world.

The corporate naturalization of growth at the expense of the world has many precursor forms that link the colonial era to racialized labor forces to imperial projects of extraction. The foreigner who shows up to "help" is the central concern of Louisa Lombard's chapter on humanitarian profiteering in the Central African Republic. International peacekeeping, global health, counterterror, and global finance now all have a "boots on the ground" logic of intervention, proliferating self-constituting caring experts who arrive with missionary zeal to improve local conditions. These multifaceted organizations and projects ride on the long legacy of colonization and missionary work, which cloaked a desire for control in the guise of dispensing aid. Becoming a site for raiding by Muslim polities to the north in the nineteenth century, the Central African Republic was subjected to colonization and ruthless resource extraction in the first half of the twentieth. Since independence in 1960, its fortunes have only declined. Armed groups have taken on larger roles in the country's politics. Since 2013 they have controlled most of the country's territory, while a class of government officials get rich from the perquisites of statehood, and everyone else lives off humanitarian handouts. Today, the international community labels the country a "humanitarian crisis." In the context of over a century of colonial, postcolonial, Cold War, and war on terror interventionist projects, the flooding of the Central African Republic with humanitarian workers after 2013, involving thousands of foreigners representing more than one hundred organizations, raises obvious epistemological questions for a divided and warring public. Lombard examines the rumors about theft, tracking the diagnostic practices of locals who see in these foreign projects not a helping hand but the latest round of extraction. Crucially, Lombard also raises the question of who is allowed to have conspiracy theories in a postcolonial state—reinforcing how the term *conspiracy* can function in the twenty-first century as a way of foreclosing both thought and debate. The emblem of local concerns about peacekeeping profiteering, Lombard shows, is perhaps the new modernist high-rise tower built in the capital for aid workers—providing high-end housing to those who have moved from distant shores into the conflict zone. The glass and steel structures offer a constant visual provocation to locals about the goal of foreign humanitarian intervention. For how exactly is it that a country so spectacularly rich in gold and diamonds remains, generation after generation, so ferociously locked in poverty?

To be accused of being a conspiracy theorist, as we have argued, is often to be dismissed as illegitimate, irrational, or corrupt. But what happens when the accused conspiracy theorist is correct and, in fact, blowing the whistle on an unfolding disaster? In his chapter on the financialization of higher education, Robert Meister walks us through his experience as the head of the faculty union at a major public university at a moment of unannounced corporate restructuring. Publicizing the surprising use of total tuition revenue as collateral for bonds to fund other projects, Meister attempts in real time to draw attention to the conversion of students into debt vehicles—a fundamental shift in the logics of higher education. This linkage of tuition to debt explains in part the fantastic rise in tuition over the past decade, as student fees are converted into collateral for ever greater indebtedness. For Meister, the vociferous official denial of his claim (that tuition was being raised to fund construction projects via student debt financing) reveals how powerful the conspiracy theorist allegation can be in shutting down debate and demonizing those who challenge institutional power. The episode raises, for him, fundamental questions about the fate of the contemporary university, the veracity of public debate, and the normalization of financialization to hide radical structural reform. The "invisible hand" of the market here positions students as a source of cash to be massively leveraged for projects other than education. As Meister shows, the steady financialization of higher education means that even the public universities that were once tuition-free and committed to expanding social access now function more like hedge funds, profiting off the escalating debt load of students—a conspiracy against all future generations and a fundamental code-switch in the mission of the university from education to profit.

Part IV. The Politics of Enmity

If there is a primary conspiracy against the world, many would identify it as racism, a foundational violence that continues to organize capital and politics in the twenty-first century. W. E. B. Du Bois (1935, 714) theorized what he called the "propaganda of history" in his assessment of the techniques of white supremacy after the Civil War, linking a project of false memory to a wide range of material forms of voter suppression and physical coercion. In doing so, Du Bois showed how organizing fictions and direct repression could be fused, creating the terms of a counterrevolutionary everyday coded by those in power as normal. In the course of his work in Philadelphia, for example, Du Bois kept track of the laws regulating Black bodies, including one making it illegal for Blacks to "carry arms without special license" or for four or more "to meet together without lawful business of their masters or owners" (Du Bois 2007, 287). Similarly, in her theorization of surveillance as a historic form of anti-blackness, Simone Browne (2015, 25) assesses the "lantern laws" in New York City, which required all nonwhites to carry lanterns at night "so that they could be seen," an early precursor form to "stop and frisk," in which policing is based explicitly on race. We can see in such laws a fundamental elite white fear of the conspiratorial agency, communication, organizing, and potential stealth of the subaltern. For this reason alone, it is important to attend to how accusations of conspiracy function ideologically in any historic moment or social context.

Part IV of *Conspiracy/Theory* examines conspiracy's implications in the politics of demonization, a theme threaded through several of the volume's contributions, but which comes into bold relief in analyses of racist thought. This part tracks racism's psychosocial dynamics, narrative recruitments, and willful misrecognitions. "The Politics of Enmity" considers how the politics of "othering" creates forms of social reproduction in which the powerful self-represent as perpetually injured and in danger, warranting violence—physical, emotional, exclusionary, preemptive—of various sorts.

Faith Hillis, in her chapter on Russian efforts to hack liberal democracy, explores the historical force of a global miasma of disinformation. In light of the widespread accusations that the Russian state manipulated US and British elections in 2016 (leveraging the surprising British vote to leave the European Union and the equally surprising Trump presidency), Hillis focuses on a precursor form from the late nineteenth century, one that continues to have influence today. Like the Russian FSB and the hacking accusations in 2016, the Okhrana, the nineteenth-century Russian secret service, sought in the 1880s to promote the tsarist state across Europe by discrediting its critics. Planting stories demonizing revolutionary subjects led eventually to the invention of an elaborate narrative of a Jewish conspiracy to overthrow the Russian state. This propaganda technique would be repurposed by many states across the twentieth century. Hillis tracks the evolution of specific disinformation campaigns in France to cast Russian émigrés as subversives, leading up to the production of one of the most consequential conspiratorial texts of the twentieth century, the *Protocols of the Elders of Zion*, which first appeared in a Russian newspaper in 1903 and which has been in global circulation ever since. Hillis not only considers the political production of this notorious forgery but also the ways in which the tactical propaganda products of a specific historic moment endure, creating resources that link the *Protocols* to later racist projects (e.g., in Nazi Germany and in subsequent texts like *The Turner Diaries*; see Belew, this volume). The counterrevolutionary project of demonizing activists via deception has a life cycle worthy of serious scholarly review,

Hillis suggests, and in the case of the *Protocols*, unfortunately, more than one.

The politics of terror, and the reactionary formations that can be organized around that label, is also the subject of Darryl Li's chapter. Li carefully unpacks the production of a legal fiction, one that by now has accumulated a high body count around the world as well as a set of "experts" willing to testify to its veracity. At stake is the original designation of al-Qa'ida as a global conspiracy, responsible not only for the suicide-hijacker attacks in the United States in September 2001 but also for actively coordinating violence around the world. This now commonplace claim—the very basis for the constitution of a US counterterror state apparatus and global military mobilization—resides, in large part, in a set of legal documents of curious origin and disposition. Li tracks a set of handwritten documents in Arabic, found in Bosnia in 2002, that were used in US federal court to establish the origins of al-Qa'ida and to link seemingly disparate acts of global violence (going back to the 1980s) to the organization. Li examines the legal trajectory of the file itself, a proffer that was never accepted as evidence in court and that has never even been completely translated, but which has nevertheless been invoked repeatedly in mass media, legal hearings, and national security debates to assert claims about al-Qa'ida's origins, goals, and global history of violence. Tracking the conspiratorial details of a legal case formally detailing a global conspiracy, Li lays bare the production and deployment of a national security fiction, one that has been used to justify a US counterterror response across the Middle East and Africa. As Li shows, a crucial aspect of this project was the testimony of "terrorism experts," sometimes with no Arabic language skills or regional experience, who would cite the proffer documents on television or in court as definitive proof. Thus, the circuit of projections and misrecognitions is completed when unverified documents become the de facto basis for war, predicated on the statements of self-styled experts with no understanding of the communities they are targeting. Here is a conspiracy of the state in action—one in which national defense rides on the production of fictions, which accrue power over time simply via citation, rather than on the basis of intellectual curiosity, factual veracity, or cross-cultural understanding.

While the US war on terror seems to suggest that the configuration of these concerns is contemporary, Hussein Ali Agrama finds them operative across the twentieth century, linking British Imperial politics to the current reliance on military authority in Egypt. Finding a conspiratorial core in the logic of the modern liberal state, Agrama interrogates the ever-present but undertheorized reliance by state actors on secret knowledge and the ways in which that knowledge is deployed to create a collective social imaginary. Crucially, this power has been used to demonize a vast and diverse global Muslim population as inherently threatening. Concerned with the foundational contradictions within the liberal state form, Agrama chronicles the ease with which claims for inclusion and transparent political processes ride alongside the machinations of intelligence agencies, including the force of espionage, plausible deniability by state actors, and covert actions. Considering a specific kind of racism that is marked in Europe and the United States as "Islam," Agrama demonstrates how political demonology works by equipping political commitments with the elements needed to undermine religious and social movements by coding them as inherently other. The "Muslim," rather than designating an individual, becomes a category that carries an existential threat to the liberal democratic form, one that when exposed undoes the claims of the liberal state to authority and legality. Agrama questions the basis for such generic (and consequential) suspicions and argues that the growth of covert intelligence agencies over the past century is co-implicated in the production of such enemy formations. This co-constitution of a dangerous other and an intelligence agency devoted to fighting it in perpetuity raises a fundamental challenge to the liberal idealizations of law, security, and authority.

If manufacturing enemy formations is a key to imperial state power, then what narrative practices support violent domestic counterformations, those devoted not to a collective future but to racist purification? The white power movement in the United States has long been a source of violent conspiratorial modes of thinking, attributing malicious intent to fictional organizations and promoting race war to purge the United States of nonwhite others. In her chapter, Kathleen Belew examines *The Turner Diaries*, a core white power text, showing how a poorly written science fiction set in the year 2099 has been deployed since the 1970s as a guidebook, an inspiration, and a coordinating device for the present-day racist revolutionary movement. In depicting the final war for America, *The Turner Diaries* details in fictional terms how to run an insurgency, organize cell groups, master sabotage techniques, and destabilize a political order. Belew tracks its production and reception among white power groups, detailing its influence on perpetrators of violence against banks, state institutions, and citizens in the 1970s and 1980s. Most prominently, Timothy

McVeigh had a copy on him when he was arrested for the Oklahoma City bombing in 1995. Belew shows how *The Turner Diaries* collects conspiratorial ideas from different periods, playing on feelings of antisemitism and anti-blackness to constitute an idea of the political order as a system that needs to be destroyed in order to be saved. Here, revolutionary thought is connected to end-times thinking, with accelerationist aims—that is, the goal is to reproduce the idea of America through mass violence, an idea that is as long-standing in American popular culture as conspiracy is itself. If *The Turner Diaries* offers a blueprint for insurgency and violence, Belew unpacks how its narrative form—its clumsiness and fictional character—has also allowed agencies like the FBI to discount the seriousness of the white power movement, treating it as a set of not very sophisticated lone individuals rather than as a highly organized group utilizing cell structures with a specific project of waging war on the federal government. Belew explores the power of whiteness in American life, often identified as the unmarked social category, but transformed via *The Turner Diaries* into an enduring invitation to would be terrorists/revolutionaries to embrace the very end-game of politics.

Conspiracy/Theory concludes with an epilogue focused on the stakes of conspiratorial reason in the twenty-first century. Considering the range of conspiratorial practices that infused the violent insurrection against the certification of the 2020 presidential election on January 6, 2021, in Washington, DC, it argues that developing a sophisticated reading of conspiratorial thought is vital to contemporary politics. Separating the authoritarian ambitions from the political disinformation projects, the white supremacy militarism, the money-making schemes, and the QAnon mythmaking allows different modes of accountability as well as an appreciation of the range of preexisting aggrievements that were so successfully mobilized in the attack on Congress. Powerful narratives—of a stolen election, a deep state, a race war—were powerfully merged in the service of an attempted authoritarian coup d'état. Understanding the informational tactics and histories behind the violence on January 6 is also a map of a politics of enmity in which political rivals are cast as evil, rage is cultivated, and existential danger is felt as the central motivating political strategy. To assume that simply branding these forces as unreason is enough to blunt their power in the contemporary world is to miss the argument of this book, which has asked for a careful evaluation of psyops campaigns as well as of individual efforts to theorize what they are experiencing in everyday life. In short, *Conspiracy/Theory* argues that careful attention must be paid to the reality-making power of narrative, in order to allow a broader and richer space for collective assessment and the testing of claims and evidence, all while acknowledging the proliferation of multifaceted disinformation campaigns that seek to recruit and activate all those who are able to hear the call.

NOTES

1   For a detailed engagement with contemporary online misinformation campaigns, see Joan Donovan's *The Media Manipulation Casebook* project at https://mediamanipulation.org/definitions/media-manipulation (accessed February 23, 2023).
2   See the Google Books Ngram Viewer's citational rate comparison of "conspiracy theory" and "critical theory" from 1900 to 2019, available at https://books.google.com/ngrams/graph?content=conspiracy+the ory%2Ccritical+theory&year_start=1900&year_end=2019&corpus=en -2019&smoothing=3.

PART I
ORGANIZING FICTIONS

GEORGE SHULMAN

01 IMPASSE AND GENRE IN AMERICAN POLITICS AND LITERATURE

This chapter analyzes Richard Hofstadter's critique of "the paranoid style" and its influential impact on the terms of liberal and left engagement with the event of Donald Trump. Hofstadter's analysis of the structure and appeal of a paranoid style of thinking and narrative politics has been invoked to address Trump's political appeal and electoral success in 2016, the "Big Lies" that animated his presidency, his "Big Steal" reelection campaign and its QAnon corollary, the coup attempt to save democracy from a conspiracy to steal it, and the bitter opposition to vaccines and mandates during the COVID-19 pandemic. Exploring Hofstadter's argument and how it has been taken up to address these phenomena also entails asking how critics understand the relation between factuality and fiction in politics. At present, that question is intensified and fateful because upward of 70 percent of the Republican Party truly believe that a conspiracy of elites, the deep state, and the "radical" Democratic Party "stole" the election and are stealing "our country." To assess the terms and implications of Hofstadter's critique also requires that we ask: What kind of political "style," to use his felicitous term, constitutes an effective and durable remedy to the paranoid style gripping virtually half the adult American population?

My claim will be that Hofstadter's argument bespeaks a genre of criticism that pits rationality and expertise against the irrationality and populism of a mass public and that remedies the public's ignorance, indignation, and fantasy by defending empirical factuality and specifying true interests. Originating in the Federalist Papers, this genre of criticism bespeaks a modern rationalism that dichotomizes fact and fiction, minimizes the necessity of narrative in politics, and takes empirical factuality and material interests as self-evident to rational minds. As a result, it prevents us from responding adequately to the manifest crises of our republic. The dangers in fantasy and fiction are obvious, and the anxiety to posit an impermeable border between them is understandable; but it should be clear by now that any wall imprisons those seeking protection. If we assume instead that facts and interests are not self-evident but become intelligible only through interpretation, that interpretations inescapably bespeak a passionate frame of reference as their background condition, and that specific interpretations and broader frames entail opposing worldly implications, then we can see and politicize the constructive but fraught interplay between fiction-making and world-building in all our social practices.

One lesson of the political theory canon, after all, is that the arguments and actions constituting political life are shaped by "organizing fictions"—narratives, paradigms, perspectival frames, visions, or "noble lies" as Plato says. We hold a deep, visceral attachment to the organizing fictions by which we have learned to make sense of reality, to conceive our interests, define justice, frame identity, envision a good life, imagine futurity, justify antagonism, posit (im)possibility, and stipulate action. Political theorists repeatedly trace how worldly reality is at once elastic—as it is reshaped by the fictions (of race, gender, sovereign individuality, or nation) by which we organize the world—and yet can also stubbornly resist and indeed defeat those projects. More specifically, we can trace how fiction-making and world-building unfold *differently*, depending on the genres we bespeak, enact, and rework. Whereas the heirs of Hofstadter draw on what I call a *realist* or *rationalist* genre to expose paranoid fantasy and speak as if they inhabit reality as the ones who know, I propose that we draw on the example of American novelists, who use genres of fabulation—including what Thomas Pynchon calls creative paranoia— not to escape American reality but to confront the deranged, destructive, and indeed paranoid fictions that animate it. Their truth-telling through self-exposing fictions enables us to digest the ways that fiction-making is not only inescapable and dangerous but valuable and generative. My goal in this chapter, therefore, is two-sided: to analyze Hofstadter's text in a way that explicates the limits, even the inevitable failure, of criticizing Trump and the right through a rationalist frame; and to propose that a generative political alternative to political crisis requires facing the limits of realism as a genre and undertaking the *poesis* of fiction-making. Here I am inspired by novelists of the American condition. My immediate object, then, is Hofstadter's essay as a genre of criticism, but my aim is to deepen reflection on the relation of fiction (and genre) to politics.[1]

HOFSTADTER'S ARGUMENT

Hofstadter first developed his argument as a lecture given at Oxford, literally on the eve of the Kennedy assassination; he first published "The Paranoid Style in Politics" in *Harper's Magazine* in the fall of 1964, shortly after the Warren Commission concluded that no conspiracy was involved; and a 1965 volume of his essays then featured it (Hoftstadter 1996b). Hofstadter uses the term *paranoid* because "no other word adequately evokes the qualities of heated exaggeration, suspiciousness, and conspiratorial fantasy" that characterize what he also calls a "style" or "mode" of expression. He uses the word not in a clinical sense to denote "a certified lunatic"; rather, "it is the use of paranoid modes of expression by more or less normal people that makes the phenomena significant" (1996b, 4). By style he means to connote "a way of seeing the world and expressing oneself," and he thus claims to focus on "the way in which ideas are believed and advocated," not "the truth or falsity of their content." Indeed, he notes that "paranoid writing begins with certain defensible judgments"—about organized powers, inequality, and social change—that are translated into a "grandiose theory of conspiracy" and an "apocalyptic and absolutist framework" (4, 17). As Hofstadter identifies the features of the paranoid "style," we see him introduce aesthetic and affective dimensions into the study of politics.[2]

The paranoid style begins with what he calls a "defensible judgment" about a conflict or crisis; but this judgment is organized in a certain way. First, "the central image is that of a vast and sinister conspiracy, a gigantic yet subtle machinery of influence set in motion to undermine and destroy a way of life" (29). A *narrative* of imminent danger is thus organized around an *image* of malevolent power. The paranoid style turns a history that includes specific conspiracies or conflicts into a narrative in which "history *is* a conspiracy, set in motion by demonic forces of almost transcendent power" that provoke an *apocalyptic* conflict that will determine "the birth and death of whole worlds, whole political orders, whole systems of human values" (29).

Second, the narrative framework includes "an elaborate concern with demonstration," a "heroic striving for 'evidence' to prove that the unbelievable is the only thing that can be believed." The paranoid style is thus "intensely rationalistic" in its "accumulation of factual details as constituting overwhelming proof," and therefore, "what distinguishes the paranoid style is not the absence of verifiable facts . . . but the curious leap in imagination . . . from the undeniable to the unbelievable." Unbelievable, for Hofstadter, is a depiction of reality "far more coherent than the real world, since it leaves no room for mistakes, failures, or ambiguities" (37).

Third, the narrative produces a protagonist who "constantly lives at a turning point," feels that "time is running out," and takes on heroic and redemptive action (30). Accordingly, fourth, the character of the narrative and its protagonist entail a style of politics, or rather, what Hofstadter deems a refusal of politics: "He does not see the social as something to be mediated or compromised, in the manner of a working politician. Since what is at stake is always a conflict between absolute good and absolute evil, the quality needed is not a willingness to compromise but the will to fight things to the finish. Nothing but complete victory will do." In turn, Hofstadter points to the "the fundamental paradox" that the paranoid protagonist, facing a "free, active, demonic agent," embraces "imitation of the enemy," taking on its secrecy and plotting, its extra-legal action and violence, its suspension of the liberal norms that the paranoid professes to defend. As demonizing involves projection, it justifies actions that mirror the enemy; comparing the paranoid to a "sadomasochistic Puritan" punishing Catholics, Hofstadter sees him enjoying the very desires and practices he professes to condemn (32).[3]

But there are deep ambiguities in his account. For Hofstadter depicts a social referent provoking or summoning a paranoid response: "The paranoid disposition is *mobilized* into action chiefly by social conflicts that involve ultimate schemes of value and that bring fundamental fears and hatreds, rather than negotiable interests, into political action" (39). It is *aroused* by a confrontation of opposed interests that are (or are felt to be) "totally irreconcilable" and so "not susceptible to the normal political process of bargain and compromise" (39). He thus hovers between saying a paranoid "style" or "disposition" is provoked by real and even existential conflicts of value, which make normal politics seem insufficient to a crisis, and saying that an exaggerated *perception* (of existential danger) generates a polarization that *precludes* a normal politics mediating conflicting interests. Rather than avow or enter this space of irresolution between paranoid subjectivity and worldly crisis or conflict, which puts at risk his sense of the adequacy or rationality of normal politics as "negotiation and compromise," he depicts a paranoid style that converts social circumstance into an apocalyptic—inherently exaggerated and destructive—narrative of history *as* a conspiracy involving totalized conflict. "We are all sufferers of history, but the paranoid is a double sufferer, since he is afflicted not only by the real world, with the rest of us, but by his fantasies" of "a world of power" that is "omnipotent, sinister, and malicious" (39).[4]

This translation occurs, he proposes, because of status anxiety. Whereas in Europe, paranoid politics occurs at the level of and through the state, as demonstrated by Hitler and Stalin, Hofstadter argues that "in the American experience, ethnic and religious conflicts with their threat of the submergence of whole systems of value, have plainly been the major focus for militant and suspicious minds of this sort"; but he also insists that "suspicious discontent" has been "the preferred style *only* of *minority* movements" (9). And whereas nineteenth-century proponents of the paranoid style "were fending off threats to a well-established way of life in which they played an important part," the modern right wing already "feels dispossessed; America has largely been taken away from them and their kind, though they are determined to try to repossess it and prevent the final destructive act of subversion" (23). At the same time, "the growth of mass media and their use in politics has made politics . . . an arena into which private emotions and personal problems can readily be projected." Accordingly, the paranoid style recurs in history and cannot be abolished; especially because of modern media, political leaders "are forced to deal, as an element in their calculations, with the emotional life of the masses, which is not something they can altogether create or manipulate, but something they must cope with" (63).

Hofstadter rejects this style for several obvious reasons. First, because the fuel or motive of this rhetoric is a wounded sense of *displacement*, the style justifies, projects, and channels *ressentiment*. Like Ahab's monomania, this style posits a demonically malevolent object—King George, the state as Leviathan, the slave-power conspiracy, the trusts, Wall Street, the Jew, communism, globalist elites—and "plots" how this willful agent and author covertly *controls* life, causing our servitude and suffering. Giving resentment a cause and object, this "way" of seeing and "style" of expression moralizes conflicts, demonizes adversaries, and personalizes history in contrast to what Hofstadter deems a "political" (and also rational or "defensible") perspective on history, which emphasizes impersonal institutions and social processes.

Moreover, if a conspiratorial narrative purports to seamlessly explain every coincidence, accident, and event in a vast design, it displaces both the complexity and the contingency that are crucial to a political sensibility toward social actuality. As fiction replaces rather than illuminates reality, melodramatic and apocalyptic simplification displaces politics. Hofstadter thus foregrounds affective and aesthetic dimensions in politics—how motivation and style constitute political action—but in a wholly negative or pathologized sense. Seeing history *as* a conspiracy shows the danger in fiction as fantasy: if we imagine an omnipotent and malevolent author masterminding a plot, then art replaces life, and our rancorous projection of an enemy displaces mediated forms of engagement with complex institutions. Timothy Melley thus echoes Hofstadter when he says that "rather than a more complex theory of social control, the conspiratorial model projects the ideal qualities of the individual—rationality, intentionality, and self-control—into the social order itself, eventually seeing it as a willful and malevolent being." As a demonic agent is endowed with "a total and magical control," the "disenchantment" that Max Weber identified in modernity is overcome, and the world is re-enchanted (Melley 2020a, 431).[5]

As a "way" of "seeing the world and expressing ourselves," therefore, a paranoid style closes the gaps between reality and interpretation, between life and narrative, between historical complexities and moral absolutes. Because Hofstadter protests the capture of the real by a suspicious symbolic, a generous reading could say he prefigures Eve Sedgwick's use of Melanie Klein to depict a "paranoid position" characterized by a hermeneutic of suspicion, demonization of power, and presumption of harm. But Hofstadter's critique enacts its own problematic and, in certain regards, paranoid displacements; as a style or way of seeing the world and expressing ourselves, it works to legitimate an elite-governed interest-group liberalism rather than the affective politics of what Sedgwick calls the *reparative position*.

Most obviously, Hofstadter locates the paranoid style only at the margin of American politics, not as a hegemonic (and thus bipartisan) common sense that organizes state power and national belonging. As what Michael Rogin (1987) later calls "counter-subversive demonology," a paranoid style in fact characterizes the white supremacy central to American history, a paranoid demonization of people marked Black and Red that is central both to local practices of popular power and to organized state violence. The racialized framing of what Carl Schmitt (1995) calls a "frontier" between "friend and enemy" is constitutive of the liberal world of pluralist politics that Hofstadter takes as his norm and ideal, which always defines, polices, and violently proscribes the impulses, practices, and people it deems antiliberal, alien, subversive.

As Rogin argues, Hofstadter's liberalism is founded on "white over red and black" not only materially, by expropriating Indian land and Black labor, but also symbolically, as European colonists make themselves "white" by projecting disowned aspects of their humanity onto demonized others. This motivated disavowal, splitting, and projection remain the deep (and bipartisan) structure organizing an expansionist or imperial state seeking new frontiers or enacting "anticommunism" and a "war on terror." As Rogin (1987, 284) puts it, "When the nation itself is imagined as an imperial self we have entered counter-subversive territory, for then the contradictions denied at the center of American life are located in the dark side of Americanism, the alien." What Hofstadter calls the paranoid style thus appears not at the margins of American politics, nor in "minority movements," for it is the necessary complement that protects an idealized, exceptionalist "American" identity. Its "Manichean division of the world, its war on local and partial loyalties, its attachment to secret hierarchical orders, its invasiveness and fear of boundary invasion, its fascination with violence, and its desire to subordinate political variety to a dominant authority" are, Rogin argues, recurring features of the *dominant* mode of American liberal nationalism. As it creates extralegal zones of exception in which liberal values are suspended, it "imitates the subversion it attacks. Practices attributed to the subversive actually depict counter-subversive aspirations; the more powerful the demonology, the more it speaks, against itself, truths about American politics" (Rogin 1987, 284). In sum, Hofstadter displaces racial domination, majoritarian phobia, and state violence when he juxtaposes a deranged and marginal minority to the rationality of a pluralist center.

Second, Hofstadter thereby displaces the role of organizing fictions in all politics, including the liberalism that is sanitized and protected by his own narrative. Finding genre (as a way of seeing the world and expressing the self) *only* in the melodramatic narrative of those he casts as marginal extremists, he does not see the genres of American politics more broadly, and he seems oblivious to the specifically paranoid (or "counter-subversive") features of his own critique. In my view, the dominant and recurring form of American political rhetoric joins what the literary critic Leo Marx (1964) once called "pastoralism," which conjures an idealized America unmarked by history, inequality, or conflict, to a "paranoid style," which conjures monstrous powers and alien threats that subvert this ideal of harmony and plenitude. An idealized America (in one genre form) is protected by a counterinsurgency war (against various reds and terrorists) and culture war (against the forms of "blackness" that disorder the normative codes of a propertied, masculine individualism). Pastoral idealization is the systole and paranoid demonology is the diastole that drive the beating heart of American nationalism. The liberal principles of civic nationalism that Hofstadter celebrates (formal equality, rule of law, pluralism, and representative government) live inside a frontier of phobia marking the dangerous, un-American outside, which is always already inside. As D. H. Lawrence (1990) said, white Americans repeat pious rhetoric of "love and produce, love and produce," while underneath this liberal and Christian surface is a "hum of destruction" audible to those who would listen.[6]

In genre terms, we could also follow Hayden White (1973) to depict a dominant "mode" of "romance," which promises mastery over circumstance and time to an individual subject or national protagonist seeking to achieve or defend self-determination against despotic or malevolent powers that threaten captivity or emasculation. The modes of romance that narrate sovereign freedom involve an idealization that entails a melodramatic or gothic rendering of danger. Narratives with such pastoral and paranoid features authorized the American Revolution, the Civil War, the late-nineteenth-century populist insurgency against corporate power, and since Richard Nixon, a right-wing project that depicts elites using the state to benefit Blacks and women at the expense of white men. Rather than propose a taxonomy to distinguish specific genre features, though, I would emphasize the entwinement of vernacular idioms, inherited narrative forms, and habitual expectations in the highly charged images and tropes that recurrently organize American politics. Those plots of freedom endangered can be symptoms not only of declining or threatened status but also of atomized individualism and idealized exceptionalism; such plots can be mobilized by the state, but also against it, by established elites, or against them. If we say that no one simply stands outside of genre, and that all political speech and criticism occurs through genres we bespeak and enact but also rework, then I can ask: through what genres do critics address the inflated and split character—at once idealized and paranoid—of American political romance?[7]

By asking this question, I fold Hofstadter within the politics of genre and cast his effort to exempt himself as characteristic of the still prevailing genre of criticism initiated by Alexander Hamilton and James Madison in the Federalist Papers. In that genre, critics typically invoke the empirical and pragmatic against the ideological, extremist, and irrational. Rather than own their realism as itself a genre, as a convention of thought and expression that mediates our relation to reality, critics in this genre claim to inhabit the real, as the ones who know, compared to those captured by ideology and emotion. At American origins, for example, a revolutionary period of pervasive democratic participation involved what Bernard Bailyn (1967) called paranoid rhetoric, depicting a dangerously centralized and conspiratorial power corrupting and enslaving a free people. Denouncing this exuberant enthusiasm for democracy as the irrational attachment of backward-looking farmers to an archaic political form, Madison and Hamilton invoked progress, science, and modernity as they endorsed a powerful central state, cosmopolitan elites, machinery to contain pluralistic factions, and highly mediated—mostly indirect—political representation. Such a system would prevent majoritarian movements and assure rule by rational elites to save "the people" from their regressive instincts and from demagogues exploiting them. Hofstadter inhabits this genre of critique when he defends New Deal liberalism, ethnic pluralism, and a new elite of experts against the paranoid style of a nativist, populist "New Right."[8]

The displacement of the paranoid style from the center to the margin, and the displacement of genre from liberal nationalism to an inflamed antiliberal minority, enables a style of criticism that makes liberal "realism" and "pragmatism" the only valid genre of a "politics" conceived narrowly as negotiation—"bargaining and compromise"—over material resources by elites adjudicating group interests. Hofstadter secures this realism by positing boundaries—between illegitimate and legitimate forms of politics, between merely personal issues and properly political considerations, between emotional excess and rational faculties, between ideological militancy and pragmatic bargaining, between symbolic expression and instrumental action. The counter-subversive features of his critique appear in policing these distinctions not only against Goldwater-supporting "pseudo-conservatives" in the Republican Party but also against New Left, antiwar, and abolitionist activists. The terms of his critique of the right not only authorize liberal critique of the left, though it is not the explicit object of his analysis, but also displace attention from the paranoid style of a white majority and the imperial state that speaks in its name.

Hofstadter therefore enacts a third displacement as he pathologizes *democratic* aspirations unless contained within the form of interest-group liberalism. His critique is directed against an emerging "new" right, but by anchoring their style in the populists, he echoes Madison and Hamilton as he reverses the right's antistatist and counter-subversive narrative by construing only the right, and not (also) the state, as the paranoid problem. He thereby equates the populist and democratic and reduces both to rancorous resentment and irrational yearning for an impossible coherence. The price of his critique of the paranoid style is thus two-sided: it defines organizing fantasy and fiction-making as the betrayal of proper politics and not what all politics necessarily traffics in; and it forecloses rather than recovers the radically democratic.[9]

FROM HOFSTADTER TO TRUMP: IMPASSE AND GENRE

When Democratic Party and media elites use this genre of analysis on Trump and his supporters that Hillary Clinton famously called "deplorables," these displacements are repeated. These critics make Trump's paranoid style a scandalous anomaly as they deny its historic roots and systemic function. Enacting a counter-subversive narrative to protect the liberal nationalism they idealize, they deny their own involvement in status politics and their own investment in genre as they righteously reject the rancorous fictions of adversaries. They displace the failures of a liberal regime by making the paranoid style of Trump and his base a problem external rather than internal to it. To make a pluralist and constitutional interest-group liberalism the *remedy* for Trump, they must sever it from its violent history and from the long political impasse and crisis of confidence that produced him, and figures like him, across the Euro-Atlantic world.

We can trace the path from Hofstadter's argument to its use now by noting the powerful strand of popular reaction to neoliberalism and globalization in the Euro-Atlantic world. By targeting immigrants, cosmopolitans, and elites, this politics expresses the anxiety and rage of enfranchised white citizens suffering increasing precarity, inequality, and displacement in a globalizing economy. But these citizens do not acknowledge the even starker inequality and disproportionate suffering created by a global "color line," the afterlife of slavery, and the racial state of exception these entail. Deep structural forces—uneven globalization, automation, and the ongoing legacies of colonialism in Europe and slavery in the United States—have thus created conditions of suffering and racial division that seem intractable and never-ending. Significant political change would depend on enough whites joining rather than rejecting a multiracial coalition to transform a regime historically wed to economic inequality, climate catastrophe, and racism. What organizing fictions are available to imagine, justify, and engender that possibility? Do we have a theoretical/critical language to perceive, let alone amplify, their emergence?[10]

On the one hand, in the face of right-wing populism, media pundits and Democratic Party elites tend to link their technocratic liberalism to the reality principle, and racial nationalism to fantasy, nostalgia, and rage. Their default logic equates fiction and fantasy with ideology, as radically contrasted to "reality," as if the real were self-evident and could be apprehended without the mediation of imaginative structures. This technocratic and progressive liberalism remains ameliorist and presumes a supposedly meritocratic, but really oligarchic, elitism that has provoked rage against a "rigged system." On the other hand, left critics of the Democratic Party rightly object to the displacements by which liberal normality is idealized, protected, and minimally reformed. But the left remains oblivious to its own genre of criticism. Insofar as it assumes that white workers will cross racial lines and enact a radical politics if only they are told the truth (or given the facts) about capitalism, this genre at the very least minimizes the grip of race and gender—of whiteness and masculinity—as organizing fictions inseparably entwined with the meaning of class in America. As long as it devalues so-called identity politics, as if it merely divided "working families" who otherwise would be united, the left will be unable to name and address the real racial codes and gender norms that white men and women are attached to and anxiously defend, and it will be unable to forge a coalition that can address the intersectional injuries of a vast, multiracial majority of precarious women and men without college degrees. Trapped by its own organizing fiction of a 99 percent made conscious of their true interests, it repeats the national romance that recurrently promises to redeem white men.

Because the neoliberalism of the Democratic Party (since Bill Clinton) created an opening for—and indeed called forth—the paranoid style invested in a melodramatic, nostalgic, and conspiratorial racial nation-alism, we inhabit a structural impasse in which the politics of class identity and economic precarity remain organized by white supremacy and toxic masculinity; and we are stuck in this impasse because the left has not articulated a credible, alternative narrative. The political problem is not only structural but discursive: the romance of civic nationalism—the genre organizing American politics around inclusion, prosperity, and progress—is in grave crisis; but in mass media, popular culture, and ac-ademic discourse it has seemed impossible to imagine a future "beyond" neoliberalism and white supremacy, let alone the nation-state. Instead, we see projections of an imaginary past to restore or resume, whether a 1950s moment of white prosperity and privilege on the right, or a new New Deal on the left. Surely, labor nationalism is more just, inclusive, and reparative than the right's despotic project, but climate catastrophe and endemic racial domination require not just more and higher paying wage labor but a radical reconstruction of sustainable livelihoods, forms of belonging, credible futures, and meaningful democracy.

Frames of reference and organizing fictions undergo such crises, and in such moments in the history of a community, or religion, or organization, people may "know" in an inchoate way that the assump-tions and expectations framing their practices and sense of the good life are no longer credible. My view is that whites across class lines do "know," in *tacit* and inarticulate(d) ways, that our historic form of life is failing them, unjust to others, and destroying the earth; yet, they lack a salient way to *acknowledge* what they know and cannot yet conceive the possibility of living otherwise. Absent such language, human beings remain gripped by their inherited vision of the good life despite its manifest failures: we seem driven by what Lauren Berlant (2011) calls "cruel optimism," we "res-urrect the dead," as Marx put it, or we undergo despair and its nihilistic symptoms instead of articulating and investing in what Marx called "a poetry of the future."

But how does an imaginative framework shift, or a new organizing fiction emerge? Not because we are exposed to facts that remedy our ig-norance, to the fallacies in our logic, or to experts who explain our true interests, thereby revealing the truth that would finally enable us to face reality instead of being captured by fantasy. Theory in this cognitive or epis-temological form always fails to be persuasive. Instead, we become open to change if, as, or when we are inspired by others enacting a different practice of living and horizon of futurity, or as our own struggles engender that incipient sense of possibility. What Cornelius Castoriadis (1975) calls "radical imagination," and the "figures of the newly thinkable" it offers, does not appear *ex nihilo*, nor as the exclusive possession of those Percy Bysshe Shelley calls "poets as legislators"; but rather, it emerges in and by what Fred Moten (Moten and Harney 2013) calls "socio-poetic insurgency." In this regard what changed between Trump's election in 2016 and the election campaign of summer 2020 was the conjunction of a devastating pandemic and the murder of George Floyd, which created an unprecedented synergy as whites—perceiving the limits of neoliberalism, the value of essential workers, and the racial disparity harming them—crossed the color line to support protests against police violence organized and led by M4BL (the Movement for Black Lives). By connecting the state's willful and depraved indifference to life, and the deranged, ongoing targeting of Black life, activists not only promoted paranoid assumptions about power, and connected the dots to depict a system or regime, but also expressed the dream of living otherwise in another world that is ignored by Hofstadterian analysis of paranoid suspicion and anger in politics. And that fiction-making, to conjure a democracy to come, was inseparable from—both a cause and consequence of—world-building by fugitive organizing and flagrantly public protest. In speech and action, an opening beyond impasse was newly imagined and prefigured, even if not (yet) taken up or generalized as a hegemonic alternative. By this brief account of impasse and genre, then, I mean to have set the stage to explore in more detail how a "paranoid style" is not (only) a pathology for political realism to "cope with" but (also) a democratizing resource. For a "creative paranoia" can both problematize the dangers Hofstadter feared, and yet also bear a generative poesis and praxis.

FICTION AND POLITICS

Since the "hermeneutic turn" in critical theory, it is a commonplace that facts do not speak for themselves, and that it is through paradigms and frames of reference that we select empirical evidence and endow it with both significance and worldly implications. In this sense, "theory" comes "before" the realities it makes visible or important, even as it reveals how phenomena long taken as given and real are invented, contingent, and changeable artifacts. In turn, I am conceiving the trope of an "organizing fiction" not in referential terms of true and false, to be (in)validated by self-evident empirical evidence that precedes it, but rather in a mythopoetic and constitutive sense as a "passionate frame of reference" in Wittgenstein's (1972) phrase, that is materialized in social practices and instantiated as collective identities. The issue we face now is less one of fake facts and ignorance—though these are real and indeed grave problems—and more one of the energy invested in what James Baldwin (1984) called a willful innocence, a defiant energy elicited and mobilized by organizing fictions that people defend violently and self-destructively against the evidence of their senses and the claims of others. As literary artists have dramatized by protagonists like Ahab, Gatsby, and Sutpen, we are trapped by the fictions we invest in, live out, and make real at great cost to others and ourselves; like these characters, we bring doom on ourselves because our fictions disavow crucial aspects of reality, which return to haunt and cripple if not to destroy us. And because these organizing fictions are inscribed and embodied at visceral and unconscious levels, they are undone neither by reason, facts, and logic, nor by events or even catastrophes.

Rather, our capacity to undertake change, or alternatively, to accept change we did not initiate or welcome, is elicited, inspired, and supported only when an alternative frame of reference composes our suffering, ambivalence, and aspiration into a compelling narrative that not only dramatizes what we already know, feel, and wish for but inflects that tacit knowledge and inchoate desire by new figurations of possibility that we invest in making true and real. Just as literary artists create fictions to dramatize the animating power and fatal costs of the fictions that organize us, so too does a creative politics not so much replace the fictive or fantastical with the real and prosaic as mobilize people around an organizing fiction that depicts not only the grip of the reality they inherit but also its contingency and their capacity to change it. A politically salient counter to political mobilization by what William Connolly (2017) calls the "aspirational fascism" of the Trumpian right thus requires not exposure of facts to remedy ignorance or false consciousness, nor the pragmatic assembling of extant interests into an electoral coalition—though these are crucial—but compelling counterfictions that, like good metaphors, carry our imaginations from the familiar toward the unexpected, to open an incipient possibility for new possibilities. In literature and in politics, such truth-telling not only exposes fiction-making but requires it; rather than dichotomize reality and fiction, let us face the disturbing truth that fictionality is at once inescapable, dangerous, and generative.

In these terms I return specifically to "paranoia" as a trope for thinking both theory and politics. I hope I have been clear that I am invested not so much in redeeming paranoia as in acknowledging the necessity and value of fiction-making. The dangers in fantasy and fiction—and thus in paranoia—are manifest today in such intensely antidemocratic and violent ways that critical and political anxiety about illusion, self-deception, and disavowal—about seduction by narrative and fantasy—is surely justified. In another context and with more space for elaboration, I would respond to such anxiety by depicting the dynamic interplay between fiction and reality in our social practices and in our discursive conventions for making sense of the world. I would parse how social reality is elastic in response to our fictions and yet also a stubbornly confounding limit, a mocking return of the disavowed. I would invoke Alexis de Tocqueville and Hannah Arendt to emphasize that a shared "common sense" about the (f)actuality of the world is possible among otherwise atomized and isolated citizens only if plural and democratic spaces enable them to discover the world as a common object by compelling them to confront contrasting experiences of it and perspectives on it. The "literacy" of citizens and readers alike, I would argue, means judging unreliable narrators and adjudicating contrasting narratives, and that involves contestable claims that invoke evidence to argue about the way the world is. The goal of such arguments is not to devalue reality or factuality but to revalue fictionality in the service of a truer, complex, sense of the real. Though my focus on genre has suggested the staggering degree to which life follows art, I would follow Friedrich Nietzsche to ask whether our art serves life or impoverishes it, and I would follow Baldwin as he composes fictions that bear witness to what has been unspeakable and unsaid, inaudible and invisible. As Nietzsche said of those practicing a "gay science," we contest the "will to truth" in its dominant forms, but because we still love truth, only differently than before.[11]

Let me conclude, then, by invoking canonical political theory as well as the examples of Herman Melville, Pynchon, and Sedgwick, to creatively rethink the value of the so-called paranoid style as a kind of fiction-making. First, I propose viewing paranoia neither as necessarily pathological, nor as a merely individual and psychological condition, but rather as implicitly or potentially *political* in its capacities as an organizing fiction and dramatic narrative. After all, political theory since Sophocles, let alone Plato, has presumed the necessity of making sense of a world and emplotting a history whose structure and meaning, causes and fate, are not self-evident. As C. Wright Mills argued in 1959, we must identify and name "public causes" if we are to politicize what otherwise would remain merely private (individual or psychological) "troubles." As Sheldon Wolin argued in 1960, "political theory" is a practice that composes apparently discrete features of social life into an "architectonic vision" of a whole or regime and that emplots its history as a dramatic narrative of crisis and fateful choices. They grasped that the core of both theory and politics is a dramatization of social control, a plotting of how power works, a forging of protagonists, and a figuration of both agency and possibility. As Ahab's plotting of a whale—taken by critics to signify objects like the state, the slave-power, and whiteness itself, and not only a demonic metaphysical agent—is dramatized by Melville's plotting of a novel, we can see the intimate and complex connection between literary, theoretical, and political practices that try to make sense of the constitutive and destructive ways people make sense. In turn, readers and citizens are wise to ask: What are the designs of the theorists, artists, and leaders who would interpellate us by their art?

If "connecting the dots" between appearances, events, and structures is the very premise of literary art, theoretical paradigms, and organized political action, then perhaps paranoid styles appear on a kind of spectrum that runs from Ahab, say, to Freud and Marx, de Beauvoir and Du Bois, and on to their contemporary heirs. For if we are dominated by powers and plots, those committed to democratic forms of life need to name them to oppose them; insurgent politics entails weaving the disparate and discrete into wider forms of sense that name circumstances, identify danger, designate causation, dramatize meaning, and indicate "what is to be done," as Lenin put it. As critical and political theory thus values a hermeneutic of suspicion, traces the dialectic of structure and agency, and endorses organized, public forms of contest or antagonism, we can see the outlines of a politicizing paranoia committed to expanding democratic agency against visible, and invisibly invasive, forms of modern power. A politics invested in democratic empowerment weds forms of knowledge, suspicion, and aggression to struggle against a world organized in life-denying and murderously unequal ways, which poses the Ahabian danger of whom insurgents become in their quest to contest injustice.

Second, therefore, I put the *arguments* of theory in conversation with the *dramatizations* of American literature. On the one hand, novels such as *Moby-Dick; The Great Gatsby; Absalom, Absalom!;* or *Beloved* show how an organizing fantasy—of sovereign freedom and masculine mastery, of new frontiers, of productivity as progress, of full belonging, of redeeming a traumatic past—drives a protagonist toward self-destruction. But paradoxically, to really see and feel—to acknowledge—the reality and consequences of such an impasse can be liberating, not imprisoning. On the other hand, therefore, such novels do not leave readers—and citizens—with the false choice between grim reality or escapist fantasy; rather, they place us at a threshold: we must ourselves take up a capacity for fiction-making that is wholly entwined with our sense of the real and with our worldly practices. To take on that authorship or authority is surely to risk the danger of inventing a "true world" by which we devalue the actual one, as Nietzsche (1997, 23) warned, to inflict on ourselves the misrecognition and disavowal dramatized by tragedy. However, to not only disclose such dangers in vivid ways but also to conjure ways to live otherwise, we still must compose counterfictions. Indeed, if people cannot be, before they act or legislate, what they (hope to) become by way of it, our inventive capacity for imaginative projection is crucial. By shifting our attention from the epistemological problem of validating claims about the world to the rhetorical register that traces the generativity of speech-acts, literary art can help us foreground the affective and worldly difference between the rationalism of critical theory and the visceral and symbolic registers at which political action is motivated.

It is notable that in the era of Hofstadter's essay, American writers thematized paranoia, though it was also a concern of Edgar Allan Poe and Melville. Novels by Norman Mailer, Don DeLillo, and Pynchon gave dramatic form to the perception (and so the premise) that all dimensions of reality are related, that human beings are deeply connected to each other and to nature, and that these connections are not so much invisible as hidden in plain sight if only we had the vision to see them. As Pynchon (1973, 188, 703) put it in *Gravity's Rainbow*, paranoia is both "the Puritan reflex of seeking other orders behind the visible," and "the leading edge of the discovery that everything is connected." Such paranoid visions offered no new facts or information but made connections visible by dramatizing how protagonists come to see the familiar differently. Still, like the Greek tragedians they also dramatized its danger of denying the space between art and life, between narrative coherence and rampant contingency, as if to deny "the joke between appearance and reality," as Ralph Ellison (1964) put it. Then we entrap ourselves in an organizing fiction; by presuming a degree of knowledge and certainty no one can possess, and we risk repeating a tragedy of self-destruction. To discern power and its impact, to make sense (and art) out of chaos, to emplot temporality, and to conjure collective action, fictional protagonists (like their readers) must run that risk; but it can be mitigated by the ironic distance these texts practice to engender self-reflection in readers and citizens.

I credit the concern of critics who diagnose paranoia as a symptom of what Melley (2016) calls "agency panic," whereby we try to protect a fantasy of sovereign agency by identifying (and killing off) threats to it, as we see in injured Ahab's enraged monomania, or in Trumpian politics now. Just as contemporary social life seems characterized by increasingly diffuse, circulating forms of power—as in neoliberalism and institutional racism—so too we see paranoid styles of theorizing or narrating distorting reality by designating intentional authors, simplistic (and seamless) plots, and malevolent purposes. Such arguments rework Hofstadter to criticize a paranoid style that salvages ideas of integral agency and coherent meaning rather than face how modern forms of social control and mediatization undo them. But we also might test this critique by asking: Did Occupy Wall Street or Bernie Sanders bespeak a paranoid style by naming "the 1 percent" or "Wall Street" the source of American decline? Is that style modified but still enacted by naming neoliberal globalization our object? Likewise, Ta-Nehisi Coates's account of Trump as "the white president" personifies white supremacy rather than traces its impersonal dimensions. Are such counterfictions—including vivid memes and personifications and simplifying narratives—only a danger to renounce or a political necessity to own but complicate?

I echo Pynchon's view that features of the paranoid style narrative are crucial to making visible and visceral the dangers in modern surveillance, the extent of corporate power, the insidious impact of marketing designs, and the presumptions and violence of a racial state. The greatest analysts of the paranoid style—Freud and Pynchon—recognized that it is not irrational in any simple sense, and they acknowledged their own implication in it by the practice of both diagnosis and writing. Freud said that "the compulsion not to let chance count as chance" was the interpretive bond relating religious narrative and paranoid projection to his own theory of systemic symptoms (quoted in Melley 2002, 71). For Sedgwick, therefore, a "hermeneutic of suspicion" has been inseparable from radical critique and radical politics to identify and oppose forms of power that invade, shape, and control us. Like Freud and Pynchon, she tries not to eliminate or abolish the paranoid but to engender an antidote to its dangers, and she used Melanie Klein to depict the "reparative (depressive) position" to hold in tension with it. That position signifies and fosters affective shifts: from rage at injury to gratitude for life, from anticipation of harm to surprise at contingency, from investment in purity and antagonism to acceptance of contamination and ambivalence, from splitting the absolutely good and absolutely evil to a reparative ethos that dwells in the imperfect.

Many critics read Sedgwick in a paranoid way, however, as if she replaced a merely pathological paranoid position by a reparative position deemed wholly benign and the only ethical way to live; but in fact she saw both positions as imaginatively conjured fictions, and she even said that politics requires us to sustain both positions in a complementary tension. If theorists propose a reparative ethics that makes deflation and ambivalence the only antidote to dangerously inflated affects, I see an example of (paranoid) splitting that (like the Federalists and Hofstadter) would save politics from excessive enthusiasm and fiction-making, or save reason and civility from inflamed politics. I would respond by saying there is no vibrantly *democratic* politics without drama—inflation, intensity, desire, and poetry, if not melodrama—which means we need to sustain tensions between creative paranoia and its reparative other. Pynchon's early novel *The Crying of Lot 49* (1965) suggests one way to do that.[12]

In that novel, Pynchon dramatizes the necessity of paranoia as a political and aesthetic practice of identifying power and making sense; but the plot of the novel and the self-reflection of the protagonist— "Oedipa Mass"—also problematize the effort to finalize a plot, stabilize or fix meaning, and gain certainty about the truth of a representation of the world. As we readers identify with or as Oedipa, as she (like her namesake) struggles to make sense of the powers and plots that ensnare her, we infer or project a coherence the text continually confounds or defers, and we end up feeling that the author is conspiring or plotting against us, not with us. Our longing for certainty, for knowing what to count as evidence that proves definitively what is true, is elicited as the text both demands practices of interpretation but withholds closure. But in this way, the text also suspends us between deracinated disenchantment that sees no connections and an uncanny sense of wonder at the vast inter-indebtedness connecting all things. Making readers into coauthors, Pynchon's text thus models and nurtures democratic citizenship as a practice that requires suspicion, but also suspicion of our suspicion, sense-making but also acknowledgment of ambiguity, disenchantment about power but also pleasure in making connections.

But the text is not just an epistemological exercise in enigma, for the political education of this suburban white woman occurs as she discovers a counterculture or undercommons, called Trystero, not so much secret as hidden in plain sight, sustained as alienated people practice ways to communicate and affiliate that refuse formulaic language and sanctioned institutions. As Pynchon puts it:

> For here were god knew how many citizens, deliberately choosing not to communicate by U.S. mail. It was not an act of treason, nor possibly even defiance. But it was a calculated withdrawal from the life of the Republic, from its machinery. Whatever else was being denied them out of hate, indifference to the power of their vote, loopholes, simple ignorance, this withdrawal was their own, unpublicized, private. Since they could not have withdrawn into a vacuum (could they?), there had to exist the separate, silent, un-suspected world. (1965, 101)

They are paranoids, for sure, but *therefore* engage in an alternative world-building to engender the reparative pleasures of meaningful speech and mutual aid. Oedipa feels so powerfully drawn to this alter-world that she fears she may herself be a paranoid, inventing Trystero out of the depth of her desire to escape the "exitlessness" of the America she knows. As she enters the ambiguous space between a possibility she needs and imaginatively projects, and the risks of action that make it real, she reaches a threshold of politicization or a moment of decision, where the novel leaves its readers. In these ways, Pynchon writes in a paranoid style that remains underdetermined in its democratic possibilities.

Imagine, then, that Hofstadter positions himself as Starbuck to a wounded, enraged Ahab, as if to speak sober prose to dispel Ahab's intoxi-cated poetry, as if to defend the prosaic against the lure of fiction-making, as if to disenchant those ensnared by such magic. In contrast, Pynchon's text positions us not with a Starbuck invested in reestablishing the rule of normal but somewhere else in the spectrum between Ahabian projec-tion and Ishmaelian perspectivism, as it were, between heroic protest and quotidian resilience, between drama and irony, between paranoid theory and reparative ethics. From the perspective of the novel, a demo-cratic politics needs to navigate *through* the paranoid, by tracing plots and power, and *draw out* the reparative, by enacting impulses to seek con-nections if not reconciliations. Melville's and Pynchon's literary art thus situates a democratic politics between protesting injury to our dignity and acknowledging the limits of our sovereignty, between angry demands for justice and forbearing hopes for healing, between the value of antagonism and the irreducibility of ambivalence. Can the way they contain these tensions within their dramatic counterfictions inspire or model the value of sustaining parallel tensions in our political practices of democratic insurgency and world-building? As their texts vindicate while problematizing fiction-making, so must we, if we are to reanimate our diminished collective life.

NOTES

1 These claims about fiction echo the European theorists who argued that fascism—and, by extension, American racial politics—can be understood and opposed only if we shift from the language of interest and reason that characterizes the rationalism of liberal and Marxist theory to foreground instead desire, motivation, longing, and anxiety as well as dreaming, fantasy, and symbolization, which drive and shape investments in collective identity, submission to authority, and violence against perceived threats to the integrity of the self. I am also echoing European theorists, like Ernesto Grassi, who recovered the tradition of rhetoric, and Cornelius Castoriadis, who foregrounded the generative role of imagination in the construction of society and psyche. But I learned to focus on motivation and meaning, on rhetorical form and narrative, by reading American literature as a form of political theory.

2 Excellent critical accounts of Hofstadter's argument, running parallel to mine, can be found in Fenster (2008); Butter (2021); Melley (2016); and Melley (2020a).

3 Hofstadter (1996b) identified this dynamic in those he called "pseudo-conservatives" in an essay he first published in 1954. Pseudo-conservatives express overt support for establishment values but depart from the temperate spirit of "true conservatism" in their "profound if largely unconscious hatred of our society and its ways." He took the term from Theodor Adorno, for whom a "pseudo-conservative" is "a man who in the name of upholding traditional American values and institutions and defending them against more or less fictitious dangers, consciously or unconsciously aims at their abolition" (Adorno et al., 1950, 675, quoted in Melley 2021).

4 Hofstadter says he is not taking an epistemological approach, which would focus on the "truth or falsity" of a vision or narrative, choosing instead to focus on "the way" it is believed; but in fact, his concern is that the "paranoid" way sacrifices reality to fantasy as it translates a "defensible judgment" into a conspiratorial narrative. In addition, he is confident that a paranoid narrative can be readily or easily separated from a rational (or defensible) alternative.

5   Melley (2020a, 431) attributes the paranoid style of conspiracy theory not to status anxiety but to what he calls "agency panic" by liberal individuals anxiously but inchoately feeling the impact of social control. He agrees with Hofstadter that a "defensible judgment"—about the reality of social control—is translated into a form of perception and understanding that is "melodramatic" in the way it simplifies and moralizes social control, while confirming outdated and misleading assumptions about individual agency that we need to question and relinquish. Melley thus credits the truth about social control in the paranoid suspicion, even as he would complicate it.

6   On melodrama, see Anker (2014). Rogin's most developed account of "counter-subversive demonology" is "American Political Demonology"; see Rogin (1987).

7   The extent to which other historians locate a paranoid style at the center of American history is striking. In his foreword to *Pamphlets of the American Revolution*, published in 1965, Bernard Bailyn argued that "the fear of a comprehensive conspiracy against liberty . . . lay at the heart of the Revolutionary movement" (x), and this idea then organized his justifiably influential *Ideological Origins of the American Revolution* (1967). David Brion Davis's *The Slave Power Conspiracy and the Paranoid Style* (1970) addressed the antislavery movement. In a 1982 essay, "Conspiracy and the Paranoid Style: Causality and Deceit in the Eighteenth Century," Gordon Wood argued that the pervasive conspiracy thinking, assuming both plots and intentional action, reflected the dominant epistemology, "a mode of thinking neither pathological nor uniquely American" but rather "a rational attempt to explain human phenomena in terms of intentions" (419, 429) (quoted in Butter 2021, 40).

8   In this regard, Hofstadter's unreflective "we" about "them"—not unlike Hillary Clinton's depiction of "deplorables"—enacts but denies status politics: he reverses the accusing nativist gaze by making *them* the problem threatening the rational center; he enacts his own paranoid presumption of harm in the very way he claims to discredit it. As Rogin (1987, 277) puts it, "It is as if the children of immigrants were saying to their old-family targets: 'You had the fantasy that our parents were dangerous to you; that fantasy made you dangerous to them. When America belonged to you, you tried to exclude us. Now with the New Deal it belongs to us as well. But whereas you had only superstition and religion to de-legitimize us, we can use modern, scientific methods to discredit you.' Paranoid style analysts were thus participating in the same status politics they analyzed."

9   Hofstadter's defense of ethnic immigrants suggests the romance of an inclusive pluralism in a civic nationalism—the progressive, inclusionary romance that Barack Obama affirmed. Though I have called Hofstadter's critique a genre of realism, it still rests on an organizing fantasy that

partakes in and indeed depends on a romance about state and nation, even if that presumption cannot be owned explicitly or the identity of the cool critic is jeopardized. As anticommunism, the war on terror, and a history of anti-blackness indicate, interest-group (or multicultural) pluralism rests on an exclusionary premise—the embrace of propertied individualism—that may be relaxed in some moments but that is vividly revealed in moments of felt danger. Hofstadter's critique suggests that the exclusion of the nonliberal as an intolerable excess is the inescapable and anti-democratic premise of the pluralism he defends.

10   In his book of essays on the paranoid style, Hofstadter concludes a discussion of Goldwater and pseudo-conservative politics (1996a), with this statement about the future of rightwing politics:

> The largest single difficulty facing the right wing as a force within the Republican Party is its inability to rear and sustain national leaders, but on the other hand, even the seemingly minority position of the Republican Party, which in a sense sets a limit to the operation of the far right, is in another sense one of its assets. . . . The very destruction that Goldwater has wreaked within the party has its compensations for the right-wingers . . . so long as the party continues in its present helpless minority position, the possibility remains that, even without a repetition of the Goldwater takeover, the right-wingers can prevent the moderates from refurbishing the party as a constructive opposition. But above all, the far right has become a permanent force in the political order because the things upon which it feeds are also permanent: the chronic and ineluctable frustrations of our foreign policy, the opposition to the movement for racial equality, the discontents that come with affluence, the fevers of the culturally alienated. . . . As a movement, ironically enough, the far right flourishes to a striking degree on what it has learned from the radicals. Their forces have been bolshevized—staffed with small, quietly efficient cadres of zealots . . . while it spends the money it gets from conservatives. Finally, it moves in the uninhibited mental world of those who neither have nor expect to win responsibility. Its opponents, as men of government, are always vulnerable to the discontents aroused by the manifold failures of our society. But the right-wingers, who are willing to gamble with the future, enjoy the wide-raging freedom of the agitational mind, with its paranoid suspicions, its impossible demands, and its millennial dreams of victory. (140–41)

11   On the one hand, all our basic concepts are a kind of fiction and rest on metaphor, whether conceptions of gender and race, free markets and contracts, nations, gods, sovereign subjects, and so on. As Althusser argued in his generative revision of ideology, these are not false ideas compared

to reality, but rather are materialized in and as social practices, so that at intuitive and visceral levels the world seems to validate our conceptions. Feminism has also emphasized the degree to which "reality" is elastic in this sense. On the other hand, however, we typically "fail" to fully embody our fictions, and we constantly face the gap between "the truths we hold self-evident" and the realities that exceed it. That gap can be catastrophic, as Arendt argued in her essay on lying and the Vietnam War and as scientists now argue about climate change. As Arendt showed, the gap can be theorized through forms of realism that make specific evidentiary claims about what our representations mistake, or the gap can be dramatized by forms of tragedy depicting the intractability of a reality that consistently resists and defeats our efforts to make sense and meaning. The gap can also be theorized ironically and comically. Ralph Ellison (1964) thus calls the fiction of race a cruel and absurd joke, and he locates both American humor and Black life in this gap between fiction and reality. Even as he condemns those who build public policy—indeed the American social world—on the basis of melodramatic fictions of blackness as pathology, he also condemns those who reify and fix "blackness" as if to close the gap between language and life. What we call ideology names the fictions we have reified or naturalized, but for Ellison the alternative is "forging" (in both its senses) another figuration, another mask, in speech-acts that others may take up, contest, or revise.

12 It is important not simply to dichotomize the reparative and paranoid, as if one did not include the other. After all, Freud saw Daniel Schreber's paranoia (as Melville saw Ahab's monomania) as a step toward recovery from catastrophic loss, as a libidinal reengagement with the world, that is, as enabling a form of repair—though also a form of self-defeat. Conversely, Klein's argument was that the reparative position is initiated and animated by our ongoing and paranoid fears that our aggression will provoke punishment and abandonment, and those feelings of love or gratitude cannot ever simply erase—but rather continually stimulate—feelings of disappointment and rage.

_____

02 WHERE DID AIDS COME FROM?

INTRODUCTION

For all intents and purposes, the issue of HIV/AIDS's origins has been resolved. The cut hunter, or natural transfer theory, based in phylogenetic mapping, concludes that the contemporary epidemic started when simian viruses spread from primates to humans in the early twentieth century (Worobey et al. 2003, 2016; Gilbert et al. 2007; Sharp and Hahn 2011).[1] A series of coincidental, unspecified accidents, such as monkey bites or the eating of undercooked meat, conjoined with the circumstances by which the virus could take hold and spread. African truck drivers and gay men in America took center stage in this AIDS-origin narrative. These men were aided by social structures, such as prostitutes and bath houses, and medical interventions, such as needle sticks and blood transfusions. Virtually anyone, if they know anything about it at all, will recite some version of this viral modeling combined with light social history. The press and scientific literature ubiquitously present the natural transfer theory as demonstrable fact, despite the impossibility of independent verification and many unanswered questions.

I have been curious about the lack of debate over the natural transfer theory as the origin of AIDS. Even a cursory nod toward twentieth-century bioscience, chockablock with cross-species blood and tissue experimentation, often between apes and humans, reveals multiple possible routes by which viral transfers could have—and indeed did—occur. The mystery of AIDS's origins combined with the severity of the disease would, one might expect, raise some serious, painstaking investigation into those cross-species transfers. And yet, one finds the opposite: not only have biomedical practices involving interspecies fluid transfers virtually *not* been studied for potential side effects (such as viral transfer), but those few studies that have been done have been dismissed with a nearly casual disregard. Somehow the question of how HIV might be linked to medical experimentation with animal blood and tissue is not only unanswerable, it has been unthinkable. The recent attention to the lab leak hypothesis for COVID-19 indicates a shift in attention toward the possibility of accidents and side effects. In this chapter I revisit the AIDS origins debate and suggest that it has been prematurely resolved.

An intriguing path dependency can be tracked in light of early explanations for HIV and their continued impact on later assumptions. The first explanations of its quick and wide spread play on stereotypes of oversexed gay men and Central Africans. Surely there was a lot of sex in these communities, but more evidence would be needed to prove it as the sole route of transmission. Later discoveries about the virus, such as its long latency period, did not lead to a reinvestigation of early findings that were based on an assumption that latency was a matter of months. Even the collapse of the Patient 0 myth in which an airline pilot was blamed for spreading the illness has not led to a rigorous revisiting of those early explanations.

It's relatively easy to see why this enormous task has not been broached. One would need to revisit the difficulties and controversies in identifying the virus through the 1980s, including the impact of variously efficacious testing methods on how the earliest cases were identified. These diagnostic confusions still muddy the waters, specifically relating to the earliest cases, the "Manchester Sailor" and Robert Rayford, both of whom are now considered not to have been AIDS cases, and yet whose early positive testing laid the framework for the acceptance of certain explanations for the epidemic's etiology. Since HIV presents through a patient's infections with more common diseases such as pneumonia and Kaposi's sarcoma, the record has been pockmarked with much confusion over the verifiable cases and their relevance.

Add to this the sheer complexity of the task: the amount of information to be parsed, from human mobility (laborers, traders, tourists, aid workers), to the global animal trade and export business (probably millions of primates in global circulation for research and to make the tissue cultures for vaccine preparation), and a global market in human blood, including imports to the United States from Africa and the Caribbean. Much of that information, undocumented anyway, is simply not available at the granular level required to track the mobility of a virus. If such complexities account for why AIDS origins have not been thoroughly investigated, they also seem to counter the rather vicious dismissal of another origin theory, one that quite reasonably suggests that the cross-over event resulting in HIV was the result of a polio vaccine trial in the 1950s.

The oral polio vaccine (OPV) theory of the origins of HIV remains worth considering for the fascinating details of the theory and the light it sheds on biomedical attitudes and practices of the mid-twentieth century. The short-lived debate it spurred in the late 1990s, and its "resolution" in favor of the cut hunter theory, also reveals much about how scientists adjudicate questions of the past and our own mistaken trust in such forms of scientific resolution.

In 1999, British journalist Edward Hooper described the OPV hypothesis (Hooper 2000c). Over the course of nearly one thousand spellbinding pages, Hooper unfurls an account of an OPV trial undertaken by American scientists in the Belgian Congo and Ruanda-Urundi between 1956 and 1960 (Hooper 2001; Courtois et al. 1958; Plotkin et al. 1961). He finds a stunning correlation between the geography of the earliest cases of HIV and the OPV trials, presents a detailed reconstruction of the chimpanzee lab in Stanleyville (the base location of the trials), and details a history of the development of the vaccine by Hilary Koprowski at the Wistar Institute in Pennsylvania and its testing in several American states, Europe, and the Congo. Given that scientists from the Wistar Institute sprayed or spooned live polio vaccine grown with animal tissue cultures into the mouths of about a million Congolese, a simian immunodeficiency virus (SIV) could, in theory, by this route cross over into humans through oral cuts or abrasions. This OPV theory, Hooper argues in detail, makes more sense than natural transfer theories, and it works from the same data beginning from the first known case of HIV-1 in Kinshasa (Léopoldville) in 1959.[2]

The River immediately received laudatory reviews in major press outlets (Cimons 1999; Altman 1999; Trivers 2000; B. Martin 2000). Praise, however, came to a swift end after a conference at the Royal Society in London (held September 11–12, 2000), which was convened to discuss the OPV theory. The precipitous and, I believe, premature closing of the debate with a widely reported press conference led to the near-universal labeling and dismissal of the OPV hypothesis as a "conspiracy theory" (rather than, say, as a plausible counterfactual hypothesis). Despite, or perhaps because of, the unusual way in which a conference came to be the arbiter of the OPV proposal, Hooper and his remaining supporters were excluded from subsequent discussions in the scientific press. In light of that, Hooper continues to publish his and other's doubts and rejoinders on a website, AIDS Origins (http://www.aidsorigins.com).

In what follows, I will not argue that the vaccine trials launched the acquired immunodeficiency syndrome (AIDS) epidemic, nor will I recite Hooper's account. Rather, I analyze how the genealogy of the dismissal of the OPV hypothesis demonstrates that the closure of the debate precluded discussion, fact-finding, and uptake of the key, and very much needed, contributions of Hooper's research. Specifically, *The River* offers one of the very few analyses of the massive global infrastructure of post–World War II vaccinology, one that includes highly mobile geographies of human experimentation involving interspecies and viral fluid exchanges on a scale nearly unimaginable to a lay reader. This infrastructure relied on the importation and sacrifice of millions of primates and other animals, particularly monkeys from India, Africa, and the Philippines (Kalter and Heberling 1971); local animal trade and care networks; Cold War and colonial politics; technologies of refrigeration, preservation, and shipping; exchange networks for biomaterials among Europe, the United States, and Africa; and high-stakes, fragile, competitive, and collegial power struggles among scientists committed to controlling how debates were framed and what information was documented and shared. By literally opening vectors for the transmission of pathogens among human and nonhuman bodies, this biomedical and technological infrastructure, which elsewhere I have called the "The Wetnet," choreographed a zone that fundamentally altered potential and real viral dynamics, spillovers, and exchanges.[3] Inter- and intraspecies viral transfers became possible in entirely new and unpredictable ways. Along with this infrastructure arose logics—such as the promise of vaccines—by which new risks were made to seem normal and justifiable; these rhetorical means became the foil and norm against which other possibilities have been judged. I argue that the OPV hypothesis can be understood in this context not exclusively for its truth or provability but as a plausible counterfactual that reveals much about how belief structures underpin what comes to count as truth.

To make this argument, I consider questions of historical reconstruction in conditions of uncertainty. Catherine Gallagher (2018) theorizes "what if" and "but for" scenarios as counterfactual histories. Such modeling, when applied to possible vectors of disease, can identify the architecture of trust relied upon: *If an iatrogenic spillover event had occurred, how would* we know? What kinds of information, not included in scientific reports and publications, would be necessary to reconstruct such possibilities? If a counterfactual method offers another way forward, enabling consideration of the multiple possibilities that may have resulted from complex biological exchanges in the context of uncertainty and naivete among scientists, it also offers a way to practically understand how allied practices, such as record keeping and shared archives, impact how the origins of emerging diseases can be reconstructed. Given how little research there is in this enormously complex and crucially important area of vaccinology, and given the burgeoning interest in medical anthropology on zoonosis (Keck and Lynteris 2018), I believe the OPV-HIV story provides insights that increase awareness of and languages for describing the complex global bioformations constituted by midcentury vaccinology.

I base this historical ethnography on the recording of the meetings archived at the Royal Society Library in London; interviews with two spectators (Elizabeth Tilly and Vinh-Kim Nguyen); interviews with participants Edward Hooper, Stanley Plotkin, and Robin Weiss; a comprehensive analysis of *The River* and the papers from the conference published in a special issue of the *Philosophical Transactions of the Royal Society of London* (Hamilton, Weiss, and Hobson 2001); a review of the scientific literature on the hypothesis published before and after the controversy's closure; and study of primary and secondary literature in vaccine history.

HOOPER'S HYPOTHESIS

The River parses an astonishing array of primary and secondary documents; Hooper's materials range from flight schedules to chimp behavior to dozens of interviews with scientists and others who were involved in, or adjacent to, the vaccine trials. The hypothesis sets forth two distinct components. First, Hooper provides arguments and evidence about why routes of HIV transmission based on human mobility proposed by other scholars lack credibility. He also documents the uncanny geographic correlations between the vaccine testing and the earliest cases of what would become known as AIDS, whereby "all 46 documented instances of HIV-1 infection from Africa through 1980 come from within 140 miles of CHAT [the OPV vaccine] vaccination sites" and "70% of these earliest AIDS cases come from a town or village where CHAT had been vaccinated" (Hooper 2001, 806). This and other data provide circumstantial evidence for the vaccines as a plausible source of the initial spillover events. Second, the tissue cultures on which the polio virus was grown offer a plausible explanation for the *mechanics* of a spillover. For instance, the seed lots of vaccine made at Wistar could have been, at the lab's base in Stanleyville, either attenuated (further developed) with chimpanzee kidney tissue cultures or, alternatively, contaminated with fluids from chimpanzee dissections.

In the United States and Europe in the 1950s and 1960s, the renal tissues of various monkey species were used for a range of medical and virological purposes, requiring the sacrifice of vast numbers of animals (Ahuja 2013; Bookchin and Schumacher 2004). Hooper interviews several experts who verify that animal kidney tissue cultures would contain lymph and other fluids that could harbor viruses. Chimpanzees and other apes generally did not contribute organs for tissue cultures in the United States; this was due not to any biological barrier but rather because the animals were expensive and dangerous. However, in Congo, chimpanzees were in plentiful supply, and the Stanleyville lab housed between four hundred and six hundred chimpanzees (in 1956–58), many of which were sacrificed without explanation (Hooper 2001). Hooper has identified these chimps, tracked where they might have been captured, and interviewed a local African lab technician who had worked in the lab and claimed that they had been making OPV with chimpanzee tissues.[4] Additionally, Hooper located a Belgian scientist, Alexandre Jezerski, who was at the time growing tissue cultures from the kidney cells of various primates (including chimpanzee) at a rudimentary lab nearby, and with whom Koprowski had met during one of his visits to Congo.

If a chimpanzee virus *had* contaminated the vaccine and instigated a crossover event, contemporary circumstances would have militated against recognition of it. For one thing, as Koprowski himself readily admitted, follow-up with trial participants was lax. Koprowski had selected rural, medically underserved areas for testing a vaccine containing strains of live polio virus whose key danger was the risk of spreading polio, yet he had no formal plans for keeping records. Tracking side effects of the vaccine was, in any case, curtailed by Congo's unexpected independence in 1960, which resulted in the expulsion of most Belgians and other Westerners— although, to be sure, the United States maintained covert operations in the country (perhaps including the Stanleyville lab) for political and economic strategic reasons (van Reybrouk 2014).[5] In addition, researchers at the time would not have linked a vaccine to early AIDS cases if, as would have been the case, AIDS-related illnesses had presented as familiar pneumonia or TB. If the virus had to be transmitted one or more times before it became virulent to humans, recognition of any causal link between the vaccine and virus would have been beyond the ken of any clinician or researcher.

The discipline-wide, broad-based intellectual framework necessary to have recognized the possibility that a virus could have contaminated tissue cultures and then have been spread through vaccines and have gained virulence after spreading almost certainly simply would not have existed—even if the trial had taken place in the United States under tighter regulations. The sv-40 case explained below details some of the resistance in the scientific community to acknowledging the dangers of animal viruses in tissue cultures. And as examples such as the synthetic estrogen diethylstilbestrol (DES) and Thalidomide have shown, scientific methods and interests tend not to be oriented toward understanding multigenerational and long-term effects of medical and industrial interventions.

While Hooper relays conversations with a number of the scientists he interviewed who found his theory plausible, he gained only one strong ally willing to speak out for the possibility of the OPV hypothesis during the course of his research. Bill Hamilton, a well-respected professor of evolutionary biology at Oxford University, became a proponent of the OPV theory and proposed the Royal Society conference. He never made it to the event that he initiated: he died in March 2000 from an illness contracted in the Congo while conducting research on the OPV question. One can speculate that his death had ramifications for the direction that the Royal Society conference took, as it left Hooper with no one inside the establishment with an interest in the theory. While this point speaks to science and technology studies' (STS) debates about controversy resolution, the existential overtone hints at the potentially significant ramifications of coincidental events in the course of history.[6]

The complexity, detail, and novelty of Hooper's theory cannot be overstated. While arguably the length of the book may deter casually interested readers, it would have had to have been hundreds of pages longer than any of the scientific reports related to the oral polio trials for it to have effectively tracked and explained to a nonspecialist audience the history of the vaccine and the various ways in which the trial, the virus, and the cross-species contamination might have played out. Indeed, as I argue below, the controversy highlights how conflicting demands for and requirements of evidence and burdens of proof measure against assumptions about normative and reasonable behaviors and expectations in the construction of historical truths.

THE CONFERENCE

The Royal Society meeting participants fell into three main groups: (1) four of the scientists involved in the Congo Trials (Paul Osterreith, Jan Desmyter, Hilary Koprowski, and Stanley Plotkin) and allies, including a group of phylogeneticists; (2) Hooper and allies; and (3) a varied group of speakers addressing zoonosis generally and epidemics broadly related to HIV. This last group added to the notion and milieu of a "conference," but it did not address or contribute to the debate at hand.

The agenda was skewed from the get-go. No one but Hooper could bolster the OPV hypothesis with additional facts or evidence. Since he had the same time allotment as every other speaker, he simply could not address the many dimensions of the theory. His main allies consisted of the Australian sociologist of science Brian Martin (2001), who gave a paper on the notion of proof in science, and Walter Nelson-Rees (2001), a well-known scientist active in publicizing cell-line contamination, who gave rather damning testimony on the believability of the Wistar scientists.

Hooper's paper, dense with detail, tracks among other things the numbers of chimpanzees at different research sites; it documents interviews with the scientists and lab technicians working in Central Africa in the 1950s; and it offers circumstantial evidence suggesting both that chimpanzee kidneys were being extracted and sent to the Wistar Institute and that batches of the polio vaccine were being made in Africa.[7] His paper addresses further issues related to chimpanzee subspecies, the geography and timelines of the OPV theory versus phylogenetic modeling, and other possible arguments against the theory.

Stanley Plotkin, who would become a giant of twentieth-century vaccinology, had in the 1950s just launched his career at Wistar as a junior researcher and had traveled to Africa for the trials. His paper refutes the OPV theory not with independent records of how the vaccine was made, but with the flat denial that any chimp tissues had been sent to Wistar. He writes: "I was in the laboratory from August 1957 to June 1961, and never saw or heard of chimpanzee cells" (Plotkin 2001, 816). He concludes, "*The River* has been praised for its precise detail and wealth of footnotes, but one can be precise without being accurate" (Plotkin 2001, 822). By contrast, Belgian scientist Paul Osterrieth worked at the lab in Stanleyville where the Wistar scientists did efficacy and other testing on chimpanzees. He claims in his paper: "It is true that six minced chimpanzee kidneys were sent to the Wistar Institute" (Osterrieth 2001, 839). Such discrepancies in personal recollections stand in lieu of records, with no wider or structured attempt at rebuttal or reconciliation. As a result, the reader has no way to judge the veracity or likelihood of the different narratives.

The means by which the Royal Society meeting hammered the first nail into the OPV theory's coffin has received a rigorous STS work-up by Brian Martin (2010), the STS scholar who also presented at the conference. He portrays the form of the rather stunningly rancorous proceedings, and he suggests that the Royal Society meeting and subsequent events demonstrate the ways in which "supporters of orthodoxy have a tactical advantage over challengers" (B. Martin 2010, 215). He compares the Royal Society meeting's tactics, one for one, to other dominant political movements such as those of the Indonesians' justification for violently quashing protestors in East Timor. Martin's observations about the mechanics of justification asks his readers to see the violence behind, and enabled by, the epistemological and aesthetic front of the conference—one behind which all kinds of reasonable and normative people and assumptions can scurry.

The most crucial point made at the conference all but sneaked out of the building via a fire escape; certainly, it was not reported in the press. At the meeting's conclusion, long after the reporters had left, the chair and convener of the meeting, Robin Weiss, an expert in retroviruses and cross-species viral transmission, stated that experimental vaccines *could* credibly have been the cause of the zoonosis that resulted in HIV. He later wrote: "To reduce the argument over the origins of HIV to the OPV hypothesis versus the cut hunter hypothesis is an over simplistic and false antithesis. Both natural and iatrogenic transmission of many retroviruses, including HIV, have been thoroughly documented and are not mutually exclusive" (R. Weiss 2001a). *Surely Hooper's challenge is worth truly understanding*, we can hear Weiss intimating. And yet, closure on the OPV-HIV debate had already been achieved—not based on the evidence (which was inconclusive) but because the politics of certainty in science demanded it. Certainty in this case came down to the insistence of the scientists in the room.

A close reading of the Royal Society meeting reveals an event mired in the confusing intentions of the organizers who at once claimed to want to investigate the OPV hypothesis while making that structurally impossible. Many of Hooper's key points were not taken up or addressed at all by the speakers and the resulting collection of essays. No other formal structures for investigation—such as through law or a third party—were or are available to address questions of this kind or scale, and no independent researchers emerged to take on the considerable effort and risk of continuing, or verifying, Hooper's research.[8]

Even a cursory reading of the Royal Society's conclusions, which are presented in an essay by conference convener Robin Weiss, renders problematic any ready acceptance of the notion that universally emerged from it: that the OPV hypothesis is debunked. Weiss's paper can be read as a clear warning about the possibilities of zoonosis, and his prevarications relay an ambivalent conclusion. Indeed, Weiss explicitly echoes journalist Tom Curtis, who had originally introduced the OPV hypothesis in a 1992 article: "If the Congo vaccine turns out not to be the way AIDS got started in people, it will be because medicine was lucky, not because it was infallible" (T. Curtis 1992, 108). It is telling, and certainly a result of Weiss's rhetorical approach, that while Koprowski sued Curtis for libel, Weiss's finding flew under the radar (Hooper 2000a; Plotkin and Koprowski 1999; R. Weiss 1999).

One final epitaph to the OPV hypothesis bears noting. Hoping to confirm his hypothesis, Hooper had advocated for any extant vaccine to be tested by a neutral third party. After the conference, samples provided by Wistar tested negative for chimp DNA and SIV/HIV. The Wistar scientists claimed absolution, and the press once again declared the case closed. For his part, Hooper pointed out flaws in the testing, most specifically, "There is no evidence that any of the CHAT samples produced at the Wistar Institute and Wyeth Laboratories . . . have any relevance to the vaccinations conducted in Africa." He added: "It is now apparent that the vaccine used in Ruzizi and along Lake Tanganyika did not comprise one homogeneous preparation of CHAT pool 10A-11 [the pool that was tested], but rather several different CHAT preparations, made at different times and originating from different laboratories" (Hooper 2001, 807). While even Koprowski had claimed that samples of the vaccine used in the trials no longer existed (Vaughan 2000), this testing was the final nail in the coffin.

If this strategy of consensus science worked, it was because scientists have a great deal of cultural and economic capital that they used to guide the debate, and journalists and historians have generally fallen into line. It remains true, however, that the free and open debate of the OPV theory would have required institutions, record-keeping practices, independent peer review, and modes of interrogation that simply did not and do not exist. Despite good reasons to critique legal reasoning and practice, the legal system does offer a structure for determining the likelihood that events occurred in particular ways based on evidence and testimony.

Clearly if capital-S science, or capital-M medicine *had* wanted to develop a means of self-regulation, ample opportunities have been presented over the decades. With no formalized way to handle a narrative such as Hooper's, however, personal responses and judgments took on an outsized role, and major slippages stood uncontested.

THE FINAL REPORT: AMBIVALENT INTENTIONS

Academic conferences typically gather independent researchers to present work on overlapping interests, and as such they are not intended to resolve controversies in any structured or rigorous way. Thus, a conference offers a curious format in which to tackle a subject of such complexity, and Robin Weiss's published paper assessing and summarizing the proceedings similarly offers a problematic finale, one that provides neither the evidence nor the logic to adequately conclude the debate, despite its presentation as such.[9] In his essay and in person, Weiss represents the two-day Royal Society meeting as an open and rigorous debate whose aim was to "lay open all the arguments and counterarguments."[10] One can only guess at the reasons for this rush to closure in a mere two days. He had already reviewed *The River* for *Science*, where he described it as "a towering achievement; right or wrong in its main conclusion, there is much to learn from Hooper's exposition" (R. Weiss 1999). As such, Weiss's focus was on a second tier of "important lessons to be learned from Hooper's analysis," which he lists as "our complacency over 44 years' use of primary monkey kidney cells as a substrate for live viral vaccines" and the use of litigation to shut down debate, as Koprowski had done in suing Tom Curtis.

Weiss's conclusion to the proceedings uses an intriguing rhetorical method to leave the door ajar for future consideration of the OPV theory while still appearing to reject it outright (Weiss 2001a). After each point he makes in favor of the cut hunter theory, he curiously loops back to note that none of his points actually disprove the OPV hypothesis. Such rhetorical skill, I would argue, was a crucial factor in the closure of the debate over OPV as a source of HIV, and it suggests that subsequent commentators did not closely read the document. His argument consists of a series of subjective assessments: his trust in the scientists' testimony; his view that the OPV theory seems "contrived"; and his belief that the burden of proof lies with Hooper. Weiss finds no motive or evidence for a cover-up on the part of the scientists: he finds them believable and reasonable, falling squarely into a kind of old-school notion of reasonableness as described by Steven Shapin and Simon Schaffer in their classic work on experimental science (Shapin and Schaffer 2017). Weiss also discusses what he considers to be the unassailable reputation of the pharmaceutical industry. Both of these points are irrelevant to the OPV theory, unless one believes they preclude the need for further confirmation of events.

Notably, given the stakes of the argument, crafting objectivity was a personal and rhetorical accomplishment. As a result, the entire edifice of the conference depended on the believability and characterization of the OPV scientists as disinterested bystanders, genuinely wanting to engage a debate that put them at the center of a poorly run trial on medically underserved colonized people, and may have been the cause of the HIV epidemic that had killed tens of millions of people.

Weiss clarified to me in an interview his reasons for believing the scientists. In the mid-1950s, he explained, it would have been completely acceptable for the scientists to have used chimpanzee tissues for vaccine manufacture.[11] This ironic twist of reasoning (they are honest because it was standard practice to do the very thing that is purported to be a root cause of the HIV cross-over event) enables him to both embrace the possibility of OPV transmission and retain the credibility of the scientists involved in these trials. Weiss offered another confusing premise equally unproblematically. He writes, "Neither does the polio vaccine industry have a particularly bad record of cover-up" (R. Weiss 2001a, 952). Leave aside that no unitary "polio vaccine industry" existed at the time: What industry there was had virtually nothing to do with Koprowski's trials. Still, Weiss gives two questionable examples of the "success" of the industry. He cites the Cutter incident, in which an improperly made vaccine was found to have given some forty thousand people polio, resulting in five deaths and fifty-one cases of permanent paralysis, and which was aggressively defended by Cutter Labs in subsequent personal injury cases.[12] Then he mentions SV-40, a monkey virus that contaminated Salk's polio vaccine and that was spread to millions of Americans. Weiss praises the "quick response" to SV-40 by describing the replacement of kidney cell substrates derived from rhesus macaques with that of African Greens in polio vaccine manufacture. To describe these incidents as successes is simply bad faith.

The take-away from Weiss's points is emphatically not that there were no cover-ups, but that the whole infrastructure of vaccine development, testing, and administration was highly experimental in the 1950s and early 1960s, with an adventitious simian virus, sv-40, being spread to large populations; lax manufacturing protocols; unethical experimentation; little regulatory oversight; and, ultimately, the likelihood of sivs "on rare occasions" slipping into vaccines.

....

Questions relating to subtypes and recombination lie beyond this chapter's purview. Amid complexity and speculation, Weiss turned to Occam's Razor. This problem-solving principle asserts that the simplest explanation is generally the correct one, and Weiss used it to argue that the opv theory is "unnecessarily complicated" (2001a, 949). Specifically, the diversification date of the virus according to phylogeneticists would have been the date that it entered the human species, whereas for Hooper, it would have diversified in chimps and then been transferred to humans.

Turning to medieval philosophy to adjudicate an issue of this magnitude offers an intriguing strategy. Surely, the "simplest" explanation depends on one's basic disposition or knowledge base. For many Black Africans and colonial subjects, the simplest explanation would be that white people have hated and murdered Black people for centuries. Here again Weiss prevaricates and allows the possibility of multiple routes of cross-species transmission. In other words, despite going through the motions of describing Occam's razor and finding Hooper's more complex, he admits that both theories of the crossover could be true.

Ultimately, Weiss's essay (both brilliantly and disappointingly) offers a conclusion that implies that the conference had properly adjudicated and dismissed the opv theory. Only by engaging the text does one see what little evidence this conclusion rests on. Barely discussing Hooper's findings, he relies instead on a strong belief in the good of science and its spokespeople. The writing may well be in bad faith, as Martin's (2010) broader reading of the conference suggests. Hedging also offers an effective form of manipulation. Weiss might have been eager to close the debate for good reasons superseding the implications of the debate: fears of an anti-vaxx movement, the challenge of an accomplished journalist-historian "outsider" who was unpopular with Weiss's powerful (and, not incidentally, senior) scientific colleagues, and the consequences of acknowledging the magnitude of the possible events. Difficult as it is to know what to make of this document, it offers an intriguing method of closing a controversy, one that surely evinces a missed opportunity to do exactly what he seems to want to do: that is, open debate on the risky practices of the era.

In the aftermath of the conference, scholars have gone some way to reinforce the idea of the debate's closure. For example, in *The Origins of AIDS* (Pepin 2011), a book that has emerged as the model for the explanation for AIDS, physician and historian Jacques Pepin devotes three pages to *The River*. Pepin wrongly bases his dismissal of Hooper on Plotkin's argument and accused Hooper of a rookie mistake in confusing local dilution of concentrated vaccine stock with local production or amplification (Pepin 2011, 52; Gellin, Modlin, and Plotkin 2001). This caricature of the OPV hypothesis belittles both the hypothesis and Hooper's research, making him an easily dismissed strawman.

Like the post–Royal Society conference press, Pepin relies solely on the word of the scientists who ran the trial. But instead of addressing this question about evidence and objectivity head-on, Pepin accuses anyone who would doubt his reliance on the defendant scientist's account of conspiracy thinking. In considering the vaccine that tested negative for chimpanzee DNA, he writes, for example: "Conspiracy theorists could argue that [Wistar] had a vested interest in supplying vials which they already knew were not contaminated" (Pepin 2011, 52). He resorts to an anti-intellectual ad hominem attack rather than engaging Hooper's hypothesis raising the question of why Pepin himself is so dependent on, and ready to accept, the scientists' word.

I am not claiming that the OPV theory is correct. But it is notable that a book that serves as the go-to resource for the origins of the epidemic resorts to mischaracterization and name-calling, and it is equally noteworthy that this tactic flies under the radar of reviewers. A discussion of Pepin's article by physician and science historian Howard Markel (2011), patronizingly titled "It's the Science, Stupid," illustrates the latter point. Markel briefly parodies Hooper's book as "insisting" on a "fanciful thesis." He then poses Pepin's breakthrough based on "meticulous scientific analysis," that "a viral strain called SIVcpz, which infects large numbers of . . . chimpanzees living in central Africa, was the central source of HIV-1." This point is definitively not a breakthrough, and it is actually one that both Hooper and Pepin agree on. They differ in their hypotheses of *how* the species jump took place. But despite Markel's assertions to the contrary, no evidence marks Pepin's account as specifically more "convincing" or "brilliant" than Hooper's, aside from Markel's own ability to be convinced. Both accounts require the reader to fill in details and gaps with what they consider to be reasonable.

WHAT CANNOT BE ASKED

It is obvious why Koprowski and Plotkin would want to kneecap the theory and the messenger. However, it is not as clear why others have not taken an interest in the deeper story-behind-the-story of the OPV hypothesis either as a legitimate possibility for zoonotic events or as a fascinating story of the complex intertwining of human, animal, and viral interspecies transmissions quite apart from HIV.

The late scholar of historiography Hayden White makes the point that a discipline is constituted by what it forbids its practitioners from doing. He writes that "the so-called 'historical method'" consists of little more than the injunction to "get the story straight" (without any notion of what the relation of "story" to "fact" might be) and to avoid both conceptual overdetermination and imaginative excess at any price (1978, 126). This useful insight reflects on the OPV debate, since "the science" relied on in its resolution consists not of provably true facts, but rather, as I have outlined, finds its truth in a historical narrative based on what commentators assume as plausible, sensical events. Pepin, Markel, and others (Nattrass 2012) who dismiss the OPV hypothesis out-of-hand indicate precisely what is "forbidden" in historical scholarship about science: historians cannot disagree with "the science" *as constituted by scientists*. It does not help that Hooper's account is organized not as a lucid explication of his results but as a narrative of his decade of interviews, discoveries, and hypotheses; few casual readers would put in the time it takes to get through *The River*. But the same could be said for numerous historical and academic texts and archives that historians manage to closely parse and analyze.

Looking back at vaccine production in the 1950s and 1960s certainly gives the sense that if there was no species jump it was pure luck. In fact, the focus on what *actually* happened has left a major gap in the history of science, STS, and medical anthropology. Namely, biomedical infrastructures, such as tissue cultures, vaccines, and blood products, created the new routes for zoonotic and intraspecies viral transmissions that need to be better understood.

One example of an iatrogenic zoonotic transfer of a monkey virus occurred in Jonas Salk's killed polio vaccine in the 1950s. Revisiting that story opens some larger questions about the history of vaccinology infrastructures, risk, and regulatory infrastructures.

Salk completed his 1954 field trial of a vaccine consisting of killed polio virus on 1.8 million American children. The vaccine, subsequently used in a mass effort to eradicate polio, was made by growing polio virus on the kidney tissues of rhesus macaques that were imported from India by the tens of thousands per year. The polio virus was killed with formaldehyde, with the assumption among vaccinologists that any extant monkey viruses would thereby also be killed. It was further surmised that monkey viruses would not cross the species barrier, and therefore, that potential cross-over events need not be seriously studied (Bookchin and Schumacher 2004, 79).

A complicated and relevant story ensued. A brief version is as follows. Bernice Eddy was a scientist, working at the Laboratory of Biologics Control (LBC) since 1936, who had completed award-winning work devising potency and safety tests for gamma globulin and developing influenza and polio tissue cultures. With Sarah Stewart, a National Institutes of Health (NIH) scientist, Eddy received international recognition and founded the field of viral oncology with her codiscovery of the SE-polyoma virus (Eddy and Stewart 1959). Having shown that a mouse virus could cause cancer in small mammals, she began to wonder whether a monkey virus could cause cancer in other primates, including humans. While the occasional virologist had raised misgivings about the possibility of vaccines as a possible vector of zoonosis (Hull, Minner, and Mascoli 1958), no one raised the possibility that simian viruses could cause cancer. Not finding anyone at the LBC willing to collaborate on what was considered politically sensitive and possibly career-hijacking work, Eddy began research on this question, and soon found that 109 of 154 hamsters injected with a rhesus kidney cell extract developed tumors and eventually died. She suspected the tumor-causing "substance" was hardy and virulent, had a long latency period, and maintained oncogenicity over time and through passage from animal to animal. And it originated in the monkey tissues.

At this point Eddy presented the results to her boss, the head of vaccine safety testing at the Division of Biologics Standards (DBS), Joe Smadel. Smadel discouraged Eddy's work, eventually forbidding her to publish without his permission (which he rarely gave) and moving her into a tiny lab, "stripping her of all her vaccine responsibilities" (Bookchin and Schumacher 2004, 67). While Eddy did ultimately publish her work, Debbie Bookchin and Jim Schumacher (2004), in their detailed history of sv-40, explicitly labeled Smadel's response a "cover-up," a point to which I return below.

Smadel eventually admitted to Eddy's discovery of sv-40 when Ben Sweet and Maurice Hilleman (Hilleman 1998) disclosed their simultaneous detection of the same agent contaminating rhesus and cynomolgus monkey tissues.[13] The debates that followed among virologists over what to do about sv-40 were confounded by a morass of competing interests: the USSR was winning the "polio gap" with a more effective, cheaper, and painless oral polio vaccine developed by Albert Sabin (Bookchin and Schumacher 2004, 70); there was competition between Hilleman and Sabin for their respective killed and live polio vaccines; the manufacturers had questions regarding liability; there were real concerns about sv-40's dangers; and fear about losing public trust in a vaccine already widely distributed and celebrated.

Koprowski himself thought it best not to exaggerate the significance of viral contamination: "If an adequate number of persons exposed to these agents have been shown to develop specific antibodies without any clinical disease, the evidence should be regarded as overwhelmingly in favor of the harmlessness of these agents" (Koprowski 1960, 975). Once Koprowki's lab developed a human diploid vaccine strain made of fetal tissue, his opinion changed, and he subsequently advocated against the use of monkey tissues (Wadman 2017); this later advocacy was fore-grounded in the Royal Society meeting.

My point is that the sv-40 scare could have led to a reconsideration of the fundamentals of the vaccine program: the conditions of monkey importation, including gang caging, sacrifice, and sterilization; the pool-ing of tissues; and the testing of tissue cultures for contaminants. It did not. While vaccine companies were allowed to use up their stocks of sv-40-contaminated vaccine, no plan was made for long-term testing of the ten to thirty million Americans who now carried sv-40; and the press did not cover the virus. The scientific literature since then has generally ac-cepted that sv-40 was benign to humans, or at least that no immediate and noticeable effects were evident. Significantly, those who have care-fully tracked the studies on sv-40's potential impact on humans find that the research done was insufficient to rule out rare or chronic illnesses, or those that present later or in future generations (Lewis 1973).

CONCLUSION

Eve Sedgwick began her famous article on paranoid thinking by asking what we would know differently if we knew the origin of AIDS—if we knew, say, that AIDS was a result of medical or military experimentation. Sedgwick quotes the noted historian Cindy Patton, who argues: "Even suppose we were sure of every element of a conspiracy: that the lives of Africans and African Americans are worthless in the eyes of the United States; that gay men and drug users are held cheap where they aren't actually hated; that the military deliberately researched ways to kill noncombatants whom it sees as enemies. . . . Supposing we were ever so sure of all those things—what would we know then that we don't already know?" (Patton, as quoted in Sedgwick 2003a, 123).

From the perspective of Patton and Sedgwick, there is nothing surprising about the general contour of the events tracked here, from the conditions of the vaccine trial itself to the virtual, and multi-sited cover-up of even the possibility that a viral transfer could have, in theory, taken place. In that view, racism and homophobia are so intractably part of the way that the events and their entry into the historical record took place that even to uncover the truth of those biases cannot change the narrative of the science history. Based on my reading of the events, this analysis is plausible. It's hard to find another explanation for why the research has not been undertaken to more thoroughly investigate the origins of AIDS, albeit in academic systems that reward short turn-around times and at best semi-controversial findings.

Still, the labeling of the OPV hypothesis as "conspiracy theory" has resulted in a missed opportunity to read *The River* as a detailed account of the conditions of possibility underlying the vaccine project writ large, and the immense social, political, technological, and interspecies infrastructure on which the vaccine project relied in its reorganization and intercalation of animals, humans, and viruses. At the very least, Hooper's magnificent research gives us a starting point from which to attempt to trace the complex fragility and the enormous risks that were undertaken in twentieth-century vaccinology. In the late 1990s, potential failures seemingly had to remain invisible. This is no longer the case. And so, while the origin of the HIV epidemic is not particularly controversial, perhaps it should be.

Acknowledgment: This chapter formed the basis for "The WetNet: What the Oral Polio Vaccine Hypothesis Exposes about Globalized Interspecies Fluid Bonds," *Medical Anthropology Quarterly* 34, no. 4 (2020): 504–24, https://doi.org/10.1111/maq.12587.

1 The explanation relies on an enormous coincidence—that crossovers happened around the same time as at least five main cases of HIV, with at least two types of primates and in different areas of the continent—despite thousands of years of butchering and eating primate meat during which such crossover did not occur—and that HIV then lay dormant or unnoticed for decades.

2 I use cut hunter and natural transfer theories here interchangeably as the main hypothesis of phylogeneticists.

3 Lochlann Jain, "The WetNet: What the Oral Polio Vaccine Hypothesis Exposes about Globalized Interspecies Fluid Exchange," *Medical Anthropology Quarterly* 34, no. 4 (December 2020): 504–24.

4 Edward Hooper, "The Origin of HIV-1 Group M: The CHAT Polio Vaccine Theory," presentation at the Origin of HIV and Emerging Persistent Viruses conference, Accademia Nazionale dei Lincei, September 28, 2001, https://pages.ucsd.edu/~jjmoore/publications/hivhooper2001b.html. Hooper explains why Paul Osterreith's claim that the lab was not sophisticated enough to make tissue cultures is inconsistent with other evidence.

5 American interests and activism in the Congo remained heightened both because of Cold War strategic reasons and Russian presence in the region, and because of the mineral-rich geography. Neil Ahuja suggests that the involvement of the chimpanzee lab in Stanleyville may have been a Cold War pawn in the early 1960s (Ahuja 2013).

6 Koprowski, on the other hand, lived to be ninety-six and vigorously and litigiously shut down debate on the OPV hypothesis.

7 Hooper discusses his method of triangulating information sources. For example, he quotes an interview with a worker from one of the research labs who said he vaccinated locals in Butare with Wistar's vaccine in 1957. Hooper corroborates this with interviews of community members in eight villages around Butare, finding "two old men [who] independently told us that they recalled oral vaccinations against *mbasa*, or polio." These data are then linked to the epidemic: in 1984, 88 percent of prostitutes in Butare were HIV positive, "an extraordinary percentage for so early in the AIDS epidemic" (Hooper 2001, 806).

8 My own efforts to gain funding for such a project were unsuccessful.

9 "In 2001, I jumped off the fence on the polio vaccine hypothesis in favour of 'disproved.' . . . But I am open to persuasion that my conclusion was premature" (Robin Weiss, email to the author, November 12, 2017).

10   Robin Weiss, interview by the author, December 13, 2017.

11   Robin Weiss, interview by the author, December 13, 2017

12   Gottsdanker v. Cutter Laboratories [Civ. No. 18413 and 18414. First Dist., Div. Two. July 12, 1960.] 182 Cal. App. 2d 602 (Cal. Ct. App. 1960). https://casetext.com/case/gottsdanker-v-cutter-laboratories.

13   The monkeys, imported from India, were gang caged in transportation, thus enabling the sv-40 virus to spread among the monkeys. Vaccine companies used different techniques to make the vaccines. Vaccines made with one kidney had a 20 percent contamination rate; those made with kidneys from two to three animals had a 70 percent contamination rate; and when ten or more animals' kidneys were used, the resulting vaccines had a 100 percent contamination rate. "Studies estimate that the vaccine infected between 10–30 million adults" (in itself a tellingly vague estimate), and that "potentially contaminated vaccine had been administered to almost 90% of individuals under 20" (Shah and Nathanson 1976, 5).

_____

03 A FALSE FLAG

If only we could see the report. You know the one: the official statement connecting the dots, the detailed narrative that reveals who did what and when, describing the collusion, the disinformation campaign, the covert actions and corrupt profits, the authoritative revelation of the deception, the cover-up, the fraud. I am talking of course about the unfinished second 9/11 report on the George W. Bush administration's actions leading up to the 2001 suicide-hijacker attacks and the role of the Saudis, or perhaps the full version of the Senate's report on US torture,[1] or the one on the number of police killings in the United States,[2] or maybe the one explaining the true purpose of Nixon's War on Drugs,[3] or the one on what happened to all the fossil fuel moneys the Department of the Interior collected for indigenous nations over the past century that were never distributed,[4] or maybe the one about the twelve billion in cash sent to Iraq directly from the Federal Reserve in 2003 in perfectly shrink-wrapped one-hundred-dollar bills, the twelve billion that somehow got lost along the way . . .[5]

With an official report in hand, the structures of a democratic society can be activated, making accountability possible, correcting failed policy, overcoming corruption. In the absence of official documentation—the perfect paper trail—political life becomes a sea of conflicting messages, of claims and counterclaims, of _InfoWars_-style manipulations of emotions and disinformation campaigns, creating an inability to mobilize collective life to correct forms of violence that are structural, long lasting, and amplifying.[6] The ongoing reliance on declassification and transparency to create the confessional grounds for the political has a long history and is a key technique of counterrevolutionary politics in the United States, a means of discounting what citizens see, experience, and know in favor of a perfect but always out-of-reach paper trail.[7] Public focus on the declassified official report also provides citizens with an ever-present alibi for nonaction—even while implicitly assuming that perfect documentation exists for all the crimes and mistakes of a hyperviolent political order—creating a fetish form out of official narratives to the exclusion of other forms of civic engagement, consideration, and public activism (see Dean 2002).

The vital question of how one comes to know, of how one comes to understand collective conditions in the twenty-first century arrives at a moment when the epistemological terms of public life, the utility of theory as well as of logics of conspiracy, touch directly on the kinds of worlds that are desired and on the kinds of worlds that are unavoidable. Critical narratives—whether labeled conspiracy or theory or a combination of the two—all promise up front that the world can be rendered coherent and known, that deception will not win out, that with the right point of view, insight, or understanding, one can see clearly the dangers lurking all around as well as identify the allies that matter and the possibilities that can still be activated. This assumption of a one-to-one correspondence of interpretation to reality, of signifier to signified, belies people's actual experience of social life and is perhaps the primary form of what Lauren Berlant (2011) calls "cruel optimism"—a culturally coded promissory note for positive futurities that inevitably fail and disappoint.

The promise of theory as the perfect diagnostic is beautifully illustrated by John Carpenter's ever more astonishing 1988 film, *They Live*, in which a homeless, out-of-work journeyman, John Nada, finds a pair of sunglasses that allows him to see society as it actually is, to see the world within the world of print capital, mass mediation, class, and species. The sunglasses not only reveal the ever-present, subliminal messaging-surround of a control society but also expose the truth that those inhabiting positions of economic power are literally from another planet. Via the cognitive interface of the sunglasses, Nada comes to understand that earth has been taken over by aliens who now occupy the elite strata of society and control all markets, while relying on unrelenting propaganda, mind control, and deception to keep human beings pacified and asleep. Through the sunglasses, he now sees the embedded messages in advertisements and on television, and is radicalized by the discovery of this highly successful colonization of everyday life by a covert alien presence—which is trying to superheat the earthly climate to enable the next wave of its ongoing alien invasion (see figure 3.1). The sunglasses stand here not only for technology but also, I think, quite explicitly for the promise of critical theory, which offers a transformative way of understanding social conditions. That is, as one discovers the methodological and conceptual insights of critical-theory concepts (surplus value, alienated labor, interpellation, libidinal desires), one comes to see the world differently, gaining a new attention to its hidden depths and violence, understanding the lived consequences of commodity fetishism, dehumanization, fantasy, misrecognition, and engineered consensus. The direct promise of critical theory is a form of emancipation through insight; it is a mode of interpretation that assumes that people build their own reality and that inequalities are not just material; they are layered with culture, language, historical forms, and psychosocial investments. As Walter Benjamin (2007) might put it, the revolutionary project of the critical thinker is to "brush history against the grain": that is, to expose the naturalized perceptions, narratives, and practices that code violent conditions into an everyday that could still always be rendered otherwise. From this perspective, the conceptual interface between perception and material conditions is the crucial node, the formation that both holds the potential for a revolutionary insight and, more commonly, acts as the normative opposite, a way of consolidating—through repetition and nonattention—existing violent relations as the only possible social order.

Conceived a full decade before the advent of the web browser and two decades before the invention of the smart phone and social media platforms, the sunglasses in *They Live* are a one-way portal—a strictly visual technology. For those in the film who are armed with this technological interface, the goal becomes the dismantling of a broadcasting antenna that transmits deception globally and enables subliminal social control of people. Today the sunglasses would need to be reimagined as a two-way portal—allowing access not only to the hidden world of an economy run by extraterrestrials to advance their imperial agenda but also to the technological co-constitution of the self, as attentional hacking, digital surveillance, and perception management are at the center of the business model for Google, Facebook, Twitter (now X), and a host of related social media companies (see Zuboff 2019). The screen interface (via computers or smart phones) promises infinite modes of critical insight (the ability to see things differently, to globally communicate and travel while staying in the same place, and to collect information on an unprecedented scale); but it also facilitates sophisticated forms of cognitive capture. The misinformation of a corporate machinery (e.g., the Big Oil disinformation campaign against climate science), a political machinery (the Trump

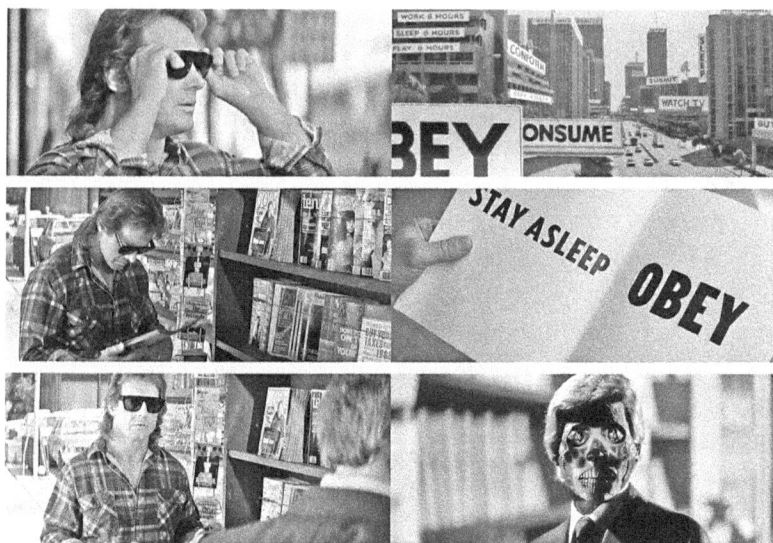

3.1 Eyeglass revelations from John Carpenter's *They Live* (1988).

administration's war on public health in the midst of a global pandemic or its demonization of asylum seekers as rapists and economy killers while deregulating toxic industries and giving billionaires tax cuts), or a for-profit disinformation machinery (*InfoWars*, *The Rush Limbaugh Show*, or Fox News, which lie and demonize every day for financial advantage) seeks via multiple new media techniques to flatten the world into yes or no propositions, refuting complexity in the pursuit of affective, rather than intellectual, intensity. The value of conspiracy theory is precisely its combination of harm identification and intuition, a value that is lost in a world of such binary absolutes. Thus, one important part of a conspiracy/theory project is to assess the goals of explanatory narratives, to consider whether the aim is to misdirect and agitate (as part of a disinformation effort or for-profit entertainment) or a more serious effort to locate the problems in social life and gather resources to them. At a historic moment when harm comes from direct and dispersed origins, where official agencies have agendas that are antidemocratic—making war, environmental destruction, and inequality infrastructural to current conditions—the diagnostic role of narrative is vital to both understand and cultivate, which is why conspiracy theory has become so politicized an accusation.

John Carpenter's 1988 film is also notable for casting a professional wrestler—Roddy Piper—in the lead role of John Nada, which enhances the flattening out of the story into two simple modes—truth or falsity, color or black and white, human or nonhuman—with the sunglasses as mediator. This effect is worth interrogating as a crude rendering of interpretation itself, one for which conspiracy theory is often derided but that also powers the pleasurable force of narrative. Wrestling has for years entertained its audiences by flattening the contest down to a good-versus-evil confrontation with formal characters—the heel (or bad guy) and the face (or good guy). The heel expresses the illiberal, performing antisocial liberation, while the face works to reconstitute the idea of righteous justice through physical power. This binary underscores one of the dangerous pleasures people find in conspiracy stories, namely, the entertainment value of paranoid narratives that flatten out the complexity of contemporary society into a set of propositions that allow an easy moral judgment and either/or framings via affective amplification. The elimination of complexity in wrestling, as Barthes (2012, 5) notes in *Mythologies* is, in fact, its great psychosocial achievement: "Each sign in wrestling is thus endowed with an utter clarity since everything must always be understood on the spot. Once the adversaries are in the Ring, the public is entrusted with the obviousness of the roles. As in the theater, each physical type expresses to excess the role assigned to the combatant."

Thus, for Barthes, the obese aging body of a wrestler who cheats in the ring recruits the contempt of the crowd, while the youthful wrestler body signals virtue, both in its power and beauty, and in its adherence to the rules until provoked. The excessive world of wrestling is one of overt simplification and emotional recruitment, offering a kind of template for a world of social interaction that is not about transformation but about confirmation, not about risk but about certainty, and where the affective circuit that is formally coded into the structure of the event is a good-versus-evil binary matchup.

Barthes, however, offers us an even more vital insight about enjoyment, one that I think raises an important qualification to the work of theory:

> But what wrestling is especially supposed to imitate is a purely moral concept: justice. The notion of payment is essential to wrestling, and the crowd's "Make him suffer" signifies above all "Make him pay." What is involved, then, of course, is an immanent justice. The viler the "action of the bastard," the more satisfied the public is by the blow he receives in return: if the villain—who is of course a coward—takes refuge behind the ropes, claiming his

right to do so by a brazen gesture, he is pitilessly cornered there, and the crowd roars its approval at seeing the rules broken for the sake of a deserved punishment. Wrestlers are good at flattering the crowd's powers of outrage, going to the very limits of the concept of Justice, this farthest zone of confrontation, where it takes only a trifle to open the gates to a frenzied world. (Barthes 2012, 10)

Barthes concludes by suggesting that the only justice people have reliable access to comes in this entirely theatrical, temporary form, one where the flattening of the world down to good-versus-evil offers a kind of momentary—but highly pleasurable—emotional release, a desire not only for their wrestler to win the match but to humiliate the bad-acting adversary. It also, of course, allows people to hate virtuously and to practice doing so, which is why wrestling finds such an easy alliance with authoritarian politics.

Donald Trump spent years not only in faked reality television but also in staged wrestling contests, becoming a formal member of the World Wrestling Entertainment (WWE) Hall of Fame in 2013. Attentive viewers of his presidential performances have noted his use of the same narrative tactics of the WWE, evidenced in his focus on dominating the news cycle through outrageous accusations, his use of demeaning nicknames for opponents, and the constant sorting of people into opposing camps (including the declaration of "good people" who might also be neo-Nazis and offering a near daily list of rivals to be humiliated and beaten). After contracting COVID-19 in the fall of 2020, President Trump sought to stage his exit from Walter Reed Hospital as a WWE-type stunt, proposing to his staff that he shuffle out of the building pretending to be frail and infirm before ripping open his dress shirt to reveal a Superman costume underneath (Karni and Haberman 2020). This kind of fakery is central to WWE events, where crafted injuries, planned humiliations, and obvious cheating are the vehicles for unlocking emotions in the crowd and creating the terms for redemptive acts of violence. In WWE, the heel and the face occasionally switch roles, revealing the constructedness of the event but also allowing the audience to feel the pleasure of revelation and conversion while maintaining the structure of a fight. It also creates a foreground/background distinction between the performance in the ring and the actual lives of the performers—who work out their roles in advance and often travel together, despite their staged animosity for the audience. Signaling the fakeness of the match is thus key to its psychosocial recruitment, allowing the crowd to play out unrestrained emotions as play rather than to consider the implications of unlocking social passions through violence.

I draw attention to the affective circuit produced by this staged good/ evil binary because it underscores the inherent danger of a world flattened into opposites. For example, rich people and corporate executives in *They Live* are literally not human, which allows John Nada to hunt them without remorse, staging an ever-increasing violence on the occluded world of alien oppressors. Depending on your viewpoint, he is either the heroic subject protecting humanity from an invading army devoted to human subservience that only a few can see, or the lone white male gunman shooting up public spaces because he has no place in society (a scene that has become so terrifyingly recurrent in the United States since the high school shooting in Columbine in 1999). Perhaps not surprisingly, illiberal talk-show host Alex Jones, a proponent of the idea that mainstream media is fake, has identified *They Live* as his favorite movie and has spent years talking on *InfoWars* about how the "globalists" controlling the world are not actually human and that school shootings are staged. Concurrently, QAnon supporters claimed that former president Donald Trump was masterminding a war against a highly secretive and all-powerful cabal of pedophiles hidden within the federal government, finding in his every word, error, and strange behavior a coded message about the latest stage of the covert conflict that only he could win.

These forms of political demonization foment an either/or world (and can become national frameworks as in the anticommunism of the Cold War, or the counterterror of the war on terror). Such rehearsals also create an animosity circuit that can be easily directed and redirected. At Trump's political rallies, for example, the chant of "lock her up" (first aimed at Hillary Clinton but then repurposed for a wide range of political targets) recruited followers not to an engaged political deliberation but rather to an all-or-nothing fight against an always already known duplicitous other. The opposition in this kind of political frame is cast as an overwhelmingly malevolent entity that cannot be understood or trusted and needs only to be crushed and, preferably, humiliated. Trump rallies mimic the structure of WWE events where the heel cheats and steals and ridicules to provoke the audience. In this way, the "lock her up" chant manifested the kind of affective politics of control that George Orwell powerfully depicted in *1984*, in which the authoritarian state demands citizens perform a daily "two-minute hate" of a designated, but constantly changing, state enemy, a ritual that foments an "undirected emotion which could be switched from one object to another like the flame of a blowlamp" (Orwell 1949, 14). The public face of the Trump administration may have been all WWE and may have functioned by generating both distraction and outrage, but the actual work of his administration has been the deregulation of petrochemical and financial industries, attacks on immigrants and on civil rights movements, and the further rewriting of the tax code to consolidate billionaire capital. But if in the Trump era many Americans seem to be experiencing the desperate conditions depicted in *They Live*, it is not because of the novelty of the WWE tactics or Trump's understanding of the power of playing the heel, but because deception, misinformation, and confusion have a deep political history in the United States.

Consider, for example, Neil Harris's assessment of fraud in nineteenth-century American society in his remarkable study of the life of P. T. Barnum, titled *Humbug*. An entertainer who made things up and produced trickster events for profit, Barnum became one of the most well-known huckster figures in nineteenth-century American life, Harris argues, precisely because his staged spectacles allowed visitors to exercise their judgment as to veracity versus hoax. Harris notes that the late nineteenth century was a time of accelerating technological revolution—the railroad, telegraph, electrical lights—weak federalism, and widespread fraud (much like the early twenty-first century, where accelerating technological change, the globalization of financial capital, and the emergence of social media have also radically transformed the terms of everyday life). Harris argues that Barnum's genius lay in recognizing the dizzying social effects of technological revolution and urbanization, offering spectacle and entertainment as opportunities for paying customers to exercise their analytic judgment about the objective possibilities of the world. Harris (1973, 79) calls this "an aesthetic of the operational, a delight in observing process and examining for literal truth. . . . Barnum's exhibitions concentrated on information and the problem of deception. Onlookers were relieved from the burden of coping with more abstract problems." Barnum's hoaxes required no research or expertise of the audience, suggesting to viewers that people's innate capacities to observe and judge were all that was necessary to distinguish between a hoax and the genuine article. In this way, they relied on an idiom of self-reliance, reinforcing an American variant of possessive individualism in a world riddled with deceptions and inequalities that was also undergoing rapid technological and social change.

Much of what is traditionally identified as conspiracy theory in the United States today falls under Harris's notion of an operational aesthetic. The 9/11 truthers—people who do not believe that the World Trade Center was destroyed by two hijacked jets flying into the buildings—mobilize observations and claims about the melting temperature of steel and building strength to dispute the official record. As a term, *truthers* is also a deliberate effort not to use the term *conspiracy theorist*. It is powerful because, like the operation aesthetic and WWE-style wrestling, *truther* suggests that a singular truth is to be had in public life—that clarity and objectivity are rendered difficult only because of a deliberate effort to deceive and confuse. Indeed, the most common truther claim is that the 9/11 attacks were not perpetrated by foreign nationals but were instead an inside job, a "false-flag" operation—the work of federal agents seeking to unlock wartime powers and operate in antidemocratic terms.

In the worlds of state-sanctioned espionage, a false-flag operation is one that attributes responsibility for a violent act to an uninvolved party. It is an accusation that is contagious today across the political spectrum, informing discussions of elections, news, and bombings in many parts of the world, and it is a key accusation in projects of political disorientation. It, too, has a deep history in American thought, one that was most clearly recognized during the Reagan era by the political theorist Michael Rogin. Rogin theorizes American political demonology, a tradition he claims is essential to the American project. By this he means:

> the creation of monsters as a continuing feature of American politics, the inflation, stigmatization, and dehumanization of political foes. These monsters—the Indian cannibal, the black rapist, the papal whore of Babylon, the monster-hydra United States Bank, the demon rum, the bomb-throwing anarchist, the many-tentacled Communist conspiracy, the agents of international terrorism—are familiar figures in the dreamlife that so often dominates American politics. (Rogin 1987, xiii)

In considering these forms, Rogin notes that the countersubversive tradition relies on crafting an image of the dehumanized, monstrous other committed to excessive violence in order to indulge forbidden desires, which ultimately allows "the countersubversive, in the name of battling the subversive, to imitate his enemy" (xiii). Thus, the constitution of a demonic other becomes a way to psychosocially justify otherwise immoral or illegal activity—a mobilization of existential defense against the image of an all-powerful other, a kind of interiorized false flag to enable an un-provoked attack. Rogin traces this practice from the colonization of North America (Indigenous genocide and dispossession) to the management of the Jim Crow South (anti-blackness) to the logics of the Cold War (anti-communism). I would extend it into the war on terror, with its dual pivot to construct a "terrorist with a WMD" as unmarked category and de facto anti-Islamic implementation (Masco 2014). In other words, US police actions at home and abroad have relied on willful misrecognition and projection for a long time. They operate by fomenting a false reality filled with demonic others as a core project in US settler-colonial/imperial culture. US national culture has a long history of racist recruitments to fantasy, a project that social media has amplified in new ways, allowing anyone with a social media channel on YouTube, Facebook, or X to conduct powerful campaigns in political demonology for political or financial gain or, in some cases, just for illiberal enjoyment.

For example, longtime right-wing dirty trickster Jerome Corsi has participated in a series of false-flag delegitimation campaigns against Democratic presidential candidates, most prominently by arguing that Barack Obama was secretly born in Kenya (not Hawaii) and thus could not legally be elected president (Corsi 2011). In addition to this "birtherism" campaign, Corsi played an active role in an effort involving hacked emails, Russian cyberoperations, WikiLeaks, and the Trump campaign to discredit Hillary Clinton in 2016. When challenged on his serial lying on a cable news talk show, Corsi replied: "I've been trained in public relations by Edward Bernays. British Petroleum becomes BP and now they are 'Beyond Petroleum'—is that a lie? It is a repositioning. In politics there is a lot of repositioning that goes on. If that were a lie, if people were guilty of a crime for doing that, there would hardly be a politician alive today."[8] Evoking Edward Bernays, Freud's nephew and a founding figure in a version of public relations focused not on facts but on engaging emotions and libidinal desires, Corsi declared that a lie is not a lie if you believe it, before finally concluding to the news host, "What you call lying, I call politics."[9] The reveal here is in the willfulness of the deception and the commitment to informational warfare as the basic form of politics, which, in an ever more mass-mediated age filled with proliferating opportunities and platforms for misinformation and psyops, raises important questions about how citizens can come to know or trust anything at all.

In their counterintelligence textbook on deception, Robert Clark and William Mitchell identify the false flag (or what they call "pseudo-operations") as a basic military tactic, a way of creating false appearances and hiding responsibility for actions. They argue that false flags are particularly powerful in twenty-first-century digital worlds:

> What began as simple deceit about identity in chat rooms and blogs has expanded with the rapid expansion of digital social networking possibilities. Social media such as Facebook, Twitter, and Instagram have become vibrant battlespaces for pseudo-operations. Fake profiles, groups, and avatars operated relatively unhindered until several of the larger firms began applying policies that are more restrictive. However, social media today is an acknowledged battlespace domain that is inherently permissive for pseudo-operations. (Clark and Mitchell 2019, 23)

The advent of the World Wide Web has collapsed the military distinction between foreign and domestic information operations, amplifying the power and reach of false-flag politics. Zuboff's (2019) helpful theorization of social media as "surveillance capitalism" is essentially a recognition that the largest companies in the world are committed to false-flag politics, offering free technologies under the guise of enabling an open exchange of information and ideas that are actually embedded in a financial model devoted to extracting information from users for future manipulation and exploitation.

False-flag politics are deeply informed by the relationship between US capitalism and warfare, a constellation that at least dates to World War I. The traumatized subject as well as the intentionally mobilized subject were coproduced in this moment, opening the interior life of the individual up in new ways to corporate and state-based manipulation. Looking back on his experience producing successful anti-German propaganda during World War I, Walter Lippmann concluded he had uncovered a fundamental weakness in the democratic state form, namely, that it assumes a rational citizen-subject that can be informed via media on the important matters of the day and exercise sound judgment:

> The private citizen today has come to feel rather like a deaf spectator in the back row, who ought to keep his mind on the mystery off there, but cannot quite manage to keep awake. He knows he is somehow affected by what is going on. Rules and regulations

continually, taxes annually and wars occasionally remind him that he is being swept along by great drifts of circumstance. Yet these public affairs are in no convincing way his affairs. They are for the most part invisible. They are managed, if they are managed at all, at distant centers, from behind the scenes, by unnamed power. . . . In the cold light of experience he knows that his sovereignty is a fiction. He reigns in theory, but in fact he does not govern. (Lippman 1993, 3-4)

Pondering whether, under such conditions, one could potentially build a subject capable of democratic reason, Lippman concludes that the public is ultimately nothing but a "phantom," making the only reasonable course for a democratic state a reliance on elite, expert control of policy. Otherwise, he argues, the serious matters of state would be turned over to subjects that could be easily manipulated via propaganda techniques (such as the ones he deployed in World War I) or swayed by advertising or other local influence operations, or who might simply be irrational. By the start of the Cold War the mechanisms for influencing American thought Lippman was worried about were highly institutionalized, both expertly designed and multiple. As Hugh Wilford (2009) documents, by the time Hofstadter (1996b) is identifying the "paranoid style" in American thought as a social pathology in 1964 the CIA is running a wide range of front operations in the United States and internationally. The CIA covertly funded student groups, arts projects, and activist groups without their knowledge, and managed mass media campaigns (across radio, newspapers, and magazines) inside the United States in violation of the agency's legal charter, even while also working to overthrow democratically elected governments on three continents.

This is to say that the Cold War was not only an arms race, it was also a serious multigenerational governmental commitment to foreign and domestic information warfare. The US Cold War state was deeply invested in gaslighting, psychological operations, and emotional-management campaigns using nuclear fear, images of demonic communist others, and covert media campaigns to create Americans as Cold War subjects and the United States as a covert imperial power (Rogin 1987; Oakes 1994; Masco 2014). It is important to note that the classic conspiracy theorist in the American imaginary for the past half century has been the UFO believer, the person who sees a vast government denial and cover-up of the arrival of extraterrestrial beings. This narrative has many sources, among them the CIA and the Pentagon, who used UFO stories for decades to misdirect the public from domestic aeronautical research, preferring citizens to see unverifiable visitors from another world in the night sky and have their sanity questioned than to acknowledge the state-of-the-art US aircraft in development in North America (see Haines 1999).

Given the prevalence of false-flag politics as an instrument of modern political power, what is the right interpretive mode? How can citizens learn to read between the lines, to anticipate the alternative projects, in Eve Sedgwick's (2003a) sense, embedded in the public ones, acknowledging that at least for some, paranoia is a vital mode, one that can anticipate reparative modes and forms of collective life? Thus, it is important to ask: What would constitute a critical theory of this kind of official deception, where misdirection is authorized as normalized statecraft? Or, alternatively, what would constitute a mode of inquiry that acknowledges this practice as ever present? Political theorist Leo Strauss would say that deception is nothing less than the very basis of expert knowledge. In *Persecution and the Art of Writing*, Strauss argues that great philosophers are necessarily involved in a life-and-death game of deception in their writing. Indeed, he details the challenges of writing under conditions of political censorship, concluding:

> Persecution, then, gives rise to a peculiar technique of writing, and therewith to a peculiar type of literature, in which the truth about all crucial things is presented exclusively between the lines. That literature is addressed, not to all readers, but to trustworthy and intelligent readers only. It has all the advantages of private communication without having its greatest disadvantage—that it reaches only the writer's acquaintances. It has all the advantages of public communication without having its greatest disadvantage—capital punishment for its author. But how can a man perform the miracle of speaking in a publication to a minority, while being silent to the majority of his readers? (Strauss 1952, 24)

Strauss details and advocates for a method through which a writer, while seeming to agree with the necessary opinions of the times or regime, also laces the writing with small signs for the knowing reader, with a set of clues that take back the officially sanctioned view and offer some kind of subversive truth telling. Indeed, he argues that such writers offer two teachings: "a popular teaching of an edifying character, which is in the foreground; and a philosophic teaching concerning the most important subject, which is indicated only between the lines" (Strauss 1952, 36). Thus, he suggests that to be a serious philosopher is to "lie nobly" in order to smuggle truths for a future reader into one's text (36). Here, a false flag is the very condition for offering up important philosophical knowledge. Strauss advocated to generations of students and readers a technique of close reading designed to locate the hidden truth in great philosophical texts. Some of his key students would take these lessons about noble lies—truth telling only to the anointed few alongside the necessity of public deception—to a new level. Undoubtedly breaking with the intent of Strauss's teaching, they constituted the neoconservative revolution that has structured much of US geopolitical and national security debates since the 1970s. For example, arguments about noble lies figured prominently in the White House deliberations about a potential US invasion of Iraq in 2003, as proponents sought to craft a narrative to gain public support rather than evaluating facts on the ground (see Mann 2004). For Strauss and his self-proclaimed neocon students, the most skilled writers, the most serious philosophers, the most important strategists, are false-flag artists of the highest order. Indeed, the false flag is vital to ambitions for empire.

The perhaps long-standing commitment to deception within empire was supercharged by the advent of the atomic bomb and the resulting configuration of "existential danger." The logics of nuclear production and deterrence in the twentieth century relied on a serious game of perception management, requiring a regular demonstration of both technological capacities (that is, nuclear explosions at test sites) and overt statements of political resolve to go to nuclear war to constitute the Cold War logic of mutually assured destruction between the United States and Soviet Union. But defense intellectuals, despite decades of energetic work, were never able to define the minimum nuclear capabilities needed to create deterrence, nor, for that matter, were they able to identify what "political resolve" looked like. The four decades of Cold War were about building not only a technological infrastructure for global nuclear war but also a theater for the projection of antagonisms and fears in pursuit of national advantage. Deception was a basic element in the geopolitical tool kit. There is much to say on this point, as domestic politics as well as geopolitics were remade via nuclear fear after World War II (Masco 2014, 2021).

Taking one key example, the phantom threat of Iraqi weapons of mass destruction and imminent danger of Iraqi attack on the United States in

2002 pulled on a script, going back to the missile gap of the late 1950s, in the form of a US expert assessment that the Soviets had secretly achieved superiority in ICBMs. The move was successful in mobilizing a significant military buildup despite the lack of evidence of the material existence of the ICBMs or the reality of any such technological breakthrough on the Soviet side. Indeed, satellite photography would soon document that the United States maintained a vast numerical superiority in both ICBMs and warheads, a fact that was not made public. Faking nuclear vulnerability was subsequently installed as a basic part of the military industrial and defense strategy tool kit. Indeed, assessing not only Soviet technological capabilities but imagining Kremlin desires became a way of continuing to expand US militarism through the end of the Cold War, allowing a state-of-the-art US program in nuclear weapons science to be frequently cast domestically as a much smaller and merely a reactive undertaking, requiring a desperate effort to catch up in the name of national survival. For example, in 1974, a nuclear strategist and teacher of future neocons in the George W. Bush administration, Albert Wohlstetter, wrote a highly influential essay in the journal *Foreign Policy*, "Is There a Strategic Arms Race?," in which he recovered and repurposed the missile gap argument, stating that the United States continued to systematically underestimate Soviet capabilities and was vulnerable to a surprise nuclear attack. The entire logic of the Cold War system was based on a misreading of Soviet systems and interests, in his view, posing a direct challenge to experts at the CIA devoted precisely to these issues and doing yearly assessments and forecasts of Soviet capabilities. Wohlstetter's challenge was fierce enough to create the context for a world-class bit of false-flag politics in the form of the CIA Team B reports of 1976.

Team B arose as a right-wing effort to challenge the veracity of official CIA assessments of Soviet capabilities by creating a second, independent review process of Soviet nuclear technologies and desires; and it was made up of the soon-to-be-ascendant neoconservatives who would eventually become key members of the George W. Bush administration. Team B did indeed conclude that the CIA systematically misunderstood Soviet intentions and capabilities. They accused established CIA Soviet experts of "mirror imaging"—that is, assuming that the Soviets approached nuclear weapons identically to the United States and thus had similar values, when they were in actuality a different political, and inherently malevolent, species. According to Team B:

> Since in the United States nuclear war is generally regarded as an act of mutual suicide that can be rational only as a deterrent threat, it is assumed that the USSR looks at the matter in the same way. . . . [But in reality] the Soviets believe that the best way to paralyze U.S. strategic capabilities is by assuring that the outcome of any nuclear exchange will be as favorable to the Soviet Union as possible (as) . . . the Russians seriously believe that if, for whatever reason, deterrence were to fail, they could resort to the use of nuclear weapons to fight and win a war. (CIA 1976, 2)

Thus, Team B replaced deterrence (i.e., preventing nuclear war) with "winning" as the terms of the Cold War standoff, advocating a significant arms buildup to gain that elusive (and ultimately nonexistent) capability.

The centerpiece of the Team B assessment was a discussion of Soviet research on a stealth submarine—a *non-acoustical* nuclear-armed ship that could evade US radar and that might already be sitting silently just off the Atlantic coast waiting to blast New York and Washington, DC, to smithereens (see Cahn 1998). The beauty of the Team B argument was that the lack of material evidence of the submarine was marshaled to create urgency about its reality. Thus, when Secretary of Defense Donald Rumsfeld (2002) said of terrorist threats, in the buildup to the 2003 invasion of Iraq, that "absence of evidence is not evidence of absence," he was drawing directly on the lessons he learned from Team B three decades earlier. The emerging portrait of Soviet military and nuclear superiority in the mid-1970s empowered the coalition that would soon be supporting President Ronald Reagan, who mobilized concern about a new "window of vulnerability," fomenting the start of what some now call the second Cold War—a period of trillion-dollar US military expenditures, military confrontation, and ideological amplification with the Soviet Union even as it fell apart. The never-found weapons of the Team B exercise (like the Soviet ICBMs of 1960 or the Iraqi WMDs of 2003) were nonetheless hugely productive, promoting war with an imaginary existential danger over opportunities for diplomacy while diverting vast sums of money to existential "defense."

Mobilizing political demonization and threat projection (that is, amplifying imagined threats over verifiable capabilities), the Team B project helped secure a massive increase in the arms race across the Carter and Reagan administrations. The role of deception was not just strategic, however, as it also mobilized true believers to the cause who could be convinced despite the lack of evidence. A little-known US military exercise in

1983, called Able Archer, can be seen as the culmination of Team B's radical reassessment of Soviet capabilities and thinking, and it reveals how this kind of narrative project can capture belief, becoming something more than a political tactic. In November of 1983 the Reagan administration staged a worldwide nuclear war exercise timed to accompany the president's designation of the Soviet Union as an "evil empire" and the launching of the Strategic Defense Initiative (a fanciful effort to create a network of space-based satellite lasers to shoot down Soviet intercontinental missiles). The "exercise" involved a global simulation of DEF CON 1 conditions (that is, global nuclear war) by mobilizing tens of thousands of troops in Europe, Navy maneuvers around the world, and Air Force bombers, some armed with nuclear weapons, to fly at Soviet territories simultaneously from all directions. While large military exercises were a staple of the Cold War system and the nuclear war machine had been on minute-by-minute readiness for launch for decades, the Able Archer exercise remains exceptional. Soviet leadership, for example, thought it might be an actual attack hiding within an exercise (i.e., a false-flag peaceful military exercise), leading to worried discussions about end-game retaliatory measures in the form of global nuclear war. Afterward, Reagan and his national security team acted for domestic audiences *as if* their global exercise had been peaceful, expressing shock that the Soviet leadership—confronting a global mobilization of US forces with live ammo and nuclear weapons—might actually have been worried about a surprise US nuclear attack, even after having taken every conceivable step to make the global nuclear war "exercise" realistic (see Nate Jones 2016).

Evoking, and at times faking, existential danger in this manner has been massively successful for the defense industry in the United States. Indeed, one can follow some key figures from the original Team B project (Wolfowitz, Rumsfeld, Cheney) through successive administrations into key positions of authority at the start of the war on terror. Thus, we could think seriously about the nonexistent Soviet missiles of 1960, the invisible non-acoustical Soviet submarine of 1976, and the absent Iraqi WMDs of 2003 as part of a theatrical politics of American power—a serious false-flag geopolitics. The war on terror as an affectively organized concept, structured around preemption of the potential WMD, is the normalization and expansion of these exceptional moments in Cold War policy (see Masco 2014). Increasingly today, the threats monitored by the national security apparatus are not derived from measurable dangers in the world but produced out of games and exercises designed to identify worst-case scenarios and "what ifs" that do not need evidence to activate state power. The shift from risk to threat here allows the imagination to play an ever-greater role in distilling dangers from the future (see Masco 2014)—it also allows fiction, fantasy, and forms of deception to take a formidable place in planning.

With this context in mind, we might now ask via a conspiracy/theory analytic: How is it that in 2003 some 70 percent of Americans understood that Saddam Hussein was involved in the 9/11 attacks and had weapons of mass destruction poised for a imminent second attack on the United States that might produce "mushroom clouds." The American public learned after the US invasion of Iraq that none of this was true, having nonetheless set in motion the death of hundreds of thousands of Iraqis while displacing millions more to other countries.[10] So how did such a mistaken and massively consequential understanding reach the majority of Americans? It was a serious piece of statecraft, a domestic use of psychological operations, one never properly interrogated or investigated, perhaps precisely because it indicts so many aspects of American society—the White House, Pentagon, Congress, and reporters, as well as, ultimately, a public that was willing to believe. In part, it involved White House officials leaking information to major newspapers and then going on television citing those statements as nonpartisan facts that they had nothing to do with. It also involved the Pentagon placing retired generals still under contract to military firms on 24/7 cable news to offer "objective" assessments of the need for war. In fact, these retired military figures were coordinated directly from the Secretary of Defense's office and were told what messages to amplify to enable the invasion (see Barstow 2008). As then Secretary of Defense Donald Rumsfeld put it, the goal leading up to the invasion was to create a media surround in which American citizens encountered the same incendiary narrative about imminent danger from Iraq at every turn—a classic propaganda goal that assumes that the background informational noise is as compelling as the direct messaging. The domestic psyops project list promoting the invasion of Iraq is long and required a lot of work (see Draper 2020; and Althaus and Largio 2004), including a series of stacked deceptive maneuvers in US media to convert the 2001 attacks organized by a Saudi citizen, Osama Bin Laden, into a morally righteous, and retaliatory, invasion of Iraq, an uninvolved country.

This ability to craft perceptions on a national and even global scale is key to imperial projects that hide as collective defense. An adviser to President

George W. Bush in this moment of US military ambition, widely believed to be Karl Rove, explained to Ron Suskind the reality-making power of the White House:

> The aide said that guys like me were "in what we call the reality-based community," which he defined as people who "believe that solutions emerge from your judicious study of discernible reality." I nodded and murmured something about enlightenment principles and empiricism. He cut me off. "That's not the way the world really works anymore," he continued. "We're an empire now, and when we act, we create our own reality. And while you're studying that reality—judiciously, as you will—we'll act again, creating other new realities, which you can study too, and that's how things will sort out. We're history's actors . . . and you, all of you, will be left to just study what we do." (Suskind 2004)

This White House commitment to "creating our own reality" (see also Suskind 2006) involved not just the global counterterror state's ambitions but, increasingly, has also overtaken right-wing politics in the United States, more generally producing the conditions of possibility for President Donald Trump's illiberal commitment to rejecting scientific facts (on public health, environmental sciences, and vote counts) and lying to foment a strategic disorientation of the public and to test the constraining powers of state and federal institutions.[11]

BY WAY OF A CONCLUSION

While conspiracy, political demonology, and forms of political speculation have a long history in the United States, and while the intensities of each era matter and are different, I would argue that the contemporary twenty-first-century moment is unusually organized by what I have called false-flag politics. This is a mode of deception that covertly attributes the violence of the age to nonresponsible third parties and that operates now as a basic attribute of power. The prevalence of the false flag today (as both practice and accusation) is diagnostic of a larger set of conditions that underpin how the military industrial sector, corporate finance, and environmental disruption are intertwined and involved in managing the foundational contradictions within American society. This mode of politics recognizes real suffering and worries about the future but redirects public attention away from the foundational causes—namely, racism, inequality, and militarism—which amplifies the distorting effect they have on public life. Consider the commitment of major oil companies to simultaneously promoting scientific study of the global warming effects from petrochemical emissions while also funding major antienvironmental disinformation campaigns (Oreskes and Conway 2010). We could also discuss the counterrevolutionary stealth project of plutocratic billionaires to limit American access to the vote and courts—a formal democracy-reduction project taking place in the United States—as a means to consolidate capital, and their doing so in a way that is in direct alignment with white supremacy (see MacLean 2017). These are corporate false-flag operations—modes of doing politics via stealth and deception and division. Consider, for example, the presentation of Rhode Island Senator Sheldon Whitehouse at the 2020 confirmation hearings for Judge Amy Coney Barrett to the Supreme Court, in which, rather than ask questions, he revealed an extraordinary false-flag strategy to stack the courts with pro-corporate, anti–civil rights judges.[12] Whitehouse started with the creation and funding of a "nonpartisan" NGO—the Federalist Society—to preselect conservative judges for nomination to the Supreme Court. This was followed by the creation of fake citizen groups (such as the Judicial Crisis Network) to support the designated candidates chosen by the Federalist Society, and then linked to a series of staged lawsuits and accompanying friend-of-the-court briefs to bring matters that do not have public support to the Supreme Court for the preselected judges to rule on. Whitehouse argued that massive dark money (at least $250 million) enabled this operation to put Barrett and others on the Supreme Court, positing that a single individual with investments in polluting industries might be covertly controlling US federal policy on reproductive rights, civil rights, voter rights, environmental protections, healthcare access, and corporate regulation. Whitehouse presented Amy Coney Barrett's nomination as a multigenerational achievement of billionaires who could not win a popular vote for their policies, but who have captured the courts to do that work for them. Whitehouse depicted a corruption of the American judiciary to the detriment of democratic majority interests on a vast set of issues. Ultimately, Whitehouse made the case that false-flag politics are at the absolute center of American politics today—determining the quality of the air and water we all breathe and drink, the robustness of the vote, the details of the tax code, matters of war and politics, and even the version of truth that informs federal policy (for more, see Mayer 2016; MacLean 2017).

In his remarkable 2016 film *HyperNormalisation*, Adam Curtis argues that increasingly authoritarian states are now involved in a strategic production of confusion as a means to maintain and expand power. The reliance on a mass-mediated public sphere to debate the terms of everyday life and policy is, in such cases, systematically replaced by an official effort to destabilize citizens' sense of reality, to make perception itself untrustworthy and thus politically unaccountable. On this point, Masha Gessen (2018) explains the differences between US and Russian state influence campaigns this way:

> Russian propaganda is cacophonous. This is its single most important distinguishing feature, and it is the one that never fails to confound Americans. Americans assume that propaganda serves a clear, actionable objective: campaign propaganda is intended to make you vote a certain way, and war propaganda is intended to make you hate the enemy and support the troops. The same assumptions, Americans think, hold for totalitarian propaganda: it is probably intended to make everyone support the regime. In fact, the purpose of totalitarian propaganda is to take away your ability to perceive reality. . . . Totalitarian propaganda is overwhelming and inconsistent. It bombards you with mutually contradictory claims, which often come packaged in doublethink pairs.

With this context in mind, I do not see how one can afford to not be a kind of conspiracy theorist today, mobilizing all one's faculties and resources to engage a national, corporate, political project that is structured by violent deceptions and that has never really developed a robust social commitment to public accountability. Conspiracy theory has been weaponized by states, by corporations, and by individuals interested only in provoking outrage, to be sure. But conspiratorial narratives today can also reveal genuine fears about the contemporary moment as well as represent efforts by individuals experiencing something painful to make sense of that suffering. Current media and political worlds are increasingly organized around exploiting such pain rather than preventing it or responding to it. The prevalence of false-flag operations and accusations today also underscores the necessity of building collectives and positive futurities, of acknowledging existing conditions but also maintaining the capacity to imagine a world that responds differently to people—which is the ultimate conspiratorial act. Conspiracy theory, from this point of view, needs to retake its full spectrum of meanings, acknowledging the negative effects of paranoia while avoiding simple binary formations, embracing modes of collective self-fashioning and investment that make breathing together, and dreaming together, the essential project of future-making. No one needs the declassified report for that.

NOTES

1   In 2014 the Senate released a 500-page selection from the 6,700-page report on the use of torture by American troops and agencies during the first years of the war on terror. The Senate's effort to research and write the report was subject to hacking by the CIA, that involved spying on congressional investigators and manipulating their access to federal information. While the report attempted a comprehensive review of the torture, black sites, and prisons after 9/11, the full congressional review has still not been released.

2   In 2015 the *Washington Post* began collecting state-by-state statistics of police shootings, after realizing that there were no comprehensive federal accounts. See "Fatal Force," *Washington Post*, last updated February 15, 2023, https://www.washingtonpost.com/graphics/investigations/police-shootings-database/.

3   Dan Baum (2016) reports a 1994 interview with John Ehrlichman, Assistant to the President on Domestic Affairs in the Nixon administration, about the covert logics behind the War on Drugs. He quotes Ehrlichman as saying:

> The Nixon campaign in 1968, and the Nixon White House after that, had two enemies: the antiwar left and black people. You understand what I'm saying? We knew we couldn't make it illegal to be either against the war or black, but by getting the public to associate the hippies with marijuana and blacks with heroin, and then criminalizing both heavily, we could disrupt those communities. We could arrest their leaders, raid their homes, break up their meetings, and vilify them night after night on the evening news. Did we know we were lying about the drugs? Of course we did.

4   The federal government took on a trust role for Native American communities in the nineteenth century, collecting moneys (upward of $175 billion) from land transfers and extractive industries for redistribution back to the tribes. The money was never returned, leading, after years of activism, to a settlement in 2010 for a fraction of the collected funds. See Friends

Committee on National Legislation, "Native American Trust Fund: Massive Mismanagement," September 29, 2016, https://www.fcnl.org/updates /native-american-trust-fund-massive-mismanagement-131.

5 See Javers (2011) and Pallister (2007).

6 See the *Frontline* documentary "United States of Conspiracy," which interviews key members of the *InfoWars* staff that details how, the more outrageous the claims they made on YouTube.com, became the more money they made. Alex Jones and Roger Stone turned *InfoWars* into a major vehicle for the Trump presidential campaign by suggesting that school shootings were staged events and that there was a deep state manipulating everyday life against citizens. For a transcript of the interviews, see "United States of Conspiracy" (transcript), *Frontline*, PBS.org, accessed April 27, 2023, https://www.pbs.org/wgbh/frontline/documentary/united -states-of-conspiracy/transcript.

7 See Gellman (2008) for a detailed study of Vice President Cheney's disinformation efforts, including leaking materials to the *New York Times* and then quoting those leaks as part of the "factual" publicity campaign around the invasion of Iraq.

8 See "Trump Open to Manafort Pardon" (transcript), *The Beat with Ari Melber*, MSNBC.com, November 28, 2018, https://www.msnbc.com/transcripts /msnbc-live-with-ari-melber/2018-11-28-msna1170051.

9 "Trump Open to Manafort Pardon."

10 For an ongoing account of the costs of the war on terror, see "Costs of War," Watson Institute of International and Public Affairs, accessed February 27, 2023, https://watson.brown.edu/costsofwar/.

11 For a numerical assessment of the daily lying of President Trump, see Kessler, Rizzo, and Kelly (2021).

12 For Senator Sheldon Whitehouse's presentation during the Supreme Court Nominee hearing for Amy Coney Barrett on October 13, 2020, see PBS *NewsHour*, "Sen. Sheldon Whitehouse Speaks during Hearing for Supreme Court Nominee Amy Coney Barrett," YouTube.com, accessed February 27, 2023, https://www.youtube.com/watch?v=cjcXVKg43qY.

_____

04 CONSPIRACY ATTUNEMENT AND CONTEXT / THE CASE OF THE PRESIDENT'S BODY

On December 11, 2009, the body of Tassos Papadopoulos, former president of the Republic of Cyprus, was stolen from his grave. The theft transpired one day before the first anniversary of his death and thus his one-year memorial—an important day of remembrance for any deceased person in the Greek Orthodox tradition but especially for one who had lived such an outsized public life. For the rest of that December and for several months following, the identity of the thieves and the motive for their crime attracted intense speculation. On December 19, a little over a week after the theft, Anastasia Papadopoulos, Tassos's daughter, published an essay entitled "The Rape of Our Dignity" in *Philelevtheros*, an independent, Greek-language newspaper with the highest circulation in the Republic. In a blow-by-blow account, she described what it had been like to receive the news of the theft, the horror and pain her family had felt and were still feeling, the outpouring of love they had received from some (but not all) members of the political class, and the onslaught of "conspiracy theories"[1] about the crime:

> And after the memorial, too, all those thoughts remained. The attempt to understand why. To feel something other than the rage that flooded me. The scenarios were making us crazy. Was it for ransom? They didn't leave us alone even at the memorial. Was it extremists? For what reason? What did they hope to achieve? What were they doing to him? Where did they have him? And to the

scenarios we imagined ourselves were added other, obscene ones: [that] we took him, [that] he planned it himself. . . . I laugh so that I don't cry. (Papadopoulos 2009, 3)

Long before the theft of his body buried his legacy in "conspiracy theories," so to speak, Papadopoulos was understood among progressive Cypriots as the very embodiment of political paranoia. Konstantina Zanou, a Cypriot intellectual historian, observed in an essay published shortly after the theft that the period of Papadopoulos's presidency was the "golden age" of "conspiracy theory" in Cyprus (Zanou 2010). For decades before he assumed the presidency, from the time of his earliest political activity in the 1950s, Papadopoulos was intimately associated with the movement of Greek-Cypriot ethnonationalism that sought the union of Cyprus with Greece—against the wishes and interests of the minority Turkish-Cypriot population—and that ultimately led to the division of the island in 1974. That summer, a coup led by Greek-Cypriot extremists, backed by the Junta government in Greece, provoked the invasion of the island by Turkish military forces; the fighting that ensued caused mass casualties and massive displacement, as Greek Cypriots evacuated to the south of the island and Turkish Cypriots to the north. The division put a provisional end to two decades of intercommunal, paramilitary, and state violence, both before and after Cyprus's independence from Great Britain in 1960.

Although a political settlement for reunification has persisted as a dominant issue (if not *the* dominant issue) in Cypriot politics since then, the division between north and south—between Turkish-Cypriot and Greek-Cypriot communities and regimes—remains in place today. It survived an island-wide referendum on the only reunification plan ever proposed to Cypriot publics in April 2004. Known as the Annan Plan, after Kofi Annan, then secretary-general of the United Nations, this proposal was supported by most Turkish Cypriots but rejected by most of the much larger population of Greek Cypriots, who were encouraged to vote "no" by a broad coalition of political leaders in the south headed by then president Tassos Papadopoulos. The division has since been normalized by the opening of checkpoints for pedestrian and automobile traffic between north and south in 2003 and Cyprus's accession to the European Union in 2004 as a divided country.[2] UN-mediated negotiations between the Greek-Cypriot and Turkish-Cypriot authorities in 2008–10, 2010–12, 2014, 2015–17, and 2021 opened and closed without a settlement.

Today, critics and supporters of Papadopoulos alike draw a line of continuity between the stance in favor of Cyprus's union with Greece that he took in the early years of the Republic and the stance against the reunification of north and south that he took as president in the last years of his life. This stance committed him to the villainization of Turkey and of the small community of peace-minded Greek Cypriots and Turkish Cypriots who pushed for bicommunal reconciliation and a political settlement. These Cypriots were among the chief targets of his "conspiracy theorizing." In a bitterly comic essay published in the left-leaning Greek-language newspaper, *Politis*, in February 2005, journalist Makarios Drousiotis (2005b) offered an account of Papadopoulos's conspiracy-theory mongering, reflecting at length on the pervasive "political paranoia" among Greek-Cypriot politicians during the lead-up to the referendum on the Annan Plan and following its defeat. Excoriating President Papadopoulos and Demetris Christofias, president of the House of Representatives at the time, Drousiotis framed their "preoccupation with conspiracy theories" as a "curse" "bequeathed" by former president Spyros Kyprianou, whose own "conspiracy theorizing" during his tenure (1977–88) was notorious; among other theories he promoted publicly, Kyprianou claimed that a fascist movement called the Black Internationale was conspiring to undermine his political power and possibly to kill him. In a tape recording he made of himself and then released to the media in 1978, Kyprianou named members of the conspiracy, including a German diplomat in Cyprus, an Israeli soccer coach, and Tassos Papadopoulos himself, whom he suspected of acting on orders from Kikis Constantinou, a hotel owner in the southern resort town of Ayia Napa, identified by Kyprianou as a former chief of EOKA-B, the terrorist organization that staged the coup in 1974 (see also Psyllides 2011 and 2016).

In his article, Drousiotis was intensely critical of the newspapers—from both the left and the right—that actively advanced Kyprianou's "conspiracy theory" about the Black Internationale and his many other "conspiracy theories" in the 1970s. These same newspapers, he contended, did the same decades later with the "paranoid" theories, promoted by Papadopoulos and Christofias, about the "unseen hand" of foreign conspirators against Cyprus. Specifically, during the lead-up to the referendum, these papers published a series of claims made by Papadopoulos and his allies that certain individuals in Cyprus, supporters of the Annan Plan, were "paid agents" of the United States and the United Nations (Drousiotis 2005a, 7, 10). The defeat of the referendum is widely attributed to Papadopoulos's strenuous encouragement to Greek Cypriots to vote "no." Regarding the accusations made by Papadopoulos and Christofias about this "foreign conspiracy," Drousiotis (2005b) observed, "[T]his government is possessed by a persecution complex, and automatically blames everything that goes wrong for it on the foreigners."

The theft of Papadopoulos's body in 2009 provoked rampant speculation in both the north and the south about the culprits in the Cypriot press. In order to study this public discourse, some years after the fact, I consulted four Greek-language newspapers in the south and six Turkish-language papers in the north, as well as one English-language paper published in Nicosia, the divided capital city. These spanned the political spectrum; I also selected several independent papers (not associated with political parties) published in each regime. Theories in the southern press pointed in many directions: to Turkish nationalist groups like the Grey Wolves, or Turkish intelligence agents attempting to sow chaos in the south, or Turkish Cypriots and Greek-Cypriot leftists angered by Papadopoulos's role in defeating the Annan Plan. The CIA and MI6 also made a few appearances. The northern press was more creative and wide-ranging in its coverage; these papers proposed the Russian or Romanian Mafia as culprits, a global network like the one behind the DaVinci code, the president of the regime in the north, grave robbers working for medical schools in Turkey, and even Papadopoulos's own wife, Fotini, a figure of long-standing intrigue herself.[3]

My friend N., a Greek-Cypriot artist and historian, remembered the theft of the president's body very well, years after the event: "The big story after the theft was that it was Turkish Cypriots or Turks who'd done it," he told me. The supposed proof for this theory was quicklime found around the desecrated grave that was tested and found to match samples from mountainous terrain in the north. N. laughed at the absurdity of this theory. "Where do you think the soil and stone and building materials come from, for all the construction projects you see in the south?" he asked. "It all comes from the north, all of it, right across the border in trucks, legally—that's the border economy." He reminded me that Papadopoulos's son, Nikolas, who had become head of his father's political party after his death, had supported the theory about Turkish Cypriots publicly in the press. "The other suspects were people like me—the 'Nainaikis,'" N. said. This term, he explained—"the yes-men," which also means "traitors"[4]—referred to those (relatively few) Greek Cypriots who had voted to support the Annan Plan in 2004. "So, after the theft, my friends and I, we all went around whispering, 'Where did you put them?' meaning, the bones. 'Where are you hiding them?' It was hilarious."

The hilarious quality that my friend identified in the responses of people (like himself) suspected of the theft to the theories that circulated in the weeks after its discovery marks an acute awareness among Cypriots of the prevalence of "conspiracy theory" in Cypriot public discourse. I found that awareness expressed in many dozens of news items, op-eds, and letters to the editor in Cypriot newspapers published in the aftermath of the theft. While I cannot claim to read tone accurately in all the press coverage, I do register the knowingness with which Cypriot journalists marked their participation in a time-worn and very explicit public discourse about "conspiracy theory" as such: a discourse with a characteristic vocabulary, style of expression, and range of performative affects, from cynical to rueful to playful.

Almost three months after the theft, in March 2010, Papadopoulos's remains were found by the Greek-Cypriot police, acting on an anonymous tip, and conclusively identified by DNA analysis. One of the alleged thieves, Sarbjit Singh, an Indian national, was ultimately identified as the source of the anonymous tip; he confessed his involvement and named his employers as the key players in the plot. His employers were two brothers, Antonis and Mamas Kitas, who were rumored to be running a criminal organization based in Nicosia, the capital city. In this case, prosecutors alleged that the Kitas brothers had planned to ransom Papadopoulos's remains, or leverage their return, for the release of Antonis, who was already imprisoned for the rape and murder of two women in the 1990s. The three defendants were charged with different combinations of overlapping crimes, including conspiracy to commit a felony, illegal entry into a cemetery, desecration of a grave, exhuming a body without a relevant court order, insulting religion, insulting the memory of the dead, and extortion (Evripidou 2010). The defendants all pleaded not guilty; Antonis Kitas, in fact, tried to implicate a series of other people as the real masterminds. They were tried in July 2010 and convicted the following April on the charges of conspiracy, illegal entry, and illegal exhumation (Pantelides 2011).

This resolution of the case did not, however, settle the matter for many Cypriots, including supporters of Papadopoulos and members of his family, who were very critical of the police investigation and the conduct of the trial. I have heard many alternative theories over the years since then—theories that have survived the conviction of the Kitas brothers and Mr. Singh, and that may even have been energized in some ways by the failures of the official story in which they played starring roles. I have heard, for example, that it was Papadopoulos's own family who committed the crime in order to generate attention and sympathy for him as he faded in importance and as his reputation decayed after his electoral defeat and death. I have heard that it was a member of Papadopoulos's administration—the skilled architect of his "No" campaign to defeat the Annan Plan—who orchestrated the "scam" in order to redeem Papadopoulos's career in the public mind. I have also heard that the two men fingered by Antonis Kitas for the theft had indeed assisted in the crime but were given an immunity deal by the police in exchange for information that helped solve a high-profile murder case. Every time the story of the president's body comes up in my conversations with people in Cyprus, I hear another theory about what really happened.

And so, the story of the president's body has stuck with me over the years. Among other reasons, I think this is because the story epitomizes the kind of "conspiracy theorizing" of which Cypriots are so often accused, readily and most insightfully by Cypriots themselves. A good example of this insight comes from Yiannis Ioannou, a Cypriot professor of comparative literature at the University of Cyprus and author of *Conspiracy Theory and the Culture of Partition: Essay on the Political Culture of Cyprus*. This book was published in 2009, on the eve of the sixtieth anniversary of Cyprus's independence; it takes as parameters the period from 1950 to 1974, when histories of modern Cyprus often begin. In his book, Ioannou uses concepts such as "political culture" and "culture of division" to theorize how the division has fostered Hellenic and Christian conservatism in the south, not in the form of ultra-right-wing factionalism but rather in the form of mainstream Greek ethnonationalism. Ioannou associates this transformation in Cypriot political culture with widespread "belief" in what he calls "satanic conspiracies" behind the division of the island from 1974 through to the present—a period when many Greek Cypriots were displaced from their ancestral lands, radically isolated from Turkish Cypriots, and entrained in long-term processes of urbanization and middle-class formation. His diagnosis is despondent and even bitter as he considers what Greek Cypriots have allowed themselves to become; his bitterness, which isolates him from mainstream society in the south, is grounded in what he calls "rationality" (ορθός λόγος), which, on his reading, has been absent from the Cypriot political scene for generations.

Ioannou's book takes pride of place in a vast and growing literature on "conspiracy theories" in Cyprus that seek to account for the division. The "conspiracy theories" of the division that Ioannou dubs "satanic" variously depict the control of Cyprus by outside forces, or forms of secret governance within Cyprus, that have remained invisible and unaccountable to democratic processes since Cyprus's independence. They refer to secret deals between foreign powers and Cypriot authorities; interventions by the CIA, KGB, and MI6; and the covert orchestration by the "deep state" in Turkey and the "para-state" in Greece under the Junta (1967–74) of irregular insurgency and counterinsurgency groups that perpetrated much of the violence during periods of inter- and intracommunal conflict in 1963–64, 1967, and 1974. They trade in and comment on Cold War geopolitics, characterizing the roles played in Cyprus by the United States, the United Kingdom, Greece, and Turkey by way of their socialist or anticommunist ideological alignments. In conserving this geopolitical framework, such theories can be seen as a kind of Cold War haunting, but they also have a contemporary purchase on political life in Cyprus; they are wielded as weapons to influence or undermine the ongoing peace talks, among other ends (Psyllides 2009a). Perhaps for this reason, "conspiracy theory" also appears as a distinctive feature of Cypriot politics to critics, like Ioannou, who attribute the chronic failure of these talks to the regressiveness of the (Greek-)Cypriot political class, or more broadly, to a "culture of conspiracy" (Ioannou 2009, 14).

Since I began spending time in Cyprus in 2007, I have been reading this discourse on conspiracy published in Greek, Turkish, and English, the country's three official languages. Especially intriguing is a recent surge in journalistic and academic research by both Cypriots and foreigners, who aim either to corroborate "conspiracy theories" about the division or to disprove them definitively using newly available materials from British and American intelligence archives that were declassified in 2005.[5] In other writing, I explore how different kinds of evidence are used by these differently positioned theorists to substantiate their claims: evidence such as hearsay and rumor; news stories without named authors or sources; interviews with state and para-state actors; and declassified intelligence documents, including diplomatic letters and reports. Disputes in this discourse over what counts as evidence, and over specific pieces of evidence, indicate to me the influence of an ideology of transparency that actually reproduces secrecy and doubt, although many authors avowedly aspire to establish historical facts according to knowledge-making procedures compatible with democratic norms of open dialogue and accountability.

In this chapter I do not directly examine "conspiracy theories" about the division in Cyprus, but I do consider how they have served as a context for the story of the president's stolen body. *That* story is, therefore, more than a case study in Cypriot conspiracy theory, though it is certainly that. At the same time, it enacts a meta-epistemology of conspiracy theory more generally: it spins and unspins narrative and evidence, time and place, context and knowledge. It begins in the recent past, but it encompasses and recontextualizes the division of Cyprus and its theorization as conspiracy in a way that sheds light on what I will call *conspiracy attunement* in Cyprus: a shared sensibility of knowingness about "conspiracy theory," promoted and cultivated in a dialogic context of public talk about "conspiracy theory" that is historically deep and recursive in nature. In this light, I consider such public talk as a performative discourse in which self-representations, and representations of others—in the form of accusations and attributions, jokes and insults, stories and legacies, habits and weapons—operate as stakes in a field of power.

By way of motivating this conception of conspiracy attunement, in the next section, I critically engage *conspiratology*, a body of general theory about "conspiracy theory," to demonstrate the impossibility of "conspiracy theory" itself as an analytic object in this literature.

CONSPIRATOLOGY AND CONSPIRACY ATTUNEMENT

Readers who are not on intimate terms with the modern history of Cyprus might have difficulty assimilating the explicit and implicit contexts entailed and created by the public talk about "conspiracy theory" that I discussed in the previous section. This difficulty is not incidental; the close-to-the-ground quality of talk about "conspiracy theory" in and about Cyprus is an artifact of the way locale operates, both geopolitically and theoretically, as I hope to show in this section. My subject here is the vast and growing literature of *conspiratology*[6]—a body of theory about "conspiracy theory"—which is characterized by a great deal of intertextuality, cross-referencing, and self-conscious intervention into ongoing debates. In this section I draw a few key points from a few key pieces in this literature, dismantling a series of distinctions that most conspiratologists conserve while laying the groundwork for thinking differently about contexts of "conspiracy theory." I am guided in this venture by four key principles:

(1)   First, the term "conspiracy theory" is not a neutral, merely descriptive term. Its normative usage is to dismiss the truth of the theory in question, often without any evaluation of the evidence. Cultural studies scholar Jack Bratich (2008) contends, "Conspiracy theories . . . in a neutral marketplace of ideas . . . *could be* one kind of descriptive narrative among many. But this is not the case. Conspiracy theories exist as a category not just of description but of disqualification" (3). It is in recognition of this condition of most conspiracy talk that I place scare quotes around the term "conspiracy theory" with every usage in my own writing. This is a practice of documenting the attributions others make of "conspiracy theory" without gauging the referential truth of any theory in particular. It is also a means of foregrounding the unexamined premises and implicit presumptions of mutual understanding that characterize so much conspiratology—presumptions such as "we know it when we see it," a form of inductive reasoning that, as Bratich notes, aspires but fails to position us to draw definitive distinctions between "conspiracy theory" and other kinds (3).

One of the procedures commonly used by conspiratologists to disqualify specific "conspiracy theories" in the way Bratich indicates is to diagnose those theories, or their proponents, as paranoid—to offer, that is, a "symptomatic reading," as Best and Marcus (2009) describe the dominant mode of literary analysis from the 1970s onward that "took meaning to be hidden, repressed, deep, and in need of detection and disclosure by an interpreter" (1). To be sure, most scholars of "conspiracy theory" are careful to specify that they do not operate the diagnostic term "paranoia" in a clinical mode; its generalization beyond mental pathology is a key to the liberality with which these scholars accept and explain the meaningfulness of particular "conspiracy theories" while denying their referential truth. The appealing notion of "paranoia within reason" was popularized (if not coined) by George Marcus in his introduction to the *Casebook* he edited with that title. Riffing on Richard Hofstadter's famous 1964 essay, "The Paranoid Style in American Politics," Marcus is interested in paranoid tendencies of thought that remain within the orbit of plausibility. His introduction operates a distinction between "exotic and excessive" forms of paranoia and those that are merely "distorted, even playful," and indeed, he observes, "commonsensical in certain contexts" (G. Marcus 1999a, 5, 2). The primary such context he identifies is the post–Cold War era globally and, more specifically, scenarios of regime change in postcommunist and other postconflict states, as Cold War legacies of "paranoid social thought and action" and "paranoid policies of statecraft and governing" reverberated in the growth of "wild capitalism" and organized crime (2–3).

The other main context Marcus identifies is social theory itself, indexed to the same Cold War legacy of paranoia that he finds in social and political life; dominant forms of cynical rationality such as game theory interacted, he says, with the "crisis of representation" in the social sciences and humanities from the 1980s onward to produce a situation of radical epistemological uncertainty with a paranoid tinge.[7] Marcus notes that accounts of these developments at the turn of the millennium (the moment of his writing, too) reflected the emergence of global relations of power and knowledge on such a massive scale, and of such intricate complexity, that social theorists could only grasp at fragments they found impossible to reconcile coherently within now-dismantled and discredited "metanarratives and conceptual frames" (G. Marcus 1999a, 4). Paranoid "conspiracy theories"—whether about transnational capital, the new world order, or the end of days—arose to account for the "social and ethnographic facts of the world" that demanded but defied those conventional forms of explanation (4).

Marcus's *Casebook* is by no means the only influential work to frame "conspiracy theory" as a symptom of failures in social theory to address the scale, intricacy, and complexity of post–Cold War relations of power and knowledge (see also Stewart 1999; Harding and Stewart 2003; Melley 2000). Many scholars have taken this symptomatic approach, from literary critic Fredric Jameson's glossing "conspiracy theory" as "the poor person's cognitive mapping in the postmodern age" (Jameson 1988, 356; see also Jameson 1992, 38)[8] to the cultural diagnosis tendered by anthropologists Jean Comaroff and John Comaroff, who construe "conspiracy theory" as that which has come to "fill the explanatory void, the epistemic black hole" opened by millennial transformations in society and political economy (Comaroff and Comaroff 2003, 287–88; see also Comaroff and Comaroff 1999).

Quite a few ethnographic works have made a point of muddying the distinction between social theory and "conspiracy theory" advanced by these scholars but nevertheless take the same symptomatic line. One such is a 2003 paper on millennial America coauthored by Susan Harding and Kathleen Stewart, who move swiftly from neurasthenia at the turn of the twentieth century to "conspiracy theory" at the turn of the twenty-first, taking these affective mental disorders both as vocabularies or "idioms" of social malaise in the United States and as symptoms of it (Harding and Stewart 2003, 259). Their brief case studies take them to two marginal communities in California that formed in the 1970s but that came conspicuously into public view in the 1990s: Calvary Chapel, a fundamentalist evangelical megachurch in Orange County; and the Heaven's Gate group in San Diego, which combined Christian eschatology with UFO/alien cosmology. The forms of "paranoia" Harding and Stewart find in these groups, which, in radically discrepant ways, concerned salvation at the end of days from dominant groups seeking their corruption and exploitation, are quite remote from the sort "within reason" marked out for study by Marcus; presumably this is among the reasons Harding and Stewart turned their attention to them, designating Heaven's Gate in particular as "ultra fringe" due to the mass suicide of all thirty-nine members in 1997 after the passage of the Hale-Bopp comet. Given the marginality of these groups, the authors are able easily to gloss over and dismiss their practices, but their decisive analytic maneuver is to *diagnose* those practices in a symptomatic register by connecting them to features of less marginal "hippie/drug culture," pop culture representations of space travel, and evangelical Christianity, among other sources (280). In multiplying these connections, Harding and Stewart obscure the division they themselves have drawn between the fringe groups they study and the broadly construed "therapeutic culture" of millennial America that they take as a context for understanding those groups. It is that division that authorizes their own diagnostic judgment, implicitly locating themselves in the reasonable center of American culture even if they are also subject, in some ways, to its characteristic anxieties.

In his 2004 paper on a cholera epidemic in the Orinoco Delta of Venezuela, Charles Briggs takes a subtler but nevertheless symptomatic approach, contextualizing the meanings of "conspiracy theories" of the epidemic and showing how those meanings functioned to normalize long-standing, multidimensional rifts between *criollo* and indigenous Venezuelans. Studying the circulation of all accounts of the epidemic— from theories expressed by public health officials about contaminated shellfish to those expressed by indigenous Delta residents about their deliberate poisoning by government officials and agents of oil companies—

Briggs traces the specific processes by which the latter came to be labeled and dismissed as "conspiracy theories." Focusing on the structural conditions of racism in which state power is embedded in Venezuela (and globally), he identifies with the radical doubt cast on official theories of the epidemic by indigenous residents and interprets their "conspiracy theories" as artifacts of the "unequal distribution of symbolic capital" (Briggs 2004, 178). These theories are not *only* artifacts for Briggs, however. He is ultimately interested in mobilizing his analysis of "conspiracy theories" to develop a critique of the structural inequalities across which symbolic capital is (thus) unequally distributed. For my purposes here, it is most important to note the diagnostic tenor of this critique, which positions "conspiracy theories" as symptoms whose meaning refers to social, economic, and political inequity and injustice rather than to truth.

This line of argument ultimately runs up against the approach developed by Mathijs Pelkmans and Rhys Machold (2011), although they share with Briggs a preoccupation with asymmetries in the social field. In what I am referring to as symptomatic readings of "conspiracy theory," Pelkmans and Machold find a "lingering functionalism that fails to interrogate systematically the links between power and truth" (68). This "lingering functionalism" is especially evident to them in those works that characterize "conspiracy theories" as "subaltern strategies" to "make sense of impersonal and opaque forces" (68) and other disempowering conditions of social and political life. They turn their attention instead to "conspiracy theories" that have what they call a "use value" other than "sense-making" (68). Focusing on a counterexample, namely, the theory that Saddam Hussein was amassing weapons of mass destruction and "conspiring with Al Quaeda" to attack the United States in the early 2000s (67)—which, they point out, was universally discredited but never labeled a "conspiracy theory," even though it entailed a conspiracy on the part of Bush administration operatives to misinform the public—they identify its use value as "serv[ing] the political status quo" (68). Their analytic approach—shifting the frame from "conspiracy theories" to *theories of conspiracy*—has the benefit of backgrounding the truth or falsity of "conspiracy theories" and foregrounding instead how all theories move through "asymmetric fields of power" and come either to be labeled as "conspiracy theory" or, by contrast, to be accepted as true or false representations of reality (73).

The focus Pelkmans and Machold (2011, 66) train on the fields of power in which "truth and untruth are created" puts them at quite a distance from symptomatic reading, but rather closer to the approach developed by Jack Bratich in his book, *Conspiracy Panics*. In this work, Bratich (2008, 6) does not attempt to find the deep meaning of "conspiracy theory" but rather presents it as a "metaconcept signifying the struggles over the meaning of the concept." From this metaperspective, he examines the process by which theories are disqualified as "conspiracy theories" in favor of hegemonic knowledge claims, and how those processes of disqualification produce meaning and reproduce power. He therefore shifts his analytic sights from "conspiracy theories" to conspiracy *panics*—that is, to fretful and despairing discourses about "conspiracy theory" that have surfaced at particular historical moments. In this, Bratich criticizes but also aligns himself with what he calls the "symptomatological" approach, according to which "conspiracy theories are taken as a sign of something else" (14)—some kind of collective dis-ease, malaise, anxiety.[9] What sets Bratich's "symptomatology" apart from others, on his own account, is that he takes conspiracy panics rather than "conspiracy theories" as his object, and thus renders an "immanent diagnosis," probing the "'unstated presuppositions and problematics'" of conspiracy panic discourse (16), rather than a transcendent diagnosis of "conspiracy theory," in which a special position of authority is reserved for those who know better. Indeed, the truth of the matter and whether people believe the truth are not Bratich's concerns. He examines how truth claims operate in conspiracy panics to "define the normal modes of dissent" by relegating "conspiracy theories" to the irrational fringes of society and framing them as "a symptom of a culture or a climate of paranoia" (11). In substituting the "diffuse threat" of "conspiracy theory" for any clearly defined object of fear, he argues, conspiracy panics mobilize generalized anxiety that reveals "presuppositions" about rationality and morality that are not "articulated" explicitly within conspiracy panic discourse (11, 16). While Bratich is, thus, very interested in collective dis-ease, he sees it as a product of conspiracy panics rather than as a cause of "conspiracy theories."

(2) Although this second principle is entailed and encompassed by the first, it is worth highlighting in its own right: "conspiracy theory" cannot be categorically distinguished from social or any other kind of theory. There is only theory: good and bad, well-evidenced and not, persuasive and not, enlightening and not, desirable and not. The questions about expertise and legitimate authority that are often raised by critics of "conspiracy theory" are equally raised by

social theory—a point to which many social theorists are comfortable acceding when engaging in critique, but often less comfortable when rejecting "conspiracy theory." Likewise, as conspiratologists readily acknowledge, there are actual conspiracies in the world, and (therefore) a conspiratorial form of causal agency—a multiple, collusive, secretive agency (Keeley 1999, 116)[10]—is sometimes at work in the social, economic, political, and cultural phenomena conspiratologists study. These conclusions are shared by many "conspiracy theorists" and social theorists; Durkheim's theory of social cohesion around ritual elites, Marx's theory of primitive accumulation, Althusser's theory of ideology, even John L. Jackson's theory of race-thinking as a conspiracy (of anthropologists, among others),[11] stand as obvious, if contestable, examples. The prospect of contesting the classification of these theories as "conspiracy theories"—as in Karl Popper's defense of Marx as "one of the first *critics* of the conspiracy theory [of society]," for instance (Popper 1963, 167 n2)—is precisely what lures some conspiratologists into drawing categorical distinctions between "conspiracy theory" and social theory that are not warranted on epistemological grounds.

Critics who try to establish such a distinction between illegitimate "conspiracy theory" and legitimate social theory on epistemological grounds—such as a priori definitions of agency, or "leap[s] in imagination" in linking together pieces of evidence—are thus engaged in a process of begging the question (see Jackson 2017). What they offer as the conclusion of their argument—namely, that a particular theory is in fact a "conspiracy theory"—is actually its premise. Denouncing or dismissing a particular theory by reclassifying it as one *kind* of theory obscures other more stable and compelling grounds for critique. To the extent that the "conspiracy theory" label is used by critics to distinguish it from legitimate theory, the term can only be a red herring and its use a muddying of the waters.

In my reading of conspiratology, it is rare to find a social scientist or social theorist willing to offer an explicit and stable definition of "conspiracy theory." These writers tend to take an implicitly nominalist stance, identifying "conspiracy theory" as that which their subjects in the social field say it is; or they take the inductive approach criticized by Bratich, assuming a consensus among writers and readers as to what we all mean by the term. Philosopher Brian Keeley (1999, 116), on the other hand, in a widely cited piece, offers just such a definition: "A conspiracy theory," he writes, is "a proposed explanation of some historical event (or events) in terms of the significant causal agency of a relatively small group of persons—the conspirators—acting in secret." He presents this as a "bare bones" and neutral definition that may apply to theories of conspiracy in which we ought to believe as well as of those we ought not. He helpfully assumes that we are and may always be in a position of limited knowledge of the truth; the question as to how we might distinguish between "conspiracy theories" and legitimate theories is, therefore, a question of what it is reasonable to believe.

The distinction Keeley pursues between warranted and unwarranted "conspiracy theories" (UCTs) maps quite cleanly on to the distinction Marcus and others operate between reasonable and unreasonable paranoia. Rather than relating "conspiracy theories" to their context in order to arrive at that judgment, however, as Marcus and others do, Keeley proceeds to discount UCTs by identifying and discrediting their characteristic epistemological features. These include their contestation of a "received" or "official" account, their stipulation of secrecy and "nefarious" intentions, their connection of "seemingly unrelated events," and their reliance on "errant data" (Keeley 1999, 117). Keeley moves beyond these distinguishing features of UCTs—which are not, for him, reason enough to reject them in advance—to a consideration of the "outdated" picture they hypostatize of an ordered world in which everything fits. He implies that belief in these theories constitutes a moral choice to inhabit *that* sort of world instead of "an irrational and essentially meaningless" one, a position he characterizes as "absurdist" (125). The distinction between warranted and unwarranted "conspiracy theories" thus ends up resting on how much "skepticism . . . we can stomach" (126).

Keeley is admirably clear by the end of his paper about the moral nature of the distinction he has developed between warranted and unwarranted "conspiracy theories." His relativism is grounded in his assumption of our limited access to truth. Judgment of a theory's legitimacy therefore takes the following form: *this theory is more plausible than that one*. It is an epistemological relativism rather than a contextual one, and thus does not entail any assessment of the effect that one's context may have on one's judgment about the plausibility of a particular theory. Pelkmans and Machold (2011, 69–70) point to this problem in their careful reading of Keeley: "One peculiarity of the attempt to pinpoint the epistemological characteristics of conspiracy theorizing [as Keeley does] is that these presumed epistemological characteristics turn out to be sociological ones when scrutinized.

The issue of the fundamental attribution error is ultimately about the relation between theory and theorizer—about how data are interpreted and given weight by social actors." Following Pelkmans and Machold in this line of argument against Keeley, we circle back to the first principle articulated above. "Conspiracy theory" can be attributed socially but not defined epistemologically, and thus it cannot be distinguished on epistemological grounds from any other kind of theory.

(3) "Conspiracy theory" does not have a specific time or place. Epoch and locale operate as unexamined premises in much of the conspiratology literature: as the parameters of contexts that "make sense" of theories that would not make sense elsewhen and elsewhere. From these unexamined premises follow all the distinctions operated by conspiratologists: between reasonable and unreasonable paranoia, primarily, as well as between the dichotomies rejected by Harry West and Todd Sanders (2003, 6) in their volume, *Transparency and Conspiracy*: "[T]he west and the rest, the global and the local, modernity and tradition, rationality and conviction." Rather than start from epoch and locale as contextual parameters, I start instead from the question: What is a context?

One way to begin examining this problem is to observe a division of analytic labor common in conspiratology between the various epochs and locales of "conspiracy theory." In Marcus's *Casebook*, for example, part I of the book, "Paranoia within Reason," comprises papers on theories and knowledges developed by reasoning experts of various kinds—philosophers, quantum physicists, attorneys, psychotherapists, climate scientists—based in European or North American locales that are not thematized as contexts for the theories and knowledges being examined. Part II of the book, "Paranoid Histories," shifts toward what are styled as Cold War "legacies" of fascism in Italy, dictatorship in Brazil, Stalinism in Russia, and Yugoslav socialism in Slovenia. The contributions in part III, "Paranoid Presents," engage the same "present" as those in part II—that is, the 1990s—but, in Marcus's framing, rather than the past, they address "what may be emerging" in the form of "visceral and immediate responses to contemporary events and experiences," such as a Mafia trial in Italy, a neofascist movement in London, Gulf War illness, and evangelical millennialism in the United States (G. Marcus 1999a, 8). This split in the present moment between legacy and emergence seems to be a function of the specific geocultural locales in which the "conspiracy theories" in each chapter are examined. What is more striking to me about the arrangement of material in the *Casebook*, however, is the division between part I and the rest of the book—between, that is, theories and knowledges whose locale is not thematized or addressed explicitly at all, and "histories" and "presents" whose locales form the central explanatory context.

In their edited collection on transparency and conspiracy, West and Sanders (2003) advance a more expansive understanding of locale, assembling case studies in South Korea, Nigeria, Mozambique, Indonesia, Tanzania, and China as well as post-Soviet Russia and the United States. In the introduction, reflecting explicitly on the problem of locale, West and Sanders warn us not to reproduce the dichotomies we have inherited between "the west and the rest" and all those connected with it—dichotomies that they find undergirding a more specific split in conspiratology between "conspiracy theory" and occult cosmology. They ground their own distinction between these two genres of theory in the scope and scale of the beliefs in question; cosmologies, in their view, regard the entire world and its operations, whereas "conspiracy theory" may concern itself only with specific domains or fragments. While this distinction may not be tenable in all cases, it stands as a very useful reminder—as Jean Comaroff and John Comaroff (1999) point out in their now-classic paper on occult economies—that "local" and "global" are heuristic rather than descriptive concepts that always raise "a problem of scale" (294).

This problem of scale has attracted much attention in the conspiratology literature. Yet the thematization of scale as an analytic problem has not emboldened many anthropologists to radicalize their own orientation as observers or analysts toward what they take to be "local" or "particular" epistemologies—which is to say, epistemologies they do not share. In much of this literature, thus, writers already know that the "conspiracy theories" they examine are false, but they seek to understand why and how people are nevertheless compelled by them by placing them in local context (see Comaroff and Comaroff 1999; Fassin 2011). In Harding and Stewart (2003) discussed above, for example, notions of scale and context are essential to their approach but taken for granted rather than worked out conceptually; Calvary Church and Heaven's Gate remain local groups whose beliefs and practices can be contextualized in terms of American therapeutic culture but not shared by anyone outside their communal boundaries. Even Pelkmans and Machold (2011) ultimately take a somewhat localist approach, characterizing "organizational features of societies" (71)—such as hierarchy and secrecy—or collective situations of "conflict or political transformation" that make it reasonable for ordinary people to be paranoid, skeptical, or cynical. While they are agnostic with respect to potentially distinctive epistemological or rhetorical features of "conspiracy theory," then, they assent to sociocultural criteria for distinguishing "realistic" theories from "fantastical" ones (72), maintaining the implicit premise of sociocultural boundaries that create a local context in which the distinction between reasonable and unreasonable "conspiracy theories" can usefully if not durably pertain.

As for place, so for time. One of my aims in examining the story of the president's body in Cyprus is to show robust continuities and recursive entanglements between this story and those surrounding the division of Cyprus in 1974 and other times besides. There is no historical-cultural threshold or discontinuity dividing conditions of knowing and feeling between Cold War "conspiracy theories" and those circulating in 2009–10; the former condition the latter as historical contexts that can be dated but not periodized. I therefore work against the epochal tendencies that characterize so much writing on "conspiracy theory," especially the body of literature that grew around the turn of the millennium, connected with the rise of finance capitalism, the internet, and the so-called New World Order forming in the wake of Soviet collapse (see Comaroff and Comaroff 1999, 2003; Dean 1998; Harding and Stewart 2003; G. Marcus 1999b; Stewart 1999; West and Sanders 2003). The apparently special moments in historical time when "conspiracy theory" has flourished, like the millennial turn and the ongoing Trump-times, are better described, in Bratich's (2008) terms, as conspiracy *panics*: "historical conjunctures" in which "conspiracy theory" has been overtly problematized (8). "Conspiracy theory," on the other hand, the ostensible object of these panics, does not share these conjunctural parameters.

Neither, however, is Bratich's rubric of conspiracy panics as comprehensive or generalizable as we might wish it to be when specifying a relevant historical context for particular "conspiracy theories." Panics, as he describes them, entail a periodic or resurgent crisis temporality that breaks into normal times, dismantling the reigning social consensus and inaugurating a new epoch. The temporal logic underlying such notions of crisis and panic is a sort of naive historicism, implying a linear temporal ordering that is not in play in Cyprus, for example, where "conspiracy theory" has been a routine matter of public talk continuously since at least the mid-1960s; and it may not, in fact, exist anywhere. A deeper historical contextualization, by contrast, would trace how "conspiracy theories" emerge and change, fragmenting and morphing, overlapping with other theories and changing again, in people's talk about them. This is the sort of meta-discursive historical contextualization I have in mind with recursivity—the concept that I think best describes the ordering process by which people apprehend apparently "new" theories and thereby reframe "old" ones.

"'Meaning is context-bound, but context is boundless,'" Roy Dilley reminds us in his reflections on "the problem of context" in anthropology (Culler 1983, 123; as cited in Dilley 1999, 22, 36). Noting that context can shift, expand, and regress infinitely, depending on the delimiting choices made by analysts, Dilley (1999) characterizes context as a conceptual device that defines the interdependence of relativism and universalism in anthropological knowledge: "One of the purposes of anthropological contextualism—the invoking of local cultural contexts—has been to produce a counter to universalist, context-free knowledge. Both approaches to knowledge—via contextualism or 'context-freeism'—are mutually implicated and necessary, for one makes little sense without the other" (36).

If context is conceived *only* as "local," and if, moreover, "local" is conceived in fixed and narrow cultural terms in which linear temporal ordering is utterly taken for granted, then contextualization is tantamount to exoticism. It is in this sense that I see the localist approach to "conspiracy theory" (in which its meaning is relativized to local context) as intrinsically connected to the symptomatic approach (in which its meaning reflects deeper disorder or malaise within that context). Distinctions between reasonable and unreasonable paranoia, like those between social theory and "conspiracy theory," are tethered to boundaries between here and there, and between now and then, which are neither warranted nor desirable so long as they demarcate such discrete and stable contexts. Boundaries rest on and also generate distinctions. They are not to be avoided for that reason, of course; the task at hand is rather to ascertain what kind of distinctions are entailed by the boundaries we observe, and vice versa, when we are defining a context for analysis.

(4)   "Conspiracy theory" is not a distinctive feature of any particular epoch or locale, but conspiracy attunement may be. For that reason, among others, I see conspiracy attunement as a much better avenue for analysis, and especially for cross-contextual comparison. With the concept of conspiracy attunement, I am interested in theorizing context in general, and analyzing the Cypriot context

of conspiracy discourse in particular. I am interested in how Cypriots reach for shared symbols to articulate a sense of collective solidarity in relation to their division; in whether they in fact experience that sense of a collective; and if they do, in how satisfying and how durable it is, and in what sense it is indeed collective. These questions—which move away from assessments of "reasonable" vis-à-vis "excessive" paranoia—probe what it means to belong to a social body or to be excluded from it, and they are questions that I think many Cypriots often ask themselves. To answer them, I cannot look only at academic and public discourse on "conspiracy theory" in Cyprus; I must also examine how Cypriots relate to their characterization as "conspiracy theorists" and how they wield that characterization against others.

One example of the characterization I have in mind is this: On January 1, 2011, the left-leaning Greek-language newspaper, *Politis*, gave its award for "best conspiracy theory of 2010" to Giorgos Perdikis, head of the Green Party in Cyprus, for promoting the theory that the British air force had been "spraying the clouds" over Cyprus to disperse them in order to prevent rain, and/or to enhance signals coming to and from the massive radar facility in the Troodos mountains near the British Sovereign Base Area on the southern coast (*Politis* Staff 2011, 1). I have heard this theory—several different versions of it, in fact—so many times in my everyday conversations in Cyprus that I can attest personally to its wide circulation (see also Zanou 2010). In February 2016, several years after this item appeared in *Politis*, the minister of agriculture in the Republic, Nicos Kouyialis, ordered an official investigation into these allegations of "geoengineering," charged with assessing the chemical composition of the cloud cover and requesting information about Royal Air Force activities from the British Foreign Ministry. An earlier report, issued in 2010, had been dismissed by Perdikis and others as a "whitewash" (Hazou 2016).

My point in offering this example is not that the cloud theory is both widespread and silly, but rather that the author of this news item in 2011 found it funny and knew that his readers would appreciate the award because they were already well aware of the theory in relation to many other "conspiracy theories" of which they were also aware. In other words, the *Politis* piece expresses not "conspiracy culture," as Peter Knight (2000) has it, but rather conspiracy attunement. On this point, I have learned much from Jodi Dean's analysis of UFO-logy in the 1990s. Considering an array of TV shows, online discussion groups, and other pop culture forms, she notes, "Their insight into the themes and anxieties just below the surface of American society in fact presupposes a general cultural awareness of this discourse. 'Getting it' requires prior knowledge of UFOs and alien abduction" (Dean 1998, 29). It is not the "anxieties below the surface" that I think are explanatory—these can only be hypothesized via symptomatic diagnoses of cultural forms—but rather the cultural processes Dean indicates, by which such a "prior knowledge" may be developed and recursively applied in new cultural productions. It is the acute awareness among Cypriots of the prevalence of "conspiracy theory" in Cypriot public culture, and the need perceived by many to position themselves in relation to these theories in order to speak publicly about matters of political significance, that I find distinctive of the Cypriot context of conspiracy attunement. Studying any particular "conspiracy theory" in Cyprus requires deep knowledge of the recursive learning process by which "conspiracy theory" has been and continues to be transmitted in Cyprus as a legacy or, as Drousiotis (2005b) put it, as a "curse."

The long duration and open-endedness of this cultural process preclude any periodization of "conspiracy theory" as an expression of the Cold War, post–Cold War, millennial, or any other epoch. Such epochal tendencies derive, I think, from the narrow focus in cultural studies of "conspiracy theory" on popular culture in the United States, a locale that is not marked as one cultural context among others so that it might be compared with those others. The unmarkedness of this context makes it fertile terrain for the production of general theory about "conspiracy theory": argumentative claims that it is a generic thing with generic traits that work in generic ways for generic reasons.

Theory about "conspiracy theory" in Cyprus, on the other hand, a locale that seems to require dense description in order even for Cypriots to grasp it as a context, operates much closer to the ground—at least as close as what Geertz (1973, 24) had in mind with "thick description," contrasting the "theoretical development" of "cultural interpretation" to the "imaginative abstraction" of other sciences. Thus Yiannis Ioannou attributes "conspiracy theory" to a Cypriot "culture of conspiracy" that developed out of the division and that persists as a filter or contaminant for the interpretation of everything that has happened since: "It is clear how the culture of conspiracy [in Cyprus] is fortified and strengthened, and how it counteracts any lucid, rational comprehension and analysis of phenomena. It favors a comforting interpretation of developments that renders all Cypriot heroes innocent, and attributes tribulations, failures, and catastrophes to factors outside Cyprus. A persecution complex and xenophobia replace substantive political analysis. The terrorization of the people activates their survival instinct, prodding them to rally around their leaders and return them to office time after time" (Ioannou 2009, 119–20).

Ioannou is an avowedly symptomatic reader of "conspiracy theory" in the Cypriot context. In his analysis, the Cypriot "culture of conspiracy" is Greek-Cypriot culture, defined by its separation from and antagonism toward the Turkish-Cypriot community (there is no question here of a unified and coherent pan-Cypriot culture). His approach is densely localist, bound to a locale that serves, implicitly, as context. The fact that locale does not (or not necessarily) serve as context in this way for conspiratologists of the United States is to be expected, perhaps, given the geopolitical position of Cyprus (a specific, peripheral somewhere) vis-à-vis the United States (a general, imperial anywhere and everywhere). The frequent invocation in public talk in Cyprus about its victimization by the Great Powers, to which Ioannou alludes in the passage above, speaks to this geopolitical-theoretical asymmetry, which has been a condition of anthropological theorizing from the beginning, if also a challenge to it. Approaching conspiracy attunement in Cyprus—or anywhere—demands scrutiny of the terms by which locality is identified, and especially those terms by which the local is contrasted with the global, the particular with the general or universal, and vice versa. Only by rethinking context itself in this way can we obviate the unwarranted distinctions between reasonable and unreasonable paranoia, as between social theory and "conspiracy theory," that I have been arguing against in this chapter.

My central aim here is to dismantle the ethnocentrism that stabilizes a diagnostic position for *us*, who know the truth, in relation to *them*, who believe in "conspiracy theory." This aim is not a liberal or relativist proposal to make sense of and accommodate radical difference; rather, it is motivated by the sense that "conspiracy theorists" are not so different after all, and that, in fact, *we* might appear to be the "conspiracy theorists" if the boundaries—the contextual parameters—around *us* were drawn differently. This redrawing of boundaries might also help to disrupt the desire for a general theory of "conspiracy theory" that so many conspiratologists seem to be after. A place like Cyprus, as seen through an ethnocentric lens—small, exotic, insular in all senses, stuck in the past, remote from world centers of knowledge production—is as good a place as any, and perhaps a better place than most, to start such a disruption.

1 As I explain later in this chapter, I place *conspiracy theory* in scare quotes as a tactic to forestall the naturalizing common sense that so easily forms around this term, though I acknowledge that this tactic may be experienced by readers as distracting or onerous.

2 See Bryant (2007, 2010); Trimikliniotis and Bozkurt (2012). See also Demetriou (2008) on how the process of EU accession formed a space for opponents of reconciliation in the south to consolidate political and social support.

3 See the case study of this press coverage as well as an extended reading of the conspiratology literature, in E. Davis (forthcoming).

4 The term "ναιναίκοι" (yes-men, yes-sayers) uses the Greek word for "yes" (ναι) to make a homonymic play on the derogatory term, "νενέκοι," connoting "traitors"—a reference to Dimitris Nenekos, the chief of Patras in the Greek revolutionary war era (c. 1825), who "sold out" to Ibrahim Pasha, an Egyptian general, during clashes between Egyptian and Ottoman forces in parts of what are now Crete and mainland Greece.

5 See, for example, Asmussen (2008); Constandinos (2009); Dimitrakis (2010); and Drousiotis (2014).

6 My usage of this term differs from that of Bratich (2008, 5), who thus describes researchers of conspiracy seeking scientific legitimacy rather than (as I do here) researchers of conspiracy theory.

7 Jean Comaroff and John Comaroff (1999, 292) gloss this juncture slightly differently as the "Age of Futilitarianism . . . in which the rampant promises of late capitalism run up against a thoroughly postmodern pessimism."

8 Best and Marcus (2009, 3, 5) identify Jameson as the preeminent "symptomatic reader" of the late twentieth century.

9 Among the cultural analyses of conspiracy theory that Bratich considers symptomatological are Melley (2000); Fenster (2008); and most of the pieces in G. Marcus (1999b), along with many others.

10 Melley observes an "all-or-nothing conception of agency" in his examination of conspiracy narratives in American culture: that is, "a view in which agency is a property, parceled out *either* to individuals like oneself *or* to 'the system'—a vague structure often construed to be massive, powerful, and malevolent" (Melley 2000, 10).

11 This phrase, originally in Hofstadter 1964, has been cited or reproduced frequently in conspiratology literature (see, for example, G. Marcus 1999a, 1; Oushakine 2009, 106).

TIMOTHY MELLEY

05 CONSPIRACY, THEORY, AND THE "POST-TRUTH" PUBLIC SPHERE

On November 16, 2016, eight days after the election of Donald Trump, the editors of the *Oxford Dictionaries* declared *post-truth* the 2016 international "Word of the Year" (Oxford Languages 2016).[1] A host of prominent critics soon sketched the features of what they called "post-truth America," the "post-truth climate," and the "post-truth crisis." They associated this new climate with resurgent ethnonationalism and authoritarianism, the totalitarianisms of the twentieth century, and the punctuation of political discourse by regular allegations of "fake news," "alternative facts," covert operations, classified leaks, and disinformation. Nothing, however, marked the post-truth moment more than conspiracy theory—and nothing signaled the ascendancy of conspiracy theory more than President Donald Trump. In "an age of post-truth politics," the British sociologist William Davies wrote in the *New York Times*, "conspiracy theories prosper"—and by all accounts, the Trump era seemed to mark "conspiracy theory's big comeback," the dawn of "a golden age of the conspiracy theory."[2]

Even before Brexit and Trump, the supposedly marginal phenomenon of conspiracy theory had become surprisingly central to western political discourse. In 2015, the British prime minister David Cameron launched an attack on the "ludicrous conspiracy theories" that he saw as the root of violent extremism and terrorism (Dearden 2015). The next summer, Cameron was drummed out of 10 Downing Street by Brexit enthusiasts enraged about Brussels-based "plots" against Britain. Meanwhile, the president of France, François Hollande, seemed to toy with a ban on conspiracy theory—or as he put it a "legal framework" to "manage [the] social networks" through which "conspiracy theories are disseminated" (Hollande 2015).

If Cameron and Hollande were concerned about the persuasive power of violent subversives, then the election of a conspiracy theorist-in-chief in the United States must have been a surreal inversion of their fears. Donald Trump, it turned out, also wished to manage the social networks through which fake news is disseminated—although not at all in the ways Hollande or Cameron had in mind. If Trump seemed the very emblem of post-truth culture, he represented himself as its chief victim. "I want you all to know," he shouted to a seething mob at one of his post-election rallies, "we are fighting the fake news. It's fake, phony, fake"—a product of "terrible, dishonest" journalists, "the lowest form of life" and "the enemy of the people" (Media Matters Staff 2017).

It is scarcely possible to catalog the litany of wild allegations that tumbled out of candidate Trump's mouth: that President Barack Obama was Kenyan by birth, that global warming was a strategic Chinese hoax, that Obama was the creator of ISIS, that Hillary Clinton was the creator of ISIS, that the Democrats would steal the elections, and eventually that *Hillary Clinton* had originally started the rumor about Obama's Kenyan birth. Trump's election and inauguration did little to stay this torrent of outlandish assertions. In a striking departure from centuries of tradition, Trump jettisoned even the veneer of interpretive caution for a whirligig of fact-free allegation, rumor-mongering, and contempt for expertise. Although victorious at the polls, he continued to claim that the election had been "hacked," that British and American intelligence agencies were spying on him, and that a "deep state" faction within the US intelligence community was plotting his downfall, possibly on secret instructions from Barack Obama (Lester 2016; see also Leonhardt and Thompson 2017). He seemed, in all these regards, the very model of the conspiracy theorist in its most pejorative sense.

Pundits and journalists of all stripes deplored Trump's assertions, but they seemed even more disturbed by their own inability to correct the record with clear evidence, rational argument, "truth-o-meters," "live fact-checking," investigations and disclosures, and stories about historical demagoguery. Like so many earlier opponents of conspiracy theory, the entire American punditocracy found itself flummoxed by the remarkable resilience and viral power of outrageous claims in the face of something like Habermasian public reason. Had a new form of irrationality, a resistance to truth itself, settled over the democratic public sphere?

There is no doubt that Trump's presidential style represented a stunning departure from the traditions of the office or that Western democracies are realigning in worrying ways. Yet there is also reason to be skeptical that the "post-truth era" is a radically new formation. Both its features and its periodizing claims are eerily similar to earlier claims about the "postmodern" erosion of Enlightenment certainties. Indeed, Habermas developed his classic 1962 account of the "rational-critical" public sphere partly out of a concern that it was *already* in crisis—"refeudalized" by new forms of mass culture and institutional secrecy.[3] It is no accident that "post-truth" discourse so often points to the nexus of these two threats—the transformations of mass media and the growth of state and corporate secrecy. Trump's conspiratorial claims, for instance, focus squarely on the dangers of clandestine institutions and the "dysfunction" of the public press.

What is perhaps most strange about the 2016 election coverage, then, is that the tumultuous battle over "post-truth politics" seemed completely unrelated to the more matter-of-fact reports on state and corporate plots. As the press expressed alarm about a rise in conspiracy theories, it also calmly reported on a host of alleged, but ultimately unknowable, secret plots—government surveillance programs, state-sponsored hacking, classified leaks, corporate influence schemes, and covert operations. In reports that were notably *not* called conspiracy theories, for instance, US intelligence leaders took the rare step of publicly alleging state-sponsored Russian *conspiracies* to steal and "weaponize" politically embarrassing emails from Democratic operatives, to hack into US voting machines, and to influence American voters through social media. These humdrum reports unfolded amid the seemingly endless quasi-scandal about the propriety of Hillary Clinton's use of a private email server during her tenure as secretary of state. Though Clinton's initial fault was an alleged failure to guard the sanctity of state secrets, the criticism soon became that she had failed to disclose to the world all her private correspondence over four years as secretary of state. The all-or-nothing logic of these criticisms—the contradictory demand for both total transparency and total secrecy—points to the paradox of what might be called the democratic security society. On the one hand, western democracies continue to laud the ideals of the public sphere—participation, openness, free speech, and the marketplace of ideas. On the other hand, they are increasingly organized around the biopolitical regulation of life, the mitigation of threats to public health and safety, and the restriction of liberties as a way of securing liberty itself.

This paradox was everywhere visible in the 2016 US presidential election and its aftermath. Trump's widely ridiculed position on Syria, for example—that he had a foolproof *secret* plan that he could not disclose to the public—was politically inept, yet it also precisely articulated the central paradox of US foreign policy since the Cold War: that the public need not and *cannot* know the operational details of US policy. Clinton, meanwhile, offered a more transparent set of policy prescriptions on Syria, but in a secretly recorded Seattle fundraising event, she said she would "intervene [in Syria] as covertly as is possible for Americans to intervene." These episodes were reported but largely ignored by both the press and the candidates themselves, presumably because they reaffirmed covert action as a core element of US foreign policy since the Cold War. There was little sense, moreover, that the epistemology of state secrecy had anything to do with the post-truth moment, with the plague of conspiracy discourse, or with Donald Trump's outrageous assertions about democratic institutions, foreign nations, immigrants, women, and racialized others. And yet an unaccountable security apparatus and a dysfunctional public sphere were the defining concerns of Trump's presidency. While his administration was organized against a broader array of demons, Trump repeatedly cast himself as a maligned hero battling the specters of a "traitorous" press, a vast liberal scheme to falsify election results, and an intelligence community plot to undermine his will.

How can we understand these extraordinary allegations? What is their public appeal, especially in the face of withering criticism by the guardians of the public sphere? Are we really in a golden age of conspiracy theory? What is the history of this form of political suspicion? And what, if anything, is to be done about it?

The answers to these questions will require an approach that looks beyond individual psychology—tempting as it may be—to institutional and discursive contexts. In the pages to follow, I examine how conspiracy theory became a recognizable form of cognition, seemingly distinct from legitimate social theory, and why it continues to flourish as a way of imagining social power. Conspiracy theory, as it is now called, is an age-old, global phenomenon, but the idea that there is something called "conspiracy theory" seems to have emerged in the Cold War era. This chapter concentrates on the way this concept developed in the United States in tandem with the cultural imagination of a burgeoning national security state.[4] As a feature of post–World War II American culture, conspiracy discourse is both a symptom of and a response to the conditions of knowledge in a democratic security society—a regime in which secrets are the objects of insistent public speculation, expert knowledge struggles to keep pace with technical innovation, and risk mitigation is the stuff of everyday life. Conspiracy theories are more than individual allegations; they are elements of a cultural imaginary that incessantly circulates representations of institutional corruption, secrecy, and public deception. Much of Trump's success as a conspiracy theorist lies in his ability to rearticulate as propaganda the central propositions of this conspiratorial imaginary.[5] Combating this form of conspiracy mongering will require more than a redoubling of Enlightenment rationality—more fact-checking, more debunking, more transparency. It will also mean "working the dark side" of the public sphere (to repurpose Dick Cheney's haunting strategy), for propositions that seem ludicrous in the bright light of the rational-critical public sphere make strange sense in the lurid shadows of the conspiracy imaginary—the "nonserious" space of mere entertainment that turns out to be the home turf of national and state fantasy (see Mayer 2008, 10; Berlant 1991; Pease 2009).

THE INVENTION OF CONSPIRACY THEORY

Conspiracy theory would seem to be the simplest of discursive objects—and the most simpleminded. It consists, as everyone knows, of the unproven allegations of cranks who line their homes with tinfoil and devote their sad evenings to the revelation of arcane plots. On this view, it is the epitome of illogic and unreason—often comical, sometimes outrageous, and occasionally dangerous. This view of conspiracy theory makes several assumptions: first, that conspiracy theory is easy to identify and segregate from normative political discourse; second, that it is a marginal phenomenon stemming from individual psychopathology, irrationality, "identifiable cognitive blunders," or "crippled epistemologies" (Sunstein and Vermeule 2008, 1, 8); and third, that it is easily dismissed because we have already established a legitimate narrative that contradicts its wild assertions. Underlying these assumptions is a faith that the organs of the public sphere have done their work: we *know* the truth, and attacks on established social narratives needn't be taken seriously.

But conspiracy theory, so-called, is more complex and recalcitrant that it might first seem.[6] It is notoriously hard to define and difficult to disprove. Conspiracy theories are not theories at all in the doctrinal sense; they are historicist narratives alleging secret agency behind social events. They take many textual forms—from social media posts and watercooler comments to pamphlets, letters to the editor, essays, government reports, novels, histories, and films. They are often intertextual, relying on evidence circulating in other places and forms. They rarely concern conspiracies in the original sense of small cabals of plotters who "breathe together" (*conspirare*). Rather, like academic social theory, conspiracy theories often aspire to explain grand social events and structures, and they frequently assert a general dysfunction in the public sphere. Indeed, for all their putative irrationality, they are fueled by the same hermeneutics of suspicion that Paul Ricoeur finds behind the philosophical systems of Marx, Freud, and Nietzsche. As Bruno Latour notes, there is a scandalous likeness between conspiracy theory and academic critique, and many conspiracy theories are strikingly akin to expert discourse (Latour 2004, 229). More scandalous still is how many people seem to accept conspiratorial explanations—although here, too, the matter is more complicated than it seems. Surveys reporting levels of belief (and disbelief) in one or more conspiracy theories are probably registering a more complex array of positions, including skepticism, agnosticism, openness ("it might be true"), and committed belief (Butter and Knight 2016).

Conspiratorial explanation is not a new feature of public discourse. Historians have repeatedly found it a pervasive, even normative, feature of earlier periods and other societies. In the eighteenth- and nineteenth-century United States, for instance, suspicions about foreign agents, powers, banks, and secret societies were widely held by the general public and elites (Butter 2014; Bailyn 1967; D. Davis 1971). As Gordon Wood (1982) explains, conspiratorial explanation thrived in eighteenth-century America:

> as nineteenth-century society became more interdependent and complicated . . . attributing events to the conscious design of particular individuals [came to seem] increasingly primitive and quaint. By our own time, dominated as it is by professional social science, conspiratorial interpretations have become so out of place that . . . they can be accounted for only as mental aberrations, as a paranoid style symptomatic of psychological disturbance. (441)

In other words, if the form of thinking we now call conspiracy theory is old, the tendency to see it as "conspiracy theory" is new. The phrase *conspiracy theory* only gained salience in the late nineteenth century, when it was used in legal and forensic discourse. It became briefly popular in the sensational 1875 adultery trial of Henry Ward Beecher, whose legal team presented what came to be known as a "conspiracy theory defense."[7] The term was revived in connection to President Garfield's assassination and other public cases, often with a sense of disapproval at a legal maneuver that seemed self-serving.

But the contemporary sense of conspiracy theory—the notion that it is a special type or style of thinking, one that is aberrant, pathological, and threatening to democracy—emerged during the Cold War. The term "conspiracy theory" first came into widespread usage between 1945 and 1972, and it has steadily grown in popularity since 1979. As the Google Books Ngram tool suggests, the biggest surge in the term's usage came amid widespread debate over the *Warren Commission Report on the Assassination of John F. Kennedy*.[8] By 1979, a huge body of discourse on Kennedy's murder—two massive federal investigations, many smaller state and local inquiries; several thousand essays, articles, and books; scores of novels, films, and plays; and more than five thousand newspaper and magazine articles—had framed the case as an interpretive contest between a "lone gunman" and "conspiracy theories."

The scholarly discourse on conspiracy theory developed in precisely the same twenty-year period. Indeed, the most influential scholarly description of conspiracy discourse—Richard Hofstadter's classic 1964 essay, "The Paranoid Style in American Politics"—was given as a lecture at Oxford the night before Kennedy's murder. If Hofstadter firmly established the idea of conspiracy theory as a problematic rhetoric, it was Karl Popper who first theorized it as an interpretive error. In his popular 1945 treatise, *The Open Society and Its Enemies*, Popper ([1945] 1962) dismisses what he calls "the conspiracy theory of society":

> It is the view that an explanation of a social phenomenon consists in the discovery of the men or groups who are interested in the occurrence of this phenomenon . . . and who have planned and conspired to bring it about.
>
> This view of the aims of the social sciences arises, of course, from the mistaken theory that, whatever happens in society—especially happenings such as war, unemployment, poverty,

shortages, which people as a rule dislike—is the result of direct design by some powerful individuals and groups. (94–95)

Notably, Popper sees this type of explanation not as deliberate propaganda but as populist error—what Fredric Jameson (1988, 356) would later call "a poor man's cognitive mapping" of social relations. The conspiracy theory of society, Popper ([1945] 1962, 95) argues, is "widely held" because most people cannot think structurally. They comprehend social developments through a secularized religious framework that attributes quasidivine agency to powerful groups. Popper's primary example is vulgar Marxism (101), which explains inequality as a capitalist plot rather than a product of ideological and structural determinants. The intellectual error here is the attribution of human intentionality to a social system—which Popper calls "the very opposite of the true aim of the social sciences" (94). Although Popper does not say so in this context, conspiratorial interpretations are often resistant to the criterion of "falsifiability" that was at the heart of Popper's program for distinguishing science from pseudoscience.

It was thus Popper who inserted the slash between *conspiracy* and *theory*, naming conspiracy theory the illegitimate other of academic social theory. Two decades later, in "The Paranoid Style in American Politics," Hofstadter more forcefully delegitimated conspiracy discourse. Like Popper, Hofstadter (1996b, 3–40) faults the paranoid's sense of causality—the absence of an "intuitive sense of how things do not happen"—and defensive resistance to contradictory evidence. Yet Hofstadter's primary concern is not interpretive error; it is what Michael Rogin (1987) would later call "demonology"—the conservative American tendency toward paranoid scapegoating—and paradoxical imitation—of the putative enemies of state. The elements of the paranoid style, in fact, are notably the elements of melodrama (Melley 2021). And the occasion of Hofstadter's essay, it is important to remember, was the "post-truth" crisis of his own age—the rise of Cold War demagoguery from Joseph McCarthy to Barry Goldwater. Hofstadter (1996b, 25, 29) connects this Cold War "pseudo-conservatism" to a long-standing "paranoid imagination" that sees "a 'vast' or 'gigantic' conspiracy as *the motive force* in historical events."[9]

Between them, Popper and Hofstadter put conspiracy theory into discourse just as a new form of political suspicion began to dominate American culture. I will return to this historical shift, but here I want to highlight several important consequences of their accounts. First, they defined conspiracy theory as a form of bad social theory. Neither of them is much interested in allegations of conspiracy, strictly speaking—that is, in secret plots by a small group that "breathes together." On the contrary, their examples concern mostly large social institutions (the Catholic Church, the Illuminati, the Masons) and economic structures (capitalism and communism). Popper is explicitly concerned with the "conspiracy theory *of society.*" Hofstadter (1996b, 3, 26) associates the paranoid style with the "conspiratorial fantasy" that an organization seeks to control the entire "apparatus of education, religion, the press, and the mass media . . . in a common effort to paralyze the resistance of loyal Americans." Conspiracy theory, in short, is about *institutional* power—and thus it is a species of social theory, no matter how ham-handed. Notably, conspiracy theory is often an account of a *corrupted public sphere* itself, of democratic rationality undermined by control of "the press, . . . 'managed news,' . . . brainwashing, . . . a special technique for seduction, [or] a stranglehold on the educational system" (32). Interestingly, then, the most "grandiose theories of conspiracy" (3) attempt something like ideology critique. That they do so in a form that does not require (and often explicitly rejects) Marxian determinism is one reason for their popularity in the Cold War United States (see Melley 2012, ch. 1).

Second, many conspiracy theories involve a nostalgic fantasy of sovereignty. They are animated by an all-or-nothing conception of agency in which individuals lack autonomy but *social systems* possess the coherence, willfulness, and intentionality of individual agents (Melley 2000). For Popper, the central error of the "conspiracy theory of society" is its attribution of intentions to social processes. Combating this tendency was a major task of the interpretive social sciences throughout the twentieth century. Popper's 1945 volume, for example, appeared only a year before W. K. Wimsatt and M. C. Beardsley (1946) reoriented literary studies with their attack on "the intentional fallacy." Yet banishing intentionality from social theory proved difficult and perhaps undesirable. "Power relations," as Michel Foucault (1978) wrote, are "*intentional* and *nonsubjective*":

> There is no power that is exercised without a series of aims and objectives. But this does not mean that it results from the choice or decision of an individual subject; *let us not look for the headquarters that presides over its rationality.* . . . The rationality of power is characterized by tactics that are often quite explicit at the restricted level where they are inscribed . . . yet it is often the case that no

one is there to have invented them, and few who can be said to have formulated them. (94–95, second emphasis added)

Foucault's problem with the idea of a "headquarters" to power is its reliance on an anachronistic model of sovereignty—a power imagined to reside in the secret chambers of the prince rather than in modern discourses and institutions. This notion—that power lurks in a smoke-filled room—is, of course, the starting assumption of conspiracy theory, which imagines a willful, sovereign agent or agency behind important social developments. Foucault suggests the persistent appeal of this notion, warning that in our thinking about power "we have still not cut off the head of the king" (88–89). Conspiracy theory's powerful nostalgia for sovereignty helps explain why Donald Trump is so drawn to it. Trump's deep state theory, for instance, reflects his sense that being president of the United States is like being a boss or a king (*l'état, c'est moi*). Trump's deep state allegations arose out of frustration that his early policy statements did not immediately spin the administrative *Titanic* on its axis. To Trump and his minions, any failure to instantly implement the sovereign will of the new president was not an artifact of bureaucratic complexity or communicative inefficiency but a secret plot of a competing sovereign.

Third, despite an emphasis on the logical or psychological problems of conspiratorial explanations, both Hofstadter and Popper constructed conspiracy theory as an irrationalist threat to democracy. For Popper, the very idea of powerful cabals covertly shaping social outcomes is inconsistent with the promise of "the open society." For Hofstadter, the demonological tendency to imitate the putative enemies of state erodes democratic institutions. Between 1945 and 1964, a number of other American sociologists and historians—including Daniel Bell, Seymour Lipset, Talcott Parsons, and Edward Shils—expressed similar concerns about Cold War–era conspiracy mongering. The stakes seemed high during the Cold War for maintaining an idealized account of the US public sphere as a model of rationality, openness, and transparency.

Paradoxically, as Shils (1956, 77) brilliantly observed in *The Torment of Secrecy*, it was this American ideal of transparency and openness that made Americans overreact to the "threat of secret machinations." The "paranoid style" was one such overreaction. Stamping it out seemed a reasonable way of protecting democratic institutions. But—and this was the heart of the problem—the Cold War National Security State was itself built as a hedge against the perceived weaknesses of the open society. The architects of the National Security State took seriously the major external threat Hofstadter associated with the paranoid style—international communism. In so doing, they imitated the secret agency they attributed to their communist enemies. To put it another way, if Popper and Hofstadter seemed concerned about the irrationalism of conspiracy theory, the major architect of the security state, George Kennan, was concerned about the perceived irrationalism and paranoia of the Soviet regime, and his proposed solution was to advance a new American form of "strategic irrationalism" (Melley 2012, 31–40). *They have fought us with unreality, with irrationalism,"* Kennan complained. "Can we combat this unreality successfully with *rationalism*, with truth?" The implicit answer was no, and so Kennan set to work on what he called "the necessary lie" (Harlow and Maerz 1991; quoted in Saunders 2013, 38). Crucial to this effort was NSC-10/2, the dull-sounding memorandum that became the secret constitution of the Cold War Security State. Signed by President Truman in 1948, it granted the newly chartered CIA the power to conduct covert warfare and specified that covert operations must be conducted so that "any US Government responsibility for them is not evident to unauthorized persons and that if uncovered the US Government can *plausibly disclaim any responsibility for them.*"[10] By conceptualizing American citizens as "unauthorized persons," Kennan revived Machiavelli's notion of a deceptive sovereignty exercised over an immature people.

Following this principle, the United States erected a massive new national security apparatus charged with the conduct of covert operations, propaganda, and psychological operations around the world. Over seventy years, what began as a small exception to democratic practice would become a vast clandestine apparatus: 17 intelligence agencies, 28 other federal agencies, 1,271 sub-bureaus, and almost 2,000 private corporations now perform "top secret" work in 10,000 US locations at a cost of $75 billion annually, more than any other domestic discretionary budget category and all other world spending on intelligence combined (Priest and Arkin, 2011). "Instead of enabling a system in which knowledge is power," Joseph Masco (2014, 123) observes, this system produced "a world in which knowledge is always suspect." As the structure for state suspicion grew, it stimulated public suspicion about its activities, particularly as its work became a *public secret*—operationally clandestine but widely understood to include plots of global political significance.[11] One of the high-water marks in public awareness about the security state came in 1964—the year of Hofstadter's "Paranoid Style in American Politics"—when the reporters

Thomas Wise and David Ross published their prominent critique, *The Invisible Government* (1964).

It is, at the very least, ironic that the apparent irrationalism of conspiratorial explanations was delegitimated at the very moment that the American public began to recognize and worry about an "invisible government" whose major activities would seem to require precisely the form of suspicion cast into doubt by the critique of the paranoid style. These agencies were deeply interested in conspiracy discourse and sometimes used it to shield their own activities from the "rational-critical" public sphere. The Atomic Energy Commission, for instance, went out of its way not to combat reports of UFO sightings and allegations that the US government had concealed evidence of alien contact. This major strand of Cold War conspiracy discourse served as a valuable cover for decades of advanced weapons and aircraft testing in the Nevada Test and Training Range, which contains Area 51 (Jacobsen 2012).

But US agencies aggressively combated conspiracy theories that undermined US policy—such as claims that the Apollo moon landings were a hoax—or that might provoke public inquiry into clandestine matters. In 1967, for instance, the CIA issued a dispatch to all station chiefs worldwide, attacking anti-CIA conspiracy theories about the Kennedy assassination. The fifty-three-page memo, "Countering Criticism of the Warren Report," notes that "a new wave of books and articles criticizing the Commission's report . . . have speculated as to the existence of some kind of conspiracy," and it expresses alarm that "a public opinion poll recently indicated that 46 percent of the American public did not think that Oswald acted alone."

> Conspiracy theories have frequently thrown suspicion on our organization by falsely alleging that Lee Harvey Oswald worked for us. The aim of this dispatch is to provide material for countering and discrediting the claims of the conspiracy theories, so as to inhibit circulation of such claims in other countries. Background information is supplied in a classified section and in a number of unclassified attachments. (CIA 1967)

To this end, the memo offers a series of talking points and action steps, as well as a prospective article for *The Spectator*, to be drafted by a CIA staffer, offering a point-by-point refutation of Edward Jay Epstein's 1966 *Inquest*. It directs all CIA station chiefs to reach out to "friendly elite contacts (especially politicians and editors)" and to "employ propaganda assets to answer and refute attacks" on the findings of the *Warren Commission Report*.

I cite this document not as the smoking gun in what might be called "the conspiracy theory of conspiracy theory" (the CIA *invented* conspiracy theory in order to discredit radical critiques of state secrecy!), but to suggest the continuous entanglement of post–World War II conspiracy discourse with the Cold War state. It is notable that the CIA not only deployed the notion of conspiracy theory as a subversive form used by "anti-American, far-left, or Communist" agitators but also developed a comprehensive list of now-standard debunking arguments: that a grand conspiracy is impossible to conceal; that apparent anomalies are statistical regularities; that conspiracy theorists narcissistically close their systems to falsifiability; and so on.

Most ironic of all is that Hofstadter mounted his critique of the paranoid style at a moment when US cultural narratives of suspicion radically changed character. Whereas Hofstadter's major examples all concern *external* threats to the nation—the Masons, the Illuminati, and communists—the major American conspiracy theories after 1960 focus on the deceptions and dangers of the security state itself. They assert serious government deception and malfeasance in the assassination of John F. Kennedy, the Apollo moon landings, alleged UFO cover-ups around Area 51, and the attacks of 9/11.

PUBLIC SPHERE HEROES

What are the implications of this brief genealogical sketch? To begin with, the term *conspiracy theory* is less innocent and simple than it seems. In popular usage, it is a pejorative, like "fake news," that labels politically unpalatable claims improbable, silly, or insane. The term *conspiracy theory* is almost never applied to descriptions of actual conspiracies in the original sense of that term. Nobody, for instance, calls the *9/11 Commission Report* a conspiracy theory. A conspiracy theory is made a *conspiracy theory* by its political opponents. Over the past sixty years, the term has become a rhetorical weapon deployed against a wide array of ideas, ranging from Donald Trump's late-night tweets to Noam Chomsky's structural critique of media. There is, of course, nothing surprising about this, but it should disabuse us of the idea that conspiracy theory is some stable, objectively identifiable category of discourse.

More important, conspiracy discourse is a discourse on the public sphere. It stems from a sociological impulse, a desire to explain the effects of a secretive or mystified social institution—"the banks," "Big Pharma," "the media." It usually critiques an "official" narrative (for example, that the United States won the space race by landing *Apollo* 11 on the moon) and thus impugns the apparatus of legitimation itself (for example, a co-opted press spread the lie that the United States actually landed on the moon). In some cases, conspiracy theory pushes such a claim so far that it essentially offers an account of ideology as false consciousness. If it begins with the assumption that the public knows much less than it thinks it knows, in other words, it often suggests that the entire public sphere is a deceptive spectacle. (In many right-wing online communities, the realignment of belief is called "taking the red pill," a reference to the scene of ideological unmasking in the 1999 sci-fi thriller *The Matrix*.) But even such extreme cases only become "conspiracy theories" by being marked as such by the guardians of the system of legitimation. Thus, assertions of conspiracy should be understood as components of a discursive system that includes *both* "revelatory" accounts of covert power and also rationalist dismissals and debunking of such accounts.

Seeing conspiracy theory as part of a discursive system of public reason helps to explain its surprising resemblance to its apparent opposite, debunking discourse. As Latour (2004) notes, the popularity of conspiracy theory reflects the centrality of debunking to academic critique. In addition to their common intellectual assumptions, *both* conspiracy narrative and debunking discourse are often motivated by a desire to heal the dysfunctional public sphere with therapeutic transparency. To be sure, some conspiracy theories (and some debunking claims) are circulated as deliberate disinformation, disorientation, and political manipulation. As Joseph Masco and Lisa Wedeen point out, we live in "an age of propaganda, of wall-to-wall psyops, disorientation campaigns, and attentional hacks" (this volume), and both conspiracy theories and attacks on conspiracy theories are often politically weaponized. Yet, it is important to note that many claims dismissed as "conspiracy theory" seem to be motivated by what might be called "public sphere heroism." They are the work of self-appointed guardians of the public interest, amateur journalist-scholars intent on exposing malfeasance and public deception. Indeed, both conspiracy theorists and debunkers often act in defense of democracy—on the one side, against the irrationality of sovereign secrets, and on the other side, against the irrationality of subversive conspiracy mongering. Both approaches aim to restore public reason with therapeutic demystification. This common commitment to an ideal of the public sphere helps to explain why so many conspiracy narratives resolve through a fantasy of publication (Melley 2020b).

Many narratives of conspiracy seem to get the particulars of their claims wrong, but they often point to serious structural problems of public knowledge, as many of the chapters in this volume attest (see, for example, the contributions by Joseph Dumit, Darryl Li, Louisa Lombard, Joseph Masco, and Lisa Wedeen). While this chapter has stressed the effects of US state secrecy, it is important to note that there are other important stimuli for conspiracy discourse. These include the curation of news feeds by social network algorithms; the emergence of what Ulrich Beck ([1986] 1992) has called the "risk society," in which threats are everywhere but cannot be understood without special technical expertise; and a regime of corporate public relations that includes attempts to corrupt public knowledge. In the Trump era alone, to take notable examples, investigations revealed the sugar lobby's fifty-year effort to manipulate scientific evidence in order to promote carbohydrate consumption through the creation of the USDA Food Pyramid; and Monsanto's attempts to influence studies of its weed killer, Roundup, which is widely used on genetically modified "Roundup Ready" crops (O'Connor 2016; Singer 2009; Hakim 2017). These stories join a torrent of "news we can use," telling the public whether helpful—or harmful—to eat fat, take a daily baby aspirin, have a mammogram, use a proton pump inhibitor, drink red wine, and so on. This regime of quotidian risk mitigation produces uncertainty and skepticism about "expert knowledge" and guidance.

Skepticism is also heightened when state secrets ooze into the public sphere: Eisenhower's public lie about U-2 flights over the USSR, Kennedy's Bay of Pigs fiasco, fabricated revolutions in Iran and Guatemala, the release of the Pentagon Papers, falsified intelligence about Iraq, the Snowden files. It is easy to misunderstand the effect of these regular dramas of secrecy and revelation. They draw our attention to the *content* of secrets, but their *form* matters more—and that form is *public secrecy*, the widespread awareness that the state is doing things *we think we know but cannot know in detail* (see Melley 2012, 19–23). In the parlance of Donald Rumsfeld, the once philosopher-king of US intelligence, security society is a place with a surfeit of "known unknowns," and in this strange epistemology, the savvy citizen can hardly be blamed for suspecting government and corporate speech to be deceptive or for imagining the kinds of secret operations the state's giant security apparatus must be conducting. After all, the starting assumption of conspiracy theory—*there's something they're not telling us*—seems an accurate description of the US national security arrangement since the Cold War.

It is important to note how ubiquitous and normalized this assumption has become. Consider, for instance, that in May 2018, Michael Hayden, the former CIA and NSA director, joined the chorus of voices deploring Donald Trump's apparent inability to "distinguish between truth and untruth" as part of "post-truth . . . erosion of Enlightenment values." Hayden dismissed Trump's belief in a deep state conspiracy and expressed sensible concern that his erratic proclamations were undermining US national security and diplomatic relations. Strangely missing from Hayden's analysis, however, was any sense that the CIA or NSA might play a role in fostering worries about a "deep state." Most Americans have not read enough of the 2014 US Senate report on the CIA torture of detainees to know that it cites Hayden scores of times for "appalling" misrepresentations to Congress.[12] But many Americans are aware of the stunning post-truth moment in which NSA director James Clapper flatly lied to the US Senate about the existence of massive NSA programs of domestic surveillance (Hayden 2018). More generally speaking, the "informed citizen" has been aware for a long time that, as Wise and Ross (1964, 4) put it, "the foreign policy of the United States often works publicly in one direction and secretly through the Invisible Government in just the opposite direction."

Informed citizens need not read congressional reports to get this impression, for the deceptions of the security state are the sine qua non of a robust American conspiracy imaginary. Countless films, novels, television series, comic books, games, and other media since the Cold War have eroticized the elements of conspiracy theory—its discovery of minor anomalies and coincidences in the official record, its ceaseless desire to reveal secrets, its fantasy of agency and sovereign power under the veneer of social life. Conspiracy melodramas normalize the assumption of corruption, malfeasance, and brutal sovereignty lurking within democracy. In so doing, they provide some of the "evidence" and narrative glue for conspiracy allegations. Indeed, one reason conspiracy theories can be so free of evidence and explanation is that their foundational assumptions about power are already widely available to consciousness in popular fiction.

The effect of the conspiracy imaginary lies less in its representation of particular plots than in its recirculation of a generalized suspicion about state and corporate power. But perhaps no threat is more common in conspiracy melodrama than what Donald Trump and his supporters call the "deep state"—a group of plotters unaccountable to their democratically elected leaders and feverishly crafting their own diabolical policy deep in the bowels of the "administrative state." Trump and company fear this sort of plot in part because it is *the* master narrative of conspiracy thrillers from the Cold War to the present. Rogue bureaucrats are a dime a dozen in the fictions of the security state, including sophisticated conspiracy novels by Don DeLillo and Norman Mailer, and popular thrillers from *Three Days of the Condor* to 24. While fears of a deep state conspiracy seem crazy to security officials and mainstream journalists, they feel like natural laws in the lurid shadows of the conspiracy imaginary. Consider, for example, *Jason Bourne* (2016), the fifth in a series of films about an amnesic assassin struggling to overcome his CIA brainwashing. In this espionage melodrama, the CIA is running numerous programs of assassination and total surveillance, and its director calmly orders globally placed assassins to kill Americans just to keep espionage programs secret. These assassinations are not shocking revelations of the thriller plot; they are just starting assumptions—facts of life presented with humdrum cynicism. In Hollywood's deep state, murdering scores of coworkers is all in a day's work.

The conspiracy thriller purports to reveal this terrible knowledge, and it promotes paranoia as a healthy antidote to the duped stupidity and cowed compliance of the general public. The narrative's hero is often quixotic in the original sense of the term: a self-appointed knight in the service of a mocking and ungrateful public. But the hero of the conspiracy thriller is always right—and the narrative's tension is usually not relieved until a doubting public accepts the hero's seemingly nutty allegations. In Richard Donner's 1997 thriller *Conspiracy Theory*, for example, a taxi driver's wild allegations are not only validated but greatly exceeded by the revelation of a sinister covert program of mind control and assassination. In the face of such terrible knowledge, heroism becomes a matter of revelation, publication, and dramatic disclosure. While some conspiracy thrillers end with an unsettling sense of unknowability and state or corporate domination (*The Conversation, The Parallax View, Syriana, Body of Lies*), many end in a fantasy of triumphant revelation that promises to heal the corrupted public sphere. Since *Three Days of the Condor* (1975), heroic publication has become a staple denouement of films like *The Insider, The Firm, The Package, Michael Clayton, The Green Zone, Fair Game, Safe House*, and many others.

In the conspiracy imaginary, paranoid reason seeks to *imitate* the putative work of the covert state. Conspiracy fictions require their heroes to adopt the suspicion and tactics of an intelligence agent, and they encourage their audiences to do the same. Jack Lovett, the spy in Joan Didion's (1984) brilliant novel *Democracy*, gives a good sense of this thinking.

> Jack Lovett did not believe that accidents happen. In Jack Lovett's system all behavior was purposeful, and the purpose could be divined by whoever attracted the best information and read it most correctly. A Laotian village indicated on one map and omitted on another suggested not a reconnaissance oversight, but a population annihilated. . . . A shipment of laser mirrors from Long Beach to a firm in Hong Kong that did no laser work suggested not a wrong invoice but transshipment, re-export, the diversion of technology to unfriendly actors. (36–37)

Generalized suspicion is what makes Lovett such an effective agent, but it is also the mode of Didion's narrator, a journalist who adapts Lovett's approach to a broader understanding of the Cold War public sphere.

This mode of reading lies at the heart of "serious" conspiracy theory. The most durable post–World War II US conspiracy theories—the faked moon landing, the Kennedy assassination, the claim that the United States planned the 9/11 attacks—have grown from fine-grained analyses of the public archive in a search for missed clues. An army of amateur forensic specialists regularly pore over images of World Trade Center 7 or helicopter footage of the Newtown elementary school massacre. In doing so, they rehearse the work of state officials and dramatic public revelations, like the Kennedy administration's U-2 images of nuclear weapons being deployed in Cuba in 1962, or US Secretary of State Colin Powell's 2003 UN presentation about Iraqi weapons of mass destruction. Iraqi trailers revealed in satellite images, Powell told the world, were actually mobile chemical weapons platforms. Powell's photographs were an interesting sort of evidence: they pointed to an anomaly (large trailers moving around in the desert) and purported to document a secret; but the secret was never revealed, only publicly asserted. That this argument proved entirely wrong only strengthens its resemblance to the public testimony of the thousands of self-appointed guardians of the public sphere who fill blogs with arcane analysis of the Zapruder film of President Kennedy's assassination, footage of the World Trade Center falling, and NASA photographs of the *Apollo* 11 mission.

Such would-be public sphere heroes return us, finally, to the case of Donald Trump. Trump's conspiracy discourse, too, has been a relentless attack on the organs of the public sphere, and it has at times asserted that the entire representational apparatus of US society is fundamentally deceptive. At a certain point in the 2016 presidential campaign, he even seemed to cast himself as Morpheus in *The Matrix*, revealing that what others saw as a prosperous, functional democracy was in fact a miserable "desert of the real"—a nation of "third-world airports," urban hellscapes, and murdered citizens. "The American dream," he shouted at the Detroit Economic Club, "long ago vanished. . . . Our inner cities are a disaster. You get shot walking to the store" (Wachowski and Wachowski 1999; Ferris 2016; Charles 2016; Chicago Tribune Staff 2016; Covert 2016).

This was not all, however. As he slipped behind in public opinion polls, Trump began to claim that the election was rigged. Experts and leaders of both parties deplored these baseless assertions, perhaps forgetting that they were already central themes of notable serial political dramas of the day *Scandal*, *House of Cards*, and *Mr. Robot* (the tagline of which is "our democracy has been hacked"). In the final weeks of the campaign, as polls suggested a Clinton victory, Trump pushed his critique further, suggesting that not only the electoral system but the entire system of publicity—"the media"—was "rigged" (Weigel 2016; Yuhas 2016). Trump had already attempted an end-run around the mainstream press with his outraged late-night tweets, Facebook news platform, and personal YouTube channel, the Trump TV Network. But as he contemplated a humiliating defeat, Trump sensed a way to refashion himself one last time as a public sphere hero. Members of his team began to leak that Trump's "endgame" was the launch of a new cable television empire with "Trump News" as its anchor (Ellison 2016; Haberman and Steel 2016; Detrow 2016). Faced with a rigged system as corrupt as that in any Hollywood thriller, there was only one way out: Trump would pour his personal fortune into the tireless work of reforming the corrupt public sphere, correcting injustice, and revealing conspiracy wherever it hid—all on Trump TV.

NOTES

1   On the 2016 ten-word short list were *alt-right* and *Brexiteer*, the latter of which was cited, along with Trump's nomination, as a major source of post-truth's popularity.

2   See "The Post-truth Issue" (2017) of the *Chronicle of Higher Education*; Glasser (2016); Florido (2016); Davies (2016); Szklarski (2017); Freeman and Freeman

(2017); R. Marcus (2016); Todd, Murray, and Dann (2017); Rosenberg (2017); and Mariani (2016).

3 For a longer treatment of this idea, see Melley (2012).

4 This is not to suggest that conspiracy theory itself is particularly American. As more comparativist studies have demonstrated (Butter and Knight 2016), conspiracy theory is a persistent, cross-cultural phenomenon. That the scholarship on conspiracy theory, including my own (Melley 2000) has focused on the United States is part a legacy of the genealogy of conspiracy theory, which I explain in detail below, and of the fact that many influential studies of the early twenty-first century were done by Americanists.

5 Trump's position gives his conspiracy mongering a propaganda value and totalitarian potential. Whether it is deliberate disinformation or the genuine articulation of grievance, it is nonetheless tapping into a set of national and state fantasies.

6 See Fenster (1999); Melley (2000); Knight (2000); and O'Donnell (2000).

7 The *discursive concept* of conspiracy theory is relatively new. The *Oxford English Dictionary* dates the term to a 1909 book review in the *American Historical Review*. The reviewer calls the author's thesis a "recrudescence" of an 1880 "conspiracy theory" about the origins of the Missouri Compromise. On the history of the concept of conspiracy theory, see McKenzie-McHarg 2019 and Thalmann 2017.

8 See the Google Books Ngram Viewer's citational rate of "conspiracy theory" 1900–2019, available at https://books.google.com/ngrams/graph ?content=conspiracy+theory&year_start=1900&year_end=2019&corpus =en-2019&smoothing=0.

9 Hofstadter explains "pseudo-conservatism" more fully in *The Paranoid Style and Other Essays* (1996b).

10 National Security Council, "NSC 10/2," June 18, 1948, Document #43; cited in Warner (1994, 215–16); emphasis added.

11 On public secrecy, see Taussig (1999). For a brilliant account of public secrecy and US national security structures, see Masco (2014, 113–44). See also Melley (2012, 1–31).

12 US Congress 2014113–288. For sample comments on Hayden, see 14n25, 14n28, 113n665, 170–71, 201n1168. "Senator Feinstein wrote a separate letter to CIA Director Michael Hayden stating, 'I want you to know that I found the October 17, 2008 reply . . . appalling'" (210n1213).

PART II

ATMOSPHERES OF DOUBT

LISA WEDEEN

06 ON UNCERTAINTY AND THE QUESTION OF JUDGMENT

The proliferation of websites disseminating purported news; the ease with which digital photos can be doctored; the accelerated cycles in which "news" gets circulated, absorbed, and then superseded by the next catastrophe; the tension between rival discourses registering moral outrage from different angles—all play a role in how we apprehend the condition of generalized uncertainty that is evolving and metastasizing throughout the networked world today. And although it is easy to point to instances of direct manipulation, there are also less overtly directed forms of uncertainty and doubt—ones that come into circulation acephalously, independent of propagandistic strategy. Competing images, rumors, and conspiracy theories, alongside the divisive testimony of "eyewitnesses" regarding real or alleged events, make for a consequential if sometimes unwitting collusion between commercial media outlets and political regimes.

This chapter takes the example of war-torn Syria as a window into our contemporary world of epistemic murk. In Syria, we see the media's demand for sensational content driving both regime supporters and well-meaning citizen-journalists from the opposition to massage (if not manufacture) purported evidence of all kinds, leaving Syrians at home as well as observers abroad doubting the validity of what otherwise might be regarded as authoritative news reports or the claims of international fact-finding missions. We also see in the post-March 2011 example of Syria that such conditions of generalized uncertainty significantly aided the frayed state's counterinsurgency campaign—not so much by helping it maintain credibility in its own version of events as by casting doubt on all reporting, enabling the regime to seize critical advantage in an oversaturated high-speed information environment.

My argument about ideology and its relation to judgment bears on the concerns of this volume in the following three ways. First, and this is a lesson that citizen-activists learned at tremendous cost: too much information can generate the very uncertainty that circulating it is intended to allay. Over the course of the uprising, the Syrian state's ideological apparatus, no longer able to brand the regime as a kinder, gentler version of autocracy, learned how to use conditions of fear and insecurity to counter human-rights activists' and citizen-journalists' attempts to document "the truth." By disseminating its own claims and counterclaims, and by exploiting the political inexperience of the fractious opposition, the regime has not always been able to establish its own authority over the facts, but it has been repeatedly successful in sowing doubt among a variety of possible addressees regarding the nature of evidence and the credibility of oppositional narratives.

Second, as scholars of American politics have pointed out, information overload and the uncertainty it generates may induce people to seek out opinions reaffirming their own; and this tendency toward balkanization can lead to polarization (see, for example, Sunstein 2001, 11–21). Internet users (taking an oft-used, contemporary example) tend to isolate themselves into echo chambers, relishing the sound of stories they are telling themselves anyway—and the stories they tell themselves about the stories they tell themselves. The atmosphere of uncertainty cultivated by an excess of information can create siloed publics, where the confinement of debate within narrow communities of argument allows interlocutors to take pleasure in exclusively encountering views that confirm their own.[1]

Third is a possibility that the Syrian conflict illuminates especially well: conditions of generalized uncertainty make it easy for people to find alibis for avoiding commitment to judgment at all. In circumstances of information oversaturation, and perhaps particularly when feelings of present danger extrude a "remainder of surplus threat" (borrowing Brian Massumi's formulation), uncertainty can provide a potent rationale for inaction in situations where action might otherwise have seemed morally incumbent (Massumi 2010, 60). Over the course of the intensifying violence of the Syrian uprising, reasons for hunkering down and staying safe overwhelmed. But at the beginning, this recourse to nonjudgment had consequences. It put what came to be referred to as the "gray people" (*al-ramadiyyin*)—moderates, or those in the "silent middle"—at odds with activists and ultimately with the project of political transformation. An atmospherics of doubt nurtured a self-satisfied ambivalence, which justified political paralysis and withdrawal. This political resignation mattered in the early years of Syria's neoliberal autocracy, as I have noted elsewhere (see Wedeen 2019, especially chapters one and two). In the context of outright protest, the professional, managerial elite's silence in particular helped the regime navigate the changing circumstances of its rule.

As the product of novel technologies of information dissemination and the not-new circumstances of war, this generalized uncertainty exists in the Syrian context alongside certainties that are well entrenched—sometimes cleaving along demographic lines and sometimes registering something more on the order of a mood or position within a single person. My effort here is to move beyond a commentary on the paradoxical effects of the so-called digital revolution by demonstrating how the opening in Syria to reflexive questioning, the supposed hallmark of the liberal public sphere which defined experiences of civic solidarity at the beginning of the uprising, got shut down as a form of revolutionary mobilization.[2] Syrian activists were under no illusions as to whether the regime itself was liberal, and they were adept readers of the structuring guidelines for public speech and action that characterize autocratic rule. A great many Syrians did, however, share the expectation that their own work would help bring into being a world of public debate and reflection. This chapter is about those expectations and how they were stoked and then extinguished, managed and then deferred—or in some cases recalibrated in exile. It is also more generally about the logics of autocratic retrenchment and how they converge with market mechanisms of social control.

In contrast to one common conception of authoritarianism, in which it is the withholding of information that enables domination, Syria exemplifies a regime exploiting an excess of information and accelerated conditions of dissemination for authoritarian political gain.[3] But the Syrian case does more than that. It invites a renewed exploration of the always fragile relation between truth and politics, exposing in particular how the specter of immediate danger works when danger has, in fact, become immediate. By way of getting at these matters, I want to unpack two exemplary moments. The first involves an extended controversy about who might have been responsible for the murder of a prominent local singer, whose mutilated body had been left on the bank of the Orontes River in the city of Hama, presumably as a warning to activists—unless, that is, the victim was someone else entirely, or, as was conceivable at one point in the twisting tale, no one had been murdered at all. The story marks an important turn in the uprising, when it became apparent that activist expressions of countrywide solidarity, outrage, and creativity were starting to encourage forms of rhetorical overreach, exaggeration, a willingness to rush to judgment, and people's eagerness to express clear political positions based on the murkiest of facts.

The second moment is the seemingly incommensurable example of the chemical weapons attack in eastern al-Ghouta in August of 2013, a devastating event in which the "evidence" seemed to point in different directions, stirring a global debate, with politicians, activists, and scientists all weighing in on what might actually have happened and who was to be held accountable. These conflicting accounts in the Western press also circulated in Syria, where they were often translated into Arabic or excerpted in Arabic on Twitter and Facebook. At the same time, local eyewitness accounts, rumors, and images appearing on Arabic websites were being translated into English and circulated accordingly. The effect was to polarize Syrians whose positions were already firm, even while intensifying uncertainty for others less sure of their commitments. Bringing these two examples together allows us to see in events local and world historical the ongoing speculative reproduction of an affective and epistemic insecurity, the operation of which conduced to favor the beleaguered Asad regime's counterinsurgency project—contributing substantively to its survival.

Throughout, the chapter is informed by the thinking of Hannah Arendt and Ludwig Wittgenstein. In the closing pages, I briefly engage with the work of the Syrian collective Abounaddara, whose work attempts to unsettle the conventions of documentary representation; I put its cultural production into conversation with Arendt and Wittgenstein, drawing out mutual points of relevance for our understanding of politics. These artistic efforts bypass the impasse produced by an intensified atmospherics of doubt. In an overly saturated information environment, no preponderance of evidence becomes credible enough to convince those whose minds are already made up that an alternative account might be the right one. Nor does more or better information serve to allay the ambivalence of those in the "gray area," whose ideological investments become framed by forms of nonjudgment encapsulated by the famous phrase of disavowal "I know very well, yet nevertheless . . ."[4] By producing works that are orthogonal to expectations associated with conventional documentary film, artists such as these acknowledge uncertainty without succumbing to political paralysis—allowing ambiguity, contingency, and competing views to thrive, and thereby reopening possibilities for political judgment—for the considered reflection in and ongoing assessment of complex political circumstances.

ATMOSPHERICS OF DOUBT

In the early days of the uprising, a new anti-Asad song became a political phenomenon, widely recorded on cell phones and uploaded on YouTube. Marked by a catchy rhythm, the song's simple rhyming lyrics enjoined Syria's president to step down and leave the country. Stanzas opened and closed with the repeated chorus "Go on, leave, O Bashar" (*Yalla irhal ya Bashshar*), while the song zeroed in on familiar allegations of first-family corruption. Exhilarating in its irreverence and leveling crude insults directly at Bashar, Bashar's notoriously brutal brother, and his venal cousin, the song was at once angry and joyful, challenging the self-evidence of tyranny while paying homage to lives lost. By performing a newfound sense of solidarity, the lyrics invited popular participation, which came in the form of extemporaneous add-ons expanding and adapting the song—giving license to each singer, writer, and listener to act in concert with the acoustics of revolutionary change. The proliferating stanzas surpassed the abstractions of typical, more elitist political songs, not only perpetuating defiance but working to air publicly what had hitherto been predominantly private grievances (see Abdo 2013).

Initially, it was widely thought that the song's original singer had been one Ibrahim Qashush (or Qashoush), a firefighter in Hama, who was said to perform occasionally with another local, ʿAbd al-Rahman Farhud, or as he was more popularly known, Rahmani (or sometimes Rahmuni). On July 4, 2011, Qashush reportedly turned up dead, his corpse left on the bank of the Orontes River with the larynx carved out. Many understandably interpreted the murder in terms of the crude symbolism, presumed at the time to have been the work of regime thugs who had punished the subversive singer in the most graphic way possible.

In making these assumptions, people were probably wrong. First of all, the singer of the song was most likely Rahmani, not Qashush; and Qashush, far from being a beloved singer of subversive tunes, may have been a police informant. In (likely) being mistaken about who Qashush was and what role he may have played in the events in question, a multitude of Facebook postings, featuring new songs and videos made after his supposed demise, ended up paying tribute to a possible double-crosser, whose body it may or may not have been that was found, missing its larynx, by the side of the river. Moreover, as suspicions spread that Qashush was guilty of traitorous complicity, the matter of whether responsibility for the mutilated corpse indeed lay with regime thugs was also cast into doubt. Stories quickly emerged claiming that vigilante activists had executed Qashush (or someone else) for collaboration.[5] Finally, as if scripted, sightings of Qashush surfaced in 2013, accompanied by articles and Facebook photos attesting to his continued well-being in exile, and culminating in a *GQ* article in 2016. This piece, reported a few days later in Arabic, purported to reveal that the "real singer" was not Qashush but Rahmani—the latter still alive and well in Spain. The article stated that Qashush had, in fact, been slain on the bank of the Orontes River, and that he had been a guard (not a firefighter) at the fire station. He was not the singer of revolutionary songs or, for that matter, of any songs at all (Harkin 2016).[6] The article dealt with issues ranging from the circulation of rumors to sins of omission (by both Rahmani and opposition outlets); to an effort by the late Anthony Shadid of the *New York Times* to report the factual truths; and tellingly, to the failure of Shadid's story to "stick" in the context of the "avalanche of new media propaganda." The Qashush story thus exemplifies a conflict in which truth claims, rather than accumulating into a collection of established facts, recall something more like a shifting kaleidoscope of putative alternatives—registering both the uprising's complexities and the multiple efforts to paper over them.[7]

The regime not only helped produce these conditions of uncertainty— for example, by barring professional journalists from entering the country—but also repeatedly capitalized on them, seizing on moments of exaggeration and misrepresentation to discredit opposition positions, polarize communities of argument, and disorient worlds in which truth claims might have led to action. That is, the regime's advantage lay not in its exercise of strict control over an ideological state apparatus but in not having to be believable in order to be powerful. From the inception of the uprising, the burden of proof lay on activists taking the moral high ground, in calling for an end to tyranny and advocating for dignity and a civil state. It fell to citizen-journalists to provide a discursive corrective to autocratic dissembling, whether in the blatantly fictitious terms reminiscent of the cult of personality surrounding Bashar's father, Hafiz al-Asad, or in the subtler forms of market-oriented spin characterizing the urbane élan of Bashar and the glamorous first lady.

Ludwig Wittgenstein (1972) teaches us that "the truth of certain empirical propositions belongs to our frames of reference. When we first begin to *believe* anything, what we believe is not a single proposition, it is a whole system of propositions. It is not single axioms that strike me as obvious, it is a system in which consequences and premises give one another *mutual* support" (12e, para. 83, emphases in original). What we have seen in Syria is the collapse of these frames of reference and, at the same time, the annihilation of truth in Wittgenstein's sense—not the truth of philosophical a priori principles but the political truth of empirical propositions, by which I mean what counts, for purposes of politics and political discourse, as fact. Wittgenstein's insistence that what allows our beliefs to make sense is the relational system in which they are embedded points to the difficulty that was involved in judging evidence or ascertaining the nature of truth-claims circulating in Syria's "media wars" since the uprising began in March 2011. In this respect, the story of Qashush is more than an isolated incident of mistaken identity. The mystery about who might have murdered a well-known singer or indeed whether he was a well-known singer or even dead, his contradictory deployment as a symbol of oppositional courage and regime brutality, and then later as a symbol of regime co-optation and opposition revenge—all this is but a single complex example, both symptomatic of and contributing to an entire economy of uncertainty that works to dilute moral outrage among addressees who otherwise might be available for political activation. This economy of uncertainty causes what would be political judgments to come unmoored from the conceptual systems in which they are situated.

In this context, the curious lack of follow-up articles and interest by opposition activists initially so invested in the song and in the purported singer's purported murder could be read ungenerously as indicating a cover-up of journalistic failings. Or it could be seen as indicative of reading and writing habits cultivated in conditions of high-speed eventfulness and information overload. But this silence relative to the commotion caused by the initial discovery of the corpse by the river also speaks to a collective disappointment born from the uprising's ongoing-ness, the forms of depredation that have squelched revolutionary exhilaration. The song had originally beckoned ordinary people to take part in something momentous, to participate in events charged with the embrace of political responsibility, to sing what they meant. New forms of sociality made possible in the moment, the resonances embodied in the musical invitation to action, and the fleeting sense of political promise worked together to summon into being what Kathleen Stewart (2007, 20) in a different context calls "a solid ephemerality," a sense of something graspable, temporary, promising—a potential something.[8] This potentiality is precisely what had dissipated even before questions of mistaken identity or sightings of a healthy Qashush made their lackluster appearance. The revolutionary idea of Qashush had already "been assassinated," as one activist put it, taken down not only in conditions of uncertainty but, in part, by them.[9]

POLITICAL IMPASSE

The chemical weapons attack on August 21, 2013, in eastern al-Ghouta on the outskirts of Damascus was a devastating event. My purpose in revisiting the incident here is to extend our exploration of the work uncertainty does by looking at a particularly dramatic and painful case in which the whirl of excessive information called into question prevailing relational systems and their frames of reference. A pared-down timeline of the attack looks like this: In the early morning of August 21, Syrians in the area began to report mysterious deaths. Circulating on social media were stories of children whose faces had turned blue, who were foaming at the mouth, or who had stopped breathing; entire families being discovered dead; and still other civilians suddenly falling ill, with eyewitness accounts proliferating as the day went on. On August 24, Doctors without Borders confirmed that three days earlier, on August 21, staff had observed at least 355 deaths from "neurotoxic symptoms" at three medical centers in eastern Damascus. On August 25, regime forces agreed to a cease-fire to allow inspectors from the United Nations (already in Syria examining cases of an earlier alleged use of chemical weapons) to conduct on-site investigations; these took place during a series of five-hour periods from August 26 to 29.[10]

It was during this period of cease-fires that US Secretary of State John Kerry issued a statement seeming to commit the country to some form of direct military intervention against the Asad regime, which in Kerry's narrative was the undoubted perpetrator of the atrocity. Unsurprisingly, given recent instances of high-level US officials lying to the American public and in testimony before the UN Security Council, Kerry's statement would itself generate doubts and speculation about cynical US motivations. It was in attempting to forfend just such a reaction that Kerry described his certainty about the regime's responsibility as "grounded in facts," but "informed by conscience and guided by common sense." He also alluded to classified information that would settle the matter, once and for all, which he promised would be revealed in due time (see Kerry 2013). This statement was translated into Arabic and circulated widely through multiple media outlets within Syria and across the Middle East. Four different kinds of warrants—the factual, the moral, the sensus communis, and the classified—converged to produce what Kerry claimed was "undeniable" evidence. But as time wore on, Kerry's failure to produce decisive proof generated the very conditions of deniability that his assertions of incontrovertability sought to discount.

Despite Kerry's insistence on certainty, or perhaps in some instances because of it, what was supposedly "already clear to the world" became increasingly difficult to discern amid the inundation of claims and counterclaims prompted by the secretary of state's statement. And as more information emerged, the more it seemed to generate uncertainty both in and outside Syria. Many reports basically confirmed Kerry's allegations—citing eyewitness accounts, relying on the circulation of information and images on social media sites, and producing a plethora of articles translated from Arabic into English and vice versa.[11] Other reports attempted to complexify what counted as the Syrian regime. An example here would be Phil Sands's (2013) article in the Abu Dhabi daily *The National*, claiming the following:

> There were indications that some of the army officers involved had tried to distance themselves from what happened, and insisted they were not told the rockets they were firing were loaded with toxins. "We have heard from people close to the regime that the chemical missiles were handed out a few hours before the attacks," said a source from a well-connected family, with contacts both with the opposition and with regime loyalists. "They didn't come from the Ministry of Defence but from air force intelligence, under orders from Hafez Makhlouf [a relative of President Asad's]. The army officers are saying they did not know there were chemical weapons. Even some of the people transporting them are saying they had no idea what was in the rockets—they thought they were conventional explosives."

Barely a week later, however, a counternarrative began to emerge, one that placed ultimate accountability with the opposition.[12] As ʿAdnan ʿAli in the opposition-oriented magazine *Al-Araby Al-Jadid* pointed out in a 2016 article looking back on the massacre, the regime typically operates in ways consonant with such a dynamic: it first denies that anything has happened; then, when news stories attesting to the occurrence of an event achieve a certain prominence, it fabricates evidence and manipulates images to blame the opposition for what has occurred (Ali 2016). Although early reports accusing the opposition of the chemical attack lacked the more obvious authority or credibility of sources like the ones holding the regime to account, they nevertheless became increasingly susceptible to uptake. These latter reports were less a way of anchoring an alternative certainty than of questioning the empirical propositions on which existing frames of reference relied. Some expressed uncertainty about who was behind the attacks; others engaged in heated exchanges of polarized beliefs; and still others justified inaction or suspended judgment on the grounds that the truth of what happened was impossible to know.[13]

The story took a technical turn on September 4, 2013, with the publication of an article in the comparatively reputable (if sometimes wrong) *New York Times*. Entitled "Rockets in Syrian Attack Carried Large Payload of Gas, Experts Say," the report drew on a study by Richard M. Lloyd, an "expert in warhead design," and Theodore A. Postol, a physics professor at MIT (Broad 2013). The study promised a scientific resolution of the accountability question by addressing a previously unnoted problem at the heart of the investigation: How could what were initially thought to be rockets with minimal carrying capacity deliver enough gas to kill so many people over such a large area? Basing their analysis on photographs publicly available on the internet, Lloyd and Postol concluded that the munition in question was designed to carry "about 50 liters (13 gallons), not the one or two liters (about half a gallon) of nerve agent that some weapons experts had previously estimated."[14] The question of the quantity of gas involved in the attack was significant because it raised technical issues about prevailing US government assertions of clear-cut culpability. Lloyd claimed that the opposition, not just the regime, had the capacity to manufacture the rockets used, while admitting that it remained unclear (at the time) how the rebels might have acquired that much nerve agent (again, as reported by William J. Broad in the *Times*). Other experts interviewed were explicit about their doubts that the opposition could have acquired so much gas, in effect advocating on behalf of the opposition while producing an even greater sense of uncertainty that largely bene-fited the regime (Broad 2013).

Subsequently, Lloyd and Postol published a second report, this time casting doubt on UN and US calculations of rocket trajectories, rather than carrying capacity, and further generating skepticism about the re-gime's role in the attack. Based on photographs of the remains of what appears to have been the wreckage of rockets that had delivered the toxic nerve gas to al-Ghouta on August 21, Lloyd and Postol now argued that the rockets could not have been launched from regime-held territory, because from that distance they could not have reached the target. All these find-ings appeared also in Arabic translation. As C. J. Chivers (2013) of the *New York Times* wrote in a sober update on December 28, "The new analysis [of Postol and Lloyd] could point to particular Syrian military units involved, or be used by defenders of the Syrian government and those suspicious of the United States' claims to try to shift blame toward rebels."

Memorable among those participating in what became a discursive jostling with high-stakes consequences bearing on foreign direct military intervention, and thus on regime survival, was the Syrian presidential spokesperson Bouthaina Shaʿban. In a statement given on Septem-ber 4 to Sky News (2013; in English and then reiterated on many Arabic-language sites), Shaʿban held the opposition responsible for the attack: "They kidnapped children and men from the villages of Lattakia and they brought them here, put them in one place, and used chemical weapons against them. That's the story that the villagers in these villages know."

In this narrative, the ones killed were, by implication, ʿAlawis from areas supportive of the regime, not the opposition. At the cost of concoct-ing a narrative involving the transport of pro-regime victims to opposi-tion territory, a five-hour bus trip away from home, Shaʿban accounted for what would seem to be the central problem the regime had in telling its story: Why opposition forces would victimize civilians in territories they controlled. Especially interesting in our context, however, is how Shaʿban—who had just offered "the villagers in these villages know" as definitive evidence for her claims—concluded: "But why don't you leave it to the UN Commission to investigate, to analyze?" Or again, "Western countries are always very scientific, they go by the law, they investigate. Why when it comes to something concerning our countries, they say 'it is believed that the Syrian government used chemical weapons'? Why don't you wait for the specific, scientific results of a neutral UN committee that is investigating?" (Sky News 2013).

The incoherence of her appeals and the sheer outlandishness of the story nevertheless produced its own rejoinders, including reports noting that the regime's kidnapping scenario would have required a large caravan of buses passing unhindered and unnoticed through a large number of enemy checkpoints. In other words, the story could be simultaneously dismissed and addressed, with each new interpretation producing its own extended labor of fact-checking efforts, which themselves contributed to the work uncertainty does in turning what could be the object of ethical-political judgments into confusion, with implications for global actors as well.

One more aspect of Sha'ban's preposterous statement is worthy of note: namely, her appeal to science. And here, too, science worked less to establish truth (or falsify fallacious claims) than to convert what might have been provisionally consensual knowledge into entrenched political conviction, including the conviction that we can never know what happened. The scientific democratization of expression personified by internet activists such as the famous opposition-oriented Eliot Higgins (who previously wrote under the pseudonym Brown Moses) operated alongside the views of experts like Lloyd and Postol whose MIT-authorized science backgrounds were also tarnished by a history of questionable speculations. And in this case, everyone was operating in a world saturated by conflicting claims. These were not conspiracy theories of the caliber that Sha'ban and others brought to the fore, but their very existence as disagreements enabled those whose minds had been made up in advance of circulating evidence, which was itself confusing, to stay that way.[15]

US President Barack Obama's prime-time speech on September 10, 2013, and Russian President Vladimir Putin's *New York Times* op-ed the following day looked like a matched-set throwback to Cold War politics, in which political posturing trumped all curiosity. Facts, already hard to adjudicate, became pared down to an acknowledgment that something bad had happened—a chemical attack—while attributions of responsibility broke along classic political fault lines, with Obama assuring the American people that the Syrian regime was behind the attack and Putin (2013) recommending caution by placing the blame on the opposition: "No one doubts that poison gas was used in Syria. But there is every reason to believe it was used not by the Syrian Army, but by opposition forces, to provoke intervention by their powerful foreign patrons, who would be siding with the fundamentalists. Reports that militants are preparing another attack—this time against Israel—cannot be ignored." Putin's invocation of Israel may have been a cynical attempt to curry favor with American readers, given their particular Middle Eastern commitments and anxieties. More interestingly, his closing rhetorical gambit provided a more plausible motive than Sha'ban's for why the rebels, if they were the ones accountable, had timed the attack when they did. In doing so, he demonstrated how privileged access to state knowledge (even when the specific knowledge of a case does not exist or is not supportive of the claims being made) can be used to convert uncertainty into an anxiety that then reproduces another set of certainties—that is, these militants must not be supported.

The UN's own authority as a fact-finding team and its careful language regarding what it could and could not ascertain was undercut by past mistakes. Its reputation as a partial international body, as opposed to an objective arbiter of truth claims, produced doubts about its conclusions— however tenuous and carefully worded they might have been. And in some cases, appeals to science and skepticism about the UN's neutrality could converge, as in MIT researcher Subrata Ghoshroy's (2013) September 26 analysis, "Serious Questions about the Integrity of the UN Report." Ghoshroy charged that there had been "communication between the UN team and the analysts outside, which prejudiced the UN's report." That report supposedly confirmed various aspects of the divergent analyses by Lloyd and Postol and by Higgins. Additional expert assessments were released after the end of the UN inspection but before the publication of the UN's report, suggesting some sort of leak. Ghoshroy continued, "Secretary of State John Kerry dismissed the UN inspectors as irrelevant because they would not bring to light any new information that the US did not already know. He was right. The purpose of my analysis is not to prove or disprove anything. The sole purpose is to raise questions about the integrity of the UN team's report. Decisions on war and peace depend on it." Ghoshroy also accused Higgins of "interspersing" photographs and video from another area where a chemical attack had occurred with images of the massacre in al-Ghouta, not to demonstrate that the same sorts of munitions were used in both cases but to deliberately "mislead" the reader.[16]

The December appearance of Seymour Hersh's "Whose Sarin?" in the *London Review of Books* raised additional doubts. In this investigative report counteracting Obama administration claims, Hersh (2013) contended that the president "failed to acknowledge something known to the US intelligence community: that the Syrian army is not the only party in the country's civil war with access to sarin, the nerve agent that a UN study concluded—without assessing responsibility—had been used in the rocket attack." Faulting various studies circulating online and through conventional news channels, Hersh maintained that it was known that the opposition force and Al-Qaʾida affiliate Jabhat al-Nusra had access to the necessary ingredients to make sarin and had demonstrated interest in using it. In a follow-up piece published in April 2014, Hersh went further, suggesting that Turkey was in fact behind the al-Ghouta attacks. These claims then showed up in Arabic-language media and made up the bulk of what a reader received when she Googled in Arabic (in Chicago but also Beirut), "Who is responsible for the Ghouta chemical weapons attack?"[17] This remained the case until April 2017, when arguably, the attack on Khan Sheikhoun (Khan Shaykhun), the most devastating one since 2013, supplanted queries about responsibility for the earlier massacre. And importantly, a similar logic of regime denial characterized this attack—sowing doubts about the timing of chemical spread, alleging doctored images of damage, and shifting ultimate responsibility to the opposition by claiming that the devastation was not caused by an "air launched chemical attack."[18] Aided by its Russian allies claiming that the deadly chemicals were dispersed as a consequence of a preemptive strike on a munitions factory controlled by the opposition group Hay'at Tahrir al-Sham (previously known as Jabhat al-Nusra), the regime could reproduce ambivalence among those who remained uncertain about the murky facts while stoking loyalist claims. Ardent supporters, like the official Russian statements, came to justify the attack on the grounds that the opposition would have otherwise used these weapons against innocent civilians. Such reliance on a form of hypothetical, anticipatory reasoning to explain state violence had been a strategy of regime management from the start.[19]

Moreover, the still popular question of who bore responsibility for these attacks, not to mention so many others like them, is made to order for conspiracy theorists, who view seemingly disparate happenings as connected, as intentional products of a force whose interests are ultimately served by and organized through another's victimization or ruin. And they are not always wrong, as this volume stresses. Hersh's investigation into the 2013 attack was potent because it was plausible (at least to some). So, too, were reports suggesting that Hersh had been hoodwinked by his contacts in the Pentagon—to help avoid direct military intervention or to limit the US mission to eliminate the Islamic State (Saliha 2014). In structuring arguments in terms of what some scholars have termed a "paranoid" functionalism that posits effects as the product of purpose,[20] the question as to who was responsible for the chemical weapons attack in al-Ghouta was easily harnessed to a familiar regime narrative of national vulnerability and threat—in which the "national" becomes, once again, coterminous with regime-oriented.

Questions of "who is behind" a specific act need not reduce to a conspiratorial narrative, of course. For others, the very posing of the question conveyed a sense of collaborative unknowability in which doubt could modulate affective registers like outrage and disgust, along with the political judgments that might ensue. Phrasing like the following was typical: "The chemical weapons attack was sickening. But who was responsible? Was the regime really worse than the opposition? They were both awful, of course." The regime and opposition groups could plausibly deny responsibility—at least for those open to skepticism. It was not simply that camps were polarized, with staunch loyalists and people in the "gray area" following regime-oriented sites and tracking investigative reports such as Hersh's, while official opposition sources called for US intervention because the regime clearly had "crossed [Obama's] red line." As young people identified with the uprising became increasingly disillusioned by both regime and opposition, as the impossibility of adjudicating truth claims came to apply to virtually continuous acts of unspeakable cruelty, some in exile sought to redefine and radicalize the terms of debate, conceding to a situation in which facts were especially vulnerable and everyone might lie.

A surplus of information, even better information, it turned out, did not necessarily lead to truth. Circulating truth claims were vulnerable to counterspin from the get-go, generating difficulties of adjudication that augured poorly for the establishment of anything like a democratic or revolutionary consensus. A combination of autocratic politics, outside intervention, and high-speed news dissemination had worked to cultivate forms of uncertainty that were unlikely to be resolved by any amount of reporting conducted in accordance with standards of journalistic evidence suitable for political deliberation. In conditions of violence and discursive disorientation, the very conceptual projects of verifiability, eyewitness reporting, and objectivity had themselves become grist for the mill. And meanwhile, more people had died—notwithstanding the technical debates and political posturing of all involved.

FROM IMPASSE TO BYPASS:
MAKING OPENINGS

The loss of what Arendt in various writings calls "a common world" is dramatized in Syria by the relentless soul-crushing violence, but it is also characterized by an atmospherics of doubt in which recourse is made to forms of certainty that polarize some people based on what they think they already know while providing others with the grounds for disengagement and disavowal—in that they know that they do not know. Such a situation profoundly complicates possibilities for political judgment. We see in Syria today the constellation of mutually related rules, propositions, experiences, techniques of reasoning, everyday practices, and mental images through which we are "trained" to judge—in Wittgenstein's sense—having been undermined by a world in which information is paradoxically both incomplete and overwhelming.

This is not simply von Clausewitz's proverbial "fog of war," where military commanders know exactly what they would say given perfect information, which is made impossible by the fog. Rather, this is a condition in which what is lost is faith in the efficacy of what until then had been understood as valid informational currency. As Arendt (2006a, 227) acknowledges in her rich essay "Truth and Politics," the "politically most relevant truths are factual"—and they are, as Linda Zerilli (2016, 135) underscores, also the most easily imperiled, the most vulnerable to "human mendacity" and to the "pursuit of [narrow] political interests." Politics is a domain of plural contingent opinions, argues Arendt, where the understanding of freedom is rooted in an appreciation of the human capacity for speech and other kinds of action. Intriguingly, even lying for Arendt is expressive of a kind of freedom, although it cannot be the freedom of an affirmative politics; for prerequisite to the political in a salutary sense is a contingent, open-to-revision factual truth-telling that helps establish a common world.[21] We have already seen from Wittgenstein how such a world is made up of frames of reference that are subject to collapse. Some Syrian filmmakers share this appreciation, showing us the death of politics that occurs when a common world in formation is crushed by dissimulation and violence.

The work of the anonymous film collective Abounaddara, made up of "self-taught and volunteer filmmakers" engaged in "emergency cinema," likewise suggests that when the conventions of the documentary are challenged, something radical or at least out of the ordinary might happen in their stead.²² For the most part, the collective's short films hint at prospects that are left vaguely defined, gesturing toward experiences of self-assertion as well as of self-dissolution and unpredictability, offering accounts of events or situations in which there may be room for reclaiming judgment as a political activity.

One powerful example is *The Trajectory of an Unknown Soldier* (Abounaddara 2012), a four-part series of two- to three-minute films chronicling the evolution of a soldier fighting for the opposition—his decomposition in the face of gruesome wartime intensities and his ultimate struggle (in part 4) to recalibrate his relation to the world. Filmed with the soldier always in silhouette, the visual in-shadow effect not only protects his anonymity but underscores, like a photograph's negative, how light reveals darkness and darkness, light. The clanging of unseen pots and pans contributes to a low-key, ambient ordinariness, the sound an invitation to reinhabit the familiar in marked contrast to the soldier's story of violence and, until part 4, despair. Part 1 establishes the soldier's first realization that he is capable of killing. Faced with the need to take another's life, he is scared, but he feels that he has no choice. That refrain—that he has no choice—provides the central animating theme of this short, a testimony to judgment's suspension, or at least compromise; to the simultaneous recognition and evasion of responsibility; to an emotional catastrophe that leaves the social fabric torn. He has to protect his family. He knows it is wrong to kill. But he has no choice. He fears God but he has no choice. The regime has left him with no choice.

Part 2 describes his experience entering a home and finding children who had been lying dead for some days. There is no obvious cause of death. The soldiers were looking for food and water and just happened into the dwelling. In describing his search through the house, he bears witness to a mother's love for the son she "holds against her"—both dead. He tells us that the buildings behind the house, where he and others had been fighting, were besieged by the regime army, and he cries as he recalls the terrifying experience, part of a relentless nightmare in Syria's central city of Homs. It is a war that is both disorienting and suffocating. The remaining inhabitants of that embattled area were "as afraid of us as they were of the Syrian [regime] army," he admits, wiping tears from his eyes and noting how "truly frightening" it was. Residents could not open a window for fear of being shot; there was literally and figuratively "no breathing allowed."

In part 3, the soldier has become self-consciously "dissociated" or "split" (his word, *infisam* means both in Arabic) from himself. Here he recounts killing "someone" by cutting the person's throat. In the soldier's retrospective lamentation, he notes that while his body slaughtered the victim, his soul was crying. Now he can scarcely imagine himself having done it. No level of resentment or desire for revenge can make that "legitimately right." The filmic strategy is to narrate the dissociation while at the same time diagnosing it as such, to suture the diegetic and the extradiegetic in an effort to repair cinematically what cannot be healed practically. Politically, the soldier begins by saying that he does not want to be like the other soldiers in the Free Syrian Army, an opposition military force. But then he confesses that he has indeed acted like them. This acting of the body in violation of the soul suggests a specific horror of wartime, an experience of splitting in which an otherwise moral self is cleaved from his orienting ethical world. His anonymity, like that of the victims he encounters, or the ones he kills—or Abounaddara's insistence on its anonymity as a collective, for that matter—suggests a kind of national substitutability, in which each soldier or victim is both fungible and exemplary, as is each director. This gesture of interchangeability also suggests an interpretive generosity in which the soldier appeals to multiple audiences, perhaps including regime soldiers themselves.

Part 4 shows the haunted soldier's effort to regain a sense of the world that might make politics possible again. He prays to God for a secular state, the seeming contradiction not really one at all but rather an assertion of the right to private piety and a public "civil state." He identifies himself as Sunni but champions a multisectarian Syria, claiming half-jokingly even to like "Christians more than Muslims." He is careful, when speaking of 'Alawis, to qualify his willingness to generalize by underscoring that it is only "some" 'Alawis that oppress. And he treats as ludicrously unpatriotic the idea that Syria would be "dismembered," carved up into sectarian enclaves. In short, he recovers himself by imagining politics that make good on the regime's vision of national integration and multisectarian accommodation—indulging in the hope that despite the bloodshed, or perhaps because of all the sacrifice, dictatorship can be, indeed must be, replaced with a liberal, tolerant, Asad-free nation-state. This hope is not offered in the register of the uprising's early days of exhilaration. The soldier is deflated, but not fully destroyed. And in his worries and wishes for Syria's future, there is something tentative and stale, exhausted.

But not only that. There is also an acknowledgment that any politics going forward will necessarily involve mutual engagement between those who fought for the regime and those who fought for the opposition. Recorded in 2012, the soldier's address is shockingly early, for members of the opposition tended not to register criticisms of their own actions until 2014–15. That prescience is part of what makes the soldier's gesture of self-scrutiny so important. And although, like the rest of the Abounaddara corpus, its circulation was initially limited—the audience made up mainly of western and Syrian intellectual types sharing an interest in activism and film—the shorts live on, accessible on Vimeo to anyone who wants to watch and reflect. In making unfashionable judgments about the conflict, the soldier and the filmmakers are modeling interpretive generosity for adversarial counterparts (among activists and regime soldiers) in the apparent hope of inducing reciprocity. Adumbrated in this effort at reciprocity is an aspect of what Arendt (2006a, 237) called "representative thinking," to be myself in a place where I am not.[23] This is a call to a kind of political judgment that is based neither on an overidentification with suffering others nor on conformity to a popular position. It is an instance—and there are so many—of creative estrangement that operates inside ideology but at a distance, opening up imaginative possibilities for reclaiming some kind of ameliorative agency in the world.

In distinction to official opposition and regime proponents alike, with their polarizing answers always at the ready, the collective embraces the ambiguity of the situation—extending it even to questions of what the national community might look like, given what the war has done to what could conceivably be Syria. In doing so, Abounaddara gives up on a certain kind of knowing, without giving up on judgment and political intervention as such.[24] Whereas both the regime and the multiple oppositions demand that people take sides for or against, the collective's commitment to complexity is not the same as the frame-breaking uncertainty that provides an alibi for nonjudgment. On the contrary, the recognition of the fragility of subject positions allows viewers to embrace a temporal lag between perception and action without abandoning the latter, to counter the temptations of ideological disavowal, to be humble and befuddled without being abject—an invitation to revitalize judgment with the full albeit paradoxical knowledge that nothing is ever fully known.

CONCLUSION

The forms of discursive oversaturation described in this chapter come from what I have called the temporality of "high-speed eventfulness," or the sheer velocity with which information is transmitted and apprehended in the internet age. The unceasing whirl of (over)information makes it easy for people to move on to something new the instant a favored narrative fails. The Ibrahim Qashush controversy brings into bold relief the conundrums for judgment posed by these new conditions, showing how the Syrian regime's media manipulations—a shorthand here for both direct propaganda efforts and an ability to exploit issues put into circulation by others (whether Russian diplomats, investigative reporters like Seymour Hersh, or scientists such as Lloyd and Postol, or for that matter, missteps by the Obama administration)—interfered with activists' capacity to maintain or develop a revolutionary narrative. This means that stories were easily knit into the narrative fabric of stories people were already telling themselves, or that political exuberance was flattened, the latter ending up, like Abounaddara's unknown soldier, mired in doubt and disillusion. In the context of heightened uncertainty, both ambivalence and oppositional deflation thrive. Such an atmospherics of doubt is part of what Slavoj Žižek (2008, 9) calls "systemic violence," which in the Syrian case operates in cahoots with other forms of overt regime brutality to extinguish or dampen what began as incendiary political excitement. In this context, the artistic efforts showcased here in Abounaddara's shorts are like embers: a trace of light and heat, a past-bearing invitation to begin anew.

NOTES

1 The online organizer Eli Pariser calls this phenomenon the "filter bubble." For him, the problem lies less with consumers and more with web companies that tailor their services, including news and search results, to personal predilections, limiting exposure to alternative ways of seeing the world. See Pariser (2012).
2 For some striking parallels with the digital revolution in another authoritarian context, see Humphreys (2012).
3 For conventional political science examples of authoritarian disinformation practices, see King, Pan, and Roberts (2017); on China, and on Russia, see MacFarquhar (2016); and Ostrovsky (2016).

4 *Je sais bien mais quand même* (Mannoni 1985).

5 An article, published in October 2013 by the opposition website hunasotak .com, claims that the singer was not Qashush, but Rahmani, and that he was killed by the regime. The *GQ* article by James Harkin (2016) discussed later in this chapter supports some key assertions of this earlier—but generally unknown or ignored—report.

6 See this Arabic-language piece reporting on Harkin's *GQ* article: Syrian Press Center, "What Is the Degree of Truth about the Nightingale of the Syrian Revolution Being Alive" [Ma Sihhat Khabar Wujud "Bulbul" al-Thawra al-Suriyya ʿala Qayd al-Hayat?] Markaz al-Sihafa al-Ijtimaʿiyya, al-Markaz al al-Suri Social Press Center, December 29, 2016, https:// tinyurl.com/y889bbu2.

7 See also Zaina Erhaim's (2022) account of the challenges facing Syria's independent media outlets. She suggests that "perhaps the biggest lie of all since the uprising" began is "the story surrounding the killing of Ibrahim Qashoush."

8 Conjuring up Walter Benjamin, Stewart (2007, 21) notes that "potentiality is a thing immanent to fragments of sensory experience and dreams of presence. A layer, or layering to the ordinary, it engenders attachments or systems of investment in the unfolding of things."

9 Phone conversation with Yahya al-ʿAbdallah, July 2016.

10 For a more detailed timeline, see Wedeen (2019, ch. 3).

11 See Wedeen (2019, ch. 3). See also the opposition-identified Syrian Observatory for Human Rights' extensive reports. See also "The Office for Documenting the Syrian Chemical Attack: The Regime Has Not Handed Over Any Shipments in a Month," [Maktab li-Tawthiq al-Kimawi al-Suri: al-Nizam Lam Yanqul Ayy Shahna Mundhu Shahr], April 3, 2014, https://www.syriahr.com/%d9%85%d9%83%d8%aa%d8%a8-%d 9%84%d8%aa%d9%88%d8%ab%d9%8a%d9%82-%d8%a7%d9%84%d9% 83%d9%8a%d9%85%d8%a7%d9%88%d9%8a-%d8%a7%d9%84%d8%b3 %d9%88%d8%b1%d9%8a-%d8%a7%d9%84%d9%86%d8%b8%d8%a7%d 9%85-%d9%84%d9%85/19600/ and "The Russian Campaign in the Security Council to Change the Story of the Chemical Attack" [Hamla Rusiyya fi Majlis al-Amn li-Taghyir Riwayat al-Kimawi], December 17, 2013, https://www.syriahr.com/%D8%AD%D9%85%D9%84%D8%A9 -%D8%B1%D9%88%D8%B3%D9%8A%D8%A9 -%D9%81%D9%8A-%D9%85%D8%AC%D9%84%D8%B3 -%D8%A7%D9%84%D8%A3%D9%85%D9%86-%D9%84%D9%80%D8%AA%D 8%BA%D9%8A%D9%8A%D8%B1-%D8%B1%D9%88%D8%A7%D9%8A/16436 /. Previous URLs have ceased to work but these were accessed on May 7, 2023. Thanks are owed to Jeson Ng for his research help.

An article a year later reiterates these findings: "One Year after the Chemical Massacre: What Do Syrians Remember and What Do They

Forget?" ['Am 'ala Majzarat al-Kimawi: Madha Yatadhakkar al-Suriyyin wa], Madha Yansawn?], *Orient News*, August 17, 2014, http://www.orient-news.net/ar/news_show/80599. A comprehensive list with short introductions to most of the reports/articles/videos and images accusing the Asad regime is available at "Al-Asad Perpetrates Genocidal Crime, Killing 635 People with Poison Gas" [Al-Asad Yartakib Jarimat Ibada Jama'iyya wa-Yaqtul 635 Shakhsan bi-l-Ghazat al-Samma], *Muntada Madinat Tumayr*, https://tinyurl.com/y7ttkf74.

For official responses to the attack from various sides, see "Response to the Chemical Bombing of Aleppo by Asad's Troops," [Rudud al-Fi'l 'ala Qasf 'Isabat al-Asad Halab bi-l-Kimawi], *Markaz al-Sharq al-'Arabi li-l-Dirasat al-Hadariyya wa-l-Istratijiyya, al-Mamlaka al-Muttahida, Landan Arab Orient Center for Strategic and Civilization Studies London*, https://tinyurl.com/ycduff4m, last accessed May 7, 2023. The Violations Documentation Center, a human rights website well regarded by opposition activists, produced a report on August 22, 2013, one day after the attacks. This circulated vigorously among Syrian- and Arabic-language global activists on social media outlets and is available here: Center for Documentation of Violations in Syria, "A Special Report on the Use of Chemical Weapons in the Province of Rural Damascus, Eastern Ghouta" [Taqrir Khass hawl Istikhdam al-Silah al-Kimawi fi Muhafazat Rif Dimashq, al-Ghuta al-Sharqiyya], August 22, 2013, https://tinyurl.com/y9nmmz98.

An archive of videos and commentary from human rights activists, as well as some comments accusing both parties of the atrocity, is available through the Internet Archive: "The Ghouta Massacre 21 August" [Majzarat al-Ghuta 21 Ab], *Al-Mindassa al-Suriyya The Syrian Infiltrator*, https://web.archive.org/web/20160917170322/http://the-syrian.com/archives /102020, last accessed May 7, 2023.

12 See the regime-oriented "Al-Ghouta Chemical Weapons: How Three Armed Factions Came into Possession of Chemical Weapons" [Kimawi al-Ghuta: Hakadha Imtalakat Thalathat Fasa'il Musallaha Asliha Kimi-ya'iyya Mundhu Sanawat], *Almersad*, October 31, 2013, https://tinyurl.com /y9p75emt. For a similar but less detailed account, see "Three Years after the Chemical Attack on al-Ghouta: The Secrets of the Massacre" [3 Sanawat 'ala Kimawi al-Ghuta: Khafaya al-Majzara], *Ad-Diyar*, August 23, 2016, https://tinyurl.com/y7qrxnaz.

13 See "Bandar ibn Sultan Is Responsible for the Chemical Weapons Attack in al-Ghuta" [Bandar ibn Sultan Mas'ul 'an al-Hujum al-Kimawi fi al-Ghuta], *Associated Press*/Damas Post.

The following link no longer works: https://tinyurl.com/y9de7mwe; it was last accessed successfully in November 2014 and was defunct as of December 4, 2018. But it is now available by way of the Wayback Machine, accessed on May 7, 2023: https://web.archive.org/web/20130903070334

/https://www.damaspost.com/%D8%B3%D9%8A%D8%A7%D8%B3%D8%A9
/%D8%A3%D8%B3%D9%8A%D9%88%D8%B4%D9%8A%D8%AA%D8
%AF-%D8%A8%D8%B1%D8%B3-%D8%A8%D9%86%D8%AF%D8%B1
-%D8%A8%D9%86-%D8%B3%D9%84%D8%B7%D8%A7%D9%86
-%D9%85%D8%B3%D8%A4%D9%88%D9%84-%D8%B9%D9%86-%D8%A7%
D9%84%D9%87%D8%AC%D9%88%D9%85-%D8%A7%D9%84%D9%83%D9%
8A%D9%85%D8%A7%D9%88%D9%8A-%D9%81%D9%8A-%D8%A7%D9%84
%D8%BA%D9%88%D8%B7%D8%A9.htm.

My claims here are also based on ongoing conversations with Syrians
in exile from August 2013 through August 2022.

14 The quote is from Broad (2013); the original report seems to be available
only as a PowerPoint presentation.

15 For a fuller account of Higgins's investigations, see Wedeen (2019, ch. 3).
Human Rights Watch also holds the Syrian regime responsible in a report
that is accessible in Arabic at https://www.hrw.org/ar/report/2013/09/10
/256469. Subsequent articles in newspapers, on television and radio, and
on internet sites likewise implicate the regime. This one from Al-Jazeera is
typical: "Ghouta: The Planned Attack" [Al-Ghuta: Al-Hujum al-Mudabbar],
Al-Jazeera, August 23, 2014, https://tinyurl.com/y9sho8z7.

16 The UN Mission released its final report on December 13, 2013, addressing wider claims of chemical weapons use: "United Nations Mission to
Investigate Allegations of the Use of Chemical Weapons in the Syrian Arab
Republic," December 2013, https://tinyurl.com/pkzrbey. For a list of all the
cases under scrutiny, refer to the discussion in Wedeen (2019, ch. 3).

17 See Hersh (2014). For opposition sources presuming the regime's culpability and decrying the world's inaction, see below, and see also Wedeen (2019,
ch. 3).

18 See, for example, the following article from the state-owned international
news and current affairs television network based in Paris: "Bashar al-
Asad: The Khan Shaykhun Chemical Attack Was Fabricated 100 Percent"
[Bashshar al-Asad: al-Hujum al-Kimiyaʾi ʿala Khan Shaykhun
"Mufabrak Miʾa fi al-Miʾa"], *France 24*, April 13, 2017, https://www
.france24.com/ar/20170413-%D8%B3%D9%88%D8%B1%D9%8A%D8%A7
-%D8%A7%D9%84%D8%A3%D8%B3%D8%AF-%D8%AE%D8%A7%D9%86
-%D8%B4%D9%8A%D8%AE%D9%88%D9%86-%D8%B3%D9%84%D8%A7%
D8%AD-%D9%83%D9%8A%D9%85%D9%8A%D8%A7%D8%A6%D9%8A.

See also Asad's interview claiming that the attack was a conspiracy
against his regime: Presidency Syria, "President Asad Interview with the
French Press," YouTube, April 13, 2017, video, 23:28, https://tinyurl.com
/kxd8wkz (no longer available as of September 2018).

Additional Arabic-language articles from *Russia Today*, in its typical
short format: Arabic RT, "A Former US Intelligence Officer Determines
Who Is Responsible for the Khan Shaykhun Chemical Attack," April 20,

2017, https://tinyurl.com/y9c3y8yd. The following *Russia Today* article is based on information from a purported CIA expert: Arabic RT, "CIA Director: We've Gathered Compelling Evidence on Khan Shaykhun in One Day!" [Mudir CIA: Jamaʿna Adilla Damigha Hawla Hujum Khan Shaykhun Khilal Yawm Wahid!], July 12, 2017, https://tinyurl.com/ybbrrfrp. See also a recent UN report accusing the Asad regime of responsibility: Enab Baladi, "UN Declares the Regime Responsible for Khan Shaykhun Massacre" [Al-Umam al-Muttahida Tajzim bi-Masʿuliyyat al-Nizam ʿan Majzarat Khan Shaykhun], September 6, 2017, https://www.enabbaladi.net/archives/171441, last accessed May 7, 2023.

19 See, for instance, "Russia Says Syria Gas Incident Caused by Rebels' Own Chemical Arsenal," *Reuters*, April 5, 2017, https://tinyurl.com/yb3kcppf; Martin Chulov and Kareem Shaheen, "Syria Chemical Weapons Attack Toll Rises to 70 as Russian Narrative Is Dismissed," *Guardian* (US edition), April 5, 2017, https://tinyurl.com/m9lh8q8; Ole Solvang, "Russia's Claim on Alleged Chemical Attack in Syria," *Human Rights Watch*, April 6, 2017, https://tinyurl.com/yb6mkmge; Danielle Ryan, "Why Is US Media Ignoring All Dissenting Expert Voices on the Khan Sheikhoun Attack?," RT, April 20, 2017, https://tinyurl.com/y9gp3hre; and Ammar Abdullah, "Chemical Incident in Khan Shaykhun Deliberately Staged by Militants, Syrian Probe Finds," RT, August 17, 2017, https://tinyurl.com/y7rlby93. Accounts of the attack that place the onus on an aerial bombardment include well-regarded opposition sites: an article from the online bulletin all4syria is available through the Internet Archive, "Chemical [Attack] Kills the Children of Khan Shaykhun: Victims in the Hundreds While Those Counting the Dead Stand By Helpless" [Al-Kimawi Yaftuk bi-Atfal Khan Shaykhun . . . al-Dahaya bi-l-Miʾat wa-ʿAddadat al-Mawt Taqif ʿAjizatan], April 4 2017, https://web.archive.org/web/20171029121408 /http://www.all4syria.info/Archive/400043 in all4syria, last accessed May 7, 2023; another is "Hundreds of Victims without Blood in a Chemical Bombing on Khan Shaykhun" [Miʾat al-Dahaya bi-La Dimaʾ bi-Qasf Kimawi ʿala Khan Shaykhun], *Step News Agency*, April 4, 2017, available via the Wayback Machine: https://web.archive.org/web/20170404121650/https://stepagency-sy.net/archives/139340. There was also horrifying video about the same brutal event: Assi Press, "Scenes from the Chemical Massacre in the City of Khan Shaykhun Caused by the Regime's Aircraft by Targeting the City with Chemical Gases [Mashahid min Majzrat al-Kimawi fi Madinat Khan Shaykhun Alladhi Sabbabahu Tayran al-Nizam bi-Istihdaf li-l-Madina bi-l-Ghazat al-Kimawiyya]," YouTube, April 4, 2017, video, 0:40, https://tinyurl.com/y6wafjhc. Some videos chronicled the death of an entire family: Assi Press, "Chemical Bombardment of the City of Khan Shaykhun by the Syrian Regime," [Qasf bi-l-Kimawi ʿala Madinat Khan Shayhum min Qibal al-Nizam al-Suri], YouTube, April 3, 2017, video, 0:51, https://tinyurl.com

/y83s76wr. A helpful timeline was produced by Eliot Higgins, "Summary of Claims Surrounding the Khan Sheikhoun Chemical Attack," *Bellingcat*, July 4, 2017, https://tinyurl.com/y94gadfc. Higgins refuted Hersh's efforts to sow doubt about this attack, claiming that he had been hoodwinked: Eliot Higgins, "Will Get Fooled Again—Seymour Hersh, Welt, and the Khan Sheikhoun Chemical Attack," *Bellingcat*, June 25, 2017, https://tinyurl.com/ybaxukm2.

20 See Hofstadter (1964); and Harper (2008). Harper argues, much like James Scott, that conspiracy theories and rumors are "weapons of the weak." See Scott (1985). But Michael Rogin's early work on the McCarthy era, as well as his subsequent analysis of political "demonology" in the American context, suggests otherwise. See Rogin (1967, 1987). For recent work in this vein, see Masco (2014).

21 For a discussion of the difference between Arendt's and Wittgenstein's view and Jürgen Habermas's notion of communicative rationality or reason, see Zerilli (2016).

22 Abounaddara, Vimeo profile, https://vimeo.com/user6924378; see Abounaddara 2012. The collective's name is commonly transliterated as Abounaddara and I have followed that convention here, although the Vimeo profile is abou naddara.

23 For a more in-depth discussion of "representative thinking" and for an account of other Syrian films that operate in this mode, see Wedeen (2019, esp. ch. 4).

24 Others, such as the site Takkad [Verify, https://verify-sy.com], are attempting anew to produce journalism with professionally recognized standards of objectivity. Their work has generated some important retractions, including from BBC Arabic. See also Brian Whitaker's investigative journalism, including a self-published book entitled *Denying the Obvious: Chemical Weapons and the Information War in Syria* (2021); and Stefan Tarnowski's illuminating work (which is in conversation with arguments made here and also deals with both Verify and Abounaddara), "Struggling with Images: Revolution, War, and Media in Syria" (PhD diss., Columbia University, 2022). As Arendt (2006a, 236) has also pointed out, facts are not only fragile, but also stubborn, and this obstinacy might be a source of political hope in the context of ongoing challenges posed by conditions of epistemic murk.

07 RESONANT APOPHENIA

UFOS, aliens, lizard people, secret networks of unworldly abductors working with the government, technologies of the sinister . . . Stories of uncanny conspiracy tell their audience about many and various things. But their themes keep circling back to a sense that life in America is shaped by some ineffable, enormous power, a power that can be seen only in the patterns of its effects.

Fantastic conspiracy stories, like ordinary personal memories, arise amid experiences of class, loss, race, gender, and the body's unmoored location in a world of accelerated technological change. But those experiences are not always articulated. Their shapes as stories are only partially visible from wherever one stands.

During the Trump presidency, outraged conspiracy theories were tweeted relentlessly from the dead center of power. Many liberal Americans regard the political deployment of far-right conspiracy theory as the inevitable fallout of conspiracy theory itself, critiquing its mood of paranoia, its failures of rationality, or its faulty notions of evidence. But the meaning of any conspiracy theory is inextricable from the situation that generates it: conspiracy theory issued as official propaganda means something different from theory emerging from the social margins, where histories of violent and insidious plots; experiences of invasion, theft, and destruction; experimentation and abduction by powerful agencies against Indigenous people, Black people, poor people, and vulnerable people, underscore the fact that some conspiracies by the powerful are not "theories," but histories and memories. The meanings of conspiracy narratives are inseparable from their situated position.

Many current conspiratorial themes are alive and blooming across the internet now—stories of sinister governments and their secret dealings with aliens, uncanny surveillance, and terrifying plots by the shadowy powers that be—and always, the impossibility of knowing any final verdict about what the truth might be—have been growing for decades. Such theories and stories were common during a time I was listening carefully to them, for years, over a long stretch of the 1990s. There is a restless, germinating affect to note, a gathering intensity, when one looks back in time there—a stirring, still-inchoate, gathering affect—something that was even then already ripe to multiply and circulate, something that decades later could be sucked up into new media technologies and transformed, moving from the margins into official narrative, from late-night radio into major news channels, supercharged from vernacular talk into propaganda, shifting in its new situation from a restless, endless figuring out into the potential reifications of policy. The necessary affect was already there. In many small stories, people always theorized and felt conspiracies from the sidelines of political and economic power, and—because this is how modern power works—the injury those stories spoke of was recognized as something that might, in fact, be taken up and used, in resonant forms, redeployed from the center itself.

The time I want to think about here, though, is like an eye in a hurricane. The First Gulf War was over and the next wars against Iraq and Afghanistan had not yet begun. The twin towers of the World Trade Center were standing unmarked against the skyline. No one could yet have theorized that it was government bombs and not the planes that caused the towers to collapse, or that Flight 93 was completely staged, or that all the Jews stayed home that day. All the fraught events that quickly followed in the aftermath of the towers' destruction—the medicalized terror of anthrax scares, the secretive "code orange" days, the arguments for public safety through the erasure of civil liberties, and even years later, the growing uneasiness over the government's ability to read one's email or listen in on one's phone calls—all these still lay in the future. And yet, for some people, when these anxious events did occur, they did not seem so very unfamiliar.

A sense of trauma fills many of the stories I am relating here. Its source is often elusive, not just for a skeptical critic but also as an element of the story itself. People telling these uncanny stories can only wonder about what really happened; but they just know *something is wrong*. Lauren Berlant (2011, 80) wrote that "the trauma produces something in the air without that thing having to be more concrete than a sense of the uncanny—free-floating anxiety in the room, negativity on the street, a scenario seeming to unfold within the ordinary without clear margins, even when a happening is also specific." Here you can explore the intense elaboration of this affect as it moves from a fleeting sensation into the center of things.

In the period during which most of the ethnographic stories here arose, the Tea Party did not yet exist. Antigovernment conspiracy theory was commonly described in dominant media, if mentioned at all, as marginal or kooky. Before the mid-2000s, it was hard to imagine antigovernment conspiracy theorists achieving the empowered political base that Donald Trump activated first in the birther movement, and then in the claims of election fraud. Yet in many ways, libertarian discourses and movements based in the conspiratorial sensibility that achieved political ascendancy in the early twenty-first century were already latent, not just in the common populist strand long-standing in America, nor in some quintessential "paranoid" quality of American character, but specifically in the uncanny talk that intensified in the 1990s.

To remember a sense of the public sentiment during the time frame I invite you to explore here, you might think of it as beginning at the first year of the Clinton administration and ending in 1999, as confusing predictions began to haunt the media with visions of an apocalyptic Y2K, when "the computers" would all break down and society would fall apart. My friends in rural Nevada were gearing up for Y2K with extra stores of canned food and ammunition; my friends in New York City laughed at how ridiculous the doomsday rhetoric in the media was, how technophobic, but still they filled their bathtubs with water on December 31, 1999. *You never know*.

In 1992, when I first met UFO believers in the midsize southern city I call here by the pseudonym Hillview, *The X-Files* had not yet appeared on television. Master narratives about American history—its settlement, genocide, captivities—were shifting in public culture, uneasily for some people, as old themes of triumph and destiny began to lose claim to a monologic real.

There were still yellow ribbons hanging raggedly in some trees, leftovers from the Gulf War. In 1992, the country was in a recession. By 1998—when Hillary Clinton was mocked for accusing her husband's opponents of a "conspiracy"—there was an economic boom. But for many people, talk of booms and busts did not necessarily make a difference, except to the way they thought of themselves in relation to master narratives of class mobility. There was a sense that the true driving force of economic and political life in this country, and in the world, was not to be found in the surface ups and downs that might be declared on the news (see Dean 2009). Instead, there was a sense of occult and sinister operations, something that went far beyond the moment's booms and busts and elections, back thousands of years, forward into the future, beyond America, beyond Europe, beyond the earth itself. There were forces of good and evil, forces that became manifest in our politicians but that transcended them by far. *They* gained power through their links to each other, building up strength and intensity through subterranean connections. All these were things people did not name directly, calling them connecting forces and the powers that be.

APOPHENIA

Apophenia refers to the experience of perceiving connections between random or unrelated objects. This definition, though, already contains within it a specific point of view, an assumption of power. Who decides what is really related or unrelated? Who defines whether the relations between objects—or between events, or between spectacles of dominance across various contexts—are random and arbitrary?

In mainstream psychology, apophenia is called an "error of perception," in "the tendency to interpret random patterns as meaningful" (Hoopes 2011). But the people I write about here cultivate apophenia not as an "error" but as a way to begin seeing those things that have become invisible. They foreground the naturalized patterns that normally go without saying. It is in one sense an endless bricolage (Lévi-Strauss 1966), but rather than building something concrete from the "odds and ends" at hand, here the product is never finished; you select the part for the rush of its echo to another part. Here each found or revealed sign leads on to other resemblances, other openings.

People who feel uncanny conspiracy as a rush of the real pay close attention to parallels and resemblances between stories. And the parallels produce a feeling and an aesthetic sense of resonance. I argue that the resonance itself becomes another story. More than a story, too: the sense of uncanny resonance becomes an expressive modality, a vernacular theory of power, a way of seeing the world, an intimation of the way it all makes sense. It becomes both performance and theory, creating a sense of an occult design that might someday be apprehended below the jumbled surfaces of the ordinary. Accumulating and recursive images and the felt connections between them reveal how historical trauma gets lodged in the bright, broken bits of fantastic things.

I use the term *resonance* to mean the intensification produced by the overlapping, back-and-forth call of signs from various discourses. The uncanny narratives here acquire affect, intensity, and meaning through their resonance and dissonance with other more familiar cultural narratives, those that can seem like the inevitable shape of the real and that are less overtly marked as constructed narratives. Resonance describes the social, affective, and aesthetic dimension of a perspective based in apophenia, finding connections between signs and often understandings that process as political. Here those connections are based on resemblance and repetition. This effect entails mimesis; but the resemblance is partial and fluid. It is felt. And the intertextual connections feel vertically layered rather than horizontally bridged.

Resonance is not an exact reiteration. Rather it is something that strikes a chord, that inexplicably rings true, a sound whose notes are prolonged. It is the just-glimpsed connections and hidden structures that are felt to shimmer below the surface of things. It attunes to anxieties in the atmosphere (Stewart 2011). It is what makes people say, "Now it all fits together" and "Something just clicked" and "My whole life I just felt like something was going on, and this explains it."

ABDUCTIONS

People I met in Hillview and at UFO conferences in the Southwest in the 1990s often told the same origin story: it was about how their lives shifted into a register of thinking and talking about aliens when they discovered Whitley Strieber's 1987 book *Communion: A True Story*. Some people said just seeing the book changed their lives. (Strieber was already a successful writer of gothic fantasy fiction when he described his own weird alien abduction experiences in *Communion*.) The book flooded people with feelings and half-memories. Even before they identified with Strieber's strange narrative and its tone of anguished questing, the cover image struck people with the immediacy and intensity of revelation. It was the first time they saw a picture of that iconic alien face dominated by enormous black eyes like a giant insect, or like a Nazi in a gas mask, or a surgeon peering down at you as you veered in and out of awareness on the operating table. But also like none of those things exactly, not specifically one of them alone. People I met said it was that cover—and then the book—that made them remember things they had already known and, over time, forgotten.

Throughout that decade, alien abduction discourse intensified. People passed around battered paperbacks by Budd Hopkins telling abduction stories from his work with abductees. Hopkins's books widely circulated the now-familiar abduction narrative: how aliens come to your bedside, paralyze you, silence you, and float you out of the room and into their nightmarish clinical surgeries. His colleagues in abduction research added repeating elements: How "abductees commonly feel that data of some sort is being extracted from their minds" (Jacobs 1992, 97). How the aliens steal not just your thoughts and feelings but your eggs and sperm, the babies in your womb; how they put trackers up your nose, silently follow you year after year, so you can just feel that presence.

The image, the idea, the word, the story, struck a chord: *abduction* seemed instinctively, uncannily real. People felt an organizing convergence of a vaguely ominous sense. The word itself, *abducted*, with its Latinate sound and hard split as your lips pop between its consonants, was somehow more clinical and official than *kidnapped*, the *duct* inside it a rushing force, a channel that carries you away. *Abduction* expressed an overspilling sensation of captivity and containment by something you can't control; it communicated a feeling about the unseen forces that inscribed your mind and body . . . it just *made sense*, it *fit in* with what people said they had already known and felt. Some people acted on this feeling and underwent hypnosis with therapists sympathetic to the abduction experience to see if they might unearth a whole memory. Many people have, through hypnosis, recalled alien abduction. Many others remain in the liminal space where the haunting feeling of abduction brings together a nagging, familiar sense of a *something* that was already there.

You could say all that in different words, a new vocabulary, perhaps now, in words that make that same kind of intuitive sense to me. Another way of describing an image or idea that seems to organize a whole range of feelings and social experiences, that appears in stories of different kinds and links them together, that makes a pattern out of things you never before knew how to pull together is to see it as a trope. The more I heard over the years about things *just fitting together*, the more it seemed clear to me that abduction itself was a greatly capacious and affecting trope, one that was changeable and alive. It spoke to the nagging, unresolved underside of the dominant national trope, freedom.

And abduction was only half of it. The other half of abduction was release, the coming through containment to the other side.

Some people tried to reduce the stigma of UFO belief; as they put it, they wanted UFO investigations to "go mainstream." But other people identified with its marginality. The proliferating UFOs in television shows and movies and books didn't sit well with those who felt intuitively that UFOs belonged to the unincorporated realm of the *weird stuff*. They didn't want UFO belief to "go mainstream." And they didn't trust "science" to approach the mystery of UFOs without killing something irreducible in what that mystery meant to them. For these people, the fact that most *folks just didn't get it* was the point.[1]

Many people in American UFO discourse communities of the 1990s arranged their political, social, and emotional affinities not around ideas of a "left" or a "right" political wing but around ideas of invisible centers of power (Dean 2009). In this specific structure of feeling and imagination, the margins oppose that occult, sinister center, a black hole that invisibly sucks people into its gravitational pull. My closest friend in the UFO support group where I did fieldwork eventually drifted into a social world that actively sympathized with the militia movement. It was sometimes difficult to understand her support for right-wing militias along with her intense championship of gay rights and gender nonconformity. Many UFO believers plucked stances from both traditional right- and left-wing ideologies, relating not to traditional activist political lines but instead to a sense of distance from the powers that be (see Dean 2009, 1998). The prepper bookstore I visited in Nevada displayed militia manifestos and apocalypse-preparedness handbooks next to Noam Chomsky's *Manufacturing Consent*.

My friend Carla could smell appropriation and incorporation from miles away. She hated the way "the UFO thing is everywhere now." For Carla, talking about UFOs expressed her distance from a sinister power that tried to control ordinary people. The power came in various manifestations, emerging from bloody centuries of the past. As the powers that be, it was always present in some form. If you were not careful, it incorporated you into its zombified center where you could no longer think for yourself.

Carla had politicized her distance from the *powers that be* in a way that would soon itself become "mainstream" in populist public culture, forcing her to move on yet again. After a while she was no longer talking so fervently about UFOs, inner dimensions, or unusual spiritual experiences, but more and more about the New World Order, the threat of worldwide socialism, and the plots that global networks were secretly planning with then-attorney general Janet Reno, the Trilateral Commission, and wealthy powers that be across the brutalized body of the world. After a few more years, she left the UFO group and got caught up elsewhere. She and her new intellectual companions saw that the world as they knew it was ending.

Another community of uncanny storytellers emerged in central Nevada, a land of both drifters and homesteaders.[2] Rachel, Nevada, is a rural hamlet located on the border of the vast military-industrial complex of Nellis Air Force Bombing and Gunnery Range, the Nevada Test Site, and the secret military base called Groom Lake, or Area 51, the hugely funded dream of the Cold War come to life in the desert.[3] There, what you more vividly heard was the restless interplay between uncanny and ordinary stories. This was a place not just for "conspiracy theorists" but also for hardworking western people with strong community bonds, people who valued the decency of everyday accomplishments and had a fierce attachment to a legacy of independence. The inextricability of the uncanny and the ordinary expressed a particular blend of desire and nostalgia—a mix of otherworldly displacement and the deep specificity of a heavily textualized, lived-in place in the American West. The ways these discourses of settlement—uncanny and historical—came together suggested other kinds of anxiety about colonization and the earth, secrecy and theft, nature and loss, and the vulnerable boundaries of the human body. I had heard these same themes in Hillview.

The central meeting point in Rachel was a UFO-themed café called the Little A'Le'Inn. Joe, who owned the café with his wife, Pat, believed in many of the same things as my friend Carla from Hillview. Both Joe and Carla were charismatic storytellers with abandoned origins in charismatic churches. And they were both driven by the partial designs they saw: architectures of conspiracy, webs of the powers whose hidden strands you could tease out, a bit at a time, through talk. Like the other people I write about here, their sense of hidden meaning was an "occult cosmology," the term used by Todd Sanders and Harry West (2003, 6) to describe the "ontological dimensions" of covert systems; it was a cosmology expressing a vernacular theory of power.

Like Carla, Joe had always just felt it in his bones: *something was wrong*. And one day for him, too, he said, it "all clicked," it "all came together," "everything just made sense" as a plot by the powers that be. But Joe, who had a poor childhood, was now making a good living at his café. Though he liked to keep life simple, he owned his mobile home, and he had bought land. By midlife he was in a stable, long-term third marriage. Carla, by contrast, was moving around. She had nothing fixed in place but her convictions, her fierce intellect, and her ability to meet new people who, for a while, formed a world with her, based on a feeling that there was always *a something more*.

VULNERABILITIES

For some people, the ominous powers in the world came into sharpest relief as a coherent belief when the Bureau of Alcohol, Tobacco, Firearms and Explosives raided David Koresh's Branch Davidian compound in Waco, Texas, in 1993. The Waco incident crystallized an already-developed feeling of *how things are* and played out this sense of subterranean sinister developments in an overt, concrete display of government violence against civilians. There it was on the news: the government was killing people who did not toe the line. They could raid anyone who wanted to live the way they saw fit. The media was part of it, showing things in the news from only their own side. *They* demonized Koresh and let the government off the hook, keeping the public in a perpetual state of deception. It was maybe even worse than Ruby Ridge the year before, because now it seemed the government was going after not just overt independence and freedom but also spiritual belief.

The day of the fire in Waco, Carla called me in sorrow and outrage. I had been watching the television news about Koresh stockpiling weapons, but I was too stunned by the whole disaster to make any immediate judgment (although soon afterward I came to agree with Carla about the criminality of the raid there). "What do you *think?*" she asked, in a slow voice of controlled anger, testing me, testing my position on an invisible line. I did not yet know what I thought. She heard the newscaster brand the Branch Davidians a cult. She said:

What is a cult?
A cult is a culture.
A cult is a culture
That they don't like.
And she added:
We are supposed to have religious freedom in this country. . . .
It's all a lie.

For Carla, watching the Waco complex burn was at once a terrible revelation and a confirmation of what she already *just knew*: that unseen powers, consortia of the media, the government, and covert groups of the rich, elite, and powerful were intentionally testing the American people. In her view, they used a rumor of Koresh's crimes of sexual abuse to play on easy American sentiment. The Waco compound was a lethal *experiment* they conducted on ordinary people to see *what they could get away with*. And, she noted, they did get away with it. No one watching the news revolted. To Carla, and to many other people who thought like her, the Branch Davidian fire was a declaration of war by the powers that be.

There is much to say about the ways that such incidents, especially the raids on Ruby Ridge in 1992 and Waco (and to some extent before that, the 1986 bombing of MOVE in Philadelphia), helped catalyze militia movements and talk of the New World Order in the United States (see Fenster 2008; Barkun 2013; Sanders and West 2003). But here I want to focus on Carla's way of speaking, as a way into what she saw and felt in the discourse about Waco.

She said: *A cult is a culture !*—And this poetic register best expressed the truth. For Carla (and for many of her intellectual and political companions), it was vital to avoid being duped by the television anchor's authoritatively referential register, which he used to intone about Koresh. Listening with her point of view in mind, you can hear it with ears attuned to the pervasive performance of power. The voice of the news broadcaster was a monologic appropriation, a performance that justified *their* actions by claiming the singular point of view.

This referential-based register—the performance style of the powers that be—denied the hidden, piled-up connections between things in favor of painting a lulling picture of rational cause and effect. But perhaps you could discover the deep structure of things in verbal parallelism and hints of hidden relationships. *They* rationalized their violence by calling Koresh's group a "cult," defining it in a totalizing move. But attending to the verbal resemblance between *cult* and *culture* gave Carla the insight that what *they* called a "cult" was in fact a coherent entity of meanings and traditions, which is what she thought of as a "culture." The Koresh compound was an autonomous culture that deserved its own sovereignty—but one that the authorities did not like. Noticing the parallel between the words *cult* and *culture* allowed her this swift insight into the validity of difference.

Just as there are overlaps between various sources of power, then—among the media and the government and other hidden groups—there are resonating overlaps in words. You glimpsed a grammar of "the real" here, through iconicities of language. *Culture* containing *cult* pointed to a larger etymology of things beyond language itself, a structure glinting through the words that represented it. Cult and culture clicked. For Carla there was always a sense of the inextricably poetic and political hidden structure in the world. There really was no separating the poetic from the political.

RESONANT APOPHENIA

But what was abducted from a person, and who was doing it? What in the experience of power fit so well with stories of uncanny abducting forces? What is the inarticulate and half-forgotten material that adds the resonant urgency and feeling of depth to stories of alien abduction and uncanny conspiracy? Though it is never a one-to-one kind of symbol, the accumulated stories that point to a forgotten *something* do suggest what that something might be. There are stories of class and its invisible, unmarked limitations; and stories of race and gender; and stories of the small, multiple ways that a life is disappointed by master narratives of progress and success. There are stories of nuclear fear, resonating in scattered and displaced effects within everyday life, the "psychic effect" that Joseph Masco (2006) has illuminated as the "nuclear uncanny." There are stories of the federal government's mid-twentieth-century experiments on poor people: giving children plutonium-laced cereal, feeding them radioactive snacks after luring them to join the Science Club at school, and giving pregnant hospitalized women plutonium in what were said to be vitamins (Welsome 1999). There are images of the body's containment in what feel like strange new medical developments, cloning, and surrogate pregnancies of poor women for rich women. There are images here that echo the medical experiments done in Nazi concentration camps. There are images of slaves in America, of the Middle Passage in a strange ship going to a strange new world. There are images of centuries of colonial genocide of Native American people, abductions into boarding schools and reservations, in a quick afterimage that flashes in the cowboys and Indians movie that you went to as a white kid decades ago, when for a second you rooted for the wrong side and did not register anything except a feeling of *something wrong*. . . . Linked up with the variable infinite experience of class, race, gender, and loss, it is the parallels between these stories about power that *become the subject* of many uncanny stories. The original stories of historical trauma do not always make it up for air. (If they did, they would no longer haunt.)

Instead, the uncanny story itself is about the resemblances between the unspoken originals. The urge toward apophenia begins to resonate and hum. And that resonance is something to notice too, because it is a story of power on its own.

RESONANT CONSPIRACIES

Some guys were working on our house in Hillview, and Junior, the handyman with a missing leg, was going progressively insane. It took me days to notice that anything might be amiss, because it seemed everyone was talking about things from other worlds. Junior's smart, pragmatic partner Eddy came into the kitchen because he was thirsty; he talked about his dreams of going underground, about storing what you need down there to survive when this government shit hits the fan. Eddy said he was planning to buy *invisible land*. It was chitchat while he drank instant iced tea at the table.

But Junior was really unraveling. He'd seen the saucers in the desert himself; he'd seen them spin into underground bases. He implied unspeakable dangers. At the kitchen table, he drew diagrams, charts and graphs, and quick loops and loops of the spinning. But to some extent these were the same stories and the same kinds of drawings I knew from ordinary, very sane people who were into UFOs—city employees who entered data in clean white offices, busy mothers, short-order cooks, secretaries, and tech workers—people who had no mental illness. The UPS man, hearing about my interest in UFO stories, stood on the porch and described seeing a UFO as a kid. "Man, it just took off, just like that." Talking about this was part of a discursive world, and it did not mean one lived outside the ordinary boundaries of quotidian, practical life.

But then Junior said *they* stole his leg because he knew too much. *It's a warning*. Next, he said, they would take his life. He became aware of sinister electronic codes. These were tones that would kill whoever heard the right combination. He beeped the lethal sequences into his phone and pager, thinking he could kill the sinister listener on the other end by remote control. We could overhear the poor guy Junior had called, yelling, "Hello? Hello?" to the sound of the pushbutton beeps, and when the beeps didn't kill the guy, Junior grumbled, *Jeez, nothing works anymore.*

My housemate and I hastily drove Junior to his brother's house across town. It was his only family. We explained to the sister-in-law what had happened and advised her to get Junior some help. We thought we'd done what we could for Junior, telling his family about his spiraling down, figuring they'd find a way to save him. But a couple of days later he stolidly walked the five miles back to our house, in the hot southern sun, on his one leg. The stump was bloody and sore over the prosthetic. There was obviously nowhere left for him to go.

But what makes me remember Junior forever is this: he brought me a gift when he returned. It was a filthy, single nylon leg cut off from a pair of panty hose. He said it would help make a powerful tea; herbs brewed inside this stocking would cure you of anything and give you perfect health. *Cures everything*, he promised.

We stood outside the house with its still unfinished work. I accepted the single magic stocking that unfurled and flapped in the slight breeze like a tiny shadow of a perfect leg as he limped off on his missing one; and I do in fact remember him by it. I remember him limping and fretting about *them* and the powers that be, and wonder at the other, missing life—the potential, the phantom life, what was once supposed to be but had never existed. . . . And there are plot fragments here that ache like phantom limbs, the resonating of something that lives on in the imagination, whether or not it once was really there.

....

Intricate hidden structures, traumatic abductions, and immobilizing powers are the ground tropes for uncanny conspiracy theories. But what makes a conspiracy a "theory?" When it comes to the powers that be, any conspiracy you find is always incomplete, always still a theory.

Something is wrong, but no one knows what. No one talks about power as class in these stories, nor national foundation of slavery and genocide at the base of American colonization; but disturbing free-floating afterimages of enslavement and colonization remain, flashes of historical abductions gathering in distorted forms, in discourses from people with no direct birthright to those traumatic histories. Uncanny conspiracies find cracks in the order of things, then wedge themselves into those cracks and shape them with the resonance of other stories.

On the sliding American uncanny landscape, the real is not what you can finally prove but what you just know—that aliens are burning the world in ire. Or that you are an alien yourself, or a hybrid. Or that you have a child out there somewhere who was tracked and ripped from your body. They are tracking you with an implant in your brain. They stole your eggs and sperm. They leave their signs in body scars that have no ordinary source. There are signs that won't close in on referents, in spreading terrors of invasion. One day you are pregnant, the next day that baby is just gone. They stole it. They take you out of bed while you're still sleeping. They put foreign things inside you—embryos and half-born thoughts—then rob them back. We can't see them, but they see us; they know where we are at every minute of every day.

And—"I don't know what's going on," says Fern, "but I know it is not right. *They* don't care about human rights."

These accounts of the body's inhuman invasion and the earth's unnatural violation open into more stories, conspiracy theories, perhaps, which also unfold around omniscience and defilement.

In 1996, a few months before the group suicide of the religion known as Heaven's Gate, which took the Hale-Bopp comet as a sign of the impending end of the world, people across the country were calling late-night uncanny talk radio, saying a comet is heading straight for us, and behind that comet is a terrible thing four times the size of our planet, a thing made of metal and mud and guided by intelligent eyes. It will swallow us up, and *they know*; their scientists have the data in secret logs. And *they* have underground bases filled with crashed ships. *They* make deals with the aliens. *They* offered us up as guinea pigs; *they* are watching and *they* know . . . until the alien *they* and the government *they* converge into an allegorically felt figure of unseen power and agency, an overwritten, unfinalized *they* who invade and track ordinary experience from oblique, omniscient heights.

The uncanny late-night radio show, hosted by Art Bell from his home in "the Nevada desert," flourished and became a hit. Everyone knew his talk about the escalating signs of apocalypse, what he called "the quickening." *They* were outed on his show in the voices of 4:00 a.m. insomniacs bursting with elaborate theories of the universe and signs of the world's destruction. *They* know the earth is whispering its last breath under radiation and piles of trash.

Look around. Listen, the callers said, hearing their voices go out across a nation. You know they are hoarding secret piles of bubonic plague to spread on the population. It's time to prepare. The frogs are deformed, born without legs, or with extra legs that are withered and useless. There are uncanny limbs that show what's going to vanish. They are crawling now from the cleanest headwaters. The pelicans are dying because the fish they eat are poison. I heard the manatees are going, and the honeybees are dying out too, and soon the other insects will follow; and there will be no more food. The invasion is sneaking in the borders of the earth and penetrating the margins of the body with clinical ease. And they are building themselves mansions and resorts underground where they will be safe and hiding the truth from us.

Fern was my friend in Hillview who got the feeling *there was more going on*. She started to *make connections*. She had been getting restless and wary as more and more things she knew were becoming incorporated by them. She emailed me:

Dear Susan,

There is so much going on that you have to be careful. Are you sure you want to find this out? They are devious and brilliant and work through lies and deceit. They were back in Biblical times, they caused the fall in the garden. Their greatest accomplishment is to convince people that they do not exist. I think they've taken over the world monetary and political system. . . . The thugs in this world who push us tax-slaves around and make laws that only apply to us—not to them. . . . They are using mind-control technology perfected through CIA programs . . . through TV, and movies—in *Independence Day* notice how everyone comes together and obeys the government. We are being set up for a fake extraterrestrial invasion. They will use the Blue Beam and other technologies to scare people to death and make them accept world-wide socialism. World money will be issued, and a global police force will enforce their orders. Yes, we really have been invaded, but since "they" are guiding the education system, the media and the field of psychiatry, they make the rules. Little people like me are discounted—I'm a crackpot. But this is what I think is really happening. Watch for a fake "invasion." . . . The ones who aren't fooled by it have places prepared for them in "collection centers" and new prisons all over. . . . This is scary stuff, are you sure you want to go any further?

There are plot fragments here that leave trails, the ghosts of peripherally glimpsed effects of power, desire, and fear. It was hard to know whether they illuminated dangers no one wanted to see, or whether, in all their intensified distortions, they made those dangers easier to ignore.

NOTES

Acknowledgment: This chapter is adapted from my book, *The Resonance of Unseen Things: Poetics, Power, Captivity and UFOs in the American Uncanny* (Ann Arbor: University of Michigan Press, 2016).

1 Hillview is a fictional name for the town where I met UFO experiencers. I have changed the names and at times the identifying details of people I knew from the Hillview UFO Experiencers Support Group and in its parent group, the Mutual UFO Network (MUFON). MUFON is an international organization whose mission is to make UFOs a credible topic of scientific investigation, and Hillview has an active chapter. There were some intellectual and strategic differences between the two local groups in Hillview (though people often participated in both), but the Experiencers Support Group was my primary ethnographic home base in the overlapping Hillview UFO worlds. I did fieldwork in these groups, though primarily in the support group, for a total of two years; and I maintained friendships with a few members for many years afterward.

2 I first went to Rachel in 1997. I do not use a false name for the town of Rachel (nor for the owners of the café there) as I do for Hillview and its citizens, because Rachel is already public, a well-known destination for UFO tourism.

3 Although the US government finally admitted its existence in 2013, Area 51 in the 1990s was, literally, an enormous open secret: four million acres of unacknowledged bomb range (Patton 1998). In the 1990s and early 2000s, as uncanny stories of the government hiding UFOs were accumulating and thickening in the air, Area 51 was just beginning to grow notorious beyond the world of conspiracy talk. There were regular organized protests at the base demanding the release of information. But before the era of social media, the scale of the mass-organized attempt to "Storm Area 51" that began on Facebook in the summer of 2019—and then the rapid transformation of that joyful fury into a Burning Man-type music festival called Alienstock—would have been impossible and inconceivable.

DEMETRA KASIMIS

_____

08 THE PLAY OF CONSPIRACY IN PLATO'S *REPUBLIC*

Does the *Republic* depict a conspiracy? The ostensible impetus for discussing profound political change behind closed doors is a desire to discuss the meaning of justice, not to replace a political order with a new one. But the dialogue takes place during the Peloponnesian War, when fears of plots sporadically consumed an eroding Athenian democracy. Arguments about political instability and instances of plotting reverberate throughout the dialogue that takes shape in this suspicious climate. Whether Socrates makes us privy to a conversation about a political world that does not exist or presents us with a strategy for talking about revolution undetected remains unresolved. I argue that Athenian fears of secret power and revolution express themselves in the style and arguments of the *Republic* and suggest that already at the origins of democratic practice, critics like Plato were concerned with theorizing the subtleties of democratic erosion.

At first glance, Plato may seem like a surprising figure to enlist in this volume's efforts to probe links among democracy, conspiracy, and critical theory. Famous for writing works like the *Republic*, which criticizes democracy, endorses government mendacity, and praises rational discourse, Plato is still routinely credited more for providing arguments against democracy, political upheaval, and epistemic confusion than he is for offering salutary explorations of these urgent themes.

Yet Plato sets the so-called founding text of Western political theory in a classical Athenian world beset with conspiratorial plots, public mistrust, and instability. And like the "critical theory" outlined in the editors' introduction to this volume, the conversations that Plato writes onto this democratic context distrust "surface forms in favor of excavating depths" and revealing "greater truths" (this volume 10). A conspiratorial atmosphere also frames the narrative action. The *Republic*, after all, is Socrates's first-person account of a long night he spent with other men designing a regime radically different from the democracy in which they live. The apparent impetus for that conversation, however, is a desire to explore the meaning of justice, not to replace a real political order with a new one. Yet Plato's framing casts a specter of plotting over the dialogue nonetheless: the private, secluded, and nocturnal setting inside a home infuses the group's activity with a "quasi-illicit" quality, gives the meeting "the look of conspiracy," and evokes circumstances that Plato's fourth-century BCE readers would have recognized as the initiation of a potential "coup" (Ober 1998, 221; Zuckert 2009, 429–430; Ferrari 2000, xii; see also Strauss [1964] 1978).[1] That Plato sets the *Republic* in a conspiratorial atmosphere is widely acknowledged, but what is the actual significance of this framing for the meaning of the text? What heuristic possibilities does a "conspiratorial" reading of the *Republic* offer contemporary theory?

In this chapter, I argue that the *Republic* enacts the "speculative appraisals" of a conspiratorial democratic climate (this volume 13). I show how, in Plato's hands, theory emerges from a scene that not only belongs to a political moment of conspiratorial possibility but is *itself* impossible to distinguish from a conspiracy. I propose that the *Republic* offers us the instructive insight that democratic instability is not just a problem to solve but a starting point for a particularized as well as a general analysis of politics in which conspiracy is a permanent question for the study and practice of democracy, if not all regimes.

To develop this argument, I foreground the sense of conspiratorial possibility subtending the dialogue and connect the conspiratorial atmosphere to the instances of collective plotting and conspiratorial thinking that emerge from it. I argue that these rhetorical and doctrinal elements work together to produce the *Republic*'s "play of conspiracy." With "the play of conspiracy," I mean to establish an interpretive frame for capturing the performative, allusive, and dynamic senses in which a topos of conspiracy operates in Plato's text, none of which are unserious or trifling.[2] First, *performative* refers to the *Republic*'s staging and dramatic action, which enact a potential conspiracy the way a play might. Insofar as this enactment fails to establish a conspiracy with any certainty, however, I argue that the *Republic* is only ever "alluding" (*ad* "toward" + *ludere* "to play") to an illicit activity. Second, this *allusiveness*, or playing at a conspiracy, invites us to hold open, rather than to reconcile, two different interpretations of the dialogue's impetus the whole time we read. Finally, instead of my suggesting that it is either rhetorical features, such as staging, *or* doctrinal concerns, such as the dialogue's conspiratorial proposals, that establish a topos of conspiracy, I read the *Republic* through its "dynamic" interplay of the rhetorical and doctrinal registers. Foregrounding this dynamism enables me to treat the conspiratorial proposals of the dialogue as emanations of the distrustful and eroding democratic realities in which they are imagined and voiced.[3]

This argument—that analyzing the *Republic*'s play of conspiracy holds the key to unlocking its instructive insights into plotting and democratic decay—is due in no small part to the fact that Plato pulls his fourth-century audience back into the recent Peloponnesian War (431–404 BCE), a time of increasing polarization, waning confidence in democratic institutions, and mounting public concern over real and perceived plots against democracy (Roisman 2006, 68; Carugati 2019).[4] A conversation that recommends the routinization of collective deception by the ruling class in order to keep the regime just and stable over time takes shape, in other words, against an Athenian backdrop in which plotting and instability have become everyday political concerns. Socrates finds that the best deterrence against the dissent, faction, and instability that enable conspiracies by revolutionaries is a series of conspiratorial acts performed by wise and just rulers. Yet he finally admits that none of these efforts could, in practice, eliminate the possibility for change and regime breakdown.[5] Even the *kallipolis*, a regime expressly designed to achieve stability at all costs, would begin to succumb to corruption as soon as the rigged marriage "lottery" was improperly administered by the guardian class (546a). Restored to the convulsive political realities of their Athenian setting, these arguments for arresting change and preventing *stasis* through plotting no longer simply reflect the peculiar needs of the ideal city. They double as creative and immanently Athenian responses to a suspicious democratic world that had "never before" experienced "such peril" from the inside.[6] Seen through this interplay of form and content, the dialogue's core arguments take on new meaning: they offer a still-relevant cautionary tale about the fantasy, particularly alluring in unstable and conspiratorial times, of designing a constitution to stop change and dissent once and for all.

Here, a few words about how I understand conspiracy may be in order. My working and flexible definition is inspired by everyday political usage to refer to a secret collaboration whose participants share an agenda to acquire or maintain political power. This means that "conspiracy" does not carry an exclusively insurgent or illicit valence, though this is certainly the sense invoked by the performative features of the *Republic*, as readers have noted. "Conspiracy" also functions polemically in political speech to refer to the covert activity a government may undertake to resist social change and conserve power, purportedly in the name of justice and stability.[7] I propose that we think of the plotting that the *Republic*'s characters recommend for the just city in this light. The interpretive choice to call these activities "conspiratorial" rather than merely secretive or deceptive has the benefit of capturing, rather than obscuring, the collective dimension that Plato gives the guardians' machinations. For while a conspiracy may require secrecy to achieve its ends, it is not the same as a secret or a deception as such. Neither a secret nor a lie has to be shared.

This brings me to the final sense of conspiracy that I see at work in the *Republic*. So long as a conspiracy must remain hidden to accomplish the aims of its practitioners, its signs may, in practice, appear indeterminate to those on its outside. The secret clubs of elite men who gathered in private houses like the one in the *Republic* were organizations for political networking within Athenian democracy, as I elaborate below. But they also, from time to time, coordinated to overthrow democracy in Athens. For this reason, their gatherings could, especially in times of crisis, provoke rumors and accusations of plotting, even in the absence of additional or certain proof. A convincing narration of a conspiracy in real time would therefore need to convey this indeterminacy while provoking a desire in the reader to decipher it. To say that the *Republic* invites us to confront the ambiguity of a real-time conspiracy, however, is not to call Plato a conspiracy theorist or to claim that his text produces meaning conspiratorially. I do not advance a version of Leo Strauss's (1941) argument that Plato's writing style hides his (or Socrates's) true ideas between the lines, whether to avoid "persecution" or to reach the very few able to decode his hints. Rather, my performative reading suggests that the *Republic* enacts the indeterminacy of a yet-to-be-proven conspiracy in plain sight. To take seriously the illicit staging, then, is to see that it is impossible to settle, once and for all, whether Socrates is relaying an innocent conversation about a political world that could not exist or presenting a strategy for talking undetected about a practicable revolutionary conspiracy. The claim that he joined with other men to find "an example of a good city in speech" might just as easily sound like an alibi—the group stayed up all night for the sake of (the) argument, nothing more (427d–e).

The stakes of this reading for the history of political thought and for the contemporary study of political erosion are not insignificant. Modern readers are accustomed to downplaying the suspiciousness pervading the registers of the *Republic*, but there is little reason to presume Plato's initial audience would have. Plato wrote the *Republic* (ca. 375 BCE) during a period of new democratic stability following Athens's defeat in the Peloponnesian War, its five constitutional transitions, and its descent into civil war. He and his readers were deeply familiar with the polarization, mistrust, plotting, and periodically open violence that had characterized Athenian democracy just a few decades earlier. Socrates had been tried and executed as part of this political context. Yet many Athenians at the time of the *Republic*'s dissemination seem to have hoped that the postwar redesign of the democracy's constitution, which granted law and legislation a central role in mediating conflict, had successfully resolved the deep conflicts of the past (Carawan 2013; Carugati 2019). The *Republic* suggests otherwise. Plato returns his readers to the problems of the recent past precisely because they point to the potential problems of the future. Erosion, and the plotting that often attends it, may not be uniquely democratic problems from the *Republic*'s vantage point. But if the endemic and underlying condition of every "real" polis is conflict, as the dialogue suggests, then Athenian confidence in the postwar solution to *stasis* was dangerously impairing. For like any real-world regime, Athenian democracy still harbored the conditions of its own degeneration.

The chapter proceeds by exploring the Athenian dynamics of democratic erosion in the period of the *Republic*'s setting. I suggest that conspiracies, both real and perceived, were generated by and generative of an erosion of public confidence that made coups in Athens viable. Subsequent sections adopt this sense of the *Republic*'s context as a lens for reconsidering aspects of its rhetorical dimensions and arguments. I show how these features of the text can be read as vehicles for analyzing democratic dynamics of instability and attempts at influencing Plato's fourth-century audience. I conclude by suggesting that if an imperiled, plot-ridden, and uncertain democratic context is not "mere" background to the so-called founding text of political theory but the catalyst for its arguments, then a conspiratorial reading of the *Republic* has the power to unsettle the familiar terms in which thinkers typically approach the question of political decay today.

CONSPIRATORIAL FRAMING
AND FOLDED TIME

Scholarship on the *Republic* regularly acknowledges that the text stops short of incorporating allusions to the period right after the Peloponnesian War, when the Thirty, a Spartan-backed junta that came to power without stealth or struggle, imposed violent, tyrannical rule over the city (404–403 BCE).[8] At the same time, readers tend to adopt the impending regime collapse as an explanation for the *Republic*'s conspiratorial mood, which is assumed to establish dramatic irony for a fourth-century reader.[9] There are some good reasons for holding these views. The reign of the Thirty entangled many of the figures in the *Republic.* Socrates's reputation suffered from his exchanges with oligarchic sympathizers, which made him vulnerable to accusations of forbidden political activity associated with plotting. Athenians tried and executed him, unofficially at least, for guilt by association with a former student, Critias, who was Plato's relative and a member of the Thirty. As Ferrari (2003, 11) argues, Plato is "certainly at pains to lay the shadow of the Thirty and its bloody failure over the *Republic*'s opening pages, most obviously by staging the discussion at the house of Cephalus. Both sons of this wealthy metic were to suffer under the Thirty, with Polemarchus murdered for his money and Lysias escaping into exile."

Athenian readers encountering the *Republic* decades later would have known this recent history. They would also have known that the historical figures Plato puts in the home that night ended up on opposite sides of the *stasis* that divided the city during the coup of 404–403. They would have recognized, in other words, that the hypothetical plot to found the *kallipolis* was hatched by, or at least conceived in the presence of, an ideologically diverse group of soon-to-be suspected conspirators, oligarchic sympathizers, and pro-democrats.[10] Although the *Republic* is not the only Platonic text to resemble the sorts of meetings convened by aristocratic fellowships (*hetaireiai, synōmotai*), its approximation to one is especially charged because the dialogue concerns the alteration and founding of a polis.[11]

In Athens, these informal "dining or drinking clubs of congenial men, usually of roughly the same age and social standing" were "small enough to plan or act in confidence" because they gathered in private houses (Connor 1971, 26, 27).[12] While these meetings were not "essentially or inevitably political, still less conspiratorial" early in the Peloponnesian War, they came under increasing suspicion of fomenting oligarchic revolution and, as the war dragged on, did in fact facilitate "sedition, assassination, and conspiracy to overthrow the government" (27). Yet, as Nicholas F. Jones (1999) argues, the "antithesis between innocent socializing and subversive conspiratorial political machination may be a false one." It is not clear that associations belonging to the aristocratic elite, who "had predominately oligarchical ideological tendencies," were ever "in any sense nonpolitical" (226–27). But by the time of Athens's failed campaign to Sicily in 415, a period to which the *Republic*'s setting alludes, demagogues had come to emphasize the oligarchic associations of the *hetaireiai* as a way of stoking citizen fears of radicalization and plotting.

The conventional view that the *Republic* winks at a real conspiracy only to distance Socrates from it is therefore supported, on the one hand, by the scene's approximation to an *hetaireia* and, on the other hand, by the diverse range of political leanings of the characters and the "merely" philosophical impetus for their discussion. For Strauss (1978), this ambiguous framing was Plato's way of suggesting that the difference between a private, philosophical discussion and an antidemocratic plot could be easy (if not strategically useful) to elide in moments of democratic crisis. As Socrates claims in Plato's *Apology*, he socialized with antidemocratic conspirators but condemned their plots and beliefs. Yet this tension—that Socrates disparaged politicized private meetings while nevertheless celebrating private exchange about political questions (36b)—also made it impossible for him to dispel definitively the rumors that linked him to the Thirty's machinations.

One effect of the standard view of this ambiguous framing, then, is to mark the scene's difference (as presented in the *Republic*) from that form of potential illicit power. The setting, ideologically diverse characters, and utopian goals of the dialogue function, on this view, to reopen the gap Athenian politics closed between a theoretical conversation and a revolutionary plot and to present that disparity as an object of interpretation and contestation. But this approach does not attend to Plato's use of folded time, which establishes the text's historical setting through asynchronic references. As Debra Nails (2002, 325) has carefully shown, Plato "presents a series of reactions to the Athenian democracy that characterize a period from the beginning of the war through its formal end in 404—not a snapshot."[13] Textual allusions to persons, places, and events point to different, incommensurate years during a thirty-year period. The narrator reenacts a single night's conversation, of course, but he establishes the setting for that conversation by calling to mind historical events figuring different chronologies as if they were contemporaneous with each other. Readers can *assume* beginning and end points, in other words, but any effort to use some textual details to fix the action to a specific historical year immediately renders others anachronistic.

That the *Republic* does not provide a historical recording of a singular moment in fifth-century Athens, however, does not mean that its being set in that time provides no specific interpretive context or produces no political content in its own right. M. M. Bakhtin ([1981] 2008, 84–85) used the term *chronotope* to denote the way narratives construct their own "time space" by assimilating isolated aspects of "real historical time." As Carol Atack (2020, 16) writes, "Plato uses the reversals of Athenian politics at the end of the Peloponnesian War and the trial and execution of Socrates to generate an unreal kind of time for his dialogues, subject to acceleration and deceleration, temporal collapses and incursions, and, with its moments of stillness, resistant to linear narrativization." A feature of Plato's writing more generally, this blurring of time is an "affective" and historical way of constructing meaning: Plato's style expresses a "sense of political and social crisis" that produces "a distinctive experience of temporality, the recognition of a foreshortened future" (11, 12).

But asynchronicity and unverifiability also work to specific political effect when analyzed alongside the rhetorical features and thematic concerns of the *Republic*. I argue in the next section that in the chronotope of the *Republic*, an open-ended and anxious democratic world is animated by a private conversation focused on regime change. In this Athens, private discussions are suspected to double as plots to overtake democracy. Plato's general use of folded time produces some uncertainty and disorder in the reader, but this disorientation is also an affective feature of democratic erosion in particular.

SUSPICIOUSNESS, PLOTTING, AND DEMOCRATIC UNCERTAINTY IN ATHENS

In 415, the Athenians decided to invade Sicily under the command of Alcibiades. To support the doomed venture and ensure that a larger number of poor citizens would have access to arms, the Athenian assembly made an unprecedented commitment to taxing the propertied. Some wealthy citizens saw the decision and the impending Sicilian expedition as a bellwether of the poor's increasing influence over democratic politics. In this climate of shifting dynamics, two events took on particular political significance: the mutilation of the Herms, sacred stone images that populated public spaces in Athens; and the circulation of rumors that some men, including Alcibiades, had parodied the Eleusinian mysteries in private homes (Thuc. 6.27.1–29.3, 53.1–2, 60.1–61.7; Andoc. I.11–70). These transgressions appeared to some Athenians as signs of antidemocratic sentiment, if not outright oligarchic plotting, and the demos took preventive action in response (Thuc. 6.53, 6.60). The council appointed a commission of inquiry to investigate the events, with the assembly offering a reward to citizens and noncitizens who could identify perpetrators.

A culture of increasing distrust took over the city. Athenians were "always in fear" and perceived everything "suspiciously" (Thuc. 6.53.3).[14] In this state, "recalling everything they knew by hearsay [akoē] on the subject [of past tyrannies]," the people "grew cruel [chalepos]," Thucydides writes, and they convinced themselves that the events around the Sicilian expedition were part of an "oligarchic and tyrannical conspiracy [synōmosia]" (Thuc. 6.60.2).[15] Once exposure and accusation based on weak evidence, if not rumor, came to constitute the activity of a judicious demos protecting its rule from the disaffected, guilt could, and often did, adhere to anyone who refrained from making denouncements (Thuc. 3.82.4–5; 8.66).

In the years of the *Republic*'s setting, the demos sought to avert regime collapse by exposing hidden acts. The signs of conspiracy, however, were not "the scandals" (of the Herms or the Profanation of the Mysteries) themselves, which transpired in the dark, but rumors and hearsay accounts—the sort of reporting that, in the absence of further investigation, amplified doubt and fear. The demos's injunction to provide, in public, reports about speech (in some cases heard to have been) performed elsewhere suggests that speculation came to supplant the familiar practice of "actively listening to and judging the merits of complex, competing arguments" that distinguishes democracy as a regime (Ober 1989, 79). As power was perceived to permeate, if not wholly reside in, the dark and interior spaces of a democratic city, the need to rely in public on what was said in private grew, eventually foreclosing the forms of political speech and contestation thought to constitute democracies in particular. An unstable democracy, deeply distrusting and invested in its own impotence, attempted to reconsolidate itself by means that accelerated the conditions of its own erosion.

It is within this climate that the oligarchs briefly suspended Athenian democracy in 411. Thucydides alleges that, unlike the later junta of the Thirty, secret clubs (*synōmosiai*) coordinated to overthrow democracy in this case, following a two-step plan that included public intimidation and political propaganda (8.47–48.2; 8.54.4; 8.65).[16] Aristotle invokes these events when arguing that deceit (*apatē*) causes a change in regime from the inside: a faction legally and strategically manipulates a democracy's institutions, and, finding no resistance to its efforts, circumscribes the citizenry's power to rule. In Athens, he explains, conspirators tricked the demos into "consenting to a change" to their own constitution, an alteration that was subsequently maintained through force, which, he says, is the other way *stasis* can come about (*Pol.* 1304b; see also Thuc. 8.65–66). Thus, while the Athenian assembly and council continued to meet after their decision to place power in the hands of five thousand men, they were in reality controlled by the conspirators (Aristotle 1996, xxx–xxxiii).

READING THE *REPUBLIC* IN A CONSPIRATORIAL MOOD

The previous sections trained attention on the *Republic*'s chronotope to privilege the volatile and conspiratorial political realities of the narrative's time-space over the tyranny and regime collapse that lie outside it. This different approach constitutes the hermeneutic horizon in which I engage the *Republic* here. Such recontextualizing, along with the serious attention to rhetorical structure it entails, enables me to show that the *Republic* figures the conspiratorial in ways that exceed its much-noted setting to unexpected interpretive effect: an unreliable, informing narrator; a plot relayed as hearsay; an unverifiable historical timeframe; an unidentified addressee; reported dialogue; and, within that dialogue, the fantasy that a just regime would work ideally, stably, and most effectively if the ruling class's machinations remained hidden from the public through the dissemination of a big, founding lie, which is but one of the many conspiratorial mechanisms the group advocates using during the night.[17]

In her reading of the *Republic*, Arlene Saxonhouse (2009, 731) notes that "we do not know who the audience is for the long, long speech of Socrates. It certainly must be someone willing to listen to all ten books without apparent stop."[18] She then pauses to ask, "Is the *Republic* the long answer to his wife's question: 'Where were you last night?' What would it do to our reading of the dialogue if we read it as a sheepish excuse for a long night of carousing?" (731). For Saxonhouse, the underappreciated matter of the unspecified addressee is one way the *Republic* draws our attention to the narrative's multiple meanings. Though she has a domestic infelicity in mind, her proposal bears on the question of conspiracy. One effect of the unknown audience, Saxonhouse suggests, is that it gives us reason to suspect the philosophical conversation might constitute an alibi for something (more) illicit.

I argued earlier that the folded time of the narrative tropes the uncertain atmosphere of Athenian democracy during the Peloponnesian War. The narrator's unspecified addressee and reporting style work with that chronotope to establish the unreliable informant's account of a private nighttime gathering.[19] Whether read or recited, in other words, the recollected dialogue of the *Republic* also belongs to the category of *akoē*, the hearsay reporting that, according to Thucydides, dominated democratic politics in moments of crisis, threatening to overtake a different kind of *akoē* as a sign of citizenship, namely, the public speech heard and judged in the assembly and law courts. From this angle, it is not only the setting of the text but also the form of the narrative that evokes the political tendencies of its atmosphere, in which an increasingly anxious demos came to treat uncertain testimony as evidence of conspiracy. For, what the narrator conveys cannot really serve as empirical or corroborating proof for something that "really" happened. Yet, in taking us behind the scenes of a plot with no sense of who might be listening in, the narrative simultaneously draws critical attention to the inadvertent, messy circulation of rumor to which it is contributing. The practice of evaluating existing relations of power and imagining new ones is performed by an informant in a conspiratorial mode. The narrative conditions that cannot alleviate doubt thus do more than provoke suspicion. They provide the terrain for analyzing democratic flux, and its attendant atmosphere, in immanently critical terms.

Explicit instances of conspiratorial thinking are frequent in the dialogue's elaboration of the structure of the *kallipolis* and its susceptibility to failure. That such thinking might reflect the suspicious mood of its setting rather than simply the peculiar needs of the *kallipolis* is perhaps clearest in Book VII's cave allegory (514b). The much-studied passage constitutes Socrates's last attempt to explain the rulers' education in philosophy, requiring of the group that they imagine the fundamental conditions of reality to be constructed and maintained by puppeteers. When we stress the underappreciated point that Socrates presents this allegory as a *more* accessible way to explain the study of the good to his Athenian audience, we see how conspiratorial thinking is not only a strategic necessity for the *kallipolis* but also a familiar (Athenian) expression of a conspiratorial mindset.

The literal terms denoting a conspiracy (*synōmosia*) and an aristocratic fellowship (*hetaireia*), however, appear only once in the *Republic*. The references are crucial nevertheless because they lay out the basic parameters of the text's subsequent and wide-ranging concern with plots. In particular, they introduce conspiracy as a permanent feature of political life (even for the just city). They appear in Book II, before the dialogue has turned to a discussion of the *kallipolis*. Adeimantus aims to clarify how Athenians typically understand and practice justice. He parrots a conventional young man who believes a mere "reputation for justice" brings a "wonderful life" and advocates forming "secret clubs [*synōmosias*] and societies [*hetaireiai*]" to gain political influence and to shape the perceptions of others (365b–c, 365d; see *Ap.* 36b). His remarks insinuate that a quotidian practice of clandestine politicking does not so much endanger as preserve Athenian ideas about politics. Democracies may claim to constitute themselves through public acts of speech, but they also condone, by defining themselves against, private gatherings that risk (being mistaken for) becoming cabals.

A permanent interplay would seem to pertain between what is said *es meson* (to the middle) and what is said behind closed doors. That one of the major claims of the dialogue—justice consists in being, not seeming, just—emerges partly in response to this critical depiction of Athenian life deserves attention. For, despite the attempt to distance its own Athenian gathering from a political meeting by denouncing the latter, the dialogue does not go on to ban secret plotting from the *kallipolis*. Nor do the characters claim that collusion may be peculiar to democracies. The discussion maintains instead that large-scale practices of political deception will be necessary for organizing a new political world and deterring the *stasis* that (unauthorized) conspiracies typically signify.

The *kallipolis* will retool this dynamic to serve its own ends, most famously by contriving the basic terms of its political realities to predictable, totalizing, and undetectable effect. The *kallipolis* will work best, and most stably, if the machinations of the founding generation and, if necessary, those of the future rulers are concealed by people's belief in a "noble lie" (*gennaion pseudos*) (415 c–d). Socrates grants hidden forces a necessary and official role to play when he suggests that the city should propagate a myth to keep citizens believing that their places in the tripartite membership hierarchy are pre-ordained and fixed. Obscuring the artifice and political work (e.g., testing, selecting, and breeding) required to naturalize this state of affairs deters *stasis* because it prevents competitiveness among inhabitants (Bakewell 2019). Redeployed to serve the supposedly beneficent ends of the *kallipolis*, in other words, secrecy makes possible the pursuit of this conception of justice, too. What makes the use of conspiracy neither insurgent nor illicit in the case of the *kallipolis* is the further condition that only those formally vested with the power to rule (or in some cases to found) may undertake it. This prohibition is key. It marks the dialogue's dual interest in eliminating plots *against* the ideal regime and managing political flux. Socrates repurposes the conspiratorial to neutralize the threat of political change that conspiracy otherwise signifies and, in the case of the *Republic*'s Athenian setting, evidently inspires.

Upon closer inspection, however, things may not be so simple. Rarely analyzed by critics is the curious invocation of rumor (*phēmē*) that follows the myth of the metals and that conjoins the two political matters, conspiracy and unverifiable speech, which Thucydides's picture of Athenian politics linked in the previous section. After explaining the myth, Socrates asks Glaucon whether he thinks the rulers might be persuaded (*peisthein*) of the contrivance (*mēchanē* [415c]) they will employ in the city. Glaucon answers negatively, suggesting that only their children or children's children might be (415c). Nothing less than the feasibility of the *kallipolis* regime would seem at stake in the exchange (415d). And though Socrates says he thinks he sees what Glaucon is "getting at," the meaning remains opaque. "Anyway," Socrates abruptly declares, "let that turn out in whatever way rumor [*phēmē*] might lead it."[20]

Given the dialogue's concerns with strategic management, the recourse to rumor (and chance) stands out. Power relations are initially imagined as the effects of deliberately conspiring founders. The instantiation of their rigid hierarchy, however, apparently depends on the fluid and unreliable workings of rumor, which has a life of its own. The entrenchment of an elite conspiracy relies in practice on a sticky, egalitarian form of speech of "uncertain and mysterious origin" that travels not from top to bottom but from "mouth to mouth."[21] It is obvious that the *mēchanē* of the noble lie signifies an intentional effort by the city's founders to safeguard the city against the change that (always) menaces a political regime.²² What is less clear is why rumor's uncontrollable power of dissemination should be called on to supplement an already supplemental mechanism for staving off *stasis*.

That rumors spread (myths) while effacing the question of their original source seems appropriate for the *kallipolis*, which is designed to conceal the traces of its willfully constructed political relations. Rumors work "independently of demonstrable intention or purpose" because they circulate "acephalously" (Wedeen 2019, 150). Like myths, they do not count as verifiable discourse, which means they acquire their potency not through proof but through retelling (Brisson 1998, 90). Rumors are therefore not only received but also passed along. They can generate feelings of "solidarity" and make residents complicit in (the conspiratorial effort at) upholding the regime (Wedeen 2019, 152). For the same reason, however, rumors are also open to alteration, strategic adaptation, and doubt by the people who circulate them. To leave the myth of the metals to rumor is therefore to reintroduce the issue of contingency and the problem of *stasis* that the noble lie was meant to foreclose. We saw something like this double bind in Thucydides's account of the demos, whose efforts to reconsolidate their rule ended up courting *stasis*. Whether rumors that serve the regime in power gain political traction or fade out would seem to depend, however, on how well other everyday practices in the city are working to uphold the city's order.

A similar insight underlies Socrates's recommendation that the rulers use an additional subterfuge to regulate kinship relations in the *kallipolis*. If the myth of the metals aims "to reduce the danger of *stasis* among the various social classes in Kallipolis," the "subsequent move" by Socrates "to outlaw traditional families and private property among the guardians" attempts to "reduce *stasis* in that [particular] group as well" (Bakewell 2019, 103; *Rep.* 424a). Book V's famous reconfiguration of kinship—"no parent shall know its own child" and "no child its own parent" (457d)—serves the overarching goal of fixity because it encourages the guardians' identification with the (family of the) city over their biological kin. In connecting the use of hidden contrivances to the problem of political change, the discussion of marriage and procreation mirrors the noble lie passages: "the rulers will need to employ a good deal of falsehood (*pseudei*) and deception (*apatē*) for the benefit of those they are ruling" (459c8–d2).

Securing unity and order (*homonoia*) necessitates an elaborate set of covert sexual and eugenic regulations—the "feasibility" of which Socrates again suggests, though this time explicitly—poses a problem best taken up at another point (458b; see 5.449c8). In arranging that "the best men should have sex with the best women as often as possible" and the "worst" as infrequently as possible, the rulers will maintain the "quality" of the classes so that the "herd of our guardians" can be "as free as possible from dissension" (459e). These practices, as Peter Rose (2019, 354) points out, assume that excellent qualities "observable in parents are normally trans-mitted to offspring by the process of sexual reproduction," adding that "the most elaborate precautions" of surveillance are taken at the same time against the breakdown of this inheritance principle.'" To those listening in, the proposals have the additional effect of conceding genealogy's inability to guarantee membership performance in practice (Kasimis 2016, 343).

Like the regulation of the membership order, the policing of inter-course and reproduction must appear unintended. Concealing the will-fulness of the rulers' breeding system ultimately demands additional stealthy machinations to supplement the lies, festivals, sacrifices, poems, and hymns Socrates initially proposes (459e–60e). "We must have lot-teries, I think—and pretty ingenious ones—so that every time there is a marriage the inferior type we want to exclude will blame chance rather than the rulers" (460a). The lottery will deflect attention from the rulers' deliberate practices of selecting and breeding by compelling the selected and bred to blame "chance" (*tychē*), rather than a deliberate system, for their fate in marriage and procreation (460a). The dialogue proposes that inclusion in (and exclusion from) a given membership class in the *kallip-olis* should appear to be the consequence of birth, that is, as natural and random, while stipulating that, in reality, the randomness is rigged by powerful agents conspiring from within. It is not insignificant that Soc-rates appropriates the Athenian language of lot-drawing (*klēroi*) in this passage. The democratic institution taken to actualize, if not express, the political equality of citizens is repurposed here to present randomness and the equal conditions it signifies as a hoax geared to maintaining unequal relations behind the scenes—a suspicious, if fitting, thought to voice in an eroding political context.[23]

We soon read of the need for more subterfuge. Using the same term for contrivance (*mēchanē*) that he uses for the noble lie (414c), Socrates proposes additional practices for concealing the truth about biological ties: officers will employ "every means they can think of to prevent" a woman who has recently given birth from recognizing "her own child," including the use of other nursing women to serve as maternal decoys (460c).[24] When Socrates finally does address the problem of feasibility, the verdict, predictably, is not very good. The recursive quality of the conspiratorial mechanisms has alerted us to the *stasis* threatening the *kallipolis*. In the end, Socrates concedes, the rulers will err in their regulation of marriages and unite people who are undeserving of each other. However safeguarded this city, "destruction awaits everything that has come to be," he claims. "It will fall apart" (546a3–5).

CONCLUSION

Socrates pauses frequently to acknowledge the implausibility of the *kallipolis* plan and to ask whether it is foolish to continue pursuing it (in discussion). The few vocal interlocutors in the room that night always respond with a dutiful "no." These asides are important. They afford opportunities to emphasize the noninstrumental value of theory—an ideal arrangement is worth exploring despite its unlikelihood in practice, and so on. Read through and against the play of conspiracy, however, the "fantastical" character of the *kallipolis* begins to carry another meaning (Ferrari 2000, xvi).

When Socrates reaches for the allegory of the cave or suggests that political power would ideally work in a systematic and secretive way through the use of a noble lie, he expresses the idealizing, comforting, and conspiratorial thought—appealing in times of great uncertainty—that power really could work with "exactness and efficiency" (Marasco 2016, 238). But to claim, as he also does, that politics on the ground does not work this way is ultimately to present the desire for permanent fixity as a fantasy. The *Republic* suggests that an eroding democratic world can and often does induce a desire to seek solace in totalizing political explanations, certainty, and repressiveness. On the preceding reading, the text takes a further step to offer the more salutary point that an eroding democracy affords critical terrain for seeing that permanent stability is illusory.

Does Plato help us theorize the present, then, without being "presentist"? By the end of the Peloponnesian War, Athenian democracy had finally "succumbed to the joint pressure of coups and institutional erosion, the two leading causes of contemporary democracies' death" (Carugati 2019, 7). Whatever the differences between ancient and modern democracy, the symptoms of contemporary political decay—severe polarization, waning confidence in public institutions, and a pervasive interest in conspiratorial explanations for political life (McCoy, Rahman, and Somer 2018, 18; Runciman 2018)—are all present in the democratic context Plato uses to stage the *Republic*. The narrated dialogue provides a heuristic rendering of what some people living under different eroding democratic conditions might sound like, talk about, desire, and fear.

In recent years, political scientists have sought to understand the gradual and seemingly imperceptible changes that lead democracies in advanced liberal societies to break down or backslide from the inside into "political systems that are ambiguously democratic or hybrid" without showing "manifest signs" that they are eroding (Bermeo 2016, 5, 6; Przeworski 2019, 15). Although understandably worried that democracies may be exhibiting an "incipient decline" worldwide, some thinkers still appear wedded to the notion that democracy, as a regime type, moves along a "progressive arc" (L. Diamond 2015, 142; Rosenblum and Muirhead 2019, 166). Democracies are "vulnerable to crises" on this view because democracy is a "recent and still rare" regime type (Przeworksi 2019, 16). In time and with the right design, real-world democracies would inoculate themselves once and for all against the kind of change that induces erosion from within.

A reading that places the *Republic*'s play of conspiracy at its center and that restores the dialogue to its volatile Athenian setting directly contravenes this view. Plato's dialogue does not furnish a practical solution for eradicating change, polarization, plotting, and breakdown. No matter how well or prolifically a regime crafts and re-crafts its institutional mechanisms, constitutional design cannot rid political life of its inherent contingency or the possibility of dissent. Why might that be? Each of the mechanisms designed as a bulwark against change is shown over the course of the conversation to constitute an independent form of action with indeterminate effects. Each act, a life of its own. Regardless of what these mechanisms are intended to do, their proliferation does not so much reduce as multiply the forms of contingency at play. With this, the *Republic* offers an important warning about the tendency, still prevalent in contemporary studies of democracy, to regard a regime as a static or progressively ameliorating political form. The desire to exert total mastery over political life appears in Plato's hands as a wishful fantasy, born of a conspiratorial moment, that fails to realize itself in practice. In the end, what the conspiracy to stop all conspiracies makes clear is that there can be no end to political change.

1   Translations of Plato's *Republic* are by Tom Griffith (Plato 2000) unless otherwise noted.

2   The term "play" has been used in different ways to describe Plato's writing by other readers including Voegelin (2000) and Blondell (2002).

3   Roisman's (2006, 66) argument that Athenian anxieties about conspiracy dominated public discourse and reflected a suspicious worldview focuses on the fourth century BCE in which Plato wrote; but he also argues that Aristophanes's earlier comedies also express "the rhetoric of political conspiracy" in fifth-century Athens. This is good reason to consider that throughout the classical period, a *topos* of political conspiracy is available for strategic redeployment by writers like Plato.

4   I discuss the complications of historically situating the dialogue in the next section.

5   The routinization of deception includes the invention of the noble lie, a deliberate conspiracy in its first undertaking by founders and even possibly in its subsequent telling by rulers, as well as a range of mechanisms, like the rigged marriage "lottery," which all aim at keeping the city's membership order stable.

6   Shear (2011, 2) is referring here to the decade following the first coup in 411, a span of time to which Plato's setting incorporates allusions.

7   A modern example of covert governmental activity in the United States is COINTELPRO, which aimed at neutralizing political groups like the Black Panther Party.

8   Here I adopt the position of Roisman (2006, 78), whose reading of the major historical sources on 404–403 (Xenophon, Aristotle, and Plutarch, among others) leads him to the conclusion that "there was no oligarchic conspiracy" preceding the city's surrender to the Thirty. See *Lysias* (12.43–47), the extant source to claim that *hetairiai* played a pivotal role in coordinating the coup of the Thirty, which has had an outsized influence on scholarly depictions of how the coup occurred.

9   Howland (2004) treats Plato's *Republic* as an engagement with this tyrannical violence. He reads the first book of the *Republic*, with its emphasis on Polemarchus's character, as a "Platonic reply" to *Against Eratosthenes*, a speech, written and delivered by Lysias, that "calls for revenge against the murderers of his brother Polemarchus." Howland stresses dramatic irony, writing that "Plato's Athenian readers were doubtless well aware of these facts and of the oligarchy's execution of Niceratus and possibly also of Cleitophon," who are also present in Socrates's account of the evening (180, 181).

10 For an in-depth discussion of the figures in the house and their participation in the tyrannical coup, see Howland (2018); and (Nails 2002).

11   See Plato's *Symposium*. Roisman (2006) points out that the terms for a se-
     cret plot are not necessarily pejorative—the most common is a *synōmosia*,
     literally, "a swearing together," which serves metonymically to designate a
     conspiracy.

12   Historical studies of Athenian *hetaireiai* also include the definitive account
     by Calhoun (1913), and shorter discussions in Gottesman (2014) and Jones
     (1999).

13   Nails (1998, 385) argues that the *Republic*'s folded time is an unintended
     consequence of Plato's writing practice. More fruitfully, Moors (1987) con-
     siders it a rhetorical strategy that calls attention to the *Republic*'s difference
     from history: "Stated simply, this dialogue, as Plato writes it, cannot have
     actually taken place" (6). Strauss (1978, 62) finds this cloudy yet recog-
     nizable picture of a wartime Athens overwhelmed by political instability
     worth considering in its own right. Yet he ultimately retreats from this
     view. His interpretation of the political conditions in terms of imminent
     decline collapses the difference in perspective between a fifth-century
     character and a fourth-century reader.

14   Athenian preoccupations with plotting had drawn Aristophanes's atten-
     tion a decade earlier in *Knights* and in *Wasps*. Thucydides's account of the
     first half of the war generally supports this picture as well.

15   I have altered Crawley's translation of *chalepos* from "uneasy" to "harsh"
     to convey the severity of the Athenian conduct that followed from their
     suspicions, and I have rendered *tyrannikē* "tyrannical" (rather than
     "monarchical").

16   See also the discussion in Teegarden (2013, 17–18).

17   In the proposal that the founders ought to banish anyone over the age
     of ten from the *kallipolis* at its founding, Sagan (1994) sees a "powerful
     paranoid anxiety," which he takes as a response to a climate of oligarchic
     violence (145). The dialogue does not provide "an actual political program"
     but instead expresses a "paranoid" "cast of thought" (146).

18   As Rosenstock (1983) notes, besides the *Republic*, only the *Charmides* and
     the *Lysis* are narrated by Socrates. But only the *Republic* and the *Charmides*
     "make explicit the relative time of the narration" (221).

19   For a reading of Socrates as the "unreliable narrator" of Plato's *Lysis*, see
     Planeaux (2001, 63), who argues that we are "carefully drawn into an elabo-
     rate game of hide-and-seek between what Socrates said he was doing and
     what he appears to be doing." The "overt" pattern of inconsistent state-
     ments and "selective half-truths" ultimately leads Planeaux to argue that
     Socrates is drawing attention to the artifice of his story. Plato "stages his
     character staging the conversation—part of the fictive power of a master
     craftsman" (62, 67).

20   This is my translation, which attempts to preserve the sense of *phēmē*.

21   Here I am quoting and combining two different senses of *phēmē* as defined
     in the Liddell-Scott-Jones Greek Lexicon.

22   Frank (2018) argues that in the *Republic*, the term *mēchanē* "refers consistently to exactly those things that make people see and believe what is not true" because they are designed to deceive (64).

23   On lot as a constitutive feature of democracy, see Otanes's contribution to the debate over regimes in Herodotus, which uses the different term *palos* (III.80–82). Aristotle describes the use of sortition (*klērountai*; *Ath. Pol.* 43.2) for the Athenian Council and courts. Staveley (1972, 116) notes that Athenians made sortition much more complex in the fourth century, when they used a *klēroterion*, or allotment machine, and probably "eliminated" opportunities to tamper with the operation (see also Aristophanes, *Eccl.*, 681). Before this, in the fifth century, efforts at fraud "must have been common" and would have been less difficult to accomplish if one colluded with the "presiding official": "[H]ad two or three persons in authority been brought into the conspiracy it would have been perfectly feasible for one or more of the lots to have been so marked as to be discernible to the touch of those in the know. Admittedly, the sources preserve no concrete examples of the use of methods such as these, but for proof that it was common . . . look [at] those provisions in the jury selection" (Staveley 1972, 115, 116).

24   These passages propose a range of other practices of concealment, such as child exposure, that exploit oppositions of seen/unseen in the making of kin and hence the reproduction of the *kallipolis*'s membership order (461a–c). See the "Ring of Gyges" as well (359a–2:360d).

_____

09 AN ECONOMY OF SUSPICION / ON THE "MILITARY-CIVILIAN DIVIDE" AND THE NEW AMERICAN MILITARISM

Standing in the White House briefing room in October 2017, White House Chief of Staff John Kelly delivered a defense of his commander in chief. Responding to criticism of Donald Trump for his allegedly insensitive comments on a phone call to the wife of a soldier killed in Niger, Kelly's remarks were steeped in references to the "military-civilian divide," even as he did not name it as such. And his was no simple empirical description:

> Who are these young men and women? They are the best one percent this country produces. Most of you, as Americans, don't know them. Many of you don't know anyone who knows any one of them. But they are the very best this country produces, and they volunteer to protect our country when there's nothing in our country anymore that seems to suggest that selfless service to the nation is not only appropriate but required.

At the end of his prepared statement, Kelly was willing to take questions only from "someone who knows," a Gold-Star parent or sibling or someone who knew one.[1] He closed the briefing with the following words: "We don't look down upon those of you who haven't served. In fact, in a way we're a little bit sorry because you'll have never experienced the wonderful joy you get in your heart when you do the kinds of things our service men and women do—not for any other reason than they love this country" (*New York Times* 2017).

In the shadow of the ongoing "wars on terror," the US public domain is saturated with references to the military-civilian divide. So, too, is it replete with talk about soldier trauma. Combat's psychological afterlife has emerged as a powerful and pervasive framework through which the American invasions and occupations of Iraq and Afghanistan appear in the public domain, that is, the framework through which they are discussed, collective responsibility is articulated, and the obligations of citizenship are fashioned. Talk of a military-civilian divide and the discourse of soldier trauma operate in concert to interpellate American civilians to the call of war, I argue, and they do so, in part, by creating an economy of suspicion that haunts the civilian citizen: she who is tarnished by a moral and epistemological lack, she who must support those citizens who have gone off to war and sacrificed themselves in her name.

In *The Image before the Weapon*, Helen Kinsella (2011) develops a genealogical account of "the civilian." While the meaning of "combatant" has been quite stable since the twelfth century, she argues, that is not so for the civilian. Only in the nineteenth century did the word come to refer to someone "who is not a member of the armed forces" (29). And, as Kinsella rightly insists, the focus on *who* a civilian is belies the more fundamental question as to *what* a civilian is. That question cannot be answered by any simple reference to an individual who is a noncombatant. Kinsella traces the emergence of the figure of the civilian—in different times, in different contexts of warfare—out of "threads" that weave together discourses of gender, innocence, and civilization in distinct ways (7). As my argument unfolds, I will focus on the matter of "innocence."

If, at the most basic level, a civilian is she who is not a combatant, that means something quite specific in the context of a state that can conduct its wars on someone else's soil. In the American vernacular and, more specifically, with reference to the "war on terror," "civilian" refers not to a noncombatant in a war zone but to someone who has never experienced war (the term is often modified in reference to civilians in a war zone, as, say, Iraqi or Afghan civilians). Nor is this civilian simply someone with no experience of war. She is someone *who can never truly know* war. Among citizens are those—soldiers, veterans (and in a different way, their families)—who know war, and those who do not. And the divide is stark. These two kinds of citizens are separated by an epistemological and moral abyss, and all sorts of work about national obligation, responsibility, and civic value and virtue gets done in the space in between. American civilians are innocent. But theirs is an innocence with a twist. Their innocence is suspect, even pernicious. It is a guilty innocence. The innocence of American civilians operates as an accusation: civilians are naive about the evil that exists in the world, ignorant about what war is really like. Their innocence signals a privilege that those sent off to fight wars on their behalf do not have.

In what follows, I explore this figure of the (American) civilian through a reading of three intersecting phenomena: an emerging public discourse about "moral injury" (a rearticulation of the trauma of combat), the gesture of thanking soldiers for "their service," and a call being issued to the civilian public to care for soldiers and help them "heal." I trace discursive practices and demands through which the suffering soldier appears as the only meaningful, the sole *acknowledged* "object" of concern and action (Cavell 1969; Zerilli 2016) in the public domain. Drawing on Hannah Arendt's writings on representative thinking, judgment, politics, and collective responsibility (1958, 1967), I explicate and question an American political common sense in which "we" *must* "support the troops." And I do so by exploring the forms of care that the support is supposed to take as well as the grounds—epistemological, moral, and political—on which the demand is being made.

In so doing, I shift the terrain of much public political critique. I do not focus on the role of state secrecy in sustaining American militarism and war, that is, that the US security state lied to the American public about weapons of mass destruction in Iraq, or that it insisted that the American military was making progress in the war in Afghanistan, even though that was far from the truth (Ackerman 2021; Whitlock 2021). For that matter, I query the foundational assumptions of projects such as Wikileaks, that is, that the conspiratorial nature of the US state—the enormous labor that it puts into keeping secrets from its citizens—ensures the impossibility of a robust democratic politics. No doubt, the US security state believes in its own high-stakes game of state secrecy, presumably, that it ensures the American public remains "ignorant" about much of what the United States does in the world. Nevertheless, rather than understanding state secrecy as the only—or even, the primary—obstacle to a critical and participatory democratic citizenship, I suggest it can operate as an alibi for political inaction. The American public, I maintain, knows *more than enough* to engage in a robust critique of American militarism, if only it would choose—and were authorized—to do so.

Caring for soldiers is a constitutive labor of American militarism in the post-9/11 era. The demand to care for the troops functions as an ideological mechanism that attaches American civilians to the war (Terry 2017) and relies on a fundamental misrecognition. While presented as a politically neutral act and an unequivocal ethical good, caring for traumatized (and injured) soldiers captures the American civilian—liberal and conservative, pro- and (presumably) antiwar—in its distinctly imperial gaze. The post-9/11 wars appear only in and through their costs to American troops; no one else, it seems, is of any ethical or political concern.

SOLDIER TRAUMA

In giving an account of stories of soldier trauma in the public domain, I focus here on a particular emergent trauma frame. In 2009, several Veterans Administration (VA) psychologists published a paper questioning whether post-traumatic stress disorder (PTSD) was the suitable diagnosis for many combat veterans coming in for treatment (Litz et al. 2009). PTSD's etiology resides in "life-threatening trauma," they wrote; it describes a fear-based response. But many soldiers suffer from something other than the lingering aftermath of existential threat. According to the VA psychologists, soldiers suffer the psychological consequences of having violated their own moral standards. Killing women and children, of course—but also prescribed killing and the handling of dead bodies, even simply witnessing the depravity of war, can precipitate moral harm. Brett Litz, Nathan Stein, and colleagues proposed "moral injury" as the name for this (other) syndrome and began developing distinct clinical protocols to respond to this particular wound of war.[2]

While not formally recognized as a distinct diagnostic category, the concept of *moral injury* has traveled beyond the medical domain. As described by Tyler Boudreau (2018), a Marine who served in Iraq and later became critical of the war, "It's a term being used more frequently across the medical community and among political activists, various faith groups, and others. 'Moral injury' is capturing attention in the media and veterans' organizations" (53).

In March 2014, the *Huffington Post* published a three-part essay by David Wood on moral injury among American troops returning from the wars in Afghanistan and Iraq. It opens with the following words: "How do we begin to accept that Nick Rudolph, a thoughtful, sandy-haired

Californian, was sent to war as a 22-year-old Marine and in a desperate gun battle outside Marjah, Afghanistan, found himself killing an Afghan boy? That when Nick came home, strangers thanked him for his service and politicians lauded him as a hero?" Wood continues,

> Can we imagine ourselves back on that awful day in the summer of 2010, in the hot firefight that went on for nine hours? Men frenzied with exhaustion and reckless exuberance, eyes and throats burning from dust and smoke, in a battle that erupted after Taliban insurgents castrated a young boy in the village, knowing his family would summon nearby Marines for help and the Marines would come, walking right into a deadly ambush.

In case we cannot imagine it, Wood does it for us:

> Nick . . . spots somebody darting around the corner of an adobe wall, firing assault rifles at him and his Marines. Nick raises his M-4 carbine. He sees the shooter is a child, maybe 13. With only a split second to decide, he squeezes the trigger and ends the boy's life.

As for Nick himself, he concedes the problem: "He was just a kid. But . . . I'm trying not to get shot and I don't want any of my brothers getting hurt. . . . You know it's wrong. But . . . you don't have a choice." Wood tells his readers that Nick is haunted by the boy's death. It has left him "mired in the swamp of moral confusion and contradiction so familiar to returning veterans of the wars in Iraq and Afghanistan" (Wood 2014a). That is the essence of moral injury, which is common among those who have fought these latest American wars.

In choosing to describe this particular case, Wood is able to depict a young American Marine's moral injury as rooted in his actions during a battle instigated by a barbaric act. Stories of barbaric acts, culturally incommensurable values, and an enemy who does not recognize the laws of war characterize many accounts of the wars on terror and their "signature wound," moral injury.[3] But there are also other kinds of stories, some providing more politically critical accounts, like the one told by an army veteran at a training workshop on moral injury, about how he was shaken to his core by his own cruelty toward an Iraqi child. An adult rushed over to protect the child and this army veteran said he did not recognize himself in the man's terrified eyes. Who had he become? There are the moral injuries caused by the everyday acts involved in carrying out an occupation—

kicking in doors, scaring the family, finding no insurgents at home (see Boudreau 2018). Soldiers tell of mistaking noncombatants for insurgents in the heat of battle or at a checkpoint with a car speeding toward them that fails to stop (see, for example, Fallows 2015). For the most part, these narratives are framed by a conversation about the inevitable moral ambiguities of counterinsurgency wars. Occasionally they are offered—almost exclusively by veterans—as a political critique of America's wars and its global reach, which they now oppose.

IN OUR NAME

In the preface to a well-reviewed book on moral injury an ex-general asks, "What does the nation owe its citizens-who-become soldiers?" (Sherman 2015, xiii–xiv). That question organizes the discourse about moral injury as it appears in the public domain, often tethered to the "fact" of the growing military-civilian divide. National Public Radio (2011) reported 2,226,883 Americans serving in the US military as of March 31, 2010, less than 1 percent of the total US population (309 million in 2010).[4] But the divide is not simply a matter of numbers. As of 2015, according to a report in the *Los Angeles Times*, "Some 49% of the 1.3 million active-duty service members in the U.S. are concentrated in just five states—California, Virginia, Texas, North Carolina and Georgia" (Zucchino 2015). In addition to being highly concentrated, "as many as 80% of those who serve come from a family in which a parent or sibling is also in the military." And "[t]hey often live in relative isolation—behind the gates of military installations such as Ft. Bragg or in the deeply military communities like Fayetteville, N.C., that surround them" (Zucchino 2015; see also Sherman 2015, 29).[5] It is not surprising, then, if the "US military today is gradually becoming a separate warrior class . . . increasingly distinct from the public it is charged with protecting" (Zucchino 2015).[6]

Talk of the military-civilian divide indexes far more than straightforward statistical facts, however, as Kelly's performance at the White House press conference makes clear. It speaks to the question of political judgment, in which a virtue attaches to military personnel, and, by way of comparison, a critique of citizens who have not served. Moreover, it stages a call to citizens who have not gone to war to step up to the plate and support those who have. As Nancy Sherman, a philosophy professor at Georgetown University, put it at a conference, "Even in a city like ours, those who wear uniforms are exotic. . . . So my work is in a sense helping us to come out of the bunker on both sides. I don't think you can only talk to your fellow buddies over a beer if you're coming home from war."[7]

What is involved in coming out of these respective bunkers? More specifically, in this discourse about war, troops, civilians, and moral injury, what kinds of practices, obligations, and responsibilities are called into being? Let me return to David Wood's (2014a, 2014b, 2014c) essays in the *Huffington Post*. He does far more than elaborate the contours of moral injury. A second theme structuring his narrative is the chasm of knowledge and understanding he sees dividing civilians from soldiers. His articles are an effort to bridge that divide. He notes several distinctive features of life at war. For example, there is a particular closeness and love among the members of a combat unit. Given that intimacy, the "traumatic loss of someone you love [a fellow soldier] is not fully understandable by a civilian." He quotes Amy Amidon, a psychologist who works with active-duty Marines, saying that "civilians are lucky that they still have a sense of naïveté about what the world is like. . . . The average American means well, but what they need to know is that these [military] men and women are seeing incredible evil, and coming home with that weighing on them and not knowing how to fit back into society" (Amidon, as quoted in Wood 2014a). Or, as Timothy Kudo (2018) recounts in his essay, "On War and Redemption":

> When I returned from Afghanistan this past spring, a civilian friend asked, "Is it good to be back?" It was the first time someone had asked, and I answered honestly. But I won't do that again. We weren't ready for that conversation. Instead, when people ask, I make it easy for everyone by responding, "It's fine." That's a lie, though. It's not fine. (79)

"Thank you for your service." Critiques of this (presumably) prevalent gesture occupy a lot of space in the literature on war, soldiers, civilians, and homecoming. While no doubt received and interpreted in various ways by (ex-)military personnel in practice, *as a trope* the act stands for the fraught relationship between soldiers and civilians the way the image of civilians spitting on Vietnam veterans or calling them "baby killers" did for that earlier war. Thanking soldiers and veterans for their war service is treated as a sign of support, a signal that the American public has learned the lessons of Vietnam. As argued by Elizabeth Samet (2011):

> Whether anyone ever spat on an American soldier returning from Vietnam is a matter of debate. . . . Apocryphal or not, this image has become emblematic of an era's shame, and of the failure of civilians to respond appropriately to the people they had sent to fight a bankrupt war. The specter of this guilt—this perdurable archetype of the hostile homecoming—animates today's encounters. . . . "Thank you for your Service" has become a mantra of atonement. (787–89)

Nevertheless, according to many, this supposed gesture of thanks tends not to be all that well received. As Matthew Richtel (2015) explains, the "thank you for your service phenomenon," more often than not, "comes across as shallow, disconnected, a reflexive offering from people who, while meaning well, *have no clue what soldiers did over there* or what motivated them to go, and who would never have gone themselves nor sent their own sons and daughters" (emphasis added). Being thanked "can feel self-serving for the thankers, suggesting that he did it for them, and that they somehow understand the sacrifice, night terrors, feelings of loss and bewilderment. Or don't think about it at all."[8] David Finkel's (2013) book, *Thank You for Your Service*, now a major motion picture, is an intimate account of veterans who have returned from fighting in Iraq, a portrait of broken lives, of psychological and physical pain that stands in glaring contrast to the book's title. What precisely are we thanking them for? And what are the afterlives of war for soldiers who civilians feel compelled to thank?[9]

In *Afterwar*, Nancy Sherman (2015) unpacks what she calls the "ritual" of thanking men and women for their service. Sherman asks, "How can gratitude be substantive when its expression is so trivialized in a pat, easy-to-say 'Thank you'" (39)? In contrast to many other commentators, she refuses to dismiss the gesture out of hand, instead thinking about what a civilian is doing when she thanks someone for their service. The ritual is "a public enactment and recommendation of a norm," Sherman insists. "Our gratitude shows others how to respond" and "in showing gratitude, we ourselves come to feel gratitude" (44). Thanking soldiers for their service is a practice of ethical self-fashioning, the cultivation of a morally appropriate disposition on the part of civilians in the face of those who "have served." In this spirit, Sherman stages her book as a call to (civilian) readers to engage with those who went off to war. It is "a manifesto for how to engage in moral repair, one on one, with individual service members and veterans so that we can begin to build a new kind of integrated community" (19). "We've been at war while the country has been at the mall," Sherman reports being told by soldiers, invoking a well-rehearsed trope—or accusation.[10] "Each side feels the distance" between the military and the society in whose name, presumably, it went off to war (19). And in response, Sherman argues for "the moral necessity for each of us to be personally engaged in the largest reintegration of American service members into civilian society since Vietnam. The mil/civ walls have to come down. It is critical for the moral healing of soldiers" (19).

Developing her argument, Sherman asks civilians to step up in the face of a widespread "resentment" on the part of (ex-)military personnel. Rather than recoil from tense encounters, she wants American civilians to understand veterans' resentment and to fashion a productive response. This is not Friedrich Nietzsche's critique of *ressentiment*, Sherman makes clear. Resentment involves "holding another to account, of demanding respect, of calling out another for due attention and recognition as part of a shared moral community. It is a way of saying another is responsible *to you*" (26). Implicit in it is the "complaint that civilian fellow citizens . . . fail to assume an adequate degree of moral responsibility for the wars that they (indirectly or directly) help wage, and for the afterwar—the arduous veteran recovery that follows in the wake of going to war" (32).[11]

I want to unpack Sherman's account of resentment, civilians, responsibility, and moral healing. She demands that civilians recognize a national collective responsibility for (some of) the afterlives of the ongoing American wars. But what does a "one-on-one" obligation to help soldiers heal entail? And what does it preclude?

CIVILIAN RESPONSIBILITY AND THERAPEUTIC CITIZENSHIP

In *What Have We Done: The Moral Injury of Our Longest Wars*, David Wood (2016) insists that healing from moral injury will never happen within a purely clinical setting. Instead, he writes, "True healing of veterans with war-related moral injuries will only come from community . . . peers, neighborhoods, faith congregations, service organizations, individuals. That means it's up to us" (260).

Whether moral injury is best treated by clinicians, or even framed in medical-psychiatric terms, is far from a settled question. As the concept circulates beyond clinical practice, many find in it possibilities for re-building community and repairing a divided citizenry by getting civilians to engage with and take responsibility for American soldiers returning from war.[12] For others, for example, Tyler Boudreau, the ex-Marine who fought in Iraq and later became a critic of US global military power, the concept opens a space for political engagement. In contrast to PTSD that tends to "depoliticize a veteran's disquietude and turn it into a medical issue," Boudreau (2018, 55) argues, moral injury "takes the problem out of the hands of the mental health profession and the military and at-tempts to place it where it belongs—in society, in the community, and in the family. . . . It transforms 'patients' back into citizens, and 'diagnoses' into dialogue."

There is nothing inherent in the concept of moral injury that precludes the possibility of radical political critique.[13] Nevertheless, Boudreau's is a rare voice in the public discourse about moral injury. Wood's (2016) ac-count is far more typical. After arguing that healing needs to come from community, Wood instructs his readers on how to get involved. "*Let's set aside the question of war itself*," he begins (264, emphasis added). Even if war is a "criminal waste," he states, he has "found harmony with those who have fought in combat, for they have the keenest appreciation of the ugly de-pravity of mass state-justified bloodletting" (265). Criminal waste, deprav-ity, evil: many writers describe the horrors of the wars on terror in such general terms. Others point more specifically to the inherent depravity and ambiguity of (these) counterinsurgency wars. Far less common than either are *political* critiques of the kind Boudreau offers. And when such critiques do appear, they tend to come from the mouths—or pens—of those "who have served" (see also D. Anderson 2018).

Despite the variety in how the "horrors" of these wars are framed, however, there seems to be (near) unanimity on the particular "lesson" of the American war in Vietnam. "We have learned that we are supposed to separate the war from the warrior," writes Sherman (2015, 3); "we have a sacred obligation to those who serve, whether or not we agree with the cause of those wars and whether or not those who serve agree with them." In turn, that sacred obligation is to be enacted through a practice of listening. Take the following account by Bill Edmonds (2018), an Amer-ican adviser and trainer at an interrogation center in Iraq where prison-ers were tortured. He asks, "Can warfighters who are unable to reconcile what they've seen or done with the person they once were, ever fully come home? That is, can wounds to moral identity ever truly heal?" (49). They can, although "the obstacles are daunting." He advises his readers, "listen. . . . Provide for them . . . a safe, nonjudgmental, and compassionate space in which to share their experiences, and an environment where they can, possibly, [engage in] self-forgiveness" (49–50). For his part, Wood (2016) recommends a program developed by a clinical psychologist at Harvard University. "Her idea was to match veterans with volunteer civilian listeners for a long session of uninterrupted, intentional listening" (267), writes Wood. Intentional listening is "listening with validation." It is "listening without judgment; saying, 'Yeah, *that was fucked up*. But also . . . *I honor your service*'" (268, emphasis added).

Listening without judgment: What are the political effects of enacting a one-on-one obligation to listen to soldiers and veterans not just regardless of our own position on the wars but also, as Sherman requires, *regardless of theirs*? And what can it possibly mean to take collective responsibility for (a) war and yet simultaneously to "set aside the question of war itself"?

Listening without judgment is fundamental in a therapeutic context, and it takes a specific form in clinical protocols designed to treat moral injury (see Litz et al. 2016). Listening without judgment is also the foundation of pastoral care (see Werber et al. 2015). And that makes sense. But listening without judgment—in contrast, say, to Tyler Boudreau's call for "dialogue"—may not be as salutary when extended to the demands of (civilian) citizenship. In that context, the admonition speaks of a broad valuation of the soldier as ideal citizen that characterizes the new American militarism Andrew Bacevich describes (2005; see also Lutz 2001). Moreover, as a demand, it indexes a problem of epistemology and thereby returns us to the question of civilian innocence and the problem of—or the obstacles to—political judgment.

There is an unresolvable tension at the heart of this call on civilians to listen. At the same time as civilian-citizens—generally interpellated in this discourse as "we"—are being called upon to listen, the prevailing conviction among psychiatrists and psychologists, among journalists and philosophers, and among many a soldier and veteran is that civilians will never *really be able to hear*, at least not if hearing implies the possibility of actually coming to understand, let alone to know. "The difference between what the . . . soldiers know about the world and what most American civilians know about the world is often at the center of their encounters with each other," notes Zoe Wool (2015, 192). Or, to return to Amy Amidon, "civilians are lucky that they still have a sense of naïveté about what the world is like" (Amidon, as quoted in Wood 2014b). This "common sense" echoes through the writings of Wood and Sherman, in accounts by veterans and the psychiatrists who work with them, and in a growing canon of war literature emerging out of these still ongoing wars. As Roy Scranton (2015) has argued, only the soldier knows war, and that truth—his truth—is that of the "trauma hero."

Joan Scott (1991, 776) has written critically of historiography that attempts to "enlarge" the picture by "rest[ing] its claim to legitimacy on the authority of experience, the direct experience of others." If orthodox history as a field is typified by its referential understanding of evidence, then "when the evidence offered is the evidence of 'experience,' the claim for referentiality is further buttressed—what could be truer . . . than a subject's own account of what he or she has lived through" (777). But, Scott cautions, "When experience is taken as the origin of knowledge . . . [q]uestions about the constructed nature of experience, about how subjects are constituted as different in the first place—about language (and discourse) and history—are left aside" (777). And as a consequence, "the evidence of experience . . . reproduces rather than contests a given ideological system" (778).

A parallel invocation of the truth of experience characterizes calls upon civilians to listen to those "who have served." In contrast to historians who firmly believed in their capacity to understand and present experience as history, however, the evidence of experience operates here to reinforce the dividing line. "You who never was there," to borrow Walter Benn Michaels's (1996) turn of phrase, can never know. Civilian citizens are called upon to attend to the "individual suffering" of returning troops, to listen to their suffering, all the while refraining from judgment (Was it a war crime? Was the war itself just?) in part, at least, because they cannot know.

What kinds of stories must civilians be willing to listen to? Or, more precisely, what are civilians being encouraged not to judge? If civilians are to support the troops regardless of "our"—or *their*—political position on the wars, are we also enjoined from expressing any political judgment on the war(s)—that perhaps the wars are wrong—even if that judgment is not directed at the soldier per se? And what, precisely, in the things that soldiers and veterans have done or have desired to do should civilians not judge? Killing a thirteen-year-old child holding a gun that Nick Rudolph had "no choice" but to do? Kicking in doors and raiding homes as part of the everyday work of carrying out an occupation? The torture at Abu Ghraib? Does it also include not judging the pleasure some soldiers take in the work of war and the act of killing? "War is a gift from God," one of the veterans interviewed by Wood declared one day. "In Iraq we were killing people every day. There's a lot of satisfaction in the hunt, getting a target, going after a specific person, which I did many, many times, and like I said, I enjoyed it a lot" (Wood 2016, 149–50). And now, he tells Wood, he suffers moral injury.

Many decades ago, Hannah Arendt faced an onslaught of criticism for her coverage of Adolf Eichmann's trial in Jerusalem. One criticism spoke to Arendt's willingness to hold Eichmann to account: "There was a whole chorus of voices that assured me that 'there sits an Eichmann in every one of us'"(Arendt 2003b, 59). Under the repressive and terrifying conditions produced by the Nazi regime, can anyone be sure that they would have acted differently? Is any of us sure that we, in contrast to Eichmann, would not have "followed orders"? That same logic structures the demand for civilians to refrain from judging US veterans, and it divides citizens into two (national) kinds: those who "serve," and those who do not; those who may speak and explain, and those who must listen (at least, when face-to-face with a soldier or veteran); those who really know, and those who cannot know and therefore must not judge. If politics presupposes an obligation to think from someone else's point of view, as Hannah Arendt has insisted, to have the "willingness to imagine how the world looks to people whose standpoints one does not necessarily share" (Zerilli 2016, 1), in the injunction to listen to soldiers, the obligation is borne by civilians alone. Pace Boudreau's call for dialogue, this civilian-military encounter is not imagined as real conversation. Soldiers/veterans have the right to talk; civilians have but the obligation to listen.

While calling for one form of accountability, this moral injury discourse renders another ever more difficult to mount and sustain. It dismisses from consideration alternative, antinationalist, and anti-imperial forms of accountability. If we are to exit the national-imperial frame, at the very least we need to maintain one basic distinction. Returning to Wood's anecdotes, we might want to separate out the "Yeah, that was fucked up" from the "I honor your service." Certainly, it is plausible to express compassion for someone's suffering—even if that suffering is born of *what he has done*—without simultaneously honoring his service. Also plausible, appropriate even, is not being able or willing to feel compassion for someone who speaks of the pleasure he took in killing or who believes that the wars are politically or morally right.

The call to "support the troops" and to honor their service regardless not just of our position on the wars but also of theirs is not the correct "lesson" learned from the American war in Vietnam, contrary to what Sherman and so many others insist. That mantra is a consequence of the conservative reconstruction of the US military defeat in Vietnam that framed, in part, Ronald Reagan's rise to power in 1980 (see Hagopian 2009; Abu El-Haj 2022). It is a consequence of the reconstruction of the military as a professional military with the discipline, virtue, respect, and abilities needed for winning wars. The valuation of the soldier as ideal citizen has become a political common sense, continuously inter-pellating the American public—right and left, liberal and conservative— into the new American militarism (Bacevich 2005). As Robert J. Lifton put it in an interview, it is "as if serving in a war is the highest and bravest activity a young person can engage in, even if often the kids who serve have nowhere else to go," and this is regardless of what one "thinks of the wars themselves."[14] This attitude echoes through articles and books writ-ten about moral injury, most of which begin by insisting that the US mili-tary is a moral institution, perhaps more moral than any other domain of American society today (see, for example, Litz et al. 2009, 697; Litz et al. 2016). It echoes through the ritual of thanking someone for their service, during which, as Sherman puts it, "we are recognizing character—*courage tied to public service*" (Sherman 2015, 3, emphasis added).

This "common sense" relies not only on a militarist ideology requiring civilians to respect, be grateful for, and thank the troops. It also relies on a fundamental slippage and misrecognition. Despite what are some-times explicit claims to the contrary, American civilians are being asked to respond to soldiers and veterans as if they occupy the subject position of the victim. Sherman (2015, 49), for example, elaborates her argument about the political value of resentment via an essay by Jean Améry, a Ho-locaust survivor famous for refusing to relinquish his resentment, argu-ing that only a victim of the Nazi regime can possess "the moral truth of the blows." Sherman does not draw a simple parallel between what she names Améry's "moral injury" and what American soldiers and veterans are suffering. And soldiers and veterans tend not to appropriate the vic-tim identity, at least not in any explicit or coherent sense.[15] Nevertheless, as Scranton shows, Sherman fails to recognize that, "if you map Améry's situation onto the last fourteen years of war, Améry's 'moral truth'" lines up not with American soldiers but with orange-suited, force-fed detainees at Guantanamo Bay and naked, tortured Iraqis in Abu Ghraib" (Scranton 2016, 154–55).

For all the talk of killing and moral transgression that talk of moral injury has brought into the public domain, as a discourse it largely skirts the question of US military aggression, overlooking the acts through which "one person"—the American soldier—"violates another" (Bernstein 2015, 4)—the Iraqi or Afghan individual on whose lands the war is being fought. For Iraq War veteran Tyler Boudreau (2018, 56), "without the Iraqi people, the troops can have no moral injuries to speak of. And the only way Americans can fathom the meaning of this term, 'moral injury,' is to acknowledge the humanity of the Iraqis." Unfortunately, Boudreau's interpretation does not mirror the prevailing discourse. Only rarely does talk of moral injury move to the humanity of the Iraqi, the Afghan, or, for that matter, the Pakistani, the Yemeni, the Syrian, and the ever-proliferating list of Others on whose territory the so-called war on terror is being waged. Those Iraqis and Afghans whom American soldiers and Marines have wounded or killed, whose villages the Americans destroyed and whose families they have decimated, do appear in this discourse. Their injuries, in short, *are not secrets*; they are hidden in plain sight. The injured Other emerges as but an object lesson in a drama that revolves entirely around the American self. American troops are the (suffering) subjects here. We are told stories of Iraqi doctors shot at checkpoints, children killed, people humiliated, Afghan villages flattened, but we are supposed to hear them for the purpose of understanding what US soldiers and veterans have suffered. The stories call on civilians to identify with—and to care for—the ones who committed the violence.

To be clear: the "facts" of the suffering Other are *known*. Talk of moral injury requires—it presupposes—that US military personnel have injured, killed, and destroyed people and communities elsewhere. After all, moral injury appears only insofar as soldiers speak of—*confess to*—acts of (perceived) moral transgression.[16] The facts are unmistakable. But they do not emerge as objects of public concern; that is, they do not appear in such a way as to merit consideration and judgment (see Arendt 2003b; see also Zerilli 2016). To use Stanley Cavell's (1969) distinction, the reality that Iraqis and Afghans—and people of all the other countries on the receiving end of American military violence—have suffered the effects of military violence is well-enough *known*.[17] What those who have suffered most are not is *acknowledged*. They remain insignificant facts in the discourse that frames the "war on terror" in the American public domain.[18]

The stories of "evil shit" (Scranton 2016, 152) recounted by some veterans and soldiers are often presented as narratives that need to be heard, even revered. For example, a military chaplain at a conference on moral injury instructed the audience to "put down your pens and listen with your hearts," in his introduction of a panel of veterans. "This is not an interrogation," he said. "They are making a gift to us." In bestowing their "gifts," it is important to emphasize, two veterans expressed profound remorse for what they had done to Iraqi civilians, and they spoke critically of American imperial violence. But throughout the three-day conference those two Iraq War veterans were the only ones to bring up "the Other" with any sense of remorse for what had been done *to them* rather than as part of a call for the rest of "us" to empathize with and listen to the American veteran now suffering moral injury stemming from his own acts (or failures to act). The role of civilians, we learned, was "to bear witness and to validate their [the veterans'] loss and pain," in the words of one workshop leader. And to be clear, the organizers and most participants at this conference were positioned on the liberal-left of American society. It was not a particular *political* position on the wars that produced the deafening silence about the damage caused abroad by US militarism. The focus instead was on our shared "respect" for those who had served and the unquestioned assumption that those who had never gone to war had no authority or right to judge, or really even to speak.

CARING FOR THE WORLD

In her essay "Collective Responsibility," Arendt (2003a) sketches the philosophical and theological genealogies on which distinctions between the political, the legal, and the moral rest. I want to focus on the distinction she draws between the moral and the political. For centuries now, Arendt argues, the moral has spoken to a concern with the self; the political, in contrast, has indexed a care for the world. Arendt's exploration of political and moral standards was driven by a particular history. Writing in the aftermath of Nazi Germany, she was interested in "collective and vicarious responsibility in which the member of a community is held responsible for things he did not participate in but which were done in his name" (154). In a similar vein, the talk of moral injury speaks to the question of collective and vicarious responsibility. But other than in exceptional speech acts—spoken almost exclusively by veterans—moral injury is talked about as a call for collective and vicarious responsibility on the part of civilians *for those Americans who fought the war*. This is a morality play all about the US imperial self.

It is not just one self being referenced here. There is the self of the soldier who must learn to live with himself. Whether articulated in secular or theological terms, moral injury is understood to signal an unbearable split within the self, echoing Arendt's description of moral conduct in seeming "to depend primarily upon the intercourse of man with himself; . . . not a matter of concern with the other but with the self" (Arendt 2003b, 67).[19] And there is the self of the nation: of restoring unity to a divided house. There is no talk of reparations. There is no talk of a moral responsibility toward others whom American soldiers have harmed.[20] The suffering Iraqi or Afghan is mentioned, if at all, as an afterthought, as someone to be gestured toward and then set aside (see, e.g., Wood 2016).[21]

In *The Order of Evils*, Adi Ophir (2005, 26) rightly argues that (any) moral discourse frames "only some of the existing evils and let[s] only some of its victims come into presence and assume their own voice." In the discourse of moral injury, existing evils appear through the figure and voice of the suffering American soldier, and the responsibility for disrupting that order of evil is displaced onto an American civilian public that needs to care for those "we" sent off to war. There is no call for a *jus post-bellum*, an obligation toward those whom "our" troops harmed and whose lands "our" military destroyed. That, after all, would require judgment. We would then not be able to set aside the question of (the) war itself.

The problem of responsibility, both individual and collective, dominated much of Hannah Arendt's thinking, especially in the aftermath of covering the Eichmann trial and the pushback she received for that work.[22] However, Arendt did not address collective responsibility from within a moral framework; she did so through the language of the political. Responsibility "is always political," she writes, "whether it appears in the older form, when a whole community takes it upon itself to be responsible for whatever one of its members has done, or whether a community is being held responsible for what has been done in its name" (2003a, 149). And from an Arendtian perspective, collective responsibility requires an act that Wood and Sherman preclude a priori. Along with the many others who call upon "civilians" to just listen, they evade the human responsibility to judge. Yes, we must try to think from others' points of view, which is an *imaginative* rather than an impossible act; but then we also need to deliberate and evaluate together, and in public, with (imagined) others.

The risks of not doing so, for Arendt, were monstrous: "Out of the unwillingness or inability to choose one's examples and one's company, and out of the unwillingness or inability to relate to others through judgment, arise the real stumbling blocks. . . . Therein lies the horror, and at the same time the banality of evil" (146).

What emerges in and through all this talk of war, moral injury, and civilian obligation is what Miriam Ticktin (2011) has named a "moralist anti-politics." Civilian citizens are called upon to attend to the "individual suffering" of returning troops. Civilians are told they cannot possibly understand—or know—the experiences military personnel have been through. "We" are asked to receive their words as "gifts." Civilians are told to set politics aside, to set aside the question of war itself. In effect, civilian citizens are called upon to disregard what Arendt calls the "care of the world." Instead, the (re)engaged citizenship that is presumed to result takes the form of the therapist's couch.

It is certainly possible to support the need for institutional care for (ex-)military personnel and yet reject the therapeutic model and the moralist antipolitics that undergird the call to civilians to just listen, to help heal those who fought, who perhaps did horrible things, and who may well still think what they did was right. Even if Stacey Pearsall, a combat photographer in Iraq, cannot get herself to say "that Iraq was not worth it, because then I would be diminishing the sacrifices my friends made on the battlefield" (Pearsall, as quoted in Wood 2016, 272), I have no problem saying it. It was not worth it. And it was not worth it not simply, or even primarily, because of the American troops who suffer(ed) and died. It was not worth it because of the tens (the hundreds) of thousands that American troops killed and wounded (directly or indirectly) and because of the everyday worlds they shattered, and that are still in disarray today, two decades on. By any measure, there is absolutely no statistical equivalence between the harms suffered by the Iraqi and Afghan populations and those suffered by American troops. Perhaps there is no moral equivalence either.

This moralist antipolitics is not always what is being asked of the American public by ex-military personnel. And I do not want to imply that there is no space or call for political critique or judgment in the public domain today. As a former Green Beret told Matt Richtel (2015), it is not only that civilians have no skin in the game but that they seem not to have any "real opinions either. . . . 'At least with Vietnam, people spit on you and you knew they had an opinion.'" For that matter, many of the same writers—journalists, scholars, veterans—who call upon civilians to step up and listen also ask "us" to step up and take a position on the wars (We are a democracy after all!), just not, it seems, when one is face-to-face with someone "who has served." There is a profound, perhaps irresolvable tension here: the (figure of the) American soldier cannot be elevated while decrying (the) war. And the truth of war cannot be taken to be the truth of the soldiers' experience while articulating a robust critique of (the) war. For a nation that has the privilege of fighting its wars on someone else's soil, the soldier's perspective is inherently imperial in its epistemological conceit. The war of the other combatants does not appear within its gaze. Neither do the lives, experiences, and perspectives of the other civilians—that is, civilians, subjects in their own right, who are caught in the vortex of the violence of US invasions, occupations, and counterinsurgency wars who certainly and constitutively "know" what war is.

Tim O'Brien, a novelist and antiwar activist who fought in Vietnam, has argued that the ritual of thanking troops for their service is mere "patriotic gloss"; "we're thanking without having the courage to ask whether the mission is even right" (O'Brien, as quoted in Richtel 2015). But courage is not all that is lacking. Nor is it a matter that the American public is ignorant of the horrors American militarism and war has wrought around the world; or that the expanding domain of state secrecy renders the possibility of a robust democratic politics ever more tenuous. American civilians may not know all the details, but they certainly *know more than enough*. Instead, a constitutive obstacle to judgment, to the possibility of politics—and more specifically, to the possibility of a radical, political critique of American militarism and war—is the lack of epistemic and moral authority among those American "citizens" who are now commonly referred to as "civilians." In the contemporary American public sphere, combatants are the privileged witnesses to war. They are the nation's super citizens toward whom the rest of us are obliged. The overriding commitment to care for the troops (rather than, say, to "do no harm to Iraqis") speaks to the virtue of national "unity" at the expense of all else; and the responsibility for restoring that unity resides with "civilians" who must act in particular ways to re-suture the nation across the abyss that is the military-civilian divide. The citizen responsible for the re-suturing is an always already suspect civilian subject (she who does not serve, she who cannot know), who must listen and never judge, who must care for and console the soldier. The new American militarism has found—and forged—the civilian citizen that it needs.

1 "Gold star" refers to the loss of a family member in military service.
2 There is a far more complex history of PTSD than their account suggests. But by the 1990s, PTSD had become very much a condition of victimhood (see Fassin and Rechtman 2009, although they date the linking of PTSD to victimhood earlier than would I).
3 For example, see Goldstein (2015). See also Edmonds (2018). In an account of his work as a special operations soldier training Iraqi troops in inter-rogation techniques, Edmonds notes that he arrived in Iraq on the heels of the "Abu Ghraib scandal." He then proceeds to write about his struggle with the different "rules" and "culture" in Iraq, ones in which torture is ac-ceptable. He also confesses that he came to realize that he was "torn about torture myself" (Edmonds 2018, 39). The essay is an account of Edmonds's struggle with and recovery from moral injury.
4 That number includes active duty, National Guard, Air Guard, and the Reserves.
5 As of 2015, Sherman (2015, 30) reports, 20 percent of members of Congress were veterans; by way of contrast, post-Vietnam that number was over 75 percent. Following the 2018 mid-term elections, 18 percent of people serving in Congress were veterans. See Leo Shane III, "Veterans in the 116th Congress, by the Numbers," Military Times, November 20, 2018, https://www.militarytimes.com/news/pentagon-congress/2018/11/21 /veterans-in-the-116th-congress-by-the-numbers/.
6 Rita Brock (fieldnotes by author) noted at a workshop on moral injury held at the Union Theological Seminar in New York that while when she began working with military veterans she assumed it was a class draft, she had come to realize how much more complex the sociology of the military actually is: the "bulk are middle class," she said; there are very few people who come from either real poverty or real wealth. "They want to go to college; they are aspirational." Moreover, about 60 percent come from families with a history of military service. It's "a family business."
7 Listening to Trauma: Insights and Actions conference, George Washington University, Washington, D.C., October 20–22, 2016.
8 Richtel (2015, 15) then notes, "The issue has been percolating for a few years," elucidated memorably in *Billy Lynn's Long Halftime Walk*, a 2012 National Book Award Finalist about a group of soldiers being feted at halftime of a Dallas Cowboys game. The soldiers express dread over people rushing to offer thanks, pregnant with obligation and blood lust and "their voices throbbing like lovers."
9 A staff writer for the *Washington Post*, David Finkel embedded with an infantry battalion of the US army in Iraq in 2007. After that unit came home, Finkel decided to write a follow-up book about those whom he knew

from Iraq who were struggling psychologically at home. In effect, he re-embedded with some of the same soldiers, now veterans at home.

10　See, for example, Ben Fountain's (2012) award-winning novel (and now Hollywood film) *Billy Lynn's Long Halftime Walk*.

11　Sherman (2015, 28) points out that the "'you' who is addressed" by these feelings of resentment is "a generic civilian, a 'personation' for a group."

12　I deal with this at length in my book *Combat Trauma* (2022).

13　The concept of the trauma of perpetration is not new (nor, for that matter, is the name "moral injury"; see Shay 1994). The psychological and moral pain wrought by perpetration was central to what was initially named "post-Vietnam syndrome," by radical, antiwar psychiatrists working with antiwar Vietnam veterans. And the concept of post-Vietnam syndrome, in contrast to the concept of moral injury, was a decidedly political intervention, even as it was also a clinical one.

14　Robert Lifton is a psychiatrist whose work was key to developing "post-traumatic stress disorder" as an official psychiatric diagnosis. He was an antiwar activist who developed his understanding of combat trauma through his work with the organization, Vietnam Veterans Against the War. See Lifton 1973.

15　I do want to argue, however, that the subject position of the soldier/veteran is emerging as a new form of identity politics, with all the complexities of *ressentiment* attached to it that Wendy Brown (1995) has explored at length (see Abu El-Haj 2022).

16　The language of "confession" is central to theorizations of moral injury as a medical concept. As one of its architects referred to therapy for moral injury: it is "secular confession" (interview with the author, Boston, MA, October 2018).

17　While I don't have the space to go into it here, I want to push back against what I see as an overemphasis on the problem of secrecy—and lies—in the conduct of the post-9/11 wars. Yes, the American public does not know *everything* (although after the Wikileaks document dumps, one could argue that there is an overwhelming amount of information publicly available, if one is interested enough to delve into it). But do American citizens not *know enough*? What else might Americans need to know in order to take a stand, to evaluate the wars—to judge them—and get involved? Secrecy and lies become alibis for inaction.

18　According to the Costs of War Project at the Watson Institute at Brown University, by 2018, over 480,000 civilians had died due to "direct war violence, and several times as many indirectly"; the war had produced 12 million war refugees and displaced persons, and the US is carrying out counter-terror missions in 80 countries. See "Costs of War," Watson Institute, accessed May 11, 2023, https://watson.brown.edu/costsofwar/.

19 Arendt is elaborating Kant's discussion of the moral in his *Critique of Pure Reason*.

20 I am mapping here the grammar of a prevalent and powerful discourse, but I do not mean to imply there are no exceptions. See, for example, the Islah Reparations Project (http://www.reparations.org/). One of the founders is a former marine who fought in Fallujah during the second siege.

21 Note that in Wood's (2016) description, he draws a moral equivalence between US military personnel on the one hand, and Iraqi and Afghan *civilians* on the other. This is a common move, one that is crucial to maintaining the virtue of the American soldier in contrast to combatants on the other side.

22 Arendt (2003a) insists on the distinction between "guilt" and "responsibility." She argues that one can be responsible for things one has not done but that "there is no such thing as being or feeling guilty for things that happened without oneself actively participating in them" (147). "Guilt, unlike responsibility, always singles out; it is strictly personal. It refers to an act, not to intentions or potentialities . . ."; "'We are all guilty' is actually a declaration of solidarity with the wrongdoers" (147–48).

PART III
THE FORCE OF CAPITAL

ROSALIND C. MORRIS

10 CONSPIRACIES OF THEORY / OF GOLD IN THE SHADOW OF DEINDUSTRIALIZATION

Few subjects have given rise to more conspiracy theories than has gold. Tales of buried treasure and of international cabals hoarding the precious metal in order to subvert local financial systems are legion, as are myths of alchemical fabrication and magical gold-spinning maidens. Often, such tales imagine the conspirators to be members of religious or ethnic minorities. Nonetheless, the affinity between gold and conspiratorial thought is not confined to any specific national tradition. Wherever gold has functioned as the signifier of true or absolute value and as a store of wealth, wherever it has, *at the same time*, permitted the symbolic conversion of other values, it has been the object of theoretical speculation and, with it, an anxiety about the limits of knowledge. This particular combination—of speculation about what is not immediately or empirically apprehensible, and anxiety about the finitude of the subject as the bearer of knowledge—is the epistemological core of conspiratorial thinking. As such, it cannot be categorically distinguished from the practice of scholars. Nor is it to be found only among populists or paranoiacs.

I am not the first to observe the repeating connection between gold and conspiratorial thought. It was noted in passing by Richard Hofstadter (1964), in his notorious text, "The Paranoid Style in American Politics." In that essay, Hofstadter quotes an 1895 tract of the American Populist Party, about the putative "gold gamblers of Europe and America," who were said to have used "every device of treachery, every resource of statecraft, and every artifice known to the secret cabals of the international gold ring" to thwart "the prosperity of the people and the financial and commercial independence of the country" (78). Although there were innumerable prior examples, and several contemporary ones, Hofstadter was not centrally concerned with the fact that the fantasized conspiracy of 1895 was centered on gold, however.[1] He was trying to explain the root causes and transformation of a political disposition, namely, populism.

Much can be said for Hofstadter's diagnosis of American populism, but such discourse is also common elsewhere—especially in its connection to gold. Indeed, gold seems to provide a peculiarly apt currency for conspiratorial thought in general. Nor is this coincidental. The fear and loathing directed by the populists against the political elite in the 1890s, described by Hofstadter, had everything to do with the belief that the Goldbugs were going to demonetize silver and establish gold as a privileged medium and bearer of value, thus elevating it to the status of master signifier and making those with only silver coin or paper currency and other notes dependent on gold and indebted to its owners. In other words, the gold standard was thought of as a usurpation and a displacement. It was for this reason that John dos Passos ventriloquized the great orator of the populists, William Jennings Bryan, and referred to him as the man with the "silver tongue." Dos Passos (2000, 136) quotes Bryan as saying, "You shall not press down upon the brow of labor this crown of thorns, you shall not crucify mankind upon a cross of gold." His narrator then makes the connection, as many opponents of the gold standard did, between Goldbugs and the mining engineers and Randlords of South Africa. The narrator laments, "But McArthur and Forrest, two Scotchmen in the Rand, had invented the cyanide process for extracting gold from ore, South Africa flooded the gold market; there was no need for a prophet of silver."

In South Africa, itself, conspiracy theories also abounded, as they still do, although the ground for them was not bimetallism. To the contrary, the ascendancy of gold as master signifier and privileged bearer of value was not opposed, but access to it was fought over, and conspiracy theories were concerned about the possible withdrawal of gold from circulation. Thus, for example, a belief that President Paul Kruger (of the Boer Republic) buried gold in the Highveld of the Transvaal as he fled the conquering British troops in 1900, during the Anglo-Boer War, persists today. Sometimes this story is reinflected and the gold is said to have been hidden not by Kruger but by Ernest Oppenheimer, the founder of the Anglo-American mining corporation and one of the heads of the de Beers diamond empire.[2]

If gold is the currency for an apparently general tendency toward conspiracy theorizing—partly, as I shall show, because gold is a key signifier of the process of generalization—it also hides within its own dazzling image the logic that Hofstadter attempted to identify. In the recent South African case, Oppenheimer stands for a corporate elite whose extractive processes are associated with the dispossession and immiseration of the (mainly Black) subjects whose land and labor were so integral to the fortunes of the Randlords and mining capital. That is to say, the narrative form of the conspiracy theory particularizes and encodes an analysis that would appear to escape the accusation of paranoid or conspiratorial thinking if read from a critical-theoretical perspective and in terms of its structural logic rather than its narrative aspect. In this case, the narrative of a literal concealment of gold in the Highveld encodes and encrypts a story about originary accumulation and the repression of wages. However, this very appreciation of the theory's truth depends on reading the narrative *as a metaphoric displacement* and on distinguishing between surface appearance and hidden meanings. Thus, to the extent that the narrator-theorist recognizes the metaphoricity of the narrative, he or she escapes the charge of conspiratorial thinking. To the extent that the interpreter literalizes the narrative, she or he succumbs to the charge. Conspiracy theory partakes, therefore, of the logic of fetishism's discourse.[3] It is a form in which surface and depth, signifier and signified, collapse in the image-sign. And like all discourses on fetishism, that on conspiracy theory works in the mode of accusation and self-(defensive)-consolidation. The designation of thought as conspiratorial or paranoid marks out a space within which to preserve the authoritative claims of the one who pronounces the name (or the accusation) of conspiracy theorist or paranoid style. At stake is the problem of knowing how to read and, indeed, of the necessity for such a reading of the narrative code of the metaphoric displacement.

In 1964, Hofstadter believed that those most likely to commit the literalist sin and, thus, to exhibit a paranoid style were the politically disenfranchised. He thought that the provision of information and better access to political decision-making would mitigate what he described as the double suffering of the newly dispossessed, that class of people who, feeling themselves to once have been masters of their fate but now resenting their loss of command, indulge in totalizing explanations of an apocalyptic sort (and in this description he distinguished the paranoid style of the 1960s from that of the 1860s). I do not share this belief about the efficacy of information-based consciousness raising. Nonetheless, Hofstadter offers an important insight when he suggests that the paranoid style is also characterized by an incapacity or refusal to think by means of counterexample, or negativity. The historian, he says, "teaches us to think how things do *not* happen" (1964, 86). This kind of awareness is lacking in conspiratorial thought or the paranoid style, he claims, as it appears among people who are ignorant of and excluded from the actual operations of power. In other words, the conspiratorial thinker does not contemplate the possibility that his own analysis could be subject to falsification, and this failure is commensurate with his belief that the conspirators have unlimited powers to realize their malevolent schemes.

Here, an abyssal space opens. For the very diagnosis of conspiratorial thought seems to immunize itself against precisely this kind of self-falsification. Indeed, Hofstadter's essay elides the difference between access to and knowledge about political-institutional processes, and he assumes that the disenfranchised are ignorant of that which excludes them—a highly dubitable proposition. It is on this basis that he secures the perimeter of the intellectual's territory: by positing an identity between ignorance that results from exclusion, on one hand, and the fact of exteriority to power, on the other. Although he claims to merely be "borrowing" the diagnostic language of psychoanalysis in the mode of analogy when invoking "paranoia," we can recall that Freud had attempted to distinguish true psychoanalysis from other forms of psychotherapy by remarking on the necessity for a real science to "admit the imperfections of our understanding, to learn new things and to alter our methods" (Freud 1955, 159). There is thus some continuity between their styles of reasoning; both argue that science depends on its willingness to admit error.

Not incidentally, Freud metaphorized the distinction between the science that submits itself to falsification and the therapeutic practice that must focus on effectuating a remedy for patients—and that is, of necessity, less concerned with advancing science—via an analogy with gold and copper. Freud did not disavow the virtue of an alloy in a symbolic system where gold signified both truth and purity. For, in this analogy, that alloy would permit psychoanalysis to be extended to the poor (via state support). However, it would also encourage overly expeditious treatment via the technique of "direct suggestion," and this would inhibit the scientific (generalizable) knowledge to be generated otherwise. By contrast, Freud (1919, 168) likened the pure and unalloyed form of his science to pure gold. In doing so, he simultaneously avowed a form of knowledge that is capable of negation (and dialectical self-overcoming) and expressed certitude that this form of knowing is superior to others. His certitude about his self-doubt, then, is rendered in the figure of gold. So, too, Hofstadter reposes in the confidence of science's own capacity to survive self-negation—*in an augmented form*. Historical modesty is here the mask of teleological assurance.

The dream of symmetry between power and knowledge, and also between ignorance and interpretive excess, has a long history, and I will consider some examples of it below. Already, however, we can discern in Freud and Hofstadter the trace of a form of Enlightenment thought, most identified with Kant, according to which the perception of subjective or epistemic finitude is the occasion for an act of self-consolidation. In both authors' works, conspiratorial thinking is characterized by a lack of epistemological self-restraint. The double bind that these thinkers express, more or less self-consciously, cannot be easily circumvented, however. Nor, in my opinion, is it to be disavowed; certitude about one's own epistemic limits may well be one of the most enabling contributions of Kantian philosophy.

In what follows, I consider these questions through reference to the world in which gold functions as the scene and object of both thought and practice: more specifically, the world of informal gold mining in the deindustrializing spaces of South Africa. I do so because, as already mentioned, gold is a broadly prevalent currency of conspiratorial thinking, something like a general metaphor of the absolute, of the universal, from which marked individuals and groups or special interests are recursively excluded. But this role as metaphor for a universality that excludes individuals is also grounded in the particular processes by which gold functions as money in exchange-oriented economies. Taking the metaphor seriously, which is to say, literally, enables one to confront the affinity as well as the differences between conspiratorial thought and scholarly analysis. The task that I have set myself, then, is twofold: to analyze the forms of practice in the informal gold-mining world that are subtended by conspiratorial thinking; and to provide a reading of them as the effect of and exposure to a history in which gold's production is the locus of a vast and systematic conspiracy *because* of its role as the privileged signifier of value. What I want to demonstrate is that the richly narrated practices that generate gold, even in an era of so-called digitality and long after the formal demise of the gold standard, including its modified form under the Bretton Woods system, also partake of the metal's strange status as both commodity and medium of exchange, as both signified and signi-fier. Informal miners are captive to this oscillating and often mysterious process in which gold appears only to disappear—as wealth, as money, as power, as access to mobility, and as token of futurity. The movement between appearance and disappearance is as important to understand-ing conspiracy theory—of both populists and scholars—as the more frequently remarked tendency to find hidden or occulted meanings in mundane circumstances. It is the corollary of that epistemic contradiction that I have briefly described above. And it is nowhere more visible than in the eloquent efforts that informal miners make to grasp the forces that shape their world. Let me then turn to that scene, somewhere on the Witwatersrand.

THE SCENE, SEEN

To a certain extent, of course, all underground mining for gold is a pursuit of buried treasure. It is the attribution of an agency responsible for the interment or concealment of that treasure that differentiates conspirato-rial from other kinds of causal explanation—to the extent that they can be distinguished. If gold is found in the earth (either in an alluvial form or in a deep-level conglomerate), its specific emplacement may be understood in popular discourse as an effect of divine forces (a creator god or ances-tral spirits) or natural causes (such as the meteoric event that created the Vredefort Impact crater in South Africa two billion years ago, which gen-erated the specific angled geological structures in which gold is found).[4] Its relative accessibility as well as its hiddenness may also be explained by such events, but insofar as this hiddenness is conceived as a blockage of what would otherwise be either naturally accessible or divinely revealed, it is the object of conspiratorial speculation. What requires explanation in this case is not merely the location of the gold in spaces that are other-wise invisible on and from the surface of the earth, but what forces might prevent people from discovering or accessing it. Hence, if there are sto-ries about Kruger and Oppenheimer actually digging holes in which to bury their hoards (and many such stories have been recounted to me over the decades during which I have conducted research in South Af-rica), these are few compared to those that accuse mining capital and the state of organizing its extraction in a manner that keeps those who mine from obtaining that which they extract *and* produce through their own labor—not merely gold but that which it signifies: productivity, surplus value, wealth, and the capacity to access other material things. This is one reason why the informal miners in South Africa, called *zama-zamas*, do not often speak about gold, whether referring to the metal in its purified form or when it is embedded in a vein of rock; rather, they almost always speak of it in the terms for a generalized value, namely in the idiom of *imali*.[5] Before examining what is at stake in this rhetorical practice, it is necessary to describe the scene and something of the drama that takes place on its stage.

The area of which I speak, not far from Johannesburg, was once the site of intensive and highly industrialized gold mining. It is now a loose set of townships, informal settlements, and squatter communities. In the vacated spaces created by the closure of large-scale mining operations, which included vertical shafts descending more than 2.5 miles below the surface and elaborate networks of tunnels that traverse many tens of miles, self-trained miners continue to seek gold. These activities once depended on capital-intensive and highly mechanized processes. After drilling in the industrial mines, shafts were typically finished with reinforced cement; the tunnels underground were buttressed with supports bolted with flexible steel and various synthetic materials (resin and polyester); and the artificially cavernous spaces were illuminated by electric and battery-operated lights. The mining itself was aided by pneumatic drills and refined blasting technology; ore was transported using automated removal equipment and electrified rail transport. Functioning deep-level mines also make use of complex dewatering and oxygenation systems as well as of cyanide and mercury-based communition processes and industrial smelting. Yet, today, alongside these large-scale processes, *zama-zamas*, most from the neighboring states of Zimbabwe, Lesotho, and Mozambique, perform all these functions manually. They enter the earth with no more than picks, hammers, battery-operated headlamps, and on occasion, rubber boots and protective clothing woven from jute sacks. They follow the same routes as the industrial miners did, but without the assistance of electric transport vehicles and in the absence of industrial ventilation or dewatering. Upon finding what appears to be a potential vein in the rock, they assay samples by panning, and they use sausage-sized sticks of dynamite purchased on an illicit market to blast rock that they then sort by hand and ultimately carry to the surface on their backs in bags that once held rice or cornmeal. Working in small groups of friends and relations or with men from the same region who share a language, but sometimes in larger groups under the authority of international but ethnically coherent gangs, the miners stay underground for days and weeks at a time. The more self-organized groups are both work teams and protective units, their conviviality leavened by the need for self-defense in the event of attack by armed bandits underground or at the shaft exits.

Above ground, women or, in some areas, young men, perform the Sisyphean labor of transforming rock into powder, breaking stones with other stones to produce a fine sand that can be mixed with water and then poured over ribbed towels on makeshift sluicing tables. This intensive manual labor takes over what was performed by enormous stamp machines when the industrial mines were in operation (as many still are). Nonetheless, the women make use of the remainders of that industrial process, working on the smoothed surfaces of the cement foundations, where once mine offices or dwellings stood, to ensure the efficiency of their grinding and to mitigate the loss of material in the natural crevasses of the earth. The women in the area where I conducted fieldwork are organized in teams under the possessive gaze of the men who have borne the rock and who temporarily claim both the territory and the women's labor as their own. These same men gather the visible gold nuggets and flakes from the sluicing tables before consolidating and sifting the runoff, amalgamating it with mercury. The remainder constitutes the payment for the women's work. Women receive no cash payments, only a residue that may or may not contain gold. The women reprocess this residue, transforming the mud into mineral cake by drying it in the sun and then repeating the process.

At the end of these gendered processes, which differ in both the time they take and the amount of gold they generate, tiny nuggets are sold into the market via local middlemen, who keep track of spot prices on the international commodities market and who pay in cash.[6] Organized and armed gangs play their part and are increasingly active in the region, focusing their attention on the choke points in the system (shaft entries and exits, or grinding sites) or areas where modest capital accumulation has begun to occur. But they do not monopolize all the production in this world. Whether sold independently or brokered by gangs, the gold will travel along the capillary networks that extend from Johannesburg to China and Pakistan, the United States and Europe. It will adorn the bodies of the wealthy, be incorporated into dowries, and clad the fixtures of the ultra-rich. It will be used to hedge financial bets, to secure or repay loans, and also to signify a capacity for excess.

THE NAME OF THE GAME: CONSPIRACIES OF LANGUAGE

Zama means "to try" in isiZulu and isiNdebele, and the reduplicative phrase, *zama-zama*, means "to keep on trying" to "persist." It also means to gamble. The term acquired some of its current valence in 1994, when it was introduced as the name of a lottery game that featured daily draws of up to 25,000 ZAR on tickets that could be purchased for 2 Rand (Mapoma 1994). Today, it designates both the activity of informal mining and the miners themselves.

Now, informal miners are gamblers, and they wager their lives on a daily basis; but they are also conspirators. Underground, they breathe together. Spending days beneath the surface, they inhale the air that is contaminated by crushed rock and the smoke of dynamite. They take in the scent of each other's bodies—a scent that, they say, approaches the rank odor of death with each passing day. They also conspire together as illegalized scavengers: evading the police, strategizing self-defense, planning their activities, distributing functions, sharing tools and food supplies, warning each other of blasting dangers and rockfalls, or sending word to the surface when an accident has occurred. As in the formal mines, the greatest danger underground is falling rock, and it claims lives on a weekly basis.[7] Always skirting the possibility of such collapse, self-organized *zama-zamas* work in groups whose members typically speak a common language. The groups provide security in the face of armed gangsters who occasionally bypass the above-ground security systems established by the miners themselves, to press-gang those whom they capture underground, or who expropriate their ore when they bring it for crushing. In large mines, there may be dozens of such small groups, some of whom know each other, many of whom do not. Upon entering the shafts, they greet each other with terms of respect and amity, implicitly announcing their intention to seek gold peaceably. This is their first gamble: this communication of the desire for communication, this gift of discourse in the underground, where death is a mute but constant companion. It is not always received, of course. There is much conflict underground, and even in peace, the specter of what the men call war is as threatening as that of the serpent spirit whose rage they frequently adduce to explain the rockfalls.

The gestures of salutation both offer and seek recognition, but they are made in the absence of any sure knowledge of the one who receives the gesture. Above all, what language will the other speak? There are hundreds of men underground, temporarily grouped together, on schedules that are never integrated except by aspiration to return above ground at dawn on any given day, so that the women who will do the work of crushing the rock and readying it for sluicing will be able to work in the light of day, and in advance of the expected raids by police or attack by *tsotsis* (thugs). The tiny lances of light emanating from headlamps do not illuminate the faces of the men, so those who call out to them do not recognize them—even if they know them—until they are within a few feet. Until then, the echo chamber of the mine is filled with whistles and shouts, and calls of friendship: Hello, friend, chief, boss. Greetings, my man, my boy, my brother, my uncle. The terms for these relative forms of possible solidarity vary by language. What follows them are bursts of polyglot politesse and the quick or curious exchange of information about how long someone has been down, with whom he has been working, whether or not he has seen one or another possible mutual friend, if the ancestors have been generous, if gold has been found. The sentences are a jumble of languages, which are themselves hybridized. Thus, any exchange may commence in Sesotho, slide into isiZulu, incorporate a few words of Shona or Chitonga, move into isiNdebele, and then revert to Sesotho or Setswana, or abandon itself to English or Afrikaans. There are many shared lexical units in these languages, but also many *faux amis*. Sometimes, misunderstanding arises as rhymes across languages give the impression of shared meaning but dissolve into mutual incomprehension. Sometimes, people imitate the sound of each other's languages, especially those of people who speak relatively minor languages and dialects, their accent giving them away as much as the tone of mockery. An overheard expression may be repeated jokingly and uncomprehendingly.

I recall one such episode because it contains within itself something of the logic of conspiratorial thinking as well as the means by which it might be averted. Two groups of miners had met and stopped to share a meal together. One group consisted of isiNdebele- and isiZulu-speaking men from Western and Southern Zimbabwe, the other of Chitonga speakers from the north. Chitonga is spoken by relatively few miners in this area, but it had been overheard by one of the young Zulu men in a story about a fight. No matter what was being discussed, the Zulu man jokingly interjected "Jati magonkwe." Whenever the Tonga men conversed together, he would cast this phrase in their direction. The expression means "to grab and cut," or "grab him and slit his throat." It can also mean "to fuck him (over)." After the young man had repeated this expression several times, and for no apparent reason, one of the older Tonga men asked him if he knew what he was saying, what it meant. "Yes," the young Zulu man affirmed, cockily: "I know this Tonga language." The Tonga-speaking miners laughed, and one of them retorted with sardonic condescension, "Oh really." And then he added, in Chitonga, "I could destroy you with words and you wouldn't even know it." With this act of verbal bravado, more laughter erupted, but now it was tinged with triumph. The parody of the Tonga men by the Zulu miner had been overturned, the joke inverted as a collective audience cohered in their opposition to the exposed ignorance of the other. The Tonga men thus affirmed themselves not as the object of ridiculing imitation but as the bearers of a secret, as possible conspirators. In this manner, they also invited the Zulu man to imagine a possible intent, and thus to become a conspiracy theorist.

This expression, "I could destroy you with words and you wouldn't even know it," describes a kind of agency that the conspiracy theorist, as understood by Hofstadter and others, fears. An invisible force is felt to operate, and if it is detectable as such—as a force—its particular operations and intentions remain opaque. In this context, one can say that the conspiracy theorist is someone who is constantly "overhearing."[8] And, as already discussed, much conspiracy theory assumes that there is a hermeneutic excess in the conspiracy theorist's analytic practice. He both apprehends a message that may or may not exist, or that was not addressed to him, and invests it with a surfeit of intentionality and efficacity. In this case, however, the fact of linguistic difference constitutes a more radical veil and, quite possibly, the veil of a more radical difference. The man who surmises a conspiracy implies that something might be being said. Something malevolent, perhaps something that could kill. However, because the threat is made in the form of a joke, which is announced as such, the threat is mitigated or at least suspended in a kind of subjunctive mode. The structure is nonetheless clear: vulnerability consists of ignorance of the discourse *coupled* with exposure to its effects. In this scenario, the exposure and the vulnerability that arises from it does not derive from magic or from other invisible powers but from linguistic limitations. The announcement of the joke does something like the announcement of a metaphor; it curbs the violent force of language. In this manner, if it holds open the possibility of a future exercise of force while announcing a knowledge that can deploy such force at will, the revelation of the joke also momentarily attempts to mollify the conspiracy theorist. It is a mode of suspension.

Now, the neutralizing gesture has a form, which might be encapsulated thus: 'It's just a joke, don't worry, I mean no harm.'[9] To be sure, such professions, even if implicit, can summon a long chain of further, suspicious readings and countertheorizing, some of which take the form of a reverse accusation: 'What you call a joke is in fact the expression of hostility, which you nonetheless pretend is nonexistent.' The irreducible aggressivity of the joke, even when partially neutralized via a confession, is acknowledged by *zama-zamas*, for whom the capacity for violence is itself admired, *especially* when it is metaphorized or sublimated in a verbal duel.[10] However, what holds the threat of this joke in play, as it were, is the fact of linguistic opacity, of not knowing what is being said when it is known that something is being said.

Nor should this come as a surprise. Anyone who knows anything about the histories of counterinsurgency and intelligence in the United States knows that it is suffused by a paranoia that is inseparable from the monolingualism that subtends every discourse of the public sphere in the United States. This is why the national security institutions are always cultivating translators, and it is why they are always subjecting them to surveillance, fearing their capacity to mutate from informant into Trojan horse. It is also one of the reasons why they have relinquished intelligence gathering based in reading in favor of one that registers the magnitude of communication and the noise in the system—but that is an issue I cannot pursue here.[11]

In its crudest liberal formulation, the public sphere is a space in which successful communication entails the transmission of messages in which intended meaning is received without loss or surfeit. Its paradigm is thus not language but code. There are numerous critiques of this formulation, which remark the exclusions that are constitutive of its operations or which attend to the agonistic nature of the exchanges.[12] But such critiques rarely attend to the fact that messages traverse public spaces and are heard and overheard in ways that can accrete meaning by virtue of the associations that interlingual rhymes and the histories of communicative practice make possible in contingent and idiosyncratic ways. Such associations do not need to imply any "understanding" at all. The product of sensuous apprehension, they take place in an aural domain, in the ear, and beyond cognition even when they lead to speculative readings.

Now, verbal combat is a source of enormous pride underground. Beyond the pleasure in expertise, the sense of accomplishment in labor, the relief of surviving danger, or the hatred of the exhaustion and humiliations of eating and defecating in the same place, there is a love of verbal dexterity, multilingual play, and rapier wit. The laughter that erupts in this context is not unrelated to the thrill of gambling itself—as Freud well knew. He likened manic laughter to the kind of expenditure made by the "poor wretch," who, "by winning some large sums of money, is suddenly relieved from chronic worry about this daily bread" (Freud 1914–16, 253). In any case, the combative verbal play is almost always multilingual in the mines; it entails a movement across the boundaries of language and acquires its force because of those boundaries, which are not so much transcended as skirted, tarried with, and multiplied. It is therefore important to recognize that there is no lingua franca in the informal mines, unlike in the formal mines where the artificially constructed *fanakalo* functioned as a pseudo-language of commandment and regulation. A mixture of Afrikaans and isiZulu, *fanakalo* was the language of the gold industry under apartheid, and it ensured that Black mineworkers could understand the instructions of their white bosses while facilitating safety.[13] In the informal mines, of course, it is imperative that miners communicate to each other when they are about to set off dynamite or when they have sensed shifting rock. They depend on each other like all coconspirators do. But this is not because they will keep each other's secrets. Rather, they commit to keep none when it comes to safety. For they share a situation of exposure to risk—the radical risk of death in the underground. The transience and instability of populations in the informal mines, which entail constantly shifting composites of language, mitigate against the sedimentation of a creole (a general currency of communication) even though there is also constant creolization at work.

What kind of power, then, accrues to one who defeats another who nonetheless remains ignorant that he has been vanquished? "I could destroy you with words and you wouldn't even know it." It is at this point that the story from the world of *zama-zamas* reveals something about the operations of conspiracy theory as the basis of a social formation rather than as an epistemological problem. For the laughter of this gambler is not merely the expenditure of the poor wretch who has struck gold at last. It is the expression of an exclusive intimacy with those who can precisely hear and bear witness to the verbal mastery that takes the form of having the last word. The very fact that the verbally assailed man would not know he has been devastated constitutes the basis for recognition of the speaker by his ethnolinguistic peers. This is the flip side of that wondrous substitution of the word for violence that promises the means for evading or resolving conflict.[14] For there is no *word*, per se. No language in general. Only languages, which, when rendered isomorphic with ethnic identity, threaten to both materialize and undermine that awful boon that the gamble on communication—the polyglot greetings sent into the unknown abyss—seeks to transform into knowledge and wealth.

The cathecting of language and ethnic difference and the mobilization of that (reified) difference in the development of political and economic strategy oriented toward the preservation of white dominance was, of course, the ground and purpose of apartheid ideology in South Africa. It led not only to the division and cultivation of preexisting enmities between different language-based communities in southern Africa but also to the ascendancy of one or another European language as the idiom for accessing and signifying the universal, functioning as a medium or currency of general equivalence. Ultimately, English achieved the upper hand, subordinating Afrikaans (except in specific enclaves) and becoming what we might refer to as the "gold standard" of political discourse in the newly democratic state. The notion of a language-as-gold-standard expresses the belief that it is a medium or currency of total translatability. This is why Marx (1973, 162–63) insisted that money be understood by analogy to language only insofar as it implied translation.[15] So, I need to make clear that this dream of universality is both invested in English in South Africa today and recurrently cast into doubt. Access to upward and international mobility is presumptively linked to competence in that tongue, which is nonetheless thought incapable of conveying many of the concepts and affects that are felt to reside in one or another African vernacular.[16] If miners play and conspire in vernacular tongues, if they revel in the power of a given language's nonuniversality and inaccessibility (its capacity to enable secrecy), they also accede to English's status as the tongue of globality. Compared to bimetallists, they appear to be (and are) multilingualists (multimetallists?); but they also know they cannot escape the power of the One.[17]

Like that of English, the fetish of gold does not merely imbue it with a capacity to translate, and to thereby conserve both meaning and value, however. The fetish of gold, that justifies the horrendous risks that miners take and that promotes its reckless pursuit, derives from the fact that it is not merely a currency of total convertibility but also, at the same time, potentially more than itself: a self-fecundating substance. And this is why the conspiracy theories about gold as a signifier of value, concealed or withheld, buried or secured in vaults, or merely sold for a price that is not transferred to its producers (made the medium of surplus value in Marx's idiom), abound and repeat, solicit and seduce.

THE DREAM OF A PARKED CAR: GOLD, MONEY, AND SURFEIT

As mentioned earlier, the oddity of zama-zamas' linguistic practice with respect to gold is the rarity of the term's use. In fact, zama-zamas almost never speak of gold. It is always already money. At every step of the process, that which is being sought is referred to in isiNdebele and isi-Zulu as money, imali or, in Sesotho, chelete. The gold lodged in the rock is referred to as imali. The sludge that is produced by mixing powdered rock and water and that will be poured over sluicing tables is called imali. The runoff of the sluicing tables that will be given to the women as payment for their crushing work is called imali. The drying cakes of the runoff, which will be reprocessed in the same manner, is also called imali. The lump of gold, still black with soot, is called imali. The polished nugget, too, is imali. And the brilliantly colored notes bearing the images of Mandela and the animals of South Africa share this name: imali. This word designates the capacity for it to become something else.

Zama-zama miners are gamblers, and they take both calculated and incalculable risks in the pursuit of gold, and thus of money. But they also believe that the risks they take constitute a form of labor that, if immeasurable in quantitative terms, nonetheless has a relative intensity. It is this relative intensity rather than any abstract labor-time that permits them to compare themselves favorably with those who are the heirs to luck (rather than to ancestral favors) and thus undeserving of their good fortune. What differentiates zama-zama mining from other games of chance is the certitude of outcomes—either money or death, but never nothing. "Zama-zama is like gambling, but the better part of gambling. If you go in the mine, you are sure that you may come up with something. Maybe 200, maybe 300, maybe 100." The reason for this is quite simply that you will stay underground until gold is found. The fact that miners must pay entrance and exit fees to the security guards that they themselves have appointed means that they cannot leave the shafts empty-handed. "You go there to look for money," they say. "But sometimes, you can't find money" right away. "So . . . you have to sacrifice yourself, stay underground for three, four, five days, until you get what you want."

The one who sacrifices himself in this way is, of course, hoping to avoid death. And yet, he must risk it. "If you're risky, at the end of the day, you'll get rich."

Miners often talk about what might happen if they strike it rich. And what they aspire to is often less the satisfaction of need than the valorization of desire's apotheosis. Consider the following monologue, spoken underground while sampling, and translated from isiNdebele: "If I hit it big, I am going to park a car. Then I'm going to buy groceries. After that I'm going dancing. That will be the end of my Christmas." It elicited both approval and then ridicule from other men underground. And it initially confused me. Why would you park a car if you struck gold? Wouldn't the first thing be to buy a car? Perhaps a very fancy car? Often enough, these men talk about their poverty as being indexed by their lack of a car, of being dependent on their legs. In this land of automobility, in which cars and other vehicles have for decades provided the symbolic infrastructure within which racialization and class differentiation takes place, the car is an index of wealth and the medium of spatial and social mobility (Morris 2010). So, it is significant that the young miner describes his hoped-for wealth in an image of parking and repose. Not speed, or the thrilling velocity that violates the laws of the highway, not the rush of acceleration, or the cinematic sequence of the passing trees. The dream of a parked car is a dream of economy's transcendence. It is a dialectical image of a stasis achievable only after having entered and exited the world of movement—including the movement *out* of the immobility that acute poverty entails.

The other men understood this. But they scoffed when the young man said he would buy groceries. "Why are you always talking about groceries?" sneered one. "I want money! Everything!" If, however, the miners derided the descent into practicalities, actual exchanges, and the consumption of use-values, which is to say the satisfaction of needs, their own dreams typically followed the same sequences. Only secondarily did they enumerate the purchases they would make, typically starting with new cell phones. (Women, by contrast, tended to plan their expenditures in the opposite direction, beginning with necessities and only at the end, when all needs had been satisfied, to dream of luxurious consumption.) Cristiano Ronaldo's fabulous wealth beguiled the men from afar. The elder cousin of the duo I described above frequently invoked the soccer star as the personification of absolute wealth. And he sometimes speculated on what it would be like to occupy a place of such seemingly limitless means: "If I can be Cristiano, I can do *mati* [make a carpet] of money. Even my blankets can be made of money." His conversation would then become a reverie about a world fabricated from money: of beds, tables, and chairs made out of cash.

The literalization of the idiomatic metaphor provides the inverse image of that parked car, in which the lucky man expresses his freedom from need as repose—rather than frenzied consumption. Here, money is not only that which buys the carpet or the bed, it *is* the carpet and the bed. One is hard pressed to imagine a more perfect expression of the fetish-character of the money commodity, of its coming to appear identical with that which it buys. The image has banished from its body the memory of exchange, while disclosing a truth about money's capacity to transmogrify into absolutely anything. At the same time, it reveals gold's promise to ground that potential in the order of the real.

The men knew that this is what they were doing. They laughed with deep and self-satisfied irony as they slid between the idiom of "walking on cash" and the fanciful depiction of real blankets woven from paper currency. Their line of flight into the absurd was no more or less self-conscious than that of any surrealist. And their laughter, as Freud would see it, traversed the boundaries between dreaming and waking life, bringing back into the impoverished everyday world the momentary experience of a surplus wasted in joyous abandonment. Were the men dreaming of gold, or were their minds bedazzled by money? And was gold the image of money or was money the representation of gold? We speculate that gold is "invisible" or perhaps, to follow Foucault's (1970) incisive distinction, "unsayable" underground not because it is abstract but because *it must be abstracted* in order to achieve its status as money.[18] In his writings on money, Marx vacillates between a defense of gold as naturally predestined for its function as the medium and symbol of value (by virtue of its density, divisibility, permanence, and stable luster), and an analysis of it as a pure product of ideas.[19] And he noted that, as both a measure of value and as a medium of exchange, it could be replaced by tokens or symbols. It is by virtue of its separation into body and shadow, matter and sign, that the precious metal can serve as money. The result is a strange immateriality: "It is only a *semblance* . . . which disappears as soon as the process [of exchange] has ended" (Marx 1973, 209). It is only when loans are converted or payment is demanded in hard cash, that gold must be present in its materiality (Marx [1867] 1992, 221–27).[20] This is the moment that Jean-Joseph Goux ([1973] 1990, 48) describes as the turn to the real, which occurs, in his analysis, in the order of the fetish.

At the time of Marx's writing, gold was not yet the exclusive commodity-anchor for national currencies. Indeed, Marx acknowledges that he treats gold as the representative of the money commodity, only "for the sake of simplicity" (Marx [1867] 1992, 188). And, as we have already seen, bimetallism was opposed to gold's relative valorization as the signifier of general equivalence until the end of the nineteenth century. As Goux notes in his gloss of Marx's analysis, the two potentialities of gold—that it can be substituted for by tokens and that it can provide access to other valued objects—derive from the fact that it is only "a *connecting link*" in a "chain" of infinite concatenations, or what he terms abstract *textuality* (Goux [1973] 1990, 48). It is this very capacity, along with the promise of unlimited access to everything that can be valued quantitatively, that underwrites the fetishist's love of money. But not his love of gold-as-commodity. The fetishist of gold who withdraws the metal from circulation—to adorn his body, to plate the fixtures of his boudoir, to embroider the fabric of his cloak—that person "sacrifices the lusts of his flesh to the fetish of gold" (Marx [1867] 1992, 231). And insofar as money is the representation of gold, including its function as money, this fetishization can take place with regard to banknotes, too. A mat or a bed made of money, dreamed of by a miner, would constitute direct hoarding in relation to which Marx described the possession of gold commodities as an aesthetic form (231).

There is nonetheless a fetishism of the abstract, of exchangeability per se, that can also arise in relation to money and that is the fetishism that Walter Benjamin identified in the Paris Arcades, where it was practiced most expertly by gamblers—those who could throw money into circulation without any effort to anchor it in the order of the real, whether as the purchase price of an object or the recompense for labor time. Walter Benjamin felt that the fetish of money, once the prerogative of the aristocracy, had become bourgeois in the time of the Arcades at the end of the nineteenth century, the time of the great gold rush in South Africa, and of the bimetallist panic in the United States. And he made a note on Edouard Gourdon's *Les faucheurs de nuit* as an exemplum of this attitude: "I see it in terms of the joys which gold procures, and I savor them to the full. . . . I live a hundred lives in one. If it is a voyage, it is like that of an electric spark. . . . If I keep my fist shut tight, and if I hold onto my banknotes, it is because I know the value of time too well to spend it like other men. To give myself to one pleasure alone would cause me to lose a thousand others."[21] This attitude is also expressed in the ridicule of a purchase of groceries, and is only intensified in a post-wage world that is nonetheless not entirely digitized, once gold has lifted off from its function of signifying labor time. As suggested above, time has not vanished as an axis of value, but it is not rationally measured in abstract units so much as conceived as a threshold or a limit toward which one submits oneself and that is governed by the capacity of the body to expend itself in the pursuit of gold or, to be more precise, *money* (what the men call "sacrifice"). Recall that for the *zama-zamas* gold is always already money, even when it is metal embedded in rock. And if they, too, wear gold rings to announce marital status or take pleasure in a glittering necklace, they know that even the shimmering item of jewelry can be cashed in and instantaneously transformed into a medium for accessing another commodity: a cell phone, for example. (The many pawn shops in the local towns are never without gold.) This is why the other *zama-zamas* revile the man who would spend his money on groceries, the most consumable of all commodities, the least perduring store of wealth. They want "everything," and the means to have permanent access to everything. And there's the rub, for in the desire for permanent access to everything, the risk of hoarding arises. The two desires, for everything and for an eternity of wealth, contradict each other in a world where circulation is everything.

The *zama-zamas'* infrequent recourse to the term for gold, their polyglot play across languages in the absence of a lingua franca, and their simultaneous reveries of beds made from banknotes suggest their persistent inhabitation of a Real that resists abstraction *at the same time* that they long for and participate in a world of exchange, where Money—as connection—is also an object of desire and the dreamed-of medium enabling or sustaining both social and material transformations. Perhaps their practice is a repudiation of the teleologies and epochal historiographies within which so much analysis—materialist and structuralist, Marxist and psychoanalytic—remains mired.[22] Certainly, Goux's ([1973] 1990) analysis is captive to teleology. He describes a progressive movement "from fetish to symbol and from symbol to sign" that is "gradually taken over by transcendence," such that the "materiality of value [is] abandoned for the abstraction of value in a hypostatized sublimation" (49). In this schema, the recurring turn to gold as the real and proper guarantor and symbol of value has to be figured as a regression, a falling back into fetishism, whereas the evidence suggests that it is an irreducible, if spectral, dimension of the global economy even today. And not only among *zama-zama* miners. When Russia purchases gold and sells its US dollar reserves in an effort to evade sanctions, as it did in September 2018, it demonstrates the force of a (gold) standard that has been neither completely abandoned nor transcended, but that constantly appears, disappears and reappears. It is to explain this mysterious movement between appearance and disappearance of gold both as commodity and as that which it signifies when abstracted as the medium of exchange that conspiracy theories are so frequently adduced. Is it any wonder that the moments in which gold's status as commodity relative to its function as sign, that is to say, moments of socioeconomic transformation, are so apparently rife with conspiracy theories (on the part of those who are being marginalized or excluded or exploited by the transformation) and accusations of conspiracy theorizing (on the part of many who have acceded to or who are their beneficiaries)?

I began this essay by noting that wherever gold has functioned as the signifier of absolute value *and* has functioned as a store of wealth, wherever it has permitted the settling of debts with hard currency and *at the same time* has permitted the symbolic conversion of other values in a chain of infinite substitutions, it has been an object of theoretical speculation while also representing an anxiety about the limits of knowledge. And I have repeatedly discerned evidence of both poles in this vacillating economy, in which the real and the symbolic have been mediated in and through a fetishistic imaginary of gold, in locations far removed from each other in space and time, such as the nineteenth-century world of the Paris Arcades described by Benjamin and the contemporary world of postindustrial mining. This is because there is a structural affinity between the moment of the Arcades, or rather of their demise, which is what Benjamin was addressing, and that of the ruined mines of which I write. This affinity can be discerned not only in the material spaces that dominate and emblematize them but also in the forms of collective life that inhabit them—in moments that might be described as post- or pre-revolutionary, but that are in any case characterized by a certain fragmentation or inhibition of class formations and the proliferation of efforts to forge them.

In his essay on "The Paris of the Second Empire in Baudelaire," the Second Empire being the era of the Arcades, Benjamin (2003) recalls Marx's distinction between occasional and professional conspirators, the former being those who plotted conspiracies in their spare time, the latter being those who devoted themselves completely to conspiracy. They were not a class rooted in labor, in any typical sense, but were rather brought together by circumstances, in the venues where they could gather, namely, taverns. These taverns nurtured the ready-to-hand masses (the populists) that sustained the demagogic Napoleon III in his rise to power. The space that they anchored is what Benjamin called *la bohème*. The superficiality of the political commitments of the bohemians is a well-worn trope, of course. What remains interesting in Benjamin's analysis, however, is the co-emergence of the bohemian with the figure of the ragpicker, the scavenger on the slagheaps of industrial life, in whom, he says, all the bohemians recognized a part of themselves. The ragpicker was one of several figures that Benjamin offered as counterparts to nineteenth-century physiologies—the descriptions of social types so beloved of Balzac. Among the others were the gambler and the flaneur, and, of course, the conspirator.

We may say that the *zama-zama* is a contemporary figure in whom these three social types are transformed and subsumed. And the *zama-zama* dwells, like the ragpicker, on the peripheries of those ruins where industrial life once worshipped itself. The cavernous underground of the abandoned mines is graspable as a negative image of the Arcades in the moment of their vanishing. In their heyday, the illuminated tunnels of functioning mines were like vaulted alleys except that what was on display was industry and technology itself. Today's ragpicking conspirators and conspiracy theorists come together more or less spontaneously in groups of shared language, place of origin, and ethnic affiliation, dispersing almost as spontaneously along the flight-lines of both opportunity and its foreclosure—as already described. Like the conspirators of *la bohème*, they are not bound by anything like class-consciousness. Both the transience of these populations and the residual and even reinvigorated force of ethnicization, which the colonial and apartheid regimes cultivated to obviate this very possibility, intervene in and defer that process. Yet, when these conspirators and conspiracy theorists recall those shimmering days, when all that glittered seemed to be gold, they do so with a double question. Why are they not the beneficiaries of that grandiose economy, whose abandoned underground altars they now prop up with old timbers, and whose cathedrals still illuminate the Johannesburg skyline, a dreamworld of consumerism that nonetheless remains as remote for them as any biblical "city upon the hill"? Or, to phrase the matter in a more Marxian idiom: Who extracted and then withheld that wealth born of their forebears' labor from them? And, Why do these dark tunnels in which the precious metal was said to have been exhausted, and whose exhaustion supposedly led the mines to close, now seem, once again, to harbor the returning promise of gold, called money? Recall that conspiracy theory wants to understand not only what causes the world to be as it is, but why this cause is being withheld from the one who would know. Let us then consider the question of how people understand the "return" of gold, in the aftermath of industrial mining. In doing so, we want to bear in mind not merely the discourse of those who seek an explanation but also the analytic gesture that attempts to fix this discourse in a manner that makes it representative of a particular cultural understanding, an ontology, and/or a conspiracy theory.

THE MENACE IN THE MACHINE: FOREIGN ORIGINS

Many people who live and work in the vicinity of the abandoned mines say that the gold is "growing back" or "germinating." How else, they ask, can you explain the persistent presence of gold when everyone knows that the mining corporations—which sought with such tenacity and singularity of purpose, which expended such vast quantities of capital on technology and ordered the workforce to labor so relentlessly, which mobilized ethnic difference as an obstacle to class-based solidarities—would not relinquish even an ounce of the precious metal? If there is gold now, it is not because the mining corporations neglected or overlooked it, but because the earth has restored it.

Is this a metaphor? And if it is a metaphor, is it grasped as such? In what sense? By whom?

On the surface, this explanation for gold's residual existence in the mines appears to express an ontology in which the division between inorganic and organic, inanimate and animate, is either nonexistent or radically differently construed from how it is in Western metaphysics. Often miners have asked me to look at the horizon near a shaft and to observe in the late afternoon or early morning light, when the temperatures rise or fall, the gentle clouds of moisture that rise from underground. They are what many miners refer to as the evidence of the earth breathing. The possibility that the earth is animate is quite distinct from the set of beliefs, also widely expressed in this area, that associates rockfalls with the vindictive rage of a serpent spirit that is said to reside in the deepest recesses of the earth and to be covetous of men's obsequies. The serpent resides in the earth but is not of it. The idea of a living, breathing earth, in which even metal breeds, exceeds this older understanding.

Now, before reading these narratives as evidence of an ontology—rather than a belief that can be disputed—or as a representative expression of cultural alterity, it is important to recognize that many people also dispute the existence of gold's autogenerativity. These more skeptical people insist that gold is not that which can germinate, that the earth is not only mute but inanimate, and that the clouds of steam that rise from the shafts are simply a function of the changing temperatures and the fact that the mines are, in this area, full of water that evaporates in the clouds that otherwise can appear like an exhalation. Some also point to the fact that "smoke" is generated by the miners' activities and rises through the openings, that it is a mere simulacrum of breath. Still others remark, sagaciously, that breath is merely a "way of explaining" appearances.

But the figuration of the moist clouds as breath is not exclusively the property of African mythologies, however partially shared. The vents of the industrial mines, tall chimney-like structures that can still be seen in many of the ruins, were and are also referred to as "breathers." And it is impossible to know whether it was the industrial mines coding the vents through an analogy with respiration or the recoding of the earth as a pneumatic being within an animist framework that originated the chain of metaphoric substitutions by which the shafts came to acquire their appearance as organs of a terrestrial inhalation and exhalation. The undecidability of this metaphorization should not detain us; what is important here is the fact that the explanation (for why gold is present) is summoned precisely because a historically prior agency had been attributed to the corporations. More importantly, the recourse to an idea of gold's own autogenerativity, its fetishization, arises only because that prior agency is thought to have withheld or concealed the gold, or at least used it up and converted it into money and surplus value, ensuring that it would not be available to the men and women who now scavenge in the ruins. Thus, the capitalist fetishization of gold as money and the medium of exchange summons its own substitution in a displaced set of images and metaphors (which are nonetheless not completely generalized). In the most literal but also literary sense, one conspiracy (theory) is summoned by the other, and neither can be granted the status of origin.

This is not to say that the attribution of autogenerativity to gold today is simply a result or mimetic reproduction of industrial capitalist history; it is, rather, a part of the narration of that history *and* of the resistance to it. Moreover, it is not merely the earth but the technology specularized in the mine-as-arcade that has been accorded these animate qualities in the act of resisting capitalism's commodity fetish. There is, in fact, a long tradition in southern African literature of according animacy and even personhood to mining technology, as part of an effort to describe and explain the predicament of colonial dispossession.

The persisting belief in gold's power and the belief in the persistence of gold are also legible in the anachronism with which people today speak of the mines in the national economy. Among those who live near the mines as well as among many others, the belief persists that the mines are the primary source of the country's wealth. It is not uncommon to hear people say that 75–80 percent of the country's GDP is generated in the gold mines. Nor is it uncommon for people to imagine that the gold mines employ today as many as they did in the 1980s, although the number of directly employed individuals in the sector is only about 24 percent of what it was then (only 95,130 as of 2019, just before the pandemic, compared to about 480,000 in the peak year of 1988).[23] In 2016, the Chamber of Mines estimated that, with conventional mining methods, gold mining in South Africa will cease by 2033 (Chamber of Mines 2016, 30). Thus, if the mining corporations structure their operations and calculate payable gold with reference to a future of closure, ordinary people remain captured by an image of the mines as they were half a century ago. This may be one reason why people feel compelled to explain the closure of the mines through recourse to an intentional and, indeed, malevolent agency. The unevenly shared notion of gold's return is thus paired with a narrative of its withdrawal.

How do *zama-zama* miners explain that withdrawal? Once again, there are many competing explanations. But one widely circulating narrative in the area that I have described here attributes the closure of the mines to white capital flight. An elderly resident and squatter in the abandoned mine compound described above explained the matter thus: "There's still a lot of money in the mines and . . . [t]hese mines were just closed when a black man came into power. They just shut down." Answering questions posed to him about the area's history by another long-term resident, he mused, "They were upset because a black man was in power." The other man repeated, "Oh, they shut down when they heard freedom is coming." His elder interlocutor agreed: "Freedom. And they closed."

The context for this statement was a conversation about life under apartheid—understood to have been both a source of abundance for the employed, expressed mainly in dream-images of plentiful food, and a scene of brutal exclusion for those who, having lost their jobs or sources of income (however forcibly they were included in the waged regime to begin), were regularly evicted by mine management for failure to pay rents. After the closure of the mines, when squatters reoccupied many of the abandoned buildings, conflict erupted between the informal residents and the corporation that owned the mine at that time, its security forces, and state-sponsored removalists called "Red Ants." It culminated in a series of fire-bombings and the near-total destruction of the remaining facilities, including a hospital and several office buildings. This is the space now inhabited by the *zama-zamas* and other squatters, ragpickers, and scavengers.

For the men who narrated the closure of the mines as a function of the mining corporations' anxiety about a Black-majority government and possible nationalization of the resource sector, the post-apartheid conflagration was merely the belated finalization of a process that had begun decades earlier. These mines had closed in 1993, shortly after ethnicized hostel violence on the property had claimed the lives of a number of Mozambican migrants. As is well known, such ethnicized hostilities, colloquially described as the hostel wars, were fulminated by the apartheid regime during the last years of its reign, exploiting divisions that had been constitutive of mining's administrative practice throughout the century. Not only were residential spaces allocated on the basis of ethnolinguistic identity but, as revealed in the Myburgh Report of 1996, many mines based their division of labor, including the assignation of tasks and thus both remuneration and rank, on the pseudo-anthropological attribution of different skill sets and propensities to different ethnicities ("Report of the Commission of Enquiry" 1996). Rising above and descending below those ethnonational divisions, however, was a more general racial distinction.

The story of gold's rejuvenation in these ruins begs the question of metaphor. But this only returns us to the question of the analytic position whence the designation of metaphoricity emanates. If, as was discussed earlier, the recognition of one's own metaphoricity permits an escape from conspiracy theorizing, it need not demand the literalization of others' metaphors (in, for example, the attribution of ontology, despite the evidence of disputed belief). Nor must it entail the accusation that others do not grasp their own dependency on metaphor. But the recognition of metaphoricity is not yet the submission to falsification, which is what Hofstadter and Freud both advocated as the gold standard of science. Perhaps, what one may learn in the abandoned mines and the discourse of those who inhabit them is that analysis must acknowledge what can only be called the multidimensionality and nonlinearity of historical process. The linguistic forms and postindustrial practices of *zama-zamas* testify to the simultaneous drive to abstract totalization and the failure to achieve it. The vacillation between them is repeatedly incarnated in gold's changing status as commodity and signifier; in the effort to transcend ethnolinguistic difference as well as in the effort to contain that transcendence through racialization; in the aspiration to exchange and in the dream of stasis in hoarding; in the desire for mobility and in the hope for return. If, in the end, this series of vacillations leaves one breathless, that predicament may provide an occasion to reflect on how and why it is that, in times of economic instability and massive social transformation, conspiracy theories—of both populists and scholars— seem to offer such solace.

Benjamin suggested that conspiracies—and not merely conspiracy theories—arise in the spaces where class solidarity seems obstructed or without ground (in shared ongoing experiences of work and life together). Groups of coconspirators are not communities, and their forms of sociality are always premised on their own self-exceptionalization, their clandestine collectivity, and their detachment from the broader society. Insofar as the postindustrial situation is marked by a similar lack of ground due to the instability of its communities, the temporariness of work that would otherwise form the basis of shared experience, and the internal divisions created by language and place of origin, it may provide an especially fertile soil for these alternative forms of collective social action, for conspiracies and for theories about possible conspiracies. In my experience, there is much mutual suspicion in the transient worlds of the mines, despite the many forms of solidarity that exist there and that sustain its polyglot individuals. What is true in South Africa is also true in the United States, and the story of postindustrial life in one place may illuminate its possible future unfolding in another. The mark of conspiracy in both places, it seems to me, is always that it entails *both* a collective dimension (a breathing together) and a limiting structure (a suffocating tendency to secrecy), both a movement toward generalization and a withdrawal into particularisms. The task of theorizing conspiracy, then, is to understand the concepts and conditions that enable the movement between these poles rather than to resolve them into a structure of surface appearance and hidden truth.

NOTES

1 Shortly after Hofstadter published "Paranoid Style," Joel A. Tarr proffered a reading of Ian Fleming's *Goldfinger* as a contemporary reinvigoration of the populist paranoia that had infused bimetallists' discourse about the so-called Goldbugs' efforts to demonetize silver. For Tarr, the mark of populist paranoia, recursively attached to the specter of gold, was that of attributing structural events to personalized power. See Tarr (1966).

2 For a relatively recent story of a supposed rediscovery of Kruger's gold, see Munnion (2001).

3 On this element of fetishism's discourse, see Morris (2017b).

4 I am not concerned here with the specialist knowledges of geologists and mining engineers but with the commonsense explanations that traverse everyday speech among people who inhabit the areas around mines without being employed by them.

5 The term *imali*, in isiZulu and isiNdebele, means money, and it is etymologically linked to the word for wealth and/or property. Also found in Kiswahili, it is lexicalized across most of the languages spoken in this area and used to refer to almost all forms of wealth that can be exchanged for cash.

6 On a visit to the area in August 2023, I learned that the women performing manual crushing labor had vanished from the process, having been displaced by men using small-scale mechanical devices called *Penduka*. Mechanization has, in fact, meant a more general transformation in the gendered dynamics of this economy and a concentration of masculine power, with increasing poverty for, and marginalization of, women as a result.

7 Industrial accident prevention strategies in the formal mines have led to a significant reduction in injuries and deaths due to rockfalls, but the accident rate is still highest in the gold sector (compared to coal and platinum extraction), and rockfalls still account for about 35 percent of all underground accidents. Nonetheless, lung disease remains a significant source of industrial hazard. In the area described in this chapter, the women who grind the stone inhale as much dust as the men beneath the earth.

8   I am indebted to James Siegel for the analysis of overhearing. See Siegel (1997).

9   I use single quotation marks to indicate possible speech, and full double quotation marks to indicate actually reported speech.

10 On the aggressivity of jokes, see Freud (1905).

11 On the substitution of quantitative assessments of communication, or noise in the system, for the actual reading of messages, see Morris (2004); also Apter (2006).

12 I have written about the limits of this position and its critiques and offered a theory of the public sphere as a space of mistranslation in Morris 2013.

13 In recent years the insurgent militant union, the Association for Mineworkers and Construction Union, has begun using *fanakalo* again as an alternative lingua franca to English or Afrikaans. This is in contrast to the National Union of Mineworkers, which operates largely in English.

14 There are many versions of the philosophy that opposes language to violence, from liberal political theory to structuralist anthropology to Lacanian psychoanalysis. In anthropology, its most eloquent proponent is perhaps Pierre Clastres. See Clastres (1998). Arguments to the contrary, about the performative force of language and the impossibility of definitively opposing it to violence, are also numerous and various. See, for exemplary treatments, Derrida ([1967] 2016) and Butler (1997).

15 On the difficulty of translating Marx's analogizing of money, blood, and language in translation, see Parker (2012, 102).

16 The most notable case of this is the discourse on *ubuntu*, a term used to refer to social entanglements and structures of mutual obligation that mitigate against possessive individualism. But the concern with vernacular language–specific knowledge also subtends much of the discourse on indigenous knowledge as well. On *ubuntu*, see Krog (2008); see also Praeg (2014).

17 For an account of the ways in which speaking in English is made a litmus test of political sophistication, see Morris (2017a).

18 Foucault's distinction between the visible and the sayable is well-explicated by Deleuze in his theoretical biography (Deleuze 1988).

19 With respect to the capacity to signify quantity, Marx ([1867] 1992, 192) argued that, if gold is divisible by nature, it can signify the variability of value because it is "itself a product of labor and therefore potentially variable in value."

20 This ended in 1971, with the Nixon Administration's severance of the dollar from gold.

21 Eduoard Gourdon, *Les faucheurs de la nuit: Les jouers et les jouesses*, 14–15; as quoted in Benjamin (2002, 495). Benjamin often invoked this quotation in his writings on Baudelaire.

22 One form in which people attempt to skirt this teleology only to restore it is in the nomination of postindustrial mining as artisanal. For a critique of his tendency, see Morris (2018); see also Hull and James (2012, 5).

23 Current numbers are from Chamber of Mines (2016) and Stats South Africa (2023). Historical figures from Harrington, McGlashan, and Chelkowska (2004). I have used the 2019 numbers to indicate employment levels prior to the pandemic, during which period employment rates in most sectors dropped radically. However, it is notable that the gold sector lost relatively few employees during the most severe period of the pandemic, dropping at the end of 2021 to 93,998. See https://www.statista.com /statistics/981151/people-employed-gold-mining-south-africa/, accessed April 20, 2023.

JOSEPH DUMIT

_____

11 ADRIAN PIPER AND ALIEN CONSPIRACIES OF BULLYING AND WHISTLEBLOWING

INTRODUCTION

> Only human beings are capable of self-destruction, of suicide, of acts
> that have our own self-obliteration as a conscious purpose. Human
> beings must view themselves as alien enemies to be able to do this.
> They must believe that if they allow this alien enemy to exist, it will
> destroy them. And so to avoid destroying themselves, they destroy
> themselves.
>
> **Adrian Piper, *Portrait*, 1983**

    I had always been a fan of conspiracy theorists, those who take a felt insight about the world and use a heightened sense of apophenia (pattern-seeking) to flesh out its potential, more or less willing a world into existence in which their feeling becomes tangible. This geeky ability to pattern-match is a kind of antidisciplinary strategy. If disciplines tend toward paradigms that stick with specific forms of data and ignore anomalies, conspiracy thinking keeps adding things in, keeps looking deeper and elsewhere to find more and more in the world that might relate. The other power of conspiracy theorizing is the ability to embrace scale changes across potential connections fluidly, from personal, to political, to institutional, to global connections (Horton 2019). This ignoring of "proper" channels is a powerful form of analysis, where the very small and very large are linked and trafficked. This understanding was

PORTRAIT

All sentient species are biologically programmed to attack alien enemies. Some species are programmed to attack their own members as alien enemies. Rats, for example, will attack, kill or even cannibalize one another under conditions of overcrowding and deprivation. But human beings are more unique still. Only human beings are capable of self-destruction, of suicide, of acts that have our own self-obliteration as a conscious purpose.

Human beings must view themselves as alien enemies to be able to do this. They must believe that if they allow this alien enemy to exist, it will destroy them. And so to avoid destroying themselves they destroy themselves.

We can see why this might be so. We do not know ourselves very well. Often we feel assaulted by unacceptable thoughts and impulses, and move to suppress them; or shamed by unacceptable physical features, and work to remove them; or threatened by others' unacceptable behavior or appearance, and so attack or reject them. We view these things as alien enemies, not as the familiar ingrained parts of ourselves they are. And so we are constantly moved to destroy and reconstitute ourselves in conformity with our truncated and distorted self-image.

In all these cases, and others like them, we fail to recognize that we are destroying ourselves. And so our centrally motivating urge to self-destruction itself goes unrecognized. Perhaps we wouldn't recognize this particular facet of ourselves if it stared us in the face.

© Adrian Piper 1983

Nagasaki, August 9, 1945, three minutes after the bombing. The smoke column has reached 20,000 feet. (Hiroshima–Nagasaki Publishing Committee, U.S. Army returned materials.)

11.1 Adrian Piper, *Portrait*, 1983. Photostat, 40 × 30 inches (101.6 cm × 76.2 cm). Private collection. © Adrian Piper Research Archive (APRA) Foundation Berlin.

helpful for learning from those who suffer from illnesses that medicine ignores (Dumit 2006). Their conspiratorial grasp of how the system was against them provided basic insights into how structural inequalities could be built into corporate and state institutions as tools of "efficiency," tools whose harm could be denied and disavowed. This is perhaps best summed up with the phrase a sufferer was told when trying to get care from a hospital: "We don't even have a code for this disease, so we're not going to pay you" (H. Johnson 1997).

This was my starting point when I started teaching a conspiracy/theory course with Joe Masco in the fall of 2016: How to take conspiracy theories seriously as practices of seeing differently? Trump's election and the elevation of "conspiracy theory" as a tool of political manipulation shifted the focus. These mass social media practices of seeding, manipulating, and trolling conspiracy theories are taken up by other chapters in this volume. In what follows, I redouble my efforts to learn how the institutionalization of structural inequalities traffics in conspiracies and conspiracy theories.

Encountering the work of artist and philosopher Adrian Piper changed again how I understand and work with conspiracies. Piper questions how humans become alien to themselves in a conspiratorial way that leads to mutual destruction. How can we claim to care about communities and worlds and yet stand by as our everyday, institutionalized practices destroy our own future and all our children's futures? Piper ceaselessly probes this paranoiac and xenophobic paradox in her conceptual art and scholarly writing. Born and raised in New York and currently living in Berlin, she has achieved eminence in both art and philosophy for her investigations, which are inspired by Kant and the promise of transcendent rationality in the world. She is an optimist regarding the possibility of a transpersonal ethics and a lifelong keen ethnographer (as artist and philosopher) of the practical ethics of racism and capitalism. She has lived within the effective conspiracy of these processes, which she calls "bully systems," in markets and at universities (2013b, 211). These systems convinced people to participate in them, rendering structural and specific violences onto nonnormative, anomalous people. And yet she also strove to understand the choices that we all have, every day, when we witness inequality and harassment: the choice to withdraw into individuality (as a pseudo-neutrality), becoming bystanders who amplify the system, or to do the right thing, to blow the whistle and stand up for a transpersonal world, even if that choice increases one's own suffering (2013b, 394–415; 2018, 76, 99–127).

Piper works from what she calls "the indexical present," pointing to this moment here-now that I am in, the moment that you are in, a moment that is interpersonal and ongoing, here and now and actively making "our" future (Piper [1990b] 1996). Piper says of her art that it offers a reflection of this moment, and that each person will take it differently. I think the word "we" in an essay like this can be offered this way: "We" is not a claim about a universal subject but an indexical pointing to a question of who I, the author, and you, the reader, are becoming; what you are including yourself in, right now, and whenever something happens and you are standing by. This becoming is transpersonal when it is not about the past or other people but about attending directly to our care-full future making of the institutions we are inhabiting.

For Piper, aliens are real, real enough to destroy the world. And we are simultaneously part of the plot and of the denial that the plot is unfolding. In this chapter, I share my ongoing questioning of how to take conspiracy theorizing seriously. Is capitalism a conspiracy? Is race a conspiracy? Is man a conspiracy? Are there aliens? Do they live among us? These seem like trick questions, but they are not. Inside them is a serious inquiry into the conspiratorial nature of reality. On the one hand, we like to think that conspiracy theorists are crazy, while we critics justly accuse them of irrationality because they get the "cause" wrong. We know there are no super-secret cabals of men in smoke-filled rooms plotting the control and destruction of others. We know that the world is not great, but okay, made up of fallible humans. We are trying. Rationality will save us from misguided conspiracy theorists.

This is the stance taken by Richard Hofstadter (1964) in his now-standard reference article, "The Paranoid Style in American Politics." Hofstadter treats humans as rational subjects while claiming that too many of them are susceptible to fantasies, which prevent their proper apprehension of historical truth. Hofstadter engages in a bioclinical framing of paranoia precisely to hierarchize his own style of thought as the only normal, sane, and proper one, and to declare his position as neutral, above the fray of the world, merely observing it. He is not paranoid, and he thinks no one should be.

On the other hand, is this notion of crazy conspiracy theorists not itself a distraction from the deeper truth: that something really is out to get us, and that it is controlling our perceptions and behaviors; hurting people right in front of us as we stand by; destroying our world, planet, lives, souls, and livelihoods. Maybe we need to recognize conspiracy theories as specific kinds of propositions whose investigation risks our subjecthood and the way we understand the world. We need to ask how the way we live might be contributing to larger systems that are rigged against us and others. We need to continually question how we can stand by, be bystanders, when we see people being hurt and harassed in front of us. How can we turn away or pretend that it is someone else's problem when we know that the systems we are in have perpetuated this very happening? How can we protect a system when our very defense of it amplifies the problems we know will repeat again in the next generation?

The power of conspiracy/theory is how it scales reality—from the interpersonal moment right in front of us, through institutions and media, all the way to social systems and world history. Conspiracy/theory disobeys disciplines, questions what it means to be human, asks about secret causes, and is willing to consider that we do not already know what is out there. It does not rule out aliens. A conspiracy theory is material-existential, systemic-individual, socio-psycho-biogenic. It is comprehensive; it does not leave loose ends. And isn't this what theory should do?

This chapter shares my ongoing homework. I investigate the extent to which we can theorize our so-called self-destructing world through an amplified form of conspiracy theory that refuses to purify and separate socio-psycho-biogenic processes, that refuses to keep the university outside of theory, that refuses to separate corporations from knowledge, whiteness from psychology, aliens from institutions. Capitalism, racism, humanism, alienation, and aliens: the question is perhaps not whether there is a conspiracy, but which conspiracies we are in, how "we" are differently in those conspiracies, and how we are reinforcing the very things that we claim to be against. Can we contemplate or even consider a world without capitalism or innocence? Can we abandon or destroy "our" comfortable world in favor of one that is nonracist and nonhyperviolent? Maybe that is what changing the world means: asking "What needs to go?" and learning how to let go.

CONSPIRACY CAPITALISM

> Money has spent us.
>
> **Tanya Tagaq, "Retribution," 2016**

Is capitalism a conspiracy? The situation is bleak. I have spent the last twenty years tracing some of the many modes through which large, often multinational corporations, organized to grow as their primary directive, pursue actions that are directly antihuman. We are mostly familiar now with the fact that oil companies like Exxon and Shell used science to predict climate change in the 1970s, building their oil platforms higher in anticipation of sea-level rise to come while simultaneously spending millions to create a controversy around climate change so they could ensure that policies would not prevent this predicted future from happening (Lieberman and Rust 2015; see also this volume 7). Many companies like this claim they are bound by fiduciary duty to their shareholders and other owners not to do anything contrary to growth, even when it is evil but legal (or illegal but affordable). It is not intentional; anthropomorphism does not apply. Corporations are not persons, no matter how many legal rituals we perform as though they were. If helping humans have more health, happiness, democracy, and so on enables more growth, corporations pursue them; if hurting humans, killing them, and destroying democracy enables more growth, corporations pursue them. Growth is the sole directive and, unfortunately for all of us, for the last fifty years, antihuman activities have led to more growth. Here are two brief examples to show that I am not exaggerating by calling large corporations aliens who do not care if the planet is destroyed.

PHARMA

We all hope that the health care industry is different, that it is really about people. Yet pharmaceutical companies and the health care industry as a whole need to grow; this is what they keep telling us (Dumit 2012). This means growing "health" itself, which on first hearing sounds good. But on second thought, health should actually be a societal cost to be reduced, not a market to be grown. Companies will actively avoid researching new drugs if these new drugs are likely to cut into long-term profits from less helpful drugs. They evaluate clinical trials based on how many pill sales the trial will result in, not on how many people will be helped. They know this is evil, but they blame us (society and shareholders) for incentivizing them to make ineffective medicines that are given to more people who can be shown to be "at risk," rather than develop more targeted medicine for those who would most benefit from it. Even more tragically, they will actively shut down profitable research areas of health research if another area promises relatively more growth (Dumit 2017). When I put it this way, it sounds evil. It is evil if you are human. But it is also good business practice, and executives defend it as necessary when society has handed over medical research to companies.

Evil may seem a strong word. Reviewers for an anthropology journal told me to not use it. I used instead Pignarre and Stengers's notion of "infernal alternatives," describing the way that capitalism (and bureaucracy) presents agents with a forced choice: do this evil thing or the company will be destroyed. But it usually does not look so evil because it comes in the form of a growth chart, allowing the directors to make an apparently logical choice among alternatives, some of which clearly lead to more growth than others, and with most, if not all, of the ethical and social and environmental consequences absent from the chart. They will have been "cleaned" away (Dumit 2017; Pignarre and Stengers 2011).

Pignarre and Stengers (2011, 21) thus call for an "ethnology of capitalism," one that attends to recognizing the beast and how it works rather than defining it. Methodologically, I take this as a call to track the changing practical discourses and logics of the pharmaceutical market worldview—methods of counting, accounting, and being accountable to. It is part of my larger body of work, studying the ways in which companies see and make worlds, how they measure value and define what counts as health.

Many capitalists go further still and embrace the paranoia that Hofstadter decried. For them, paranoia is rational (once you are fully possessed by identification with your company) because everyone is out to get you. They are your competitors, after all. And rationality is paranoid; you are never doing enough. Where Marx detailed the genesis of this psychological subject and its naturalization, Intel's former CEO Andy Grove, author of *Only the Paranoid Survive*, developed a biological theory of human nature, embracing paranoia precisely because it is the most rational approach to identifying oneself with pure growth: "Growth is kinda built into everyone's genes. It's built into management's genes, the salesman's genes, the investors' desires. People expect companies to grow" (Grove 2001). Grove's naturalization of growth as kind-of-genetic allows him a kind-of-innocence, erasing any social role in shaping human nature. Kind-of-genetics serves as the natural cause of society and capitalism, allowing Grove and others to avoid personal or collective responsibility for the consequences of their actions, and justify their dedicating 100 percent of their time and energy into cynical and antihuman growth.

When pharma companies need to grow the number of medicines in the world and the amount consumed by our bodies every year, they choose to research chronic treatments over cures and vaccines. Back in 2003, one pharmacoeconomic analysis concluded that vaccines should not be researched by companies at all, because if a vaccine worked, it would "more likely interfere with the spread of the disease more than drug treatments, thus reducing demand for the product" (Kremer and Snyder 2003). Curing a disease sounds crucial to humans, but to companies it means destroying their markets.

When the COVID-19 pandemic happened, I hoped for a counterexample to show how corporations could care more about stopping the pandemic than about making profits. But in fact, COVID-19 showed a new way to make vaccines a growth strategy for pharma companies. In a global crisis, if companies gave vaccines to only one-quarter of the world and spent the rest of their public relations (PR) budgets on lobbying to keep the intellectual property rights away from the rest of the world, they could ensure that the market potential of their vaccines would be extended (Mookim 2021, Lerner 2020).[1] Pfizer and Moderna, as well as Bill Gates and Joe Biden, all paid lip service to the idea that it was vital to grant global access to vaccines. But future profit streams clearly took precedence in denying countries in the Global South the ability to make those vaccines, which in turn played a role in enabling variants to emerge (Stiglitz 2022; Stiglitz and Wallach 2021). We do not yet know if they actually modeled variant production in this way, but we do know that both Pfizer and Moderna had more profits during 2020 and 2021 than ever before (an approximately 70 percent profit margin) and that they did not spend their vast and powerful PR budgets countering vaccine hesitancy or misinformation about masks and ventilation because, unfortunately for humans, these would have slowed future growth of the vaccine markets.

Perhaps surprisingly, even conspiracy spy writers like John le Carré are exceeded in imagination by this investment. In an epilogue to his horrifying pharmaceutical conspiracy thriller *The Constant Gardener*, le Carré (2004) writes, "As my journey through the pharmaceutical jungle progressed, I came to realize that, by comparison with the reality, my story was as tame as a holiday postcard." He learned this from a pharma whistleblower (Olivieri 2020). Not only do pharma companies take advantage of ethical variability across the world to pit governments against each other, allowing them to engage in deadly clinical trials with few consequences, as they conceal deadly side effects behind ghostwritten articles to manipulate public, governmental, and medical knowledge of them (Petryna 2009; Sismondo 2009; Healy 2012). They will extort people and countries to unbelievable limits if they have something that saves lives (Davies et al. 2021), and they will do what they can to prevent new research into better treatments if it endangers ongoing profits from less effective ones (Dumit 2017).

FRACKING

From most human perspectives, fracking is about as stupid an industry as can be imagined. In its most basic terms, fracking is a technique of fracturing rock deep below the earth's surface to release oil or natural gases such as methane. These fuels rise to the surface through a drill pipe and are subsequently sold as energy. Fracking-derived oil and gas power 31 percent of current US electricity production, with the market growing worldwide. Along the way, fracking terraforms the planet at an almost unimaginable scale. The practice requires a carpet of drilling pads on land secretly bought out from underneath most farmers and homeowners, with each pad requiring hundreds of trucks and men, tens of millions of gallons of fresh water that is rendered poisonous but whose disposal remains unregulated, and leaves in its wake squashed environmental regulations, sick families, tap water that can be set on fire, earthquake swarms in areas that have never before had earthquakes, and laws that outlaw protests against the practice (Wylie 2018).

Yet the "need" for fracking may be entirely fake. It exists because energy consumption needs to continue to grow. Alternative energy often has the paradoxical effect of growing energy consumption rather than substituting one form for another (Zehner 2012). Degrowth is "not in society's best interest." "Society" here is a euphemism for government reelection (in Euro-America), which is so messed up, we often refuse to contemplate it. But to quickly summarize: the core axiom of democratic politics is that the economy indexes society's success, so that (unfortunately) economic growth has come to stand in for social progress. Growing the economy therefore becomes the basic aim of most politicians and political parties. And although they may balk at certain forms of destruction—of the environment, urban health, and so on—they have become subservient to a notion that growth is good; and growth means more energy consumption, more health care consumption, more surveillance, more police, more war—more of almost everything that can be privatized or sold is necessarily good (or at least has the benefit of doubt).

When we step back, this all is suicidal, as Greta Thunberg and others remind us. Growth for growth's sake is destroying the planet, corrupting facts, sacrificing lives for growth. It is obviously an out-of-control logic based on a stupid set of values. One task of conspiracy/theory is to understand how this has become a kind of unquestioned common sense—at least for some—and how it survives even when it is in no one's long-term interest.

One of my approaches to make sense of this is to make a game about it. In a class I taught, we created *Frack: The Game*, in which each participant plays as a fracking company, trying to grow as big as possible before the world ends (Dumit 2017). The idea was that in playing as a company a participant experiences first-hand the tension between trying in some way to steer a company to do good while trying to beat the competition. Almost immediately, players' desires to be good actors are overcome by the gleeful paranoia of anticipating what the others might do, outfoxing them, outgrowing them, and using whatever means are available in the game to do so. In modeling the game as much as possible on how companies actually behave, perhaps players notice that this is how the world is ending. Or perhaps, they do not look up.

CORPORATE CONCLUSION

In these examples, corporations are knowingly and actively destroying land and our planet's habitability, all the while openly admitting that their goals have nothing to do with human welfare and that they will manipulate facts and knowledge as much as they can get away with, even if it means accelerating the end of the world. These accounts presume an underlying subject who is rational yet abducted; that is, capitalism has "reduced [our] intelligence" (Pignarre and Stengers 2011, 28) by providing us instead with a type of limited common sense. With my work in this area, I hoped to account for the apparent conspiracy of capitalism that many of us participate in without full awareness. I have depended in this analysis on a form of enlightenment rhetoric: that by pointing out how stupidly we are acting, we might learn to act differently.

Yet rather than appearing as a conspiracy, it seems almost banal. This is where most alien invasion movies pick up. Only in the face of an alien invasion would we then band together to overthrow the inhuman overlords. Alien movies are often about corporations with their own antihuman missions—bringing back from outer space the creature that is infecting everyone and keeping it alive so that profit and/or a war machine (and profit) can be made. We know these plots and call them science fiction or horror. We call them entertainment precisely to deny and unsee the ways in which we already live with aliens we pretend are natural. We are surprisingly loyal to our institutions even as they harm people in front of us and the planet. Is this our future? Here is a transcript:

> Texas 2020. We were once mankind. We were humanity. And now we are no more than pests. Vermin. They came here to extermi-nate us. They took our history and culture. They covered our land-marks with dying humanity (images of buildings destroyed by alien spacecraft). They killed us in waves when they first arrived. They built these megastructures that spew methane, manufac-turing their atmosphere. They've sown their crops, snuffing out our plant life, raising the global temperature, causing our cities to flood. They waged war on Earth, they set fire to our forests. It's already hard to breathe. Impossible to breathe if you are close to the stacks. . . . They know it's just a matter of time before the entire planet is theirs. . . . But we're survivors. Scrounging enough to eat, gathering enough morale to fight . . . (Oats Studios 2017)

This transcript is of the opening lines of a 2017 short film. I thought it was an ironic take on corporations or colonial America, based on the new Intergovernmental Panel on Climate Change (IPCC) reports, that corpo-rations treat us like pests, transforming our history and culture, building factories that create greenhouse gases, changing our atmosphere, indus-trializing our crops at the cost of forests, climate change, fires, floods, pollution, and how we need to stop being bystanders and stand up. But it was serious; the film short was about the aliens (Lambie 2017). The film showed images of humanoid-insect aliens with guns walking among people, whipping them and collecting them, followed by the images of kids loading rifles, women picking them up and heading to battle. It was the cookie-cutter scrappy-but-smart militia will-save-the-day arc. It was only ever a story about humanity, innocent of the changes to the planet; a story about the need to prepare for war by making better weap-ons; a story of a few who see what is happening to save humanity by sav-ing themselves; a story about heroes who look everywhere but at them-selves; a story in which tremendous sacrifice returns us to the present, where the aliens are all dead and we are safe and have shopping malls.[2]

However, just attending to the world-destroying capacity of corporations does not account for how benefiting from them pairs with not only denial but viciousness among institutions or persons. It does not account for why capitalism's violence is also deeply sexualized, racialized, colonial, and normalized against disabilities (Robinson 2020; Piepzna-Samarasinha and Lakshmi 2018). But in making a different account, it is imperative not to fall into Grove's form of denial, in which evil is essentially justified as a side effect of a natural kind-of-genetic propensity, or that of Steven Pinker and so many other sociobiology apologists, who describe human nature as naturally evil or self-interested or individualist. Each of these worldviews treats racism and sexism as secondary to other problems, or as not a social problem at all. The question for conspiracy/theory then is: How to make vicious, tenacious, willfully blind inhumanity accountable without naturalizing it? How to see structures not as fixed or inevitable but as maintained and participatory? Answering these questions means starting at home, in our own institutions.

ADRIAN PIPER AND BULLYING INSTITUTIONS: IS THE UNIVERSITY A CONSPIRACY?

> We do not know ourselves very well. Often we feel assaulted by unacceptable thoughts and impulses, and move to suppress them . . . or threatened by others' unacceptable behavior or appearance, and so attack or reject them. We view these things as alien enemies, not as the familiar ingrained parts of ourselves they are. And so we are constantly moved to destroy and reconstitute ourselves in conformity with our truncated and distorted self-image.
>
> **Adrian Piper, *Portrait*, 1983**

As an academic, my institutional home is the university. As an anthropologist who studies the effects of capitalist growth decision-making on humans and the planet, I could not help but find the same effects deeply present in academia. When asked in 2014 to teach a five-hundred-student class on "Introduction to Cultural Anthropology," I organized it around debt. It was full of cross-cultural ethnographies of the abuses of debt in different places and times; but we also, every week, examined with the students how their collective student debt was worse than their parents' debt; how academia itself was structured at every level by artificial scarcity, economic growth pressure, and an amplification of inequalities actively producing more class and race injustice, including an ever-increasing student-teacher ratio as "efficiency" (good for university capital growth, terrible for student learning). The very class we were in together was one for which some students incurred hundreds of thousands of dollars in debt, as rules were being changed to make the force and longevity of that debt worse, while others incurred none. We discussed how conspiracy theories seemed inadequate relative to the actual deep state corporate lobbying-effects taking place in plain sight. These effects were clear enough if you looked, and were reported on repeatedly; and yet, that never quite made a difference.

Adrian Piper's *Rationality and the Structure of the Self: A Two-Volume Study in Kantian Metaethics* is a groundbreaking metaethical analysis. It achieves its power by not taking the social practices of power for granted, as so much of philosophy does. Piper explained in a talk that "Kant has a model of rationality and a model of the self, which I think is just ideal for giving a complete analysis of xenophobia, racial discrimination, gender discrimination, you name it, there's really a good solid model in the text" (Piper 1992, @2:02:40).

Piper therefore draws on ethical cases from real life, the interpersonal moments we live in daily life, the problems we face and the decisions we make. This is where rationality should intervene. She gives an example: a young untenured female professor is harassed in a variety of explicit ways by a senior male colleague (2013b, 394). The professor informs her chair of this behavior, who explains away the behavior, saying that the senior colleague is a "good guy," that being untenured is stressful, that she might have misheard or misunderstood, and in any case the department is relatively well-functioning, and one should not rock the boat. Regardless of the chair's idea of ethics, in practice he is engaging in what Piper analyzes as denial and disavowal. The chair's "dissociation of [the female professor's] pain from the domain of moral significance is a pseudo rational attempt to protect his social network at the expense of social justice" (2013b, 442).

Piper uses this important moment in academia, the harassment and bullying of relatively disempowered members, to inquire into the perpetuation of bullying. She describes a specific situation and the words-as-actions that enact worlding via dismissal and denial, what Piper calls a "bully system" that functions to maintain itself in no small part by keeping anomalous individuals (those who do not conform to norms of appearance, behavior, argument, deference) out. Institutions, she explains, "are composed of individuals, and that institutional manifestations of racism are composed of interpersonal ones" (Piper [1990b] 1996, 236). These systems are in fact processes taking place now, in "the indexical present," between people, between us, in the decisions we are now making.

Piper draws out this systemic process from within Kant's work on aporias and how people respond to anomalies, as well as from the work of Thomas Kuhn's (2012) historical work, in *The Structure of Scientific Revolutions*, that introduced the notion of "paradigm change" into popular consciousness. Kuhn's strength was in charting just how hard it was for new facts that challenged existing theories to be accepted by most of those in power. Institutions such as journals made it relatively easy for the challenging facts to be dismissed as anomalies. Kuhn charted the tenacity with which senior members of departments, conference organizers, and journal editors refused to allow anomalous facts into print, insisting on the old, standard, normal way of doing science and talking about science. He repeated Max Planck's half-joke about how "science progresses one funeral at a time," noting that most journals changed their recognition practices only once those in power died. Many disciplinarians would rather die than change. They would rather abuse science and fellow scientists than admit their own role in retarding it.

Piper then extends Kuhn's account as an object lesson in rationality's humanness in context. Constrained within systems that enforce hierarchy, inequality, and scarcity, persons come to believe that they are egocentric individuals, they behave as if their survival depends on defending the system, and they act in inhuman ways toward others who challenge the system. As they come to feel that anomalous facts are to be denied, they also come to feel that people who espouse those facts are anomalous and less deserving of respect. They also feel disrespect for others who are demographically anomalous (e.g., in the academy, women and persons of color). The anomalous are actively attacked as (dangerous) aliens, "but what counts as alien, what counts as fearful and unfamiliar, is entirely a matter of social context" (Piper [1993] 1996, 256). And Piper is clear that those behaving inhumanely are not completely wrong about survival—given their socialization and environment. First, there are rewards for accepting the normative "descriptive theory of social reality as factual, in the form of a feeling of cognitive stability and inclusion in social community. . . . The *authority of reward* consists in the approval, status, goods, resources, and favorable treatment bestowed on us for 'toeing the party line'" (Piper 2013b, 361; see also Piper 2014).

In the case of perpetrators of bullying, they bully by not following the rules they otherwise enforce, that is, by making exceptions for themselves, conspiring together against their own fears of otherness. The bullying institution in turn supports these strategies even as it destroys the spirit of its defenders. Piper's analysis is confirmed by the parallel and extensive work of Sara Ahmed (2012, 2021) describing these mechanisms of refusing and defusing complaint. Like Ahmed's attention to the experience of the harassed, Piper attends to the dispositions and decisions of the enablers. Ahmed builds on experience, interviews, and Edward Said's definition of professionalism as "not rocking the boat, not straying outside of accepted paradigms of limits," which she notes reproduces so much violence in "keeping things steady" (Ahmed 2019; Said 1996, 74). Piper (2013b, 390) ties it directly to conspiracy/theory: "The proscription of moral commentary is, more usually, a conspiratorial proscription of boat-rocking."

Piper describes how institutions and wider parts of our societies come to be conspiratorially organized: how we come to behave as if we are sharing breath in a room to the point that individuals are correct in believing they have a lot to lose if they respect the anomalous in others (or in themselves), even if they know that behaving in this way betrays the work to which they contribute. We condemn ourselves: the result, Piper (2013b) writes, is that "one's preoccupation with external events or anticipated external events is so all-encompassing that one fails to notice one's own internal discomfort at all. This is an abdication of the present self to an anticipated future scenario" (281). Rationality can be bullied, in other words, precisely through power because power shapes values, and those who have power do not have to recognize certain truths.

Piper looks at these professionalizing decisions with *both* understanding and judgment. *Understanding* that their job can be on the line, that their benefits might be diminished if they do not "toe the line" (2013a, @14:30; cf. 2013b, 361). She works to *understand* that they might not want to know, that they might defend the system and its benefits to themselves and others, rather than working to change it and make it into a different system. And she *judges* their effects on the moment and the future. She shows that those who allow this to happen are *amplifying* the system's harm to the anomalous. By protecting themselves now, they are condemning their own future and that of future colleagues and students who will suffer more for having to defend themselves from a clearly harmful system.

Bully systems thus do not just reinforce power hierarchies and inequality; they reward people for taking advantage of the system. Research into academic bullying confirms that it "becomes a career tool," one that that can force out promising scholars and that facilitates mediocre scholarship and even establishes some bullies as citationaly central (Täuber and Mahmoudi 2022). This irony is not lost on Piper. In her memoir she describes the process of getting a PhD in philosophy at Harvard and witnessing graduate students learning to betray their ideals in order to fit in, in part by attacking anomalous others. Over time, they ascended to professorial positions in which they were philosophically compromised and so participated in the advancement of bullying institutions that were the opposite of what they taught. Their bitterness increased even as they pretended, even to themselves, to be polite (Piper 2018).

The tragedy from a conspiracy/theory perspective is that it is the system that is a truly inhuman alien running something like a *Squid Game* (Tan 2021), using metrics of reward and punishment to enforce artificial scarcity (Biagioli and Lippman 2020). These systems reward some humans to the extent that they choose to treat other humans as less-than-human, as dangerous alien threats, destroying both their flourishing and the possibility for positive change.

BYSTANDING IS NOT INNOCENT: IT AMPLIFIES BULLY SYSTEMS

> We often assume the stance of what amounts to disingenuous innocence. The things that I don't know, I don't have to deal with. And please don't tell me about them. Because if you do, I won't be able to deal with anything. That's the attitude.
>
> **Adrian Piper, Interview, 2013a, @37:10**

The real tragedy of the academia we operate within (and corporations and other institutions as well) is the way in which we engage in self-deception regarding the role of bystanders. Thus far we have stayed at the level of malicious people (harassers) and direct enablers (chairs and administrators). We might even feel okay for not having been such a bad actor ourselves. And yet we too often stand by or move out of the way as something happens, when someone looks for help. The practice of bystanding is to actively identify with and to claim being passive and nonparticipating. We say to ourselves (and often to others, too) that we did not do anything. That the system will take care of it. We might even care about the injury to the harassed, but from a distance. We will not do anything.

Piper again sympathizes with this position: it is complex; our survival, the world we know, is at stake. Disingenuous innocence is a survival strategy. It is not fragility, as a psychological reaction (DiAngelo 2018), because it knows. It pretends to be innocent of that knowing, even as it *actively* refuses to learn more. Thus, it is "well-intentioned" colleagues who can be the most disingenuous when faced with the task of responding to injustice when it is right in front of them. Their self-esteem and their egocentric sense of their own survival produce a breathing together, a conspiring together, emitted as a thinly veiled viciousness against those who threaten it. And they stay docile in this fashion precisely because they know that if they speak up, they too will be subjected to the same subtle and overt sanctions that they are perpetuating. This active refusal to learn more contributes, however, to the conspiracies of silence that those who make complaints describe, a conspiracy that Sara Ahmed describes as a "wall of investment" in institution, person, and identity (Ahmed 2021, 117). It is as if we are bribed for complicity with a job, with an institutional home that gives us an identity, with friends (people who would leave us if we were to leave the institution or betray it). We academics might even defend our institution as a necessary evil to protect knowledge making from the greater evils of pure capitalism, even as we reinforce a system that creates massive student debt and that exploits most of its staff and adjuncts.

Innocence, even disingenuous innocence, promises to save our souls a little, but here conspiracy theory helps us to understand our complicity. Being a bystander is not actually standing by and staying out of the way. Piper (2018, 119–25) insists that we notice how bystanding amplifies the bully system, protecting it and making it worse. For instance, the act of bystanding often encourages others to bystand. It implies that what is happening is okay, is right, even a normal part of culture. Bystanding is telling the person being harassed that they are on their own (betraying any sense of solidarity as a false promise). It is reinforcing the idea that the current system is doing what it is supposed to be doing, and bystanding implies that damage might result from not bystanding, from intervening in the harm. In other words, we reinforce the institution as a zero-sum competition for limited resources, in which the privilege to perpetrate or ignore harm is something to be taken advantage of.

All enablers together are the bully system: institutions are made of interpersonal interactions, all those moments when another is there and treated pseudo-rationally, as less deserving. Piper describes how "racism is not an abstract, distant problem that affects all those poor, unfortunate other people out there. It begins between you and me, right here and now, in the indexical present" (Piper [1990b] 1996, 248). In other words, bully systems and conspiracies are not on paper, even if we can see it in data and stats (and while metrics are helpful, we should not become dependent on them, since once data are made the target of regulation, those metrics are immediately "gamed" by those in power [Griesemer 2020]). Bully systems are the actions we are always taking with others, even if we claim they are nonactions. We can see, too, how our bystanding is a performative claim that nothing important, nothing needing action, is happening. How bystanding is a form of gaslighting, buttressing the accusation that someone is making up a conspiracy theory. The perpetuation of bully systems and disingenuous innocence means that everyone really is out to stop complaints from being heard. This is felt directly by everyone in the form of so-called survival tips (often called mentoring): you should really ignore that problem person, let the issue go, let the system take care of it, that person just does not get it.

I belabor the figure of the bystander because in talking with colleagues and students about these issues, it is clear that *we want the possibility of neutrality and innocence*. We want to believe in the idea of a resting place in the middle of complexity and overwhelming conditions. It matters, then, to understand that in bystanding we are further *amplifying* this system and its behavior for our future selves and our colleagues, that we are helping make sure our students behave in similar ways in their futures. But our survival strategies will backfire. By claiming to fear future harm while letting current harms persist, bystanders create the context for more and more future harm. By bystanding, we become part of the very conspiracy that we pretend to analyze, acting like innocents in front of those we care about. But there are no innocent bystanders. Even children are learning in each moment how to behave from those around them. The hardest part of conspiracy/theory is realizing that you are part of it, that you are not innocent at all, you are engaging in self-deception, and that the wool over your eyes is actively held in place by your own hands.

IT GETS WORSE: MEAN-SPIRITED AND ANOMALOUS INDIVIDUALS

> People who shut their eyes to reality simply invite their own destruction, and anyone who insists on remaining in a state of innocence long after that innocence is dead, turns himself into a monster.
>
> **James Baldwin, *The Fire Next Time*, 1984**

Bystanding (and more, active enabling) is fake believing that the bad stuff will stop after this. This very thing that you wish you did not have to be part of. This thing that you wish would only happen once, even though you know in your bones that it will continue, which is precisely why you are in denial of this future even while seeing the present which you cannot deny. You can dissociate. You can become cruel. You can lose your soul. You can deny your participation with justifications and rationalizations that only ruin your soul even more. You become vicious to yourself and others. Especially to the others who remind you of your guilt. This is worse: we become mean-spirited toward others.

> Mean-spiritedness . . . evinces poverty of spirit. It is a condition of emotional deprivation, in which inner integrity is violated by the other's felt distress—i.e., in which one is vicariously possessed by that distress; and in which the demand for relief of that distress is met by desensitizing and fortifying the self against it—i.e., in which one is self-absorbed by one's own. Thus the spiritually undernourished or mean-spirited self swings between vicarious possession and self-absorption relative to the other's distress. It is bereft of the inner resources both for preserving the integrity of the self against incursion by the other, and for extending those resources beyond the self to the other. (Piper 2013b, 261)

Piper thus shows the pseudo-rational ways in which we bystanders become mean-spirited as a result of being exposed to others' distress. Piper describes this process as keeping the egocentric gains of indulgence and power rather than developing the character of "transpersonal rationality." My gloss on this is that because we are connected, we do care; therefore, we do not want to hear too much. We would prefer that we had not seen it. Sometimes we do not even want to read or hear the whole complaint. Yet we bystanders are already entangled, our very statement to ourselves that we are not doing anything is already a (secret) acknowledgment that we feel the other's suffering (and would not want it to happen to us). In claiming not to be entangled we separate ourselves from this transpersonal communion with them. In telling ourselves a story about our own noninvolvement, we cut off our involution, our connections *that we feel*.

We try to forget our tiny but active contributions to the problem, the times in the past when we also looked the other way. We try to imagine ourselves as individuals who are truly separate, not involved. But this active noninvolvement itself becomes oppressive. And in so doing we suffer both from our separation from community and from our need to deny that we are not innocent. Because we do care, we turn away, so we are not pulled into the risky act of caring enough to change the system. Piper's analysis of privileged subjects is precisely one in which transpersonal ethics are foundational but covered over, which results in a pseudo-separate self who suffers from separation. Discomfort rules. Piper emphasizes that this is a mode of survival, but survival only in an egocentric individuality that protects the system rather than people.

Most tragically perhaps, the harassed other is the one reminding us of our guilt. Having cut ourselves off from feeling *their* suffering, we cement our separation by seeing them as causing our discomfort. Their difference from us becomes a category that pseudo-rationally explains our suffering. They become anomalies in our world, aliens, and we become xenophobic toward those "alien" like them (see Piper 2013b, chs. 10 and 11, esp., 428). Even if we are like them. And it eats us from within. Whether we actively have helped to hurt others, or passively abstained from stopping the inequality and harm that we benefit from, we are haunted by our complicity, increasing our separation. The eruption of mean-spiritedness is literally the climax of alien horror films like *Invasion of the Body Snatchers*: the moment when a friend or mentor turns on someone they have promised to protect, opening their mouth and pointing. It is the moment when we turn on, by turning away from, those we have promised to protect.

In one of her art pieces, *Vote/Emote* (1990), Piper gave people the opportunity to anonymously list their fears about what others might say and do.

> The privacy and the anonymity of the situation was really fascinating. Most people expressed a fear of retribution. People said things like, I'm afraid that you will treat me as I have treated you. I'm afraid that you think of me in the ways I've thought of you is very moving. And there were also lots of other confidences in these texts. I've transcribed them and hope to eventually publish them. (Piper 1992, @1:45:48)

This projection of one's own thoughts onto one's own victims (individually and collectively) is a critical aspect of understanding the vicious intensity of colonial and settler states and institutions. These projections enable these respondents to participate in ongoing violence and avoid even trying to understand the pervasive violence of states and institutions.[3] Piper notes *one* of the ways in which racism can become alien conspiracy: "The ultimate racist fear is the loss of self through coercive interpenetration by an omnipotent alien invader. Racists secretly worry that black people will do that to them" (Piper [1991] 1996, 253–54). This capacity to see others as dangerous aliens is a distraction from the actual aliens trying to run the world: corporations and bullying institutions, racial capitalism and white supremacy. Conspiracy/theory has to confront this doubled alien.

On the one hand, institutions are inhuman aliens seemingly/actually controlling our thought and behavior by setting up artificial scarcity and survival needs that we mistake for natural conditions. We explicitly disavow our own involvement in perpetuating systems of bullying and inequality because we want to keep our jobs. Bystanding deeply enables more than inequality in society, from sexism and racism to other forms of ableism and norms governing etiquette. Bystanding amplifies its viciousness. In bystanding we render difference categorical and dangerous and reinforce hierarchies of humanness. We do not want "others" to speak so loudly, to remind us so clearly of the problems of the system that we are trying to put up with (because we have put up with it so far). On the other hand, because we think we have these anomalous individuals among us and fear them in our fantasies, we do not see the real alien institutions and ourselves as their perpetuators. We do not want to be reminded that not changing the system will make it worse for everyone in the future, maybe even destroy the actual world . . .

WHISTLEBLOWING IS THE ONLY WAY FORWARD EVEN IF IT HURTS YOU OR DESTROYS THE SYSTEM

> Anyway, all I ever meant by "the institution cannot love you" was this: whether the institution makes you feel great or horrible, it isn't about you. Institutions aren't choosing NOT to love you. They are choosing to reproduce themselves. I'm just a widget.
>
> **Tressie McMillan Cottom, tweet, 2022**

If to be a bystander is to not just stand by but to actively reinforce and amplify the situation, then there is no meantime, no waiting. If to stand by is to demonstrate to all present that what is happening is okay, to help it happen more in the future and upon future generations, and for one to become more and more mean-spirited, then we need to become whistle-blowers, both for the future and for ourselves. I read Piper as always having been imagining something beyond the world as is described. That is what she finds in Kant: a categorical imperative to whistleblow! She further reasons why none of us is free if we all aren't (echoing Hamer 2013).

Of the bully systems we are in, Piper maintains their "very stability depends on permitting the infliction of unjustified harm" (Piper 2013b, 411). Bystanding is so common as to seem natural precisely because it is rewarded, and it reinforces the system of rewards. Bully systems are the immediate worlds we live and breathe in. To be ready, to stand up, to become a whistleblower, is to risk losing one's world, to destroy it, and to put oneself at risk. Piper's memoir narrates her own personal world's destruction when she blows the whistle on racism at Wellesley and ends up having to flee the resulting violence, escaping the United States to Berlin. Yet she writes about there being no other real choice for any of us. We really are given a choice: destroy one's own (socially bulwarked bullying) world or continue with the destruction of our social future and the entire planet.

The threatening claim of the system and its enablers, that we are destroying something good (or good enough), is something felt within us as well as something said to us. We too feel the risk of losing the world. Saying and doing something can catch us in our throat, feel impossible, seem too much for anyone to do. Piper explains that this is in part a limit in how we see ourselves (as isolated) and how we see the world (as given), and the leap we need to make is what Kant describes as "willing the super-sensible world" (Piper 2013b, 378, citing Kant, *Critique of Practical Reason*, Ak. 44). "We will this 'world' into existence by instantiating its principles in our own actions, regardless of the corrupt behavior of others" (378). Piper goes into beautiful detail on this process of willing, more than I can address; but I will summarize.

I feel that Piper arrives at aliens, speculative fiction, and conspiracies in her art and philosophy precisely because of the narrative-nervous capture that she analytically and empirically sees and experiences. All need to be changed together—narrative-and-somatics, self-and-collective. This can sound like wishful science fiction, but we are up against aliens in so many ways. Yet while whistleblowing may be rational and necessary, it is also hard and risky. It is by no means easy to stick your neck out; often everything in your habits, sense of etiquette, and nervous system seriously tell you not to. And yet, "Regardless of the advantages or attractions [emotional investment] a bully system may offer, it deserves neither our respect nor our acceptance but rather our condemnation" (Piper 2013b, 413).

Whistleblowing is a practice of instantiating a world that we want to live in, one that identifies with a (speculative) humanity, loved because it is alien. One can work to will an otherwise world into existence, as a transpersonal community whose values of mutual aid and xenophilia, and outweigh any choice to further amplify a bullying world despite what Piper calls "the overwhelming attractions of comfort, convenience, gratification, and self-deception" as well as "profit and safety" (Piper 2013b, 32, 377). "In order for that to happen. We need to work real hard on exercising our imagination" (Piper 2013a, @31:24).

My conspiracy/theory understanding of Piper's analysis is that humans are going to see others as aliens (this is a lesson of history). But this does not mean we have to choose to see those aliens as dangerous and engage in xenophobia, bullying, and war. Xenophilia can also be chosen. This is an underrated and *practically* dismissed idea in my (our?, your?) world, which is materialized through artificial scarcity. Xenophilia is actually an indexical practice of responsibility that rejoices in being changed by others. It resists the "training," socialization, and professionalization that emphasizes system reproduction and that tells us stories of dangerous aliens. Xenophilia rejoices in being changed by others. "I want viewers of my work to come away from it with the understanding that their reactions to racism are ultimately political choices over which they have control" (Piper [1990a] 1996, 1).

Piper's choiceless-choice position is thus echoed by those who take a stand against injustice; it is strikingly illustrated today in Greta Thunberg, who stopped going to school in protest of inaction on climate change. "Why," she asked, "should we study for a future that may not exist anymore?" (Brockes 2019). That the head of OPEC declared the campaign Thunberg stands for "the greatest threat" to the fossil fuel industry (Watts 2019) indicates simultaneously the conspiracy of inaction by all of us who want to keep the world that is destroying us and the actual transpersonal ethics that are possible if we are willing to see beyond this world. Despite the apparent enormity of climate change, capitalism, and racism, we are still in this moment, our interpersonal interactions are the tissue that makes up the system, no matter how big. We can continue to realize this choice.

UTOPIA OR ETIQUETTE?

> The idea that to be the one willing to disrupt and become disoriented in the ways we've embodied harmful structures (for important reasons related to survival) is to be willing to be disobedient and disloyal—to be willing to, as someone shared, prioritize authenticity over attachment.
>
> **Karine Bell, Tending the Roots, 2022**

What does it mean to think that bystanding is okay, that it takes time to figure out whether to fight against injustice or against systemic vicious inhumanity? On the one hand, it implies someone privileged enough to think that they benefit from it or that it is not their problem. On the other, it implies someone who is deeply delusional, brainwashed, and suffering. Either way, that someone is part of a conspiracy of injustice. Inequality is not just a side effect but a conscious production of certain types of others. Piper's micropolitics of the everyday behavior of bullying shows how it connects and inhabits the larger politics of racism and capitalism, resulting in viciousness that is not random but incredibly targeted, perpetuating "the inequitable consequences of a market economy" (Piper 2013b, 24).

As in all conspiracy theories, the world is at stake—in its biological, psychological, and social coherence, no matter how uncomfortable or apparently impolite it may be (for some of us) to write about capital and race together, or about the ways in which our privilege and institutions are part of the production of violence. We can begin to understand the conspiratorial nature of the world by continually working to understand how our everyday ways of life, academia, capitalism, corporatism, antiblackness and nationalisms have reproduced a scorched-earth approach to culture and the planet. The world, our world, hides its own alien brutality within the notion that it would rather destroy all humans than give up the hierarchy that many perceive as natural and their natural right. It fascinates me that etiquette is one of the switch-points where the interpersonal and structural interact; etiquette is how we know we have a choice to act in each moment in order to protect people and to prevent the system from amplifying itself.

The core accusation against conspiracy theorists is that they are stupid because they misunderstand structure and causes. But this is itself a misunderstanding of how to act in the face of structural violence. Conspiracy theorists could be seen as finding ways (no matter how misguided) of not losing the affective insight about harmful structures and of maintaining motivation in the face of complexity. By sticking to the indexical present, they cannot unsee the interpersonal interactions that are part of the structure, a structure so vast that almost everyone is part of it! And despite not being able to imagine system change, they are willing to act beyond their imagination. Conspiracy theories are one set of strange cracks in this world: those who understand that the world is out to get them—they are grasping at a terrifying structure, one that everyone participates in. It is part of how they/we think and reason. Because the world, our world, is structural and part of the structure is bio-socio-affective denial, it can easily be a xenophobia that excuses the theorist as innocent, that pretends that the world is not actually cracked. How to hold on to a conspiracy/theorizing that refuses innocence and embraces aliens?

Piper's fascinating proposal is to embrace etiquette.

> In an ideal society of healthy and nonegoistic values, the prevailing response to racist social conventions would be anger, resentment, and moral outrage on the part of all concerned and reflective individuals, not only those directly victimized by them. In a society governed by an etiquette of acceptance of cultural and ethnic others, racism would be the faux pas, not anger in response to it. In conceiving particular pieces, I work from the standpoint of a community, however small, governed by such norms of etiquette. (Piper [1990b] 1996, 251)

Etiquette, Piper argues in her philosophical texts, is more important (more an indexical present, I would even argue) than ethics (2013b, 22–23, 355–56). Ethics has wiggle room, whereas etiquette is a conspiracy—precisely, a shared-breath "sense" of what is proper. Proper behavior, propriety, politeness, and so on, have gotten a bad rap because of how they are used to uphold bullying and denial, "not speaking out of turn," "toeing the line," and so forth. Can we instead practice the end of this world and an unimaginably different world? One in which whistleblowers are the norm? This is Piper's cosmically optimistic proposal. Willing a supersensible world means speculatively working beyond the world that is trying to kill all of us by targeting some of us. If we want to talk ethics or policy, we must measure "our willingness to act on the practical consequences of a particular moral interpretation the theory prescribes; this willingness is what distinguishes the whistle-blower from her co-workers" (Piper 2013b, 391–92). This means something other than creating new policies. Piper goes on to detail the ways in which antidiscrimination policies, DEI (Diversity, Equity and Inclusion) offices, and so on, are granted symbolic positions but no real power to change institutions indulging in "fantasies of tolerance and generosity" (Piper 2013b, 453; see also Ahmed 2012, 2021, for detailed examples). By offering the whistleblower as a properly embraceable subject, one who values the transpersonally based community that should exist over the current one that devalues everyone, our habits, and etiquette itself, can develop cracks.

We need conspiracy/theory to understand how they (and most of us are they) come to value protecting and preserving a morally corrupt bully system more than protecting people. This also means something other than having the right ethics; it means living a different etiquette, one in which you are impolite if you are not angry and making a scene. Piper proposes that we write and make art from this worldview:

> In an ideal society of healthy and nonegoistic values, the prevailing response to racist social conventions would be anger, resentment, and moral outrage on the part of all concerned and reflective individuals, not only those directly victimized by them. In a society governed by an etiquette of acceptance of cultural and ethnic others, racism would be the faux pas, not anger in response to it. In conceiving particular pieces, I work from the standpoint of a community, however small, governed by such norms of etiquette. (Piper [1990b] 1996, 251)

Bullying institutions are those whose very mechanism is to obfuscate the direct role they play in oppression and to hide those who benefit from others being targeted. In contrast to Kuhn (2012) or Ludwick Flook (1979) (who implicitly draw upon Rousseau and so many others; see Graeber and Wengrow 2021 for this problem), who take bully systems for granted as a naturalized part of the world we must learn to live within, and in contrast to those who advocate a step-by-step reformist approach, Piper arguably proves that one must blow the whistle on the conspiracy, including one's own role in it, despite the effects that the conspiracy will have upon one-self: "Because there are things that we do that conflict with our desires that require that we sacrifice our desires. And we do them wholeheartedly" (Piper 2013a, @22:02).

In doing so we can perhaps speculate ourselves to be part of a conspiracy of whistleblowers, breathing a future into being, whether or not we are there to enjoy it.[4]

NOTES

1   See also the sources on "KEI Blogs and Research Notes on COVID-19/ Coronavirus," Knowledge Ecology International, accessed March 3, 2023, https://www.keionline.org/coronavirus.
2   To add to the colonial irony in this Canadian film: Sigourney Weaver—the one who tried to kill the "Alien" in the eponymous movie about a corporation who wanted to harvest it as a weapon—plays here the resistance leader in this fictional world without corporations.
3   Anti-blackness and libidinal economy; police and lynching; settler violence and residential schools; compulsory monogomy; and so on. Much of our privileged willingness to go along with and be bystanders to violence in society is tied to our ongoing enabling of bullying systems at this interpersonal, indexical level.
4   I really cannot figure out whether to end on an up or down beat.

LOUISA LOMBARD

12 HUMANITARIAN PROFITEERING IN THE CENTRAL AFRICAN REPUBLIC AS CONSPIRACY AND RUMOR

I first traveled to the Central African Republic (CAR) in 2003. A new president had taken power in an armed coup three months earlier. I experienced the capital, Bangui, as a city in waiting. Like during an equatorial downpour when everyone finds a roof to duck under, immobilized by the deafening sound of water on tin, everyday life both went on and was held in suspension. People were waiting to see if this new president would remain in power and if schools and offices and other institutions of daily life would reopen. Only barely a handful of humanitarian organizations were present in the country, all with just a few staff members and focused on small-scale development and health projects. In the following years I came back to CAR many times, including for dissertation research in 2009–10. A number of rebel groups had emerged in the country's rural areas in the intervening years, but none reached the capital. Then, in 2013, another armed takeover of power occurred, and the violence and upheaval metastasized into a war. When I returned to the country at the end of 2014, I expected to find a situation similar to that of 2003: a destroyed city whose residents were collectively holding their breath. Instead, I found traffic jams and roads full of potholes due to the patrolling of UN armored personnel carriers. Luxury condo towers by the still-beautiful river had been quickly built to house UN employees and diplomats. Generators growled twenty-four hours a day in these com-pounds, and the city's two supermarkets now stocked French ice cream. At the same time, all my Central African friends had wrenching stories of tragedy, or for the lucky among them, tragedy narrowly averted. Prior to the installation of the humanitarians, geography, visa regimes, and the cost of plane tickets meant that few Central Africans had direct ex-perience of the wealthy world's life. Now, prosperity had been transposed onto their own world, but still with impermeable cordons preventing them from enjoying it themselves.

To me, these were striking juxtapositions. They are striking juxtaposi-tions to Central Africans too. In all my trips to CAR since "the crisis" (as the post-2013 period is known, despite the inexactitude of this term; see Roitman 2013; Carayannis and Lombard 2015) set in, people have been developing theories about who is profiting and who is suffering from the violence and disorder. Through the years, many more Central Afri-cans have gotten jobs in humanitarian organizations and are themselves carrying out humanitarian projects; yet, many are all the more vocal about the ways that such organizations are on the side of antisocial forces and fighters. After all, only if fighting continues will the interveners remain in business; therefore, they have a vested interest in secretly fomenting violence. The evidence of a wealth-violence link was both obvious and in need of uncovering. It was the conspiracy on everyone's minds, and it circulated socially as a rumor. Paying attention to the social context of this conspiracy highlights that conspiracies are good stories (L. White 2000) that explain misfortune and assign blame. They channel histo-ries of dispossession that at this point are very difficult to redress and present them as current practices with living, apprehendable perpe-trators. Conspiracy is not just a matter of truth, whether that truth is understood to be factual or social. It is also always moral in ways that entangle a researcher, too. Yet while conspiracy stories are compelling and convincing to many people, the people telling them or nodding along to them do not necessarily change their actions as a result. The number of Central Africans who have acted upon their conviction that humanitari-ans are immiserating them is very small and mostly limited to a subset of those who have joined armed groups and have other reasons to target humanitarians.

FROM RUMOR TO CONSPIRACY
IN CENTRAL AFRICA

The Central African Republic has seen more than its share of armed violence, particularly during the colonial period and over the last two decades.[1] In the twenty-first century more than a dozen rebel groups have emerged in the country, and they include men-in-arms from CAR as well as from beyond its borders (Chad and Sudan; Debos 2016). In tandem with the armed groups' appearance, since the late 1990s, CAR has also hosted a dozen interventions by regional and international organizations (the African Union and the United Nations, among others) and by other states (Chad, France, Russia, and Rwanda) with the stated objective of helping to reduce the extent of violence in the country's politics (Olin 2015). Since 2013, the violence has become more acute. In response, international interventions have also ratcheted up to a new scale. The country currently hosts a massive UN mission, about thirteen thousand people strong. As the fighting peaked, the number of humanitarian organizations in the country rose from about twenty to nearly 150, some with staffs of dozens of expatriates and hundreds of Central Africans. These organizations and their employees make for a diverse lot of interveners, whom I refer to elsewhere as the "good-intentions crowd." They are often competing and do not get along, and they see themselves as different from each other, although they share being present at the same place (being a crowd) and generally understand themselves in terms of their self-professed good intentions (Lombard 2016a). From the Central Africans' perspective, the good-intentions crowd's self-description as altruistic is at odds with their individual lives of material privilege, as are the claims to be building peace, given that Central Africans have experienced unending unrest and decline. The divergences observed among the good-intentions crowd between ideology and material reality require explanation, and Central Africans suspect they help explain their country's plight more broadly.

A Central African friend living in the United States sent me a few photos on WhatsApp during a period of heightened violence in 2015. The first showed uniformed Caucasian soldiers standing in a hole in the ground, holding small boxes in their hands. The next photo showed chunks of gold. My friend messaged, "French soldiers in CAR. What a shame!" He wanted a moment of commiseration and shared outrage, but I mostly let him down. He saw the photos as visual proof that French soldiers were illicitly exploiting the country's mineral wealth, carting away box after box of it.

I was not so sure that the meaning of the photos was self-evident. Maybe the soldiers were digging some other kind of a pit—perhaps a latrine? And maybe the photo with the gold was a stock photo? Or maybe not. But I still had questions. My concern—and my inability to join in his declaration despite sharing his critique of the French soldiers[2]—was about how he and others passing on similar information linked clues. It seemed obvious that he was making connections and drawing inferences a bit too quickly about nefarious forces behind seemingly everyday practices.

Linking clues to identify antisocial hidden forces is, of course, a definitional move of a conspiracy theorist. And yet rarely are Central Africans' claims about profiteering described as conspiracy theories. Far more often they are termed rumors. Partly, this may be an issue of language. Few in CAR speak English, and the working language among Central Africans and interveners tends to be French (though the use of English has expanded rapidly over the last five years). *Rumeur* is simply easier and more expansive than *théorie du complot*. Partly, it is probably due to the ways Africa gets constructed as Other. The rest of the world has data and the ability to verify stories (or so people like to think), while in Africa, reliable statistical data are limited or inherently misleading (Jerven 2013), and therefore what is left is mostly rumor. Prominent explanations for the birth of conspiracy as a concept tie it to the development of states and capitalism, using the particular history of Western Europe as a model (Boltanski 2014), while the historicity of African states is quite different (Bayart [1993] 2009). Others make a culturalist argument: African culture is more orally based than European culture, so that recounted stories—a variety of rumor—have a larger role in public discourse (Ellis 1989); or the role ascribed to invisible-yet-active forces is greater in Africa than elsewhere (Marchal 2015). These factors then become intertwined with area studies' vernacular preoccupations. Rumors are much studied in Africa (e.g., L. White 2000; Geissler and Pool 2006; Bonhomme 2009; Musila 2015), and participating in the debates about these issues is made easier by retaining that conceptual frame.

Asking why Africans only rarely get to have conspiracy theories is ultimately less interesting than seeing what we can learn by examining this Central African concern about humanitarian nefariousness, which is usually described as rumor, to see what it shows us about conspiracy theories, a category to which it clearly could belong. And vice versa: What might the concerns attached to conspiracy theories teach us about rumors?

I argue that the conspiracy frame foregrounds the cognitive aspects of invisible ontologies; conspiracies are generally treated as convictions (explanations the holders of the theories are convinced of). Thinking with rumor allows people to better attend to the fundamentally social aspects at play, which is to say, to whatever extent these processes are about belief, they are also about enunciation in the context of interactions and the kind of social reality that emerges from them. Thinking with conspiracy, on the other hand, draws attention to evidence and materiality in ways that rumor often overlooks.[3]

Supported by the methodological and conceptual insights from the literature on conspiracies and rumors, this chapter demonstrates the moral conviction and social productivity of Central Africans' conspiratorial thinking about humanitarian profiteering. But while joining the conviction-centered (conspiracy) and social interaction–centered (rumor) frames allows for a fuller conception of what conspiratorial thinking consists of, the approach also raises questions that require further exploration. The two questions this chapter takes up both concern moral-ethical considerations: First, What is the relationship between conspiracy/rumor and what people do (or how does the conspiracy affect interactions beyond those involving the telling of conspiratorial tales)? And second, How do researchers get drawn into ontologies that involve an important but invisible element, as conspiracy explanations always have, both during the process of research and in trying to write about it afterward? That there are moral implications to explanations, too, cannot be escaped.

BELIEF AND SOCIAL TRUTH IN INVISIBLE ONTOLOGIES

As Lisa Wedeen summarizes usefully elsewhere in this volume, "Conspiracy theorists view what can easily be regarded as disparate happenings as connected, as intentional products of a force whose interests are ultimately served by and organized through another's victimization or ruin." (162). There are a few key elements in this definition. One is the fact of connecting things that other people would not see as functionally related. A second is the nefarious intent behind these hidden but discoverable connections. And a third rests with the helpfully broad word "view," which highlights that conspiracies are about perception or belief.

Beyond those three points, some scholars of conspiracy wend in the direction of functional arguments about groups and power. For instance, studies of conspiracies in the contemporary United States highlight the groups that conspiracy creates. To take one example: "Americans periodically have *organized themselves* around narratives about hidden, malevolent groups secretly perpetuating political plots and social calamities to further their own nefarious goals, what we would define as a 'conspiracy theory'" (Oliver and Wood 2014, 952; emphasis added). Others connect the "group" aspect of these processes to power dynamics, arguing that to label something a conspiracy is to delegitimize it.[4] The powerful label the claims of the less powerful as "conspiracy" in order to focus attention away from the content of those claims or the sense of grievance or injustice that often underlines them, granting them instead a "social-psychological status" (Aistrope and Bleiker 2018, 171). But these approaches move too quickly from observation of people's expressed affinity for a conspiracy to functional outcomes and relational positions. They tend to present conspiracy as an idea that can be analyzed and dissected in isolation from actual social interactions, which are inherently messier and unpredictable processes.

Scholars of rumor, another kind of subaltern truth, cannot forget that rumor is inherently a social process. Rumors are defined as ideas that spread quickly by word of mouth or its electronically mediated forms. Telling stories in this manner is not so much an endorsement as a popular research technique. It is a way to invite a reaction from a listener, which itself becomes part of one's assessment of the information as well as one's assessment of that person. Perhaps an essential trait of a rumor is that rather than a "pure idea" that could exist in some kind of idealized intellectual ether, it implicates events, gestures, and affects—interactions and enunciations (Bonhomme 2009, 35). Rumors do effective social work, in other words, by allowing people to gather and share clues, explanations, and worries, and to gain succor and privileged insight from others in the process. In CAR, conspiracy theories of humanitarian profiteering acquire a social life through exactly these kinds of rumor processes. But people studying rumor have perhaps not paid enough attention to evidence and clues, particularly to their materiality—which conspiracy theorists have shown is crucial. This case from CAR therefore allows us to explore both the ways that conspiracy can be about a belief and the ways that belief is rooted in social processes and rituals, which have their own kind of meaning.

Nevertheless, the problem of verifiability continues to cast a shadow over professions of the value or meaningfulness of social truths. That is, some kinds of truth are visible and verifiable, and thus are easily assimilated to the scientific methods of assessment that have become a gold standard for rigorous research. Others are inherently "invisible"; they rely on truths that cannot be studied in the same way. Historian Carlo Ginzburg (1992) describes this tendency to differentiate among generalizable/scientific/verifiable and particular/experiential/subjective realms as having forced an "unpleasant dilemma" on the more interpretive accounts of social life:

> The quantitative and antianthropocentric orientation of the natural sciences from Galileo on forced an unpleasant dilemma on the human sciences: either assume a lax scientific system in order to attain noteworthy results, or assume a meticulous scientific one to achieve results of scant significance. . . . The question arises, however, whether exactness of this type is attainable or even desirable for forms of knowledge most linked to daily experience—or, more precisely, to all those situations in which the unique and indispensable nature of the data is decisive to the persons involved. (124)

Ginzburg makes a compelling case that understanding the world requires immersion in social life, not just natural scientific truth. This general view has provided succor to those caught in the "unpleasant dilemma," because what it poses is not actually a dilemma after all: understanding forms of knowledge related to daily experience *requires* conjectural and clue-based ways of finding out about the world, which remove evidence as verified by scientific process from its pedestal, providing space for other ways of making sense of the world.

But the realms of visible and invisible ontologies are not always so easily bridged. Or, put otherwise, it is possible that both are correct, that conjectural, clue-based, and social ways of finding out about the world allow access to insights not provided by Galilean techniques, and that those social modes of knowing the world have important limits. In particular, there are ethical and moral matters they do not, in and of themselves, address, as this case from CAR also lets us understand. But first let us see what "good stories" (L. White 2000, 30) Central Africans tell about the problems that afflict them, and especially about the stratification they experience with new potency.

HUMANITARIAN PROFITEERING

The following quote from a discussion with members of a local association in the capital city, Bangui, in March 2016, gives a sense of how Central Africans talk about the good-intentions crowd.[5] The speaker was a man in his early forties:

> For me, I am tempted to say the UN has a hidden plan. Pretty much all the actors [elites] in CAR benefit from the crisis. The hidden plan is for the UN to permit different countries to exploit our natural resources and to permit their people, who are involved in the management of the crisis, to buy gold, diamonds, animal pelts, and even parrots. The exploitation is under the cover of the UN and escapes the state's control. Is the UN providing a service to the Central African population or is it putting in place the conditions for the next crises? We do not understand anything in this.

"We do not understand anything in this," the man says, but in fact, he was fairly sure he did understand it—he saw the foreigners, and the UN in particular, as present in CAR to get rich and further eviscerate the state and the nation, just as he described. But profiteering at the expense of the weak is deeply antisocial and immoral and, therefore, incomprehensible to someone who wants to see himself as operating on the side of the good. That final expression—"we do not understand anything"—was not a statement of ignorance, but one of moral approbation: what the alleged peacekeepers are doing is wrong, and it is part of an invisible world that produces "sensible outputs" (Fields 2001, 293). The outputs are sensible in both senses of the term: they are apparent and observable, and they seem reasonable. The key thing about an invisible ontology is that the invisibility is not a reason to call into question its existence, since invisibility is a prior assumption.[6] With his statements, this man was enunciating a sense of aspirational shared values about wealth and its distribution, when in fact values centered on wealth (how much one person should accumulate and display, how much should be shared) are incredibly contested in CAR. His belief in the truth of what he was saying cannot be severed from the various imperatives he felt to verbalize moral critique. His statements can be understood only in the inherently social context of a focus group and his own status as the intellectual of the group, someone to whom others deferred for his insight and spoken acuity. His stories effectively conveyed "ideas and points" that helped explain what people experience as predicaments, as Luise White (2000) found in her study of vampire and other blood-related conspiracy-rumors in colonial southern Africa:

> People do not always speak from experience—even when that is considered the most accurate kind of information—but speak with stories that circulate to explain what happened. This is not to say that people deliberately tell false stories. The distinction between true and false stories may be an important one for historians, but for people engaged in contentious arguments, explanations, and descriptions, sometimes presenting themselves as experts, or just in the best possible light, it may not matter: people want to tell stories that work, stories that convey ideas and points. (30)

The stories "work" because they explain things according to the suspicions, presuppositions, and concerns that people have.

The Central African colleague I worked with on this research was somewhat caught in between: he, like other Central Africans, understood both why these stories were true (in moral and factual ways) and, having lived in France to study anthropology, he also understood something of my skepticism. He put me in contact with people he saw as especially insightful, often because they had been privy to insider relations with the actors known for their nefarious profiteering. One such person had had a short tenure as a high-level government employee overseeing extractive industries, but at the time we met, he was no longer employed in a salaried way. In our conversation, he took up the issue of the peacekeeper and humanitarian interest in profiteering. "These forces [peacekeepers] have morality problems. They are *businesseurs*. They are buying diamonds, gold, other stuff. They do it openly." When, eager verifier of facts that I am, I asked where, he explained:

> The days they get their salaries you will see a whole market develop around their bases. This is from about the twenty-third to the fifth of the month. They are buying all sorts of things, including diamonds. Sometimes they even get duped by the fraudsters! . . . All this peacekeeping is a game in order to give them time to go fishing [meaning get wealth]. It's a good job, and they want it to continue.

An alternate reading of these payday scenes would posit them as evidence of excellent new opportunities for Central Africans: supply and demand working efficiently and to the benefit of all. But for this interlocutor, the existence of a market *itself* was a sensible output confirming the existence of illicit profit-making at Central Africans' expense.

Around the time of this conversation, I participated in a meeting that involved a UN security briefing. "Central Africans are always watching us," the former French officer in charge of the briefing stressed. He said this in the context of a warning about all the ways Central Africans had developed to steal from foreigners. I found the concern exaggerated (I once had a watch stolen in Bangui, but nothing else). But he was correct in saying that Central Africans are preoccupied with trying to understand these new peacekeeping/humanitarian strangers in their midst, strangers who often seemed intent on avoiding the kind of contact with Central Africans that would otherwise make them seem like normal social actors. The Central African researcher with whom I collaborated for this research related his own stories about how people would socially share evidence gleaned from their contacts with the good-intentions crowd. The luxury towers that had sprouted up by the riverside, what they had inside, and how much it all cost were topics that came up repeatedly. Someone working as a cleaner or a cook in an expatriate house might overhear the cost of the house rental, when even just a room in an expatriate-standard house was going for US$1,000 per month. A housekeeper might at some point get a glance at a pay stub or other paperwork left out on the table demonstrating the vast discrepancy between his own take-home pay (perhaps US$100 per month) versus his employer's (if a UN employee, easily over US$10,000 month). A waiter does not have to trouble himself to see the total tab even parsimonious diners rack up at the elite-oriented restaurants, where main courses are generally US$20 or more. Gathering evidence, particularly in material form, is something often overlooked or underplayed in studies of rumor, which tend to emphasize the story over its sensible traces.

To a wealthy expatriate, there is nothing surprising or in need of explanation here: some places and people are rich and reap the benefits; some places and people are poor. Whether attributable to luck, divine power, or fate, such unfairness is simply the way of the world. But to many Central Africans, the inequality demands a combination of explanation and approbation. And the explanation that links all these clues and questions together is that the foreigners' real interests lie in resource exploitation and fomenting conflict so as to keep themselves wealthy and Central Africans poor. Central Africans make similar arguments about the nefarious greed of rebel leaders and local politicians, whom they also see as authors and perpetuators of the curse of being a regular Central African today. But whereas those modes of profiting are more expected, the well-intentioned interveners' profiteering is only half obvious, half hidden by their humanitarian self-justifications, and from that comes an added frisson in uncovering it: it seems like the crucial missing piece in the puzzle.

The half-hiddenness of peacekeeper profiteering also means that people who can position themselves as having credible insider knowledge and material proof become socially more important as storytellers and shapers of circulating ideas about these matters. How insights about conspiracy bolster relations of social status, expertise, and dependency became particularly clear to me through a long conversation with a captain in the Central African military in March 2016. My Central African colleague had arranged the meeting, saying that the captain was known for always having interesting things to say and for being privy to things the rest of us could never hope to directly observe but wanted to know about. We sat on the captain's porch; his house was at the back of a large but bare concession with a high wall around it. The captain, close to retirement if not already pensioned, held a folder of documents carefully on his lap. He said he had been close to the former president, Bozizé, and that "they" (he did not explain who) had even tried to assassinate him once, a sign of his importance. When I asked him about the presence of international forces in CAR, he replied:

> Things are difficult here now. There is no advantage to having the international forces here. They aren't playing their role. There has been pillaging and rapes, including by Sangaris [the French troops]. The French are the ones who give the UN mission prescriptions about what to do. And France just wants our rich subsoil. Ever since independence there was an agreement: what's over the surface is ours; what's under the surface is theirs.

Indeed, at independence, France had signed agreements with each of its former colonies securing privileged access to resources and military cooperation. By now, however, French commercial interests in CAR are vanishingly small (S. Smith 2015). At least officially. The captain continued:

> It's the French who brought this war between Christians and Muslims. They intervened. And then it's gotten worse. People killed Christians right in front of the French. Then the French fire on

us. It's not good. They themselves [the French] give weapons. It's a reality. They brought in 184 Peulh [Muslim pastoralists with both long-standing presence and long-standing national ambiguity across West and Central Africa] by helicopter to Mpoko [the capital's airport], where they eat in the cafeteria with the other soldiers. They outfit them with UN uniforms—the blue helmets—and then they send them out to wreak havoc. . . . They are mixed up with the Rwandan peacekeepers. We know this because there were some deaths and it was confirmed that a victim was in fact Peulh and not Rwandan like the uniform he was wearing.

All that, it's France. Why do they greenlight Seleka [an umbrella term for mostly Muslim rebel groups]? Why do they bring them munitions? How does Seleka get the ammunition if not from the French? How did they get stocked? Seleka does not economize when they shoot—they just shoot, shoot, shoot. So they must have been supplied. And it must have been the French. There was a UN vehicle carrying five containers of guns at the central mosque. The next day the clashes were much worse. How could that happen, when they had been out of ammunition? We [high-level officers, people in the know] got called and were informed that the provisioning was in progress. And then the next day we saw the worst attacks.

In the captain's stories and arguments, the airport played an important role as a site where some things were visible and others were impossible to effectively surveil, and as a site of power and mobility. He said, "Each time, we don't know what they [the French] hide in the boxes they put in the airplanes bound for France." And yet he knew exactly what he thought went into those planes: boxes of diamonds and gold and even ivory. When I asked how he knew, he said he had heard from General Tumenta, the Cameroonian force commander of the UN mission in CAR (who had died a few months earlier, during his tenure as force commander).[7] General Tumenta had told him, "Don't collaborate with the French. They are thieves." The issue, the captain further explained, is that there is an agency at the airport that is supposed to check what goes on any plane, but they do not really do their job in the case of the French. Military planes never get properly checked. There is, in other words, something that is constitutively invisible or opaque and that becomes constitutive evidence of profiteering interests.

The captain's overall analysis was clear. The peacekeepers in general and the French in particular were augmenting the conflict, and doing so permitted them to continue to exploit resources. His connections to insider circuits of knowledge, his claim to be able to definitively interpret statements that might otherwise seem ambiguous, the documents on his lap—all bolstered the social ways that he could be read as well-informed by his compatriots. Among Central Africans, official channels and venues of information are seen as an instrumental veneer covering what is actually going on but probably can never be definitively known.[8] Therefore, accessing at least a portion of those truths requires networks of insider knowledge as well as the ability to obtain and pass on that knowledge in particular ways—such as to people in the neighborhood who regard the possessor of the information as an important person, a status that comes in part from having such knowledge.[9] The knowledge, by definition, cannot be accessed through fact-checking, because the official facts are seen as designed to hide the real truth underneath. Being able to effectively mediate between and explain the interplay between the visible (what everyone can observe) and the invisible (what only some can access) therefore becomes key to telling a good story, one by which people will feel edified. Material evidence can be crucial in that respect: photos shared on WhatsApp or insider documents.

The captain never showed us the documents in his folder. I had another appointment, so I could only stay for two hours. My colleague said they were documentary proof of the veracity of his claims, which we would have seen if only we had stayed longer. My hunch was that they would be more mirror-like than transparent in their content, as Mariane Ferme (2001) has described what she terms "the real" being "hermeneutically encoded" in Sierra Leone:

> Truth is what lies under multiple layers of often conflicting meanings. In this hermeneutic encoding of the real, the shifting order of visibility works less as a transparent surface, through which deep intentions and knowledge become accessible, than as a mirror, which mimetically doubles what is in front without giving away what is beyond the reflection. The impossibility of appealing to the truth behind the surface makes contestation an integral aspect of arriving at the truth, despite apparent declarations to the contrary on the part of social actors. (7)

To whatever extent such "hermeneutic encoding" is a Central African cultural trait, it is augmented by the way that the official narratives of what interveners are doing in CAR ("peacekeeping as peacebuilding") are so out of tune with what Central Africans observe them to be doing, namely, making money and otherwise benefiting from material privilege ("peacekeeping as enterprise"; Jennings 2016). Central Africans analyze and interpret the evidence that surrounds them and have found a resonant way to talk about the "public secret" (Taussig 1999; Geissler 2013) of global wealth disparities and, moreover, a way to do so that foregrounds moral concerns and ensures that those concerns about morality and inequality remain part of broader conversations.

At the end of my notes from our conversation with the captain, I wrote, "Yeesh, that was a lot of blaming other people!" While no one could disagree that the interveners made princely salaries in comparison to Central Africans and enjoyed other luxuries as a result of their jobs in CAR,[10] I was less convinced that boxes of diamonds were being loaded into every French plane, hidden in plain sight. I considered the debates in the French media and diplomatic circles about the cost of the Sangaris mission (800,000 euros per day). There, the concern was not to keep the mission going but to end it as soon as possible. I saw how the captain's stories provided a way to express moral outrage over material stratification,[11] which is otherwise immensely hard to talk about, owing to its status as a public secret in the world of allegedly equal nation-states. But I also had trouble fully inhabiting the social, interactional, enunciation, and material evidence-based aspects that made the stories work for so many Central Africans.

Underlying Central Africans' concerns with humanitarian profiteers is a preoccupation: "Why are we poor?" To the good-intentions crowd and other outsiders who have interests in the country, that question seems naive or beside the point. *Obviously*, goes their line of thought, the country is poor because it had a difficult colonial history (but that was long ago, no use thinking about reparations—think of all that France and other countries have done for CAR since), and because it has had self-aggrandizing leaders since, and crucially, because warlords now profit from violence. If the country gets on the "good governance" straight and narrow, it could be fine. A bit of misfortune, a lot of Central African complicity, a need to hew more closely to capitalist-state ideal types: that is the general diagnosis and prescription. This view owes much to the post–Cold War division of the world into allegedly equal nation-states, in which the maintenance of the state system is the highest goal (Ghosh 1994). This makes it possible to "compare newly like sovereign states—suddenly Senegal was 'just like' France and could be compared as such. Rather than demonstrating the disastrous relational effects of colonialism, these tools [GDP and other state-based economic measures] were employed to demonstrate global poverty in ostensibly discrete nation-states and to intervene, now in the name of economic growth" (Appel 2017, 298). This model is easier to take for granted by those people and those countries that have been the winners of these relational histories than it is by the less fortunate.

Social scientists have often seen it as our role to champion that plane of the social, to bring back in the "relational effects" that have brought far more injustice for some than for others. In this vein, we argue for the importance of stories that account for and express outrage over material and other forms of stratification. We are interested in what counts as a "good story" and why; and often good stories are those that effectively explain the connections between the visible/speakable and the invisible/difficult to otherwise express. But it is important to consider not just what a good story *is* but also what a good story *does*. Or rather: What do people who have told or heard a story and deemed it good (informative, expressive of truth) then do? If someone understands the story to be true, does that shape how they then behave and with whom they associate? It turns out that conspiracy can be a big part of how people understand the world, while at the same time, the actions people justify in light of the conspiracy can be varied. People do not always feel the need for there to be consistency between who or what they identify as nefarious or antisocial and their own spheres of operation and opportunity. A person might share conspiracy stories, consider them true stories and even important stories, but not use them to further the goal of self-consistency in belief and behavior. Recognizing these varied pathways from conspiracy into action is also necessary to any project of taking conspiracy seriously.

WHAT FOLLOWS FROM CONSPIRACY?

I have heard many Central African critiques of humanitarian profiteering, but I have never heard of a Central African refusing a humanitarian job on principle. The Euro-American head of an international humanitarian NGO in CAR, employing some forty expatriate staff and four hundred Central Africans, brought in a psychologist to speak with the staffers after their offices were attacked toward the end of 2015. The psychologist reported that many of the Central African staff said that such attacks were understandable given how many humanitarian workers were participating in and fomenting violence in the country for their own profit. The NGO head was troubled that even Central Africans in the heart of the humanitarian enterprise (who, she assumed, should know that the allegations were false) were convinced of their truth. There are many reasons why someone who understood humanitarians to be authors of nefarious profiteering might still work in the humanitarian sector. Certain organizations or agencies get pinpointed as particularly bad, and others as less antisocial, for instance. Moreover, there are few jobs in CAR, and many Central Africans, while critical of the unequal structure of humanitarian aid, take satisfaction in earning a living while providing for the basic needs of people dealing with upheaval and desperate circumstances. They might also develop camaraderie with their fellow employees, such as during long and difficult road journeys around the country. In short, I mean no critique in pointing out that many Central Africans are both convinced that humanitarians are nefarious, conflict-mongering profiteers and nonetheless jump at the opportunity to work in that branch themselves. These divergences are interesting not because they are evidence of hypocrisy but because they demonstrate that conspiracy thinking does not lead functionally either to action or to a search for consistency between belief and action. People might relate to a conspiracy with conviction, and people might have fruitful social encounters around conspiracy— they might agree that these are "stories that work"—and yet, their actions and interactions are not determined by the conspiracy-related beliefs and encounters.

An interaction with two vocal proponents of the humanitarian-profiteering theory helped me further examine the apparent disconnect between belief and actions. In Bangui in December 2014, I attended a Saturday morning meeting between peacekeeping officers and "the community" in a borderland zone of the city that had until a few weeks prior been the site of frequent physical violence and criminality. During the meeting, military officers sat on a raised platform, while the community members (actually, a select group of invitees chosen for their positions as government officials or local organization officers; I was there at the invitation of a peacekeeper officer) sat on monobloc chairs in rows in front of them. A roof provided shade from the early dry-season morning heat. The military officers gave speeches, and then, one by one, people among the assembled audience requested the opportunity to voice their concerns and thoughts. Toward the end, a young man in a fresh, bright polo shirt (broadcasting both urban youth cool and professional cosmopolitanism) claimed the microphone and proclaimed in a vehement tone, "The origin of the crisis in CAR is the international community." He continued in this vein for about ten minutes before ceding the microphone to another.

When the meeting ended, I sought out the young man, who described himself as a rebel leader, and asked if he would be willing to expand on his ideas. We met the following week at a café of long-standing popularity (although not the current "see and be seen" spot) in the city center. I was late and had phoned to say he should order something to eat and drink. Arriving from the main street, I walked through the indoor section of the café, noting a French soldier at one table, and noting that he noted me. I continued to the back, outdoor area, where a ring of *paillottes* was in place for individual parties and found my interlocutor there. A friend accompanied him. I will call my original interlocutor Guy and his friend Henri.

Guy said he was an Anti-Balaka coordinator and attributed a similar role to Henri. The Anti-Balaka are often glossed as a rebel group, but they are neither rebels in the usual senses (Clapham 1998) nor a group. The term is instead an umbrella used to describe the many people who mobilized in the wake of the Seleka rebel alliance's takeover of power in March 2013. In their self-description, they mobilized in self-defense, but that is a matter of perspective; the people they have targeted see them as offensive fighters. Anti-Balaka do not have a coordinated structure or leadership, making it difficult to verify these men's claims to positions of prominence. Henri was a university graduate; he and Guy lacked the stable professional jobs (ideally state civil service) they desired (see Lombard 2016b).

I opened by asking who, exactly, they meant by "the international community" that was the origin of the crisis. Guy answered quickly and assertively, "France." Henri nodded emphatically. The analysis that followed mostly hewed to a "Europe underdeveloping Africa" script, with a dose of hidden deals and other obfuscations. They criticized their country's leaders too: "Our leaders play their part [meaning, they contribute to this state of affairs]. They see their own personal interests first. It's the story of families. They see only their region, and not even everyone in that region. Their families eat and that's it."

For these young men, these explanations helped answer what were pressing concerns about their country's decline and helped them imagine alternate futures.

> The first country in Central Africa to get a TV station was CAR. Today, we're the last [in every way]. The first country in Central Africa to get a university was [the University of] Bangui. Today, we're the last. We don't benefit from anything. We could be ten times richer than France with all the resources we've got if they were exploited! And yet we're so poor.

Explaining decline and imagining a brighter future can be markers of resilience. But the answers and explanations can also push in the direction of "cruel optimism"—when what one desires becomes an obstacle preventing one's flourishing (Berlant 2011). The conviction that France is a puppeteer, an invisible yet key and nefarious mover in all that happens, seemed to prevent Guy and Henri from considering the various roles they and others like them might play in the current state of the affairs and what they could themselves do to change things.

After a bit less than an hour of chatting, the French soldier from inside and a Central African man in striking, bright-purple West African–tailored clothing emerged from the café. They beckoned for Guy to join them, and all three went to the parking lot where they proceeded to converse for twenty minutes or so. When they got back, the French officer introduced himself. Then he told my interlocutors that they should watch out for me because I would write in English and they would not know what I was writing—I could write anything. (Concern about hidden, nefarious motives is certainly not a particularly Central African trait!) Henri stood up for me saying that, no, I was writing in French, and he pointed to the notebook I had in clear view of all on the table as evidence.

Once the officer departed, Guy explained what the meeting in the parking lot had been about. There was an Anti-Balaka coordinating meeting being planned in Nairobi, the Kenyan capital. The French officer was arguing to Guy and the man in the purple outfit ("Our coordinator," the self-proclaimed coordinator explained) that they should not go to the meeting because it would reverse fragile steps that had been made toward peace. My interlocutors said that they would indeed not go. Not because the officer told them not to—but because they had reasons of their own.

Soon it was time to pay the bill. I started doing quick calculations of coffees and teas and cake slices. Guy hastened to explain that I did not need to pay for them. I protested. I had invited them. No, they said, the French officer had already paid for their coffees and cakes. I could not help but reflect on this. The origin of the crisis is France, they had said.

But if a French officer bought them coffee and cake, they did not say, "No Thanks." As James Laidlaw (2013) has brilliantly explored, self-consistency is but one way of thinking about autonomy or freedom in a human life. Moreover, a French officer benefits from material and symbolic power in his relation to a not-fully-employed Central African, who may therefore feel that he cannot refuse.

But those factors do not make the inconsistencies between conviction and action meaningless. At the very least they make the point that conviction—including about conspiracy—does not always serve as a guide for action and interaction. There have been many instances when Central Africans—generally understood to be lumpen youth—have attacked interveners in Bangui, and certain members of armed groups have made interveners a focus of their attacks, both in Bangui and elsewhere in the country. These convictions about hidden humanitarian malfeasance *can* inform action, but the ways they do so are not predetermined.

A conspiracy theory or rumor can be explored for its social truths, but all the pathways leading toward the storytelling and stemming from it need a lot more scrutiny as well. Identifying conspiratorial action seems to provide moral succor for those involved in it, but the correlates of that succor—is it a kind of cruel optimism or displacement of responsibility? or is it, by contrast, an important mode of speaking truth to power?—are not always clear. And it is not clear what the answers they uncover motivate subjects to do. Conspiracy, with its focus on evidence and conviction, and rumor, with its focus on social interaction, help us understand "forms of knowledge most linked to daily experience," as Ginzburg (1992, 124) put it, particularly those accounting for potentially nefarious hidden forces. But both the conspiracy frame and the rumor frame have a tendency to unhelpfully bracket the conspiratorial *idea*, such that we forget to consider that the storytelling is but one element in longer social processes. A conspiracy skeptic might nevertheless take actions based on a "better safe than sorry" logic; an adamant promulgator of conspiracy might disregard the advice that seems to be wedded to her statements. There is an ethical (what do we do, or what should we do, now that we know?) dimension to the workings of conspiracy theories that is worth pursuing. When does the moral critique that is embedded in conspiracy require consistency in the realm of action and relations, and when not? What more can we find out about the affordances (Keane 2014) and pathways that shape the longer processes in which the conspiracy—as conviction, as social storytelling—is but one node? Whether arguing for taking an instance of conspiracy seriously because it seems to point toward worrisome social proclivities or because it seems to express a meaningful social critique, in either case, unless people's actions and practices are traced outward from the conspiracy, the treatment will fall short of the goal.

CONCLUSION: THE LIMITS OF TAKING CONSPIRACIES SERIOUSLY

And what about me? The ethical questions I have raised of those who promote the conspiracy thinking apply to me as well. What do I do, or what should I do, now that I know? Can I use the classic anthropologist's work-around, developed initially to deal with studies of witchcraft? In those cases, the anthropologist would say that the invisible ontology in question was obviously not true, but that when one approaches it from the perspective of an insider, the ideas are logical and coherent and express moral precepts. E. E. Evans-Pritchard (1937), due to his study of witchcraft among the Azande, is often cited as the progenitor of this point of view, but Max Weber preceded him in making a similar, if less elaborate, argument about Mormons.[12]

Philosopher Kwame Anthony Appiah argues that there is nevertheless a difference between visible and invisible ontologies, and that acknowledging one's own position in regard to them is essential to intellectual integrity.[13] Appiah is more interested in consistency and coherence than are most people as they work these matters out in their lives. Yet not only as philosophers, but as part of any effort to offer knowledge about the world, we must position ourselves in relation to these questions about visible and invisible ontologies. Here I have pointed out the rationality, logic, and "social rightness" of an invisible ontology, but I separate what I see as the moral truth from the literal truth in a way not shared by my informants. I argue, nevertheless, for taking it seriously because it reveals social anxieties and expresses a justified sense of injustice. Central African theories of humanitarian profiteering are a way to speak about the "public secret" of profound global stratification—a concern I share with them—despite my remaining comfortably on the wealthy side and worrying that their fixation on victimization distracts them from the things they could have control over, if they tried.

Explanation has moral dimensions, not just descriptive ones. Some invisible ontologies are more palatable for the researcher to "take seriously" than others. It is easier to say that an invisible ontology/conspiracy theory should be taken seriously when one or both of the following conditions obtain: first, the analyst agrees with the underlying critique discernible in the conspiratorial thinking (e.g., the distribution of wealth in the world is unfair); second, the analyst does not feel a primary investment with the people being described (does not feel like "one of them"). If neither of these conditions obtain, taking an invisible ontology/conspiracy theory seriously starts to look a lot more like an apologia for social destruction and oppression. Even seeing conspiracy as a genre of moral discourse that people use to criticize and otherwise talk about public secrets, and attending to the ensuing recommendation that we be more attentive to the "work of unknowing"—that is, the work of not calling attention to the public secrets (Geissler 2013), or of calling out the power relations that produce certain invisible ontological explanations as conspiracy and others as truth (Aistrope and Bleiker 2018)—these various projects are more compelling as action plans when the moral claims identified in the conspiracy align with or are irrelevant to those of the scholar. If the conspiratorial moral discourses are, say, racist, the "work of unknowing" starts to look like something else entirely.

An instance of conspiracy thinking can unfold in any number of ways and lead to any number of actions, but regardless of what happens, it is easier to justify taking the conspiracy seriously when one either shares in the grievance or fear that accompanies the conspiracy or feels unaffected by it.[14] "Classic forms of Enlightenment critique—revelation (of reality) and iconoclasm (of false representations)—have less purchase" (Geissler 2013, 30) when people must express public secrets through idioms centered on moral grievance authored by nefarious hidden forces. Figuring out what has purchase, or what should, remains to be done. Further explorations into what follows from a person's invocation of invisible yet decisive and nefarious forces in storytelling (that they are convinced of the story's content, that their actions will be shaped by that conviction in particular ways, etc.) and how the moral positions of the researcher (and not just the power relations among proponents of opposing theories) affect her interest in claiming a value for invisible ontologies, rather than debunking them, might be places to start. Both might, in different ways, bring the relationship between truth and morality/ethics to the fore and in so doing allow for an alternative to seeing truth as either objectively verifiable or the product of the workings of power or social interaction. Dealing with conspiracy, whether as a professional or popular researcher, is inescapably ethical (in light of the conspiracy, what should one do/what does one do?) and moral (what should be taken seriously and what criticized?), and not just a matter of truth, whether that truth is posited as assessable through scientific or social means.

1 For a fuller account of this history, see Lombard (2016a).
2 Notably, some among these French forces had been accused of extensive sexual violence against Central Africans (Brabant and Minano 2017).
3 For instance, Bonhomme's (2009) fascinating study of the genital-stealing rumors that swept across West and Central Africa from the 1990s into the 2000s relied on newspaper accounts, which meant that the physical or material evidence was removed from his analysis.
4 Conspiracy narratives are "legitimized or delegitimized within the hierarchies of authority and modes of knowledge production present in particular interpretive communities" (Aistrope and Bleiker 2018, 177).
5 In total, my research assistant and I spoke with about 125 people, some thirty-five in more extensive interviews, and the rest in focus groups.
6 In Central Africa, invisible ontologies have been one way of talking about the simultaneously hidden and in-plain-sight world of the antisocial. Everyone knows something about how witchcraft works, and that is both how they keep themselves safe from its dangers and know to accuse those who are using it for ill; but to profess any knowledge of it would be to situate oneself in that camp of people for whom it is familiar and normal, which is something most people would rather avoid, and this discourages extensive investigations.
7 An expatriate intervener told me that the general had used $40,000 of UN money to renovate the bathroom in his Bangui residence. She had seen the invoice, she said. Some interveners, like Central Africans, were concerned about antisocial profiteering and ways others were taking advantage of the system but felt powerless to do anything about it.
8 Musila (2015) points out that people living in a place where *official* versions of events are often concocted and would-be investigators are met with webs of obfuscation (as was the case in Kenya during the Moi years) do not enjoy the hubris of people who have easy faith in their government's good will and in the associated conviction that it is possible to "get to the bottom of things."
9 This is an important aspect of African "pavement radio" as a source of information about the world (Ellis 1989).
10 The range of salaries interveners earn is very wide, with some far more modest, in keeping with their organizations' volunteer ethos (e.g., Doctors

Without Borders) and others paid as well as professionals in the world capitals where their organizations have their headquarters (the International Committee of the Red Cross, the United Nations).

11 I use *stratification* rather than *inequality* in line with the helpful distinction drawn by Rio and Smedal (themselves drawing on the work of Louis Dumont): stratification refers specifically to "a system of unequal distribution of resources" (Rio and Smedal 2008, 8).

12 More recently, some have sidestepped the issue of "belief" in witchcraft by positing it as an alternate ontology, as something best studied as action (Ashforth 2005).

13 Appiah (1992, 135) wrote, "If modernization is conceived of, in part, as the acceptance of science, we have to decide whether we think the evidence obliges us to give up the invisible ontology. . . . The question how much of the world of the spirits we intellectuals must give up (or transform into something ceremonial without the old literal ontology) is one we must face: and I do not think the answer is obvious."

14 Karen E. Fields (2001) pointed out this discrepancy in her comparison of racecraft in the United States to studies of witchcraft in Africa:

> Following the well-established practice of most Africanists in this country, I have been granting the rationality of witchcraft, but not that of racecraft. That practice now seems to be troublesome, logically and ethically. If we judge by the dependence of both on presuppositions that are demonstrably false according to modern science, then both sets of traditional beliefs should go down together as irrational. But if we discount their falsity by that standard, then they should rise together as rational. Under our usual practice, they do neither: It is as though they were as different as cabbages and kings. (283–84)

ROBERT MEISTER

13 CONFESSIONS OF AN ACCUSED CONSPIRACY THEORIST / THE FINANCIALIZATION OF HIGHER EDUCATION

In the fall of 2009, I revealed that the University of California system (UC), where I work, had pledged 100 percent of its tuition revenue as collateral for bonds that would eventually finance over $15 billion in new construction. The UC had been increasing the revenues that could be capitalized in this way for the previous decade, starting in 1999 and 2004, when it increased in-state enrollments by 40 percent, followed by another five years during which it doubled its in-state tuition while admitting more students who would pay its higher, and rapidly rising, out-of-state rates. By 2010, the non-state component of the UC's enrollment-generated revenue would grow by 84 percent (net of returns to financial aid), but a no less important point, which the UC's leaders always understood, is that its enrollment-generated funds did not have to be spent to support the UC's instructional mission and could thus be pledged to bondholders whose claims would come ahead of the educational purposes for which tuition was presumably paid. There was, thus, no claim that this use of enrollment-generated funds had been restricted to financing, for example, the new classrooms necessitated by higher enrollments, rather than, for example, private sector partnerships with non-disclosable terms. And, unlike the project notes the UC had traditionally used to fund the parking garages and dormitories for which

California taxpayers would not pay, financial viability of the funded projects was of no concern to potential bondholders. As long as the UC could demonstrate that its nonstate revenue from student enrollments would continue to grow in both good times and bad, its bond ratings would remain high.

This is what I revealed in 2009 to be the UC's plan to securitize its rapidly growing revenue stream from students to finance on private bond markets its further diversification out of the higher education business and into health sciences, real estate development, and so forth. Since then, my concerns about the noneducational uses of the bond proceeds have been borne out, as have my concerns that the burden of debt service on those bonds would force campuses to make further cuts in tuition-funded education (Meister 2011b). My claim in 2009 was that the UC had been pursuing this financial plan for a decade, that its bond indentures had said so, and that took advantage of the budget crisis to accelerate its plan to borrow more as tuition rose and interest rates remained historically low. In doing this, however, the UC was also relying on its legal right *not* to spend increased educational revenues on reversing cuts to education, and *not* to prioritize construction projects that had an educational purpose. That, to me, was scandal enough, especially in a time of economic distress for many students. But the UC said that its more rapid tuition increases were justified by the current crisis and accused me of being a conspiracy theorist for revealing that it was following the financial plan it would have pursued anyway.

....

Was I a conspiracy theorist? Well, there was a preexisting financial plan, developed in concert with the bond markets, that the UC continued to follow, while blaming the state's financial crisis. Did this plan's anticipated deniability make it a conspiracy? As for being a theorist, I happened to be writing a politically inflected theory of capitalist financialization that could explain their plan even if it was not a conspiracy. I knew what I was talking about. But my criticism that they were persisting in that plan, despite the crisis, was also made in my capacity as head of the labor union for tenure-track faculty in the UC system and was intended to provoke the UC's leadership to deny its plan and thereby to confirm that its success depended on concealing it. The motivation here was, thus, political.

My contribution to the present volume thus frames my political work attacking the UC's financialization in the context of my broader academic work on the financialization of capitalism as such (Meister 2011b, 2017, 2021). I see financialization as having a different dominant logic than that of commoditization, and regard the financialization of universities as a response to the commoditization of educational goods and services that is also occurring outside them (Meister 2019, 2021). As I explain below, it is the logic of finance, and not of commoditization, that explains why elite public universities have been in a position to simultaneously raise prices, increase demand, and lower quality (what a business!), even as educational technology is lowering the marginal cost of delivering many instructional services.

To me, this point seemed clear, but when I wrote an open letter ("They Pledged Your Tuition [An Open Letter to UC Students]") criticizing the financialization of the UC (Meister 2009c), the leadership—from the systemwide president on down—accused me, in essence, of spreading lies and innuendo. UC's chief financial officer, Peter Taylor, wrote an op-ed response, published in all campus newspapers, entitled "Misinformation: The Enemy of Excellence and Access." It bluntly expressed the central administration's outrage:

> Misinformation is the enemy of progress toward solutions that will preserve excellence and access within all 10 campuses of the University of California. One troubling example is the claim by a UC Santa Cruz faculty union leader that educational fee increases are being implemented to allow the university system and campuses to borrow more money for capital projects.
>
> It's the kind of factually challenged distortion we've come to expect in partisan politics. What makes it troubling is that this and other misleading claims spread like viruses through the UC community. We hope students, faculty and staff recognize it for what it is: nonsense. (Taylor 2009)

Taylor went on to say, "It's misleading and inaccurate to allege, as [UCSC Politics] Professor Robert Meister has done in two open letters to students, that educational fees are the No. 1 source of revenue to pay back bonds issued for construction projects and that the purpose of tuition increases is to borrow more."

This response deliberately sidestepped what I had actually said: that tuition was the number one component of the General Revenue Fund that had been pledged as collateral for the construction bonds (ca. $3 billion out of the first $7 billion); that tuition was commingled with other revenues in the General Revenue Fund, and that, well before the state budget crisis the UC had explicitly said in bond indentures that the tuition component of the General Revenue would be rapidly increased, thereby reducing the leverage ratio, and thus the risk (leverage), of the bonds themselves. Taylor's response had essentially conceded my point, that tuition "is counted as general revenue" and that "general revenue is pledged as security for bonds," while denying that tuition "is *used* to pay debt service on our bonds" (my emphasis).

Taylor based this denial on an official press release in which he and UC Vice President Patrick Lenz had provided a list of the UC's "primary sources for debt repayment." This list did not mention tuition, but Taylor and Lenz never claimed that it was disclosed to bondholders, who might then have asked whether non-tuition revenues provided sufficient coverage. (*UC Newsroom* 2009). Clearly, tuition had been pledged as the UC's largest, fastest-growing income source because this was necessary to persuade bond-rating agencies that its revenue projections were more stable than the state's, and that its interest rate should thus be lower.

Despite this obvious truth, some UC faculty professed to take Taylor and Lenz seriously, demanding to know whether UC was monitoring the "primary revenue sources" to make sure that they were sufficient to cover the growing debt without touching tuition. Had the UC put in place an internal system for tracking enrollment-generated dollars to prevent them being used for servicing debt, thus ring-fencing its educational mission? One of the most dogged questioners was a retired Berkeley physics professor, Charles Schwartz, who pointed out that, if there were other "primary revenue sources" for tuition-backed general revenue bonds, then it should be possible for the UC to produce "debt coverage ratios" showing the extent to which those bonds put tuition revenue at risk. Schwartz pursued Taylor on this point for over a year, ultimately concluding as follows:

> I cited a letter from Taylor to Meister in which he mentioned some such ratios for individual campuses. The response I got made it official that there are no such records. Here is the precise explanation given.
>
> "The University does not record individual tabulations of each project's debt service coverage. This is because revenues generated by said projects are not the only revenues that can be pledged

toward the projects and counted toward a debt service coverage calculation."

> This seems to say: All the General Revenue funds (including all student fees) are considered to be in one big pot and we don't care which portion of the money is used to pay off the bonds. (Schwartz 2010, 6)

So, Taylor and Lenz had been bluffing when they pointed to internal records and procedures that would safeguard tuition revenues from ever being used to service its construction debt. If there were no such safeguards, then what mattered was the pledge.

CONSPIRACY/THEORY

But if Peter Taylor really thought that claiming safeguards would be a good way to justify the pledge of tuition, how could he demonize me as an "enemy" to everything good that the UC represents, both "access and excellence," for criticizing a tuition pledge that lacked such safeguards? The self-interest behind his comments was clear—he had been attacked and was fighting back. Beyond this obvious circumstance, however, he must also have been thinking that the standard economic explanations he was offering for the UC's actions in raising tuition and borrowing against it were self-evident. Any university administrator, after all, would want more money to spend, regardless of how he or she was motivated to spend it; any administrator of a *public* university would want to maintain broad public access even if the public would not pay; any administrator of a *good* university would assert its need to maintain instructional quality as a reason to raise tuition high enough to do so, even if the cutbacks already made were expected to be permanent; and any financial officer of a university with sudden growth in unrestricted revenue from its educational mission would see this as a way to fund expansion beyond that mission. There would, moreover, have been no public expectation that the UC commit new revenues from instruction to preserving or restoring academic quality when its campuses were not publicly acknowledging that their budget cuts had made them worse. Yet here I was saying that the UC was pursuing a plan to increase unrestricted revenue from its educational mission would see this as a way to fund expansion beyond that mission. There would, moreover, have been no public expectation beyond that mission. There would, moreover, have been no public expectation that the UC commit new revenues from instruction to preserving or restoring academic quality when its campuses were not publicly acknowledging that their budget cuts had made them worse. Yet here I was saying that the UC was pursing a plan to increase unrestricted revenue from its educational commitments by *means* of making itself worse, thus simultaneously exploiting and betraying its primary educational mission.

I had thus opened myself to being demonized for attacking the UC's essential goodness. According to my analysis, the UC had admitted enough new students to reduce per student instructional funding by as much as one third so that the state would allow it to subsequently double the Educational Fee charged to all of its California students: if the state wanted the UC to expand access, the argument went, it must simultaneously be allowed to raise tuition. This step toward privatizing its revenue base would allow the uc to assetize its public educational mission as a source of increased borrowing power (Meister 2011b).

The UC's strategy was, thus, not merely to make a UC education budgetarily worse (as measured, for example, by spending/credit hour), but also to exploit capital markets that its students, who were not able to borrow *for* their tuition at the low rates the UC got, by borrowing *against* it. This financial arbitrage was less likely to succeed if current and prospective students were aware of it, which could explain Taylor's vehement denial that it was in effect. But after I revealed it, his denial merely fed suspicions that part of the plan was to conceal the plan.

But Taylor's outrage at my revelation went beyond implausibly denying that the UC had a plan for ratcheting up aggregate tuition revenue that it could divert from instructional use: he seemed, especially, bothered by the fact that I called that plan *financial*, as though I had thereby impugned the motivations of UCOP [the UC Office of the President] as somehow pecuniary and self-interested. "The issue that generated the most heat," between Meister and UCOP, as Professor Schwartz (2010) accurately observed, "[was] the suggestion that University officials raise[d] student fees in order to expand their construction projects." This, he said, was "a question of motives, which I see no way of answering." Although it is often true that conspiracy theorists often allude to nefarious and hidden motives based on personal economic interests, I had never suggested that the UC's financialization strategy was explained by Peter Taylor's background in the bond industry or by the Regents' well-known business interests in real estate development and finance. Whatever personal sensitivities they may have had in these areas, I was less interested in exploring possible corruption that explained their strategies than I was in documenting the well-understood financial theories that explained actions that they were publicly justifying on other grounds.

This faculty debate over administrative motives was, in hindsight, a distraction from a deeper issue implicit in attacking me as a conspiracy theorist: whether pointing to a pre-existing plan is a good explanation of anything. The most powerful objection to conspiracy theories is not, after all, that they are false (or that motives can be hard to prove), but simply that pointing to the existence of a plan is worse, as the explanation of its outcome, than showing that the same outcome would have happened anyway, regardless of the plan. If, maybe, exposing strategies and motives—whether hidden or not—is not a good way to explain what happens in the world, then the UC's plan to raise tuition and thereby finance construction *could not* be an adequate explanation of that outcome, even if the plan was followed and succeeded.

This objection to my mode of argument was not new or surprising to me. It was central to my formation as a Marxian political theorist nearly fifty years ago. Philosophers in the 1960s and early 1970s, beginning with Karl Popper (1966), had denounced Marxism for fostering "conspiracy theories of society."[1] Popper's polemical point did not deny that a conspiracy theory could prove true; he admitted that conspiracies have occurred. It was rather that attributing a social outcome to a conspiracy is weaker scientifically than providing an explanation that could be either true or false regardless of whether an underlying conspiracy exists. The reason for this, according to Popper ([1945] 1962), was that any explanation of an outcome that relies on a conspiracy to bring it about presupposes that no unintended consequences will result from acting with conspiratorial intent, and assumes there were no intervening causes that could prevent the conspiracy from succeeding.[2] In Popper's view, the strongest explanation of any social pattern comes from showing how what actually happened would have happened anyway in the absence of intelligent design, coercion, or conspiracy. So, even if, for example, the ruling class demonstrably manipulated the state to widen economic inequality, a superior explanation is one showing that the same result could have happened without wrongdoing or nefarious intent. Models based on a purely random process would thus provide a better explanation of social structure than preexisting class power.[3]

Popper's methodological strictures and political conclusions were largely shared by Friedrich von Hayek, who thought that it is more mature—less primitive—to depict our social world as one that could have been an accidental outcome of human activity than to search for a malevolent purpose in the past that can be invoked to justify undoing its present outcome. For him, a social world that could have resulted from accident is the next best thing to one that is natural, and perhaps even better if we had not previously seen nature itself as an impersonal process and had, rather, believed it to be governed by gods imposing their will (Hayek 1967, 1978).[4] For both Hayek and Popper, "conspiracy theories" are no less superstitious than false religions insofar as they project a presumption of omnipotence onto powerful, and malign, humans whose true intentions are often hidden.[5]

The philosopher Edna Ullmann-Margalit interrogates the kind of "invisible-hand explanations" that Popper and Hayek advocate by usefully distinguishing between those that are evolutionary and those based on process (Ullmann-Margalit 1978, 1997). Evolutionary theories, she says, explain *survival*: here, something survives changes in its internal or external state because it can adapt (or performs an adaptive function in a system) regardless of how it originated or what its designer intended. Unlike such functional explanations, process-type invisible-hand theories are what philosophers of science like Carl Hempel (1965, 447–53) called "genetic" explanations: they explain origins. For Hempel, the existence of a pattern can be adequately explained only by appealing to a mechanism or story in which the inputs are previously unpatterned, or at least less patterned: otherwise, the structure and complexity of the explanation would be too similar to that of the phenomenon to be explained.

As Ullmann-Margalit points out, however, Hempel's account of genetic explanations is most persuasive when explaining something "invisible-handedly" would be seen to be a better "explication" of what happened even if its truth were only hypothetical: An explanation is "explicative," she says, only if it sheds light. It may be true, in her example, that fractional reserve banking was invented by an Italian prince and worked as he intended. But this historically provable description of what happened need not deter others from thinking it a better explication to show how and why it could have happened anyway. "There is even a sense," according to Ullmann-Margalit, "in which the fact that a cogent invisible-hand explanation proves false is felt to be peculiarly irrelevant; the fact that someone was actually smart and quick enough to have intentionally brought about the pattern in question is felt, I think, to shed but little light on its nature—indeed is felt to be almost accidental" (1978, 276–77).

An exemplary proponent of process-type invisible-hand theories was Hempel's student and my teacher, Robert Nozick, who claimed that theories using patterns (like prior class structure) to explain patterns (like subsequent class structure) are inherently weak (1974, 1997). The problem he saw with such theories is that *explanans* and *explanandum* in such theories are too much of the same type and level of complexity: that they already resemble and may even referentially entail each other. Better explanations of a pattern or structure invoke what Nozick (1981, 21–22) calls "processes" (he mentions "filtering" and "equilibrium") to show how a structured state of affairs could and would have been produced even if it did not already exist and no one intended to bring it about. This, according to Nozick, is what makes invisible-hand explanations "more fundamental" than historical explanations ascribing agency and efficacy to those who happened to benefit from previous patterns or expect to benefit from future ones. And it is also why Nozick thought that conspiracy theories (what he sometimes calls *visible-hand explanations*) may be superficially persuasive, while lacking what Ullmann-Margalit would call the "explicative value" of rigorous, scientific, history."[6] For Nozick, as for Popper and Hayek, historical explanations showing the effect of unintended processes are more "robust" against challenges than hidden-hand explanations based on the revealed intentions of conspirators whose prior ability to affect the future according to their will is supposedly demonstrated by their subsequent success.

But Nozick also says that the truth of hidden-hand explanations is the only thing that matters for the purpose of justice as what he calls a "rectification" of the past (1981, 152–55). He here makes an implicit break with the Popper/Hayek view of what counts as a good historical argument by carving out an exception for forensics. Nozick thus ends up with a seemingly paradoxical view of, for example, capitalist inequality: on the one hand it could be explicitly rationalized, and implicitly legitimated, by showing how it could have come about by accident, without anyone doing anything wrong; on the other hand, the same pattern of inequality would have to be rectified if it can be shown forensically to have come about because someone did something wrong, regardless of whether it could have happened with no wrongdoing.[7]

But why should we regard the latter form of argument as inherently more explicative in non-forensic contexts than "visible-hand explanations"? "Just so stories" about invisible hands may explain how a state of affairs survived (in the evolutionary model) or arose (in the genetic model) without having any necessary implications about the need for them to change, as a forensic argument would. But why should we always prefer these fables to forensic arguments that call for change unless we are prima facie interested in rebutting those arguments with counterclaims about the evolution and/or the origin of the status quo?

The answer is surely not about the concept of causation as such. As the philosopher Donald Davidson points out, giving someone's motivation for doing something is itself a type of causal explanation—it explains what happened *as* an action and names that action by referring to the agent's reason for it.[8] This attribution of agency rebuts the implicit assumption in Popper and Hayek that giving someone's reason for doing something cannot causally explain what happened because valid causal explanations must first rule out the possibility that what happened could have been an accident. Moreover, our statistical methods for distinguishing coincidence from correlation do not address the possibility that what happened was someone's action and the agent's reasons for it are causal explanations in Davidson's sense.

My forensic mode of argument against those in power at UCOP had the effect of renaming as their action what they would otherwise explain as a sequence of events that could have arisen by accident, and was, thus, not addressable in the register of justice. Within this register, what *makes* a present pattern unjust can depend on the history that produced it—that is, the reasons that caused it to occur. But what is thereby *made* unjust is the *ongoingness* of the present pattern, once it has been renamed as a decision point at which a strategy might be advanced or stopped. So, pointing to that strategy, whether it is conspiratorial or not, could causally explain a state of affairs if it correctly names what happened as something that someone did (which is one way of shedding light on it in Ullmann-Margalit's sense).

Thinking back on the "Meister Controversy" of 2009–2010 through the lens of a volume on *Conspiracy/Theory* has thus been clarifying to me. At one level there was, as I have said, confusion sown about whether I was criticizing the UC's financial strategy as such or the motives behind it. To what extent was my criticism that this strategy has to be concealed, in which case my critique consisted merely of revealing it? But the UC's preexisting plans were what they were, and then the Great Recession happened. So, there was a deeper question about whether its planning documents were explanatory, or, more broadly, about whether antecedent intentions can ever be causally explanatory, given all the other factors that are always at play. The real question was, thus, whether I was being paranoid in attributing the UC's actions to its prior intentions when I should have been merely depressed that in the midst of a recession it now had no alternative.[9] Is it better to disregard whatever plans and intentions were antecedently in place if there is an alternative, invisible-hand explanation of what eventually happened? Are the subsequent forensic uses of those plans and intentions merely a way of finding scapegoats for events that were in hindsight inevitable, which is, of course, the underlying objection to all "conspiracy" theories? It is also an objection to my view.

But one could also make a similarly broad objection to "invisible hand-edness" as a form of explanation: that in overstressing the contingent relation between plans and outcomes it misidentifies the phenomenon to be explained as whatever would have happened, regardless of the intentions and desires that existed in the past. This is an excessively narrow concept of causality that implicitly depoliticizes the present by effectively bracketing the ongoing character of injustice, which is often how it keeps on going. A more forensic approach to explanation would reverse this logic, which is what I hoped to do by shedding light on what the UC's business plan has been, and on why that plan must be reversed in the context of a Great Recession. An explanation of why something cannot go on now may be true or false, but it cannot be dismissed as though it were not an explanation merely because it differs in form from an invisible-hand account of how something originated, or of how it evolved, that abstract from the implicitly pragmatic role of the explanation itself in perpetuating what it purports to explain. So, whether my identification of the UC's enrollment growth, tuition increases, and construction plan as part of an ongoing financializaton strategy would be explanatory, or not, would ultimately depend on coherence of my theory of financialization rather than debates in the philosophy of science discussed above.

In 2009 I had just begun my academic study of the financialization of capitalism, where I would face similar questions about whether finance-based explanations of markets that privileged positive feedback loops, as discussed below, are superior to market-based explanations of finance that privilege equilibrium. This was not only a question about which form of scientific explanation was more fundamental and robust. It was also a question of politics—about what type of system capitalism has become and through what mechanisms it perpetuates itself. Finance-driven explanations of market crises (like the Great Recession) stress the liquidity/illiquidity of asset markets as a driver of capital accumulation that periodically destabilizes commodity markets; commodity market-driven explanations of finance regard this explanatory stress on the financial strategies of capitalists as a type of conspiracy theory that is less robust and fundamental than the invisible hand that ultimately restores market equilibrium. But *accusing* their critics of conspiracy theory is also a political strategy available to capitalists who, as cumulative beneficiaries of past injustice, do not wish to be blamed as though they were the perpetrators (conspirators?) who would have welcomed the ongoingness (continuity with the past) of what eventually occurred.[10] This would be the topic of my research for over fifteen years, and from this perspective it mattered that my argument in 2009 was not merely that the UC was acting according to a plan, but that the plan was to *financialize* itself.

FINANCE/MARKET/CONSPIRACY

Finance has always been a fruitful site to ferret out conspiracies (hidden hands) subverting the impersonal forces of Adam Smith's invisible hand in creating market equilibrium. This is because the dirty secret of market equilibrium is that transactions require funding—the discipline of payment imposes a liquidity requirement on purchases to a varying extent that depends on the purchaser's credit history and available collateral. As providers of liquidity (funding), financiers are thus in a position to influence future prices by taking advantage of asymmetric information, collusive bargaining, and so forth. And because there is no self-correcting mechanism—no invisible hand—to prevent them from doing so, the only way to stop the pernicious influence of finance has been through nonmarket means, such as anti-conspiracy law.

The deeper problem that seeing finance as a conspiracy reveals, however, is that it does not obey the social logic that we see in mainstream economics as the paradigm of an explanatory theory. Here people are presumed to have *diminishing* marginal utility—demand falls as prices rise. But the liquidity finance provides does not have the diminishing marginal value that economists associate with utility: other things equal, everyone wants to buy a financial asset because its price is rising and to sell it because its price is falling. Whatever else they may want, economic actors unanimously want liquidity, or the shiftability (optionality) that it provides. This drive toward unanimity means that in the pricing of financial assets there is no negative feedback mechanism leading to equilibrium when prices go up, and nothing to prevent a further flight to cash when they go down. What financial economists call "liquidity preference" (Modigliani 1944), then, is an example of what the cultural theorist René Girard (1996) termed "mimetic desire," in the sense that our responses to the desires of others create a positive feedback loop—a form of social contagion with no internally generated countervailing tendencies (Orléan 2014, Aglietta 2018).

In financial economics we thus have a second type of systemic explanation, positive feedback loops, which operate alongside, and can also undermine, the negative feedback loops of Walrasian market equilibrium. The reality is that financial markets are forms of social contagion that exhibit all the characteristics Girard describes, including multiple equilibria, mimetic polarization, and self-reinforcing (rather than self-correcting) expectations (Aglietta 2018; Orléan 2014). Finance can thus be seen as the subverter of stable markets to the extent that it creates price bubbles. And financial bubbles, when they finally burst, can be blamed on the secret machinations of financiers, who may be persecuted (and sometimes prosecuted) because, as Girard (1989) observes, scapegoats must be found in the aftermath of social contagion. This singling out is, however, yet another form of social contagion that can restore stability through unanimous agreement on who was to blame for past disorder.

Thinking back on the accusations against me, the UC's administrators were initially making the same objections that capitalists typically make when they are accused of being driven by financial contagion rather market rationality that is, that positive feedback loops, based on imitating others, are less fundamental than the negative-feedback explanations that end the instability to which imitation leads. But the assumption that the UCs imitation of peer public universities would be best corrected by the market would not have addressed my specific criticism of would not have addressed my criticism of its reorientation toward financial markets: specifically, the role of public higher education in increasing demand for federally backed student debt from which new credit-bases can be manufactured; the plan to assetize the expected growth in revenues from student debt-financed enrollments to become less dependent on state government; and its shorter term deception of students, who would be told each time their tuition rose that this was only because the UC was fulfilling a state mandate to expand enrollments beyond what the state was willing to fund.

This deception relates to the complaint of the UC's top administrators that in trying to burst the tuition I was scapegoating them for doing what every highly ranked state university now does. The objection here could not be that scapegoats are innocent because mimesis is a defense; it must, rather, have been a demonization of me, as its accuser, for *singling out* a specific public university that was merely following a trend. By being car-icatured as denying the trend I was in effect being recast as the conspiracy of the few. So, when I tried to burst the tuition bubble, I could be accused of being *accusatory*, which is the baseline moral criticism that can be lev-eled against all conspiracy theories regardless of their truth.

But this rhetoric deflected attention from the substance of my accu-sation. What I said—in speeches across California and elsewhere—was that, over a period of twenty years, the UC had ceased to present itself as a driver of greater income convergence resulting from the increased sup-ply of highly educated Californians; the UC was, instead, claiming credit for widening income disparities in a state economy that had transitioned from defense to tech, and was purporting to protect its graduates from being victims of those disparities. In addition to an educational service, it was thus selling an embedded financial product—its a hedge against anxieties about falling behind—that would let it raise the total price that could be charged for education even if per-student expenditure on in-struction was going down.

The underlying truth, however, is that the UC had no idea how long its opportunity to go on doing this would last. Being on the upside of rising inequality had been possible for the top 20 percent of Californians in the late 1990s, when the UC started down this path, but by 2009 the gap be-tween income growth and stagnation was approaching the top 1 percent. So, by 2009 the UC had a window of opportunity to extract revenue from its California Master Plan mission that it could then invest to diminish the role of higher education in its overall portfolio. That is what I was say-ing, and that is what UC was doing.

Most Academic Senate faculty did not see this. The few who were aware of the mimetic logic of finance mainly worried about whether a uc educa-tion would still be perceived as a luxury brand if it did *not* raise its price. Many more understood that our instructional product, was deteriorating, but still saw of our administrators as rational utilitarians and thus argued that the benefits of their respective programs were worth the cost. But financialization meant that the administration was no longer primarily engaged in cost-benefit analysis: it was more interested in which expen-ditures would raise the rankings of any given academic unit, which would not, and which units could be cut without affecting whatever rankings mattered most. This implied, or course, a decision from the top to let many areas of instruction, outside of STEM, become worse by design. But for many faculty acknowledging this would have been inconsistent with saying that the UC still stood for excellence and was getting better all the time. This implied, or course, a decision from the top to let many areas of instruction, outside of STEM, to become worse by design, but acknowledging this would have been inconsistent with saying that the uc s still stood for excellence and was getting better all the time (Meister 2009c).

Why was I so sure that this was wrong? The events I am recounting occurred at a moment of convergence between my academic, institutional, and political work. I had just begun what became a ten-year project to restate Marxist economic theory in a way that incorporates the financial models for valuing options that would explain the Great Recession and the bailout of capital markets that followed (Meister, 2021). At my own UC campus, I was coming off what had been a multiyear stint as chair of the Academic Senate Committee on Planning and Budget, which also made me a member of the UC systemwide committee. This gave me access to almost all of the UC's internal budgetary documents, and access to those in charge of its financial planning at the systemwide level. At this time I was also serving what would be a seventeen-year term as the president of the UC systemwide labor union for tenure-track faculty, which engaged in collective bargaining on only one campus (my own) but had extensive consultation rights throughout the system. The protection afforded by my status as the president of a labor union allowed me to publish without reprisal from the UC in its capacity as my employer, which was a real issue after the university had successfully defended its legal right to penalize a faculty whistleblower who had called attention to the curricular shortcomings of his department.[11]

These three roles meshed when I published "They Pledged Your Tuition." From my academic study of financialization, I understood conceptually that revenue the UC expected from tuition, unlike money appropriated by the state, could be capitalized—that it could be pledged as collateral for bonds. But I also understood, from my Academic Senate role, that, because the UC had traditionally been state supported and tuition free, the Educational Fee was specifically earmarked to support the UC's instructional mission. The Regents' 1994 policy, as amended in 2005, contained an express enumeration of its permissible uses:

> In addition to funding programs and services supported by the Educational Fee (such as student financial aid and related programs, admissions, registration, administration, libraries, and operation and maintenance of plant), income generated by the Educational

Fee may be used for general support of the University's operating budget. Revenue from the Educational Fee may be used to fund all costs related to instruction, including faculty salaries.[12] (as quoted in Schwartz 2010, 4)

Despite these explicit restrictions, however, the UC's General Revenue Fund had swept in 100 percent of the Educational Fee as though it were unrestricted revenue that could be pooled with other sources of income (including parking and dorm fees) to finance projects that were unrelated to those funding sources. As of 2009, the Educational Fees had already become the largest component of General Revenue—approximately half—and was the only component that was significantly growing. And now, the financial crisis presented the UC with the opportunity to raise Educational Fees more rapidly at a time when historically low interest rates would enable it to ramp up construction for all kinds of projects that would no longer have to be described to a bondholder or linked to any more specific funding source.

This was the basis for the Open Letter to Students in 2009. But when UC President Mark Yudof denounced it at a widely reported news conference, he specifically invoked the regents' policy on Educational Fees quoted above to insinuate that either I did not know what I was talking about or that I had deliberately lied.

> Q: . . . UCSC Professor Bob Meister has, like, written this piece, I don't know if you have heard of it, it's called "They Pledged Your Tuition: An Open Letter to UC Students."
>
> A: It is totally untrue, by the way. . . . It is untrue because we are not allowed to use student fees to pay bonded indebtedness. . . . He took two numbers that, you know, that we had pledged toward debt and when the fees were going up. [inaudible] It's just untrue. We're not allowed to use fees for that purpose. The fees are used for operating expenses of the university. The reason we made these pledges, 'cause it will lower—if you pledge the whole campuses as opposed to just the residence hall, or whatever, it lowers the interest rate, which means students pay less for their dorm rooms and the like. It's just not true, flat-out not true; misinformation.[13]

Yudof was, essentially, saying that the UC policy that allowed him to pledge the Educational Fee as collateral for bonds would also prevent him from using it to honor that pledge: that all of it could be pledged for debt service provided that none of it was eventually used for this purpose.

By the time he made this statement, I had posted the General Revenue bond indentures on our union website for all to see. Nothing in them disclosed to bondholders the existence of any legal, or other, impediment to the UC's use of the Educational Fee revenues it had pledged to service its bonds. Had the bond indentures included such a statement, the bonds would have been unmarketable. And, if the regental limitations on the Educational Fees really would preclude them from being used as pledged, this omission from the bond indentures could be said to fraudulently deprive bondholders of the primary guarantee on which they had relied.

But the bond indentures that I posted online revealed something even more important. As early as 2005—well before the 2008 financial crisis—the UC's marketing of its bonds expressly stated that it would *raise* revenues from Educational Fees by approximately as much as it would later say it had been forced to do because of state funding cuts. Its sales pitch to the bond markets was that the UC, as an elite public institution, could easily raise the Educational Fee when times were good by claiming that public higher education deserved substantial credit for widening income inequality; and, if times were bad, the UC's bondholders were assured that it could raise the Educational Fee even faster by blaming the state for forcing budget cuts, and relying on higher unemployment to bolster its enrollments despite the higher fees.[14] UC bonds would thus be a good investment when California was doing well and a much better investment than other public bond issues when state revenues are falling. This showed that UC had previewed, in 2004, the script that it followed in 2009 when it said it was forced to raise tuition by the budget crisis.

Alongside these documents, I posted Peter Taylor's 2009 slide presentations to the Academic Senate Budget Committee, showing that the dramatic growth of enrollment revenues during the state budget crisis, combined with historically low interest rates, had given the UC an unprecedented opportunity to fund capital projects that could expand its revenue base beyond public higher education. It was thus embarking on a building spree at the very moment that it claimed to be undergoing a budgetary emergency—and it expected this emergency to play a major role in funding that building spree.[15]

When I said all this in "They Pledged Your Tuition," and its three sequels, I did so as a union president protected by state labor law from speaking against the UC administration (my employer) outside the narrow channels available through the Academic Senate. I was thus able to meet with politicians in Sacramento, to consult with their staff, to give interviews to print and broadcast media, and to address large gatherings of students at building occupations and other demonstrations across the UC system. The result of their direct actions was a legislative and public backlash against the UC, which led it to freeze, until quite recently, its plans for further tuition increases.

Student opposition to UC policies was reinforced by skeptical and sometimes negative coverage of the university in statewide media,[16] and with the California story about construction bonds and tuition being picked up by elements of national media and news outlets as far away as the United Kingdom and Europe.[17] Stories in which I was quoted said that I had uncovered a conspiracy to raise tuition to finance construction. Ben Ehrenreich's (2009) headline in *The Nation*, for example, was "California Scheming." And in subsequent media events, I showed how the UC was playing a financial spread in which students borrow at 6–12 percent per annum to pay tuition so that UC could pledge the resulting revenue streams as collateral to borrow from Wall Street at a federally subsidized rate of 2–3 percent.

I also tried to stress that much of the construction being funded by instructional activities was in support of UC's effort to expand beyond its higher education portfolio.[18] This was a major theme when I was asked to respond to broadcast and print stories about the UC's specific construction projects, which in one instance I toured on TV. And an article I later published was partly responsible for prompting legislative audits of how unequally UC was allocating back to the campuses the increased revenue that it generated from the higher enrollments they were expected to absorb. (While my work was not mentioned in the legislative audit, I had made some staffers aware of what they would find, and the final report demanded transparency from the UC going forward.)

For me, the costs of such activities were small: some of the administrators targeted by my attack made the Academic Senate promise not to make me chair of the systemwide budget committee, which was really not so bad as reprisals go! Although I received no apologies from the UC administrators who insulted me, I was in the essentials proven to be right (Meister 2009b). And after seventeen years in the UC's political trenches, I returned full-time to my larger academic project, a study of the financialization of capitalism as such, which was eventually published (Meister 2021).

IS FINANCIALIZATION ITSELF A CONSPIRACY?

Was I really a conspiracy theorist? I had shown that the UC had a financial plan to securitize enrollment-generated revenue, and to increase it, without in any way earmarking those funds to support instructional activities. Part of its plan was to explain tuition increases differently to bondholders and to its students. But it was the UC's subsequent denial, and not my claim itself, that showed the importance of concealment in the implementation of its plan. In these ways I was exposing a collusive plan, the success of which depended largely on its expected nondisclosure.

But I was not mainly attacking that plan for being secret. My essential claim was also that in commingling all its unencumbered revenue for purposes the UC's leaders had *premediated* future state budget cuts and found a way to capitalize on them to deprioritize its public educational mission under the guise of expanding it. This meant that they were doing the opposite of insulating the campuses from cuts to instruction—they were simultaneously imposing and bemoaning the cuts to raise tuition while planning to leave the cuts in place. Increasing prices while lowering the budgetary quality of instruction was one part of the plan.

My focus, however, had been on the second part of the UC's plan: its creation of new financial securities—General Revenue Bonds—the value of which would be predicated upon making itself a better credit risk than the state. The bond indentures showed to the UC could raise aggregate income from tuition while state tax revenues are falling, *and* that it could use these funds from education to subsidize revenue-generating activities without any commitment to use these revenue to support its core mission. This was a strategy of which any hedge fund manager would be proud.

The fundamental problem here is that the UC's drive to financialize itself entailed an implicit acknowledgment that its core mission has changed, and largely undisclosed, repurposing of its mission. It now views higher education less as a set of commodified instructional services that non-universities may soon be able to provide more cheaply, and more as a financial product—quite simply the option to get, or stay, on the upside of a widening income distribution gap. And it now sees its ability to manufacture and sell this financial product as a function of its ranking vis-à-vis comparable institutions—a form of Girard's mimetic rivalry. As I put it then, "As long as the value of the financial asset embedded in tuition continued to grow, based on a widening income spread between those with college educations and everyone else, public universities could expect to expand their market (enrollment), raise their price (tuition), and lower delivery costs" (Meister 2011b).

This more specific analysis, which is not a conspiracy theory as such, explains highly ranked universities can become more expensive as educational technology cheapens the provision of courseware as a commodity. Here, expected income spreads (and related comparisons) are the measure of their success. And controlling costs is no longer a paramount concern because budgets can always be cut in areas that do not affect the rankings while permanent deficits can be run in areas that do.

The fact that mimetic rivalry—not cost-benefit analysis—drives administrative priorities is a truth about the financialization of higher education that every faculty member must eventually come to understand. Optionality is, as I have argued, fundamental to thinking financially, and the importance of creating and valuing options explains why in today's public universities we have so many academic plans and so few administrative commitments to funding them (R. Martin 2011).

How, then, are financial explanations of higher education policy related to conspiracy theory? In my theoretical writings, I claim that financialization incorporates both the possibility of conspiracies and the uncertainty of their success, treating them as future scenarios that can be priced, leveraged, and hedged in the present. The uc's approach to capitalizing on its sudden ability to accelerate tuition growth was clearly an example of this—creating present value in the form of a credit-rating spread over the rest of state government, while at the same time gaining greater autonomy from the state. But to hedge or speculate on long-term futures is not in itself a conspiracy to bring them about. The real conspiracy, if there was one, is more specific to the mission of public higher education.

My finance-based explanation of the uc's conduct is that it was premediating the endgame scenario of public higher education, seen as a commodity and service, in order to extract present financial value from heightened uncertainty about the timing and extent of its eventual decline or supersession. Seeing all this through lens of financial theory we need make no assumption that the uc's plans will automatically succeed to understand how the presence of those plans defines a portfolio of options the present value of which can be priced, and continuously repriced, depending on what information bearing on those plans is revealed or concealed in the course of events. Because its options are *about* its plans, the plans themselves come to function as *meta* conspiracies that might fail if they have to be fully disclosed, and thus become controversial. The concealment and revelation of its intentions can causally affect the value of its asset portfolio. So, by financializing, the UC has in a sense been making a conspiracy theorist of itself. And by revealing this through the critical use of the financial theory on which the UC itself relied, I was trying to change the present value of its options. In my view, it is thus the logic of financialization itself—not of commoditization—that we need to confront to arrive at an actionable analysis of what is happening in higher education that could potentially change the outcome.

For now, however, the UC has persuaded students to incur higher personal debt so that it can diversify into the business, for example, of providing end-of-life care to people in the generation that it was built to educate, and who are now fully insured. The irony is that the UC will have imposed debt burdens on the present generation of students that has foreclosed the ability of many to invest in future benefits, such as pensions and health insurance, that could protect them at the end of life. This is to say that their student debt has put them on the downside of the so-called miracle of compound interest.

As of 2009, the UC's financial strategy was, essentially, to take what finance theory would consider a short position on the success of the widening swath of lower-income students it expected to pay and borrow more to attend even as their future economic opportunities were narrowing. Its financial strategy was to suck more families into the interest-rate arbitrage between student-loan bonds and construction bonds, while protecting in-state families already getting full fee remission from tuition hikes. The UC did not deny my critique because I was wrong; it did so because its plan had to be deniable in order to be successful. This is, of course, a famously nefarious element in conspiracies—a reason why exposing them constitutes a criticism and why the UC's denial was an essential component of its plan. My efforts showed how exposure can impede such a strategy, and the UC's response showed how, through denial, its strategy may yet succeed.

NOTES

1. "I shall briefly describe a theory which is widely held but which assumes what I consider the very opposite of the true aim of the social sciences; I call it the *'conspiracy theory of society.'* It is the view that an explanation of

a social phenomenon consists in the discovery of the men or groups who are interested in the occurrence of this phenomenon (sometimes it is a hidden interest which has first to be revealed), and who have planned and conspired to bring it about. This view of the aims of the social sciences arises, of course from the mistaken theory that, whatever happens in society—especially happenings such as war, unemployment, poverty, shortages, which people as a rule dislike—is the result of direct design by some powerful individuals and groups" (Popper 1966, 94–95).

2. "The conspiracy theory of society is very widespread and has very little truth in it. Only when conspiracy theoreticians come into power does it become something like a theory which accounts for things which actually happen. . . . For example, when Hitler came into power. . . . But the interesting thing is that *such a conspiracy never—or 'hardly ever'—turns out in the way that is intended*. This remark can be taken as a clue to what is the true task of a social theory. Hitler, I said, made a conspiracy that failed. Why did it fail? Not just because other people conspired against Hitler. It failed, simply, because it is one of the striking things about social life that *nothing ever comes off exactly as intended*. Things always turn out a little bit differently. We hardly ever produce in social life precisely the effect that we wish to produce, and we usually get things that we do not want into the bargain. Of course, we act with certain aims in mind; but apart from the question of these aims (which we may or may not really achieve) there are always certain unwanted consequences of our actions, and usually these unwanted consequences cannot be eliminated" (Popper [1945] 1962, 123–24).

3. For Popper ([1945] 1962), the project of reversing the cumulative effects of historical injustice by a Marxist party in power is no less likely to fail—though in this case, Popper implies that such an attempt would be an actually existing conspiracy using the hypothetical existence of a previous conspiracy as a pretext for exercising unfettered political power in the present.

4. Popper's books on social science are dedicated to Friedrich von Hayek.

5. The conspiracy theory of society, "which is more primitive than most forms of theism, is akin to Homer's theory of society. Homer conceived the power of the gods in such a way that whatever happened on the plain before Troy was only a reflection of the various conspiracies on Olympus. The conspiracy theory of society is just a version of this theism, of a belief in gods whose whims and wills rule everything. It comes from abandoning God and then asking: 'Who is in his place?' His place is then filled by various powerful men and groups—sinister pressure groups, who are to be blamed for having planned the great depression and all the evils from which we suffer" (Popper [1945] 1962, 122–23).

6. This requires being able to prove both that the outcome would have happened because of the presence of the proposed cause and that would not

have happened in its absence: "To know that p is to be someone who would believe it if it were true, and who wouldn't believe it if it were false. . . . Knowledge is . . . having a specific real factual connection to the world: tracking it" (Nozick 1981, 178).

7. The conservative legal scholar Robert Bork (1978) famously applied a similar argument to antitrust law, which in the Sherman Act prohibits "conspiracy in restraint of trade." For Bork, the legal test for antitrust liability was whether an alleged conspiracy adversely affected prices—that is, whether the same prices could have been the result of an invisible hand. Here the well-functioning Walrasian market is defined as the opposite of a conspiracy in that no buyer and no seller can influence price and, thus, that price itself is the only information that needs to be known by all. Evidence that there was in fact a conspiracy to fix prices can be conclusively rebutted by demonstrating that the market itself was sufficiently robust to defeat the conspiracy. In this case, the failure of the conspiracy would be legally sufficient to prove that there was none.

8. The fact that a historical reason names an action does not rule out treating it also as a cause, and sometimes *the* cause of the action thus described. See Davidson (1963). Unlike Nozick, Davidson focuses on the explanation of actions rather than structural patterns. "Beliefs and desires conspire to cause, rationalize, and explain intentional actions. We act intentionally for reasons, and our reasons always include both value and beliefs. We would not act unless there were some value or end we hoped to achieve (or some supposed evil we hoped to avoid), and we believed our course of actions was a way of realizing our aim. . . . For we all, whether we think about it or not, make our decisions in terms of how we weigh the values of various possible outcomes of our actions, and how likely we think one or another course of action is to attain those values" (Davidson 1999, 519–20). Here Davidson is laying out the foundational assumptions of decision theory, which Nozick also embraces in other contexts.

9. The underlying point—stated with a nod to Melanie Klein—is that when something goes wrong in society you should not become paranoid and find someone to blame but rather become depressed by the thought that the problem really lies within oneself.

10. I wrote about such a mentality in *After Evil* (Meister 2011a), but for the purposes of my book *Justice Is an Option* (2021), it is worth dwelling more on Nozick's view as he applied it to economics and as I now understand its relevance to finance.

11. Hong v. Grant, 516 F.Supp. 2d 1158 (2007).

12. Perhaps in response to the controversy discussed above, this policy was soon replaced by one that renamed Education Fees as Tuition and made the use of tuition revenues discretionary for the UC administration. Prior

to this, on March 24, 2010, the UC General Counsel had recommended adding an "asterisk" to the Regents' published fee policy to clarify that "they are not intended to bind the Regents or prevent them from adopting a different approach depending on the circumstances." The proposed addition would have been as follows: "*Nothing in this policy constitutes a contract, an offer of a contract, or a promise that any fees ultimately authorized by The Regents will be limited by any term or provision of this policy. The Regents expressly reserves the right and option, in its absolute discretion, to establish fees at any level it deems appropriate based on a full consideration of the circumstances, and nothing in this policy shall be a basis for any party to rely on fees of a specified level or based on a specified formula."* (Italics are in the original.) This attempt to remove the "confusion" in press reports would have contradicted President Yudof's earlier attempt to discredit me by insisting that the UC could not possibly be using Educational Fees to fund construction because doing so would violate its published policies. The UC's eventual solution was to rename its Educational Fees as "Tuition" and to remove restrictions on their use.

13. "UC President Discusses Systemwide Financial Crisis," *Daily Californian*, accessed September 4, 2019, https://archive.dailycal.org/article.php?id =107121.

14. These representations to prospective bondholders assumed that Educational Fees revenues were not restricted to educational uses, and could permissibly be used to provide financial leverage for other UC initiatives. I have no doubt that the UC's highest-level administrators believe this assumption to be legally correct, which is why they included Educational Fees in the General Revenue Fund, but also politically unacceptable, which is why they denied my claim.

15. See Peter Taylor's "Taylor_PPT_06_OCT_2009," under "UC Bond Documents Referenced in They Pledged Part III," Council of UC Faculty Associations, accessed March 6, 2023, http://www.cucfa.org/news/tuition_bonds.php.

16. E.g., Jack Dolan "State Universities Tap Student Fees for Unintended Projects," *Los Angeles Times* (April 4, 2010), https://www.latimes.com/ archives/la-xpm-2010-apr-04-la-me-student-funds4–2010apr04 -story. html; Nanette Asimov, "Students, Cal, Both Quieter in Protest Encore," *San Francisco Chronicle*, (December 9, 2009), https://www.sfgate.com/ed-ucation/article/Students-Cal-both-quieter-in-protest-encore-3206962. php?utm_campaign.

17. Some of the relevant press releases, videos, transcripts of hearings, and so forth are still available on the "They Pledged Your Tuition Index," Council of UC Faculty Associations, accessed March 6, 2023, http://www.cucfa.org/ news/tuition_bonds.php; see also Ben Ehrenreich, "California Schem-ing," *The Nation*, November 24, 2009, https://www.thenation.com/article/ archive/california-scheming-1/; Andrew McGettigan, *The Great University Gamble: Money, Markets, and the Future of Higher Education* (London: Pluto

Press, 2013), 142–47; John Holmwood, "From Social Rights to the Market: Neoliberalism and the Knowledge Economy." *International Journal of Lifelong Education* 33, no. 1 (2014): 62–76; Holmwood, "The university, democracy and the Public Sphere." *British Journal of Sociology of Education* 38, no. 7 (2017): 927–42; Aaron Bady and Mike Konczal. "From Master Plan to No Plan: The Slow Death of Public Higher Education." *Dissent* 59, no. 4 (2012): 10–16; Andrew Ross, "Mortgaging the Future: Student Debt in the Age of Austerity." *New Labor Forum*, 22, no. 1, 23–28; Ross, "Anti-social Debts," *Contexts* 11, no. 4 (2012): 28–32; Dan Clawson, "Faculty Unions at the Crossroads: Why Playing Defense is a Losing Strategy." In *New Labor Forum* 22, no. 1 (2103), 29–35; Amanda Armstrong, "States of Indebtedness: Care Work in the Struggle against Educational Privatization." *South Atlantic Quarterly* 110, no. 2 (2011): 546–52; Lenora Hanson and Elsa Noterman. "Speculating on the University: Disruptive Actions in Today's Corporate University." *ephemera: theory & politics in organization* 17, no. 3 (2017); Michelle Ty, "Introduction: Higher Education on Its Knees." *Qui Parle: Critical Humanities and Social Sciences* 20, no. 1 (2011): 3–32; Robert Meister and Peter Taylor on Patt Morrison, KPCC (Los Angeles), 11-17-2009; Andreas Etges and Winfried Fluck, "Kann die Finanzindustrie die öffentlichen Universitäten retten?" In *American Dream: Eine Weltmacht in de Krise*, edited by Andreas Etges and Winifried Fluck, 195–215. Frankfurt: Campus, 2011.

PART IV

THE POLITICS OF ENMITY

14 CONSPIRACY AND ITS CURIOUS AFTERLIVES

At the end of his famed essay "The Paranoid Style in American Politics," Richard Hofstadter (1964) contrasts the conspiratorial style of thinking that he finds so disturbing in American life to the approach of the historian. "A distinguished historian has said that one of the most valuable things about history is that it teaches us how things do not happen. It is precisely this kind of awareness that the paranoid fails to develop" (86), he writes. As Hofstadter observes, the historical method's attachment to empirical evidence and contextualization would seem to render it an effective antidote to conspiratorial thinking. But what happens when conspiracy itself becomes the subject of historical analysis? This chapter will explore the interstices of history and conspiracy theory, analyzing the anatomy of an obscure yet consequential plot and considering the methodological challenges that it poses to the historian.

The plot reconstructed in this chapter began in the late nineteenth century, when a small circle of Russian conspirators endeavored to change Europeans' negative perceptions of the tsarist regime. Engineered by a rogue employee of the tsarist secret police, or Okhrana, who concocted an elaborate set of conspiracy theories to build support for the autocracy and to discredit its most outspoken opponents, this effort eventually evolved into a broader effort to undermine Europe's liberal regimes. With the help of a handful of well-placed European allies, Okhrana agents used the continent's nascent mass media as a field for psyops intended to influence public opinion. Eventually, they complemented this effort with influence-peddling campaigns, police provocations, and forgeries. Indeed, circumstantial evidence suggests that the most notorious conspiratorial text of all time, *The Protocols of the Elders of Zion*, may have emerged from this circle.

Echoing other contributions in this volume, this essay challenges Hofstadter's derisive dismissal of the "paranoid style" to reveal the generative capacities of conspiracy. It shows how a relatively small group of people capitalized on the real failures and injustices of liberal democracy, even as the conspiracy theories that they wove grew more and more outlandish. In the process, the protagonists of this study managed to change domestic conversations in several European countries, to shape the course of international politics, and to enhance their own power and wealth. They provide proof positive that the "paranoid style"—far from an irrational mindset reserved for the benighted, the credulous, or cranks—can be an effective means of realizing one's interests while altering the political and intellectual landscape.

The fact that the plots reconstructed in this chapter unfolded in the distant past allows us to analyze the complete life cycle of a historical conspiracy. This broad and perspectival view affirms the world-building power of conspiracy, but it also brings into clear view the world-destroying capacity of our protagonists' plots. Although they were certain that they enjoyed dominion over the conspiracies that they masterminded, this perception was not always accurate. Indeed, many of our plotters ultimately became victims of their own conspiracies, and found themselves trapped in unexpected fallout that resulted from their scheming.

The unpredictable life cycle of conspiracies raises questions about the relationship that Hofstadter posits between the history and paranoid thought. Is it really as easy as he claims for the historian to distance herself from the unruly life cycle of conspiracies? What is her best recourse if she finds herself becoming complicit in the conspiracy about which she writes—or even ensnared in its traps? Revealing the historian as an integral player in the life cycle of conspiracy, this essay challenges the notion that she can—and should—remain aloof from its creative powers.

THE PSYOPS OF THE OKHRANA

In the late nineteenth century, the tsarist regime faced a serious image problem in Europe. Notorious for its brutal treatment of political prisoners, its persecution of its Jewish population, and its unreformed autocracy, the Russian state was regarded by many Europeans as the embodiment of barbarism and backwardness.[1] Negative opinions of the autocracy in the political imagination of liberal Europeans, in turn, produced diplomatic challenges for Russia. In the last decades of the nineteenth century, tens of thousands of political dissidents and working-class Jews left Russia and sought refuge in Europe. In the liberal states of France, England, and Switzerland, at least, they usually found it. Citing the persecution and lack of freedom that tsarist subjects faced, western European nations offered asylum to the Russians living on their soil, refusing to extradite those who had been accused of political crimes.[2] Even after Russian revolutionaries embraced terrorism in the late 1870s, leading to a rapid radicalization of the emigration, public support for refugees who had fled the tsarist regime remained strong. Indeed, the execution of the radical youth who had assassinated the tsar in 1881 aroused angry protests across the continent (Collmer 2004, 323; Lord Lamington 1881).

The strength of Western asylum regimes—which were anchored in liberal political discourse that contrasted the evils of Russian despotism to the supposedly superior parliamentary democracy of the West—proved a constant frustration to the tsarist police officials working to manage the radical emigration. In the mid-1880s, P. I. Rachkovskii, who oversaw the Paris office of the Okhrana, began to formulate a novel solution to this problem. Rachkovskii had a rather unusual background for a tsarist official, which in turn endowed him with a unique perspective on policing. Born into an impoverished noble family of Polish origin in what is now Ukraine, he worked his way up through the Russian bureaucracy, beginning his career as a postal clerk and later working as a ghostwriter for several provincial governors and as a court investigator. He also briefly served as the editor of a Russian-Jewish newspaper.[3] In 1878, while working as a court investigator in the northern outpost of Arkhangelsk, Rachkovskii became friendly with a circle of exiled revolutionaries. Interrogated by the local police about these contacts, he was offered a choice between facing arrest and becoming an informant.[4] He chose the latter option. In 1879, he was dispatched on his first mission to Poland and Austrian-controlled Galicia. After a series of rapid promotions, he arrived in Paris several years later.[5]

As the director of the Paris office of the Okhrana, Rachkovskii's primary mandate was to surveil and disrupt the large populations of Russian radicals living overseas.[6] Given his journalistic experience, Rachkovskii defined this mandate more broadly than his predecessors. As early as 1880, he argued that managing public opinion served an important function in policing. In the reports he sent back to St. Petersburg from his posting in Galicia, he had included detailed analyses of the periodical press. By the 1880s, such tactics had become routine in France, where police not only surveyed the press but also founded their own revolutionary newspapers that aimed to divide and discredit radical groups (Andrieux 1885, 2:56–57). However, these techniques were far from mainstream in Russia, whose conservative regime denied the very legitimacy of public opinion. Leading police figures in Russia displayed little interest in the psy ops like the French used and at times openly disapproved of them.[7]

Once he arrived in Paris, however, Rachkovskii enjoyed greater independence and authority than he had in his previous positions. Availing himself of the benefits afforded by his distance from the bureaucrats of St. Petersburg, he launched a campaign that aimed to alter public opinion about Russia, which he hoped would in turn improve relations between the tsarist regime and its Western rivals. This effort began fairly modestly, in the form of several articles, pamphlets, and books in European languages. (Although this outreach campaign was, by definition, public, all these works were published under pseudonyms that masked their true origins.[8]) By the 1890s, Rachkovskii had organized a full-fledged press agency, which employed several agents who were directed to place articles of their own in European papers and to ingratiate themselves with journalists and editors. In the first years of the twentieth century, the Paris Okhrana opened a newspaper of its own, *La revue russe*.[9]

Rachkovskii's interventions in the European public sphere sought to alter the conventional wisdom about the Russian state and those who had fled it. Much of the work of his agents attempted to undermine the credibility of the revolutionary émigrés. Challenging the popular image of Russian radicals as long-suffering, upstanding dissidents, Okhrana propaganda aimed at Europeans portrayed revolutionary émigrés as dangerous and depraved criminals unworthy of the august tradition of asylum. One article placed by the Okhrana press agency in a British journal described Russians abroad as "the very dregs of the population, the riffraff of rascaldom, professional thieves, bullies who batten upon the shameful earnings of the weaker sex, . . . despicable desperadoes" ("Anarchists" 1894, 6). *The Confession of an Ex-Nihilist*, a pamphlet aimed at a French audience, insisted that the revolutionary emigration harbored no political ideals at all, "except for a political charlatanism sustained by force" (Ivanow 1887, 9).

Rachkovskii's campaign also impugned tsarist subjects abroad by suggesting that they were parties to an intricate Jewish conspiracy. Okhrana publicists insisted that the Russian revolutionary movement had been infiltrated by Jews whose ultimate aim was to destroy Russia. (Such claims also appeared frequently in the Okhrana's own internal correspondence.[10]) In 1887, Okhrana agents published *Jewish Russia*, which provided a book-length overview of this putative conspiracy. Drawing on Iakov Brafman's notorious forgery *The Book of the Kahal*, it claimed that the *kahal*—an organ of Jewish self-governance in Russia that in fact had been abolished in 1844—was the center of a secret Jewish plot that aimed to degrade the Russian people and to destroy their state (Wolski 1887).

By the 1890s, the putative Jewish revolutionary conspiracy described in Okhrana propaganda became even broader in scope, encompassing the tens of thousands of working-class Jews who came to Europe in search of safety from pogroms and greater economic opportunity—a group that had little to do with revolutionary politics. The Okhrana newspaper, *La revue russe*, pilloried pogrom victims, claiming that they had antagonized the Gentile population by engaging in crime and exploitation and had therefore invited violence upon themselves.[11] Okhrana publicists insisted that Russian Jews had continued their criminal behavior in emigration, seeking to connect them to the wave of anarchist violence that swept Europe in the 1890s ("Anarchists" 1894, 10–13).

The anti-Semitic conspiracy theories created by Okhrana publicists endeavored to demonstrate the otherness of Russian Jews by revealing their supposed backwardness and degeneracy. At the same time, they insisted that the culture of Russian Jews posed an imminent threat to Western culture. A short story produced by Okhrana publicists made this point in vivid fashion, recounting the story of a Jewish radical who had assassinated a tsarist official in Russia, then settled in London's East End, where he lived as a "loafer" who engaged in petty crime. At the end of the story, he returns to Russia, where he conspires with other co-confessionalists to achieve world domination.[12] The message of this work—and others—was that Russian Jews posed an existential threat to Christian civilization that could not be contained by borders.

If a great deal of Rachkovskii's energy focused on implicating tsarist émigrés in nefarious conspiracies, the Okhrana chief also labored to undermine the liberal beliefs that served as the foundation for national asylum regimes in the first place. Okhrana pamphlets insisted that in spite of liberal democracy's claims to benefit ordinary people, it had only compounded suffering, while promoting corruption and political disorder. Russian publicists reserved special wrath for Third Republic France, arguing that its claims to liberty, equality, and fraternity were nothing more than an "illusion." When the Old Regime had been toppled, they argued, a capitalist oligarchy simply took the place of the old feudal aristocracy, instrumentalizing parliamentary democracy to legitimize new abuses of power (Wolski 1887, 112–19).[13] Anti-Semitic rhetoric also played a prominent role in these attacks on the liberal system. *Jewish Russia* connected the corruption and other failings of liberal democracy to the emancipation of the Jews, whom the book branded the "charlatans of liberalism." Instead of serving the nation that had emancipated them in 1791, this work alleged, French Jews had only used the freedoms granted to them to maintain their "system of exclusive existence" and "their [separate] nationality through the shameful means of usury" (Wolski 1887, 241–42).

Challenging the notion that liberalism was the crowning achievement of modern society, Okhrana publicists presented it as a flawed and corrupt system on the verge of collapse. By contrast, they praised the autocracy as a more advanced—and more just—form of government. Far from a vehicle of repression, the strong authority vested in the autocracy had benefited the Russian people, insisted Rachkovskii and his agents. Citing the emancipation of the serfs as a reform that could not have been achieved without the tsar's unquestioned authority, one contributor to *La revue russe* insisted that the autocracy had allowed Russia to modernize while avoiding the "series of bloody revolutions" that had plagued France (de Bodisco 1903, 5; see also Un russe 1903). *Anarchy and Nihilism*, an Okhrana-produced pamphlet, went further still, arguing that the Russian autocracy was the purest incarnation of a mass "democracy" that the world had yet seen (Jehan-Préval 1892, 124–125). Claiming that the spiritual bond that supposedly united the tsar and his people produced "philanthropic ideas that often efface and reduce class distinctions," its author concluded that "the Russian worker and the Russian peasant are much happier than their French brothers" (79, 107). Okhrana publicists also touted Russia's tsars as the natural leader of the "Aryan" people against the "Semitic world" (Wolski 1887, vi). "The Russian tsar," wrote the author of the pamphlet *Russia and Liberty*, "is the only man in Europe who cannot be bought by the Jews; the Russian nation is the only that has understood, defied, and curbed the ambition of this greedy and cruel race with a will to dominate. That is why the Jews hate Russia, why they undermine and attack the autocratic principle" (Un gentilhomme russe 1889, 35; see also Jehan-Préval 1892, 202–4).

Rachkovskii's claims would have sounded outlandish to most contemporaries, but like most successful conspiracy theories, they contained more than a grain of truth. It was true that Russian radicals benefited from Europe's permissive asylum laws and that a small number had taken advantage of the protections the laws provided to plot terrorist attacks in exile. As a result of the violence and persecution that they faced in Russia, Jews were indeed well represented among émigré circles. Finally, as Rachkovskii and his agents noted, the shortcomings of liberal democracy were becoming more evident to critics on both the left and the right. Rachkovskii's great leap, however, was to suggest that there was a necessary causal connection between these discrete phenomena, collapsing a complex and multifaceted set of issues into a coherent and supposedly self-evident narrative. He presented Europe's liberal states as playgrounds for a dangerous criminal conspiracy that advanced Jewish interests, and he portrayed the authoritarian political style embodied in the Russian state as the only possible remedy for this dangerous trend.

Although it is difficult to gauge the reception of the conspiracy theories that Rachkovskii and his agents disseminated in the public sphere, it is clear that they circulated quite widely. Several of his pamphlets were published by Albert Savine, a major French publisher with a special interest in anti-Semitic materials. The archives of the Okhrana press agency demonstrate that it managed to establish warm relationships with some of Europe's most prominent news outlets, including *Le Figaro*.[14] However, Rachkovskii himself likely understood that mere exposure to his ideas would not change the minds of most Europeans. For his conspiracy theories to gain traction, they would need to be rooted in a deeper social context. By the late 1880s, Rachkovskii had begun to make the creation of that context one of his top priorities.

FROM CONSPIRACY THEORIES TO CONSPIRATORIAL CIRCLES

While in Paris, Rachkovskii appears to have maintained a rather strained relationship with his superiors in St. Petersburg. Although he sent frequent dispatches back to Russia, they contained few details about the nature or the extent of his press activities. Indeed, he appears to have self-funded most of his outreach expenses, using profits that he had earned from various business ventures he conducted in his spare time ("Kar'era P. I. Rachkovskogo" 1918, 79–81). Rachkovskii's financial independence and his willingness to circumvent formal command and control structures invested him with a great deal of power. However, it also obligated him to seek out his own allies who could amplify his work.

The Paris-based *salonnière* Juliette Adam turned out to be Rachkovskii's most valuable coconspirator. A republican activist during the Second Empire, Adam began to lose her faith in liberal ideas in the wake of the French defeat in the Franco-Prussian War. Desperate to reclaim France's lost territories of Alsace and Lorraine and to seek revenge on Germany, she began to advocate for a Franco-Russian alliance as a means of realizing this goal. By the 1880s, her interest in Russia, which at first had been primarily geopolitical, was becoming more ideological. She argued that for France to reclaim its greatness, it would need to rekindle its martial traditions of the ancient past and establish a strong state that could end the republic's perennial political turmoil (see Morcos 1962; Hogenhuis-Seliverstoff 2001). Adam's chauvinism, revanchism, and authoritarian fantasies bore a close resemblance to the ideas that Rachkovskii was then promoting in the European public sphere.

Over the course of the 1880s, Adam's salon gained a reputation as a major center of Russophile agitation that attracted a colorful cast of characters with their own interests in Franco-Russian rapprochement.[15] One of Adam's closest collaborators, I. F. Tsion (or Élie de Cyon, as he was known in France), had been born a Russian Jew but later converted to Christianity. A diehard defender of the tsarist regime and a proponent of Adam's muscular French nationalism, he acquired the conservative daily *Le Gaulois* in 1882 and became the editor of the journal Adam founded, *La nouvelle revue*, in 1886 (Kennan 1986). Olga Novikova, the heir to one of Russia's most elite families and a regular correspondent to the *Times* (of London) and the *Pall Mall Gazette*, was another frequent visitor at Adam's gathering.[16] Jules Hansen, a native of Schleswig-Holstein who had become an intelligence operative in the French Ministry of Foreign Affairs, shared Adam's antipathy toward Germany, which had annexed his native province after a brief 1864 war; in addition, he had been a childhood friend of tsarina Maria Fedorovna, who had grown up in Denmark (Hansen 1897, 18–21).[17] The anti-Semitic publicist Édouard Drumont also socialized with the circle. An admirer of Russia's illiberal politics, which he saw as a potential model for France, he repeated Okhrana conspiracy theories that implicated Jews in a plot to topple the tsar in the East and destroy Christian civilization in the West (Drumont 1886, 1894).

Although a divergent set of concerns attracted the members of Adam's salon to Russian affairs, all shared her interest in improving Franco-Russian relations—a goal that also complemented Rachkovskii's aims. Textual evidence suggests that already by the mid-1880s, the Adam circle had begun to assist Rachkovskii's press campaign, repeating and amplifying his ideas. Adam's journal, *La nouvelle revue*, featured articles by Russian agents and published glowing reviews of Okhrana-produced pamphlets ("La question juive en russsie" 1883).[18] Novikova echoed many of Rachkovskii's interventions, pointing to the criminality of Russian émigrés and to the dangerous potential of Russian Jews at home and abroad (Stead 1909, 276–95). Hansen helped Rachkovskii write pamphlets aimed at French audiences throughout the 1880s and 1890s and was appointed as editor of the Okhrana-run newspaper, *La revue russe*, in 1890 (Agafonov 1887, 34–36).[19] Drumont was perhaps the most important popularizer of the Okhrana chief's work. Indeed, at the height of the Dreyfus affair, Drumont's Anti-Semitic League republished a new edition of *Jewish Russia*, subsidizing the cost so it would be accessible to readers of the most modest social standing.[20]

The constant recycling of Rachkovskii's ideas in the mass media by members of the Adam circle imbued them with credibility through force of repetition. But not all of the group's work played out in the public sphere. By the mid-1880s Rachkovskii, Adam, and their associates had begun to engage in their own forms of conspiratorial activity. The group repeatedly used forgery to achieve its aims, leading one observer of the circle to argue that it created a veritable "cult of the false document" (Rollin [1939] 2005, 424). The first experiment in forgery conducted by the Adam circle began in the mid-1880s, when habitués of the salon collectively authored several volumes of the supposedly unpublished letters of a Russian diplomat (Morcos 1962, 286–88). Replete with gossip about the high society of Europe's capitals, these works went on to be translated into several languages and became popular best sellers. Most readers of the series were attracted by its scandalous content, but the fictive correspondence had serious ideological goals. Advancing the ideas that motivated Rachkovskii and Adam's public interventions, they drew attention to the hypocrisies of the liberal system and blamed Jews for the injustices of capitalism.[21]

Several years later, the Adam-Rachkovskii circle engaged in an even more audacious experiment with forgery that had a more elite reader in mind. In 1887, Adam hired a Belgian forger to produce documents indicating that Bismarck was conspiring to undermine Russian influence in the Balkans by meddling with the succession to the Bulgarian throne. Intended to complicate relations with Germany, with which Russia was then allied, and to encourage a rapprochement with France, Adam ultimately managed to get these documents to Tsar Alexander III while he was on vacation in Copenhagen.[22] (It is likely that either Rachkovskii, who acted as Alexander's bodyguard during his trips abroad, or Hansen, with his long-standing connections to the tsarina, gave the documents to the tsar [Kennan 1984, 167].) When Alexander III angrily confronted Bismarck, the chancellor produced documentary evidence that cast doubt on the authenticity of the forgery (Hansen 1897, 71).[23] Concerned that the plot had been foiled, Adam's forger produced a second series of documents that aimed to discredit Bismarck, and he ferried them to Russia via an associate of the salon (Smythe 1995, 76–82).

Forgery was not the only method that the Rachkovskii-Adam circle used to shape political possibilities. In 1887, Cyon approached the Russian minister of finance and offered to use his connections in Paris to explore the possibility of securing French loans to Russia (Rollin [1939] 2005, 424). Shortly thereafter, he managed to procure a major loan from the Danish-French financier Émile Hoskier, a close friend of Hansen's. Next, Cyon approached the Rothschild and Paribas houses. They, too, offered loans totaling some three billion francs. The loans are widely recognized by diplomatic historians as marking a crucial step toward Franco-Russian rapprochement (Siegel 2014, 12–49; Kennan 1984, 75–76).

At this point, Rachkovskii made his first nonliterary effort to shape European opinions about Russia. In 1890, he directed one of his experienced *agents provocateurs* to infiltrate a Paris-based circle of radical émigrés, intellectuals, students, and working-class Jews. Inciting them to build bombs, he even provided them with explosive materials. As the conspiracy neared completion, Rachkovskii instructed Jules Hansen to inform the French government of the plot; French police quickly raided the émigrés' homes and arrested them (Agafonov 1918, 37–38; Burtsev 1908, 58–64). (The *agent provocateur* managed to slip away and would go on to conduct several other terrorist acts in the 1890s; by the early twentieth century, he would be appointed the head of the Foreign Agency of the Okhrana [Brachev 1998, 64–90].) The "Paris bomb affair" and subsequent trial received extensive media coverage across the continent. Only in 1909 would the French police and public learn that the whole affair had been concocted by the tsarist secret police.[24]

The Paris provocation provided a live performance of the conspiracy theories that the Paris Okhrana had long promoted in the European public sphere. It placed new pressures on the asylum regime, dramatizing the threats that Russian radicals posed to European society. The fact that many of the targeted émigrés were Jewish sent another clear message, appearing to corroborate Rachkovskii's depiction of the Russian revolutionary movement as a Jewish plot. The event also advanced Adam's dream of a Franco-Russian rapprochement, allowing Rachkovskii to present the tsarist secret police as a valuable partner in an incipient international war against terror.

Rachkovskii's provocation played an even more important role than Cyon's loans in creating new institutional bonds that strengthened the ideological connections between France and Russia. As a result of the incident, French police officials came to regard Rachkovskii as a trusted partner, praising the "zeal" he displayed in the battle against transnational terrorist networks.[25] For their own part, the French police intensified their surveillance of tsarist subjects abroad, casting suspicion on a population once widely regarded as "refugees."[26] Republican politicians, who had once decried the autocracy as a backward and barbarian power, now welcomed Rachkovskii to their soirees; "treated as an equal by the highest French functionaries, he was even received on several occasions by two presidents of the Republic."[27] The warming of French attitudes toward Russia was further encouraged by the formal diplomatic rapprochement then underway between the two powers, which resulted in the creation of a Franco-Russian alliance in 1894. But this strategic orientation did not occur in a political or cultural vacuum: the ideological convergences and new institutions created by Rachkovskii's cooperation with Adam's circle played an important role in facilitating the rapprochement of these two formerly hostile powers.[28]

Although the effects of the conspiratorial ideas and networks reconstructed here were most pronounced in France, where Okhrana agitation was most intense, the Paris provocation also informed state practice in other European nations. Criminologists and social scientists fanned a continental panic about Russian émigrés, drawing connections between tsarist subjects abroad and the continent's incipient anarchist movement (Proal 1895, 42–43; Langhard 1891, 87–88; Langhard 1903, 312). Moved by anxiety about international terrorist networks, other nations followed France in weakening their asylum regimes in the aftermath of the Paris bomb affair. In Switzerland, which had long prided itself on the rights it accorded to refugees, Russians found themselves subjected to rigorous police checks as well as to harassment and expulsions.[29] British officials, too, began to prosecute Russian radicals in the 1890s and to share intelligence with their Russian counterparts.[30]

In addition to informing state practice, the conspiracies carried out by Rachkovskii and the Adam circle shaped public opinion. Media coverage of the Paris incident often claimed that the Russian plotters were anarchists, "mere murderers," and "bands of terrorists," which in turn generated unprecedented hostility toward tsarist subjects abroad.[31] Citizens demanded that national police forces more vigorously police the "plots of dangerous foreign revolutionaries," and some even denounced their Russian friends and acquaintances.[32] One Paris-based émigré bitterly recalled the stunning shift in public attitudes, noting that Europeans who had once lionized political émigrés as valiant freedom fighters now regarded them as "nihilists" and "bombers" (Tchernoff 1936, 22).

The anti-Semitic conspiracy theories that had been peddled by the Okhrana also began to gain greater traction in the wake of the Paris incident. Western anti-Semitic activists frequently cited *Jewish Russia* and other Okhrana-produced texts to highlight the dangers supposedly posed by Russian Jews, and praised the tsar's efforts to suppress the putative Jewish revolution.[33] Meanwhile, other fixtures of Okhrana propaganda, such as the claim that Jews dominated the ranks of Russian revolutionaries, appeared with greater frequency in mainstream outlets (Bourdeau 1892, 306).[34]

The exploits of the Okhrana and the Adam circle reveal the world-building capacity of conspiracy. Rachkovskii's novel explanation of Europe's ills provided a new framework through which citizens who were alarmed by the rising threat of terrorism, the ways in which immigration was changing the demographics of continental society, and the failures of liberal democracy could express their concerns. The repetition of Rachkovskii's conspiracy theories by European collaborators—and the real-life enactment of his narrative by the Paris "bombers"—added credibility to his ideas. The growing convergence in how tsarist patriots and European citizens thought about Russian émigrés created a climate amenable to new forms of international police cooperation and even diplomatic reorientations. The new political institutions that emerged from this process of cultural rapprochement, in turn, reinforced the basic premises of the conspiracies supported by Rachkovskii and Adam. The circle's success at crafting new narratives and using the mass media to amplify their messages endowed it with an ability to shape public opinion that was incommensurate with its relatively small size and limited resources.

Conspiratorial activity also enriched the protagonists and enhanced their political power and social status. Rachkovskii—a rogue police agent defending the interests of what was once Europe's most-reviled state— was inducted into the Legion of Honor for his supposed service to France during the 1890 bomb plot. Prussia, Denmark, Austria, and Sweden also rewarded him for his anti-terrorist mettle.[35] Cyon, as we will see, would enjoy substantial financial gain from his role in negotiating the French loans to Russia. Although Adam's gender prevented her from participating in formal politics, her behind-the-scenes actions nevertheless placed her at the center of consequential shifts in political culture. In the celebrations that accompanied the Franco-Russian rapprochement, Adam's admirers hailed her as the inspiration behind this realignment (Deschamps 1898, 119, 279, 395). For their part, the progenitors of the radical new right that swept French politics in the first years of the twentieth century credited the *salonnière* with spearheading their new and more muscular breed of French nationalism.[36]

THE AFTERLIFE OF CONSPIRACY

Although reconstructing the actions of Rachkovskii, Adam, and their associates reveals the generative potential of conspiracy, it also demonstrates the potential of conspirators to become entrapped in their own scheming. The paranoid mindset that guided many members of this circle and the boundless ambition that they showed ultimately generated intense personal conflicts that strained the coherence of the group. Cyon found himself at the center of the first clash that rocked the circle. In the early 1890s, it came to light that he had accepted large kickbacks on the French loans to Russia he had negotiated—a revelation that led to his being dismissed from his position at the Ministry of Finance (Harcave 1990, 129). In 1892, Cyon approached the new minister of finance, Sergei Witte, and asked to be reinstated. When Witte refused, Cyon declared war, denouncing the minister in *La nouvelle revue* and in pamphlets that he circulated in France and Russia.[37] Cyon's attacks focused on Witte's economic policy—in particular, his efforts to place Russia on the gold standard—but they often invoked ideas and images more closely associated with the anti-Semitic conspiracy theories that Rachkovskii and Drumont peddled (Cyon 1897a, 47–97). Cyon (1895a) implicated Witte in an international plot to undermine Russia, characterizing him as "an all-powerful Minister who has the venal press of all Europe at his disposal and is supported by the high cosmopolitan bank in every capital" (vi). He also insinuated that Witte was a servant of Jewish interests and a lackey of the Rothschilds (96–100).

In 1895, an outraged Witte convened a special commission of high-ranking tsarist officials to examine Cyon's activities abroad. That commission ultimately demanded that Cyon cease his journalistic activities and return to Russia. When the journalist refused, the tsarist government pressured France to expel him. Russia's new ally complied, forcing Cyon to move to Switzerland (Harcave 1990, 129). Undeterred, he continued to denounce Witte. The minister now turned to Rachkovskii—with whom he had established a close and trusting relationship—for help.[38] Thus began a fierce struggle between the Okhrana and Cyon. Acting on Witte's instructions, in 1897 Okhrana agents burglarized the villa of the journalist, whom Rachkovskii now called "our little Jew." The agents ransacked the house and confiscated manuscripts that they found there, including a draft version of a new anti-Witte polemic ("Kar'era P. I. Rachkovskogo" 1918, 84–85).

Meanwhile, Cyon became embroiled in a separate conflict with Drumont. Although Drumont and his supporters were strong supporters of the Franco-Russian alliance, they condemned the Rothschild loans negotiated by Cyon as a corrupt influence that had "sold" the new friendship to "Jewish kings" (Demachy 1892, 2). Yet Drumont became ensnared by contradictions in his own thought. As proof that Russia had been "sold" to the Jews, Drumont quoted extensively from Cyon's anti-Witte screeds. Drumont's call to recover a "pure" Russia untouched by Jewish influence was thus inspired by the work of the very apostate from Judaism whom the French journalist and his followers accused of mortgaging Russia's future to the Rothschilds.[39]

Although Rachkovskii's propensity for scheming had served him well in France, it did not endear him to his colleagues in Russia. As word trickled back of his unauthorized behavior overseas, he attracted several rebukes from his superiors, who urged him to desist from his provocations and attempts to meddle in foreign politics.[40] Rachkovskii's unusual style of operating also earned scorn from his colleagues within the police apparatus. In 1894, General V. D. Novitskii, the chief of the Kiev Gendarmes, penned a denunciation that accused Rachkovskii of engaging in unauthorized provocations since his first days as a police informant in the early 1880s. Ironically, this attack on the Okhrana chief echoed Rachkovskii's own conspiratorial logic. Remarking on his Polish origins, it suggested that Rachkovskii was part of a Polish conspiracy against Russia. Even more outlandishly, Novitskii claimed that Rachkovskii's provocations were entirely responsible for the emergence of the very revolutionary movement that the Okhrana chief purported to fight.[41] Alarmed by the complaints that continued to accumulate against Rachkovskii, Tsar Nicholas II finally relieved him from his position and recalled him to Russia in 1902 ("Kar'era P. I. Rachkovskogo" 1918; Agafonov 1918, 51–52). In Rachkovskii's case, as in Cyon's, his penchant for conspiracy proved his own undoing.

There is another respect in which the conspiracies of the Adam-Rachkovskii circle may have enjoyed an unexpected afterlife. In 1903, a right-wing Russian newspaper printed a description of a Jewish plot to gain world domination—a set of minutes supposedly taken by a witness to a secret meeting of the "Elders of Zion." The text, which we now know as *The Protocols of the Elders of Zion*, was reprinted several times in prerevolutionary Russia, but eventually fell into oblivion. The *Protocols* resurfaced during the Civil War that followed the 1917 revolution, and this time the world took notice. Translated into several languages, the text circulated widely in interwar Europe.

In 1921, an exposé by a British journalist challenged the authenticity of the document, proving that it was a forgery based heavily on Maurice Joly's 1864 *Dialogue in Hell between Machiavelli and Montesquieu*, a republican critique of Napoleon III. In the light of this revelation, several witnesses stepped forward to shed light on the origins of the *Protocols*. Rachkovskii's right-hand man in France and a member of Juliette Adam's salon both emerged to claim that Rachkovskii had ordered the fabrication of the text during his time in Paris (Radziwill 1921).[42]

The notion that Rachkovskii ordered the forgery of the *Protocols* immediately became the most popular explanation of the text's origins. At the Bern trial of 1933–35, in which a coalition of Jewish groups sued in a Swiss court to prove that the document was a forgery, multiple Russian witnesses testified to Rachkovskii's involvement (Hagemeister 2017, 95–97, 475–78). Later historical works reiterated this version of events.[43]

There is textual evidence to suggest that someone close to the Adam-Rachkovskii group was indeed responsible for the *Protocols*. In addition to the Joly text, there are two other literary blueprints on which the author of the *Protocols* drew, both of which are connected to the circles reconstructed here. One is an 1868 novel by the German author Hermann Gödsche that features a scene in which a rabbi gathers the twelve tribes of Israel and directs them to achieve world domination. A series of Russian pamphlets published in the 1870s were the first to pass off this fictional scene as fact (Cohn 1967, 36–39). Rachkovskii's 1887 *Jewish Russia* again affirmed that this incident had occurred, reprinting the "rabbi's speech" in its entirety (Wolski 1887, 3–19). This claim, as mediated by *Jewish Russia*, soon became a frequent fixture of anti-Semitic literature in France (Corneilhan 1889, 40–55; Puig 1897, 156; Bournand 1898, 283–302). Another preexisting source incorporated into the *Protocols* is Cyon's writing on Witte and the gold standard, which serves as the basis for the text's discussions of Jewish financial conspiracies (Rollin [1939] 2005, 450–60).[44]

But in spite of the circumstantial evidence suggesting that the forgery of *The Protocols of the Elders of Zion* might have been the most consequential plot undertaken by the Rachkovskii-Adam circle, no documentary evidence has ever surfaced to verify this supposition. Rachkovskii associates who insisted that the Okhrana chief had intentionally fabricated the text never proffered the documents that they promised would prove their claims.[45] (In any case, historian Michael Hagemeister has questioned the credibility of the witnesses at the Bern trial who testified to Rachkovskii's involvement, noting that several appear to have been motivated by financial gain and that their testimony was riddled with inconsistencies [Hagemister 2017, 90].) Furthermore, crucial documents that might shed light on the *Protocols*' origins have gone missing from Russian archives.[46]

Frustrated by the apparent dead ends to which all searches for the *Protocols* have led, several historians have recently challenged the traditional explanation of the text's origins. On the basis of a linguistic analysis of the original text, the philologist Cesare de Michelis (2004) argues that the *Protocols* were never created in Paris in the first place: instead, he contends, they were penned in the southwestern borderlands of the Russian empire in the early years of the twentieth century.[47] Hagemeister critiques the very mentality that has driven the elusive search for the document's creator. In historians' desperation to provide *the* definitive account of the text's origins, he argues, many have become entrapped by the paranoid logic of their historical subjects. "What we hear is a narrative—to be precise, a conspiracy narrative," he writes. Authors who seek to unearth the secret plot that created the *Protocols*, he explains, mirror the logic of the text itself, only they focus on the dastardly deeds of the "cunning secret agents, fanatical anti-Semites, and sinister reactionaries" who supposedly created the forgery, rather than on the Jewish cabal traditionally blamed for the text. Echoing Hofstadter, Hagemeister contends that this conspiratorial mindset is fundamentally opposed to the historical method. "The concept of conspiracy," he notes, "offers clear answers where in reality the relations are complex and opaque" (Hagemeister 2007, 94–95).

But are the tactics of the historian working to reconstruct the anatomy of conspiracy as easy to differentiate from those of the conspiracy theorist as Hofstadter and Hagemeister suggest? It is true that documentary evidence is the lifeblood of the historian's work. But when the subjects on which the historian works devote much of their energy to deceiving others—and engage in the outright forgery of texts—the task of assessing the veracity of documents (much less the claims they contain) becomes more complicated than usual. The historian can rely on context to resolve some of these epistemological difficulties. Weighing the claims of our historical subjects against the evidence provided in other sources can expose the most glaring untruths, such as Novitskii's charge that Rachkovskii's provocations were to blame for the entire revolutionary movement. But context sheds less light on crucial questions of agency and motivation. Was it ideology, a lust for power, or a playful, sporting spirit that drove Rachkovskii, Adam, and their associates? Were they truly as instrumental in shaping public opinion as the fragmentary accounts of their actions suggest? In pondering these questions, I have endeavored to connect disparate pieces of evidence into a coherent narrative and to infer motives and impute causality even when they are not made explicit. In this respect, I have resorted to the very methods favored by the conspiracy theorist.

The difficulty of distinguishing certainty from conjecture in wrestling with the life stories of professional obfuscators means that the historian might unwittingly become complicit in the life cycle of the conspiracy. Does it follow, then, that we should retreat into epistemological nihilism and abandon any hope of recovering "what happened"? Not necessarily. Paradoxically, the best means of enhancing the critical distance between the historian and the paranoid mindset is to acknowledge the alluring and productive power of conspiracy—as well as its potential to develop a life of its own that can consume its participants.

In the case of the *Protocols*, returning to the concept of the life cycle may provide an alternative explanation for the origins of the text that accounts for its apparent connections to the Adam-Rachkovskii circle without replicating the paranoid and self-aggrandizing logic of its members. It is entirely plausible that the fabrication of the *Protocols* was an accidental by-product of the infighting that plagued the Rachkovskii-Adam circle. Some scholars have contended that Cyon was the author of the text but that he was not responsible for its propagation. According to their logic, an early version of the *Protocols* was among the documents stolen during the raid of his Swiss villa. Once Rachkovskii obtained this work, he recognized its potential value, and altered the text to serve his own purposes.[48] Others, noting that the work's Russian-language title could be read as a pun on Cyon's name (*Tsionskie mudretsy*/Tsion), suggest that either Rachkovskii or Drumont created the text and tried to pass it off as Cyon's work in an effort to discredit or embarrass the journalist (Kennan 1986, 472–73; Cohn 1967, 106–7). Both these lines of argument present the *Protocols* as an unexpected afterlife of conspiracy rather than as the culmination of a linear and well-planned plot.

Drawing a thick red line between the method of the all-knowing and rational historian and the paranoid and misguided purveyors of conspiracy neither combats the allure of the paranoid mindset nor prevents the historian from unwittingly replicating its logic. Instead, the most effective way to master the epistemological challenges associated with studying conspiracy is to acknowledge its seductive—and productive—power, while simultaneously remaining attuned to its unexpected twists and turns. If the historian wishes to avoid becoming the final victim of conspiracy's curious afterlife, her best strategy is to remain attuned to its unpredictable life cycle in the first place, and to recognize conspiracy's uncanny capacity to entrap even those who believe they have achieved mastery over it.

NOTES

1 Useful surveys of European public opinion include S. Johnson (2011); Neboit-Mombet (2005).
2 For surveys of the asylum regimes in these states, see Burgess (2008, 103–34); Shaw (2015, 57–81, 162–86); Collmer (2004). On extradition refusals, see "Note sur l'affaire Hartmann," 1880, a handwritten account of

case in the Bibliothèque Nationale de France; "Tribute to Captain Rees, of the Steamship Ashlands," *The Times* (London), January 19, 1891, 7; "Arrest of Russian Refugees in Turkey," *The Times* (London), January 20, 1891, 13.

3   "Formuliarnyi spisok," State Archive of the Russian Federation (hereafter GARF), f. 102, op. 3, d. 20, ch. 18, 1883, ll. 13–21.

4   For biographical information, see "Kar'era P. I. Rachkovskogo" 1918; Brachev (1998, 11–35).

5   Records from Rachkovskii's service in these years can be found in GARF, f. 110, op. 24, d. 996.

6   On the general operations of the Foreign Agency, see Zuckerman (2002, 82–150); Agafonov (1918).

7   A. N. Nikiforaki to P. V. Orzhevskii, August 15, 1880; and P. V. Orzhevskii to A. N. Nikiforaki, August 25, 1880, both in GARF, f. 110, op. 24, d. 1197, ll. 3–4.

8   The Okhrana–produced pamphlets that I have been able to identify are Ivanow (1887); Wolski (1887); Un gentilhomme russe (1889); Jehan-Préval (1892); Denisow (1892); "Anarchists: Their Methods and Organisation" (1894).

9   For an overview, see "Russkaia okhrana i zagranichnaia pechat,'" S. G. Svatikov Papers, Bakhmeteff Archive, Columbia University. The extant records of the Okhrana press agency can be found in Hoover Institution Archives, Stanford University. Zagranichnaia okhrana (HIASU, ZO), Index iXb, Folders 1–1C Hoover Institution Archives, Stanford University, Zagranichnaia okhrana.

10 See, for example, Ivanow (1887, 14); Jehan-Préval (1892, 82–90). For examples of internal correspondence, see Undated memo to Director of Department of Police, HIASU, ZO, Index iXb, Boxes 206–7, Reel 134, Folder 1; Delevskii and Kartashev (1923, 123–57).

11 "A propos des événements de Kichinev," *La revue russe* 24, June 18, 1903, 1. The Foreign Agency's press agents conducted extensive studies of foreign coverage of anti-Semitic violence in Russia, see HIASU, ZO, Index IXa, Box 70, Folder 4.

12 "La bible et la bombe! La perfide albion?," HIASU, ZO, Index XVIa, Box 189, Folder 3.

13 For a similar argument, see Un gentilhomme russe (1889, xxii–xxv).

14 Outgoing dispatch no. 89, 16/28 June 1897, HIASU, ZO, Index XIIIb (1), Folder 1; V. A. Gol'mstrem to I. F. Manasevich–Manuilov, May 1, 1904, HIASU, ZO, Index IXb, Folder 2B.

15 For a full construction of the agitation that occurred within the salon and its agenda, see Hillis (2017).

16 For biographical information, see Baylen (1951).

17 See also "Auto-biographie de M. Jules Hansen," Jules Hansen personal file, 393QO/2006. Archives Diplomatiques, La Corneuve.

18 *La Nouvelle Revue (LNR)* 9, no. 45 (1887): 821–22.

19 See also Departament obshchikh del to I. F. Manasevich-Manuilov, January 13, 1904, HIASU, ZO, Index IXb, Box 66, Folder 1C.

20 "Bulletin officiel de la ligue antisémitique de France," no. 1, January 1, 1898, Archives Nationales (hereafter AN), Pierrefitte-sur-Seine, F7/12459.

21 See Vasili (1885, 176–89, 420–23); Vasili (1884, 154–62, 190–99).

22 The forger was named Adalbert–Henri Foucault de Mondion. For biographical details, see Morcos (1962, 286, 293).

23 Cyon 1895a, 360–61; Kennan 1978.

24 For an overview of the resulting scandal, see AN, F7/12894, dossier 2.

25 "La police russe," AN, F7/14605.

26 See, for example, the records in Archives de le préfecture de Police (hereafter APP), BA 1708–1711.

27 "La police russe," AN, F7/14605.

28 This argument is developed more fully in Hillis (2017).

29 For example, "Le parti nihiliste à Genève," January 5, 1891; and "Menées anarchistes," April 25, 1902, AN, F7/12521; Prefect of Police to Minister of Interior, May 26, 1889, AN, F7/12520A; Report of Prefect of Police to Sûreté, June 5, 1890, AN, F7/12519.

30 For example, National Archives, Kew, HO 144/272/A59222.

31 "The Trial of the Eight Russians," *The Times* (London), July 7, 1890, 9; "Arrestation de terroristes russes," *Le petit parisien,* May 31, 1890, 2; "Arrestations des anarchistes," *L'univers illustré,* June 7, 1890, 358–59; *Berliner Tageblatt,* May 30, 1890, in Politisches Archiv des Auswärtigen Amts (hereafter PAAA), Berlin, R 10609.

32 Report of Grenoble Railroad Police, June 3, 1890, AN, F7/12519. For denunciations, see Alexis Trébaux to Russian embassy, June 8, 1890; Adélaide Mathon to Russian embassy, September 18, 1890, HIASU, ZO, Index XIIIb (1), Folder 1.

33 For example, see Ligneau (1891, 323–66); Martinez (1890, 104, 127–31); Corneilhan (1889, 121); Puig (1897, 133); Delassus (1905, 631–40).

34 See "The Revival of Nihilism," *Western Daily Press,* March 30, 1889, 5; "Russian Conservative View of the Siberian Atrocities," *The Times* (London), March 14, 1890, 1.

35 "Nagradnyi spisok," 1892, GARF, f. 102, op. 3, d. 20, ch. 18, ll. 72–73.

36 "Procès du Juif Weyl," LLP, August 10, 1895, in APP, EA29; Daudet 1915, 231; see also Maurras 1898, 18–22.

37 In addition to the works cited below, see Cyon (1892, 1897b).

38 Witte described Rachkovskii as "a remarkably intelligent man, in fact the most gifted and intelligent police official I have ever met" (Harcave 1990, 291).

39 Édouard Drumont, "Le Panama russe," *La Libre Parole,* April 26, 1897, 1. See also Drumont (1891, 148–58).

40 Director of Department of Police to Rachkovskii, January 20, 1894, HIASU, ZO, Index Va, Box 34, Folder 2; Director of Department of Police to Rach-kovskii, June 22, 1886, GARF, f. 102, op. 82, d. 395, l. 11.

41 Report of Col. Novitskii to Ministry of Internal Affairs, 1894, GARF, f. 102. op. 314, d. 657, ll. 1–29.

42 Henri Bint to S. G. Svatikov, April 7, 1921, Bakhmeteff Archive, Columbia University, S. G. Svatikov Papers, Box 71, Folder 1. The exposé was penned by Philip Graves and appeared in the *Times* of London. For a detailed account of the turn of events that led up to this revelation, see Aronov, Baran, and Zubarev (2009).

43 For example, Burtsev (1938); Cohn (1967, 77–107).

44 For a full exposition of the likely origins of these connections, see Hillis (2017, 37–40).

45 Henri Bint to S. G. Svatikov, 13 October 1926, S. G. Svatikov Papers, Box 71, Folder 1.

46 Many of the archival files identified by Soviet archivists as potentially relevant to the creation of the *Protocols* are no longer available in Russian archives. For a list, see "O vyiavlenii materialov na temu 'protokoly sion-skikh mudretsov,'" 1934, GARF, f. 4888, op. 1, d. 30, l. 15.

47 It is worth noting, however, that his linguistic analysis may not preclude the work's Parisian origins: Rachkovskii was from the region's southwest-ern borderlands, and his parlance would likely have resembled that of the author of the *Protocols*.

48 A summary of this case can be found in Fox 1997. Henri Rollin and Boris Nicolaevsky, who spent much of their lives searching for the author of the *Protocols* and who advanced several theses themselves, agreed by the 1940s that this was the most likely scenario. See the correspondence between the two in HIASU, Nicolaevsky Collection, Series 248, Box 498, Folder 9. Archi-val records place one of Rachkovskii's agents in the small Swiss town where Cyon's villa was located at the time it was supposedly burglarized, but they shed no light on the theft of his documents or the result of the raid. Henri Bint to Madame Bint, 7 July 1897, GARF, f. 509, op. 1, d. 77, l. 2.

_____

15 COMEDY OF TERRORS / NATIONAL SECURITY FICTIONS AND THE ORIGINS OF AL-QA'IDA

CIA SUPERIOR: What did we learn, Palmer?

CIA OFFICER: I don't know, sir.

CIA SUPERIOR: I don't fuckin' know either. I guess we learned not to do it again.

CIA OFFICER: Yes, sir.

CIA SUPERIOR: Although I'm fucked if I know what we *did*.

CIA OFFICER: Yes, sir, it's, uh, hard to say.

CIA SUPERIOR: Jesus. Jesus Fucking Christ.

***Burn after Reading* (2008)**

One could say that 2003 was a banner year for conspiracy theory, and not only because it witnessed the US-led invasion of Iraq on the false pretext of eliminating weapons of mass destruction. There were also some lesser-known events that are noteworthy when thinking about conspiracy theorizing as a weapon of the national security state. For example, in February of that year, one of the first major legal cases of the global war on terror ended abruptly on the eve of trial when Enaam Arnaout, head of a major Islamic charity in the United States, agreed to plead guilty to racketeering conspiracy in exchange for the government dropping all the other charges, including conspiracy to provide material support to terrorists.[1] The absence of a trial meant that the government's allegations never received a thorough vetting in court. Nonetheless, thanks to notions of conspiracy in federal evidence law, the case marked the emergence into public discourse of a peculiar set of documents that would go on to shape expert and popular understandings about the history of al-Qaʻida.

This chapter traces the provenance of these national security fictions that circulate as the everyday currency of state-led conspiracy theorizing. By *fiction*, I do not mean that they are necessarily false. Rather, I wish to focus on the manner of their construction as a form of artifice and the curious twists and turns in their itineraries.[2] The national security state generates an enormous volume of materials as a necessary condition of its existence, much of it devoted to "connecting the dots" between seemingly unrelated events and people to identify and anatomize sources of threat. These narratives come not only from the military and intelligence agencies managed by the executive branch but include fictions produced by the courts as well—something that conventional critiques of the national security state that valorize the "ordinary" institutions of government over the "extraordinary" and unaccountable security apparatus may miss.[3] The national security fiction that is the subject of this chapter originates in a raid by US soldiers of an Islamic charity in Bosnia-Herzegovina (hereafter referred to simply as Bosnia) as part of the imperial mission of the global war on terror. Some materials on a hard drive seized in that incident formed the basis of a legal filing by federal prosecutors in Chicago, revealing how rules of evidence governing the use of hearsay can operate as a form of judicially supervised conspiracy theorization. Finally, this chapter will sketch the citational afterlives of these documents as they made their way into a sprawling multiyear lawsuit against entities in Saudi Arabia as well as into canonical histories of the rise of al-Qaʻida, as national security fictions continued to circulate in a broader expert ecology of think tanks, universities, and corporations (Razavi 2018).

While national security fictions are not necessarily false, there are risks that come with taking them seriously. Even earnest attempts to rebut national security fictions often normalize their assumptions, such as when critiques of a threat narrative end by uncritically imploring the state to redirect its focus to the "real" dangers. This raises a question of genre: how to write an anthropology of national security fictions and state-led conspiracy theorizing more generally? Where registers of romance and tragedy (D. Scott 2004) will not do, this chapter proposes comedy as an ethnographic genre instead. Comedy will orient a different kind of dot-connecting exercise here, one that charts the circulation of national security fictions and, by extension, the social worlds that produce them. This is not to minimize the very serious stakes involved, especially for those victimized by the national security state. But it is to refuse the epistemic gravity that state-led conspiracy theorizing demands, the acceptance of its framings, the lingering self-doubt that the state is entitled to deference for allegedly knowing things we do not and cannot fathom. While anthropologists often operate under the call for empathy, there are times when contempt and scorn can also be ethically appropriate and analytically productive. Writing about the US ruling class and its national security elite, in particular, is one such case.

With comedy in mind, the work of contextualization reveals unexpected constellations of events and personalities. Also in the spring of 2003, prominent attorney and law professor Neal Katyal published an article in the prestigious *Yale Law Journal* titled "Conspiracy Theory," one of the most widely cited works of legal scholarship on conspiracy in the United States in recent decades. Having worked previously on national security issues at the highest levels of the Department of Justice, Katyal offered an ambitious defense and theorization of conspiracy law based on a conceptualization of criminal conspiracies as akin to business corporations. Katyal reasoned that if criminal conspiracies, like corporations, are more effective and thus more dangerous because they can avail themselves of economies of scale, then their cooperative nature is also a vulnerability. One significant benefit of conspiracy law, according to Katyal, lies in its utility for extracting information. Because conspiracy charges can be relatively easy to prove—for reasons discussed below— they enable prosecutors to coerce ("flip") individuals into giving up information on others (Katyal 2003). While many of Katyal's rationalizations for conspiracy law were not new, his reliance on a corporate model and on organizational psychology resonated with a broader neoliberal moment and its various instantiations within the American legal academy. And even the supposed academic novelty of analogizing conspiracies to businesses was made possible by an overall decline in *actual* conspiracy cases against corporate actors in realms such as antitrust law.[4]

While Katyal was offering a theory *for* the criminal law of conspiracy, his biography can be easily read *through* the genre of conspiracy theorizing, in aptly embodying the technocratic liberalism and privileged insider-ism of elite American lawyering. Katyal is more than a scholar; he is a leading Supreme Court litigator and has argued a number of landmark cases. Katyal is best known for challenging the military commissions at Guantánamo Bay and the Muslim Travel Ban. But he has also represented corporate interests in predatory lending, pharmaceuticals, and securities—at long last coming into wider notoriety after successfully advancing a legal theory that would insulate corporations from liability for child slavery.[5] Among lawyers, this willingness to serve such different types of clients is often extolled as exemplifying the virtue of zealous advocacy for any client regardless of politics—but it also happens to resonate with a kind of heads-I-win-tails-you-lose unfalsifiability that fuels conspiracy theorizing (recall, for instance, anti-Semitic fantasies of Jews as the driving force behind both capitalism and communism). This is especially the case when one looks at elite connections. Katyal served as acting Solicitor General under the Obama administration but was also an enthusiastic supporter of Donald Trump's first nominee to the Supreme Court, Neil Gorsuch. Katyal's brother-in-law is Jeffrey Rosen, a prominent law professor and legal commentator who wrote frequently for the *New Republic* magazine and other prominent publications. Katyal even played a version of himself on the television series *House of Cards*—perhaps the most high-profile reminder in recent US popular culture of conspiracy-focused theorization of politics—in the years before its star, Kevin Spacey, was fired over allegations of sexual assault and harassment.

Pivoting back to the criminal case that opened this chapter, the defendant Enaam Arnaout had his own brushes with fame, or rather infamy. In the eyes of the national security state, his life must have seemed like a series of dots begging to be connected. He knew and worked with Osama bin Laden during the jihad against the Soviet Union in the 1980s, but the two appear to have later drifted apart. While bin Laden was effectively exiled from Saudi Arabia for opposing the US military presence there, Arnaout remained firmly tied to the country—he had studied there, much of his immediate family continued to reside there, and the chief benefactors of his charitable work were prominent figures in the kingdom. Arnaout supported other conflicts designated as jihad—for example, he aided Muslims fighting in Bosnia and Chechnya. But bin Laden had in the meantime moved to the far more ambitious goal of armed confrontation with the United States, orchestrating the September 11, 2001, attacks in New York and Washington. Bin Laden was gunned down in his home in Pakistan by American commandos a decade later. Arnaout completed his prison sentence and soon found himself facing government attempts to revoke his US naturalization.

What, if anything, should one make of all these connections, of Arnaout and bin Laden's acquaintance, of Neal Katyal's possible ties to Kevin Spacey? The apparent absurdity of this question and these juxtapositions gestures to the genre of comedy as an experiment in method. While this chapter shares a title with the 1963 comedy horror movie featuring Boris Karloff and Peter Lorre, a more apt source of inspiration would be the 2008 Coen brothers film *Burn after Reading*. Set against the national security landscape of Washington, DC, the film concatenates themes of ambition, vanity, and small-mindedness through a dimly horrific serendipity. A disk containing the memoirs of a disgraced CIA analyst (John Malkovich) accidentally falls into the hands of a body-image obsessed gym employee and her dimwitted sidekick (Frances McDormand, Brad Pitt), who mistake the delusional rantings for valuable secrets that can be sold to Russia to raise money for cosmetic surgery; a philandering US marshal who dabbles in building elaborate sex toys (George Clooney) believes himself to be shadowed by powerful forces who turn out to be private investigators hired by his wife. That people die for no good reason, and little makes sense—indeed, like this chapter, the movie is more absurd than it is actually funny—provides a model for testing the hypothesis that the genre of comedy may be a useful antidote to the genre of conspiracy theorizing. Like *Burn after Reading*, our story features a number of players from different parts of the national security establishment, some of whom became household names during the war on terror, but often in surprising combinations. Perhaps everything *is* connected, as the conspiracy theorist holds; but perhaps the meaning of those connections remains, to quote a CIA officer at the end of the film, "Uh, hard to say."

WHAT'S IN A NAME?

National security fictions are crafted in all sorts of strange ways. This is especially true with entities like al-Qaʻida, whose origins remain poorly understood even two decades into the global war on terror. Experts have argued as to whether al-Qaʻida is best thought of as an organization, a network, a brand, an ideology, or something else. Or rather, given the likelihood that all these understandings have been applicable at different points in time, the question is not only what is al-Qaʻida, but *when* is or was al-Qaʻida. As one attempt to make sense of the debate put it, "al-Qaeda is an epistemological challenge—a problem of knowledge—which, in point of fact, may never be solved" (Hellmich 2011, 58).

In the immediate aftermath of the 9/11 attacks, the desperation for a serviceable narrative was so great and the official ignorance of relevant histories so deep that a superficial nominalism often prevailed. Some commentators seized on decontextualized appearances of the Arabic word *qāʿida*—which means base, foundation, or rule (as in a grammatical rule) and is etymologically linked to the verb for sitting—for clues (going forward, the distinction between *qāʿida*, the Arabic word, and al-Qaʿida, the idea of a terrorist organization of that name, should be kept in mind). One particularly egregious example of misconceived origins can be found in the report of the national commission charged with investigating the 9/11 attacks, perhaps the pinnacle of performances of bipartisan governmental expertise. The report traces the creation of al-Qaʿida to an article from 1988 published in an Arabic magazine supporting the jihad against Soviet forces in Afghanistan headlined "The Solid Base" (*Al-qāʿida al-ṣulba*). The problem, however, is that this article makes no mention of Osama bin Laden or a new organization of any kind or attacking America.[6] Instead, it uses *qāʿida* in the sense of a moral or spiritual foundation for striving Muslim youth in Afghanistan, an unremarkable nationalist exhortation that quotes amply from Jawaharlal Nehru, hardly a jihadist ideologue. Moreover, the 9/11 Commission seems never even to have read the article itself, because the relevant citation makes the exact same pagination error that appears in a book by another prominent terrorism expert, Rohan Gunaratna, who does not know Arabic and who relied on a translation provided by a former Israeli military intelligence officer.[7]

Such analytical and factual mishaps are not uncommon in the world of terrorism expertise and are symptomatic of the field's epistemic precarity at the boundary between state and academic forms of knowledge (Stampnitzky 2013). Less remarked upon in the broader literature is that al-Qaʿida is a curious name for an organization of this kind: armed Islamist groups are not very different from their non-Islamist counterparts in how they nominalize themselves. They often choose names like "army of x," "front of y," "vanguard of z." *Qāʿida* lacks specific religious or militant connotation, and really, it just lacks oomph. When bin Laden made declarations of jihad or other public statements in the mid- to late 1990s, he spoke in the name of the hitherto unknown "World Islamic Front for Jihad Against Jews and Crusaders."

There is no dispute that al-Qaʿida grew out of the much broader mobilization of Muslim volunteers from around the world who joined the jihad in Afghanistan against the Soviet Union in the 1980s. But the use of the word al-Qaʿida as a self-designating proper noun only appears in public statements starting in late 2000 (Miller 2015, 7). Understanding what happened in the intervening decade has been the subject of much discussion. It is worth noting that even the United States government tended to refer more generally to "the bin Laden network" during the 1990s. It was not until 1998, just before the bombings of US embassies in Kenya and Tanzania, that al-Qaʿida was first described as a coherent organization in a federal criminal indictment filed under seal in New York.[8] The 2001 trial in connection with the embassy bombings fleshed out the narrative further, especially in the testimony of Jamal al-Fadl, a cooperating witness who had embezzled from bin Laden.[9]

These questions about the *what* and the *when* of the conspiracy known as al-Qaʿida have significant implications for how to think about the war on terror, which has been framed as a campaign against something as specific as a single elusive terrorist super-organization as well as a war on an entire affective state (Masco 2014). One dominant theory—endorsed, as we saw above, by the 9/11 Commission—is that al-Qaʿida was a clandestine organization founded in 1988 with the goal of waging jihad around the globe. This interpretation depicts al-Qaʿida as a readily identifiable enemy that can be targeted and destroyed, replete with clearly defined chain of command and bounded membership. Pushing the timeline back to 1988 also predates and therefore renders less relevant the events typically cited as grievances driving the group, especially the mass deployment of US troops in Saudi Arabia starting in 1990. Moreover, this date of origin dramatically widens the circle of suspects: in 1988 there were still large numbers of foreign Muslim volunteers in Afghanistan whose primary aim was to fight the Soviets and who were functionally US allies.

This theory of al-Qaʿida's emergence was bolstered by materials uncovered in March 2002 in Sarajevo, Bosnia, during a raid on the local branch of an Islamic charity based in Illinois, called the Benevolence International Foundation (BIF).[10] Although Bosnian police were officially the ones conducting the search, they were prodded, accompanied, and effectively supervised by a task force of US military, intelligence, and law enforcement entities overseen by an ambitious young brigadier general, David Petraeus (Broadwell and Loeb 2012, 151–52). Petraeus would go on to lead US forces in the Middle East, manage the war in Afghanistan, and serve as head of the CIA. His meteoric ascent through the ranks of the US national security state ended in an even more spectacular fashion several years later amid revelations of an extramarital affair with his biographer. After a brief time as the butt of many jokes on late-night television, Petraeus settled into the lucrative ignominy of serving on corporate boards and gracing benighted universities with his wisdom as a distinguished visiting professor.[11] Back in Illinois, the FBI had been surveilling BIF without finding compelling evidence of criminal wrongdoing; after the 9/11 attacks, the government moved much more aggressively to freeze the charity's assets. Among the materials seized in the raid was a hard drive with a folder labeled "Tareekh Osama" ("Osama's History," in Arabic), which contained several hundred pages of digitized documents, some dating to the late 1980s. Tareekh Osama was, in the words of the 9/11 Commission staff, a "treasure trove" and an "enormous break" in the investigation (Roth, Greenburg, and Wille 2004, 98, 103). As a contemporaneous set of documents, Tareekh Osama was deemed far more reliable and revealing than the description of al-Qaʿida's origins given by the government's cooperating witness in the embassy bombing trial.

Within weeks of the raid, federal agents arrested BIF's director, a Syrian-born US citizen, Enaam Arnaout. Prosecutors charged Arnaout with a series of trifling infractions that were unlikely to stick but that served as helpful pretexts to keep him behind bars while they pored over the Bosnia documents. Despite the minor nature of the charges, Arnaout was held without bail and placed in solitary confinement. According to one of his attorneys, Arnaout "was transported to and from court for his appearances in the most sensational manner possible, with the short, three block route between the jail and the court house blockaded by armored vehicles, and Mr. Arnaout, in handcuffs and shackles, escorted by US Marshals armed with machine guns" (Piers 2005, 348).[12] It was not until the autumn of that year that new and more substantive charges were ready. Attorney General John Ashcroft took the unusual step of flying to Chicago to announce Arnaout's indictment for conspiracy to provide material support to al-Qaʿida and other organizations, plus sundry counts of racketeering, money laundering, mail fraud, and wire fraud. Ashcroft mentioned the Bosnia documents as key to the case and boasted that they "provide[d] for the first time documentary proof of the founding of al Qaeda."[13] The lead prosecutor, Patrick Fitzgerald, had earlier tried the embassy bombing case in New York. In subsequent years, he would be the longest serving United States Attorney for the Chicago area, working under both Republican and

Democratic administrations. Fitzgerald would achieve even greater fame for obtaining convictions of high-profile defendants. These included "Scooter" Libby, aide to Vice President Dick Cheney; two Illinois governors (George Ryan and Rod Blagojevich); and Chicago torture cop Jon Burge. Fitzgerald was also named by *People* magazine as one of its "Sexiest Men Alive" in 2005. After 2017, he would join the #resistance of elites engaged in rearguard defense of state institutions. When Trump fired FBI director James Comey, the latter retained his old friend Fitzgerald as counsel. Both were from Irish Catholic New York families and had first met while working together at the US attorney's office in Manhattan in the 1980s.

Just four months after Ashcroft's high-profile announcement, the fanfare gave way to a much more muddled outcome. In February 2003, on the eve of trial, Arnaout pleaded guilty to a single count of racketeering conspiracy, admitting that he misled donors to BIF by failing to disclose that some of the organization's funds provided ambulances, boots, glove warmers, and other supplies to the Bosnian army and to rebels in Chechnya.[14] Arnaout was sentenced to eleven years in prison and BIF as an organization was put out of commission.[15] But this victory was widely seen as a hollow one, as the government agreed to withdraw the terrorism-related charges and failed to prove any of the allegations pertaining to al-Qaʻida. In any event, the widest impact of the case lay not in its formal legal resolution but in the fate of the Tareekh Osama documents, and their role in crafting national security fictions.

THE *SANTIAGO* PROFFER

Aside from turning one man's life upside down and closing down one of the largest Muslim charitable organizations in the United States, the broader significance of the Arnaout case stems from a single 101-page document filed by the prosecutors. The purpose of the brief was to provide a preview of evidence that the government intended to present at trial, called a *Santiago* proffer—which, though it may sound like the title of a Robert Ludlum novel, is a legal term of art whose genesis will be explained below.[16] The proffer drew heavily from Tareekh Osama to craft a capsule history of al-Qaʻida, including an origin story about how the group was allegedly founded during a secret meeting attended by Osama bin Laden in August 1988.[17] The government's interpretation of these materials is far from self-evident, but that is irrelevant to its use of them in crafting a national security fiction.[18] Because Tareekh Osama was not made available to the public for independent analysis or verification until thirteen years later, the *Santiago* proffer is cited more often than Tareekh Osama itself.[19]

To grasp the significance of this *Santiago* proffer, it is necessary to talk about conspiracy. In Anglo-American criminal law, conspiracy consists of an agreement between two or more persons to commit an unlawful act. Compared to other so-called inchoate crimes such as attempt, solicitation, or aiding and abetting, conspiracy generally has a much broader temporal scope: One can be charged far earlier in the process of planning a crime, and conspiracy remains separately chargeable even if that main crime is completed.[20] One can also be charged for the actions of coconspirators undertaken as part of a conspiracy without the need to prove specific involvement in those acts.[21] These features make conspiracy a powerful tool for prosecuting collective endeavors deemed inimical by the state, including revolutions, rebellions, criminal gangs, labor unions, and terrorist groups. It is perennially one of the most common types of charge filed in the federal criminal system.[22] Conspiracy focuses on the act of consent to a joint enterprise, hence the standard formulation reflexively recited by courts that *the agreement itself is the crime*.[23] At issue is the tension between a paradigm of individualized criminal responsibility and the state's desire to target certain kinds of sociality. While the rise of conspiracy theorizing in general may reflect a greater stress on impersonal forms of agency, state-led conspiracy theorizing nonetheless relies on the language of personal responsibility as a way to justify its targeted applications of violence.[24]

The broad scope of conspiracy, however, paradoxically raises a problem of proof. If all that is required is agreement, then short of finding a written contract to break the law or persuading one conspirator to testify against the other, what is a prosecutor to do? Separate from conspiracy as a substantive crime is how conspiracy operates in the law of evidence. Courts generally refuse to consider statements made outside of court—otherwise known as hearsay—as evidence in proving the truth of the matter asserted. The most widely cited rationale for this rule is that evidence should be subjected to the adversarial scrutiny of cross examination whenever possible to ensure accuracy and fairness. Of course, there are a great many ways around the hearsay rule. One of the most common is to allege that the statement was made by a coconspirator in furtherance of a conspiracy.[25] To take a hypothetical example, consider Joe, a defendant on trial. A government wiretap uncovers a friend of Joe's—let's call her

Lisa—implicating Joe in the crime. Ordinarily, this statement would be hearsay and not admissible as proof of Joe's guilt. But if the government can show that Lisa's statement on the wiretap was made in furtherance of a conspiracy between Joe and herself, then the evidence is exempt from the hearsay rule and can be admitted.

The crime of conspiracy and evidentiary conspiracy historically developed together and remain frequently intertwined. Evidentiary conspiracy became rooted in English common law in the late eighteenth century during the panic over the possible spread of the French Revolution across the channel (Mueller 1984, 325–29). In the nineteenth-century United States, the crime of conspiracy and evidentiary conspiracy mainly appeared in prosecutions against trade unionists. Their chief rationales were also related, in that conspiracy as a crime exists because groups engaged in nefarious activities are seen as more dangerous than individuals. And the conspiracy evidence rule is justifiable because those same groups are more likely to work in secret and enforce codes of silence on their members. As one widely cited account puts it: "Conspiracy is a hard thing to prove. The substantive law of conspiracy has vastly expanded. This created a tension solved by relaxation in the law of evidence. Conspirators' declarations are admitted out of necessity" (Levie 1954, 1166).[26]

Evidentiary conspiracy, however, raises a significant problem of circularity. To determine whether an evidentiary conspiracy exists, judges often have little choice but to rely on the very piece of evidence whose admissibility they are determining. This practice is called "bootstrapping" and became especially prevalent during the era of expanded criminal sanctions and mass incarceration from the 1970s onward and then during the war on drugs, culminating in a 1987 Supreme Court decision.[27] This circularity is compounded when both the crime of conspiracy and evidentiary conspiracy go together, as they often do, especially in drug and gang cases. To return to our example, if Joe happens to be on trial for conspiracy and the prosecutor wants to use the aforementioned wiretap of Lisa, the government needs to prove that there is a conspiracy between Joe and Lisa for Lisa's words to be admitted as proof of that very conspiracy. In *United States v. Santiago*, the Seventh Circuit Court of Appeals—the federal appellate court for the region that includes Illinois—held that a judge can decide on the existence of an evidentiary conspiracy if the finding is supported by "a preponderance of the evidence."[28] This basically means enough evidence to make something more likely than not—a significantly lower standard than "beyond a reasonable doubt," which is required for criminal convictions.

Since *Santiago*, a practice has evolved in the Seventh Circuit of prosecutors submitting so-called evidentiary proffers. These are documents in which the government previews just enough of the evidence they plan to present at trial to convince the judge to make a preliminary finding that an evidentiary conspiracy exists. In a judicial system notionally committed to principles of individual responsibility, *Santiago* proffers work to unshackle legal narration from ordinary rules of evidence and are especially useful to the state in dealing with stigmatized groups framed as gangs or terrorist organizations—situations where it may wish to rely on statements made by people who cannot or will not appear in court. A *Santiago* proffer is quite literally a theory of a conspiracy, a form of conspiracy theory generated from within the judiciary itself.

In the Arnaout case, the *Santiago* proffer that outlined a history of al-Qa'ida was a rambling narrative assembled without the restrictions of the rules of evidence. It makes allegations not only against the defendant but against any number of other people who were not and may never be charged—these people are called "unindicted coconspirators," who are essentially accused in public without having any opportunity to defend themselves before a court. Between the agency of the individual defendant and the impersonal agency of conspiracy theory, the unindicted coconspirator is a figure that is at once both conjured and pushed aside. The proffer was also produced in a context of social ties that could, from another perspective, give rise to an alternative kind of conspiracy theorizing. The prosecutor who signed the document, for example, was the son of a judge in the same federal courthouse.

The *Santiago* proffer in Arnaout's case exemplifies how national security fictions often mediate between the realms of the secret and public. Unlike the classified documents of the intelligence agencies, the *Santiago* proffer is a document generated by the judiciary's default assumption of transparency, a fiction composed for public consumption via its placement on the docket. But the underlying materials upon which it was based, namely Tareekh Osama, remained unavailable to the public. Moreover, while intelligence reports purport to embody some kind of objectivity, the *Santiago* proffer is very much a part of an adversarial process that tolerates, indeed expects, partisanship. Finally, national security fictions produced by courts are conditioned by their own distinct epistemologies as shaped by rules of evidence that we have just discussed.

It was on this last point that the *Santiago* proffer met a curious fate. The judge never considered the veracity of its allegations. She merely established that the document was too vague to establish the existence of an evidentiary conspiracy, since it failed to specify *which* of the three conspiracy counts it sought to substantiate.[29] Interestingly, the prosecution did not seek to file a more specific version that could satisfy the judge's concerns. Instead, Fitzgerald very quickly accepted a plea bargain in which most of the original charges were dropped, suggesting there were significant weaknesses in the prosecution's case.

CITATIONAL AFTERLIVES

In any event, although Tareekh Osama and the *Santiago* proffer based upon it ultimately played no formal role in the resolution of the Arnaout case, their very active afterlife was only just getting started. The proffer continued to live on the docket of the case, available to the public. Dockets are important artifacts of law: they present, in a chronologically linear format, the biography of an instance of litigation from start to finish. But the *Santiago* proffer shows how national security fictions can take on an afterlife of their own beyond their original contexts of circulation. These afterlives are the kind of narrativization and explication that draw together texts whose authoritativeness derives not only from their governmental provenance but also from the air of mystery surrounding their origins and significance.

From the moment the existence of Tareekh Osama was publicly revealed, it caught the attention of Motley Rice, a prominent plaintiff-side litigation firm based near Charleston, South Carolina. Several months earlier, in August 2002, Motley Rice and other law firms had filed a $116 trillion civil suit on behalf of victims of the 9/11 attacks and their families. The case would grow into one of the longest and most complex in US history, pitting over 6,500 plaintiffs against a staggering array of nearly 200 defendants for, among a great many other things, conspiracy. Although Osama bin Laden and the Taliban were named, the real target—those most likely to have assets that could be seized to pay a judgment—included multiple charities and banks based in Saudi Arabia as well as the Saudi and Sudanese states themselves. The suit and related civil actions were consolidated in New York and captioned under the broad heading of *In Re Terrorist Attacks on September 11, 2001.*

One of the firm's principals was Ron Motley, a flamboyant litigator who had become a legend through working on some of the largest mass torts cases in history. He played a key role in bringing about the 1998 Tobacco Master Settlement Agreement, which resulted in a nearly quarter-trillion-dollar payout to state governments across the United States. Mass product liability torts, like conspiracy, represent another area where the law has struggled with questions of causation and agency, especially in the context of the rise of industrial capitalism (Jain 2006). Moving into the underexplored terrain of treating terrorism as a tort, Motley Rice intentionally took a kitchen-sink approach. Assisting them was Jean-Charles Brisard, a self-anointed terrorism expert from France who had published a book in the immediate aftermath of the 9/11 attacks naming alleged financiers behind al-Qa'ida (Risen 2014, 78–79). Drawing from Brisard's book and media reports, Motley Rice accused almost any entity they could notionally connect to al-Qa'ida. The firm also sought to finance the suit by backing the creation of a private intelligence firm, Rosetta Stone Research and Consulting LLC. Rosetta would be used to outsource research for the 9/11 lawsuit while also selling access to the information gathered, attracting outside investors, and winning government contracts. It was run by a former US Army officer who used Rosetta's resources for unrelated freelance spying operations, including luring an Afghan drug trafficker to the United States, where he was arrested and put on trial (Risen 2014, 81–122).

The connections sketched in the complaint about al-Qa'ida and its imagined global front of charities and financial institutions would readily be dismissed as mere conspiracy theorizing in many other contexts. But this sue-first-and-ask-questions-later strategy was entirely permissible within the US legal system and points to another site where the law invites—or incites—theorization of conspiracies. While rules of evidence attempt to regulate the use of hearsay at trial, rules of pleading—the formal presentation of legal claims and defenses, often made at the outset of a case—are altogether different. In the United States, one typically need not have definitive proof in hand before initiating a lawsuit: instead, all that is required is to plead allegations with enough specificity to put the other side on notice as to the shape of the case. For factual claims, plaintiffs' attorneys must merely certify that they "*will likely* have evidentiary support after a reasonable opportunity for further investigation or discovery."[30] This "notice pleading" approach is especially important in cases where a dramatic information asymmetry is to be assumed in favor of defendants. For example, if one has to show that a large corporation knows that its activities (polluting a stream, manufacturing a dangerous product) were dangerous, it would be unreasonable to expect plaintiffs to have this proof in hand before initiating a lawsuit.[31] But in the 9/11 lawsuit, liberal pleading standards allowed lawyers to exploit ambient anti-Muslim sentiment to incite further public speculation about the defendants' ties to terrorism. Harder proof could wait until the case reached the discovery stage, when plaintiffs gambled that they would be able to extract embarrassing documents from defendants and hopefully pressure them into making a generous settlement.

For Ron Motley, Tareekh Osama must have seemed akin to the legendary Sumner Simpson papers, a cache of meticulously preserved records demonstrating the asbestos industry's knowledge of the harmful effects of its products. In discovery, Motley helped uncover the Sumner Simpson papers, turning the tide in the asbestos litigation (Bowker 2003, 165–67).[32] In particular, one of the Tareekh Osama documents stood out: a handwritten list of twenty names that the government dubbed the "Golden Chain."[33] It supposedly identified wealthy donors to bin Laden's efforts against the Soviets in the 1980s. Like the purported minutes of al-Qa'ida's founding meetings, the piece of paper had no intrinsic indicators of its origin or purpose, and any connection to the events occurring a decade later was unclear. Motley Rice nevertheless seized on the Golden Chain to implicate prominent Saudi businessmen named as defendants in the 9/11 case, including Mohammad Abdullah Aljomaih, Sulaiman al-Rajhi, and Khalid bin Mahfouz.[34] In each of these instances, however, the Golden Chain merely gave family names, so it was far from clear whether the entries on the list actually referred to these specific individuals.[35] In an English translation of the document, Brisard even took the liberty of writing "Khalid bin Mahfouz" where the original simply said "bin Mahfouz." Needless to say, Khalid bin Mahfouz was not amused and filed a series of defamation actions against Brisard, which forced him to apologize and admit having doctored the translation (Risen 2014, 80–81).[36]

Going beyond Tareekh Osama itself, Motley Rice mobilized the government's characterization of it. In one motion directed at Adel Batterjee—the financial patron behind BIF, also named in the lawsuit—Motley Rice quoted entire paragraphs of the *Santiago* proffer in the Arnaout case.[37] None of this was particularly successful: the judge noted that the proffer was hearsay and called the Golden Chain "a document with serious foundational flaws," which said nothing about who wrote it, when it was written, or for what purpose.[38] Motley Rice did not give up, even taking the unusual step of making further filings to get the judge to reconsider the document's value.[39] Rejected by two different courts, the *Santiago* proffer nevertheless continued to circulate with the imprimatur of having been used by the government. It took on a life of its own, as though by greed possessed, the muse for a new wave of national security fiction.

Motley Rice's undertaking fueled the demand for freelance terrorism expertise. Even more notorious than Brisard was Evan Kohlmann. In the late 1990s, while still an undergraduate at Georgetown University, Kohlmann began investigating alleged jihad supporters. He worked for five years at the Investigative Project on Terrorism (IPT), a private espionage outfit masquerading as a think tank whose founder, Steven Emerson, was infamous for speculating on national television about the "Middle Eastern trait[s]" he discerned in the 1995 Oklahoma City bombing before the culprits were revealed to be white Americans.[40] Among Kohlmann's targets was Adel Batterjee, with whom he corresponded by email under the false name Youcef Abdelkader, later turning the messages over to Motley Rice for use in the 9/11 lawsuit.[41] Kohlmann also recycled material from the *Santiago* proffer in an expert report he prepared for Motley Rice.[42] In 2004, Kohlmann published a book, *Al-Qaida's Jihad in Europe: The Afghan-Bosnian Network*, that would propel him to prominence among terrorism experts, including a perch as a regular commentator for the MSNBC television network (a *New York Magazine* profile of Kohlmann was optioned by a Hollywood producer, a project mercifully not realized to date). The book cites the *Santiago* proffer or other prosecution materials from the Arnaout case seventeen times.[43] Kohlmann would become the federal government's favored expert witness in terrorism prosecutions based on his experience trawling "jihadist" websites for signs of "radicalization."[44] Defense attorneys and investigative journalists have assailed Kohlmann's dubious methodology and lack of relevant credentials and linguistic competence, and they have probed his suspect ties to the government. Nevertheless, courts have generally allowed him to testify, often with seriously prejudicial effects on juries; he has helped send over a dozen Muslims to prison in the United States (W. Said 2015, 96–99, Aaronson 2015, Wheeler 2015, Goodman 2010, 659–69).

Meanwhile, Tareekh Osama and the *Santiago* proffer based upon it would later appear in some of the canonical histories of the early years of the global war on terror. The 9/11 Commission cited them six times, calling the cache "a wealth of information on al Qaeda's evolution and history."[45] Motley Rice for its part shared Tareekh Osama with prominent journalists. Peter Bergen, a former CNN producer who had participated in the network's 1997 interview with bin Laden, reprinted translations of several of the documents in his widely praised book, *The Osama bin Laden I Know*. Bergen introduced the materials to attack the documentary filmmaker Adam Curtis, whose BBC miniseries *The Power of Nightmares* had questioned the narrative of al-Qaʻida as a coherent organization. Bergen (2006) opined:

> All of these assertions are nonsense. There is overwhelming evidence that al Qaeda was founded in 1988 by bin Laden and a small group of like-minded militants, and that the group would eventually mushroom into the secretive, disciplined, global organization dominated by bin Laden that implemented the 9/11 attacks. That evidence can be found in the documents in this chapter, which were recovered in Bosnia in 2002, and can also be found in the interviews throughout this book. (76)

Bergen's dismissal of alternatives to the dominant narrative—"all of these assertions are nonsense"—carried significant weight in elite circles: he has taught at Harvard, Johns Hopkins, and Arizona State University, and is now a vice president of New America, a major Beltway think tank.[46] His rendering of the documents, however, is hardly above reproach: entire paragraphs where the handwriting is illegible are omitted without denotation, and the questionable translation choices made by the prosecutors in the Arnaout case go unchanged, most glaringly in the decision to render the phrase "new military work" (ʻamal) as "new military group" (78).[47]

Lawrence Wright, a staff writer for the *New Yorker* magazine, also used the papers in *The Looming Tower*, a bestselling account of al-Qaʻida that won a Pulitzer Prize and was adapted into a television miniseries. Although the notes from the August 1988 meeting where al-Qaʻida was allegedly founded are the foundation of an "essential scene" in the book, Wright (2006, 131–33, 36, 447–48, 52) showed more interpretive caution and noted discrepancies between the documents and some of his own interviews. The *Santiago* proffer has continued to be cited by many other terrorism commentators over the years.[48] In his memoir, Stanley McChrystal (2013), former head of Joint Special Operations Command and later the top US general in Afghanistan (who was replaced by Petraeus after disparaging remarks made about then Vice President Joe Biden and other senior officials), called the proffer "a basis for much of the public understanding of Al Qaeda's founding" (402). Secret documents used for allegations that were largely withdrawn did not fade into the obscurity of old case dockets but instead found new life in the footnotes of books and the indexes of online search engines. A judicially midwifed theory of conspiracy had matured into official history in the annals of national security.

POSTSCRIPT

The curious fate of the 9/11 lawsuit, now two decades old, reflects the strange relationship between the United States and Saudi Arabia, which excites conspiracy narratives from sectors of the right and left alike. The case languished in procedural limbo for over a decade. Many of the individual defendants were eventually dismissed from the case for a variety of reasons, including the lack of sufficient ties with the United States to justify jurisdiction.

In 2016, however, new life was breathed into the most important part of the case, namely, the allegations against the Saudi state. In that year, a classified portion of the 2002 report by the Joint Inquiry into the 9/11 attacks by the intelligence committees of both houses of Congress was finally released, albeit with some redactions. These so-called missing twenty-eight pages had excited great interest and speculation over the years. They summarized internal FBI and CIA documents concerning several men living in the United States who were alleged to have been Saudi government employees and to have had contacts with the hijackers.[49] Although vague and tentatively worded, the report constituted the strongest official statement from a US government entity linking Saudi Arabia to the attacks. While not a smoking gun, it gave plaintiffs hope of at least a Chekhovian one.

The case received a boost on the legal front in 2016 as well. Over the preceding years, the counts against the Saudi state and its agencies had been dismissed and reinstated several times. A major reason for this was the doctrine that foreign sovereigns are ordinarily immune from suit in US courts. One exception to sovereign immunity concerns states designated as sponsors of terrorism—a label that the State Department would never dare apply to Saudi Arabia for geostrategic reasons. In 2016, Congress sought to resuscitate the lawsuit's prospects by passing the Justice Against Sponsors of Terrorism Act (JASTA), which removed sovereign immunity for all acts of international terrorism against US people or persons.[50] An enraged Saudi government threatened to withdraw all its assets from the United States. The foreign policy establishment was also alarmed that JASTA would encourage other states to permit litigation against the United States in their own courts. But the pressure on legislators from both parties to lend support to the families of 9/11 victims was overwhelming. JASTA passed both houses of Congress by a voice vote. Barack Obama vetoed the law and for the first time in his presidency was promptly overridden.

The drama over JASTA reflected well the nature of the US-Saudi partnership: vociferous posturing by both sides on a firm bedrock of shared strategic interest. Saudi Arabia did not follow through on its (impractical) threat to withdraw assets from the United States, while one cannot help but suspect that members of Congress felt safer letting the lawsuit continue on the belief that it was unlikely to succeed on its merits in the end. And continue it has. In March 2018, the suit cleared a major hurdle when the judge rejected Saudi Arabia's immunity arguments and allowed the case to proceed to discovery, mostly to verify the allegations raised in the missing twenty-eight pages.[51] Over the summer of 2021, current and former Saudi diplomats were questioned under oath, although the depositions are under seal as of this writing. The notion that two close strategic allies bound together by billions of dollars of arms and oil deals and jointly committed to the cause of counterrevolution would remain at loggerheads over whether one sponsored a mass-casualty attack on the other would seem to epitomize the absurdity that often weighs down conspiracy theories. But then again, stranger things have happened.

NOTES

1 In this chapter, terms such as "terrorism" and "terrorist" refer only to the variety of offenses denominated as such under US law. The terms are not called upon here to denote a conceptual or political category.

2 Matthew Hull (2012) helpfully looks at government documents as "graphic artifacts" to call attention to their materiality. Here, I would like to highlight the relationship between artifact and artifice to shed light on how such documents contribute to worlds of fantasy that exist beyond the immediate contexts of circulation for which they were intended.

3 Such a perspective stems in part from a naïve normalization of the separation of powers doctrine (Koch 2021).

4 On the broader decline of antitrust enforcement in the era of neoliberalism, see Khan and Vaheesan (2017); Stucke (2012).
5 See *Hamdan v. Rumsfeld*, 548 U.S. 557 (2006); *Trump v. Hawaii*, 138 S. Ct. 2392
   (2018); *Bank of America Corp. v. City of Miami*, 137 S. Ct. 1296 (2017); *Bristol-
   Myers Squibb Co. v. Superior Court of California*, 137 S. Ct. 1773 (2017); *Cyan,
   Inc. v. Beaver County Employees' Retirement Fund*, 138 S. Ct. 1061 (2018); *Nestlé
   & Cargill v. Doe*, 593 U.S. ___ (2021).
6 See National Commission on Terrorist Attacks upon the United States
   (2004, 56, 467). The original article in question is ʿAzzām (1988). The author
   was a Palestinian Islamic scholar and a prominent supporter of the Afghan
   jihad who worked closely with bin Laden in the 1980s.
7 It is very likely that the Commission here was plagiarizing not from Gunaratna, but from another expert, Evan Kohlmann, who will be discussed
   below (Li 2011).
8 See *United States of America v. Usama Bin Laden*, Indictment, 98 Cr. 539
   (S.D.N.Y., June 8, 1998).
9 See *United States of America v. Usama bin Laden, et al.*, Trial Testimony, S(7)
   98 Cr. 1023 (S.D.N.Y. Feb. 6, 2001), 191–202. Journalist Jason Burke has
   noted intermittent appearances of the term "al-Qaeda" in US government
   statements throughout the 1990s, but even these suggest the functional
   notion of a base rather than al-Qaʿida as the proper name of a cohesive
   organization (Burke 2003, 7–12).
10 BIF grew out of Lajnat al-Birr al-Islamiyya, a Saudi charity founded by
   Adel Abdul Jaleel Batterjee, a businessman and philanthropist from a
   prominent merchant family in Jeddah. The US government alleged that
   Batterjee remained the main force behind BIF, added him to its list of
   Specially Designated Global Terrorists, and asked the United Nations to
   include him on its terrorism sanctions list as well. Batterjee contested
   these accusations and was removed from the UN list in 2013.
11 Early reports in 2013 that the City University of New York offered Petraeus
   $200,000 to teach a single three-hour weekly seminar—an hourly rate
   comparable to the average paid to adjunct faculty for an entire semester-
   long course—were met with outrage. Petraeus then agreed to teach for
   nominal compensation. He was also confronted by student protestors on
   campus.
12 Arnaout was initially charged with perjury. The charge was based on an
   affidavit in a lawsuit filed by BIF against the government to unfreeze its
   assets, in which he affirmed that the organization had not supported
   terrorism. After this dubious allegation was rejected by the judge, the
   government filed obstruction of justice charges for the same act.
13 "Prepared Remarks of Attorney General John Ashcroft," Press Conference,
   Chicago, Illinois, October 9, 2002, available at https://www.justice.gov
   /archive/ag/speeches/2002/100902agremarksbifindictment.htm.

14 See *U.S. v. Arnaout*, Plea Agreement, 02-cr-892, dkt. no. 178 (N.D. Ill. Feb. 10, 2003).

15 After Arnaout completed his sentence in 2011, the government-initiated proceedings to revoke his US naturalization as a first step to seeking deportation. See *U.S. v. Arnaout*, Complaint to Revoke Naturalization, 14-cv-5617, dkt. no. 1 (N.D. Ill. July 23, 2014).

16 Robert Ludlum (1927–2001), author of many best-selling espionage thriller novels revolving around conspiracy theories, had the habit of titling his books with an unusual proper noun followed by an equally catchy improper one, e.g., *The Bourne Identity, The Scarlatti Inheritance*.

17 See *United States v. Arnaout*, Government's Evidentiary Proffer Supporting the Admissibility of Coconspirator Statements 28–30, 33–37, 02-cr-892, dkt. no. 78 (N.D. Ill., Jan. 6, 2003) (hereafter cited as "*Santiago* Proffer").

18 Even without access to the original Arabic, anthropologist Flagg Miller has advanced the alternative and, to my mind, very plausible hypothesis that these documents are best understood as pertaining only to the creation of a specific training camp, al-Faruq, which would be the eponymous *qāʿida* here. Miller reads them as an attempt to marginalize bin Laden or constrain his authority rather than coronating him as the leader of a new organization (Miller 2015, 137–44).

19 The documents were posted online by Michael S. Smith II, a freelance terrorism expert who claims to have consulted for various US government agencies but who is most notable for social media feuds with fellow charlatans in the field, including Trump's openly anti-Muslim counterterrorism adviser Sebastian Gorka, whom he deemed to be lacking in "professionalism" (Smith also voted for Trump). Smith briefly held a fellowship with the New America Foundation until a racist tweet of his own, mocking Chinese accents, caused an online backlash.

20 Under the doctrine of merger, most inchoate crimes cannot be charged if the principal crime is actually carried out. For example, one generally cannot be charged with both attempted murder and murder of the same person.

21 This type of vicarious liability arises under the so-called *Pinkerton* rule established by the US Supreme Court in *Pinkerton v. United States*, 328 U.S. 640 (1946).

22 Many different types of conspiracy are listed in the federal criminal code. In December 2021, the general attempt and conspiracy statute, 21 U.S.C. § 846, was the fifth most common charge filed in the federal criminal system—and this was after dropping precipitously in relation to prior years. See TRAC Reports, "Prosecutions for December 2021," https://trac .syr.edu/tracreports/bulletins/overall/monthlyoct21/fil/. All US states and territories also include conspiracy provisions in their criminal codes.

23 In practice, however, US courts have interpreted "agreement" very broadly: not merely as an exchange of promises ("we agree to do x") but also as

assent or a harmony of opinion ("we agree that x should be done"). This effectively allows mere copresence with others discussing potential crimes to serve as the basis for conspiracy convictions, intensifying concerns about guilt by association (Sacharoff 2016).

24 Conspiracy theorizing is thus linked to a panic over the erosion of individual agency (Melley 2000).

25 In the federal courts, the coconspirator hearsay exemption is codified at Federal Rule of Evidence 801(d)(2)(E).

26 The other common rationale proffered for this doctrine draws analogously from the law governing business partnerships or agency relationships. Just as all partners in a business share legal responsibility for each other's acts carried out in the course of the business (or can be considered agents of each other), the same goes for coconspirators. The problem with this theory is that it speaks more to the substantive offense of conspiracy and has little to do with the concerns of reliability and trustworthiness that motivate the law of evidence (Levie 1954, 1165; see also Katyal 2003, 1329).

27 See *Bourjaily v. United States*, 483 U.S. 171 (1987).

28 *United States v. Santiago*, 582 F.2d 1128 (7th Cir. 1978). This standard was later confirmed nationally in *Bourjaily*.

29 See *U.S. v. Arnaout*, Memorandum Opinion and Order, 2003 U.S. Dist. LEXIS 1635 (N.D. Ill., Feb. 3, 2003).

30 Federal Rule of Civil Procedure 11(b)(3) (emphasis added).

31 Notice pleading emerged with the adoption of the Federal Rules of Civil Procedure in 1938, although a pair of Supreme Court decisions in the early twenty-first century required greater specificity and plausibility in pleadings. See *Ashcroft v. Iqbal*, 556 U.S. 662 (2009); *Bell Atlantic Corp. v. Twombly*, 550 U.S. 544 (2007).

32 One journalist refers to Motley's early infatuation with asbestos in the face of widespread skepticism as a "jihad" (Zegart 2001, 24).

33 The Arnaout prosecution team sent copies of 247 of the documents to the plaintiffs in the 9/11 litigation in March 2003. See *Burnett, et al. v. Al Baraka Investment and Development Corporation, et al.*, Plaintiffs' Motion to Enforce this Court's Letters Rogatory 2, 02-cv-1616-JR, dkt. no. 92 (D.D.C., Mar. 18, 2003). This also took place after several months of shenanigans, during which Motley Rice urged the court to compel the Justice Department to return the documents to the Bosnian authorities so that the Bosnians could then turn them over to Motley Rice.

34 See *In Re Terrorist Attacks on September 11, 2001*, Opinion and Order 40–42, 56, 03-md-1570-GBD-SN, dkt. no. 632 (S.D.N.Y. Jan. 18, 2005).

35 See "Tareekh Osama" file, folder 41, file 108. Tareekh Osama can be downloaded from https://insidethejihad.com/2016/12/al-qaida-archives-tareekh -osama-tareekh-al-musadat/.

36 Brisard also made two trips to Bosnia on Motley Rice's behalf seeking copies of the Arnaout documents. See *Burnett v. al Baraka*, Plaintiffs' Memorandum in Support of Their Motion to Enforce This Court's Letters Rogatory 3-5, 02-cv-1616-JR, dkt. no. 92-1 (D.D.C., Mar. 18, 2003).

37 See *In Re Terrorist Attacks on September 11, 2001*, Plaintiffs' Memorandum of Law in Opposition to Adel A. J. Batterjee's Motion to Dismiss with Supporting Points and Authorities 16–17, 03-md-1570-GBD-SN, dkt. no. 215 (S.D.N.Y., June 4, 2004).

38 *In Re Terrorist Attacks on September 11, 2001*, Opinion and Order 41.

39 See *In Re Terrorist Attacks on September 11, 2001*, Plaintiffs' Notice of Supplemental Authority Regarding the "Golden Chain," 03-md-1570-GBD-SN, dkt. no. 1477 (S.D.N.Y., Nov. 11, 2005).

40 In 2021, the Council on American Islamic Relations (CAIR), a leading Muslim civil rights organization in the United States, revealed that the head of one of its regional chapters in Ohio had been secretly funneling internal information to the IPT for over a decade. CAIR claimed that several other Muslim community groups had been similarly infiltrated and also published emails it obtained in which Emerson ordered his staff to conduct "research" at the request of an aide to Israeli Prime Minister Benjamin Netanyahu.

41 See *In Re Terrorist Attacks on September 11, 2001*, Exhibit 2 to Declaration of Jodi Westbrook Flowers, 03-md-1570-GBD-SN, dkt. no. 215-5 (S.D.N.Y., June 4, 2004).

42 See *In Re Terrorist Attacks on September 11, 2001*, Exhibit 16 to Affirmation of Andrea Bierstein in Opposition to Motion to Dismiss of Hamad al-Husaini 5, 03-md-1570-GBD-SN, dkt. no. 272-19 (S.D.N.Y., June 30, 2004).

43 While the *Santiago* proffer is a flawed source for the history of al-Qa'ida, Kohlmann's reliance on it introduces entirely new layers of distortion (Li 20, 34–35, 233–34n20, 234n24).

44 As of 2014, Kohlmann claimed to have been admitted to testify as an expert in nearly thirty federal court cases. See *United States v. Mustafa Kamel Mustafa*, Trial Transcript for April 23, 2014, 1163:22–25, 04-cr-356-KBF (S.D.N.Y. June 9, 2014).

45 National Commission on Terrorist Attacks upon the United States (2004, 467).

46 In later years, Bergen would maintain that Curtis's argument was "preposterous," while nuancing some of his own claims, acknowledging that in 1988, "Al Qaeda was not, in its inception, intended to be any sort of global enterprise" (Bergen and Cruickshank 2012, 2, 7).

47 This translation also appears in the *Santiago* proffer, 34. An earlier government translation accurately used the term "work," but a handwritten notation amended it to "group" (Berger 2012).

48 Among the more respectable works uncritically citing the *Santiago* proffer are Hegghammer 2010, 49–50; Tankel 2012, 39. A fuller set of government translations was published by J. M. Berger as an e-book (2012).

49   See US Congress (2002, 415–33).

50   See Justice Against Sponsors of Terrorism Act, Public Law 114–222, 130
     Stat. 852 (Sept. 28, 2016).

51   See *In Re Terrorist Attacks on September 11, 2001*, Memorandum and Order
     19–23, 03-MDL-1570 (GBD), dkt. no. 3946 (S.D.N.Y. Mar. 28, 2018).

16 AFTER MUSLIMS /
AUTHORITY, SUSPICION, AND SECRECY IN THE LIBERAL DEMOCRATIC STATE

This chapter attempts an initial, partial, and inevitably cursory exploration into some of the modern historical relations between suspicion and authority. Why explore these relations? One reason is that they are a more important feature of modern politics—and especially modern democratic politics—than we have perhaps realized. Also, these relations have profoundly shaped, and continue to shape, modern liberal social imaginaries. And finally, such an exploration may help us understand a curious feature of how Islam is commonly viewed today that one cannot fail to notice. That is, how in a wide variety of states, all around the world, Islam in one form or another has come to be seen as posing some kind of existential threat and is thus made subject to intensified state surveillance. This happens more commonly with Islam today than with any other religion, whether Muslims are a majority or minority in those states. This curious situation has sometimes been referred to as the Muslim question (see, e.g., Norton 2013).

For some, the Muslim question simply represents a none-too-soon recognition of the latent threat that has always been intrinsic to Islam. For others, it indicates a global conspiracy against the religion and its adherents. Social theorists, rightly suspicious of such thinking, would point instead to imperial and colonial secular legacies and how they have converged with current global political and economic arrangements. For me, what is especially curious is how Islam or Muslims can be seen at all as an *existential* threat to the *state*. Because, of course, they are not, and neither can they be—not least in the face of far more plausible, dire, and looming threats, including climate change, nuclear conflict, global pandemics, and the weaponization of biotechnology and AI, to name just a few. That Islam and Muslims are seen in such a wide variety of states as an existential threat therefore tells us something about the modern state itself and, more specifically, about the liberal social imaginary that historically emerged as part of it.[1] Indeed, I suspect that it indexes a structural feature of that imaginary. It is to better understand that feature that I aim to explore the modern historical relations between suspicion and authority.

Yet such an exploration presents peculiar difficulties. One of these is that suspicion seems like such a natural attitude, that anyone anywhere at any time can and typically does display in certain situations, even if it might be clothed in diverse cultural expressions. Any history of suspicion's various expressions would therefore be like a history of the different garments worn by the same body. While there is no doubt some truth to this idea, the situation is, I think, more complicated. For this idea is typically connected to the assumption that suspicion is naturally the obverse of authority, the default condition that arises when authority fails to obtain. Here authority is seen as that which needs to be actively constructed or performed, and so suspicion, which arises when that activity fails, is seen as passive in relation to authority. To put it another way: authority is what you have to work at, while suspicion is just what happens when you do not do a good job. But alongside this set of assumptions is an equally widely held idea: that suspicion, rather than being a passive condition, is an attitude that needs to be actively cultivated, especially in a world where there is too much credulity, where the presentation of authority is too easily accepted. In this latter mode of thinking, it is the suspicion that takes the hard work, against the bewildering variety of authoritative claims that stoke our fantasies, fears, and desires. Here suspicion is sometimes linked to a hard-boiled, nitty-gritty brand of realism, to an overall skepticism and demeanor of doubt that expresses a worldliness requisite to the institutional and technical complexity of the modern polities and processes in which we are embedded. Who would deny in this era of proliferating media and "fake news" that an attitude of suspicion is an absolute must? And yet, at the same time, one finds growing worries that social life is shot through with too much doubt and skepticism, too much suspicion, such that collective social life is under a clear and present threat of losing its cohesion.

Even this cursory consideration shows us that suspicion, however natural an attitude it might be, is given to much complexity and contradiction: in its senses of passivity or activity, in its paucity or ubiquity, in its relationships to fear, desire, fantasy, and authority. An initial foray into its cognates and etymologies further complicates our ideas and assumptions about it. Thus, today, suspicion, doubt, and skepticism are all seen as being of a piece—if not quite the same things, then at least as inhabiting the same semantic and conceptual field. But a look at the history of the term *skeptic* shows that it used to mean "thoughtful" or "inquiring," and that only later, in the late sixteenth and seventeenth centuries, did one find the meaning of "one with a doubting attitude." And even the word "doubt" had a very different meaning in the early thirteenth century; it meant "to dread, to fear," and it was out of these meanings that the connotations of hesitation and uncertainty were derived. Suspicion, on the other hand, seems to have emerged as a term in the early fourteenth century, and had neither to do with simple inquiry or thoughtfulness, nor with fear or dread, but with the conjecture of wrongdoing—a potentially forensic understanding—although, in being linked to the idea of "looking up" at something, it shows some historical connections with ideas of fear and awe. But it is precisely this association that disappears in the fourteenth century, replaced instead by the idea of thinking or looking "behind" something, and with the conjecture of wrongdoing. Interestingly, the translations of the word "suspicion" into a variety of Indo-European languages all show associations with the idea of thinking or looking behind something.[2]

We can see, then, how these three terms, though they might be understood to inhabit the same semantic and conceptual field today, certainly did not do so historically (or at least they expressed a very different configuration of meanings than they do today). The notion that arises in the late sixteenth and early seventeenth centuries of a "doubting attitude" could not have meant an attitude of constant dread or fear, which was the earlier thirteenth-century meaning of doubt. And while earlier, the terms skeptic and skepticism had been about thoughtfulness and inquiry—a quality, say, of a person or persons—suspicion, with the idea of wrongdoing and of looking behind something, seems to express a different concern: that of the relation between being and appearance.

The rise of the term "suspicion" coincides with an important change in judicial decision-making procedures in Europe during the thirteenth century, in response to the Fourth Lateran Council's condemnation of judicial ordeals and its prohibition of any priestly officiation over them. This required the development of judicial procedures that would protect judges and juries from using their personal knowledge (or "conscience") in judging cases involving blood punishments and thereby shield their souls from the risk of eternal damnation. As a result, criminal procedure came to be structured by a moral theology of certainty, which had four levels: *doubt*, which was the lowest level of certainty and upon the basis of which it was sinful to act; *suspicion*, which was the level above doubt, an inclination of the judge toward one or the other of the parties, which enabled him to use "no-blood" techniques to extract confession; *opinion*, constituted by grave proofs, which enabled him to order the use of torture for confession; and finally, *certainty*, the basis on which judgment could be made.[3] Here suspicion was a stage in a distinctive hierarchy, very differently related to doubt than it is today, and not an overall disposition or attitude of the self. Eventually, however, with the continual expansion of legality in European societies, aspects of these judicial procedures came to be expressed in theological works aimed first at the salvation of the self: the penitentials, or confessor's manuals, and the Protestant conscience literature. Later, with the further expansion of law and legality, these procedures made their way into a variety of dramatic genres—from Shakespearean plays to gothic literature—through which various aspects of both common and courtly life and character came to be increasingly emplotted.[4]

The point of highlighting these histories is not simply to note the elements of a contingent origin but also to underscore how the suspicion that we take for granted today involved a simultaneous expansion of legality (and hence, state) within society, along with transformations in the moral structures of the self. So, it is perhaps not the case that histories of suspicion are histories of different garments over the same body but are rather histories that structure that body differently, sometimes profoundly so. But they might also show us how our senses of suspicion as active, or passive, or partially both, are so confusing—because the presence or absence of suspicion is one of the ways that the activity or passivity of the subject (self) *comes to be defined*. Moreover, while suspicion is typically understood today to be opposed to authority, we see from the history recounted here that suspicion was fundamentally situated within authoritative structures.

As if these difficulties were not enough, we are confronted with another peculiar difficulty: the concept of authority whose relations with suspicion we want to better understand. The issue is not simply that suspicion is not necessarily opposed to authority. It is that we have lost authority—at least, according to political theorist Hannah Arendt. Here is a quote from the famous, and some ways prescient, piece "What Is Authority?" which expounds on her claim:

> In order to avoid misunderstanding, it might have been wiser to ask in the title [of this article]: What *was*—and not what is—authority? For it is my contention that we are tempted and entitled to raise this question because authority has vanished from the modern world. Since we can no longer fall back upon authentic and undisputable experiences common to all, the very term has become clouded by controversy and confusion. Little about its nature appears self-evident or even comprehensible to everybody, except that the political scientist may still remember that this concept was once fundamental to political theory, or that most will agree that a constant, ever-widening and -deepening crisis of authority has accompanied the development of the modern world in our century. . . . The most significant symptom of the crisis, indicating its depth and seriousness, is that it has spread to such prepolitical areas as child-rearing and education, where authority in the widest sense has always been accepted as a natural necessity, obviously required as much by natural needs, the helplessness of the child, as by political necessity, the continuity of an established civilization which can be assured only if those who are newcomers by birth are guided through a pre-established world into which they are born as strangers. . . . Practically as well as theoretically, we are no longer in a position to know what authority really *is*. (Arendt 2006a, 91–92)

In this piece, Arendt is concerned with what she understands to be not simply a loss of existing authorities, but more profoundly, a loss of the very concept of authority within our social lives. But this notion of a conceptual loss is quite difficult to grasp. The precious little literature on the subject is an indication of the difficulty it involves (see C. Diamond 1988; Lear 2017). What does she mean that we have lost the concept of authority, when authority seems so ubiquitous in our lives?

For Arendt, authority provided both a long-standing model on which a whole range of social relations could be forged and made intelligible; it served as an important foundation for apprehending changing experience. Part of what it means to have lost authority is that we can no longer render that model intelligible to ourselves, that we can no longer *practically* distinguish it from other associated phenomena, like persuasion, domination, manipulation, deference, servility, and violence. With the erosion of these distinctions, we have difficulty making intelligible many of our relations within our own and with other communities. This applies not just in the present but in the past, too: as we have an increasingly difficult time making intelligible many of our contemporary relations, we also begin to have difficulty making sense of what they were in the past. So, for Arendt there is an important temporal dimension to the loss of the concept of authority because, perhaps more than anything else, it provided an anchor to guide us through the past and into the present, and it enabled us to navigate the complexities of changing experience. Not knowing what authority is, *we no longer know what it was*; for Arendt, what is lost is not the past per se but a dimension that gives the past its depth.

But if we can no longer easily apprehend authority, neither can we easily apprehend its loss. How, then, might we render this loss intelligible? Where might we register its symptoms and consequences in our contemporary lives? The sociologist Richard Sennett (1993), who was a student of Arendt's, offers us some insight. He notes how this loss of authority is registered in a peculiar set of conflicting attitudes and feelings:

> The dilemma of authority in our time, the peculiar fear it inspires, is that *we feel attracted to strong figures we do not believe to be legitimate.* . . . . What is peculiar to our times is that the formally legitimate powers in the dominant institutions inspire a strong sense of illegitimacy among those subject to them. However, these powers also translate into images of human strength: of authorities who are assured, judge as superiors, exert moral discipline, and inspire fear. These authorities draw others into their orbit, like unwilling moths to a flame. Authority without legitimacy, society held together by its very disaffections: this strange situation is something we can make sense of only by understanding how we understand. (26)

To understand how we understand: that is what I seek to explore in this chapter, with respect to the relation between suspicion and authority.

And since, as we have seen, contemporary formations of suspicion were fashioned through an expansion of legality within society along with transformations in the moral structures of the self, it might make sense to look at these two historically related fronts. So we could start by asking: what might this loss of authority look like within our understanding of law, which seems perhaps more than any other institution to rely on the workings of authority? What consequences does the loss of authority have for legality, which is so historically central to the modern liberal state?

Legal theorist Marianne Constable provides us with one potentially useful way to begin thinking about these questions. She outlines a fundamental problem in contemporary historiographies of positive law: that they can never seem to find its authoritative origin, no matter how hard they try (Constable 1994). The reason for this, she says, is that, on the one hand, an ostensible origin is found in a conquering will, and yet, on the other hand, an attempt is always made to find a precedent in the previous practices and customs of the people subject to the conquering power. As a result, the ostensible origin is pushed back to another founding moment, in another conquering, yet another imposition. In the process, law comes to be seen as always potentially open to another founding. So, the loss of authority perhaps shows itself in the dilemmas of founding, that is, in an inability to ground authority in any particular present or past founding moment.

With Constable's ideas in mind, how might we understand the relations between contemporary formations of suspicion and this loss of authority beyond the simple opposition between them?

EGYPT AND THE DISCONTENTS OF THE REVOLUTIONARY STATE

To help further clarify this question, we might briefly consider some of the events that transpired in Egypt during the revolutionary period between the years 2011 and 2013, between the ouster of President Hosni Mubarak and the removal of President Mohammed Morsi.[5] Not only will these events poignantly demonstrate the dilemmas of authority and founding that Constable and Arendt speak of, but they will lead us to some broader observations on suspicion.

The fierce debates sparked in the first days after the military's forcible removal of Morsi in 2013, amid massive protests against him, cast confusion upon the nature not only of that event but of the 2011 uprising as well. Was it, as some said, a continuation and extension of the 2011 uprising and the principles it represented, which had been increasingly derailed over the subsequent two years? Or was it, as others claimed, a coup—a reversal of the principles of the 2011 uprising and the ethos that it expressed? Supporters of the military intervention drew parallels with 2011. In both cases, the heads of state were accused of having autocratic tendencies, stifling democracy, and obstructing social justice. In both cases, there were massive protests demanding that the heads of state step down. In both cases, they refused to acquiesce to the people's demands. In the face of this intransigence, the military forced their removal; the military's intervention was subsequently met with widespread approval. If anything, the removal of Morsi made evident the military's indispensable role in the removal of Mubarak, which may have been obscured due to the largely nonviolent nature of the protests at that time. Thus, supporters of Morsi's removal argued that if one supported the events of 2011, one ought to support the military intervention of 2013.

Those opposed to the military intervention argued that Morsi, unlike Mubarak, was a democratically elected head of state and that the military intervention undermined democratic processes and possibilities. But what if a head of state begins to show autocratic tendencies, assuming extrajudicial powers and stifling democratic principles? If the majority of the population believes this to be so, and if people take to the streets to demand his abdication, is it wrong for the military to intervene on their behalf, forcing the head of state to acquiesce to their demands? Does that undermine, or does that guarantee, the possibilities of democratic process? But then, would it be legitimate to forcibly remove a democratically elected head of state whenever her approval ratings dipped below 50 percent, or below 40 percent, or whatever percent and people protested for just a few days? If so, what is to prevent such removals from happening over and over again in arbitrary fashion? After all, approval ratings are highly volatile and constantly shifting. Are they enough to force down a head of state and rewrite a democratically ratified constitution? Can any new founding be so easily upended? If so, what makes any one of them authoritative?

It quickly became clear that support for the military intervention was not at all as widespread as was initially claimed. Though perhaps smaller than the protests against him, the protests and sit-ins in support of Morsi's presidency were both large and sustained throughout the country until the military violently suppressed them. People were clearly divided. While this may have strengthened the hand of those who argued for democratic process, it also raised even thornier questions. Morsi had won the presidential election with barely more than 50 percent of the vote. Many who voted for him did so only to prevent a Mubarak regime representative from winning (which raised the question of how widespread revolutionary sentiment actually was). Morsi arguably had much less than 50 percent support and certainly nothing like the mandate represented by the ostensible unity of the 2011 uprising. Under such divided circumstances, what authorized and constrained his actions? More specifically, would the legitimacy of his actions derive from previously existing law, that is, law that was enacted during the previous regime and interpreted by a judiciary still strongly associated with that earlier regime—namely, all that the 2011 uprising aimed to sweep away? Or did he have the right and the responsibility to assume the extrajudicial powers needed to wipe away past legislation and establish new law, especially in the face of stiff judicial resistance? Existing law, it could be argued, was enacted during successive autocratic regimes and sustained primarily by the coercive apparatuses of the military.

One could, in principle, extend this argument further and further back in time. Thus, if not the military regimes that began with Nasser, then why the laws that were forged under the era of British colonialism, however much an Egyptian elite might have been involved? But, in that case, could not the laws of Ottoman imperial rule in its various incarnations also be seen as an imposition on Egypt? Why, then, should any such law have been the basis for assessing the legitimacy of Morsi's actions? But if Morsi did not win the elections with the popular mandate of the 2011 uprising, if the elections threw doubt on how popular that mandate even was, then what basis did he have to enact extrajudicial powers to eliminate old regime–based law? Any such attempt could have been construed as the imposition of an autocratic will, and this was precisely how many of his attempts to enact such powers were interpreted. Indeed, many of those who criticized the judiciary for tacitly supporting the old regime and obstructing investigations against former Mubarak officials ended up opposing giving Morsi the extrajudicial powers he needed to transform the law's structure. With neither the present nor the past to rely on, it was impossible to locate a source of authority for Morsi's actions.

There is, however, one thing that remained largely unchanged throughout the tumultuous events of that period. The very same structures of coercive violence that backed old regime–law were the ones that enabled the removal of both Mubarak and Morsi: the military. What authorizes the military's violence? Is it the law? But the military's initial intervention had not been legal: the military forced Mubarak to declare, through his newly appointed vice president, Omar Sulayman, that he had transferred ruling authority to the military's ruling council. This was an instance of the military authorizing itself. Its removal of Morsi was not legal either; and as became clear, it was not met with a widespread consensus. Part of the military's public rationale was the need to forestall a potential outbreak of factional violence in the country—an admission of popular dissensus. In this case, too, the military authorized itself to act. *All* political factions in Egypt, at one point or another during the years 2011–13, turned to and relied on the military for support. But neither law, nor democratic process, nor clear consensus authorized its violence. Was it authorized, then, simply by the success of its violence?

My point is not to take sides on the contested truth of what transpired during these events. It is to show only how they boldly highlight the loss of authority and dilemmas of founding that Arendt and Constable described, in which authority seems to blur into coercive violence and in which any founding seems to render itself arbitrarily open to any other past or future one. But there is something else that is worth noting: what brought on the events of 2013 was the suspicion and fear that Morsi and his political allies sought to impose the Sharia as the law of the land, which would have been a strike against liberal conceptions of equality and rights. Morsi and his political allies, for their part, viewed liberal and left-leaning activists with disdain and suspicion, as marginal actors, unrepresentative of the wishes of the majority of Egyptians, who nevertheless sought to impose liberal principles upon them. That is, the events of 2013 and the dilemmas that came with it were brought on by the concerns and fears centered on the founding of a properly *liberal and democratic* polity.

Suspicion was therefore rampant in the aftermath of the apparent success of the 2011 Egyptian uprisings. Most peculiar is how this suspicion was directed at the military. As mentioned earlier, everyone at one point or another supported the military, yet at the same time, everyone suspected everyone else of making clandestine—and therefore necessarily malicious—deals with it. To expose such dealings was a way of revealing the hypocrisy of the parties involved. The continual shifting of alliances by all parties was equaled only by their constant mutual accusations of hypocrisy, creating an increasingly vicious cycle of fear and suspicion. Nothing appeared transparent, and every event—even every nonevent—seemed to harbor some hidden intention behind it that had to be discerned. Conspiracy and conspirators seemed to be everywhere, and the military was always in one contrasting way or another at the center of it—as though it were a flame attracting unwilling moths.

Perhaps this kind of suspicion and distrust was to be expected, it being a feature of revolutionary-style transitions. Suspicion, we might again be tempted to say, is a natural human response when long-standing social structures are undermined and replaced with new ones whose status and stability are not assured. And yet, as I have argued above, suspicion is not simply a natural attitude; and however natural suspicion might seem, this should not prevent us from studying the structures it takes and from considering what this might tell us about revolutionary transitions under contemporary statehood. Here we might return to Hannah Arendt (2006b), who offers some fascinating insights into the specific nature of the suspicion elicited by modern revolutions and, thus, insights into the relation between a complex affective orientation and modern legal-political structures.[6]

Arendt (2006b) writes that the problem of suspicion, sincerity, and hypocrisy during the French Revolution was, at bottom, a question of how to relate appearance to being. She shows how this question has elicited different answers, throughout history, in both philosophy and politics. The political question was resolved in a specific way during the French Revolution, and she contrasts that resolution with what she claims was a superior one associated with the American Revolution. While in the American case there was an attempt among the Constitutional founders to balance conflicting powers, the French case featured a constant search for sincerity, an acute awareness of and concern for the possibility of hypocrisy, and thus cultivated an incessant suspicion into one's character and convictions. For Arendt, the probing search for sincerity must always lead to failure—a failure that tends to terror—because of what she claims is the very nature of "inwardness," or the private self. The private self, she argues, is always obscure to others and partly to itself, governed by contradictory dynamics of motives, reservations, fears, and convictions. Such contradictions, whenever exposed to public scrutiny, will inevitably lead to charges of hypocrisy and corruption.

While aspects of what Arendt says here seem compelling, we should consider that inwardness and its dynamics can be profoundly historically fashioned, and often differ strikingly across place and time. It is well known that the period of the French Revolution featured emerging notions of a divided self, one that might even be divided against itself (see van den Berg 1974). And so it may be that the suspicion she speaks of here, rather than exposing inwardness, actually works to constitute it. That is, instead of construing the terror as simply a failure wrought of suspicion, we might see it as working to constitute a modality of politics together with a certain kind of self, one that remains with us today.

What about the American case? In discussing it, Arendt dismisses in a few short sentences what was then a long-standing and dominant, but declining, tradition in American historiography, as represented by the work of Charles Beard. Often cast as political-economic and focused on understanding the economic interests that motivated and facilitated political acts and events, Beard's perspective and approach purveyed a degree of suspicion of political actors, including and especially the founders of the Constitution, as acute as what Arendt attributes to the French Revolution. Indeed, Beard treats the writing of the Constitution as a successful attempt at counterrevolution, smothering popular drives toward freedom in favor of established moneyed interests. Interestingly, this interpretation was articulated at a time of deep and widespread skepticism about the Constitution and its capacity to stabilize what was then a deeply fractured polity (see Rana 2014). Faith in and loyalty to the Constitution as the guarantor of the state's stability and as the guardian of fundamental rights, which seems to us now a venerable tradition, turns out to have emerged much later than is generally realized. As legal historian Aziz Rana (2014) shows, it arises only toward the beginning of World War I and is associated with the rise of the discourse of national security. As the national-security state became more entrenched, so too did the tradition of faith in and loyalty to the Constitution. Both were fully established by the time of Arendt's writing.

Coincidentally, the dismissal and decline of Beard's historiographical style and perspective became decisive as the Cold War geared up, as organized suspicion in the form of espionage and intelligence agencies became far more pervasive than ever before, and when the concentration of power in the executive became especially pronounced. Some who continue to advocate Beard's approach argue that we need the suspicion it represents now more than ever, and that the drafters of the Declaration of Independence purveyed *precisely* that kind of suspicion against the British Crown (see deHaven-Smith 2013). For the drafters, it wasn't a single repressive policy or even several of them that motivated their declaration; it was rather that *within* the series of abusive policies they were able to evince "a design to reduce them under absolute Despotism." That is, they saw an underlying, deliberate, and malicious pattern and plan: *a conspiracy.*

But if the Declaration of Independence was indeed motivated by suspicious and conspiratorial thinking; if people deeply doubted the Constitution until at least the early twentieth century; and if Beard's historiographical approach and attitude remained so dominant until the mid-twentieth century, then maybe Arendt should not have drawn so stark a difference between the French and American Revolutions. Maybe the pervasive suspicion she identifies was strongly present in both, even if the consequences differed—though it remains perplexing how she ignores so completely the terror wrought of America's domestic, highly racialized violence, and of which she was certainly aware. It is a knowledge, however, that she seems to disavow in her writings.

At the same time, we know that Arendt's historiographical method was not so much empirically committed as self-consciously exemplary, involved in facilitating what she called "good judgment."[7] Arendt's point may have been that the suspicion she identified with the French case tends to have had adverse consequences that are paradigmatically exemplified by the way that revolution unfolded, and that an alternative approach, which she thinks may still be possible in the American case, is to focus on the balance of powers within state and society, to obstruct the concentration and monopolization of power by any one entity or conglomerate. If so, then again, this would have been an interesting coincidence, as she made this point at a time when the United States seemed to have been on the verge of a revolutionary moment, which saw both an upsurge of influential movements aimed at rectifying past injustices and obtaining civil rights *and* a vast extension of organized suspicion as a result of the growth of police and intelligence agencies, along with an increasing concentration of political and economic power as never before.

The point here, however, is that the suspicion that Arendt identified with the revolutions that established the modern state form *was not limited to the revolutionary period.* It continues to form part of the deep structure of the modern liberal(izing) state, a disposition expressed throughout its political institutions, modalities of investigation, and legal procedures; in its promotion of the subjectivities of proper democratic citizenship; and in the rise of what we call a surveillance society.

The widespread suspicion that is part of the deep structure of the modern state would seem to coincide with the loss of authority that

Arendt also speaks about. We might therefore be tempted once again to see suspicion as the obverse of authority, the rise of the one being the consequence of the loss of the other. But such a temptation is itself a consequence of the loss of authority, of our difficulty in rendering it practically intelligible in the modern world. It obfuscates how this suspicion is itself a form of binding as powerful as any conventional authority we might conceive. In the case of Egypt, we saw how suspicion worked to maintain a complex status quo throughout the volatile shifts of the revolutionary period. Indeed, it was one of the few things, along with the military and its violence, that persisted—and even became more pronounced—from Mubarak into the post-Morsi era. So, what we have here is no simple opposition between suspicion and authority; I venture that a different, more complex dynamic is at play—a dynamic of knowledge and disavowal. In particular, for those involved in the Egyptian revolutionary movement, they knew of a possibility that they could not but disavow: the possibility that the military was the enemy of the nation.[8]

SECRET KNOWLEDGE AND STATE SOVEREIGNTY

To work toward a better understanding of this dynamic of knowledge and disavowal, I would like to attend to a feature of the modern state that has become increasingly important since the end of the nineteenth and beginning of the twentieth centuries; it is a feature shared by liberal democracies, and I think it requires much more investigation than it has so far been given. I refer to the state's central need to pursue, generate, and manage secret knowledge in order to sustain its sovereignty. The capacity to do this is actually indispensable to the sovereignty that modern states claim and aim to practice today. Indeed, a state that cannot produce or manage secret knowledge—that is to say, a state that has no secrets and cannot hide its secrets simply cannot be sovereign. That is why scholars such as the historian Michael Warner[9] have defined the very notion of intelligence (as in, intelligence agencies) as the pursuit and management of secret knowledge by and for the preservation of sovereignty. And while the practices of espionage may be ancient, and not confined solely to states, Warner (2014) points to a set of fundamental transformations at the end of the nineteenth and beginning of the twentieth centuries that gave rise to what we now call "intelligence"—where it becomes bureaucratized, professionalized, centralized, institutionally independent, *and* increasingly indispensable to the modern state as it becomes the primary claimant to sovereignty. Warner shows that the institutionalization of secrecy and suspicion comes about historically with the modern state's becoming the main claimant to sovereignty, above all other entities.

Importantly, liberal democracies are not exempt from this requirement of sovereignty and, thus, from their need to constantly gather secret knowledge. Without such sovereignty, they cannot claim to be genuinely democratic, as they would then be vulnerable to both external intervention and internal subversion. And if they cannot be genuinely democratic, then their claim to being liberal is also rendered unstable (think, for example, about the hacking of elections). It might seem as though the pursuit of secret knowledge through surveillance is incompatible with liberal democracy, but in an important sense, quite the opposite is true because the *effective* generation of secret knowledge *requires* that there be a domain of privacy. If there were nothing hidden from anybody, no one could have secret knowledge or the need to generate it. For the surveillance that generates secret knowledge to yield the results it seeks, people must believe in a domain where they are unseen, where they can act "as themselves" without hindrance, without their actions being guarded. Of course, the suspicion that such surveillance is happening can make people more guarded in their private lives, and this can generate a complex, intensifying dynamics of evasion and pursuit. That is one reason why the state aims to conduct its intelligence-gathering activities in secret. What I want to emphasize here is that the liberal democratic state not only requires secret knowledge to sustain its sovereignty but is, with its commitment to personal privacy, especially conducive to the generation of that knowledge. Maybe that is why, in liberal democracies like the United States, the amount of classified information is several times larger than all the information available in the public domain (see Masco 2014).

We know that the state powerfully grounds our collective understanding and perceptions of social reality, our collective social imaginary. It authorizes and promotes the knowledge we learn and establishes the infrastructures by which it is organized and disseminated. Through its laws and legal system, the state defines and establishes an entire network of entities, agents, causalities, and responsibilities that we rely on. In its administrative capacities it regulates the basic rhythms of our daily lives, from working hours to traffic patterns. At the same time, it provides official explanations for a whole variety of domestic and international events and actions. The centrality of the state in this regard thus leads to an important question that I would like to pose here. What is the *effect* of the state's incessant, continually growing, and increasingly institutionalized pursuit of secret knowledge upon the sense of social reality that it establishes? How, in particular, does it shape the social imaginaries of the paradigmatic liberal democracies, with vibrant public spheres and multiple guarantees of privacy, as in North America and Europe? How, especially, does it structure the contemporary liberal conscience? These questions, I think, are important for understanding not only liberal democratic social imaginaries but also some of the predicaments that Muslims in a variety of states face today. One way to begin addressing these questions is to consider how the covert activities of the state inevitably seep into public awareness and the specific forms that this seepage and awareness take—in particular, how it gives rise to what the literary theorist Timothy Melley has called "the covert sphere."

"The covert sphere," writes Melley (2012, 5–6), "is a cultural imaginary shaped by both institutional secrecy and public fascination with the secret workings of the state. The covert sphere is not a set of government agencies, not what [the critical theorist] Michael Warner usefully calls a 'counter-public.' It is an array of discursive forms and cultural institutions through which the public . . . can fantasize the clandestine dimensions of the state. . . . It is a cultural apparatus," he writes, "for resolving the internal contradictions of democracy in an age of heightened sovereignty. Unlike the supposed 'rational-critical' public sphere, the covert sphere is dominated by narrative fictions, such as novels, films, television series, and electronic games, for fiction is one of the few discourses in which the secret work of the state may be disclosed to citizens."

Notably, for Melley, the covert sphere is not a domain of deliberation but of affect—that is, of specifically structured forms of fantasy, fear, curiosity, and fascination that are part of a modern liberal social imaginary. As an imaginary in which the secret activity of the state is disclosed but not revealed, the covert sphere supplements and suffuses the sphere of more conventional deliberation. Not only that, it suffuses the activities of a government's covert agencies themselves, which often do not fully know (and therefore surveil) each other's operations. More importantly, for Melley it acts as an ideological system that enables the persistence of "the internal contradictions of liberal democracy in an age of heightened sovereignty." He argues that the covert sphere has shaped contemporary liberal conscience in a specific way—one that allows for knowledge of the state's covert activities, while at the same time providing the means of disavowing that knowledge. This relationship between public knowledge and disavowal is an enduring and conspicuous feature of liberal democracies and the liberal conscience, if only because of the vibrancy of democratic public spheres and the importance placed upon public deliberation. But it is also a situation that renders the citizenry of the state, both individually and collectively, continually susceptible to the charge of hypocrisy. Melley's concept of the covert sphere helps to explain why this is so.

I want to add two thoughts to Melley's insightful discussion. First, that the phenomenon of knowledge and disavowal is intensified by an incessant, increasing demand for certainty by both the state and the public, often in the name of security. This unending demand for certainty tends to undermine itself, with one effect being that every event and action (and even every nonevent and nonaction) is turned into a sign potentially indicating something else that is open for interpretation. What I speak of here is not what is (well) known as a hermeneutics of suspicion, but a dynamic that increasingly turns social life into a hermeneutics. On the one hand, this dynamic feeds into the phenomenon of knowledge and disavowal: "We knew but we were never sure." On the other hand, it increasingly allows "state power to penetrate the density of ordinary social life" (see Asad 2007).

Second, Melley attributes both the rise of this covert sphere and the form of knowledge and disavowal it creates to the Cold War and the astonishing growth of clandestine agencies that came with it. But the sociologist Luc Boltanski (2014) traces something very much like it back to the end of the nineteenth and beginning of the twentieth centuries, with the massive reorganization and centralization of police and intelligence agencies across liberal states and their colonial and imperial territories. This occurs simultaneously with a profusion of a new literature—the genres of detective and espionage fiction—during a period of growing mass literacy. But this is also a time when conspiracy theories run rampant. For Boltanski, this is not only a moment when secrecy arises as an important idea; it is also a time when the notion of a hidden, deeper reality governing a surface, more easily perceptible, becomes a premise for the newly emerging knowledges of that era—some of which remain with us today as legitimate forms of knowledge, others as illegitimate and marginalized forms that nevertheless retain a socially palpable presence. This is a time not only of rampant conspiracy theorizing but also of the rise of social theory in the form of sociology, of psychoanalysis with its diagnoses of paranoia; and it is a time in which theorists such as Durkheim, Simmel, and Freud are theorizing secrecy as foundational to social and individual life (Masco 2014). And just as important was the need for social theory to carefully distinguish itself from the conspiracy thinking that emerged at the same time. The point is this: that conspiracy theory and social theory had the same initial conditions of emergence and existence at a moment when secrecy and suspicion were institutionalized as central activities of the state. It may therefore be impossible for social theory to subsume conspiracy theory under its particular mode of explanation, or vice versa. Where there is the one, there will always be the other, and the truth between them may seem forever undecided.

Paranoia and conspiracy theorizing (if not social theory) continue to feature largely in the public imagination today. If anything, they have taken an even more pronounced form as the clandestine activities of the state and its use of secrecy continue to massively expand. This has three connected consequences.

First, the growth and growing centrality of covert agencies for the state—the increasing importance of secrecy for state sovereignty at the end of the nineteenth and beginning of the twentieth centuries—has enabled a new form of secular blasphemy. There is an old and famous quip that heresy is no longer committed against the church but against the state. That centuries-old statement has since taken on different meanings, but since the beginning of the twentieth century it has come to have a special salience. The new form of blasphemy consists not of speaking out against the state, nor of critiquing its policies (no matter how severely), but in the betrayal of state secrets, which is seen as a fundamental threat to the sovereignty of the state and the loyalty it continues to demand. This is evidenced, in part, by the spate of espionage and state secrets legislation that were passed at the end of the nineteenth century and whose number only continued to grow throughout the twentieth. Perhaps that is why Julian Assange has been so relentlessly pursued by the world's most powerful liberal democracies—not simply because he made publicly available the classified diplomatic cables provided to him by Chelsea Manning but because his Wikileaks is an *institutionalized platform* for the betrayal of state secrets, which threatens the very practice of sovereignty. He is perhaps today's most reviled blasphemer, even as his blasphemy retains much allure. The United States calls for Assange to be tried for treason, even though, unlike Chelsea Manning and Edward Snowden, he is not an

American citizen. One of the reasons why the betrayal of state secrets—even as relatively harmless as diplomatic cables (as if ambassadors are not always making assessments of the officials they deal with)—is seen as such a seditious and venomously threatening act has to do with how the status of the secret has changed with the Cold War. As anthropologist Joseph Masco (2014) notes, with the Cold War, the paradigmatic notion of the state secret became the nuclear secret. All state secrets were subsequently seen from the standpoint of nuclear ones, and thus were seen to carry with them some degree of existential threat.

This development relates to a second consequence. The enormous growth and proliferation of covert agencies, along with the expansive suspicion that they purvey, has facilitated a mutual and intensifying embrace of secrecy and suspicion by the state, of the state, and for the state ("if you see something say something"). And with that has come an expansion of what can count as a seditious act. Whether providing "material support to terrorism" for simply translating Islamist websites in the United States,[10] or committing an "apologie du terrorisme" for refusing a moment of silence or not saying "je suis Charlie" in the wake of the Charlie Hebdo massacres in France, what can count as a potentially seditious act has broadened to seeming absurdity (according to a French official poster, a potential indicator of radicalization was if someone suddenly quit buying baguettes).[11] And as the scope of sedition has expanded, so too has an implicit demand for loyalty to the state intensified. Inasmuch as blasphemy today consists in words or deeds that betray the state, the domain of blasphemy has vastly grown. With these tightly woven affective threads of secrecy, suspicion, spying, and potential sedition, we have a set of practices as potentially broad in scope and intricate in structure as the Spanish Inquisition (see Murphy 2013). For example, in the wake of the Charlie Hebdo massacres, young Muslim children were put under scrutiny at their schools for harboring potentially seditious beliefs.[12] In other words, we have become increasingly bound to the state not through democratic process, nor through contract, but through *revelation*—of secrets and the potential dangers they conceal.

Finally, the constant generation of secret knowledge, the ongoing attempt to sustain that secrecy, the seeping into public consciousness of the existence of a guarded, hidden reality, and the (seductive) suspicion that this generates within the liberal democratic state—all this gives rise to *a conflation between the ideas of hidden truth and latent threat* in the public imagination as well as in covert agencies. In these agencies, whatever truths worth finding or having are not only those that are hidden but the ones related to potential threats, however that may be. Masco (2014) has provided us with a thoroughly insightful discussion of this conflation and of the shifts in the structure and performance of secrecy as part of state governance in the wake of the atomic bomb and the rise of counterterrorism, in what he theorizes as "a secrecy/threat matrix as a core project of the national security state" (43). I can only add a couple of thoughts to his theorization of the secrecy/threat matrix. First, within the public imagination, this conflation of hidden truth with latent threat can take many forms. For example, it can take the form of anxiety about the state itself, such as the thought that there is a deeper, shadow state that truly governs its actions, as the now numerous writings, both popular and academic, concerning "the deep state" attest. But it can also take the form of an intensified focus on particular groups seen as harboring ideas or plans that might threaten the state and the society that it claims to protect—as seen in the constant discussion in both popular and academic circles about the dangers of "radicalization." Here we see how the twin dangers—that is, the notions of the deep state and of radicalization—are structured by the same feature of the public imagination that conflates secret truths with latent threats. That is to say, both the deep state *and* radicalization *are less truths than constructs arising out of the same imaginative structure.* This is such a broad and enduring feature of liberal democratic imaginaries that we might call it structural. It is a *space* where secret truth and latent threat are conflated together, and that can be and has been occupied by different groupings, from anarchists, Jews, and communists in the past, to Muslims today.

CONCLUDING THOUGHTS

Let me summarize the suggestions I have made in this exploratory chapter. The idea that suspicion is naturally opposed to authority is itself the outcome of a complex historical development of self and polity that traces back to the modern revolutionary liberalizing state. It obscures how suspicion has been historically embedded within authoritative structures. It also obscures the role suspicion today plays in the subtle but powerful ways that society is bound together and to the state. Namely, through dynamics of secrecy and revelation, knowledge and disavowal, and through a space that continually conflates secret truth with latent threat. These are among the significant modalities of authority in contemporary times in our societies, held together, as they are, by their very disaffections. We might therefore say that under the modern state authority and suspicion have undergone a *topological inversion*: whereas before, suspicion was largely situated within authoritative structures, authority today has become situated within suspicious structures and dynamics. Or more precisely, it has *become* those suspicious structures and dynamics. Under such a situation, it is not surprising that modern intelligence apparatuses play such a significant and seemingly growing role in politics and society. We need, as Sennett (1993) would argue, healthier modalities of authority than we have now. Indeed, I would submit that this formation of secrecy and suspicion, which has become essential to the sovereignty of national security and is now almost completely entangled in corporate profit, is— alongside climate change and nuclear conflict—the biggest global danger we face today. It feeds a globally expansive space of violence that undermines any distinctions between war and peace (see Asad 2007).

This may help highlight an important fact about modern racism that we have begun to more fully apprehend. What modern racism has tended to facilitate—whether in the form of historical anti-Semitism, anti-Black racism, or Islamophobia—is an expansion in the covert intelligence-gathering activities and capacities of the state. It therefore serves to sustain and strengthen the modalities of authority I outlined above. For example, recent work has shown that the surveillance by the FBI of African American political activists and writers helped to vastly expand the intelligence capabilities of that agency (see Maxwell 2015). The surveillance also had an impact on African American literary modernism, as the FBI scrutinized African American writings for signs of sedition, and African American writers, aware of that scrutiny, encoded their critical ideas in more-difficult-to-discern forms. And this practice led to redoubled scrutiny by the FBI, which in turn led to even further encoding. Other recent work has traced the intertwined histories of anti-Black racism and the expansion of surveillance technologies in liberal societies and documented their effects on the comportment of Black bodies (see Browne 2015). Similarly, the intensity of state scrutiny of Muslims in liberal states has effected profound transformations on their everyday comportment. Covert agencies form a palpable if hidden presence in the lives of many of them—a subject that requires further systematic study. But, more than that, the state's going after Muslims today has coincided with the most massive expansion of state surveillance and big-data acquisition that has ever been seen, and that has gone far beyond what anyone expected, to encompass potentially all of humanity.

To put the point somewhat abstractly, one could say that "the Muslim" today occupies the figure of the human in a paradoxical oscillation between the universal and the particular. But we might also put it more concretely. Two prominent French scholars of Islam, Olivier Roy and Gilles Kepel, have been involved in a fierce debate about Islamism, one that has wrecked their long-standing friendship and sharply divided French public opinion (see Nossiter 2016). Kepel speaks of the dangers of the *radicalization* of Islam; he sees radicalization as a universal human tendency, but one that becomes particularly virulent when it affects Islam. Roy vehemently rejects the idea. He also sees radicalization as a universal human tendency, but he focuses instead on how it is the particular *Islamization* of radicalism makes it so dangerous. Is the problem, then, the universalization of the particular (Kepel—or was that Roy)? Or the particularization of the universal (Roy—or Kepel)? Although the debate seems astonishingly silly, it simply reiterates in yet another new form an underlying, more long-standing question: whether and how Islam can be compatible with liberalism. But if what I have said here is at all plausible, then this is the wrong question to ask. Instead of continually agonizing over Islam's potential compatibility with or danger to liberalism, we should try to understand that enduring structural space within the modern liberal imagination that conflates secret truth with latent threat, and more importantly, we should consider *how to rid ourselves of it.* For, certainly, other groups will be made to occupy that space, after Muslims.

NOTES

Thanks to Joe Masco, Lisa Wedeen, and Cameron Hu for their comments on earlier drafts of this chapter.

1 It is true that many of the states that target Muslims in this way are neither (truly) liberal nor democratic. Nevertheless, whether through their foundational constitutional documents or international political covenants, nearly all such states espouse a range of recognizable liberal rights and some degree of democracy as part of their fundamental claims to legitimacy. That is why I speak of the liberal social imaginary of the modern state.

2 All of these etymological observations can be found in any online etymological dictionary, of which there are many.

3   For a history of these transformations in judicial decision making, see Whitman (2008).

4   For parts of the story of these transformations, see Whitman (2008); Hutson (2011); Halttunen (1998).

5   A portion of the following discussion on Egypt was published previously; see Agrama 2015. It appears here in revised and expanded form.

6   Her reflections are found in Arendt (2006b), particularly the chapter "The Social Question."

7   See the excellent discussion by political historian and theorist Kirstie McClure (1997).

8   The reasons for that are beyond the scope of this chapter. Among them is the historical legacy and prestige of the military stemming from the Nasserite revolution of 1952, which ended the British occupation, but there is also the fact of military conscription, required of all male citizens. As a result, the military is intimately stitched into Egyptian family life.

9   Not Michael Warner the critical theorist.

10 One example of this is the case of Tarek Mehanna. See Akbar (2013).

11 See, for example, "'The Government Invites You to Be Wary of Those Who Do Not Eat Baguettes,'" BBC News, January 30, 2015, http://www.bbc.com/news/blogs-trending-31047810.

12 "An eight-year-old was interrogated for two hours at a police station for allegedly refusing to respect the mandatory minute of silence and join a 'chain of solidarity' on the playground in support of Charlie Hebdo. He was also alleged to have declared that he was 'on the side of the terrorists' (claims which were strongly denied by the child's parents and lawyer). About 200 incidents of that nature were reported to the Education Ministry. Even when no actual incidents took place, Najat Vallaud-Belkacem, the Education Minister, lamented that 'too much questioning came from pupils,' hinting that it was suspicious for youngsters to discuss critically what had taken place in Paris or to fail to express full solidarity with Charlie Hebdo" (Marliere 2017).

KATHLEEN BELEW

17 FLAME AND STEEL INSIDE THE CAPITOL

When a mob of rioters stormed the Capitol on January 6, 2021, it mobilized at least three conspiratorial worldviews: one about a purportedly stolen election ("Stop the Steal"), one about a ring of pedophiles in public office ("QAnon"), and one about a plot to eradicate the white race (the "Great Replacement"). Significantly, each of these theories can be mapped on to a particular social movement, each overlapping and distinct. The Trump base and Stop the Steal has been well-described; QAnon is so new that we race to understand it. But the third group, the organized white power movement and its fellow travelers on the militant right, came to January 6 with a long history, a clear ideology, decades of radicalization and interconnection, and a central text that describes an attack on the Capitol. Here, we can see clearly the way that conspiracy theory shapes real-world violence—and we can see the limitations of other kinds of conspiracy (such as prosecutions for seditious conspiracy) in curbing its lethal impact.

In 1983, the white power movement—a tightly bound social network of Klan members, neo-Nazis, radical tax resisters, proponents of white supremacist theologies, and others—declared war on the federal government and racial enemies. These activists had united a few years earlier around a common narrative of the Vietnam War, a narrative that foregrounded betrayal by the government, politicians, civilians, and the media. They saw the government as part of a cabal of malevolent internationalist forces controlled by Jews. They called this conspiracy the Zionist Occupational Government (ZOG) and, later, the New World Order. Activists believed it included government officials (the higher up, the more corrupt), bankers, the United Nations, movie and television producers, the media, and more. The movement adherents believed that these forces planned to eradicate the white race. Indeed, they described the social issues important to them—such as opposing abortion, immigration, LGBT rights, integration, and interracial marriage—as directly related to the specter of racial extinction. This rhetoric intertwined with an intensifying apocalyptic belief that moved the white power movement to declare war (Belew 2018). In other words, white power activists used conspiracy theories (about the fundamental corruption of the government) to motivate and carry out a real-life criminal conspiracy against it.

The prominence of the ZOG/New World Order conspiracy theory in the white power movement directs our attention to *The Turner Diaries*, a utopian novel that became both a manual of operations for the movement and a touchstone for the cultural frame that motivated its activists. It worked to indoctrinate believers in the threats to their racial future. It is also important to scholars because it answers a fundamental and, on its face, baffling question: How could the white power movement hope to succeed in race war when facing the hypermilitarized United States, the world power and superstate of the late twentieth century? In other words, How could they believe that they might prevail? "It seems just unreal," as the narrator of the book says, "like a gnat planning to assassinate an elephant" (Macdonald 1978, 135). Yet *The Turner Diaries* provided what white power activists would see as a feasible plan for this victory.

The Turner Diaries first appeared in 1974, serialized in the pages of *Attack!*, a periodical published by the neo-Nazi group National Alliance. In 1978, National Alliance leader William Pierce published *The Turner Diaries* in paperback, using the pseudonym Andrew Macdonald.[1] In the following years, the book would leave an indelible impression: National Alliance claimed that the book had sold some 500,000 copies by 1994. It has turned up in bookstores frequented by mercenary soldiers in South Africa, as the alias of key movement activists, in framing rhetoric across movement publications, and it is distributed free to members of white power groups from Washington State to the Carolinas. Violent activists arrested while carrying *The Turner Diaries* or excerpts from the book have ranged from members of the white terrorist group the Order to Oklahoma City bomber Timothy McVeigh. Indeed, members of the Order kept a stack of *The Turner Diaries*—twenty or thirty copies—in the bunkhouse at their training facility, where they prepared for assassinations, armed robberies, and infrastructure attacks meant to provoke race war. And McVeigh also sold the book when he traveled the gun-show circuit under an alias.

The movement ignited by *The Turner Diaries* was remarkably diverse in every way but race. However, although it spanned regions, gender, class, wealth, and social status, the white power movement was nevertheless a fringe phenomenon. One can imagine its membership through concentric circles: an inner ring included some 25,000 fully dedicated members. A second ring of those who attended rallies and bought literature numbered some 125,000 to 150,000. Beyond that were people who did not themselves buy neo-Nazi and Klan newspapers but who read them—another 450,000 (Belew 2018, 4). Although one might imagine further circles of people who would not read a white power publication but might agree with some of the movement's ideas, the movement was always small, its influence depending on appeals to the mainstream, diffusion into political discourse, and radical guerrilla action. As I have argued elsewhere, the white power movement operated in all three registers (Belew 2018). This chapter explores the final register, the one that white power activists prioritized from the declaration of war in 1983 to the 1995 bombing of the Alfred P. Murrah Federal Building in Oklahoma City. In this period, activists in the movement used the conspiratorial worldview of corrupt government authority and strategies of *The Turner Diaries*, together with the paramilitary strategies, matériel, and the legacy of violence from the Vietnam War to foment race war.

Real-world applications of strategies from *The Turner Diaries* include adopting a cell-style structure for organizing movement violence (see Belew 2018, 3; Amoss 1962; Beam 1989, 3, 47–63; Beam 1992a, 1992b), using counterfeiting as a strategy to undermine public confidence in US currency,[2] attempting to "rescue" activists from prisons,[3] a plot to blow up the FBI's national fingerprint center (Belew 2018, 232; Ridgeway 1997), and the Oklahoma City bombing itself (Belew 2018, 220–21). That act killed 168 people, including 19 children. Along the way, between the 1983 declaration of war and 1995, movement activists carried out armed robberies and assassinations of opponents and their fellow members (103–34). They obtained tons of military weapons and matériel, some stolen from armories and military posts (135–55), and they carried out paramilitary training.[4] They attacked gas lines and targeted other infrastructure like dams, and they plotted to poison the water supply of at least one major city with cyanide.[5]

The Turner Diaries shows that such acts, up to and including the Oklahoma City bombing—although it was the largest deliberate mass casualty on American soil between the bombing of Pearl Harbor and the terror attacks of September 11, 2001—were not meant to be endpoints in and of themselves. Rather, they were part of a more complex strategy, one that mirrors the events laid out in *The Turner Diaries*, in which violent action was designed to awaken the greater white populace of the United States to a state of emergency and to the presence of corrupt, conspiratorial forces in and beyond the government that threatened their lives and the future of their race. Even mass attacks with high death tolls were meant to foment further violence. They were meant to begin a long and brutal march to a white world.

Understanding the import of *The Turner Diaries* requires that one pay close attention to conspiracy theories' shadowy and imaginative narratives about corrupt power. It also requires that one pay close attention to real-life conspiracy, the grouping together of activists to effect change. Significantly, white power activists in both *The Turner Diaries* and the real-life white power movement that adopted its strategies used a *conspiracy theory* (the myth of Jewish and elite international control of government and economic institutions with the long-term goal of destroying the white race) to foment and to occlude an actual *conspiracy* (the banding together of white power activists to steal military weapons, train as paramilitary soldiers, pursue a strategy of cell-style terrorism, and overthrow the government).

That such a criminal conspiracy succeeded only in fiction pales in significance to the failure of a third category of conspiracy—*seditious conspiracy*, the legal charge leveled against real-life white power activists in a federal courtroom. The paucity of convictions of actors in this openly revolutionary campaign reveals that seditious conspiracy failed, as a category, to contain either the real-life criminal conspiracy or the antigovernment conspiracy theories of the white power movement—it failed imaginatively and also in real life and action.

The Turner Diaries

The book is presented as the diary of one white power activist, Earl Turner, from his radical awakening in the 1980s to his death in a suicide bombing for the movement. It includes an epilogue about what happens after his suicide, describing the success of the revolution and the establishment of an all-white world. The diary, in this context, is presented as an artifact and as the retrospective account of a successful revolution. Parenthetical insertions appear throughout the text to explain things that do not exist in the postrevolutionary world, including feminism, Black slang, and Black culture.

In the diary, Turner describes the state of a world as ruined by government conspiracy and corruption, where white people are threatened with property seizure—particularly of weapons—interracial rape, and the constant possibility of violence. All this is controlled by the System, a corrupt government that conspires with other malevolent forces. In this world, the Cohen Act, presumably named for a Jewish political elite, has outlawed private gun ownership and mandated state raids and seizures of firearms (Macdonald 1978, 1). The System is in the process of implementing an internal passport system run by computers and enforced by police (24, 33). Rape can be prosecuted only as a "non-sexual assault" because to do otherwise would imply a difference between the sexes (57). Jews have taken over Christian churches (64). Human Relations Councils have become police forces, outfitted with "deputized Black goon squads" (77). Jews run a sexual slave trade of white girls (84). White Americans who exhibit racism can be charged with the International Genocide Convention and tortured by Israeli Military Intelligence (91). The integrated Army is inept (40). Jewish union leaders exploit and run cities; in the novel, Turner visits the penthouse apartment of one such man, ostentatious in its luxury and replete with pornographic images of the union leader engaged in interracial sex and pedophilia (183). "We are already slaves," Turner writes. "We have allowed a diabolically clever, alien minority to put chains on our souls and our minds" (33). Each component of this System, he explains, was implemented incrementally, so that people would not rise up and fight back. Furthermore, Turner believes that the System is dedicated to the very purposeful eradication of whiteness: "The Enemy we are fighting fully intends to destroy the racial basis of our existence" (34).

The book's appeal lay precisely in the construction of the System as a reflection of other, more mainstream conspiracy theories that were popular in the historic moment of the novel's release. The fear of state seizure of firearms would become an entrenched issue on the right, gaining prominence through the 1980s and 1990s.[6] The idea of interracial sex as a threat underlay mainstream American ideologies across the nation (see, e.g., Pascoe 2009; McRae 2018; Solinger 2007). Anti-Semitism has long employed conspiracy theory to encourage hatred. The idea of abandoning all gender difference as a side effect of women's liberation appeared in more mainstream debates over the Equal Rights Amendment. Concerns over documentation and state surveillance would animate libertarians, survivalists, and a host of others who chose to sever ties with the state and live off the grid (Barkun 2013). The conspiracy theory of white slavery harkened back to the late nineteenth century. The idea of a police state that would enforce multiculturalism, the fear of the United Nations and of other internationalist forces, and the connection of both of these things with concerns about miscegenation were far from fringe ideologies and have appeared throughout mainstream political debates through the twentieth century (McRae 2018; Pascoe 2009). However, in *The Turner Diaries*, the collection of these fears into an ominous whole worked to weaponize these anxieties.

Into this terrain enters Turner, an engineer with weapons expertise. He rises through the ranks of the white activist resistance, "the Organization," and after blowing up the FBI fingerprint bank and headquarters, he is ultimately selected to join "the Order." This elite squadron works in highly disciplined cells to overthrow the System. Its members pledge to die before revealing the group or being arrested. To join, Turner has to pass both the Test of the Word (showing his subscription to the Order's ideology) and the Test of the Deed (carrying out a violent action directed by the group).

Turner engages in robberies, a brutal bombing of the FBI's database and fingerprint banks, and fragmentation grenade attacks on the *Washington Post* editorial offices and staff.

Then, although Turner is not directly involved in it, he describes an attack on the Capitol (Macdonald 1978, 60–62). In the novel, Capitol Hill is surrounded with the full power of the US military—thousands of soldiers, tanks, and armored vehicles. He describes barbed wire and helicopters whirring above. And then, as he watches, "as the TV cameras were preparing to switch from the crowded scene outside the Capitol to the speaker's podium in the House chamber, where the President would be speaking, a mortar round—although no one realized that's what it was—exploded about 200 yards northwest of the building" (Macdonald 1978, 60–62). The Order is firing from a wooded area they scouted ahead of time, and when they refine the targeting of the mortars, they are able to hit the Capitol itself. As Turner watches the attack, he is jubilant:

> We saw beautiful blossoms of flame and steel sprouting everywhere, dancing across the asphalt, thundering in the midst of splintered masonry and burning vehicles, erupting now inside and

now outside the Capitol, wreaking their bloody toll in the ranks of tyranny and treason. . . . It was the most magnificent spectacle I have ever seen. What an impression it must have made on the general public watching it on TV! (82)

But when Turner is arrested, he betrays the Order when he fails to kill himself before he is tortured for information. Instead, he is imprisoned until the Order breaks him out in a large-scale jailbreak of Organization activists from Fort Belvoir (95). The group tells Turner he will eventually be sent on a suicide mission to atone for his failure.

The novel outlines what many real-world white power activists would see as a plausible path from cell-style guerrilla warfare to the revolution's success. Immediately after the jailbreak, Turner writes, "We stopped wasting our resources in small-scale terror attacks and shifted to large-scale attacks on carefully selected economic targets: power stations, fuel depots, transportation facilities, food sources, key industrial plants. We do not expect to bring down the already creaky American economic structure immediately, but we do expect to cause a number of localized and temporary breakdowns, which will gradually have a cumulative effect on the whole public" (102). In other words, the focus on infrastructure targets, together with counterfeiting, was meant to cause larger breakdowns both in the operations of the System and in the broader public's trust in its governance (104). "Essentially, what we are doing with our program of strategic sabotage is hastening along somewhat the natural decay of America. We are chipping away at the termite-eaten timbers of the economy, so that the whole structure will collapse a few years sooner—and more catastrophically—than without our efforts" (111).

In the novel, this project is accomplished only through horrific violence. Turner's cell targets a nuclear power plant in Evanston, Illinois, one that is impervious to mortar attack but that he believes could be contaminated by causing a nuclear accident. He notes that this strategy would also raise a "superstitious" fear of nuclear contamination. As he explained, "It will horrify many people—and it will knock more of them off the fence" (117). Meanwhile, other Order members destroy the Israeli embassy with mortars, steal and stockpile military weapons and matériel, and destroy the Dallas central telephone exchange with a napalm attack (118, 122–23, 125–27).

The Order's guerrilla campaign crests on July 4 with a coordinated assault on six hundred "military and civilian targets" in and around Los

Angeles. They obliterate the water supply, electrical power, airports, gas storage, pipelines, dams, police stations, and freeway interchanges (133–38, 146). They spur a simultaneous military coup, one that inspires a Black uprising, which, in turn, provokes an even more violent white backlash (139–41). By July 10 they have seized all military bases and airfields in the area, including the nuclear weapons at Vandenberg Air Force Base (146). Although the assault continues in other places—they hit the Evanston power plant and seize the rest of coastal California—these nuclear weapons are key to the plan coming to fruition. By threatening nuclear attacks on eastern US cities and Tel Aviv, the Order stops the System from immediately retaliating against the "California liberated zone" (176).

This secured and independent white homeland is not the end goal, either, not even after the Order drives all people of color east to foment social breakdown where the System still holds power, and not even after the Day of the Rope: the execution by shooting or hanging of all mixed-race people, Jews, race traitors, professors, school officials, civic leaders, bureaucrats, and teachers (149, 153, 155, 161–62). The Order soon uses its California enclave to launch nuclear attacks. It kills 60,000 in Miami and more in Charleston, South Carolina (180). The Order threatens to continue attacks on cities until the System meets its demands—including giving them California, broadcasting the news of what has happened there, and getting Jews out of Palestine—but it also declares, "In any event, we intend to liberate, first, the entire United States and then the remainder of this planet" (180–81).

Tens of millions die in the ensuing nuclear war. When the System threatens to bomb California, the Order preempts the strike by bombing Israel and the Soviet Union, forcing the System to follow the assault with a decisive strike to eliminate the possibility of Soviet counterattack. The counterstrike the Soviets manage, though diminished, destroys Baltimore, Detroit, and Los Angeles (185–91). The Order also bombs New York City. At the end of this grim section, the Order has hobbled the System, decimated the Soviet Union's nuclear arsenal and military capacity, and destroyed "two of the world Jewry's principal nerve centers" in Israel and New York (191). Anti-Jewish riots spontaneously break out across the rest of the white world (198). Turner embarks on his long-awaited suicide mission, flying a nuclear megabomb into the Pentagon.

In the epilogue, we learn of Turner's success, followed by the Order's entrenchment in California and guerrilla attacks on the eastern United States. This provokes famine, and the Order requires white refugees to kill people of color or otherwise prove their genetic superiority to receive food. After five years of war, the Order seizes the United States following the defection of white generals. This begins the "New Era," after which it takes the Order just eleven months to seize power in the rest of the world. In four more years, they have killed all nonwhite people in the world using nuclear, chemical, and biological weapons (198–210). Theirs is not a peaceful ethnic cleansing, nor the mere securing of a white homeland, nor a bastion of resistance. It is a full-scale assault on the world.

MAKING MCVEIGH

The workings of conspiracy theory in the novel are both anticipated and contradictory. While the System is exactly what one might expect—and could easily be swapped with similar structures ranging from those appearing in *The Protocols of the Elders of Zion* to ZOG to the Deep State—the novel's real energy is devoted to laying out the very detailed criminal conspiracy of the members of the Order to overthrow the US government as well as the revolutionaries' own disavowals that they are part of any seditious conspiracy. In the book, the Order really is a secret organization with grand ambitions, wide-reaching membership, a plan of action, and nefarious ambitions both for its enemies and its future subjects, many of whom, as Turner frequently notes, will have to give up considerable rights and freedoms—or their lives—in the future world seized and ruled by the white power guerrillas.

Nevertheless, when the word "conspiracy" appears in the novel, it is in disavowal. When the *Washington Post*, a pawn of the System, calls the startling number of people who have kept their guns in flagrant violation of the Cohen Act a fascist conspiracy, Turner sees it as a failed attempt at System propaganda: "Not even the brainwashed American public could fully accept the idea that nearly a million of their fellow citizens had been engaged in a secret, armed conspiracy" (Macdonald 1978, 4). When conservatives don't fall in line, Turner notes that it's because of a "conspiracy theory" that "the Organization is actually in the pay of the System" (63). In other words, the Order is held up against a multitude of other things to assure a reader that it is *not* a conspiracy, even as its conspiratorial criminal activities unfold.

The novel's disavowal matched the real-world strategy of Leaderless Resistance, or cell-style organizing in the *Turner Diaries* mode. Leaderless

Resistance was initially implemented to foil the many undercover government informants who had become troublesome to Klansmen organizing against the Civil Rights Movement. It also worked to stymie prosecution and, perhaps more profoundly, to obfuscate its own revolutionary ambitions and therefore escape public backlash. Indeed, although the key events of the white power movement appeared on the front pages of major newspapers, on morning newsmagazine shows, and even on the late-night comedy hit *Saturday Night Live*, a public understanding of white power activism did not match its growing sophistication and dangerous intent.

In 1988, a federal court in Fort Smith, Arkansas, acquitted thirteen white power leaders and activists of charges including seditious conspiracy. The charge of seditious conspiracy was rare, having been used only occasionally through the twentieth century, most notably against Puerto Rican nationalists in 1936 and 1980. Jurors in the Fort Smith case heard ample evidence about the white power movement's attempts at revolution, including a plot to poison the water supply of a major city (Belew 2018, 140, 179; Coates 1997; "Leader Says" 1988, 7); the assassinations of a talk radio personality, fellow group members, and state troopers; and endless paramilitary training, parading, and harassment of various enemies. Jurors saw two huge hampers of the movement's military-grade weapons pushed through the courtroom.[7] Witnesses described how separatist compounds manufactured their own Claymore-style land mines and trained in urban warfare (Belew 2018, 156–86).

My book *Bring the War Home: The White Power Movement and Paramilitary America* exposes the flawed trial as an object lesson in the failures of both the US legal system and the public to reckon with the organized white power movement (Belew 2018). Elements that cast doubt on the court's impartiality and efficacy include romantic relationships between jurors and defendants; jurors who believed the Bible prohibited race-mixing; and the exclusion of large amounts of significant evidence because of chain-of-command violations. However, several of the defendants had declared their own plans for seditious conspiracy over and over. And many of the defendants, including members of the Order, star witnesses, and defendants, had read, distributed, and acted out *The Turner Diaries*. Their acquittal brings to mind Turner's glee over the failure of an Israeli torturer to get anything out of him: "He . . . found out nothing about the Order or about our philosophy or long-range goals, which knowledge might have helped the System understand our strategy" (Macdonald 1978,

93). In other words, over and over, when the state confronted the white power movement, the movement used deliberate disavowal to keep jurors and the public from understanding its revolutionary strategy.

The acquittals at Fort Smith, furthermore, led this failure of "knowledge" to be enshrined in policy. The Fort Smith trial represented an embarrassment for the federal government. The Department of Justice, FBI, ATF, and US Marshals had put enormous resources into the trial, including the fruits of years of undercover work, sting operations, plea bargains, and testimony. When none of this sufficed to prove seditious conspiracy, the FBI decided to stop prosecuting future actions undertaken as part of a social movement. Instead, they would prosecute only crimes carried out by individuals. Indeed, the FBI institutionalized a policy to pursue only individual actors in white power violence, with, according to FBI internal documents, "no attempts to tie individual crimes to a broader movement" (as quoted in Belew 2018, 211; Gumbel and Charles 2012, 262).

This decision shaped the parameters of the Oklahoma City bombing investigation, enshrining the act in popular memory as the work of one or a few men, or as an example of lone wolf violence. In neither the investigation nor the prosecution was the idea of a white power movement taken seriously. When commentators attempted to discuss the movement that clearly motivated McVeigh, it was often dismissed as conspiracy theory. However, McVeigh's actions before the bombing show that he was ideologically motivated and deeply connected with the white power movement in personal relationships and in strategy. The public-sphere disavowal of all white power ideology as conspiracy theory worked to obfuscate the real, and still unchecked, seditious conspiracy of the fringe.

The Turner Diaries gave a very specific blueprint for McVeigh's bombing in Oklahoma City. It offered the example of Turner's attack on the FBI fingerprint center using a truck bomb with around 5,000 pounds of ammonium nitrate fertilizer. In Turner's fictive bomb and McVeigh's real one, the bomber drills holes so that he can light the fuse from the cab of the truck. Each plans to drive the truck into the freight area, set the fuse, and walk away. Each does this with full awareness that his action will hurt or kill the people who work in the building. In the novel, the bomb detonates at 9:15 a.m., catching people at the beginning of their workday. McVeigh's bomb went off at 9:02 a.m.

In the novel, Turner worries about one pretty twenty-year-old white girl trapped under a steel door in the detritus of the explosion:

When I stooped to stop the girl's bleeding, I became aware for the first time of the moans and screams of dozens of other injured persons in the courtyard. Not twenty feet away another woman lay motionless, her face covered with blood and a gaping wound in the side of her head—a horrible sight which I can still see vividly every time I close my eyes. . . . All day yesterday and most of today we watched the TV coverage of rescue crews bringing the dead and injured out of the building. It is a heavy burden of responsibility for us to bear. . . . But there is no way we can destroy the System without hurting many thousands of innocent people—no way. It is a cancer too deeply rooted in our flesh. And if we don't destroy the System before it destroys us—if we don't cut this cancer out of our living flesh—the whole race will die. (Macdonald 1978, 35–42)

Even as Turner stops to help the iconic injured white woman, he insists that innocent civilians—including white women and children—must die for the good of the white race. So, too, did McVeigh refer to civilians as collateral damage in his war on the state (J. Thomas 2001; Gumbel and Charles 2012, 337; Michel and Herbeck 2002, 393).

One of several white power actors and groups McVeigh contacted just before the bombing was the National Alliance, helmed by *The Turner Diaries*' author William Pierce. Although Pierce would disavow any direct connection with McVeigh, the connection was explicit enough in his validation of the bombing itself: "If one is waging a war against the government, civilians are going to be killed," Pierce told an interviewer. "But you have to look at the bigger picture. Let's say you are trying to save our whole race, as Earl Turner was in *The Turner Diaries*. You know that there are necessarily going to be casualties in the process of doing that, including a lot of innocent people who didn't want to get involved on either side of the conflict. Under a circumstance like that, if it were part of a war, then a bombing of the Oklahoma City sort is morally justified" (Griffin 2001, 171–72).

Pierce then added a statement that might have sounded critical of the bombing, in absence of knowledge of the movement and its key text:

But if you are going to engage in a war you have to meet certain requirements. One of them is you have to have a plausible strategy, a plan that can be reasonably argued will get you what you want to achieve. If McVeigh was just throwing a single punch to send a message, then its moral justification is debatable. You might well say that this was an overly expensive message in any case. . . . But the fact of the matter is that we are engaged in a war for the survival of our people. In a war, people jump the gun, it's not unusual. Often a war is preceded by border incidents, and something like Oklahoma City could be a border incident. I feel as sorry as anyone else if a little white kid gets killed in one of these things. For that matter, I feel bad if a white kid gets killed in an automobile accident. But I don't advocate that we ban automobiles because people get killed in them . . . in the same way, I am not in favor of calling off a war because some border incidents or battles take innocent lives. Actually, the sooner the war to save our people takes place the better, because even more innocent lives will be lost if we wait. The sooner such a war, the cleaner it will be. It's going to be a mess later on. (Griffin 2001, 171–72)

"Border incident" or not, McVeigh's action was planned with precisely the "plausible strategy" that Pierce himself outlined in *The Turner Diaries*. Evidence of this comes from McVeigh himself. He anticipated being arrested, but in his car at the time of his arrest was a thick packet of extremist literature, including a quote from *The Turner Diaries*: "More important, though, is what we taught the politicians and the bureaucrats. They learned this afternoon that not one of them is beyond our reach. They can huddle behind barbed wire and tanks in the city, and they can hide behind the concrete walls of their country estates, but we can still find them and kill them" (Macdonald 1978, 83).

Although McVeigh would go to his execution claiming to have acted alone, his role in the white power movement and as its soldier could not be more clear. McVeigh had a copy of *The Turner Diaries* and showed it to his fellow soldiers while in the US Army. Later, under the alias Tim Tuttle, McVeigh traveled the gun-show circuit, reading, selling, and distributing *The Turner Diaries* while dressed in uniform or in camouflage fatigues. He carried a copy in his back pocket. Indeed, the movement had scripted the bombing and not only through *The Turner Diaries*: its members had cased the Murrah Building in 1983 and had kept it in their sights ever since. McVeigh lived with one activist who could draw a diagram of the building from memory. He also communicated or attempted to communicate with scores of white power groups and activists (Belew 2018, 209–34).

Dismissing such connections as "conspiracy theory"—rather than as social geography, ideology, and membership in a social movement—worked to utterly destroy the possibility for public reckoning with white power violence. Indeed, the disavowal of the actual criminal and seditious conspiracy demonstrated by the archive of the words and deeds of these activists worked to feed the white power movement. The failure to name and understand white power as an ideology, rather than as a "conspiracy theory" meant that its own conspiracy theory about government corruption, racial extinction, and imminent threats to white people could move from the fringe to the mainstream.

STORMING THE CAPITOL

Resonances of *The Turner Diaries* appeared at every turn on January 6, 2021. It is impossible, from the vantage point of a historian looking at such recent events, to know how many are coincidental and how many are purposeful, particularly because symbols have divergent ideological meaning to the three different groups that constituted the mob. But to white power activists, these things could not have gone unnoticed.

Someone constructed a gallows outside the Capitol on January 6, where people took selfies; others called for the hanging of politicians. Turner, after the novel's attack on the Capitol, wrote that the politicians and leaders "are all inevitably headed for the gallows" (Macdonald 1978, 83). "The gallows" also signifies the Day of the Rope and the ritualistic hanging of race traitors, politicians, communists, and journalists—hence the scrawled "Murder the Media" on January 6.

Even the action of January 6 unfolded with the same timing and on the same set as the attack in the novel, at the moment when cameras moved between the House Chamber and the building exterior (although reversed). In both actions, the point was not mass casualties (even in a movement that elsewhere sought out high body counts, both in life and in fiction). The point was the movement's ability to strike at the heart of power. As Turner describes:

> Despite all the noise and smoke and wreckage caused by our attack on the Capitol, only 61 persons were killed, we learned from later news reports. Among these are two Congressmen, one subcabinet official, and four or five senior Congressional staffers. But the real value of all our attacks today lies in the psychological impact, not in the immediate casualties. For one thing, our efforts against the System gained immeasurably in credibility. More important,

though, is what we taught the politicians and the bureaucrats. They learned this afternoon that not one of them is beyond our reach. They can huddle behind barbed wire and tanks in the city, or they can hide behind the concrete walls and alarm systems of their country estates, but we can still find them and kill them. All the armed guards and bulletproof limousines in America cannot guarantee their safety. That is a lesson they will not forget. (Macdonald 1978, 83)

Finally, both in the novel and on January 6, the Capitol attack functions primarily as a recruitment mechanism.

In the immediate aftermath of the January 6 insurrection, white power and militant right activists heightened efforts to recruit from other conspiratorial social movements that had participated as well as from a broad and interconnected network of potential recruits available to them through social media. Although it is too soon to tell how effective these efforts were and how much the movement might have grown, its reach into mainstream politics is beyond dispute. Individuals sitting at every level of government now openly proclaim their adherence to QAnon and Trumpist conspiracy theories, and at least twenty-eight have documented connections with the Oath Keepers, an unregulated private army on the militant right. When I presented the first draft of this chapter, we could think about conspiracies as largely fringe phenomena, but this has been decidedly disproven: conspiracy theory, we must know by now, cannot be allowed to stand as an endpoint of engagement or as a simple disavowal of ideology and belief. To understand the meaning of this kind of violence, and to prepare to stop future attacks, is to excavate conspiracy theory as a live current in our body politic.

NOTES

The author wishes to thank Joe Masco, Lisa Wedeen, and the participants in the 3CT Conspiracy/Theory conference for their generosity in discussing these ideas.

1   *The Turner Diaries*, as first printed as a serial in the National Alliance's periodical, *Attack!*, 1974–1976, Box 31, Folder 9, Keith Stimely Collection, University of Oregon, Eugene; Macdonald 1978.
2   See Belew (2018, 116, 122); Coates (1997, 58, 63, 73); "Jury Told of Plan" (1987, 31); "The Order's Command Structure" (1985); Testimony of Denver

Parmenter, *United States of America v. Miles et al.*, vol. 1, no. 87-20008 (W. D. Ark, 1988), F-7424, February 29, 1988, Testimonies-2, Center for Research Libraries, Chicago; "Separatists Launch New Nation" (1986, 1); Snell (1984–1985, 1); Flynn and Gerhardt (1989, 130, 134).

3   Belew (2018, 116, 172); Testimony of Randall Rader, November 1, 1985, *United States of America v. Bruce Carroll Pierce et al.*, CR-85-0001M (W. D. Wash, 1985), Box 6, at 6840, Accession 21-95-0078, Location 823306, Seattle; Flynn and Gerhardt (1989, 98); Testimony of Denver Parmenter; Coates and Franklin (1987); *United States of America v. Miles et al.* Affidavit, Farris L. Genide, Special Agent, FBI, U.S. District Court Eastern District of Michigan Southern Division, No. 86-0343, 69–70, Elinor Langer Collection, University of Oregon Libraries, Special Collections and Archives, Eugene.

4   See, for instance, Belew (2018, 33–54); "Paramilitary Training" (1982, 1); "Judge Bars Ku Klux Klan" (1982); *Vietnamese Fishermen's Association, et al., v. The Knights of the Ku Klux Klan, et al.*, no. H-81-895, 518 F. Supp. 198 (1982); 34 Fed. R. Serv. 2d (Callaghan) 875, June 3, 1982, Southern Poverty Law Center; Baker (1990); "KKK Leader Beam" (1981, B8, 13).

5   Belew (2018, 40, 171, 172, 179); Coates (1997, 153); Chriss (1988a); Testimony of James Ellison, Jury Trial, February 16–April 7, 1987, *United States v. Richard Girnt Butler et al.*, 87-2008, Council for Research Libraries, Chicago, IL; "Minister Denies Tie" (1995); Zeskind (2009, 82–83); *United States of America v. Miles et al.*; Coates and Franklin (1987); Flynn and Gerhardt (1989, 32–34); Coates (1988); "Leader Says" (1988); Hall (1986); Kifner (1995, 1).

6   On state seizure of firearms on the right, see, for instance, Gibson (1994); Faludi (1999); Stock (1996).

7   See Belew (2018, 180); Chriss (1988c); Exhibit List, *United States of America v. Miles et al.*, Box 16-2; Zeskind (2009, 61–63); Testimony of Denver Parmenter, February 29, 1988, "Increased Militancy of Supremacists Predicted"; Mathiason (1985, 6); Chriss (1988b); "Jury Told of Plan" (1987, 31); "White Supremacy Groups" (1985, 19); Coates (1997, 94); Intelligence Project Database, Southern Poverty Law Center; Morlin (1995, A1); Whiteley (1996, 1B); Flynn and Gerhardt (1989, 68, 142–44); L. J. Davis (1986, 53); Gerhardt, Accola, and Flynn (1985, 6); Opening statement of Bob Ward, September 12, 1985, *United States of America v. Bruce Carroll Pierce et al.*, Box 3, at 51; Testimony of Louis Beam, *United States of America v. Miles et al.*, November 17, 1988, Box 16, Folder 2; Testimony of Jed Martin Bridley, December 2, 1985, *United States of America v. Bruce Carroll Pierce et al.*, Box 6, at 9935–9945.

JOSEPH MASCO AND LISA WEDEEN

EPILOGUE

Conspiracy/Theory has shown from a comparative regional and historical perspective that conspiratorial reason is both an ancient practice and an ongoing one that takes on many competing forms. Recognizing the range of conspiratorial thought and action in any era beckons us to attend to epistemological claims and counterclaims with an attunement to both the messiness and the importance of judgment and discernment. To be conspiratorial is at root an attempt to breathe with others and to express a narrative interpretation of what is or ought to be. But within any conspiratorial project, the power of fiction, fantasy, intuition, and desire in social life also becomes properly political, a contested—frequently fraught and militarized but also imaginative and hopeful—domain that conditions meaningful understandings of the past, present, and future. This is to say that conspiratorial reason, along with theory itself, is a basic mechanism of world-making, a means of articulating the structures of social life, of attempting to identify unjust conditions, and crucially, of opening a space to show that the world could always be made otherwise. Peace, social justice, and environmental activists work conspiratorially to articulate a nonviolent world and to identify those institutions, policies, and practices that inform violent conditions (whether in the form of what Rob Nixon [2011] has called slow violence—i.e., poverty, climate disruption, and industrial aftermaths—or in the immediate forms of war, boom and bust capitalism, and police brutality). Conspiratorial narratives can also be used for authoritarian purposes, to counter a factual accounting of social life; to disrupt and polarize; to deceive, exploit, and agitate. Attending to the multiplicity of conspiratorial forms and tactics is one key contribution of this book. Another is to take seriously the interpretive demands put on ordinary individuals who are compelled to source harms in a twenty-first-century global order structured by multiple covert military state and corporate projects, each operating in the context of a planetary-scale climate destabilization produced by petrochemical emissions—and all this in the midst of an accelerating revolution in technologies that provide individuals with hugely powerful information warfare, psyops, and misinformation capacities. This is to say that it is vital to understand the power of narrative—of organizing fictions (see Shulman, this volume) and conspiratorial recruitments—as a complex mode of worlding, one with potentially life-or-death consequences.

Take for example the multiple conspiratorial vectors that informed the deadly January 6, 2021, insurrection in Washington, DC, involving a riot and raid on the US Capitol to prevent the certification of the 2020 presidential election.[1] An outgrowth of the Trump campaign committee's "stop the steal" strategy of contesting the authority of the 2020 election (an effort both to keep Trump in power and to delegitimize the new administration), it was an unprecedented attempt to destabilize democratic order in the United States through lies, a multifaceted conspiracy, and violence. Using the authoritarian tactic of pushing a counternarrative to observable reality, the Trump team produced a variety of unsupported claims about the election and proliferated accusations of fraud and corruption. Without offering any evidence, Trump's lawyers—Rudy Giuliani and Sidney Powell—claimed that the Dominion voting machine technology was designed by Hugo Chavez to steal elections in Venezuela and was now controlled by Hillary Clinton and George Soros. Powell also claimed there was a hidden national server that allowed all electronic votes in the United States to be manipulated after the proper vote, while Giuliani claimed there were suitcases of votes arriving and disappearing on Election Day in key voting districts. Not to be outdone, Michael Flynn, a disgraced general and former Trump National Security Adviser with expertise in US military information warfare, stated that China had manipulated the vote using satellite control of (Wi-Fi-enabled) NEST thermostats; and later he claimed that COVID-19 was created by global elites (such as George Soros, Bill Gates, and the World Health Organization) in order to defeat Trump. Flynn advised Trump to use the military to take over voting machines and to correct the election via a coup d'état. Meanwhile, John Eastman, another Trump lawyer, offered a novel legal proposition, stating that the vice president's certification of the Electoral College results was not ceremonial but absolute—ultimately leading to death threats against Vice President Pence for not attempting to decertify the election. In each of these cases, fabrication and assertion were the raw tools of information warfare, a political tactic not a theory, one that fell apart quickly on review. For example, more than sixty formal legal claims of election fraud failed in US courts, with investigators finding no substantive evidence of misconduct. But the informational warfare tactic of repetition and saturation of a media space with spurious claims was still powerful in recruiting individuals to the riot on January 6th.

Although these assertions were baseless, they nonetheless demonstrated a powerful authoritarian commitment to not being constrained by factual evidence, combined with concerted efforts to control both public perception and the mechanisms of governmental power. Much of the Trump team's attention was focused on state election officials, identifying the key players in the election process who might be corralled into influencing the 2020 election, or who might be useful in the future. In this way, the false claim of a stolen election will have ongoing consequences, allowing those in the minority to challenge the integrity of the democratic process and to demonize their political opposition. Thus, the combined informational warfare hacks of individual attention achieved through siloed media circuits on Facebook, Twitter, and YouTube were matched by a larger political strategy of hacking the mechanisms of governmental order in support of Trump by those also grifting mightily on the side. Trump raised hundreds of millions to "stop the steal" and "save the country." Steve Bannon created the top-ten ranked *War Room* podcast to sell the idea of a stolen election, to flood the media space with misinformation, and to issue calls for supporters to take over the election process at the local level to control outcomes—all while raising big money. In doing so, he was following Alex Jones, whose online *InfoWars* show attributed the 2020 election to a conspiracy of globalists against Trump, and who called for violent revolution at the January 6th rally and then afterward attributed all violence to false flag operations (by Antifa or maybe the FBI; see Masco, this volume), all while raking in social media dollars and hawking male potency supplements. Linking many of these calls is the overt promise of a restored white masculine social hegemony to be euphorically achieved via what Richard Slotkin (1998, 12) calls a "regeneration through violence." And here, we should not forget Roger Stone, who has championed a political strategy of lying and public deception, who not only coined the "stop the steal" concept for the 2016 election (queued up on the assumption that Trump would lose that election) but also worked with militia and white supremacy groups to support the raid on Congress. The Oath Keepers and Proud Boys were operating on the script provided by *The Turner Diaries* (see Belew, this volume), seeing January 6th as the long-awaited opportunity to overthrow the federal government and establish a white nation. Others in attendance on January 6 were motivated by the QAnon movement and its assemblage of long-standing racist and anti-Semitic claims about a hidden government of pedophiles (see Hillis, this volume) revealed by an anonymous military intelligent expert, "Q" (who might just be Michael Flynn), who offered online hints presaging Trump's war with the deep state.

Thus, the January 6 riot brought together a vast range of aggrieved interests and conspiratorial ideas, from those seeking to test the weakness of the democratic system in favor of authoritarianism, to those enacting a gamers vision of deciphering Q's hidden messaging, to those selling products on the side via unsupported claims of a stolen election, to those involved in long-standing Christian nationalist and white supremacist projects to overthrow the existing political order and violently impose a new regime. Trump and his allies were able to mobilize this diverse coalition only through the mechanisms of social media, which allowed direct and targeted access to individuals, a coordinating of messaging via information warfare techniques, and a siloing of receptive individuals away from other media sources. The insurrection, however, also required a willingly uncritical population, a group of people not interested in testing narrative claims or acknowledging evidence, already aggrieved and available for this kind of recruitment and mobilization. Observable reality, in this instance, became a contested field, as participants sought to shore up preexisting narratives of fraud to defend against an imagined loss. January 6th, however, was also an extraordinarily well-documented event, one that can be meticulously reconstructed on a minute-by-minute basis from cell phone footage, social media feeds, and real-time broadcasting.[2] The result has been a high conviction rate for those involved in the violence—with over one thousand individuals charged—as well as serious investigations into the key players in Trump's orbit who sought to orchestrate the attack on Congress and to stop a peaceful transfer of power. But despite this massive documentary record, mostly registered by the participants on their own phones or watched on television in real time (and resulting in a high conviction rate for rioters), many still claim the insurrection was staged, a deep state conspiracy drawing on fake actors and deep fake media, a fiction designed to demonize their position and hide the truth. This will to believe, and the pleasure in not accepting counterevidence (often by assuming that everything that is mass medi-ated is fake), is not adequately explained by the conventional conspiracy theory frame; in fact, the conventional frame misses the range of political projects and preexisting psychosocial conditions that already had to be in place to bring such a wide range of citizens into a violent attack on the center of US government.

The potent blend of ongoing crisis, populist politics, nation-state overreach, and new digital technologies of authority, influence, and sur-veillance has resulted in a profound condition of epistemic precarity. The term *conspiracy theory* is most often applied pejoratively to pathologize certain stories people tell themselves and each other when trying to make sense of their worlds. *Conspiracy/Theory* has been keen to depathologize conspiratorial thought, especially in light of an intensified sense of epis-temic uncertainty. We have also sought to expand modes of scrutiny and evidence testing to an analysis of the power of narrative, to evaluate how explanatory discourses marked as conspiratorial or theoretical actually function in the world, unpacking how such narratives are involved in ways of living and understanding the complexities of social, economic, and political orders. In recognizing that disinformation and informational warfare are active forces in political life, we have also insisted on factor-ing in the problem for many of correctly identifying the cause of their unhappiness and pain. Precarity is one key driver of conspiratorial rea-son, enabling for many a charged psychosocial space that can be ripe for political manipulation, for misrecognition, and for targeted exploitation.

The myriad conspiracy theories accompanying the COVID-19 pan-demic the world over, for example, lay bare the attractions of conspiracy theorizing as a way of making sense of contemporary predicaments. Often enough, these theories were spun out of complex and troublesome stories that ranged from denying the virus's existence to connecting it to the rollout of 5G networks. But other stories were plausible enough to re-quire further investigation, such as what to make of the WHO-sponsored trip of experts to China to assess the veracity of allegations that the virus had originated in a Wuhan lab, which ended up looking suspiciously like a coverup of its own. In China, stories that the US military brought the virus to Wuhan also gained traction, in part, possibly, because the threat of biological warfare is real and cannot be dismissed out of hand. Mean-while, Facebook users inquiring about the possibility of a COVID vaccine were often directed to antivax sites, part of an attentional hack to keep them online and to foment the negative affects productive to the company bottom line—the virality of disinformation competing with the virality of the disease in real time (see Fisher 2022, 300).

Conspiracy/Theory is the product of our attempts to navigate the complex terrain between the plausible and the implausible, the believable and the flagrantly fictitious, between knowing and not knowing; it is our effort to examine the variegated cognitive and affective experiences that interpellate subjects into our current world of epistemic insecurity. The slash in the title does a lot of work, indexing three somewhat distinct interventions. First, we have sought to underscore the affinities between conspiracy theory and critical theory—including the pleasure derived from establishing connections, unearthing dynamics of meaning and power that may or may not be immediately visible, and identifying patterns of reproduction. We also find pleasure in connecting the dots, generating solidarities in the process and with the aim of producing a political otherwiseness to conventional status-quo conventionalities. This aspirational aspect, the ultimate prospect of upending social and political structures understood in whatever terms to be oppressive or unjust, may also be a fantasy investment common to both kinds of theorizing. The difference remains, of course, between critical theory's conspiratorial mode and right-wing (and often racialized) conspiratorial thought that casts transformation as restoration, often revenant, often nostalgic for a past (e.g., Trump's "Make America Great Again"), and proceeds independently of evidence or of a polyphonic discussion capable of anticipating objections.

And herein lies the crux of a difference between critical theory and conspiracy theory, which we acknowledge in order to move beyond it. The pursuit of rigor itself, as opposed to indifference to truth and variety, is an important part of critical theorizing—and of its enjoyment. There is on the part of critical theorists an attention to and appreciation of factual truths, an awareness of their vulnerability to distortion and to the theorists' own need to be aware of updates, informed by disagreements, and reflective about the problems with knowledge production. Also of the essence for critical theory is a sensitivity to and distaste of spurious correlations, an injunction to be aware of alternative ideas and explanations, to take into consideration publics outside of the scholar's narrow communities of argument, and to engage in what Kant called an "enlarged mentality" (see Arendt 1992, 43). *Conspiracy/Theory* invites an interrogation of habits of thoughts, seeking a productive disruption in what counts as authoritative analysis in an attempt both to acknowledge the complexity of imbricated social problems and to recognize the force of narrative in collective world-making.

As Stanley Fish (1980, 14; among others) has noted, interpretations are "community" affairs and "not subjective" or from an isolated individual. Because meanings are "cultural or socially available," they are replicable, subject to ongoing investigation. Likewise for scholars' own interpretations of meanings, which make sense only in light of socially available (and *therefore* contestable) standards, including standards for what counts as a fact. For facts, as Fish also notes, "emerge only in the context of some point of view" (1980, 338). Or to put this in Hanna Pitkin's (1972, 178) words, "empirical investigation presupposes conceptual definition," and conceptual definition requires what Wittgenstein calls a "life world," which is made up in large part by replicable, iterable conventions. This attunement to multiple, overlapping life worlds, to the importance of language and its conventions, to the creative estrangements involved in scholarly world-making means that critical theory cannot be reduced to conspiracy theorizing but that it can be productively and provocatively related to it. We are arguing, in short, for an appreciation of a nuanced resemblance.

And this brings us to the second point: this volume has cultivated a scholarly curiosity for stories, even the cockamamie ones, that have animated communities of argument—online and off. What are people doing when they promote narratives about how vaccines surreptitiously inject implants that track individuals' movements, or when they embrace the preposterous claim that Hillary Clinton was operating a child sex-trafficking ring in the nonexistent basement of a DC pizza parlor? How are we to understand the semiotic, sociological, and political-economic universes in which such stories appear true to even large groups of addressees? What kind of market logics (such as in the proliferating incentives of clickbait money-making) or authoritarian dynamics (such as in sowing confusion to induce political paralysis or to dampen revolutionary enthusiasms) are at work structuring the terms of our epistemic precarity? What do we gain by abandoning an analytic that simply dismisses these narratives as insane and a product of paranoid personalities? What are the structural conditions, including the affective ones, that give them traction? Why do they seem to be proliferating as a mode of sense-making in the contemporary era? Admittedly, our volume is better at raising these questions than answering them. But we have used these questions, we hope, to organize new modes of critical attention, to cultivate our attunement to temporal and spatial similarities as well as to differences, and to unsettle prevailing modes of dismissal.

Third, this volume appreciates the kinds of hidden and not-so-hidden conspiracies that are real and that partially organize our lives. They inhere in the logics of capital accumulation (including its commodity form fetishisms, new structures of financialization, racialized and gendered hierarchies, and exploitative labor practices); in the blurry boundaries between nation-state and academic knowledge production—and increasingly in the overwhelming power of donors to influence institutions' intellectual agendas; in the efficacy of certain industries, elites, and countries to reproduce the conditions of their own flourishing at the expense of the rest. The various political, market, diplomatic, medical, and scientific coverups recounted in this volume have helped make possible, plausible, and factually true a number of conspiracies, despite their dismissal as paranoid fantasies by conventional liberal authors such as the oft-cited Hofstadter (1996b). The cynical mendacity of oil companies denying climate change while knowing themselves to be causes of it (and blithely raising the height of offshore drilling platforms to accommodate the rising sea levels they claim are not happening) underscores how important it is to take conspiracy seriously (see Dumit, this volume). The oil companies also evidence the ways in which factual truths are so vulnerable to fudging and outright lying, with potentially dire political consequences, in this case, impinging on our ability to live on planet earth. Some of these truths are hidden in plain sight. Some are secret and must be investigated or uncovered. And some operate in secret until they are exposed by the conspirators themselves mounting a public effort to upend the system. In all cases, the critical theorist's task is to cultivate modes of attunement. In some cases, this means drawing attention to things we already know but have not been able to recognize or acknowledge or think about collectively. In other cases, this means bringing to the fore new factual truths or ways of thinking or seeing that have eluded our scrutiny. And all cases require connecting the dots.

There is something admittedly discomfiting about recognizing affinities between conspiracy and critical theory—and about the assertion that we think in conspiratorial terms much of the time—whether when figuratively breathing together to create something collective and potentially new, or when baking into our arguments hidden presuppositions about how the world works, who or what has power, what kinds of collusions exist, and what logics of address or injustice or asymmetry need to be discovered, excavated, and linked to one another.

Our condition of epistemic precarity not only raises questions of plausibility, secrecy, and the existence of unseen forces, but also reinvigorates debates about truth and politics. Dueling accounts of the war in Ukraine (including simultaneous false-flag accusations by Russian, Ukrainian, and US agents) as well as anxieties about doctored photographs and staged scenes of suffering highlight the consequences of epistemic murk for our ability to judge, reviving dynamics that made the oversaturation of imagery in Syria's war so painful, at times polarizing, at other times confusing and paralyzing—and politically consequential (see Wedeen, this volume). *Conspiracy/Theory* has recognized the act of conspiracy as intrinsic to political life and has tracked how a globalized order functions to raise the stakes of interpretation itself, requiring each of us to assemble evidence and craft explanations for current conditions. As contributors to this volume have shown, narratives are not just about factual information; they are coded into modes of life, capable of organizing ambitions, affects, sympathies, and demonizations.

This social insight is well understood by both states and corporations armed with new technologies of attentional and informational capture. Consider the "Narrative Networks" project by the Defense Advanced Research Projects Agency (DARPA), a US military science research group devoted to technological revolution for national advantage. In 2011, a decade into the war on terror (see Li, this volume), DARPA sought literally to crack the power of narrative. Assembling folklorists, novelists, linguists, cognitive scientists, and brain specialists, DARPA approached "terrorism as narrative," ultimately concluding that such extremism draws on a narrative process that is simultaneously social, perspectival, and neurobiological.[3] Part of a larger US military effort to understand and control the "information domain," the narrative networks concept reveals a formal militarization of narrative. DARPA's project was coterminous with the advent of social media platforms that sought to use the same kind of neurological insights for corporate profits. To understand the stories we tell about the world as simultaneously neurobiological and world-making is not just an exploitable insight, a way to pursue imperial politics, surveillance capitalism, or misinformation campaigns; it also underscores the importance of critical thought. In the contest of informational recruitments designed not primarily to inform but to hack perception and emotion, the only adequate individual response is to develop heightened capacities to evaluate evidence and logic (see Davis, this volume), to judge motives and ambitions, and to interrogate the value system informing any narrative. This is to say that conspiratorial reason is operative in many different dimensions of social life and cannot simply be bracketed out of reasoned discourse. It is also to say that developing a sophisticated understanding of persuasion and capture operations is crucial to independent thought, to engaging those already caught, and to building a collective future not based on compounding inequality, resentment, and alienation.

NOTES

1   See the official January 6th House Select Committee investigation reports for detailed materials on the efforts to challenge the 2020 election leading up to the insurrection, available at "House Select Committee to Investigate the January 6th Attack on the United States Capitol," GovInfo, accessed March 8, 2023, https://www.govinfo.gov/committee/house-january6th ?path=/browsecommittee/chamber/house/committee/january6th /collection/CRPT.
2   For detailed reconstructions of the January 6th insurrection, see Groeger et al. (2021).
3   For more on the "narrative networks" project, see DARPA n.d.; Yirka (2011).

ACKNOWLEDGMENTS

We are grateful to the Chicago Center for Contemporary Theory (3CT) at the University of Chicago for hosting and funding the activities associated with the *Conspiracy/Theory* project. In this light, special thanks are owed to Anna Searle Jones for her extraordinary administrative support. We are also indebted to Don Reneau for his copyediting expertise and his generative skepticism of the project. Helen Galvin Ross provided excellent manuscript support. Participants at the University of Chicago's Paris Center conference on global authoritarianism offered helpful feedback on the project. We are especially grateful to Adom Getachew for her incisive remarks as discussant. At Duke University Press, Joshua Gutterman Tranen and Kate Mullen provided much appreciated production expertise. Special thanks are owed to the two anonymous reviewers for their close readings and astute comments. We would also like to acknowledge Ken Wissoker for his superb editorial care and intellectual support. We are also grateful to Lauren Berlant, Lauren (Robin) Derby, Joan Donovan, John L. Jackson Jr., and Linda Zerilli for their critical engagement at the initial conference and speaker series that inspired this volume. And a special thanks is due to Joe Dumit for co-teaching the initial *Conspiracy/Theory* seminar and for his lively engagements on conspiratorial themes throughout the conference and book. Finally, all world-making conspiracies start at home: we would like to express profound thanks to Shawn Smith and Don Reneau for both emotional sustenance and their critical engagement with the project—well beyond any paranoid turn.

REFERENCES

Aaronson, Trevor. 2015. "Doogie Huckster: A Terrorism Expert's Secret Relationship with the FBI." *The Intercept*, July 27, 2015.

Abdo, Elie. 2013. "The Impact of the Arts on the Syrian Revolution." Heinrich Böll Stiftung Middle East, February 28, 2013. https://lb.boell.org/en/2013/02/28/impact-arts-syrian-revolution.

Aboutnaddara. 2012. *The Trajectory of the Unknown Soldier* [Abu Naddara, *Sirat Jundi Majhul*]. Vimeo, November 23, 2012. Video, 1:56. https://vimeo.com/54135942.

Abu El-Haj, Nadia. 2022. *Combat Trauma: Imaginaries of War and Citizenship in Post-9/11 America*. New York: Verso Books.

Ackerman, Spencer. 2021. *Reign of Terror: How the 9/11 Era Destablized America and Produced Trump*. New York: Viking.

Adorno, T. W., Else Frenkel-Brunswik, Daniel J. Levinson, and R. Nevitt Sanford, *The Authoritarian Personality*. 1950. New York: Harper and Row.

Afrika Staff. 2009. "*Afrika*'dan mektup: Afrika'nın haberi giderek doğruluk kazanırken" [Letter from Africa: The News from Africa Gets More Accurate]. *Afrika*, December 22, 2009.

Agafonov, V. K. 1918. *Zagranichnaia Okhranka*. Petrograd: Kniga.

Aglietta, Michel. 2018. *Money: 5,000 Years of Debt and Power*. Translated by David Broder. London: Verso Books.

Agoustis, Dinos. 2009. "Βεβήλωση το Έθνος" [Desecration of the Nation]. *Simerini*, December 17, 2009.

Agrama, Hussein Ali. 2015. "Justice between Islamic Shari'a and Western Legal Tradition: Remarks on the Egyptian Context." In *A Companion to the Anthropology of the Middle East*, edited by Soraya Altorki, 361–90. Hoboken, NJ: Wiley-Blackwell.

Ahmed, Sara. 2012. *On Being Included: Racism and Diversity in Institutional Life*. Durham, NC: Duke University Press

Ahmed, Sara. 2019. *What's the Use? On the Uses of Use*. Durham, NC: Duke University Press.

Ahmed, Sara. 2021. *Complaint!* Durham, NC: Duke University Press.

Ahuja, Neil. 2013. "Macaques and Biomedicine: Notes on Decolonization, Polio, and Changing Representations of Indian Rhesus in the United States,

1930–1960." In *The Macaque Connection*, edited by Sindhu Radhakrishna, Michael A. Huffman, and Anindya Sinha, 71–91. New York: Springer.

Aistrope, Tim, and Roland Bleiker. 2018. "Conspiracy and Foreign Policy." *Security Dialogue* 49, no. 3 (June): 165–82.

Akbar, Amna. 2013. "How Tarek Mehanna Went to Prison for a Thought Crime." *The Nation*, December 31, 2013. https://www.thenation.com/article/archive/how -tarek-mehanna-went-prison-thought-crime/.

'Ali, 'Adnan. 2016. "Majzarat al-Kimmawi min al-Inkar ila al-Talfiq" ["Chemical Attack: From Denial to Fabrication."] *Al-Araby Al-Jadid*, August 21, 2016. https://tinyurl.com/y7mexgyj.

Althaus, Scott L., and Devon M. Largio. 2004. "When Osama Became Saddam: Origins and Consequences of the Change in America's Public Enemy #1." *PS: Political Science and Politics* 37, no. 4: 795–99.

Althusser, Louis. 1971. "Ideology and Ideological State Apparatuses (Notes towards an Investigation)." In *Lenin and Philosophy, and Other Essays*, translated by Ben Brewster, 127–86. New York: Monthly Review Press.

Altman, Lawrence K. 1999. Review of *The River: A Journey to the Source of HIV and AIDS*, by Edward Hooper. *New York Times*, November 30, 1999. https://www .bmartin.cc/dissent/documents/AIDS/River/NYTimes.html.

Amoss, Ulius Louis. 1962. "Leaderless Resistance." *Inform* 6205, April 17, 1962.

"Anarchists: Their Methods and Organisation." 1894. *New Review* 10, no. 56: 1–16.

Anderson, Carol. 2018. *One Person, No Vote*. New York: Bloomsbury Publishing.

Anderson, Doug. 2018. "Something Like a Soul." In *War and Moral Injury: A Reader*, edited by Robert Emmet Meagher and Douglas A. Pryer, 131–36. Eugene, OR: Cascade Books.

Andocides. 1995. *Greek Orators IV: Andocides*. Translated by Michael Edwards. Liverpool: Aris and Phillips.

Andrieux, Louis. 1885. *Souvenirs d'un préfet de police*. 2 vols. Paris: Jules Rouff.

Anker, Elizabeth. 2014. *Orgies of Feeling: Melodrama and the Politics of Freedom*. Durham, NC: Duke University Press.

Appel, Hannah. 2017. "Toward an Ethnography of the National Economy." *Cultural Anthropology* 32, no. 2 (May): 294–322.

Appiah, Anthony. 1992. *In My Father's House: Africa in the Philosophy of Culture*. New York: Oxford University Press.

"A propos des événements de Kichinev." 1903. *La revue russe* 24, June 18.

Apter, Emily. 2006. *The Translation Zone*. Princeton, NJ: Princeton University Press.

Arendt, Hannah. 1958. *The Human Condition*. Chicago: University of Chicago Press.

Arendt, Hannah. 1967. "Truth and Politics." *New Yorker*, February 25, 1967.

Arendt, Hannah. 1992. *Lectures on Kant's Political Philosophy*. Edited by Ronald Beiner. Chicago: University of Chicago Press.

Arendt, Hannah. 2003a. "Collective Responsibility." In *Responsibility and Judgment*, 147–58. New York: Schocken Books.

Arendt, Hannah. 2003b. "Some Questions of Moral Philosophy." In *Responsibility and Judgment*, 49–146. New York: Schocken Books.

Arendt, Hannah. 2006a. *Between Past and Future: Eight Exercises in Political Thought.* New York: Penguin Classics.

Arendt, Hannah. 2006b. *On Revolution.* New York: Penguin Classics.

Aristophanes. 2003. *Aristophanes: The Birds and Other Plays.* Translated by David Barrett and Alan H. Sommerstein. New York: Penguin Books.

Aristophanes. 2007. *Aristophanes: Frogs and Other Plays.* Translated by David Barrett and Shomit Dutta. New York: Penguin Books.

Aristotle. 1996. *The Politics and the Constitution of Athens.* Edited by Stephen Everson. Translated by Benjamin Jowett. Cambridge: Cambridge University Press.

Aronov, Lev, Khenrik Baran, and Dmitrii Zubarev. 2009. "Kniaginia Ekaterina Radzivill I' Protokoly sionskikh mudretsov': Mistifikatsiia kak obraz zhizni." *Novoe literaturnoe obozrenie* 96: 76–133.

Asad, Talal. 2003. *Formations of the Secular: Christianity, Islam, Modernity.* Stanford, CA: Stanford University Press.

Asad, Talal. 2007. *On Suicide Bombing.* New York: Columbia University Press.

Ashforth, Adam. 2005. *Witchcraft, Violence, and Democracy in South Africa.* Chicago: University of Chicago Press.

Asmussen, Jan. 2008. *Cyprus at War: Diplomacy and Conflict during the 1974 Crisis.* London: I. B. Tauris.

Atack, Carol. 2020. "Plato's Queer Time: Dialogic Moments in the Life and Death of Socrates." *Classical Receptions Journal* 12, no. 1 (January): 10–31.

Atran, Scott. 2016. "The Devoted Actor: Unconditional Commitment and Intractable Conflict across Cultures." *Current Anthropology* 57, no. S13: S192–S203.

Azas, Andreas. 2009. "Αναλαμβούν ξένοι εμπειρογνώμονες" Η Αστυνομία 'όργωσε' τη Στράκκα, αλλά δεν βρήκε τίποτε." *Simerini*, December 22, 2009.

Azas, Andreas. 2010. "Άλλο η σύληση του τάφου, άλλο η υφαρπαγή της σημαίας." *Simerini*, January 9, 2010.

'Azzām, 'Abd Allāh. 1988. "Al-qā'ida al-ṣulba" [The solid base]. *Al-jihād*, April, 1988.

Bacevich, Andrew J. 2005. *The New American Militarism: How Americans Are Seduced by War.* New York: Oxford University Press.

Baker, Max. 1990. "Texas's New Right." *Fort Worth Star-Telegram*, March 18, 1990.

Bakewell, Geoffrey. 2019. "Stasis, Competition, and the 'Noble Lie': Metic Mettle in Plato's Republic." In *Eris vs. Aemulatio: Valuing Competition in Classical Antiquity*, edited by Cynthia Damon and Christoph Pieper, 98 119. Leiden: Brill.

Bakhtin, M. M. (1981) 2008. *The Dialogic Imagination: Four Essays.* Austin: University of Texas Press.

Bailyn, Bernard, ed. 1965. *Pamphlets of the American Revolution, 1750–1776.* Cambridge, MA: Harvard University Press.

Bailyn, Bernard. 1967. *The Ideological Origins of the American Revolution.* Cambridge, MA: Harvard Belknap.

Baldwin, James. 1984. *The Fire Next Time.* New York: Vintage Books.

Ban, Kimberley. 2019. "Conspiracy: A Praxis." Presentation at the Conspiracy Graduate Student Conference in American Studies, Princeton University, April 11, 2019.

Barkun, Michael. 2013. *A Culture of Conspiracy: Apocalyptic Visions in Contemporary America*. Berkeley: University of California Press.

Barstow, David. 2008. "Behind TV Analysts, Pentagon's Hidden Hand." *New York Times*, April 20, 2009.

Barthes, Roland. 2012. *Mythologies*. New York: Hill and Wang.

Baum, Dan. 2016. "Legalize It All." *Harper's Magazine*, April 2016.

Bayart, Jean-François. (1993) 2009. *The State in Africa: The Politics of the Belly*. New York: Wiley.

Baylen, Joseph O. 1951. "Madame Olga Novikov, Propagandist." *American Slavic and East European Review* 10, no. 4: 255–71.

Beam, Louis R. 1989. *Essays of a Klansman*. 2nd ed. Hayden Lake, ID: A.K.I.A. Publications.

Beam, Louis. 1992a. Estes Park speech, October 23, 1992. Southern Poverty Law Center, Montgomery, AL. Video recording.

Beam, Louis R. 1992b. "Leaderless Resistance." *Seditionist* 12 (February). https://archive.org/details/Leaderless_Resistance_The_Seditionist. (Also available as part of the Intelligence Project Holdings, Southern Poverty Law Center (SPLC), Montgomery, AL).

Beck, Ulrich. (1986) 1992. *The Risk Society: Toward a New Modernity*, translated by Scott Lash and Brian Wynne. New York: Sage.

Belew, Kathleen. 2018. *Bring the War Home: The White Power Movement and Paramilitary America*. Cambridge, MA: Harvard University Press.

Bell, Karine. 2022. "Your Weekend Update to Our Bodies at the Borderlands, Tending the Roots Festival." Tending the Roots, March 26.

Benjamin, Walter. 1978. "Critique of Violence." In *Reflections: Essays, Aphorisms, Autobiographical Wriings*, edited by Peter Demetz and translated by Edmund Jephcott, 277–300. New York: Schocken Books.

Benjamin, Walter. 2002. *The Arcades Project*. Translated by Howard Eiland and Kevin McLaughlin. Cambridge, MA: Belknap Press of Harvard University Press.

Benjamin, Walter. 2003. "The Paris of the Second Empire in Baudelaire." In *Walter Benjamin: Selected Writings Volume 4, 1938–1940*, edited by Howard Eiland and Michael W. Jennings, 3–91. Cambridge, MA: Harvard University Press.

Benjamin, Walter. 2007. "Theses on the Philosophy of History," translated by Harry Zohn. In *Illuminations*, edited by Hannah Arendt, 253–64. New York: Schocken Books.

Bergen, Peter L. 2006. *The Osama bin Laden I Know: An Oral History of al Qaeda's Leader*. New York: Free Press.

Bergen, Peter, and Paul Cruickshank. 2012. "Revisiting the Early Account of Al Qaeda: An Updated Account of Its Formative Years." *Studies in Conflict and Terrorism* 35, no. 1: 1–36.

Berger, J. M. 2012. *Beatings and Bureaucracy: The Founding Memos of Al Qaeda*. Intelwire Press. https://www.intelwire.com.

Berlant, Lauren. 1991. *The Anatomy of National Fantasy: Hawthorne, Utopia, and Everyday Life*. Chicago: University of Chicago Press.

Berlant, Lauren. 1997. *The Queen of America Goes to Washington City: Essays on Sex and Citizenship*. Durham, NC: Duke University Press.

Berlant, Lauren. 2011. *Cruel Optimism*. Durham, NC: Duke University Press.

Berlant, Lauren, and Kathleen Stewart. 2019. *The Hundreds*. Durham, NC: Duke University Press.

Bermeo, Nancy. 2016. "On Democratic Backsliding." *Journal of Democracy* 27, no. 1: 5–19.

Bernault, Florence, and Joseph Tonda. 2000. "Dynamiques de l'invisible en Afrique." *Politique africaine* 3, no. 79: 5–16.

Bernstein, J. M. 2015. *Torture and Dignity: An Essay on Moral Injury*. Chicago: University of Chicago Press.

Best, Stephen, and Sharon Marcus. 2009. "Surface Reading: An Introduction." *Representations* 108, no. 1: 1–21.

Biagioli, Mario, and Alexandra Lippman, eds. 2020. *Gaming the Metrics: Misconduct and Manipulation in Academic Research*. Cambridge, MA: MIT Press.

Birchall, Clare. 2004. "Just Because You're Paranoid, Doesn't Mean They're Not Out to Get You." *Culture Machine* 6. https://culturemachine.net/deconstruction-is -in-cultural-studies/just-because-youre-paranoid-doesnt-mean-theyre-not -out-to-get-you/.

Birchall, Clare. 2006. *Knowledge Goes Pop: From Conspiracy Theory to Gossip*. Oxford: Berg Publishers.

Blondell, Ruby. 2002. *The Play of Character in Plato's Republic*. Cambridge: Cambridge University Press.

Boltanski, Luc. 1999. *Distant Suffering: Morality, Media and Politics*. Cambridge: Cambridge University Press.

Boltanski, Luc. 2014. *Mysteries and Conspiracies: Detective Stories, Spy Novels and the Making of Modern Societies*. London: Polity.

Bonhomme, Julien. 2009. *Les voleurs de sexe: Anthropologie d'une rumeur africaine*. Paris: Le Seuil.

Bookchin, Debbie, and James Schumacher. 2004. *The Virus and the Vaccine: The True Story of a Cancer-Causing Monkey Virus, Contaminated Polio Vaccine, and the Millions of Americans Exposed*. New York: Macmillan Press.

Bork, Robert. 1978. *The Antitrust Paradox: A Policy at War with Itself*. New York: Free Press.

Bourdeau, J. 1892. *Le socialisme allemand et le nihilisme russe*. Paris: F. Alcan.

Boudreau, Tyler. 2018. "The Morally Injured." In *War and Moral Injury: A Reader*, edited by Robert Emmet Meagher and Douglas A. Pryer, 51–59. Eugene, OR: Cascade Books.

Bournand, François. 1898. *Les juifs et nos contemporains*. Paris: Librairie A. Pierret.

Bowker, Michael. 2003. *Fatal Deception: The Terrifying True Story of How Asbestos Is Killing America*. New York: Simon and Schuster.

Brabant, Justine, and Leila Minano. 2017. "Les exactions impunies de l'opération Sangaris." *Mediapart*, January 3, 2017. https://www.mediapart.fr/studio /panoramique/les-exactions-impunies-de-l-operation-sangaris.

Brachev, V. S. 1998. *Mastera politicheskogo syska dorevoliutsionnoi Rossii*. St. Peters-
  burg: Nestor.
Bratich, Jack Z. 2008. *Conspiracy Panics: Political Rationality and Popular Culture*.
  Albany: SUNY Press.
Bratich, Jack Z. 2017. "If Everyone Is a Conspiracy Theorist, Is Anyone? Trumpism,
  Mutually Assured Disqualification, and Communications Warfare." Lecture
  at Pitzer College, Claremont, CA, December 14, 2017. https://www.pitzer.edu
  /mcsi/2017/12/14/jack-bratich-everyone-conspiracy-theorist-anyone/.
Briggs, Charles L. 2004. "Theorizing Modernity Conspiratorially: Science, Scale,
  and the Political Economy of Public Discourse in Explanations of the Chol-
  era Epidemic." *American Ethnologist* 31, no. 2: 164–87.
Brisson, Luc. 1998. *Plato, the Myth Maker*. Edited and translated by Gerard Naddaf.
  Chicago: University of Chicago Press.
Broad, William J. 2013. "Rockets in Syrian Attack Carried Large Payload of Gas,
  Experts Say." *New York Times*, September 4, 2013.
Broadwell, Paula, and Vernon Loeb. 2012. *All In: The Education of General David
  Petraeus*. New York: Penguin Books.
Brockes, Emma. 2019. "When Alexandria Ocasio-Cortez Met Greta Thunberg:
  'Hope Is Contagious.'" *Guardian*, June 29, 2019. https://www.theguardian
  .com/environment/2019/jun/29/alexandria-ocasio-cortez-met-greta
  -thunberg-hope-contagious-climate.
Brown, Wendy. 1995. *States of Injury: Power and Freedom in Late Modernity*. Princeton,
  NJ: Princeton University Press.
Browne, Simone. 2015. *Dark Matters: On the Surveillance of Blackness*. Durham, NC:
  Duke University Press.
Bryant, Rebecca. 2007. "Turkey, Cyprus and the European Division." *Middle East
  Research and Information Project*, February 25, 2007. http://www.merip.org
  /mero/mero022507.
Bryant, Rebecca. 2010. *The Past in Pieces: Belonging in the New Cyprus*. Philadelphia:
  University of Pennsylvania Press.
Burgess, Greg. 2008. *Refuge in the Land of Liberty: A History of Asylum and Refugee
  Protection in France since the Revolution*. New York: Palgrave Macmillan.
Burke, Jason. 2003. *Al-Qaeda: Casting a Shadow of Terror*. London: I. B. Tauris.
Burtsev, Vladimir. 1908. "Franko-russkoe shpionstvo i franko-russkii soiuz." *Byloe*
  8: 58–64.
Burtsev, Vladimir. 1938. "Protokoly sionskikh mudretsov." *Dokazannyi podlog*. Paris:
  O. Zeluk.
Butler, Judith. 1997. *Excitable Speech: A Politics of the Performative*. New York:
  Routledge.
Butter, Michael. 2014. *Plots, Designs, and Schemes: American Conspiracy Theories from
  the Puritans to the Present*. Berlin: De Gruyter.
Butter, Michael. 2021. "Bad History, Useless Prophecy: The 'Paranoid Style' Revis-
  ited." *Symploke* 29, nos. 1–2: 21–42.

Butter, Michael, and Peter Knight. 2016. "Bridging the Great Divide: Conspiracy Theory Research for the 21st Century." *Diogenes* 62, no. 3–4 (November): 17–29. https://doi.org/10.1177/0392192116669289.

Cahn, Anne Hessing. 1998. *Killing Détente: The Right Attacks the CIA*. University Park: Pennsylvania State University Press.

Calhoun, George Miller. 1913. "Athenian Clubs in Politics and Litigation." PhD diss., University of Texas, Austin.

Calik, Aydin. 2018a. "*Afrika* Suspected Attackers Detained for One Month Pending Trial." *Cyprus Mail*, January 30, 2018. http://cyprus-mail.com/2018/01/30/afrika-suspected-attackers-detained-one-month-pending-trial/.

Calik, Aydin. 2018b. "Tense Day in North after *Afrika* Article Protest (update 4)." *Cyprus Mail*, January 22, 2018. http://cyprus-mail.com/2018/01/22/crowds-surround-afrika-north-afrin-report/.

Carawan, Edwin. 2013. *The Athenian Amnesty and Reconstructing the Law*. Oxford: Oxford University Press.

Carayannis, Tatiana, and Louisa Lombard. 2015. "A Concluding Note on the Failure and Future of Peacebuilding in CAR." In *Making Sense of the Central African Republic*, edited by Tatiana Carayannis and Louisa Lombard, 319–41. London: Zed Books.

Carpenter, John, dir. 1988. *They Live*. Larry Franco Productions. Film, 94 min.

Carugati, Frederica. 2019. *Creating a Constitution: Law, Democracy, and Growth in Ancient Athens*. Princeton, NJ: Princeton University Press.

Castoriadis, Cornelius. 1975. *The Imaginary Institution of Society*. New York: Polity Press.

Cavell, Stanley. 1969. *Must We Mean What We Say? A Book of Essays*. New York: Scribner.

Central Intelligence Agency (CIA; Chief WOVIEW). 1967. "Countering Criticism of the Warren Report." Document Number 1035-960, NARA Record Number: 104-10009-10022, April 4, 1967 (released 1996). https://www.maryferrell.org/showDoc.html?docId=53510#relPageId=2&tab=page.

Central Intelligence Agency (CIA). 1976. *Intelligence Community Experiment in Competitive Analysis: Soviet Strategic Objectives an Alternative View. Report of Team B*. https://www.cia.gov/library/readingroom/document/ciardp84m00390r000300040052-3.

Ceriana Mayneri, Andrea. 2014. *Sorcellerie et prophétisme en Centrafrique: L'imaginaire de la dépossession en pays Banda*. Paris: Karthala.

Chamber of Mines. 2016. *Mining SA 2016—Facts and Figures Pocketbook*. Johannesburg: Chamber of Mines.

Charalambous, Loucas. 2004. "Does the President Have Memory Problems!" *Cyprus Weekly*, September 12, 2004.

Charles, J. Brian. 2016. "Transcript of Donald Trump's Economic Policy Speech to Detroit Economic Club." *The Hill*, August 8, 2016. http://thehill.com/blogs/pundits-blog/campaign/290777-transcript-of-donald-trumps-economic-policy-speech-to-detroit.

Cherix, Christophe. 2018. *Adrian Piper: A Synthesis of Intuitions, 1965–2016*. New York: Museum of Modern Art.

Chicago Tribune Staff. 2016. "'Chicago Is Out of Control': Trump in His Own Words on the Windy City." *Chicago Tribune*, October 20, 2016. http://www .chicagotribune.com/news/ct-donald-trump-chicago-comments-20161020 -story.html.

Chivers, C. J. 2013. "New Study Refines View of Sarin Attack in Syria." *New York Times*, December 28, 2013.

Choy, Tim. 2021. "Externality, Breathers, Conspiracy: Forms for Atmospheric Reckoning." In *Reactivating Elements: Chemistry, Ecology, Practice*, edited by Dimitris Papdopoulos, Maria Puig de la Bellacasa, and Natasha Myers, 231–56. Durham, NC: Duke University Press.

Chriss, Nicholas. 1988a. "CDR Notes on Trial." Arkansas sedition trial, February 16, 1988. Notes on *Miles et al.*, Elinor Langer Collection, University of Oregon LibrariesBox 13, Folder 9, Special Collections and Archives, Eugene.

Chriss, Nicholas C. 1988b. "Sedition Trial Acquittals Ignite Outcry over Jurors." *Houston Chronicle*, October. Elinor Langer Collection, University of Oregon Libraries, Special Collections and Archives, Eugene.

Chriss, Nicholas C. 1988c. "Witness Tells of Scheme to Topple U.S." *Houston Chronicle*, February 23, 1988.

Cimons, Marlene. 1999. Review of *The River: A Journey to the Source of HIV and AIDS*, by Edward Hooper. *Los Angeles Times*, December 23, 1999. https://www.bmartin .cc/dissent/documents/AIDS/River/LATimes.html.

Clapham, Christopher. 1998. "Introduction: Analyzing African Insurgencies." In *African Guerrillas*, edited by Christopher Clapham, 1–18. Oxford: James Currey.

Clark, Robert M., and William L. Mitchell 2019. *Deception: Counterdeception and Counterintelligence*. London: SAGE.

Clastres, Pierre. 1998. *Chronicle of the Guayaki Indians*. Translated by Paul Auster. Cambridge, MA: Zone.

Coates, James. 1988. "Plot to Poison Water Is Detailed." *Chicago Tribune*, February 28, 1988.

Coates, James. 1997. *Armed and Dangerous: The Rise of the Survivalist Right*. New York: Noonday Press.

Coates, James, and Stephen Franklin. 1987. "'Underground' of Racist Leaders Coordinated Crimes, FBI Taps Show." *Chicago Tribune*, December 28, 1987.

Cockayne, E. A. 1914. "Epidemic Catarrhal Jaundice." *Lancet* 184: 218–20.

Coen, Ethan, and Joel Coen, dirs. 2008. *Burn after Reading*. Focus Features. Film, 96 min.

Cohen, Jon. 2000. "The Hunt for the Origin of AIDS." *Atlantic Monthly* 286, no. 4: 88–104.

Cohn, Norman. 1967. *Warrant for Genocide: The Myth of the Jewish World-Conspiracy and the Protocols of the Elders of Zion*. London: Eyre and Spottiswoode.

Coleman, Gabriella. 2014. *Hacker, Hoaxer, Whistleblower, Spy: The Many Faces of Anonymous*. New York: Verso Books.

Collmer, Peter. 2004. *Die Schweiz und das Russische Reich, 1848–1919*. Zurich: Chronos.

Comaroff, Jean, and John L. Comaroff. 1999. "Occult Economies and the Violence of Abstraction: Notes from the South African Postcolony." *American Ethnologist* 26, no. 2: 279–303.

Comaroff, Jean, and John L. Comaroff. 2003. "Transparent Fictions; or, The Conspiracies of a Liberal Imagination: An Afterword." In *Transparency and Conspiracy: Ethnographies of Suspicion in the New World Order*, edited by Harry G. West and Todd Sanders, 287–300. Durham, NC: Duke University Press.

Connolly, William. 2017. *Aspirational Fascism: The Struggle for Multifaceted Democracy under Trumpism*. Minneapolis: University of Minnesota Press.

Connor, Walter Robert. 1971. *The New Politicians of Fifth-Century Athens*. Princeton, NJ: Princeton University Press.

Constable, Marianne. 1994. *The Law of the Other: The Mixed Jury and Changing Conceptions of Citizenship, Law, and Knowledge*. Chicago: University of Chicago Press.

Constandinos, Andreas. 2009. *America, Britain and the Cyprus Crisis of 1974: Calculated Conspiracy or Foreign Policy Failure?* Bloomington, IN: AuthorHouse Books.

Coplan, David B. 1994. *In the Time of the Cannibals*. Chicago: University of Chicago Press.

Corneilhan, Georges. 1889. *Juifs et opportunistes*. Paris: L. Sauvaitre.

Corsi, Jerome. 2011. *Where's the Birth Certificate?: The Case That Barack Obama Is Not Eligible to Be President*. Washington, DC: WND Books.

Cottom, Tressie McMillan. 2022. "Anyway, All I Ever Meant by 'the Institution Cannot Love You.'" Tweet. @tressiemcphd (blog), February 17, 2022. https://twitter.com/tressiemcphd/status/1494421111102230534.

Courtois, Gislain, Agnes Flack, George A. Jervis, Hillary Koprowski, and Gaston Ninane. 1958. "Preliminary Report on Mass Vaccination of Man with Live Attenuated Poliomyelitis Virus in the Belgian Congo and Ruanda-Urundi." *British Medical Journal* 2, no. 5090: 187–90. https://www.ncbi.nlm.nih.gov/pmc/articles/PMC2026116/.

Covert, Bryce. 2016. "Donald Trump's Imaginary Inner Cities." *The Nation*, November 28, 2016. https://www.thenation.com/article/donald-trumps-imaginary-inner-cities/.

Crewdson, John. 2003. *Science Fictions: A Scientific Mystery, a Massive Coverup, and the Dark Legacy of Robert Gallo*. Boston: Little, Brown, and Company.

Culler, Jonathan. 1983. *On Deconstruction: Theory and Criticism after Structuralism*. London: Routledge and Kegan Paul.

Curtis, Adam, dir. 2016. *HyperNormalisation*. BBC documentary, 167 min.

Curtis, Tom. 1992. "The Origin of AIDS." *Rolling Stone*, 626, March 19, 1992:

Cyon, Élie de. 1892. "Choses russes." *LNR* 13, no. 79: 863–69.

Cyon, Élie de. 1895a. *Histoire de l'Entente Franco-Russe, 1886–1894*. Paris: A. Charles.

Cyon, Élie de. 1895b. *M. Witte et les finances russes après des documents officiels et inédits.* Paris: Chamerot et Renouard.

Cyon, Élie de. 1897a. *M. Witte et ses projects de faillite devant le conseil de l'empire.* Paris: Haar et Steinert. https://www.google.com/books/edition/_/XYw3AQAAIAAJ?hl=en&gbpv=1.

Cyon, Élie de. 1897b. *Où la dictature de m. Witte conduit la Russie.* Paris: Haar et Steinert.

Dalgıçoğlu, Dolgun. 2009. "Papadopulos'un cesedinin düşündürdükleri" [What the Corpse of Papadopoulos Suggests]. *Afrika*, December 14, 2009.

Dalitis, Frixos. 2010. "Ξανακτύπησαν οι βέβηλοι᾿ Κατέβασαν την ελληνική σημαία τον τάφο του Τάσσου" [The Desecrators Struck Again: They Stripped the Greek Flag from Tassos's Tomb]. *Filelevtheros*, January 9, 2010.

DARPA (Defense Advance Research Projects Agency). n.d. "Narrative Networks (Archived)." Accessed March 8, 2023. https://www.darpa.mil/program/narrative-networks.

Daudet, Léon. 1915. *L'entre–deux–guerres.* Paris: Nouvelle Librairie Nationale.

Davidson, Donald. 1963. "Actions, Reasons, and Causes." *Journal of Philosophy* 60, no. 23 (November): 685–700.

Davidson, Donald. 1999. "The Emergence of Thought." *Erkenntnis* 51, no. 1: 511–21.

Davies, Madlen, Rosa Furneaux, Iván Ruiz, and Jill Langlis. 2021. "'Held to Ransom': Pfizer Demands Governments Gamble with State Assets to Secure Vaccine Deal." *Bureau of Investigative Journalism*, February 23, 2021. https://www.thebureauinvestigates.com/stories/2021-02-23/held-to-ransom-pfizer-demands-governments-gamble-with-state-assets-to-secure-vaccine-deal.

Davies, William. 2016. "The Age of Post-truth Politics." *New York Times*, August 24, 2016 https://www.nytimes.com/2016/08/24/opinion/campaign-stops/the-age-of-post-truth-politics.html.

Davis, David Brion. 1970. *The Slave Power Conspiracy and the Paranoid Style.* Baton Rouge: Louisiana State University Press.

Davis, David Brion, ed. 1971. *The Fear of Conspiracy: Images of Un-American Subversion from the Revolution to the Present.* Ithaca, NY: Cornell University Press.

Davis, Elizabeth Anne. 2023. *Artifactual: Forensic and Documentary Knowing.* Durham, NC: Duke University Press.

Davis, Elizabeth Anne. Forthcoming. *The Time of the Cannibals: On Conspiracy Theory and Context.* New York: Fordham University Press.

Davis, L. J. 1986. "Ballad of an American Terrorist: A Neo-Nazi's Dream of Order." *Harper's Magazine*, July. Elinor Langer Collection, University of Oregon Libraries, Special Collections and Archives, Eugene, 8.14.

Dean, Jodi. 1998. *Aliens in America.* Ithaca, NY: Cornell University Press.

Dean, Jodi. 2002. *Publicity's Secret: How Technoculture Capitalizes on Democracy.* Ithaca, NY: Cornell University Press.

Dean, Jodi. 2009. *Democracy and Other Neoliberal Fantasies: Communicative Capitalism and Left Politics.* Durham, NC: Duke University Press.

Dearden, Lizzie. 2015. "David Cameron Extremism Speech: Read the Transcript in Full." *Independent*, July 20, 2015. https://www.independent.co.uk/news/uk/politics/david-cameron-extremism-speech-read-the-transcript-in-full-10401948.html.

de Bodisco, Dm. 1903. "L'Absolutisme en Russie et l'Alliance Franco–Russe." *La revue russe* 8 (January): 5.

Debos, Marielle. 2016. *Living by the Gun in Chad: Combatants, Impunity and State Formation*. London: Zed Books.

deHaven-Smith, Lance. 2013. *Conspiracy Theory in America*. Austin: University of Texas Press.

Delassus, Henri. 1905. *Le problème de l'heure présent: Antagonisme des deux civilisations*. Lille: Desclée, de Brouwer.

Deleuze, Gilles. 1988. *Foucault*. Translated by Paul Bové. Minneapolis: University of Minnesota Press.

Deleuze, Gilles, and Félix Guattari. 1986. *Kafka: Toward a Minor Literature*. Translated by Dana Polan. Minneapolis: University of Minnesota Press.

Delevskii, I. U., and A. V Kartashev. 1923. *Protokoly sionskikh mudrestov: Istoriia odnogo podloga*. Berlin: Epokha.

Demachy, Édouard. 1892. "Les rois juifs et les emprunts russes." *La libre parole*, September 3, 1892.

Demetriou, Olga. 2008. "Catalysis, Catachresis: The EU's Impact on the Cyprus Conflict." In *The European Union and Border Conflicts: The Power of Integration and Association*, edited by Thomas Diez, Mathias Albert, and Stephan Stetter, 64–93. Cambridge: Cambridge University Press.

Demetriou, Olga, and Ayla Gürel. 2008. "Human Rights, Civil Society and Conflict in Cyprus: Exploring the Relationships." SHUR Working Papers Series, No. 3. Rome: SUHR. https://www.prio.org/publications/104.

Denisow, P. 1892. *Anglais et nihilistes alliés*. Geneva: Imprimerie independante.

Derrida, Jacques. 1995. *Archive Fever: A Freudian Impression*. Translated by Eric Prenowitz. Chicago: University of Chicago Press.

Derrida, Jacques. (1967) 2016. *Of Grammatology*. Translated by Gayatri Chakravorty Spivak. Baltimore, MD: Johns Hopkins University Press.

Deschamps, Philippe. 1898. *Le livre d'or de l'Alliance Franco–Russe*. Paris: A. Lemerre.

Detrow, Scott. 2016. "Did Trump TV Launch Last Night?" *NPR*, October 20, 2016. https://www.npr.org/2016/10/20/498691090/did-trump-tv-launch-last-night.

De Waal, Alex. 1997. *Famine Crimes: Politics and the Disaster Relief Industry in Africa*. Bloomington: Indiana University Press.

Diamond, Cora. 1988. "Losing Your Concepts." *Ethics* 98, no. 2: 255–77.

Diamond, Larry. 2015. "Facing Up to the Democratic Recession." *Journal of Democracy* 26, no. 1: 141–55.

DiAngelo, Robin J. 2018. *White Fragility: Why It's So Hard for White People to Talk about Racism*. Boston: Beacon Press.

Dickson, David. 2000. "Tests Fail to Support Claims for Origin of AIDS in Polio Vaccine." *Nature* 407, no. 6801: 117. https://doi.org/10.1038/35025249.

Didion, Joan. 1984. *Democracy.* New York: Simon and Schuster.

Dilley, Roy. 1999. "Introduction: The Problem of Context." In *The Problem of Context*, edited by Roy Dilley, 1–46. New York: Berghahn Books.

Dimitrakis, Panagiotis. 2010. *Military Intelligence in Cyprus: From the Great War to Middle East Crises.* London: I. B. Tauris.

Donovan, Joan. 2019. "First They Came for the Black Feminists." *New York Times*, August 15, 2019. https://www.nytimes.com/interactive/2019/08/15/opinion/gamergate-twitter.html.

Donovan, Joan, Brian Friedberg, Gabrielle Lim, Nicole Leaver, Jennifer Nilsen, and Emily Dreyfuss. 2021. *Mitigating Medical Misinformation: A Whole-of-Society Approach to Countering Spam, Scams, and Hoaxes.* Technology and Social Change Project, Shorenstein Center on Media, Politics and Public Policy. Cambridge, MA: Harvard Kennedy School.

dos Passos, John. (1930) 2000. *The Forty-Second Parallel.* New York: Houghton, Mifflin, Harcourt.

Douglas, Mary. 1980. *Evans-Pritchard: His Life, Work, Writings and Ideas.* New York: Viking.

Draper, Robert. 2020. *To Start a War: How the Bush Administration Took America into Iraq.* New York: Penguin Books.

Drousiotis, Makarios. 2005a. "The Construction of Reality and the Mass Media in Cyprus: The Obliteration of Opposing Opinion through Defamation; The Case of President Papadopoulos's Accusations That His Political Opponents Were Financed by the United States and the United Nations." http://www.makarios.eu/upload/20051111/1131713084-12865.pdf.

Drousiotis, Makarios. 2005b. "The Great Conspiracy of Brains." *Politis*, February 27, 2005. http://www.makarios.eu/cgibin/hweb?-A=727&-V=english.

Drousiotis, Makarios. 2010. "Άντης Χατζηκωστής¨ Τον σκότωσε (κι αυτόν) η μιτ" [Andy Hadjikostis: The MIT killed him (too)]. Protagon.gr, January 13, 2010. http://www.protagon.gr/apopseis/blogs/antis-xatzikwstis-ton-skotwse-ki-afton-i-mit-1053000000.

Drousiotis, Makarios. 2014. *Κύπρος 1974–77. Η Εισβολή και οι Μεγάλες Δυνάμεις¨ Η realpolitik των ΗΠΑ και το διπλό παιχνίδι της ΕΣΣΔ.* Nicosia: Alfadi. Published in English as *The Cyprus Crisis and the Cold War: USSR Duplicity versus US Realpolitik (1974–1977).* Nicosia, Cyprus: Alfadi Books, 2016.

Drucker, Ernest, Phillip G. Alcabes, and Preston A. Marx. 2001. "The Injection Century: Massive Unsterile Injections and the Emergence of Human Pathogens." *Lancet* 358, no. 9297: 1989–92. https://doi.org/10.1016/S0140-6736(01)06967-7.

Drumont, Édouard. 1886. *La France juive.* Paris: C. Marpon and E. Flammarion

Drumont, Édouard. 1891. *Le testament d'un antisémite.* Paris: Librairie de la Société des Gens de Lettres.

Drumont, Édouard. 1894. "La mort du tsar: La trahison du juif Dreyfus," and "Alexandre III." *La libre parole*, November 2, 1894.

Du Bois, W. E. B. 1935. *Black Reconstruction*. New York: Harcourt, Brace and Company.

Du Bois, W. E. B. 2007. *The Philadelphia Negro: A Social Study*. Oxford: Oxford University Press.

Dumit, Joseph. 2006. "Illnesses You Have to Fight to Get: Facts as Forces in Uncertain, Emergent Illnesses." *Social Science and Medicine* 62, no. 3 (February 2006): 577–90.

Dumit, Joseph. 2012. *Drugs for Life: How Pharmaceutical Companies Define Our Health*. Durham: Duke University Press.

Dumit, Joseph. 2017. "Game Design as STS Research." *Engaging Science, Technology, and Society* 3: 603–12.

Dumit, Joseph. 2018. "The Infernal Alternatives of Corporate Pharmaceutical Research: Abandoning Psychiatry." *Medical Anthropology* 37, no. 1 (January): 59–74. https://doi.org/10.1080/01459740.2017.1360877.

Eddy, Bernice E., and Sarah E. Stewart. 1959. "Characteristics of the SE Polyoma Virus." *American Journal of Public Health and the Nation's Health* 49, no. 11: 1486–92.

Edmonds, Bill. 2015. *God Is Not Here: A Soldier's Struggle with Torture, Trauma, and the Moral Injuries of War*. New York: Pegasus Books.

Edmonds, Bill. 2018. "God Is Not Here." In *War and Moral Injury: A Reader*, edited by Robert Emmet Meagher and Douglas A. Pryer, 37–50. Eugene, OR: Cascade Books.

Ehrenreich, Ben. 2009. "California Scheming: In the Latest Push to Privatize Public Education, Regents at the University of California Have Raised Tuition by 32 Percent." *The Nation*, December 10, 2009. https://www.thenation.com/article/california-scheming-1/.

Ellis, Stephen. 1989. "Tuning In to Pavement Radio." *African Affairs* 88, no. 352 (July): 321–30.

Ellison, Ralph. 1964. *Shadow and Act*. New York: Vintage Books.

Ellison, Sarah. 2016. "Exclusive: Is Donald Trump's Endgame the Launch of Trump News?" *Vanity Fair*, June 16, 2016. https://www.vanityfair.com/news/2016/06/donald-trump-tv-network.

Elsea, Jennifer. 2016. "In Re Terrorist Attacks on September 11, 2001: Claims against Saudi Defendants under the Foreign Sovereign Immunities Act (FSIA)." Washington, DC: Congressional Research Service.

Eminoğlu, Bilbay. 2009. "Papadopulos olayının faillerinden ses bekleniyor" [Waiting for a Sign from the Perpetrators of the Papadopoulos Incident]. *Kıbrıs*, December 15, 2009.

Erhaim, Zaina. 2022. "On the Anniversary of the Syrian Uprising, Where Does the Country's Independent Media Stand?" *Syria Untold*, March 18, 2022. https://syriauntold.com/2022/03/18/on-the-anniversary-of-the-syrian-uprising-where-does-the-countrys-independent-media-stand/.

Ersoy, Metin. 2010. "Peace Journalism and News Coverage on the Cyprus Conflict." *Muslim World* 100: 78–99.

Evans-Pritchard, Edward E. 1937. *Witchcraft, Oracles, and Magic among the Azande.* Oxford: Oxford University Press.

Evripidou, Stefanos. 2010. "Grave-Robbing Trial Opens." *Cyprus Mail*, July 15, 2010.

Fallows, James. 2015. "An Important Book on Moral Injuries." *The Atlantic*, November 23, 2015.

Faludi, Susan. 1999. *Stiffed: The Betrayal of the American Man.* New York: William Morrow.

Fanon, Frantz. 2004. *The Wretched of the Earth.* Translated by Constance Farrington. New York: Grove Press.

Fassin, Didier. 2011. "The Politics of Conspiracy: On AIDS in South Africa and a Few Other Global Plots." *Brown Journal of World Affairs* 17, no. 11 (Spring): 39–50.

Fassin, Didier. 2012. *Humanitarian Reason. A Moral History of Present Times.* Berkeley: University of California Press.

Fassin, Didier, and Richard Rechtman. 2009. *The Empire of Trauma: An Inquiry into the Condition of Victimhood.* Princeton, NJ: Princeton University Press.

Fenster, Mark. 2008. *Conspiracy Theories: Secrecy and Power in American Culture.* Minneapolis: University of Minnesota Press.

Ferme, Mariane C. 2001. *The Underneath of Things: Violence, History, and the Everyday in Sierra Leone.* Berkeley: University of California Press.

Ferrari, G. R. F. 2000. "Introduction." In Plato, *The Republic*, edited by G. R. F. Ferrari, translated by Tom Griffith, xi–xxxi. Cambridge: Cambridge University Press.

Ferrari, G. R. F. 2003. *City and Soul in Plato's Republic.* Chicago: University of Chicago Press.

Ferris, Sarah. 2016. "Trump Compares US Airports to 'Third-World Country.'" *The Hill*, September 26, 2016. http://thehill.com/policy/transportation/297935-trump-compares-us-airports-to-third-world-country.

Fields, Karen E. 2001. "Witchcraft and Racecraft: Invisible Ontology in Its Sensible Manifestations." In *Witchcraft Dialogues: Anthropological and Philosophical Exchanges*, edited by George C. Bond and Diane M. Ciekawy, 283–315. Athens: Ohio University Center for International Studies.

Finkel, David. 2013. *Thank You for Your Service.* New York: Sarah Crichton Books/Farrar, Straus and Giroux.

Fish, Stanley. 1980. *Is There a Text in This Class? The Authority of Interpretive Communities.* Cambridge, MA: Harvard University Press.

Fisher, Max. 2022. *The Chaos Machine.* New York: Little, Brown and Company.

Fleck, Ludwik. 1979. *Genesis and Development of a Scientific Fact.* Chicago: University of Chicago Press.

Florido, Luciano. 2016. "Fake News and a 400-Year-Old Problem: We Need to Resolve the 'Post-truth' Crisis." *Guardian*, November 29, 2016. https://www.theguardian.com/technology/2016/nov/29/fake-news-echo-chamber-ethics-infosphere-internet-digital.

Flynn, Kevin, and Gary Gerhardt. 1989. *The Silent Brotherhood: Inside America's Racist Underground.* New York: Free Press. Available in Western History Collection, Denver Public Library.

Foucault, Michel. 1970. *The Order of Things: An Archaeology of the Human Science.* Translated by Alan Sheridan. New York: Vintage Books.

Foucault, Michel. 1978. *The History of Sexuality, Vol I.* Translated by Robert Hurley. New York: Vintage Books.

Fountain, Ben. 2012. *Billy Lynn's Long Halftime Walk.* New York: Echo.

Fox, Frank. 1997. "*The Protocols of the Elders of Zion* and the Shadowy World of Élie de Cyon." *East European Jewish Affairs* 27, no. 1: 3–22.

Frank, Jill. 2007. "Wages of War: On Judgment in Plato's *Republic.*" *Political Theory* 35, no. 4: 443–67.

Frank, Jill. 2018. *Poetic Justice: Rereading Plato's "Republic."* Chicago: University of Chicago Press.

Freeman, Daniel, and Jason Freeman. 2017. "Are We Entering a Golden Age of the Conspiracy Theory?" *Guardian*, March 28, 2017. https://www.theguardian .com/science/blog/2017/mar/28/are-we-entering-a-golden-age-of-the -conspiracy-theory.

Freud, Sigmund. 1905. *Jokes and Their Relation to the Unconscious. Standard Edition vol. VIII.* Translated by James Strachey. New York: W. W. Norton.

Freud, Sigmund. 1914–16. "Mourning and Melancholia." Translated by James Strachey. In *The Standard Edition of the Complete Psychological Works of Sigmund Freud, Vol. XIV (1914–1916): On the History of the Psycho-Analytic Movement Papers on Metapsychology and Other Works* 237–58. London: Hogarth Press, 237–58.

Freud, Sigmund. 1919. "Lines of Advance in Psycho-Analytic Therapy." In *The Standard Edition of The Complete Psychological Works of Sigmund Freud, Vol. XVII,* 159–69. London: Hogarth Press.

Freud, Sigmund. 1955. *The Standard Edition of the Complete Psychological Works of Sigmund Freud, Vol. XVII (1917–1919.)* London: Hogarth Press.

Gallagher, Catherine. 2018. *Telling It Like It Wasn't: The Counterfactual Imagination in History and Fiction.* Chicago: University of Chicago Press.

Geertz, Clifford. 1973. "Thick Description: Toward an Interpretive Theory of Culture." In *The Interpretation of Cultures: Selected Essays,* 3–30. New York: Basic Books.

Geissler, Paul Wenzel. 2013. "Public Secrets in Public Health: Knowing Not to Know While Making Scientific Knowledge." *American Ethnologist* 40, no. 1: 13–34.

Geissler, Paul Wenzel, and Robert Pool. 2006. "Popular Concerns about Medical Research Projects in Sub-Saharan Africa: A Critical Voice in Debates about Medical Research Ethics." *Tropical Medicine and International Health* 11, no. 7: 975–82.

Gellin, Bruce, John F. Modlin, and Stanley A. Plotkin. 2001. "CHAT Oral Polio Vaccine Was Not the Source of Human Immunodeficiency Virus Type 1 Group M for Humans." *Clinical Infectious Diseases* 32, no. 7: 1068–84. https://doiorg .stanford.idm.oclc.org/10.1086/319612.

Gellman, Barton. 2008. *Angler: The Cheney Vice Presidency*. New York: Penguin Books.

Gerhardt, Gary, John Accola, and Kevin Flynn. 1985. "Informants Name 2 Berg Suspects." *Rocky Mountain News*, February 10, 1985. Western History Collection, Denver Public Library.

Gessen, Masha. 2018. "Why the Russian Influence Campaign Remains So Hard to Understand." *The New Yorker*, December 18, 2018.

Ghosh, Amitav. 1994. "The Global Reservation: Notes toward an Ethnography of International Peacekeeping." *Cultural Anthropology* 9, no. 3: 412–22.

Ghoshroy, Subrata. 2013. "Serious Questions about the Integrity of the UN Report." *21st Century Wire*, September 26, 2013. https://tinyurl.com/l835ygp.

Gibson, James William. 1994. *Warrior Dreams: Violence and Manhood in Post-Vietnam America*. New York: Hill and Wang.

Gilbert, M. Thomas P., Andrew Rambaut, Gabriela Wlasiuk, Thomas J. Spira, Arthur E. Pitchenik, and Michael Worobey. 2007. "The Emergence of HIV/AIDS in the Americas and Beyond." *Proceedings of the National Academy of Sciences of the United States of America* 104, no. 47: 18566–70. https://doi.org/10.1073/pnas.0705329104.

Ginzburg, Carlo. 1979. "Clues: Roots of a Scientific Paradigm." *Theory and Society* 7, no. 3 (May): 273–88.

Ginzburg, Carlo. 1992. "Clues: Roots of an Evidentiary Paradigm." In *Clues, Myths, and the Historical Method*, translated by John and Anne C. Tedeschi, 87–113. Baltimore, MD: Johns Hopkins University Press.

Girard, René. 1989. *The Scapegoat*. Translated by Yvonne Freccero. Baltimore: Johns Hopkins University Press.

Girard, René. 1996. "Overview of the Mimetic Theory." In *The Girard Reader*, edited by James G. Williams, 7–29. New York: Crossroad.

Glasser, Susan B. 2016. "Covering Politics in a 'Post-truth' America." *Brookings*, December 2, 2016. https://www.brookings.edu/essay/covering-politics-in-a-post-truth-america/.

Goldstein, Joseph. 2015. "U.S. Soldiers Told to Ignore Sexual Abuse of Boys by Afghan Allies." *New York Times*, September 20, 2015.

Goodman, Maxine D. 2010. "A Hedgehog on the Witness Stand—What's the Big Idea? The Challenges of Using Daubert to Assess Social Science and Nonscientific Testimony." *American University Law Review* 59, no. 3 (February): 635–84.

Gottesman, Alex. 2014. *Politics and the Street in Democratic Athens*. New York: Cambridge University Press.

Goudsmit, Jaap. 1997. *Viral Sex: The Nature of AIDS*. New York: Oxford University Press.

Goux, Jean-Joseph. (1973) 1990. *Symbolic Economies: After Marx and Freud*. Translated by Jennifer Curtiss Gage. Ithaca, NY: Cornell University Press.

Graeber, David, and David Wengrow. 2021. *The Dawn of Everything: A New History of Humanity*. London: Allen Lane.

Griesemer, James. 2020. "Taking Goodhart's Law Meta: Gaming, Meta-gaming, and Hacking Academic Performance Metrics." In *Gaming the Metrics: Misconduct and Manipulation in Academic Research*, edited by Mario Biagioli and Alexandra Lippman, 77–87. Cambridge, MA: MIT Press.

Griffin, Robert S. 2001. *The Fame of a Dead Man's Deeds: An Up-Close Portrait of White Nationalist William Pierce*. Self-published, 1st Books Library.

Groeger, Lena V., Jeff Kao, Al Shaw, Moiz Syed, and Maya Eliahou. 2021. "What Parler Saw during the Attack on the Capitol." ProPublica, January 17, 2021. https://projects.propublica.org/parler-capitol-videos/.

Grove, Andy. 2001. "Andy Grove's Rational Exuberance." Interview by John Heilemann. *Wired*, June 1, 2001. https://www.wired.com/2001/06/intel-2/.

Gumbel, Andrew, and Roger G. Charles. 2012. *Oklahoma City: What the Investigation Missed—and Why It Still Matters*. New York: William Morrow.

Gürtler, L. G., and J. Eberle. 2017. "Aspects on the History of Transmission and Favor of Distribution of Viruses by Iatrogenic Action: Perhaps an Example of a Paradigm of the Worldwide Spread of HIV." *Medical Microbiology and Immunology* 206, no. 4 (August): 287–93.

Haberman, Maggie, and Emily Steel. 2016. "Jared Kushner Talks of a Trump TV Network with a Media Deal Maker." *New York Times*, October 17, 2016. https://www.nytimes.com/2016/10/18/us/politics/donald-trump-tv-jared-kushner.html.

Habermas, Jürgen. (1962) 1989. *The Structural Transformation of the Public Sphere: An Inquiry into a Category of Bourgeois Society*. Translated by Thomas Burger with Frederick Lawrence. Cambridge, MA: MIT Press.

Hagemeister, Michael. 2007. "The Protocols of the Elders of Zion: Between History and Fiction." *New German Critique* 35, no. 1: 83–95.

Hagemeister, Michael. 2017. *Die "Protokolle der Weisen von Zion" vor Gericht: Der Berner Prozess 1933–1937 und die "antisemitische Internationale."* Zurich: Chronos.

Hagopian, Patrick. 2009. *The Vietnam War in American Memory: Veterans, Memorials, and the Politics of Healing*. Amherst: University of Massachusetts Press.

Haines, Gerald K. 1999. "CIA's Role in the Study of UFOs, 1947–90." *Studies in Intelligence*, https://www.cia.gov/library/readingroom/document/0005517742.

Hakim, Danny. 2017. "Monsanto Weed Killer Roundup Faces New Doubts on Safety in Unsealed Documents." *New York Times*, March 14, 2017.

Hall, Andy. 1986. "Secret War: 'Patriots' Have Loose Ties to Rightists Nationwide." *Arizona Republic*, December 21, 1986. Wilcox Collection, Kenneth Spencer Research Library, University of Kansas, Lawrence.

Halttunen, Karen. 1998. *Murder Most Foul: The Killer and the American Gothic Imagination*. Cambridge, MA: Harvard University Press.

Hamer, Fannie Lou. 2013. *Speeches of Fannie Lou Hamer: To Tell It Like It Is*. Jackson: University Press of Mississippi.

Hamilton, William, Robin A. Weiss, and Simon Wain-Hobson, eds. 2001. "Origins of HIV and the AIDS Epidemic." Special issue, *Philosophical Transactions of the*

Royal Society: Biological Sciences 356, no. 1410: 781–957. https://www.jstor.org
/stable/3067022.

Hansen, Jules. 1897. *L'Alliance Franco–Russe.* Paris.

Harcave, Sidney, ed. 1990. *The Memoirs of Count Witte.* Armonk, NY: M. E. Sharpe.

Harding, Susan, and Kathleen Stewart. 2003. "Anxieties of Influence: Conspiracy
Theory and Therapeutic Culture in Millennial America." In *Transparency
and Conspiracy: Ethnographies of Suspicion in the New World Order,* edited by
Harry G. West and Todd Sanders, 258–86. Durham, NC: Duke University
Press.

Harkin, James. 2016. "The Incredible Story behind the Syrian Protest Singer
Everyone Thought Was Dead." *GQ,* December 7, 2016. https://tinyurl.com
/ycyer6f4.

Harlow, Giles D., and George C. Maerz, eds. 1991. *Measures Short of War: The
George F. Kennan Lectures at the National War College 1946–47.* Washington, DC:
National Defense University Press.

Harney, Stefano, and Fred Moten. 2013. *The Undercommons: Fugitive Planning and
Black Study.* Wivenhoe, UK: Minor Compositions.

Harper, David. 2008. "The Politics of Paranoia: Paranoid Positioning and Conspiratorial Narratives in the Surveillance Society." *Surveillance and Society* 5, no. 1
(September): 1–32.

Harrington, J. S., N. D. McGlashan, and E. Z. Chelkowska, 2004. "A Century of
Migrant Labour in the Gold Mines of South Africa." *Journal of the South African
Institute of Mining and Metallurgy* (March): 65–71.

Harris, Neal. 1973. *Humbug: The Art of P. T. Barnum.* Chicago: University of Chicago
Press.

Hartman, Saidiya V., and Frank B. Wilderson III. 2003. "The Position of the Un-
thought." *Qui Parle* 13, no. 2 (Spring): 183–201.

Hartung, William. 2018. "How the Pentagon Devours the Budget." *Tom's Dispatch,*
February 27, 2018. http://www.tomdispatch.com/blog/176391/tomgram%3A
_william_hartung%2C_the_pentagon_budget_as_corporate_welfare_for
_weapons_makers.

Hassapi, Anna. 2009. "Serbian Money Laundering Victim Takes Crusade against
Cyprus to EU." *Cyprus Mail,* October 14, 2009.

Hayden, Michael. 2018. "The End of Intelligence." *New York Times,* April 28,
2018. https://www.nytimes.com/2018/04/28/opinion/sunday/the-end-of
-intelligence.html.

Hayek, Friedrich A. von. 1967. "The Results of Human Action but Not of Human
Design." In *Studies in Philosophy, Politics, and Economics,* 96–105. Chicago:
University of Chicago Press.

Hayek, Friedrich A. von. 1978. *The Constitution of Liberty.* Washington, DC: Regnery
Publishing.

Hazou, Elias. 2016. "Minister Pledges Probe into Chemtrails." *Cyprus Mail*, February 17, 2016. http://cyprus-mail.com/2016/02/17/minister-pledges-probe-into-chemtrails/.

Healy, David. 2012. *Pharmageddon.* Berkeley: University of California Press.

Hegghammer, Thomas. 2010. *Jihad in Saudi Arabia: Violence and Pan-Islamism since 1979.* Cambridge: Cambridge University Press.

Hellmich, Christina. 2011. *Al-Qaeda: From Global Network to Local Franchise.* London: Zed Books.

Hempel, Carl G. 1965. *Aspects of Scientific Explanation.* New York: Free Press,

Hersh, Seymour M. 2013. "Whose Sarin?" *London Review of Books* 35, no. 24 (December 19, 2013). https://tinyurl.com/uaamcqw.

Hersh, Seymour M. 2014. "The Red Line and the Rat Line." *London Review of Books* 36, no. 8 (April 17, 2014). https://tinyurl.com/kmelblf.

Hesk, Jonathan P. 2000. *Deception and Democracy in Classical Athens.* Cambridge: Cambridge University Press.

Higgins, Eliot. 2013. "Who Was Responsible for the August 21st Attack?" *Brown Moses Blog*, September 16, 2013. https://tinyurl.com/ybbarngd.

Hilleman, Maurice R. 1998. "Discovery of Simian Virus 40 (sv40) and Its Relationship to Poliomyelitis Virus Vaccines." *Developments in Biological Standardization* 94: 183–90.

Hillis, Faith. 2017. "The Franco–Russian Marseillaise: International Exchange and the Making of Antiliberal Politics in Fin de Siècle France." *Journal of Modern History* 89: 45–53.

Hinton, Elizabeth. 2016. *From the War on Poverty to the War on Crime: The Making of Mass Incarceration in America.* Cambridge, MA: Harvard University Press.

Hofstadter, Richard. 1996a. "Goldwater and Pseudo-conservative Politics." In *The Paranoid Style in American Politics and Other Essays*, 93–144. Cambridge, MA: Harvard University Press. 1965.

Hofstadter, Richard. 1964. "The Paranoid Style in American Politics." *Harper's Magazine*, November, 77–86.

Hofstadter, Richard. 1996b. *The Paranoid Style in American Politics and Other Essays.* Cambridge, MA: Harvard University Press.

Hogenhuis-Seliverstoff, Anne. 2001. *Juliette Adam, 1836–1936: L'instigatrice.* Paris: L'Harmattan.

Hollande, Francois. 2015. "Speech at the Shoah Memorial in France." French Embassy to the United States, January 27, 2015. https://franceintheus.org/spip.php?article6472.

Hooper, Edward. 2000a. "Commentary: Response to 11 September 2000 Press Release from the Wistar Institute Titled 'No AIDS-Related Viruses or Chimpanzee DNA Found in 1950s-Era Polio Vaccine." *AIDS Origins*, October 11, 2000. http://aidsorigins.com/commentary.

Hooper, Edward. 2000b. "Of Chimps and Men." *Science* 287, no. 5451: 233. https://doi.org/10.1126/science.287.5451.233b.

Hooper, Edward. 2000c. *The River: A Journey to the Source of HIV and AIDS*. Boston: Back Bay Books.

Hooper, Edward. 2001. "Experimental Oral Polio Vaccines and Acquired Immune Deficiency Syndrome." *Philosophical Transactions of the Royal Society, Series B: Biological Sciences* 356, no. 1410: 803–14.

Hoopes, John W. 2011. "11-11-11, Apophenia, and the Meaning of Life." *Reality Check* (blog), *Psychology Today*, November 11, 2011. https://www.psychologytoday.com/us/blog/reality-check/201111/11-11-11-apophenia-and-the-meaning-life.

Horkheimer, Max, and Theodor W. Adorno. 2002. *Dialectic of Enlightenment*. Translated by John Cumming. Stanford, CA: Stanford University Press.

Horton, Zach. 2019. "Toward a Particulate Politics: Visibility and Scale in a Time of Slow Violence." *Electronic Book Review*, December 1, 2019. https://doi.org/10.7273/9WR4-K121.

Howland, Jacob. 2004. "Plato's Reply to Lysias: *Republic* 1 and 2 and *Against Eratosthenes*." *American Journal of Philology* 125, no. 2: 179–208.

Howland, Jacob. 2018. *Glaucon's Fate: History, Myth, and Character in Plato's "Republic."* Philadelphia: Paul Dry Books.

Hull, Elizabeth, and Deborah James. 2012. "Introduction: Popular Economies in South Africa." *Africa: International Journal of the Africa Institute* 82, no. 1: 1–19.

Hull, Matthew. 2012. *Government of Paper: The Materiality of Bureaucracy in Pakistan*. Berkeley: University of California Press.

Hull, Robert N., James R. Minner, and Carmine C. Mascoli. 1958. "New Viral Agents Recovered from Tissue Cultures of Monkey Kidney Cells: III. Recovery of Additional Agents Both from Cultures of Monkey Tissues and Directly from Tissues and Excreta." *American Journal of Epidemiology* 68, no. 1: 31–44.

Human Rights Watch. 2013. *Attacks on Ghouta: Analysis of the Alleged Use of Chemical Weapons in Syria*. September 10, 2013. https://www.hrw.org/report/2013/09/10/attacks-ghouta/analysis-alleged-use-chemical-weapons-syria.

Humphreys, Laura-Zoe. 2012. "Symptomologies of the State: Cuba's 'Email War' and the Paranoid Public Sphere." In *Digital Cultures and the Politics of Emotion: Feelings, Affect and Technological Change*, edited by Athina Karatzogianni and Adi Kuntsman, 197–214. Basingstoke, UK: Palgrave Macmillan.

Hutson, Lorna. 2011. *The Invention of Suspicion: Law and Mimesis in Shakespeare and Renaissance Drama*. Oxford: Oxford University Press.

Illing, Sean. 2018. "A Princeton Sociologist Spent 8 Years Asking Rural Americans Why They're So Pissed Off." *Vox*, June 30, 2018. https://www.vox.com/2018/3/13/17053886/trump-rural-america-populism-racial-resentment.

Ioannou, Yiannis E. 2009. Θεωρία της συνωμοσίας και κουλτούρα της διχοτόμησης¨ Δοκίμιο για τον Πολιτικό Πολιτισμό της Κύπρου [Conspiracy Theory and the Culture of Partition: Essay on the Political Culture of Cyprus]. Athens: Editions Papazisi.

Ioannou, Yiannis. 2010. "Νεκροταφεία υπό επιτήρηση" Η Αστυνομία σε κινητοποίηση για τη βεβήλωση του τάφου του Σπύρου Κυπριανού" [Cemeteries under Surveillance: Police Mobilize after the Desecration of Spyros Kyprianou's Grave]. *Simerini*, January 12, 2010.

Ivanow, P. 1887. *Confession d'un nihiliste, précédée d'une étude sur les nihilistes en général.* Paris: L. Sauvaitre.

Jackson, John L. 2008. *Racial Paranoia: The Unintended Consequences of Political Correctness.* New York: Civitas Books.

Jackson, John L., Jr. 2017. "What's Love Got to Do with It? Race, Conspiracy Theories, and Contemporary Hip-Hop Culture." Lecture at Pitzer College, Claremont, CA, November 14, 2017. https://www.pitzer.edu/mcsi/2017/11/14/john-l-jackson-jr-whats-love-got/.

Jacobs, David. 1992. *Secret Life: Firsthand Accounts of UFO Abductions.* New York: Simon and Schuster.

Jacobsen, Annie. 2012. *Area 51: An Uncensored History of America's Top Secret Military Base.* New York: Little, Brown, and Company.

Jain, Sarah S. Lochlann. 2006. *Injury: The Politics of Product Design and Safety Law in the United States.* Princeton, NJ: Princeton University Press.

Jameson, Fredric. 1988. "Cognitive Mapping." In *Marxism and the Interpretation of Culture*, edited by Cary Nelson and Lawrence Grossberg, 347–57. Basingstoke, UK: Macmillan.

Jameson, Fredric. 1992. *Postmodernism, or, the Cultural Logic of Late Capitalism.* Durham, NC: Duke University Press.

Javers, Eamon. 2011. "NY Fed's $40 Billion Iraqi Money Trail." *CNBC.com*, October 25, 2011.

Jeeves, Alan. 1985. *Migrant Labour in South Africa's Mining Economy: The Struggle for the Gold Mines' Labour Supply, 1890–1920.* Montreal: McGill-Queen's University Press.

Jehan-Préval. 1892. *Anarchie et Nihilisme.* Paris: Albert Savine.

Jennings, Kathleen M. 2016. "Blue Helmet Havens: Peacekeeping as Bypassing in Liberia and the Democratic Republic of the Congo." *International Peacekeeping* 2, no. 2: 302–25.

Jerven, Morten. 2013. *Poor Numbers: How We Are Misled by African Development Statistics and What to Do about It.* Ithaca, NY: Cornell University Press.

Johnson, Hillary. 1997. *Osler's Web: Inside the Labyrinth of the Chronic Fatigue Syndrome Epidemic.* New York: Penguin.

Johnson, Sam. 2011. *Pogroms, Peasants, Jews: Britain and Eastern Europe's "Jewish Question," 1867–1925.* New York: Palgrave.

Jones, Nate. 2016. *Able Archer 83: The Secret History of the NATO Exercise That Almost Triggered Nuclear War.* New York: The New Press.

Jones, Nicholas F. 1999. *The Associations of Classical Athens: The Response to Democracy.* New York: Oxford University Press.

"Judge Bars Ku Klux Klan from Having Own Army in Texas." 1982. *Chicago Tribune*, June 4, 1982.

"Jury Told of Plan to Kill Radio Host." 1987. *New York Times*, November 8, 1987.

Kalatzis, Manolis. 2009. "Κάλεσαν τον Πρέντανγκ Τζόρτζεβιτς¨ Καταθέσεις και από πρόσωπα που βρέθηκαν ως αντίδικοι με τον Τάσσο στο δικαστήριο" [Predag Đorđević Called to the Stand: Testimony in Court from Opponents of Tassos]. *Politis*, December 22, 2009.

Kalter, S. S., and Heberling, R. L. 1971. "Comparative Virology of Primates." *Bacteriological Reviews* 35, no. 3: 310–64.

"Kar'era P. I. Rachkovskogo. Dokumenty." 1918. *Byloe* 30, no. 2: 78–87.

Karni, Annie, and Maggie Haberman. 2020. "Trump Makes First Public Appearance since Leaving Walter Reed." *New York Times*, October 10, 2020.

Kasimis, Demetra. 2016. "Plato's Open Secret." *Contemporary Political Theory* 15, no. 4 (November): 339–57.

Katyal, Neal Kumar. 2003. "Conspiracy Theory." *Yale Law Journal* 112, no. 6 (March): 1307–98.

Keane, Webb. 2014. "Affordances and Reflexivity in Ethical Life: An Ethnographic Stance." *Anthropological Theory* 14, no. 1 (March): 3–26.

Keck, Frederic, and Christos Lynteris. 2018. "Zoonosis: Prospects and Challenges for Medical Anthropology." *Medicine Anthropology Theory* 5, no. 3. https://doi .org/10.17157/mat.5.3.372.

Keeley, Brian. 1999. "Of Conspiracy Theories." *Journal of Philosophy* 96, no. 3: 109–26.

Kennan, George F. 1978. "The Mystery of the Ferdinand Documents." *Jahrbücher für Geschichte Osteuropas* 26, no. 3: 321–52.

Kennan, George F. 1984. *The Fateful Alliance.* New York: Pantheon Books.

Kennan, George F. 1986. "The Curious Monsieur Cyon." *American Scholar* 55, no. 4: 449–75.

Kennedy, Pagan. 2017. "How to Destroy the Business Model of Breitbart and Fake News." *New York Times*, January 7, 2017.

Kerry, John. 2013. "Remarks on Syria." Press Briefing Room, Washington, DC, August 26, 2013. US Department of State, Archived Content. https://tinyurl .com/y8pp9rcd.

Kessler, Glenn, Salvador Rizzo, and Meg Kelly. "Trump's False or Misleading Claims Total 30,573 over 4 Years." *Washington Post*, January 24, 2021.

Keum, Tae-Yeoun. 2020. "Plato's Myth of Er and the Reconfiguration of Nature." *American Political Science Review* 114, no. 1: 54–67.

Khan, Lina, and Sandeep Vaheesan. 2017. "Market Power and Inequality: The Antitrust Counterrevolution and Its Discontents." *Harvard Law and Policy Review* 11, no. 1 (Winter): 235–94.

Kifner, John. 1995. "Oklahoma Bombing Suspect: Unraveling of a Frayed Life." *New York Times*, December 21, 1995.

King, Gary, Jennifer Pan, and Margaret E. Roberts. 2019. "How the Chinese Government Fabricates Social Media Posts for Strategic Distraction, Not Engaged Argument." *American Political Science Review* 111, no. 3 (August): 484–501.

Kinsella, Helen. 2011. *The Image before the Weapon: A Critical History of the Distinction between Combatant and Civilian.* Ithaca, NY: Cornell University Press.

"KKK Leader Beam Says He'll Accept New Post." 1981. *Houston Post*, July 30, 1981.

Knight, Peter. 2000. *Conspiracy Culture: From Kennedy to "The X-Files."* New York: Routledge.

Koch, Insa. 2021. "Moving beyond Institutional Differences: Towards a Critical Anthropology of Law beyond the Doctrine of Separation of Powers." *PoLAR: Political and Legal Anthropology Review*, November 18, 2021. https://polarjournal .org/2021/11/18/moving-beyond-institutional-differences-towards-a-critical -anthropology-of-law-beyond-the-doctrine-of-separation-of-powers/.

Kohlmann, Evan. 2004. *Al-Qaida's Jihad in Europe: The Afghan-Bosnian Network.* Nashville, TN: Vanderbilt University Press.

Koprowski, Hillary. 1960. "Tin Anniversary of the Development of Live Virus Vaccine." *Journal of the American Medical Association* 174, no. 5: 972–76.

Kostakopoulos, Yiannis. 2010. "Πήραν τις σημαίες" Βεβήλωση και στο μνήμα του πρώην προέδρου Σπ. Κύπριανου στη Λεμεσό" [They Stole the Flags: Another Desecration at the Tomb of Former President Spyros Kyprianou]. *Politis*, January 11, 2010.

Kremer, M., and C. M. Snyder. 2003. "Why Are Drugs More Profitable Than Vaccines? *NBER Working Paper No. 9833*." Cambridge, MA: National Bureau of Economic Research.

Krog, Antjie. 2008. "'This Thing Called Reconciliation . . .' Forgiveness as Part of an Interconnectedness-Towards-Wholeness.'" *South African Journal of Philosophy* 27, no. 4: 353–66.

Kudo, Timothy. 2018. "On War and Redemption." In *War and Moral Injury: A Reader*, edited by Robert Emmet Meagher and Douglas A. Pryer, 79–82. Eugene, OR: Cascade Books.

Kuhn, Thomas S. 2012. *The Structure of Scientific Revolutions.* 50th anniv. ed. Chicago: University of Chicago Press.

Laidlaw, James. 2013. *The Subject of Virtue: An Anthropology of Ethics and Freedom.* New York: Cambridge University Press.

Lambie, Ryan. 2017. "Rakka: A Guide to Neill Blomkamp's Brand New Sci-Fi Short." *Den of Geek*, June 15, 2017. https://www.denofgeek.com/movies /rakka-a-guide-to-neill-blomkamp s brand-new-sci-fi-short/.

Langhard, Johann. 1891. *Das Recht der Politischen Fremdenausweisung mit besonderer Berücksichtigung der Schweiz.* Leipzig: Duncker and Humblot.

Langhard, Johann. 1903. *Die anarchistische Bewegung in der Schweiz von ihren Anfängen bis zur Gegenwart und die internationalen Führer.* Berlin: O. Höring.

"La question juive en Russie." 1883. *La nouvelle revue* 5, no. 22: 283–305.

Latour, Bruno. 2004. "Why Has Critique Run Out of Steam? From Matters of Fact to Matters of Concern." Translated by Antonio Arellano Henandez. *Critical Inquiry* 30 (Winter): 225–48.

Lawrence, D. H. 1990. *Studies in Classic American Literature.* New York: Penguin Books.

"Leader Says White Supremacists Considered Poisoning Major City." 1988. *Albany Democrat-Herald*, February 23, 1988. Wilcox Collection (RH WL Eph 1896), Kenneth Spencer Research Library, University of Kansas, Lawrence.

Lear, Jonathan. 2017. *Wisdom Won from Illness*. Cambridge, MA: Harvard University Press.

le Carré, John. 2004. *The Constant Gardener: A Novel*. New York: Scribner.

Legassick, Martin. 1974. "South Africa: Capital Accumulation and Violence." *Economy and Society* 3, no. 3: 253–91.

Leonhardt, David, and Stuart A. Thompson, 2017. "President Trump's Lies, the Definitive List." *New York Times*, June 23, 2017. Updated December 14, 2017. https://www.nytimes.com/interactive/2017/06/23/opinion/trumps-lies.html.

Lerner, Sharon. 2020. "Big Pharma Prepares to Profit from the Coronavirus." *The Intercept* (blog), March 13, 2020. https://theintercept.com/2020/03/13/big-pharma-drug-pricing-coronavirus-profits/.

Lester, Michael. 2016. "Donald Trump's Conspiracy Theories." *New York Times*, February 29, 2016. Video, 2:58. https://www.nytimes.com/video/us/politics/100000004236529/donald-trumps-conspiracy-theories.html.

Levie, Joseph. 1954. "Hearsay and Conspiracy: A Reexamination of the Co-conspirators' Exception to the Hearsay Rule." *Michigan Law Review* 52, no. 8 (June): 1159–78.

Lévi-Strauss, Claude. 1966. *The Savage Mind*. Chicago: University of Chicago Press.

Levitsky, Steven, and Daniel Ziblatt. 2018. *How Democracies Die*. New York: Crown Books.

Lewis, A. M., Jr. 1973. "Experience with sv40 and Adenovirus-sv40 Hybrids." In *Biohazards in Biological Research*, edited by Alfred Hellman, M.N. Oxman, and Robert Pollack, 96–113. Cold Spring Harbor, NY: Cold Spring Harbor Laboratory Press.

Lewis, James R., ed. 1995. *The Gods Have Landed: New Religions from Other Worlds*. Albany, NY: SUNY Press.

Li, Darryl. 2011. "Lies, Damned Lies, and Plagiarizing 'Experts.'" *Middle East Report* 260 (Fall).

Li, Darryl. 2019. *The Universal Enemy: Jihad, Empire, and the Challenge of Solidarity*. Stanford, CA: Stanford University Press.

Lieberman, Amy, and Susanne Rust. 2015. "Big Oil Braced for Global Warming While It Fought Regulations." *Los Angeles Times*, December 15. https://graphics.latimes.com/oil-operations/.

Lifton, Robert J. 1973. *Home from the War: Vietnam Veterans, Neither Victims nor Executioners*. New York: Simon and Schuster.

Ligneau, Jean. 1891. *Juifs et antisémites en Europe*. Paris: Tolra.

Lippman, Walter. 1993. *The Phantom Public*. New Brunswick, NJ: Transaction Publishers.

Lipsitz, George. 2006. *The Possessive Investment in Whiteness*. Philadelphia: Temple University Press.

Litz, Brett T., Leslie Lebowitz, Matt. J. Gray, and William P. Nash. 2016. *Adaptive Disclosure: A New Treatment for Military Trauma, Loss and Moral Injury.* New York: Guilford Press.

Litz, Brett T., Nathan Stein, Eileen Delaney, Leslie Lebowitz, William P. Nash, Carline Silva, and Shira Maguen. 2009. "Moral Injury and Moral Repair in War Veterans: A Preliminary Model and Intervention Strategy." *Clinical Psychology Review* 29, no. 8 (December): 695–706.

Lombard, Louisa. 2016a. *State of Rebellion: Violence and Intervention in the Central African Republic.* London: Zed Books.

Lombard, Louisa. 2016b. "The Threat of Rebellion: Claiming Entitled Personhood in Central Africa." *Journal of the Royal Anthropological Institute* 22, no. 3 (September): 552–69.

Lord Lamington. 1881. "International Law—Right of Asyldh for Political Offenders: Question, Observations." (House of Lords Debate, May 19, 1881), *Hansard* 261: 785–89. https://api.parliament.uk/historic-hansard/lords/1881/may/19/international-law-right-of-asyldh-for#column_786.

Lutz, Catherine. 2001. *Homefront: A Military City and the American Twentieth Century.* Boston: Beacon Press.

Lysias. 2000. *Lysias.* Translated by S. C. Todd. Austin: University of Texas Press.

Macdonald, Andrew [William Pierce]. 1978. *The Turner Diaries.* Hillsboro, WV: National Vanguard Books.

MacFarquhar, Neil. 2016. "A Powerful Russian Weapon: The Spread of False Stories." *New York Times*, August 28, 2016.

MacLean, Nancy. 2017. *Democracy in Chains.* New York: Penguin Books.

Mamdani, Mahmood. 2009. *Saviors and Survivors: Darfur, Politics, and the War on Terror.* New York: Three Rivers Press.

Mann, James. 2004. *Rise of the Vulcans: The History of Bush's War Cabinet.* New York: Penguin Books.

Mannoni, Octave. (1969) 1985. *Clefs pour l'imaginaire ou l'Autre Scène.* Paris: Seuil.

Mapoma, Annie. 1994. "Scratching to Make a Living." *Mail and Guardian*, September 23, 1994. https://mg.co.za/article/1994-09-23-scratching-to-make-a-living.

Marasco, Robyn. 2016. "Toward a Critique of Conspiratorial Reason." *Constellations* 23, no. 2: 236–43.

Marchal, Roland. 2015. "Being Rich, Being Poor: Wealth and Fear in the Central African Republic." In *Making Sense of the Central African Republic*, edited by Tatiana Carayannis and Louisa Lombard, 53–75. London: Zed Books.

Marcus, George E. 1999a. "Introduction to the Volume: The Paranoid Style Now." In *Paranoia within Reason: A Casebook on Conspiracy as Explanation*, edited by George Marcus, 1–12. Chicago: University of Chicago Press.

Marcus, George E., ed. 1999b. *Paranoia within Reason: A Casebook on Conspiracy as Explanation.* Chicago: University of Chicago Press.

Marcus, Ruth. 2016. "Welcome to the Post-truth Presidency." *Washington Post*, December 2, 2016. https://www.washingtonpost.com/opinions/welcome

-to-the-post-truth-presidency/2016/12/02/baaf630a-b8cd-11e6-b994
-f45a208f7a73_story.html?utm_term=.82fe2874f331.

Marcuse, Herbert. 1955. *Eros and Civilization: A Philosophical Inquiry into Freud.* Boston: Beacon.

Mariani, Robert. 2016. "The Left Is Pushing Conspiracy Theories to Feel Better about 2018." *Federalist*, December 23, 2016.

Markel, Howard. 2011. "It's the Science, Stupid." *New Republic*, December 14, 2011. https://newrepublic.com/article/98200/jacques-pepin-origin-aids.

Marliere, Philippe. 2017. "Charlie Hebdo and the Dawn of French McCarthyism." *Open Democracy*, August 15, 2017. https://www.opendemocracy.net/can -europe-make-it/philippe-marli%C3%A8re/charlie-hebdo-and-dawn-of -french-mccarthyism.

Martin, Brian. 2000. Review of *The River: A Journey Back to the Source of HIV and AIDS*, by Edward Hooper. *Science as Culture* 9, no. 1: 109–12. https:// www.bmartin.cc/dissent/documents/AIDS/River/ScienceasCulture .html.

Martin, Brian. 2001. "The Burden of Proof and the Origin of Acquired Immune Deficiency Syndrome." *Philosophical Transactions of the Royal Society, Series B: Biological Sciences* 356, no. 1410: 939–43.

Martin, Brian. 2010. "How to Attack a Scientific Theory and Get Away with It (Usually): The Attempt to Destroy an Origin-of-AIDS Hypothesis." *Science as Culture* 19, no. 2: 215–39.

Martin, Randy. 2011. *Under New Management: Universities, Administrative Labor, and the Professional Turn.* Philadelphia: Temple University Press.

Martinez, Docteur. 1890. *Le juif, voilà, l'ennemi!* Paris: A. Savine.

Martinot, Steve, and Jared Sexton. 2003. "The Avant-Garde of White Supremacy." *Social Identities* 9, no. 2: 169–81.

Marx, Karl. (1867) 1992. *Capital.* Translated by Ben Fowkes. New York: Penguin Books.

Marx, Karl. 1973. *Grundrisse: Foundations of the Critique of Political Economy.* Translated by Martin Nicolaus. London: Penguin Books.

Marx, Karl. 2010. "The 18th Brumaire of Louis Bonaparte." Translated by Ben Fowkes. In *Surveys from Exile*, edited by David Fernbach, p 143–249. Brooklyn: Verso Books.

Marx, Leo. 1964. *The Machine in the Garden.* Oxford: Oxford University Press.

Marx, Preston A., Cristian Apetrei, and Ernest Drucker. 2004. "AIDS as a Zoonosis? Confusion over the Origin of the Virus and the Origin of the Epidemics." *Journal of Medical Primatology* 33, no. 5–6: 220–26. https://doi.org/10.1111/j .1600-0684.2004.00078.x.

Masco, Joseph. 2006. *The Nuclear Borderlands: The Manhattan Project in Post–Cold War New Mexico.* Princeton, NJ: Princeton University Press.

Masco, Joseph. 2014. *The Theater of Operations: National Security Affect from the Cold War to the War on Terror.* Durham, NC: Duke University Press.

Masco, Joseph. 2021. *The Future of Fallout, and Other Episodes in Radioactive World-Making.* Durham, NC: Duke University Press.

Massumi, Brian. 2010. "The Future Birth of the Affective Fact: The Political Ontology of Threat." In *The Affect Theory Reader*, edited by Melissa Gregg and Gregory J. Seigworth, 52–70. Durham, NC: Duke University Press.

Mathiason, David. 1985. "Trial Bares Neo-Nazis' Plots and Links." *Guardian*, October 16, 1985.

Maurras, Charles. 1898. *L'idée de la décentralisation.* Paris: Revue Encyclopédique.

Maxwell, William J. 2015. *F.B. Eyes: How J. Edgar Hoover's Ghostreaders Framed African American Literature.* Princeton, NJ: Princeton University Press.

Mayer, Jane. 2008. *The Dark Side: The Inside Story of How the War on Terror Turned into a War on American Ideals.* New York: Doubleday.

Mayer, Jane. 2016. *Dark Money.* New York: Doubleday.

McChrystal, Stanley. 2013. *My Share of the Task: A Memoir.* New York: Portfolio.

McClure, Kirstie. 1997. "The Odor of Judgment: Exemplarity, Propriety, and Politics in the Company of Hannah Arendt." In *Hannah Arendt and the Meaning of Politics*, edited by Craig J. Calhoun and John McGowan, 53–84. Minneapolis: University of Minnesota Press.

McCoy, Jennifer, Tahmina Rahman, and Murat Somer. 2018. "Polarization and the Global Crisis of Democracy: Common Patterns, Dynamics, and Pernicious Consequences for Democratic Polities." *American Behavioral Scientist* 62, no. 1 (January): 16–42.

McKay, Richard A. 2017. *Patient Zero and the Making of the AIDS Epidemic.* Chicago: University of Chicago Press.

McKenzie-McHarg, Andrew. 2019. "Conspiracy Theory: The Nineteenth-Century Prehistory of a Twentieth-Century Concept." In *Conspiracy Theories and the People Who Believe Them*, edited by Joseph Uscinski, 62–81. Oxford: Oxford University Press.

McKittrick, Katherine, ed. 2015. *Sylvia Wynter: On Being Human as Praxis.* Durham, NC: Duke University Press.

McRae, Elizabeth Gillespie. 2018. *Mothers of Massive Resistance: White Women and the Politics of White Supremacy.* Oxford: Oxford University Press.

Meagher, Robert Emmet, and Douglas A. Pryer, eds. 2018. *Moral Injury: A Reader.* Eugene, OR: Cascade Books.

Media Matters Staff. 2017. "Trump at CPAC Calls Media Outlets 'Enemy of the People,' Demands They Stop Using Unnamed Sources." 2017. *Media Matters for America*, February 24, 2017. https://www.mediamatters.org/video/2017/02/24/trump-cpac-calls-media-outlets-enemy-people-demands-they-stop-using-unnamed-sources/215452.

Meister, Bob Meister. 2009a. "'Are They Saying I'm Right? They Pledged Your Tuition' III." Council of UC Faculty Associations, October 26, 2009. http://www.cucfa.org/news/2009_oct26.php.

Meister, Bob Meister. 2009b. "Response to Faculty Questions: They Pledged Your Tuition' II." Council of UC Faculty Associations, October 19, 2009. http://www .cucfa.org/news/2009_oct19.php.

Meister, Robert. 2011a. *After Evil: A Politics of Human Rights.* New York: Columbia University Press.

Meister, Bob. 2011b. "Debt and Taxes: Can the Financial Industry Save Public Universities?" *Representations* 116, no. 1 (Fall): 128–55.

Meister, Bob. 2009c. "They Pledged Your Tuition (An Open Letter to UC Students)." https://keepcaliforniaspromise.org/wp-content/uploads/2009/10/They _Pledged_Your_Tuition.pdf.

Meister, Bob. 2017. "Confronting the Corporate University: From Cold War Federalization to Financialized Higher Education." *Public Seminar* (blog), March 29, 2017. http://www.publicseminar.org/2017/03/confronting-the -corporate-university/.

Meister, Robert. 2019. "Randy Martin: Politics beyond the Commodity Form." *Social Text* 37, no. 4 (141) (December): 51–74.

Meister, Robert. 2020. *Justice as an Option: Political Redress in an Age of Finance.* Chicago: University of Chicago Press.

Meister, Robert. 2021. *Justice Is an Option: A Democratic Theory of Finance for the Twenty-First Century.* Chicago: University of Chicago Press.

Melley, Timothy. 2000. *Empire of Conspiracy: The Culture of Paranoia in Postwar America.* Ithaca, NY: Cornell University Press.

Melley, Timothy. 2002. "Agency Panic and the Culture of Conspiracy." In *Conspiracy Nation: The Politics of Paranoia in Postwar America*, edited by Peter Knight, 57–84. New York: New York University Press.

Melley, Timothy. 2012. *The Covert Sphere: Secrecy, Fiction, and the National Security State.* Ithaca, NY: Cornell University Press.

Melley, Timothy. 2016. *The Empire of Conspiracy.* Ithaca, NY: Cornell University Press.

Melley, Timothy. 2020a. "Conspiracy in American Narrative." In *Routledge Handbook of Conspiracy Theories*, edited by Michael Butter and Peter Knight, 427–40. New York: Taylor and Francis.

Melley, Timothy. 2020b. "The Public Sphere Hero: Representations of Whistleblowing in U.S. Culture." In *Whistleblowing Nation: The History of National Security Disclosures and the Cult of State Secrecy*, edited by Kaeten Mistry and Hannah Gurman, 213–42. New York: Columbia University Press.

Melley, Timothy. 2021. "The Melodramatic Mode in American Politics and Other Varieties of Narrative Suspicion." *Symploke* 29, no. 1: 57–74.

Metzl, Jonathan M. 2009. *The Protest Psychosis: How Schizophrenia Became a Black Disease.* Boston: Beacon Press.

Metzl, Jonathan M. 2019. *Dying of Whiteness: How the Politics of Racial Resentment Is Killing America's Heartland.* London: Hachette UK.

Michaelidis, Aristos. 2009a. "Ποιόν εξυπηρετεί αυτή η εξαθλίωση" [Who Is Served by This Wretched Act?]. *Philelevtheros*, December 12, 2009.

Michaelidis, Aristos. 2009b. "Μπορεί να το χειριστεί το κράτος και η ηγεσία" [The State and the Government Can Handle the Matter]. *Philelevtheros*, December 14, 2009.

Michaels, Walter Benn. 1996. "'You Who Never Was There': Slavery and the New Historicism, Deconstruction and the Holocaust." *Narrative* 4, no. 1: 1–16.

Michel, Lou, and Dan Herbeck. 2002. *American Terrorist: Timothy McVeigh and the Oklahoma City Bombing*. New York: Avon Books.

Michelis, Cesare G. de 2004. *The Non-existent Manuscript: A Study of the Protocols of the Sages of Zion*. Translated by Richard Newhouse. Lincoln: University of Nebraska Press.

Miller, Flagg. 2015. *The Audacious Ascetic: What the bin Laden Tapes Reveal about al-Qa'ida*. London: Hurst.

Mills, C. Wright. 1959. *The Sociological Imagination*. New York: Oxford University Press.

"Minister Denies Tie to Okla. Bombing, McVeigh." 1995. *Commercial Appeal*, July 3, 1995.

Modigliani, Franco. 1944. "Liquidity Preference and the Theory of Interest and Money." *Econometrica* 12, no. 1 (January): 45–88.

Mookim, Mohit. 2021. "The World Loses under Bill Gates' Vaccine Colonialism." *Wired*, May 19, 2021. https://www.wired.com/story/opinion-the-world-loses-under-bill-gates-vaccine-colonialism/.

Moors, Kent. 1987. "The Argument against a Dramatic Date for Plato's *Republic*." *Polis* 7, no. 1: 6–31.

Morcos, Saad. 1962. *Juliette Adam*. Beirut: Dar al–Maaref–Liban.

Morlin, Bill. 1995. "One Lead in Bombing Ends in North Idaho." *Spokesman-Review*, May 2, 1995.

Morris, Rosalind. 2004. "Images of Untranslatability in the US War on Terror." *Interventions* 6, no. 3: 400–23.

Morris, Rosalind C. 2010. "Accidental Histories, Post-historical Practice? Re-reading *Body of Power, Spirit of Resistance* in the Actuarial Age." *Anthropological Quarterly* 83, no. 1 (Summer): 581–624.

Morris, Rosalind. 2013. "Theses on the New *Öffentlichkeit*." *Grey Room* 51: 94–111.

Morris, Rosalind. 2017a. "Mediation, the Political Task: Between Language and Violence in Contemporary South Africa." *Current Anthropology* 58, no. S15: 123–34.

Morris, Rosalind. 2017b. *The Returns of Fetishism: Charles de Brosses and the Afterlives of an Idea*. Chicago: University of Chicago Press.

Morris, Rosalind. 2018. "Shadow and Impress: Ethnography, Film, and the Task of Writing History in the Space of South Africa's Deindustrialization." *History and Theory* 57, no. 4 (December): 102–25.

Moten, Fred, and Stefano Harney. 2013. *The Undercommons: Fugitive Planning and Black Study*. New York: Autonomedia.

Mqhayi, Samuel Edward Krune. 1982. "The Prince of Britain." In *Voices from Within: Black Poetry from Southern Africa*, edited by Michael Chapman and Achmat Dangor, 34–35. Rotterdam: AD Donker.

Mueller, Christopher B. 1984. "The Federal Coconspirator Exception: Action, Assertion, and Hearsay." *Hofstra Law Review* 12, no. 2 (Winter): 323–92.

Munnion, Christopher. 2001. "Town under Siege as Missing 'Kruger Gold' Is Found on Farm." *The Telegraph*, June 9, 2001. https://www.telegraph.co.uk/news /worldnews/1311874/Town-under-siege-as-missing-Kruger-gold-is-found -on-farm.html.

Murphy, Cullen. 2013. *God's Jury: The Inquisition and the Making of the Modern World.* Boston: Houghton Mifflin Harcourt Books.

Musila, Grace A. 2015. *A Death Retold in Truth and Rumour: Kenya, Britain and the Julie Ward Murder.* London: Boydell and Brewer.

Nails, Debra. 1998. "The Dramatic Date of Plato's *Republic.*" *Classical Journal* 93, no. 4: 383–96.

Nails, Debra. 2002. *The People of Plato: A Prosopography of Plato and Other Socratics.* Indianapolis, IN: Hackett.

National Commission on Terrorist Attacks upon the United States. 2004. *The 9/11 Commission Report: Final Report of the National Commission on Terrorist Attacks Upon the United States.* Washington, DC: National Commission on Terrorist Attacks upon the United States. https://www.govinfo.gov/features/911 -commission-report.

National Public Radio (NPR). 2011. "By the Numbers: Today's Military." *Los Angeles Times*, July 3, 2011. http://www.npr.org/2011/07/03/137536111/by-the-numbers -todays-military.

Nattrass, Nicoli. 2012. *The AIDS Conspiracy: Science Fights Back.* New York: Columbia University Press.

Neboit-Mombet, Janine. 2005. *L'image de la Russie dans le roman français (1859–1900).* Clermont-Ferrand: Presses universitaires Blaise Pascal.

Nelson, Diane M. 2009. *Reckoning: The Ends of War in Guatemala.* Durham, NC: Duke University Press.

Nelson-Rees, Walter A. 2001. "Responsibility for Truth in Research." *Philosophical Transactions of the Royal Society: Biological Sciences* 356, no. 1410: 849–51. https:// www.jstor.org/stable/3067037.

New York Times. 2017. "Full Transcript and Video: Kelly Defends Trump's Handling of Soldier's Death and Call to Widow," October 19, 2017.

Nietzche, Friedrich. 1997. *Twilight of the Idols.* Translated by Richard Pott. Cambridge: Hackett Publishing.

Nightingale, Andrea. 2004. *Spectacles of Truth in Classical Philosophy: Theoria in Its Cultural Context.* Cambridge, MA: Cambridge University Press.

Nixon, Rob. 2011. *Slow Violence and the Environmentalism of the Poor.* Cambridge, MA: Harvard University Press.

Norton, Anne. 2013. *On the Muslim Question.* Princeton, NJ: Princeton University Press.

Nossiter, Adam. 2016. "'That Ignoramus': 2 French Scholars of Radical Islam Turn Bitter Rivals." *New York Times*, July 12, 2016.

Nozick, Robert. 1974. *Anarchy, State, and Utopia.* New York: Basic Books.

Nozick, Robert. 1981. *Philosophical Explanations.* Cambridge, MA: Belknap Press.

Nozick, Robert. 1997. "Invisible Hand Explanations." In *Socratic Puzzles*, 191–97. Cambridge, MA: Harvard University Press.

Oakes, Guy. 1994. *The Imaginary War: Civil Defense in American Cold War Culture.* Oxford: Oxford University Press.

Oats Studios. 2017. *Oats Studios—Volume 1—Rakka.* YouTube, video, 21:52. https://www.youtube.com/watch?v=VjQ2t_yNHQs.

Ober, Josiah. 1989. *Mass and Elite in Democratic Athens.* Princeton, NJ: Princeton University Press.

Ober, Josiah. 1998. *Political Dissent in Democratic Athens.* Princeton, NJ: Princeton University Press.

O'Connor, Anahad. 2016. "Study Tied to Food Industry Tries to Discredit Sugar Guidelines." *New York Times*, December 19, 2016. https://www.nytimes.com/2016/12/19/well/eat/a-food-industry-study-tries-to-discredit-advice-about-sugar.html.

O'Donnell, Patrick. 2000. *Latent Destinies: Cultural Paranoia and Contemporary US Narrative.* Durham, NC: Duke University Press.

Olin, Nathaniel. 2015. "Pathologies of Peacekeeping and Peacebuilding in CAR." In *Making Sense of the Central African Republic*, edited by Tatiana Carayannis and Louisa Lombard, 194–218. London: Zed Books.

Oliver, J. Eric, and Thomas J. Wood. 2014. "Conspiracy Theories and the Paranoid Style(s) of Mass Opinion." *American Journal of Political Science* 58, no. 4 (October): 952–66.

Olivieri, Nancy. 2020. "Nancy Olivieri: How John Le Carré Changed My Life." *Toronto Star*, December 22, 2020. https://www.thestar.com/opinion/contributors/2020/12/22/nancy-olivieri-how-john-le-carr-changed-my-life.html.

O'Neil, Cathy. 2016. *Weapons of Math Destruction.* New York: Crown Books.

O'Neill-Butler, Lauren. 2018. "Opinion: Adrian Piper Speaks! (For Herself)." *New York Times*, July 5, 2018. https://www.nytimes.com/2018/07/05/opinion/adrian-piper-speaks-for-herself.html.

Ophir, Adi. 2005. *The Order of Evils: Toward an Ontology of Morals.* New York: Zone Books.

"The Order's Command Structure." 1985. *Oregonian*, December 31, 1985.

Oreskes, Naomi, and Erik M. Conway. 2010. *Merchants of Doubt.* New York: Bloomsbury Press.

"Origins of HIV and the AIDS Epidemic." 2001. Special issue, *Philosophical Transactions of the Royal Society: Biological Sciences* 356, no. 1410: 777–977. https://www.jstor.org/stable/3067022.

Orléan, André. 2014. *The Empire of Value: A New Foundation for Economics.* Translated by M. B. DeBevoise. Cambridge, MA: MIT Press.

Orphanidou, Sophie. 2010. "Μακάβριο παιχνίδι νυκτοβατών¨ Κατέβασαν και πέταξαν τη σημαία τον τάφο του Τάσσου" [The Nightwalkers' Macabre Game: They Stripped the Flag and Threw it from Tassos's Tomb]. *Politis*, January 9, 2010.

Orr, Jackie. *The Panic Diaries: A Genealogy of Panic Disorder.* Durham, NC: Duke University Press.

Orwell, George. 1949. *1984.* New York: Harcourt, Brace.

Osterrieth, Paul M. 2001. "Vaccine Could Not Have Been Prepared in Stanleyville." *Philosophical Transactions of the Royal Society: Biological Sciences* 356, no. 1410: 839. https://www.jstor.org/stable/3067034.

Ostrovsky, Arkady. 2016. "For Putin, Disinformation Is Power." *New York Times*, August 5, 2016.

Oushakine, Serguei Alex. 2009. "'Stop the Invasion!': Money, Patriotism, and Conspiracy in Russia." *Social Research* 76, no. 1 (Spring): 71–116.

Oxford Languages. "Word of the Year 2016" (Post-truth). November 16, 2016. https://languages.oup.com/word-of-the-year/2016/.

Özcanhan, Özcan. 2009. "Papadopulosu kim mezarından kaçırdı" [Who Abducted Papadopoulos from His Grave?]. *Star*, December 19, 2009.

Pagan, Victoria. 2004. *Conspiracy Narratives in Roman History.* Austin: University of Texas Press.

Pagan, Victoria. 2012. *Conspiracy Theory in Latin Literature.* Austin: University of Texas Press.

Pallikaridis, Adonis. 2009. "Ανεύθυνα δημοσιεύματα για Τάσσο¨ Δεν πήγε για λύτρα στη Ζυρίχη η Φωτεινή" [Irresponsible Reports about Tassos: Fotini Did Not Go to Zurich for Ransom]. *Simerini*, December 21, 2009.

Pallister, David. 2007. "How the US Sent $12 Billion in Cash to Iraq. And Watched It Vanish." *Guardian*, February 7, 2007.

Pantelides, Poly. 2011. "Body Snatchers Found Guilty." *Cyprus Mail*, April 5, 2011.

Papadopoulos, Anastasia. 2009. "Ο βιασμός της αξιοπρέπειάς μας" [The Rape of Our Dignity]. *Philelevtheros*, December 19, 2009.

"Paramilitary Training by Klan Is Banned." 1982. *Houston Chronicle*, June 4, 1982.

Pariser, Eli. 2012. *The Filter Bubble: How the New Personalized Web Is Changing What We Read and How We Think.* New York: Penguin Books.

Parker, Andrew. 2012. *The Theorist's Mother.* Durham, NC: Duke University Press.

Pascoe, Peggy. 2009. *What Comes Naturally: Miscegenation Law and the Making of Race in America.* Oxford: Oxford University Press.

Patton, Phil. 1998. *Dreamland: Travels inside the Secret World of Roswell and Area 51.* New York: Villard Books.

Pease, Donald E. 2009. *The New American Exceptionalism.* Minneapolis: University of Minnesota Press.

Pehlivan, Alihan. 2009. "Papadopulos'un kemikleri" [The Bones of Papadopoulos]. *Güneş*, December 19, 2009.

Pelkmans, Mathijs, and Rhys Machold. 2011. "Conspiracy Theories and Their Truth Trajectories." *Focaal: Journal of Global and Historical Anthropology* 59: 66–80.

Penzenstadler, Nick, Brad Heath, and Jessica Guynn. 2018. "We Read Every One of the 3,517 Facebook Ads Bought by Russians." *USAtoday.com*, May 11, 2018. https://www.usatoday.com/story/news/2018/05/11/what-we-found-facebook -ads-russians-accused-election-meddling/602319002/.

Pepin, Jacques. 2011. *The Origins of AIDS.* New York: Cambridge University Press.

Perikleous, Chrysostomos. 2009. "Κόψτε τα πλοκάμια της ανωμαλίας" [Cut off the Tentacles of This Mutant]. *Politis*, December 13, 2009.

Petryna, Adriana. 2009. *When Experiments Travel: Clinical Trials and the Global Search for Human Subjects.* Princeton, NJ: Princeton University Press.

Piepzna-Samarasinha Leah Lakshmi. 2018. *Care Work: Dreaming Disability Justice.* Vancouver: Arsenal Pulp Press.

Piers, Matthew J. 2005. "Malevolent Destruction of a Muslim Charity: A Commentary on the Prosecution of Benevolence International Foundation." *Pace Law Review* 25, no. 2 (Spring): 339–53.

Pignarre, Philippe, and Isabelle Stengers. 2011. *Capitalist Sorcery: Breaking the Spell.* Translated by Andrew Goffey. New York: Palgrave Macmillan.

Piper, Adrian. n.d. *Art Talk: Xenophobia and the Indexical Present.* Adrian Piper, accessed February 22, 2023. Video, 1:22:00. http://www.adrianpiper.com/vs /video_at.shtml.

Piper, Adrian. (1990a) 1996. "The Joy of Marginality," *Art Papers* 14, no. 4 (July–August). (Reprinted in Adrian Piper, *Out of Order, Out of Sight: Selected Writings in Art Criticism, 1968–1992, Vol. 1,* 233–38. Cambridge, MA: MIT Press, 1996.)

Piper, Adrian. (1990b) 1996. "Xenophobia and the Indexical Present. I. Essay." In *Reimaging America: The Arts of Social Change,* edited by Mark O'Brien and Craig Little, 285–95. Philadelphia: New Society Publishers. (Reprinted in Adrian Piper, *Out of Order, Out of Sight: Selected Writings in Art Criticism, 1968–1992, Volume 1,* 245–52. Cambridge, MA: MIT Press, 1996.)

Piper, Adrian. (1991) 1996. "Vanilla Nightmares." In *Drawing,* 34–35. New York: John Weber Gallery, 1991. (Reprinted in Adrian Piper, *Out of Order, Out of Sight: Selected Writings in Art Criticism, 1968–1992, Volume 1,* 253–54. Cambridge, MA: MIT Press, 1996.)

Piper, Adrian. 1992. "Xenophobia and the Indexical Present. Talking Art." ICA Talks, MP3, 2:17:00. http://www.europeana.eu/en/item/2059209/data _sounds_C0095X0817XX_0100.

Piper, Adrian. (1993) 1996. "Xenophobia and the Indexical Present. II. Lecture." In *Place Position Presentation Public,* edited by Ine Gevers Den Haag. Netherlands: Jan Van Eyck Akademie. (Reprinted in Adrian Piper, *Out of Order, Out of Sight: Selected Writings in Art Criticism, 1968–1992, Volume 1,* 255–73. Cambridge, MA: MIT Press, 1996.)

Piper, Adrian. 2013a. "Adrian Piper Interview: Rationality and the Structure of the Self." Interview by Robert Del Principe, APRA Foundation Berlin, May 13, 2013. YouTube, video, 1:01:43. https://www.youtube.com/watch?v= _tURuyb76XQ.

Piper, Adrian. 2013b. *Rationality and the Structure of the Self, Volume II: A Kantian Conception.* 2nd ed. Berlin: APRA Foundation. http://www.adrianpiper.com/rss/.

Piper, Adrian. 2014. "Second Wave Feminism: Unfinished Business." National Academy of Art, Oslo, November 22, 2014. YouTube, video, 1:49:41. https://www.youtube.com/watch?v=56biuP_pTuU.

Piper, Adrian. 2018. *Escape to Berlin: A Travel Memoir.* Flucht Nach Berlin: Eine Reiseerinnerung. Berlin: Adrian Piper Research Archive Foundation Berlin.

Pitkin, Hanna Fenichel. 1972. *Wittgenstein and Justice.* Berkeley: University of California Press.

Pizzi, Michael. 2014. "The Syrian Opposition Is Disappearing from Facebook." *The Atlantic*, February 2014. http://www.theatlantic.com/international/archive/2014/02/the-syrian-opposition-is-disappearing-from-facebook/283562/.

Planeaux, Christopher. 2001. "Socrates, an Unreliable Narrator? The Dramatic Setting of the 'Lysis.'" *Classical Philology* 96, no. 1 (January): 60–68.

Plato. 2000. *The Republic.* Edited by G. R. F. Ferrari. Translated by Tom Griffith. Cambridge: Cambridge University Press.

Plotkin, Stanley A. 2001. "Untruths and Consequences: The False Hypothesis Linking CHAT Type 1 Polio Vaccination to the Origin of Human Immunodeficiency Virus." *Philosophical Transactions of the Royal Society: Biological Sciences* 356, no. 1410: 815–23.

Plotkin, Stanley A., and Hilary Koprowski. 1999. "Responding to *The River.*" *Science* 286, no. 5449: 2449.

Plotkin, Stanley A., A. Lebrun, Gislain Courtois, and Hilary Koprowski. 1961. "Vaccination with the CHAT Strain of Type 1 Attenuated Poliomyelitis Virus in Leopoldville, Congo. 3: Safety and Efficacy during the First 21 Months of Study." *Bulletin of the World Health Organization* 24: 785–92.

Politis Staff. 2009. "Προβοκατόρικο δημοσίευμα της Σημερινής" [Provocation Published in *Simerini*]. *Politis*, December 22, 2009.

Politis Staff. 2011. "Και τα Αντιβραβεία, 2010 Έτος πελλότοπου πελλόκοσμου" [And the Anti-awards, 2010: The Year of a Crazy Place in a Crazy World]. *Politis*, January 21, 2011.

Pomerantsev, Peter. 2014. *Nothing Is True and Everything Is Possible: The Surreal Heart of the New Russia.* New York: Public Affairs.

Popper, Karl. (1945) 1962. *The High Tide of Prophecy: Hegel, Marx, and the Aftermath.* Vol. 2 of *The Open Society and Its Enemies.* London: Routledge.

Popper, Karl. 1962. *Conjectures and Refutations: The Growth of Scientific Knowledge.* New York: Basic Books.

Popper, Karl R. 1963. "Towards a Rational Theory of Tradition." In *Conjectures and Refutations: The Growth of Scientific Knowledge*, 165–68. New York: Routledge.

Popper, Karl. 1966. *The Open Society and Its Enemies*, vol. 2: *Hegel and Marx.* Princeton, NJ: Princeton University Press.

"The Post-truth Issue." 2017. Special issue, *Chronicle of Higher Education*, January 11, 2017. https://www.chronicle.com/specialreport/The-Post-Truth-Issue/84.

Praeg, Leonard. 2014. *A Report on Ubuntu.* Pietermaritzburg: University of KwaZulu-Natal Press.

Prendergast, John. 2015. "How to Destroy a War Economy." *Foreign Policy,* August 10, 2015.

Priest, Dana, and William Arkin. 2011. *Top Secret America: The Rise of the New American Security State.* New York: Little, Brown, and Co.

Proal, Louis. 1895. *La criminalité politique.* Paris: F. Alca.

Przeworski, Adam. 2019. *Crises of Democracy.* Cambridge: Cambridge University Press.

Psyllides, George. 2009a. "Police Visit Serbian Businessman's Home in Papadopoulos Investigation." *Cyprus Mail,* December 22, 2009.

Psyllides, George. 2009b. "When Conspiracy Stretches to the Food on the Table." *Cyprus Mail,* September 20, 2009.

Psyllides, George. 2011. "Germany's Great Conspiracy." *Cyprus Mail,* January 8, 2011.

Psyllides, George. 2016. "The Players: Spyros Kyprianou." *Cyprus Mail,* December 20, 2016.

Puig, Albert. 1897. *La race des vipères.* Paris: Delhomme et Briguet.

Putin, Vladimir V. 2013. "A Plea for Caution from Russia." *New York Times,* September 11, 2013. https://tinyurl.com/or5vtco.

Pynchon, Thomas. 1965. *The Crying of Lot 49.* New York: Harper Perennial.

Pynchon, Thomas. 1973. *Gravity's Rainbow.* New York: Penguin Classics.

Radziwill, Catherine. 1921. "Les Protocoles des Sages de Sion." *La revue mondiale,* March 15, 1921, 151–55.

Rana, Aziz. 2010. *The Two Faces of American Freedom.* Cambridge, MA: Harvard University Press.

Rana, Aziz. 2014. "Constitutionalism and the Foundations of the National Security State." Rapoport Center Human Rights and Justice, Working Paper Series, University of Texas at Austin, School of Law. https://repositories.lib.utexas.edu/bitstream/handle/2152/27527/Rana_Constitutionalism.pdf?sequence=3&isAllowed=y.

Razavi, Negar. 2018. "Secured Expertise: Washington Policy Experts, the 'Middle East,' and U.S. Foreign Policy in an Age of Counterterror." PhD diss., University of Pennsylvania.

Read, Jason. 2003. *The Micro-politics of Capital.* Albany, NY: SUNY Press.

"Report of the Commission of Enquiry into the Recent Violence Occurences at the East Driefontein, Leeudoorn, and Northam Mines." 1996. Justice J. F. Myburgh, chair. South Africa: Commission of Enquiry into the Recent Violence and Occurrences at the East Driefontein, Leeudoorn and Northam Mines.

Reuter, Christopher. 2013. "Asad's Cold Calculations: The Poisonous Gas War on Syrians." *Al Jumhuriya,* August 31, 2013. https://www.aljumhuriya.net/16517.

Richards, Paul. 2005. "New War: An Ethnographic Approach." In *No Peace No War: An Anthropology of Contemporary Armed Conflicts,* edited by Paul Richards, 1–21. Athens: Ohio University Press.

Richtel, Matthew. 2015. "Please Don't Thank Me for My Service." *New York Times*, February 2, 2015.

Ricoeur, Paul. 1970. *Freud and Philosophy: An Essay on Interpretation*. Translated by Denis Savage. New Haven: Yale University Press.

Ridgeway, James. 1997. "Tim McVeigh and the Armies of the Right." *Village Voice*, March 25, 1997.

Rio, Knut M., and Olaf H. Smedal. 2008. "Hierarchy and Its Alternatives." In *Hierarchy: Persistence and Transformation in Social Formations*, edited by Knut M. Rio and Olaf H. Smedal, 1–64. New York: Berghahn Books.

Risen, James. 2014. *Pay Any Price: Greed, Power, and Endless War*. New York: Random House.

Robinson, Cedric J. 2020. *Black Marxism: The Making of the Black Radical Tradition*. Chapel Hill: University of North Carolina Press.

Rogin, Michael Paul. 1967. *The Intellectuals and McCarthy: The Radical Specter*. Cambridge, MA: MIT Press.

Rogin, Michael Paul. 1987. *Ronald Reagan, the Movie and Other Episodes in Political Demonology*. Berkeley: University of California Press.

Rohling, August. 1889. *Le juif salon le Talmud*. Paris: A. Savine.

Roisman, Joseph. 2006. *The Rhetoric of Conspiracy in Ancient Athens*. Berkeley: University of California Press.

Roitman, Janet. 2013. *Anti-crisis*. Durham, NC: Duke University Press.

Rollin, Henri. (1939) 2005. *L'apocalypse de notre temps*. Paris: Gallimard.

Rose, Peter W. 2019. *Sons of the Gods, Children of Earth: Ideology and Literary Form in Ancient Greece*. Ithaca, NY: Cornell University Press.

Rosenberg, Paul. 2017. "Conspiracy Theory's Big Comeback: Deep Paranoia Runs Free in the Age of Donald Trump." *Salon*, January 1, 2017. https://www.salon.com/2017/01/01/conspiracy-theorys-big-comeback-deep-paranoia-runs-free-in-the-age-of-donald-trump/.

Rosenblum, Nancy L., and Russell Muirhead. 2019. *A Lot of People Are Saying: The New Conspiracism and the Assault on Democracy*. Princeton, NJ: Princeton University Press.

Rosenstock, Bruce. 1983. "Rereading the *Republic*." *Arethusa* 16, no. 1–2: 219–46.

Roth, John, Douglas Greenburg, and Serena Wille. 2004. *Monograph on Terrorist Financing: Staff Report to the Commission*. Washington, DC: National Commission on Terrorist Attacks upon the United States.

Rothstein, Richard. 2018. *The Color of Law*. New York: Liveright Publishing.

Rumsfeld, Donald. 2002. "Press Conference by the US Secretary of Defence, Donald Rumsfeld." NATO HQ, June 6, 2002. https://www.nato.int/docu/speech/2002/s020606g.htm.

Runciman, David. 2018. *How Democracy Ends*. New York: Basic Books.

Sacharoff, Laurent. 2016. "Conspiracy as Contract." *UC Davis Law Review* 50, no. 1 (November): 405–61.

Sagan, Eli. 1994. *The Honey and the Hemlock: Democracy and Paranoia in Ancient Athens and Modern America*. Princeton, NJ: Princeton University Press.

Said, Edward. 1996. "Professionals and Amateurs." In *Representations of the Intellectual*, 73–83. New York: Vintage Books.

Said, Wadie. 2015. *Crimes of Terror: The Legal and Political Implications of Federal Terrorism Prosecutions*. Oxford: Oxford University Press.

Saliha, Samir. 2014. "Man Zawwarda Hirsh bi-l Ma ʿlumat?" [Who Provided Hersh with the Information?" *Al-Arabiya*, April 16, 2014. https://tinyurl.com /ybaff92h.

Samet, Elizabeth. 2011. "War, Guilt and 'Thank You for Your Service.'" *Washington Monthly*, August 2, 2011.

Sanders, Todd, and Harry G. West. 2003. "Power Concealed in the New World Order." In *Transparency and Conspiracy: Ethnographies of Suspicion in the New World Order*, edited by Harry G. West and Todd Sanders, 1–38. Durham, NC: Duke University Press.

Sands, Phil. 2013. "Syrian Chemical Attach Spurs Finger-Pointing inside Assad Regime." *The National* (Abu Dhabi), August 26, 2013. https://tinyurl.com /y7zwab09.

Saunders, Frances Stonor. 2013. *The Cultural Cold War*. New York: New Press.

Saxonhouse, Arlene. 2009. "The Socratic Narrative: A Democratic Reading of Plato's Dialogues." *Political Theory* 37, no. 6: 728–53.

Schmitt, Carl. 1995. *The Concept of the Political*. Chicago: University of Chicago Press.

Schouten, Peer, and Soleil Kalessopo. 2017. *The Politics of Pillage: The Political Economy of Roadblocks in the Central African Republic*. Amtwer: IPIS.

Schwartz, Charles. 2010. "The Meister Controversy: How Student Fees Are Connected to UC Construction Contracts." Open Computing Facility, UC Berkeley, March 22, 2010. https://www.ocf.berkeley.edu/~schwrtz/The_Meister _Controversy.pdf.

Scott, David. 2004. *Conscripts of Modernity: The Tragedy of Colonial Enlightenment*. Durham, NC: Duke University Press.

Scott, James. 1985. *Weapons of the Weak: Everyday Forms of Peasant Resistance*. New Haven, CT: Yale University Press.

Scott, Joan Wallach. 1991. "The Evidence of Experience." *Critical Inquiry* 17, no. 4 (Summer): 773–97.

Scranton, Roy. 2015. "The Trauma Hero: From Wilfred Owen to 'Redeployment' and 'American Sniper.'" *Los Angeles Review of Books*, January 25, 2015.

Scranton, Roy. 2016. "Choosing War." *Dissent Magazine* (Winter). https://www .dissentmagazine.org/article/choosing-war-nancy-sherman-afterwar-review.

Sedgwick, Eve Kosofsky. 2003a. "Paranoid Reading and Reparative Reading; or, You're So Paranoid, You Probably Think This Essay Is about You." In *Touching Feeling: Affect, Pedagogy, Performativity*, 123–52. Durham, NC: Duke University Press.

Sedgwick, Eve Kosofsky. 2003b. *Touching Feeling: Affect, Pedagogy, Performativity*. Durham, NC: Duke University Press.

Seattle Times Staff. 2010. "Cyprus Assassination Stirs Fears of Instability." *Seattle Times*, January 12, 2010. https://www.seattletimes.com/nation-world/cyprus -assassination-stirs-fears-of-instability/.

Sennett, Richard. 1993. *Authority*. New York: W. W. Norton.

"Separatists Launch New Nation." 1986. *White American Resistance* 5, no. 3: 1. Wilcox Collection (RH WL H100), Kenneth Spencer Research Library, University of Kansas, Lawrence.

Shah, Keerti, and Neal Nathanson. 1976. "Human Exposure to SV40: Review and Comment." *American Journal of Epidemiology* 103, no. 1 (January): 1–12.

Shapin, Steven, and Simon Schaffer. 2017. *Leviathan and the Air-Pump: Hobbes, Boyle, and the Experimental Life*. Princeton, NJ: Princeton University Press.

Sharp, Paul M., Elizabeth Bailes, Roy R. Chaudhuri, Cynthia M. Rodenburg, Mario O. Santiago, and Beatrice H. Hahn. 2001. "The Origins of Acquired Immune Deficiency Syndrome Viruses: Where and When?" *Philosophical Transactions of the Royal Society, Series B: Biological Sciences* 356, no. 1410: 867–76. https://doi.org/10.1098/rstb.2001.0863.

Sharp, Paul M., and Beatrice H. Hahn. 2011. "Origins of HIV and the AIDS Pandemic." *Cold Spring Harbor Perspectives in Medicine* 1, no. 1: a006841. https://doi .org/10.1101/cshperspect.a006841.

Sharpe, Christina. 2016. *In the Wake: On Blackness and Being*. Durham, NC: Duke University Press.

Shaw, Caroline. 2015. *Britannia's Embrace: Modern Humanitarianism and the Imperial Origins of Refugee Relief*. New York: Oxford University Press.

Shay, Jonathan. 1994. *Achilles in Vietnam: Combat Trauma and the Undoing of Character*. New York: Maxwell MacMillan International.

Shear, Julia. 2011. *Polis and Revolution: Responding to Oligarchy in Classical Athens*. Cambridge: Cambridge University Press.

Shelley, Percy Bysshe. 2004. *A Defense of Poetry and Other Essays*. Project Guttenberg Ebook: https://www.gutenberg.org/files/5428/5428-h/5428-h.htm.

Sherman, Nancy. 2015. *Afterwar: Healing the Moral Injuries of Our Soldiers*. New York: Oxford University Press.

Shils, Edward. 1956. *The Torment of Secrecy: The Background and Consequences of American Security Policies*. Glencoe, IL: Free Press.

Siegel, James. 1997. *Fetish, Recognition, Revolution*. Princeton, NJ: Princeton University Press.

Siegel, James. 1998. *A New Criminal Type in Jakarta: Counter-Revolution Today*. Durham, NC: Duke University Press.

Siegel, Jennifer. 2014. *For Peace and Money: French and British Finance in the Service of Tsars and Commissars*. New York: Oxford University Press.

Simerini Staff. 2009. "Γενικότερο και σοβαρό πρόβλημα ασφάλειας" [A More General and Serious Security Problem]. *Simerini*, December 13, 2009.

Simonton, Matthew. 2017. *Classical Greek Oligarchy: A Political History*. Princeton, NJ: Princeton University Press.

Singer, Natasha. 2009. "Medical Papers by Ghostwriters Pushed Therapy." *New York Times*, August 4, 2009. https://www.nytimes.com/2009/08/05/health /research/05ghost.html.

Singh, Nikhil Pal. 2017. *Race and America's Long War.* Berkeley: University of California Press.

Sismondo, Sergio. 2009. "Ghosts in the Machine: Publication Planning in the Medical Sciences." *Social Studies of Science* 39, no. 2: 171–98.

Sky News. 2013. "Syria: US Using Lies to Justify Strikes," September 4, 2013. https://tinyurl.com/y8w4cc6h.

Slotkin, Richard. 1998. *Gunfighter Nation: The Myth of the Frontier in Twentieth-Century America.* Norman: University of Oklahoma Press.

Smith, R. Jeffrey. 2011. "The Hunt for Yugoslav Riches." *Washington Post*, March 11, 2011. https://www.washingtonpost.com/archive/politics/2001/03/11/the -hunt-for-yugoslav-riches/62113b8f-79a0-4973-99f5-eda61b46d043/?utm _term=.336aebe6987e.

Smith, Stephen. 2015. "CAR's History: The Past of a Tense Present." In *Making Sense of the Central African Republic*, edited by Tatiana Carayannis and Louisa Lombard, 17–52. London: Zed Books.

Smythe, Colin, ed. 1995. *The Autobiography of Maud Gonne: A Servant of the Queen.* Chicago: University of Chicago Press.

Snell, John. c. 1984–1985. "Militants Guided by Story of Insurrection." *Oregonian.* Elinor Langer Collection, University of Oregon Libraries, Special Collections and Archives, Eugene.

Solinger, Rickie. 2007. *Pregnancy and Power: A Short History of Reproductive Politics in America.* New York: New York University Press.

Stampnitzky, Lisa. 2013. *Disciplining Terror: How Experts Invented "Terror."* Cambridge: Cambridge University Press.

Stats South Africa. 2023. "Number of People Employed by Gold Mining in South Africa from 2011 to 2021." https://www.statista.com/statistics/981151/people -employed-gold-mining-south-africa/, accessed April 20, 2023.

Staveley, E. S. 1972. *Greek and Roman Voting and Elections.* Ithaca, NY: Cornell University Press.

Stead, W. T. 1909. *The M. P. for Russia.* London: A. Melrose.

Stewart, Kathleen. 1999. "Conspiracy Theory's Worlds." In *Paranoia within Reason: A Casebook on Conspiracy as Explanation*, edited by George E. Marcus, 13–19. Chicago: University of Chicago Press.

Stewart, Kathleen. 2007. *Ordinary Affects.* Durham, NC: Duke University Press.

Stewart, Kathleen. 2011. "Atmospheric Attunements." *Environment and Planning D: Society and Space* 29, no. 3: 445–53.

Stewart, Kathleen, and Susan Harding. 1999. "Bad Ending: American Apocalypsis." *Annual Review of Anthropology*, 28: 285–310.

Stiglitz, Joseph E. 2022. "COVID Has Made Global Inequality Much Worse." *Scientific American*, March 1, 2022. https://doi.org/doi:10.1038 /scientificamerican0322–52.

Stiglitz, Joseph E., and Lori Wallach. 2021. "Will Corporate Greed Prolong the Pandemic?" *Project Syndicate*, May 6, 2021. https://www.project-syndicate

.org/onpoint/big-pharma-blocking-wto-waiver-to-produce-more-covid
-vaccines-by-joseph-e-stiglitz-and-lori-wallach-2021-05.

Stock, Catherine McNichol. 1996. *Rural Radicals: Righteous Rage in the American Grain.* Ithaca, NY: Cornell University Press.

Strauss, Leo. 1941. "Persecution and the Art of Writing." *Social Research* 8, no. 4: 488–504.

Strauss, Leo. 1952. *Persecution and the Art of Writing.* Chicago: University of Chicago Press.

Strauss, Leo. (1964) 1978. *The City and Man.* Chicago: University of Chicago Press.

Strieber, Whitley. 1987. *Communion: A True Story.* New York: Avon.

Stucke, Maurice. 2012. "Reconsidering Antitrust's Goals." *Boston College Law Review* 53, no. 2 (March): 551–629.

Sunstein, Cass R. 2001. "A Case Study in Group Polarization (with Warnings for the Future)." In *Aftermath: The Clinton Impeachment and the Presidency in the Age of Political Spectacle,* edited by Leonard V. Kaplan and Beverly I. Moran, 11–21. New York: New York University Press, 2001.

Sunstein, Cass R., and Adrian Vermeule. 2008. "Conspiracy Theories." John M. Olin Program in Law and Economics, Working Paper No. 387. University of Chicago Law School. https://chicagounbound.uchicago.edu/cgi/viewcontent .cgi?article=1118&context=law_and_economics.

Suskind, Ron. 2004. "Faith, Certainty and the Presidency of George W. Bush." *New York Times,* October 17, 2004. https://www.nytimes.com/2004/10/17 /magazine/faith-certainty-and-the-presidency-of-george-w-bush.html.

Suskind, Ron. 2006. *The One Percent Doctrine.* New York: Simon and Schuster.

Szklarski, Cassanda. 2017. "Conspiracy Theories Blossoming in a Post-truth Climate." *Globe and Mail,* March 21, 2017. https://www.theglobeandmail.com/life /conspiracy-theories-blossoming-in-a-post-truth-climate/article34362703/.

Tagaq, Tanya. 2016. "Retribution." *On Retribution.* Six Shooter Records.

Tahsin, Arif Hasan. 2009. "Papadopulos'un anımsaftıkları ve düşündürdükleri" [Thoughts and Reminiscences of Papdopoulos]. *Afrika,* December 22, 2009.

Tan, Monica. 2021. "Squid Game: The Smash-Hit South Korean Horror Is a Perfect Fit for Our Dystopian Mood." *Guardian,* September 30, 2021. https://www .theguardian.com/tv-and-radio/2021/oct/01/squid-game-the-smash-hit -south-korean-horror-is-a-perfect-fit-for-our-dystopian-mood.

Tankel, Stephen. 2012. *Storming the World Stage: The Story of Lashkar-e-Taiba.* London: Hurst.

Tarr, Joel A. 1966. "Goldfinger, the Gold Conspiracy, and the Populists." *Midcontinent American Studies Journal* 7, no. 2: 49–52.

Täuber, Susanne, and Morteza Mahmoudi. 2022. "How Bullying Becomes a Career Tool." *Nature Human Behaviour,* February 7, 2022. https://doi.org/10.1038 /s41562-022-01311-z.

Taussig, Michael. 1999. *Defacement: Public Secrecy and the Labor of the Negative.* Stanford, CA: Stanford University Press.

Taylor, Peter. 2009. "Misinformation: The Enemy of Excellence and Access." *City on a Hill Press*, November 11, 2009. https://www.cityonahillpress.com/2009/11/12/misinformation-the-enemy-of-excellence-and-access/.

Tchernoff, J. 1936. *Dans le creuset des civilisations.* Paris: Éditions Rieder.

Teegarden, David. 2013. *Death to Tyrants! Ancient Greek Democracy and the Struggle against Tyranny.* Princeton, NJ: Princeton University Press.

Terry, Jennifer. 2017. *Attachments to War: Biomedical Logics and Violence in Twenty-First Century America.* Durham, NC: Duke University Press.

Thalmann, Katharina. 2017. "From Fears of Conspiracy to Fears of Conspiracy Theory: The Delegitimation of Conspiracy Theory in Academic Discourse." PhD diss. chapter draft, University of Tübingen.

Thiel, Peter. 2014. *Zero to One: Notes on Startups, or How to Build the Future.* New York: Crown Business.

Thomas, Deborah A., and Joseph Masco, eds. 2023. *Sovereignty Unhinged: An Illustrated Primer for the Study of Present Intensities, Disavowals, and Temporal Derangements.* Durham, NC: Duke University Press.

Thomas, Jo. 2001. "'No Sympathy' for Dead Children, McVeigh Says." *New York Times*, March 29, 2001.

Thucydides. 1996. *The Landmark Thucydides.* Edited by Robert Strassler. Translated by Richard Crawley. New York: Free Press.

Ticktin, Miriam. 2011. *Casualties of Care: Immigration and the Politics of Humanitarianism in France.* Berkeley: University of California Press.

Ticktin, Miriam. 2017. "Humanity as Concept and Method: Reconciling Critical Scholarship and Empathetic Methods." *Comparative Studies of South Asia, Africa and the Middle East* 37, no. 3: 608–13.

Todd, Chuck, Mark Murray, and Carrie Dann. 2017. "Welcome to Our Post-truth Presidency." NBC News, March 6, 2017. https://www.nbcnews.com/politics/first-read/welcome-our-post-truth-presidency-n729481.

Trimikliniotis, Nicos, and Umut Bozkurt. 2012. "Introduction: Beyond a Divided Cyprus: a Society in a State of Transformation." In *Beyond a Divided Cyprus: A State and Society in Transformation*, edited by Nico Trimikliniotis and Umut Bozkurt, 1–21. London: Palgrave Macmillan.

Trivers, Robert. 2000. Review of *The River: A Journey to the Source of HIV and AIDS*, by E. Hooper. *Times Higher Educational Supplement*, February 18, 2000. https://www.bmartin.cc/dissent/documents/AIDS/River/THES.html.

Trouillot, Michel-Rolph. 1995. *Silencing the Past: Power and the Production of History.* Boston: Beacon Press.

Tufekci, Zeynep. 2018. "YouTube, the Great Radicalizer." *New York Times*, March 10, 2018. https://www.nytimes.com/2018/03/10/opinion/sunday/youtube-politics-radical.html.

Turner, Patricia A. 1993. *I Heard It through the Grapevine: Rumor in African-American Culture.* Berkeley: University of California Press.

UC Newsroom. 2009. "Faculty Union Leader's Claim about Student Fee Increases Called Misleading." October 20, 2009.

Ullmann-Margalit, Edna. 1978. "Invisible-Hand Explanations." *Synthese* 39, no. 2 (October): 263–91.

Ullmann-Margalit, Edna. 1997. "The Invisible Hand and the Cunning of Reason." *Social Research* 64, no. 2 (Summer): 181–98.

Un gentilhomme russe. 1889. *Russie et liberté.* Paris: Albert Savine.

Un russe. 1903. "Le manifeste du Tzar." *La nouvelle revue* 3–4: 439–40.

US Congress. 2002. *Joint Inquiry into Intelligence Community Activities before and after the Terrorist Attacks of September 11, 2001. Report of the U.S. Senate Select Committee on Intelligence and U.S. House Permanent Select Committee on Intelligence.* 107th Cong., 2d Sess., S. Rept. 107–351. https://www.congress.gov/congressional-report/107th-congress/senate-report/351/1.

US Congress. 2014. *Report of the Senate Select Committee on Intelligence, Committee Study of the Central Intelligence Agency's Detention and Interrogation Program.* 113th Congress, 2nd Sess. S. Rept. 113–288.

US Department of Defense. 2003. *Information Operations Roadmap.* Washington, DC: Government Printing Office.

van den Berg, J.H. 1974. *Divided Existence in Complex Society: An Historical Approach.* Pittsburgh: Duquesne University Press.

van Onselen, Charles. 2001. *New Babylon, New Nineveh: Everyday Life on the Witwatersrand, 1886–1914.* Johannesburg, South Africa: Jonathan Ball Publishers.

van Reybrouk, David. 2014. *Congo: The Epic History of a People.* New York: Harper Collins.

Vasili, Paul. 1884. *La société de Berlin.* Paris: Nouvelle Revue.

Vasili, Paul. 1885. *La société de Londres.* Paris: Nouvelle Revue.

Vaughan, Roger. 2000. *Listen to the Music: The Life of Hillary Koprowski.* New York: Springer.

Voegelin, Eric. 2000. *Plato.* Chicago: University of Chicago Press.

Wachowski, Lana, and Lilly Wachowski, dirs. 1999. *The Matrix.* Burbank, CA: Warner Brothers.

Wadman, Meredith. 2017. *The Vaccine Race: Science, Politics, and the Human Costs of Defeating Disease.* New York: Penguin Books.

Warner, Michael. 1994. *CIA Cold War Records: The CIA under Harry Truman.* Washington, DC: CIA History Staff/Center for the Study of Intelligence.

Warner, Michael. 2014. *The Rise and Fall of Intelligence: An International Security History.* Washington, DC: Georgetown University Press.

Watts, Jonathan. 2019. "'Biggest Compliment Yet': Greta Thunberg Welcomes Oil Chief's 'Greatest Threat' Label." *The Guardian*, July 5, 2019. www.theguardian.com/environment/2019/jul/05/biggest-compliment-yet-greta-thunberg-welcomes-oil-chiefs-greatest-threat-label.

Wedeen, Lisa. 2019. *Authoritarian Apprehensions: Ideology, Judgment, and Mourning in Syria.* Chicago: University of Chicago Press.

Weigel, David. 2016. "For Trump, a New 'Rigged' System: The Election It-self." *Washington Post*, August 2, 2016. https://www.washingtonpost.com/politics/for-trump-a-new-rigged-system-the-election-itself/2016/08/02/d9fb33b0–58c4–11e6–9aee-8075993d73a2_story.html?utm_term=.8f20a9f22348.

Weiss, Max D. 2016. "Slow Witnessing: Syrian War Literature in Real Time." Lec-ture. Chicago Center for Contemporary Theory (C3T), University of Chicago, October 7, 2016.

Weiss, Robin A. 1999. "Is AIDS Man-Made?" *Science* 286 (November): 1305–6. https://doi.org/10.1126/science.286.5443.1305.

Weiss, Robin A. 2001a. "Natural and Iatrogenic Factors in Human Immunode-ficiency Virus Transmission." *Philosophical Transactions of the Royal Society: Biological Sciences* 356, no. 1410: 947–53.

Weiss, Robin A. 2001b. "Polio Vaccines Exonerated." *Nature* 410 (April): 1035–36. https://doi.org/10.1038/35074222.

Welsome, Eileen. 1999. *The Plutonium Files: America's Secret Medical Experiments in the Cold War.* New York: Dial Press.

Werber, Laura, et al. 2015. *Faith Based Organizations and Veteran Reintegration.* Santa Monica, CA: Rand Corporation.

West, Harry G., and Todd Sanders, eds. 2003. *Transparency and Conspiracy: Eth-nographies of Suspicion in the New World Order.* Durham, NC: Duke University Press.

Wheeler, Marcy. 2015. "Evan Kohlmann: Garbage In, Garbage Out." *emptywheel.net*, July 29, 2015. https://www.emptywheel.net/2015/07/29/evan-kohlmann-garbage-in-garbage-out/.

Whitaker, Brian. 2021. *Denying the Obvious: Chemical Weapons and the Information War over Syria.* Self-pub.: Al-bab.com. https://al-bab.com/denying-the-obvious.

White, Hayden. 1973. *Metahistory: The Historical Imagination in Nineteenth-Century Europe.* Baltimore, MD: Johns Hopkins University Press.

White, Hayden. 1978. *Tropics of Discourse: Essays in Cultural Criticism. World Literature Today.* Baltimore, MD: Johns Hopkins University Press.

White, Luise. 2000. *Speaking with Vampires: Rumor and History in Colonial Africa.* Berkeley: University of California Press.

Whiteley, Michael. 1996. "McVeigh Tried to Call Colony Aide." *Democrat-Gazette*, January 26, 1996.

"White Supremacy Groups Laid Plans to Assassinate Kissinger, Ex-member Says." 1985. *Los Angeles Times*, September 14, 1985.

Whitlock, Craig. 2021. *The Afghanistan Papers: A Secret History of the War.* New York: Simon and Schuster.

Whitman, James Q. 2008. *The Origins of Reasonable Doubt: Theological Roots of the Criminal Trial.* New Haven, CT: Yale University Press.

Wilford, Hugh. 2009. *The Mighty Wurlitzer: How the CIA Played America.* Cambridge, MA: Harvard University Press.

Williams, David Lay. 2013. "Plato's Noble Lie: From Kallipolis to Magnesia." *History of Political Thought* 34, no. 3: 363–92.

Wilson, John Rowan, 1963. *Margin of Safety.* New York: Doubleday.

Wimsatt, W. K., Jr., and M. C. Beardsley. 1946. "The Intentional Fallacy." *Sewanee Review* 54, no. 3: 468–88.

Wise, David, and Thomas B. Ross. 1964. *The Invisible Government.* New York: Random House.

Wittgenstein, Ludwig. 1972. *On Certainty.* Edited by G. E. M. Anscombe and G. H. von Wright. Translated by Denis Paul and G. E. M. Anscombe. New York: Harper Perennial.

Wohlstetter, Albert. 1974. "Is There a Strategic Arms Race?" *Foreign Policy* 15 (Summer): 3–20.

Wolin, Sheldon S. 1960. *Politics and Vision.* Princeton, NJ: Princeton University Press.

Wolpe, Harold. 1972. "Capitalism and Cheap Labour-Power in South Africa: From Segregation to Apartheid." *Economy and Society* 14, no. 1: 425–56.

Wolski, Kalikst. 1887. *La russie juive.* Paris: Albert Savine.

Wood, David Browne. 2014a. "Moral Injury Project, Part 1: The Grunts: Damned If They Kill, Damned If They Don't." *Huffington Post*, March 18, 2014. https://projects.huffingtonpost.com/projects/moral-injury/the-grunts.

Wood, David Browne. 2014b. "Moral Injury Project, Part 2: The Recruits: When Right and Wrong Are Hard to Tell Apart." *Huffington Post*, March 19, 2014. https://projects.huffingtonpost.com/projects/moral-injury/the-recruits.

Wood, David Browne. 2014c. "Moral Injury Project, Part 3: Healing: Can We Treat Moral Wounds?" *Huffington Post*, March 20, 2014. https://projects.huffingtonpost.com/projects/moral-injury/healing.

Wood, David Browne. 2016. *What Have We Done: The Moral Injury of Our Longest Wars.* New York: Little, Brown, and Company.

Wood, Gordon S. 1982. "Conspiracy and the Paranoid Style: Causality and Deceit in the Eighteenth Century." *William and Mary Quarterly* 39, no. 3: 402–41.

Wool, Zoe. 2015. *After War: The Weight of Life at Walter Reid.* Durham, NC: Duke University Press.

Worobey, Michael, Andrew Rambaut, Edward C. Holmes, and Oliver G. Pybus. 2003. "Sexual Transmission of HIV in Africa." *Nature* 422, no. 6933: 679. https://doi.org/10.1038/422679a.

Worobey, Michael, Thomas D. Watts, Richard A. McKay, Marc A. Suchard, Timothy Granade, Dirk E. Teuwen, Beryl A. Koblin, Walid Heneine, Philippe Lemey, and Harold W. Jaffe. 2016. "1970s and 'Patient 0' HIV-1 Genomes Illuminate Early HIV/AIDS History in North America." *Nature* 539, no. 7627: 98–101. https://doi.org/10.1038/nature19827.

Wright, Lawrence. 2006. *The Looming Tower: Al-Qaeda and the Road to 9/11.* New York: Knopf.

Wylie, Sara Ann. 2018. *Fractivism: Corporate Bodies and Chemical Bonds.* Durham, NC: Duke University Press.

Yirka, Bob. 2011. "DARPA Looking to Master Propaganda via 'Narrative Networks.'" *Phys.org*, October 20, 2011. https://phys.org/news/2011–10-darpa-master -propaganda-narrative-networks.html.

Yuhas, Alan. 2016. "The Lies Trump Told This Week: Voter Fraud and the 'Rigged' Election." *Guardian*, October 2, 2016. https://www.theguardian.com/us -news/2016/oct/21/donald-trump-fact-check-rigged-election-voter.

Yusim, Karina, Martine Peeters, Oliver G. Pybus, Tanmoy Bhattacharya, Eric Delaporte, Claire Mulanga, Mark Muldoon, James Theiler, and Bette Korber. 2001. "Using Human Immunodeficiency Virus Type 1 Sequences to Infer Historical Features of the Acquired Immune Deficiency Syndrome Epidemic and Human Immunodeficiency Virus Evolution." *Philosophical Transactions of the Royal Society, Series B: Biological Sciences* 356, no. 1410: 855–66. https://doi .org/10.1098/rstb.2001.0859.

Zanou, Konstantina. 2010. "Η Κύπρος στο επίκεντρο παγκόσμιας συνωμοσίας!" [Cyprus at the center of a global conspiracy!] *TaNea.gr Book Reviews*, March 13, 2010. http://www.tanea.gr/old-page-categories/books/article /4564870/?iid=2.

Zegart, Dan. 2001. *Civil Warriors: The Legal Siege on the Tobacco Industry.* New York: Random House.

Zehner, Ozzie. 2012. *Green Illusions: The Dirty Secrets of Clean Energy and the Future of Environmentalism.* Lincoln: University of Nebraska Press.

Zerilli, Linda M. G. 2016. *A Democratic Theory of Judgment.* Chicago: University of Chicago Press.

Zeskind, Leonard. 2009. *Blood and Politics: The History of the White Nationalist Movement from the Margins to the Mainstream.* New York: Farrar, Straus and Giroux.

Žižek, Slavoj. 2008. *Violence: Six Sideways Reflections.* New York: Picador.

Zoni, N. 2011. "Three Protagonists of B. W. Vilakazi's *Ezinkomponi* (On the Mine Compounds)." *Literator* 32, no. 2: 173–87.

Zuboff, Shoshana. 2019. *The Age of Surveillance Capitalism.* New York: Public Affairs.

Zucchino, David. 2015. "Special Report: U.S. Military and Civilians Are Increasingly Divided." *Los Angeles Times*, May 23, 2015. http://www.latimes.com /nation/la-na-warrior-main-20150524-story.html.

Zuckerman, Frederic S. 2002. *The Tsarist Secret Police Abroad: Policing Europe in a Modernising World.* New York: Palgrave Macmillan.

Zuckert, Catherine. 2009. *Plato's Philosophers: The Coherence of the Dialogues.* Chicago: University of Chicago Press.

CONTRIBUTORS

Nadia Abu El-Haj is the Ann Whitney Olin Professor in the Department of Anthropology at Barnard College and Columbia University. She is the author of *The Genealogical Science: The Search for Jewish Origins and the Politics of Epistemology* and *Combat Trauma: Imaginaries of War and Citizenship in Post-9/11 America*.

Hussein Ali Agrama is Associate Professor of Anthropology at the University of Chicago and the author of *Questioning Secularism: Islam, Sovereignty, and the Rule of Law in Egypt*.

Kathleen Belew is Associate Professor of History at Northwestern University. She is the author of *Bring the War Home: The White Power Movement and Paramilitary America* and the coeditor, with Ramon Gutiérrez, of *A Field Guide to White Supremacy*.

Elizabeth Davis is Associate Professor of Anthropology at Princeton University. She is the author of *Bad Souls: Madness and Responsibility in Modern Greece* and *Artifactual: Forensic and Documentary Knowing*.

Joseph Dumit is Professor of Science and Technology Studies and Anthropology at the University of California–Davis. He is the author of *Picturing Personhood: Brain Scans and Biomedical Identity* and *Drugs for Life: How Pharmaceutical Companies Define Our Health*.

Faith Hillis is Professor of History at the University of Chicago and the author of *Children of Rus': Right-Bank Ukraine and the Invention of a Russian Nation* and *Utopia's Discontents: Russian Exiles and the Quest for Freedom, 1930–1930*.

Lochlann Jain is Professor of Anthropology at Stanford University and the author of *Injury: The Politics of Product Design and Safety Law in the United States* and *Malignant: How Cancer Becomes Us*.

Demetra Kasimis is Associate Professor of Political Science at the University of Chicago and the author of *The Perpetual Immigrant and the Limits of Athenian Democracy*.

Susan Lepselter is Associate Professor of American Studies and Anthropology at Indiana University–Bloomington and the author of *The Resonance of Unseen Things: Poetics, Power, Captivity, and UFOs in the American Uncanny*.

Darryl Li is Associate Professor of Anthropology and Associate Member of the Law School at the University of Chicago. He is the author of *The Universal Enemy: Jihad Empire and the Challenge of Solidarity*.

Louisa Lombard is Associate Professor of Anthropology at Yale University and the author of *State of Rebellion: Violence and Intervention in the Central African Republic*.

Joseph Masco is Professor of Anthropology at the University of Chicago. He is the author of *The Theater of Operations: National Security Affect from the Cold War to the War on Terror* and *The Future of Fallout, and Other Episodes in Radioactive World-Making*.

Robert Meister is Professor of Social and Political Thought in the Department of the History of Consciousness at the University of California–Santa Cruz. He is the author of *After Evil: A Politics of Human Rights* and *Justice Is an Option: A Democratic Theory of Finance for the Twenty-First Century*.

Timothy Melley is Professor of English at Miami University. He is the author of *Empire of Conspiracy: The Culture of Paranoia in Postwar America* and *The Covert Sphere: Secrecy, Fiction, and the National Security State*.

Rosalind C. Morris is Professor of Anthropology at Columbia University. She is the coauthor of *The Returns of Fetishism: Charles de Brosses and the Afterlives of an Idea*, with Daniel H. Leonard, and with William Kentridge, of *Accounts and Drawings from the Underground: The East Rand Proprietary Mines Cash Book, 1906*.

George Shulman is Professor at the Gallatin School of Individualized Study at New York University. He is the author of *American Prophecy: Race and Redemption in American Political Culture* and the coeditor, with Alyson Cole, of *Michael Paul Rogin: Derangement and Liberalism*.

Lisa Wedeen is the Mary R. Morton Professor of Political Science at the University of Chicago. She is the author of *Peripheral Visions: Publics, Power, and Performance in Yemen* and *Authoritarian Apprehensions: Ideology, Judgement, and Mourning Syria*.

INDEX

Carpenter, John, 82–87

Carré, John le, 271

Carson, Rachel, 16–17

Carter, Jimmy, 96

Casebook (Marcus, G.), 112–13, 119–20

Castoriadis, Cornelius, 49, 57n1

Catholic Church, 40, 135

cave allegory, in *Republic*, 200–201, 205

Cavell, Stanley, 224

Central African Republic (CAR) humanitarian profiteering, 26–27; Anti-Balaka and, 307–8; belief in, 295–97; Cold War and, 304–5; as conspiracy, 291–312; France and, 301–5, 309; gold in, 293–94, 299; imperialism and, 305; Islam and, 302; knowledge in, 303; language in, 294; as rumor, 291–312; stratification in, 313n11; UN and, 291–312; witchcraft and, 310, 312n6, 313n12, 313n14

Cephalus, 195

Charlie Hebdo, 404

Charmides (Plato), 208n18

Chavez, Hugo, 426

Chechnya, 365, 370

chelete, 249

chemical weapons, in Syria, 22, 152–63

Cheney, Dick, 1–3n7, 97, 131; Libby and, 370

Chivers, C. J., 159

cholera, in Venezuela, 114–15

Chomsky, Noam, 139, 180

Choy, Tim, 12–13

Christofias, Demetris, 106, 107

chronotope, 197, 199

church bombings, 17

CIA: in *Burn after Reading*, 362, 366; in Cold War, 92–93, 137, 138–39; Cyprus and, 20, 110; deep state and, 143; false flag operations by, 92–93; Kennedy, J., and, 138–39; 9/11 and, 379; nuclear weapons and, 95; Palantir and, 24; Petraeus in, 369; UFOs and, 9; Warren Report and, 5

Clapper, James, 142

Clark, Robert, 91

Clastres, Pierre, 262n13

Clausewitz, Carl von, 164

Cleitophon, 207n9

climate change, 59n11; Big Oil and, 269; conspiracy capitalism and, 274; Thunberg and, 273, 286

climate refugees, 9

Clinton, Bill, 47–48, 176

Clinton, Hillary, 46, 58n8, 87, 176; Capitol riot and, 426; child sex-trafficking ring of, 431; emails of, 129; false flag operations against, 90; ISIS and, 128; Syria and, 130

Clooney, George, 366

CNN, bin Laden on, 378

Coates, Ta-Nehisi, 54

Coen brothers, 366

Cohen Act, 413

COINTELPRO, 14, 207n7

Cold War, 5, 16; anticommunism of, 87, 90; Area 51 and, 181; CAR humanitarian profiteering and, 304–5; CIA in, 92–93, 137, 138–39; conspiracy theory in, 124, 136–39; covert sphere in, 402–4; Cyprus and, 110, 121; democracy in, 133; false flag operations of, 90–97; gaslighting in, 92; HIV/AIDS origin and, 79n5; nuclear weapons in, 94, 138, 144; paranoid style in, 21, 113; post-truth and, 130; UFOs in, 9

"Collective Responsibility" (Arendt), 225–28

colonialism. *See* imperialism

Comaroff, Jean, 113, 120, 126n7

Comaroff, John, 113, 120, 126n7

Comey, James, 370

common sense, 273; conspiracy theory and, 126n1; Kant on, 2; with militarism, 212, 221, 223; paranoid style and, 42, 51; in Syria, 157

common world, 2, 22, 164

Communion (Strieber), 178

confession, for moral injury, 230n16

The Confession of an Ex-Nihilist, 344

Connolly, William, 50

conspiracy: afterlives of, 341–58; Benjamin on, 260–61; of Big Pharma, 269–72; burden of proof of, 371–72; capitalism as, 268–75; CAR humanitarian profiteering

DARPA (Defense Advanced Research Projects Agency), 433–34
Davidson, Donald, 323, 336n8
Davies, William, 127
Davis, David Brion, 58n7
Davis, Elizabeth Anne, 20
Dean, Jodi, 123–24
deception, 19; by Barnum, 88; in conspiracy theory, 131, 142; in false flag operations, 90, 93–101; in film, 83; in higher education financialization, 327; Machiavelli on, 137; in noble lies, 207n5; in *Republic*, 203; revelation of, 82; by Trump, 88
Declaration of Independence, 397–98
deep state: Capitol riot and, 428; CIA and, 143; covert sphere and, 405; Cyprus and, 110; false flag operations by, 103n6; post-truth and, 128, 136; Trump and, 16, 103n6, 128, 136, 142–43; 2020 presidential election and, 32, 37
Defense Advanced Research Projects Agency (DARPA), 433–34
defensible judgment, in paranoid style, 39, 57n4, 58n5
Deleuze, Gilles, 262n17
DeLillo, Don, 53, 143
De Michelis, Cesare, 356
democracy: accountability in, 111; capital conspiracy and, 269; in Cold War, 133; conspiracy of, 23; false flag operations in, 100; Islam and, 386–407; oligarchy and, 12; paranoid style in, 45–46, 52, 56; Plato on, 190–206; in Russia, 346, 347. *See also* liberalism
Democracy (Didion), 144
Democratic Party: false flag operations against, 90; neoliberalism of, 47–48; Trump and, 46–49; 2020 presidential election and, 37
demonization: in conspiracy theory, 136; in false flag operations, 84, 87–90, 96–97; in higher education financialization, 319; of Koresh, 182; in paranoid style, 40, 42–43
deplorables, of Trump, 46, 58n8
DES (estrogen diethylstilbestrol), 67

Desmyter, Jan, 68
Dialogue in Hell between Machiavelli and Montesquieu (Joly), 355
Didion, Joan, 144
digital surveillance, 83
Dilley, Roy, 122
diminishing marginal value, in higher education financialization, 325–26
disinformation: in authoritarianism, 168n3; from Big Oil, 83; by Cheney, 103n7; of Trump, 146n5
disorientation campaigns, 3
displacement, in paranoid style, 41–42, 45–46
Doctors without Borders, 156
doctrine of merger, 382n20
Donner, Richard, 143
dos Passos, John, 236
doubt, 21–24; toward Islam, 388; uncertainty and, 149–68
Drousiotis, Makarios, 106–7, 124
drug trafficking: in Afghanistan, 375. *See also* war on drugs
Drumont, Édouard, 348–49, 354, 358
Du Bois, W. E. B., 28, 52
Dumit, Joseph, 26, 141
Durkheim, Émile, 117, 403

Eastman, John, 426
Eddy, Bernice, 76–77
Edmonds, Bill, 219–20, 229n3
Educational Fee, in higher education financialization, 319, 329, 330, 337n13, 337n15
Egypt: Britain and, 30–31; revolution in, 392–98; suspicion in, 392–98
Ehrenreich, Ben, 331
Ehrlichman, John, 102n3
Eichmann, Adolf, 222
Eisenhower, Dwight, 141
Ellison, Ralph, 53, 59n11
emergency cinema, in Syria, 164–67
Emerson, Steven, 377
Enlightenment, 99; conspiracy and, 311; power and knowledge in, 239; rationality of, 131; Trump and, 129

Knight, Peter, 123

knowledge: in CAR humanitarian profiteering, 303; in covert sphere, 402;
philosophical, false flag operations and,
93–94; power and, 239

Kohlmann, Evan, 377, 384nn43–44

Koprowski, Hilary, 63, 66–77

Koresh, David, 182–83

Kouyialis, Nicos, 123

Kruger, Paul, 236, 240

Kudo, Timothy, 216

Kuhn, Thomas, 277, 289

Ku Klux Klan (KKK), 17; Capitol riot and,
409, 411

Kyprianou, Spyros, 106

Laboratory of Biologics Control (LBC), 76

Laidlaw, James, 309

Lajnat al-Birr al-Islamiyya, 381n10

language: in CAR humanitarian profiteering, 294; Marx, K., on, 248, 262n14; of
South African gold miners, 262n12

lantern laws, in New York City, 28–29

Latour, Bruno, 132, 140

Lawrence, D. H., 44

LBC (Laboratory of Biologics Control), 76

Lenin, Vladimir, 52

Lenz, Patrick, 317, 318

Lepselter, Susan, 9, 22–23

Li, Darryl, 30

Libby, "Scooter," 370

liberalism: authority and, 31; conspiracy
theory and, 364; interest-group, 42, 46;
Islam and, 386–407; oligarchy and, 47;
paranoid style against, 45–49; in Russia,
345–46, 347. See also neoliberalism

Lifton, Robert J., 223, 230n14

Limbaugh, Rush, 6, 84

Limited Test Ban Treaty, 17

Lippman, Walter, 91–92

Lipset, Seymour, 136

liquidity, in higher education financialization, 325–26

Lloyd, Richard M., 158–61, 168

Lombard, Louisa, 26–27, 141

London Review of Books, 161–62

The Looming Tower (Wright), 378

Lorre, Peter, 366

Los Angeles Times, 215

lottery: in Republic, 204; for South African
gold miners, 243

Ludlum, Robert, 382n16

Lysis (Plato), 208n18

M4BL (Movement for Black Lives), 49

MI6, 107, 110

Macdonald, Andrew, 410

Machiavelli, Niccolò, 137

Machold, Rhys, 116–21

Madison, James, 45, 46

Mailer, Norman, 53, 143

Makhlouf, Hafez, 157

Malcolm X, 17

Malkovich, John, 366

"Manchester Sailor," 62

Manning, Chelsea, 403–4

Manufacturing Consent (Chomsky), 180

Marcus, George, 112–13, 118, 119–20

Marcus, Sharon, 112, 126n8

Markel, Howard, 74–75

Martin, Brian, 68, 69, 73

Marx, Karl, 52, 117, 132; on gold, 253, 256; on
language, 248, 262n14; on money, 262n14;
on occasional and professional conspirators, 254–55; on paranoid style, 270

Marx, Leo, 44, 48

Marxism, 13, 134, 135; on conspiracy theory,
320; fascism and, 57n1; higher education
financialization and, 320, 328; Popper
and, 335n3

Masco, Joseph, 19–20, 140, 141, 184, 266,
404, 405

Masons, 135, 139

mass media: in Cyprus, 20; false flag operations and, 87; misinformation from, 84;
paranoid style and, 41; post-truth and,
129; in Russia, 349; Trump on, 145. See
also specific examples

Massumi, Brian, 150

The Matrix, 140, 145

McCarthy, Joseph, 16, 134

McChrystal, Stanley, 378–79

McDormand, Frances, 366

McVeigh, Timothy, 31–32, 410, 417–22

mean-spiritedness, in bullying systems, 282–84

mēchanē (contrivance), 202, 204, 209n22

Meister, Robert, 27–28, 316–24, 337n10

Melley, Timothy, 21, 42, 54, 58n5, 126nn9–10, 401–4

Melville, Herman, 51–57, 59n12

Michael Clayton, 143

Michaels, Walter Benn, 221

militarism: false flake operations for, 91–92, 100; as family business, 215, 229n6; pleasure in, 222; reconstruction of, 223; "support the troops," 212, 223; truth in, 221; of US, 23–24, 210–28. *See also* moral injury; war on terror

military-civilian divide: innocence in, 211–12, 220; moral injury and, 215–18, 228; in war on terror, 211–12

Miller, Flagg, 382n18

Mills, C. Wright, 51–52

mimetic desire, 326

misdirection, 19

misinformation, 433; belief and, 4; in Capitol riot, 426; from corporations, 83; on COVID-19 vaccines, 271; from mass media, 84; in Russia, 6; from Trump, 83–84, 88

"Misinformation" (Taylor), 316–17

Mitchell, William, 91

Moby-Dick, 56–57. *See also* Ahab

Moderna, 271

money: Benjamin on, 252; in false flag operations, 96; gold and, 252–54, 257, 261n5; laundering of, in Cyprus, 20; of Trump, 6. *See also* capitalism

Monsanto, 141

moral injury, 24, 212–22; accountability with, 23, 222; as collective experience, 225–28; confession for, 230n16; military-civilian divide and, 215–18, 228; therapeutic citizenship for, 218–25; from transgressions of soldiers, 224–25; truth

and, 221, 223–24. *See also* "thank you for your service"

Morpheus (fictional character), 145

Morris, Rosalind C., 25

Morsi, Mohammed, 392–98

Moten, Fred, 49

Motley, Ron, 375, 376

Motley Rice, 374–78, 384n36

Movement for Black Lives (M4BL), 49

Mr. Robot, 145

Mubarak, Hosni, 392–98

MUFON (Mutual UFO Network), 189n1

Musila, Grace A., 312n8

Muslims. *See* Islam

Muslim Travel Ban, 365

Mutual UFO Network (MUFON), 189n1

Myburgh Report, 259

Mythologies (Barthes), 85–86

Nails, Debra, 196, 208n13

Napoleon III, 255

"Narrative Networks" (DARPA), 433–34

The Nation, 331

The National, 157

National Alliance, 410

National Institutes of Health (NIH), 76

nationalism: in Afghanistan, 367; in US, 43, 46, 47–48

National Public Radio, 215

Native Americans. *See* indigenous dispossession

Nehru, Jawaharlal, 367

Nenekos, Dimitris, 126n4

neoconservatism, false flag operations of, 94, 95

neoliberalism: of Democratic Party, 47–48; Floyd and, 49; paranoid style and, 46–48; in Syria, 151

New Deal, 45, 48, 58n8

New Left, 45

New Republic, 365

New Right, 45

New World Order, 121, 180–81; Capitol riot and, 409–10; 9/11 and, 8; paranoid style and, 113; Ruby Ridge and, 183

Schumacher, Jim, 77
Schwartz, Charles, 317, 319–20
science and technology studies (STS), on
HIV/AIDS, 67, 69, 75
Scott, Joan, 221
Scranton, Roy, 221
secret clubs (*synōmosias*), 201
Sedgwick, Eve, 10–11, 42, 51, 55, 78, 93
Sennett, Richard, 391, 406
sense-making, 115
sensus communis. See common sense
SE-polyoma virus, 76
September 11, 2001. *See* 9/11
sex, in *Republic*, 203–4
sexism, 14
Shadid, Anthony, 154
Shapin, Steven, 72
Sharpe, Christina, 4–5
Shaʾban, Bouthaina, 159, 160, 161
Shear, Julia, 207n6
Shell, 7, 269
Shelley, Percy Bysshe, 49
Sherman, Nancy, 215–23, 226, 229n5
Sherman Act, 336n7
Shils, Edward, 136–37
Shulman, George, 18
Silent Spring (Carson), 16–17
simian immunodeficiency virus (SIV), 63,
70, 74
Simmel, Georg, 403
Singh, Sarbjit, 108
SIV (simian immunodeficiency virus), 63,
70, 74
*The Slave Power Conspiracy and the Paranoid
Style* (Davis, D.), 58n7
Slotkin, Richard, 427
Smadel, Joe, 76
smartphones, algorithms for, 1
Smith, Adam, 24–25, 325
Smith, Michael S., II, 382n19
Snowden, Edward, 14, 141, 403–4
Soc, 202
social media: algorithms for, 1, 141; at Capi-
tol riot, 428; democratization on, 3; false
flag operations on, 90, 91; perception

management by, 83; polarization on, 20;
revolution and, 22; surveillance capitalism on, 3, 91; in Syria, 152, 154; Trump on,
6. *See also specific platforms*
social theory, conspiracy theory and,
113–14, 118–19, 125, 134–35, 403
socio-poetic insurgency, 49
Socrates, 191–95, 199, 203–5, 208nn18–19;
cave allegory of, 200–201, 205
Sophocles, 51
Soros, George, 426
South African gold miners, 25–26, 236–49;
accident rate of, 261n6; anxiety with,
259; closure of mines of, 256–61; dreams
of, 249–56; entrance and exit fees of,
249–50; language of, 262n12; residual
gold for, 256–61
Soviet Union (USSR): Afghanistan and,
367, 368; bin Laden and, 365; collapse of,
121; as evil empire, 97; nuclear weapons
of, 94–97; paranoid style in, 137; polio
vaccine and, 77; al-Qaʾida and, 367; U-2
and, 141, 144. *See also* Cold War
Spacey, Kevin, 365, 366
speculative narratives, 1
Squid Game, 279
Stalin, Joseph, 41–42
Stalinism, in Russia, 119
Starbuck (fictional character), 56
Staveley, E. S., 209n23
Stengers, Isabelle, 270
Stewart, Kathleen, 114, 120, 156, 169n8
Stewart, Sarah, 76
Stone, Roger, 103n6
Stop the Steal, 409
Strategic Defense Initiative, 97
stratification, in CAR humanitarian profi-
teering, 313n11
Strauss, Leo, 93–94, 196
Strieber, Whitley, 178
structural violence, 4–5
The Structure of Scientific Revolutions (Kuhn),
277
STS (science and technology studies), on
HIV/AIDS, 67, 69, 75

student debt, 28, 275–76

Sumner Simpson papers, 376

"support the troops," 212, 223

Supreme Court: Barrett on, 100–101, 103n12; on conspiracy, 372; false flag operations for, 100–101, 103n12; on notice pleadings, 383n31; in US, 100–101

surveillance, 129; anti-blackness and, 28; by FBI, 406; paranoid style and, 54; suspicion and, 400; *The Turner Diaries* and, 414; in war on terror, 7

surveillance capitalism, 433; on social media, 3, 91

suspicion: in anti-blackness, 406; in antisemitism, 406; authority and, 390–91, 398–99, 406; covert sphere and, 401–3; in Egypt, 392–98; of Islam, 386–407; paranoid style and, 39; in racism, 406; with religion, 41; in *Republic*, 194, 197–98; surveillance and, 400; of US militarism, 210–28

SV-40, 67, 72, 73, 77, 80n13

Sweet, Ben, 77

synōmosias (secret clubs), 201

Syria, 22; accountability in, 158; agency in, 167; Arnaout from, 369–70; authoritarianism in, 151–52; chemical weapons in, 22, 152, 156–63; counterinsurgency in, 152; emergency cinema in, 164–67; neoliberalism in, 151; openings in, 164–67; polarization in, 167; political impasse in, 156–63; revolution in, 149–68; Russia and, 160–61, 162; social media in, 152, 154; Trump on, 130; truth in, 154, 155, 160; uncertainty in, 149–68; US and, 156–63, 168

Syria and, 160

Syriana, 143

systematic violence, 168

Tagaq, Tanya, 268

Taliban, 374

Tanzania embassy bombing, 368

Tareekh Osama, 369–78

Tarr, Joel A., 261n1

Taylor, Peter, 316–20, 330–31

Tea Party, 176

terrorism: in Cyprus, 106; defined, 380n1; from Iraq, 96; in Russia, 343, 352; *The Turner Diaries* and, 412. *See also* counterterrorism; war on terror

Thalidomide, 67

Thank You for Your Service (Finkel), 217

"thank you for your service," 23–24, 214, 216–18; as patriotic gloss, 228; veterans' dread at, 229n8

theory, 13. *See also*, critical theory; conspiracy theory

theory of race-thinking, 117

therapeutic citizenship, for moral injury, 218–25

therapeutic culture, 120

They Live, 82–88

Thiel, Peter, 24–25

Three Days of the Condor, 143

Thucydides, 198, 200, 202, 203, 208n14

Thunberg, Greta, 273, 286

Ticktin, Miriam, 227

Tilly, Elizabeth, 65

Tobacco Master Settlement Agreement, 375

Tocqueville, Alexis de, 51

The Torment of Secrecy (Shils), 136–37

toxic masculinity, 48

The Trajectory of an Unknown Soldier, 165–67

Transparency and Conspiracy (West and Sanders, T.), 119

Trilateral Commission, 181

Truman, Harry, 137

Trump, Donald, 6, 121; birthism and, 176; Capitol riot and, 409–23, 426–29; Comey and, 370; counterterrorism of, 382n19; COVID-19 pandemic and, 83–84, 86; deep state and, 16, 103n6, 128, 136, 142–43; deplorables of, 46, 58n8; disinformation of, 146n5; false flag operations of, 87–88, 90, 99; on mass media, 145; militarism and, 210–11; misinformation from, 83–84, 88; money of, 6; paranoid style and, 37, 46–49, 54; post-truth and, 21, 127–45; QAnon and, 37, 87; Russian

www.ingramcontent.com/pod-product-compliance
Lightning Source LLC
Chambersburg PA
CBHW020448270326
41926CB00008B/527